Baedeker's
YUGOSLAVIA

Cover picture: Dubrovnik – the old town from the east

162 colour photographs
56 maps and plans
1 large road map

Text:
Armin Ganser (Yugoslavia from A to Z, Practical Information)
Gerald Sawade (Climate)
Christine Wessely (Art)

Editorial work:
Baedeker Stuttgart
English language: Alec Court

Cartography:
Ingenieurbüro für Kartographie
Huber & Oberländer, Munich

Design and layout:
HF Ottmann,
Atelier für Buchgestaltung und
Grafik-Design, Leonberg

Conception and general direction:
Dr Peter Baumgarten, Baedeker Stuttgart

English translation:
James Hogarth

© Baedeker Stuttgart
Original German edition

© The Automobile Association 57312
United Kingdom and Ireland

© Jarrold and Sons Ltd
English Language edition Worldwide

Published in the U.S. and Canada by Prentice-Hall, Inc., Englewood Cliffs, N.J. 07632

Licensed user:
Mairs Geographischer Verlag GmbH & Co.,
Ostfildern-Kemnat bei Stuttgart

Reproductions:
Gölz Repro-Service GmbH,
Ludwigsburg

The name *Baedeker* is a registered trademark

Source of illustrations:

Most of the illustrations were supplied by Frau Leonore Ander, Munich. Others:

Allianz-Archiv (p. 240)
Baedeker-Archiv (p. 139)
Deutsche Press-Agentur GmbH (dpa), Frankfurt/Main (cover picture)
Renate Drescher, Munich (p. 88, left)
Prof. Dr A. Herold, Gerbrunn (pp. 49; 90, right; 193; 200, right; 226, 227, 265)
Yugoslav National Tourist Office, Munich (pp. 10, 18, 24; 59, left; 69; 90, left; 91, 99; 108, top; 109, 114; 119, both; 131; 138, top; 163, 190, 262)
Edwin Kock, Munich (pp. 80, 103, 261)
Emil Mahr, Munich (pp. 197, 198)
Austrian National Tourist Office, Vienna (p. 120)
Zentrale Farbbild Agentur GmbH (ZEFA), Düsseldorf (p. 241)

The panorama of Belgrade on pp. 44–45 was drawn by Werner Gölitzer, Stuttgart.

In a time of rapid change it is difficult to ensure that all the information given is entirely accurate and up to date, and the possibility of error can never be completely eliminated. Although the publishers can accept no responsibility for inaccuracies and omissions, they are always grateful for corrections and suggestions for improvement.

Printed in Great Britain by Jarrold & Sons Ltd, Norwich

ISBN 0–13–056184–3 US & CANADA
     0 86145 170 8 UK
     3–87504–199–2 GERMANY

How to Use this Guide

The principal towns and areas of tourist interest are described in alphabetical order. The names of other places referred to under these general headings can be found in the Index.

Following the tradition established by Karl Baedeker in 1844, sights of particular interest and hotels and restaurants of particular quality are distinguished by either one or two asterisks..

In the lists of hotels and other accommodation b.=beds. Hotels are classified in the categories shown on p. 252.

The symbol (i) at the beginning of an entry or on a town plan indicates the local tourist office or other organisation from which further information can be obtained. The post-horn symbol on a town plan indicates a post office.

Only a selection of hotels and restaurants can be given: no reflection is implied, therefore, on establishments not included.

A glossary of common Serbo-Croat geographical and topographical terms will be found on p. 251.

This guidebook forms part of a completely new series of the world-famous Baedeker Guides to Europe.

Each volume is the result of long and careful preparation and, true to the traditions of Baedeker, is designed in every respect to meet the needs and expectations of the modern traveller.

The name of Baedeker has long been identified in the field of guidebooks with reliable, comprehensive and up-to-date information, prepared by expert writers who work from detailed, first-hand knowledge of the country concerned. Following a tradition that goes back over 150 years to the date when Karl Baedeker published the first of his handbooks for travellers, these guides have been planned to give the tourist all the essential information about the country and its inhabitants: where to go, how to get there and what to see. Baedeker's account of a country was always based on his personal observation and experience during his travels in that country. This tradition of writing a guidebook in the field rather than at an office desk has been maintained by Baedeker ever since.

Lavishly illustrated with superb colour photographs and numerous specially drawn maps and street plans of the major towns, the new Baedeker Guides concentrate on making available to the modern traveller all the information he needs in a format that is both attractive and easy to follow. For every place that appears in the gazetteer, the principal features of architectural, artistic and historic interest are described, as are its main areas of scenic beauty. Selected hotels and restaurants are also included. Features of exceptional merit are indicated by either one or two asterisks.

A special section at the end of each book contains practical information, details of leisure activities and useful addresses. The separate road map will prove an invaluable aid to planning your route and your travel within the country.

Contents

Introduction to Yugoslavia

Sveti Stefan, in Budva Bay (Montenegro) ▶

Yugoslavia

**Socialist
Federal Republic
of Yugoslavia**

**Socijalistička Federativna
Republika Jugoslavija**

	Area in			
Republic	sq. miles	sq. km	Population	Capital
Bosnia-Hercegovina	19,741	51,129	4,075,000	Sarajevo
Croatia	21,829	56,538	4,532,000	Zagreb
Macedonia	9,928	25,713	1,826,000	Skopje
Montenegro	5,333	13,812	571,000	Titograd
Serbia	34,220	88,361	8,921,000	Belgrade
(Kosovo)	(4,203)	(10,887)	(1,468,000)	Priština
(Vojvodina)	(8,303)	(21,506)	(1,996,000)	Novi Sad
Slovenia	7,819	20,251	1,793,000	Ljubljana
Yugoslavia	98,766	255,804	21,718,000	Belgrade

N.B. Kosovo and Vojvodina are autonomous provinces. Area and population figures are included in Serbia.

Yugoslavia (*Jugoslavija*, "Southern Slavia") is a federal multi-national state with a socialist social structure, made up of **six republics** and **two autonomous provinces**. The constitution now in force was introduced in 1974. Since the death in 1980 of Marshal Tito, who was elected President for life, the country has been governed by a collective Presidency, one member of which is elected in rotation to act as titular head of state for a year at a time. The legislative body is the SFRY, consisting of a Federal Chamber (220 members) and a Chamber of the Republics and Provinces (88 members). The only permitted political party is the Yugoslav League of Communists.

Yugoslavia, a "non-aligned" state, is a member of the United Nations and participates in both the "western" Organisation for Economic Co-operation and Development (OECD) and the "eastern" Council for Mutual Economic Assistance (Comecon).

The four major nationalities in Yugoslavia, accounting for some 90% of the total population, are the Slovenes, the Croats, the Serbs and the Macedonians, all of whom have equal rights. There are considerable minorities of Albanians (Kosovo), Hungarians and Slovaks (Vojvodina) and Romanians (eastern Serbia, Vojvodina), as well as Turks (Macedonia), Bulgarians (SE Serbia) and Italians (Istria, and previously Dalmatia). The Albanians and Hungarians enjoy broadly the same rights as the main Southern Slav nationalities; the other minorities have certain rights of autonomy.

In the eastern and southern parts of the country the population is overwhelmingly of Orthodox faith; the majority of Croats and Slovenes are Roman Catholics. In large areas of Bosnia the population are Moslems, and so, as a rule, are the Albanians and Turks.

Yugoslavia is now one of the great holiday countries of Europe, featuring prominently in the programs of the big travel firms and attracting increasing numbers of visitors every year – primarily, it is true, to the numerous seaside resorts on the country's long Adriatic coastline and to the many offshore islands. But though the main tourist areas are predominantly in the Adriatic coastal regions the rest of the country offers a great variety of attractions – scenic, historical and artistic – as well as the opportunity to make the acquaintance of the different peoples of this multi-national Balkan state.

Yugoslavia is very far from homogeneous in terms either of physical geography or of culture. A number of provinces of very different character were brought together in the new kingdom of Serbs, Croats and Slovenes in 1918 and the federal republic in 1945, giving the country an area of 98,766 sq. miles/255,804 sq. km and a present-day population of some 22 million. The diversity of scenery and of population which strikes every visitor so forcibly is a reflection of the varied geographical structure and topographical pattern of the federal state, made up of the six republics of Serbia, Croatia, Slovenia, Bosnia-Hercegovina, Montenegro and Macedonia.

The country belongs both to Central Europe and to Southern Europe. The *Sava-Danube line*, long regarded as the northern boundary of the Balkan peninsula, runs through territory which is by no means peninsular in character. The Iberian and Italian peninsulas are clearly marked off by the Pyrenees and the Alps, on either side of which lie regions of quite different character; but the Sava-Danube line does not constitute any kind of natural barrier in south-eastern Europe. It is only S of a line running from Lake Scutari in northern Albania by way of the Morava-Vardar watershed between the Danube basin and the Aegean to the Gulf of Burgas on the Bulgarian Black Sea coast that south-eastern Europe begins to take on the geographical characteristics of a Mediterranean peninsula. On this basis the whole of Yugoslavia apart from Macedonia should properly be seen as part of continental Europe.

There was, however, some foundation for the conventional view of the Sava-Danube line as a boundary. It is true that the line formed by these two rivers is of no significance in defining the natural regions of south-eastern Europe; but it is undoubtedly of major importance in terms of human geography, being the historic frontier between the south-eastern Alpine foreland regions controlled by the Habsburgs and the southern Slav countries, which for many centuries followed different lines of political and cultural development. Thus Yugoslavia is traversed by two important boundaries, one significant in terms of physical geography, the other in terms of human geography. Macedonia, in the S of the country, belongs to the Balkan peninsula, while the territories N of the Sava and the Danube reach far into the old Austro-Hungarian possessions. The Dinaric Alps between the two areas extend from continental Central Europe to the Mediterranean and maritime regions of south-eastern Europe. This role as an intermediary between different regions which nature has assigned to Yugoslavia was no doubt one of the factors which have led it in recent years to turn to the West, as it did before the last war, as well as to eastern Europe.

The ideal situation for a country is when its geographical hub is also its political, cultural and economic heart. With such a vigorous heartland, the peripheral regions can then be incorporated into a stable national unit, in which centrifugal forces give place to the stronger centripetal forces. Yugoslavia, however, has no such favoured central region: its geographical heart is occupied by the mighty range of the **Dinaric Alps**, which starts as a narrow ridge between Trieste and Ljubljana in the NW of the country and fans out as it travels SE until it reaches a width of almost 190 miles/300 km between Belgrade and Cetinje, occupying altogether roughly half the country's total area.

The Dinaric Alps or Dinarids (named after Mt Dinara in Dalmatia) branch off the main Alpine chain and run parallel with the Adriatic coast until they encounter the Northern Albanian Alps, running inland from the coast. This mighty rampart is made up of broad ridges and plateaux but also of sharp and rugged ridges which fall down in steep rock walls to the narrow coastal strip. On the NE it slopes down more gently towards the Sava and Morava. In the wild karstic uplands of **MONTENEGRO** (*Crna Gora*, "Black Mountain") the Dinarids rear up into an almost impregnable mountain stronghold. ("Karstic" is derived from Karst – a desolate, stony, waterless region near Trieste.) The limestone massif of Durmitor, shaped by glacial action, reaches a height of 8275 ft/2522 m. When the medieval kingdom of Serbia collapsed after the Turkish victory on the Field of Blackbirds (Kosovo Polje) in 1389 there came into being in this mountain retreat the little state of Montenegro, which held out against the Turks and retained its freedom for 500 years.

Cetinje (Montenegro)

The other territories within the Dinaric Alps, **BOSNIA** and **HERCEGOVINA**, are also difficult of access. The narrow basins and longitudinal valleys, running parallel to the Adriatic coast in line with the "strike" (direction) of the Dinaric range, facilitate movement in a north-westerly or south-easterly direction but increase the difficulties of travelling inland through the mountains. Transverse valleys from one side of the range to the other are lacking, as are any deeply slashed passes. The routes through the hills have to climb steeply up from the sea, and then run over the bleak karstic plateau, avoiding the high limestone masses which rise above the plateau and the deeply cut oval basins, then usually dropping sharply down on the other side. The only river N of the Albanian River Drim, which cuts its way through the high western face of the Dinaric Alps, is the Neretva (Narenta), at Mostar, providing a passage into the valley of the River Bosna by way of the Ivan Sedlo pass (3173 ft/967 m).

This passage through the limestone gorges of Bosnia has long been an important traffic route. For the Romans it opened up the interior of Bosnia; later it provided a means of access to the Adriatic for the Turks, who built a road from Slavonski Brod on the Sava to the mouth of the Neretva, with a string of castles to provide protection. It has retained its importance in more modern times: thus it was used immediately after the Austrian occupation for the construction of a narrow-gauge railway from Slavonski Brod to Dubrovnik (1878–82). After the Second World War a line of normal gauge was built from Vrpolje to Sarajevo, and the old narrow-gauge line is now used only for goods traffic between Slavonski Brod and Teslić and between Čapljina and Dubrovnik, the line from Sarajevo through the Neretva valley to Ploče having recently been converted to normal gauge.

At the N end of the country a railway line of normal gauge, climbing to a height of 2600 ft/800 m, links Zagreb with Yugoslavia's principal Adriatic port, Rijeka. The Lika line branches off this line and, using the longitudinal valleys of the Dinaric range, reaches the coast at Šibenik and Split. Thus even today the Adriatic coastal region has only a few traffic routes connecting it with the interior of the country, particularly with the fertile plains in the valleys of the large northern rivers and with the capital, Belgrade. Macedonia has still no direct railway connection with the Adriatic, and the line from Belgrade to the Montenegrin port of Bar was completed only in the mid seventies with the help of innumerable tunnels and bridges.

There are trunk roads through the Dinaric Alps from Ljubljana and Zagreb to Rijeka, from Zagreb via Karlovac to Karlobag and Zadar and from Banja Luka to Sarajevo and Mostar, while expressways from Maribor via Ljubljana to Nova Gorica, from Zagreb to Rijeka and from Zagreb via Knin to Split are partly completed, with some sections still under construction.

Long-distance international railway lines and roads avoid the Dinaric Alps. The most important through railway line links up with the Central European railway network at Ljubljana and runs E via Zagreb to Belgrade, from where it continues via Niš and Sofia to Istanbul, with an alternative route which avoids Bulgaria branching off and running via Skopje and

Salonica to Athens or the Bosporus. Yugoslavia's most important through road, the *autoput* (highway) from Ljubljana via Zagreb, Belgrade, Niš and Skopje to Gevgelija, runs to the N of the great Dinaric mountain wedge in the Sava depression. The magnificent Adriatic coastal highway has been carried down the whole length of the country to Ulcinj, with a connecting road through the mountains from the Adriatic coast via Titograd and Priština to Skopje.

The Dinaric mountain regions, already difficult of access, are rendered still more inhospitable by the intensive karstic action in these great masses of limestone which has made the western part of the range an economic desert. In spite of its high rainfall – Crkvice in Kotor Bay is the wettest place in Europe, with an annual precipitation of 180 in/4600 mm – the coastal side of the range has few surface watercourses, since rainwater quickly sinks underground into the crevices and cavities in the limestone. In the interior of the karstic upland region the rainfall still ranges between 40 and 80 in. (1000 and 2000 mm) – fully sufficient to support a dense forest cover. Farther inland and on the E side of the mountains, where the limestones give place to schists, greywackes, serpentines and crystalline rocks, there are in fact still huge expanses of forest. Yugoslavia is the most richly wooded of the Mediterranean countries. The oak forests extend up to 2600 ft/800 m, above which there are large expanses of hornbeams and beeches, followed at still higher levels by conifers. The tree line rises from 5600 ft/1700 m in the NW of the country to 6600 ft/2000 m in the SE. Above these heights, as in the Alps, is the region of mountain pines and Alpine meadows. These forests of Central European type, interrupted by areas cleared for cultivation in earlier or more recent times, extend some distance westward into the area of Mesozoic limestones. This is the "green" or "covered" karst, so called because here the karstic processes are taking place under the surface mantle of vegetation and humus. Near the coast the "naked" karst predominates. Here the forests were felled many centuries ago to provide the large quantities of timber required by the coastal towns and villages for shipbuilding and domestic consumption, and after this deforestation the unprotected topsoil was washed away and the bare white limestone exposed, leaving the barren but magnificent landscape of the naked karst.

Karst (Slovene Kras, Italian Carso), in its original geographical sense, is a desolate stony and waterless region lying inland from Trieste. In this area the bare expanses of rock, traversed by furrows and sharp-edged ridges, are relieved here and there by shallow or cauldron-shaped depressions filled with alluvial red soil (*terra rossa*) which makes possible a modest development of agriculture. These small cultivated areas are protected by substantial stone barriers from the sheep, goats and cattle which graze on the sparse scrub growing round the fields. In summer this stony land is scorched by the pitiless sun, in winter it is lashed by the dreaded bora (Serbo-Croat bura), an icy fall wind blowing down from the mountains. The processes of karst formation were first studied by geologists and geographers in this area in the hinterland of Trieste, and the adjective "karstic" has become a general term applied to any area where these processes have been at work.

This karstic action is produced by the solvent effect of rainwater penetrating into the limestone. What are originally mere hairline cracks in the rock are gradually enlarged by the removal of the dissolved limestone into large crevices. This creates a surface pattern of clefts and ridges running roughly parallel to one another, producing large expanses of difficult terrain known as limestone pavements, with furrows which may be more than 3 ft/1 m deep. On sloping surfaces these clefts, following the line of drainage of rainwater, are usually particularly striking. The water which sinks through the various clefts and crevices forms underground rivers which flow through a system of karstic caverns and channels. The roof of such subterranean cavities may collapse, forming funnel-shaped holes in the ground; the sides of these holes are then gradually levelled down, and terra rossa is carried into them by the heavy rain. These are the characteristic karstic features known as *dolines* or swallowholes – conical depressions, usually ranging in diameter between 30 and 300 ft (10 and 100 m), with their floors lying 30, 60 or even more feet below the surrounding ground level. On the northern edge of the Imotsko Polje is a doline, formed in 1942, which looks like some enormous bomb crater, with almost

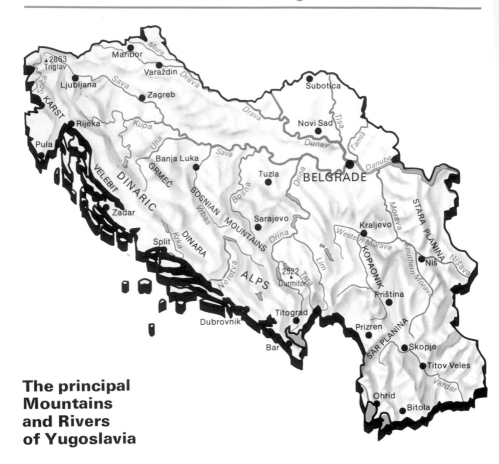

The principal Mountains and Rivers of Yugoslavia

vertical walls reaching down to a depth of some 1300 ft/400 m. Near this is a rather older crater of similar dimensions which already shows the gradual grading down of the sides. Smaller dolines can also be formed at the intersection of enlarged clefts. In many areas in the karstic upland region (for example on Mts Velebit and Orjen) one doline comes up against another, with only a narrow ridge between them; and when the intervening ridges in time disappear the dolines coalesce into a larger feature known as an *uvala*. Still larger depressions, surrounded on all sides by hills, are called *poljes*. These very typical karstic features have usually very flat floors covered with alluvial deposits of fertile terra rossa. The name polje ("field") reflects the agricultural importance of these basins of good soil in this otherwise barren upland region.

At the edges of many poljes, set at an angle to the floor of the depression, underground rivers emerge, flow through the polje and disappear again into a hole at the other end. Frequently, however, these holes (*ponori*) are too small to cope with the mass of water when the underground

rivers are swollen by heavy rain; the water then accumulates in the lowest part of the polje, and if the heavy flow of water continues the whole of the polje is transformed into a lake. In poljes lying at ground-water level this flooding can last for several months. They are usually dry again by the beginning of summer, but if the autumn rains come early they may again be flooded in late summer, and the peasants then have to make great haste to get the harvest in. The villages and hamlets in which they live naturally avoid the floor of the polje and stay out of reach of the water on the arid slopes around its edges which are not suitable for cultivation.

The water which sinks into the ground in the karstic uplands finds its way to the sea through underground channels, which have been explored only to a very small extent. Here and there can be seen sections of these subterranean "*tunnel valleys*" – e.g. the famous Postojna Caves through which the River Pivka flows, the course of the Reka in the Škocjan Caves and of the Lika in Croatia, the great resurgence at Mostar where the River

Buna emerges, etc. The underground connections of various rivers have been established by dyeing the water of one river and observing its emergence elsewhere. Many rivers, however, re-emerge after their disappearance into a *ponor* only in the form of *karstic springs* on the coast or even under the sea. Along the 250 miles/400 km of the Adriatic coast between Rijeka and Kotor Bay only four rivers reach the sea in deeply slashed, steep-sided valleys – the Zrmanja, the Krka, the Cetina and the Neretva. Surface watercourses are so rare in the karstic country that they acquire no names of their own but are known simply as Rijeka (Croat) or Reka (Slovene), "River". Only in the areas of less permeable clays and marls which occur here and there in the limestone region does a normal surface drainage system develop; but as soon as the rivers reach limestone territory they disappear underground like the others.

Human life in the karst regions is confined to the poljes, which are like oases in the stony desert. They are not large enough, however, to lead to any great concentrations of population; and the Dinaric uplands, broken up into compartments by their topographical structure, have remained thinly settled and backward by comparison with the more densely populated surrounding areas, in which some three-quarters of Yugoslavia's total population live. In these regions the Turkish thrust westward petered out: in the earlier stages of their advance they had followed the ancient traffic route which led from Byzantium by way of Philippopolis (Plovdiv) and Sofia to Belgrade, but in the Niš basin, where this road, running diagonally north-westward, ran into the N–S rift of the Morava and Vardar valleys, their westward drive lost its impetus. From Niš they dispersed their forces, moving into Serbia, Bosnia, Hercegovina and southward into Macedonia, where they met other Ottoman incomers who had travelled along the Aegean coast by way of Salonica. Here, on this "colonial" territory in the extreme W of the Ottoman empire, in the remoteness of the Dinaric mountain regions, there developed a province of authentically oriental character which has remained to this day more Turkish than Turkey itself. And yet most of the 2·8 million or so Moslems in Yugoslavia, representing 12% of the total population, are not in fact of Turkish origin but are the descendants of Slavs converted to Islam.

Thus the Dinaric uplands, in spite of their central geographical position within Yugoslavia, are not the country's economic and cultural heartland but rather a region which is under-populated, economically weak and culturally backward. The government is well aware of this and is seeking to promote the development of the area by the improvement of communications (Belgrade–Bar railway, motorway (highway) from Zagreb to Split planned), the harnessing of water-power, the working of minerals (non-ferrous metals, bauxite) and the establishment of industry (steelworks at Zenica and Nikšić, etc.); but so far these efforts have been only partly successful, to the extent that the better-off republics of Slovenia and Croatia have been ready to agree to, and to finance, a levelling-up of the standard of prosperity in Bosnia-Hercegovina, Montenegro, Macedonia and Kosovo. In spite of the often proclaimed fraternal unity of the individual federated republics, this readiness is not conspicuous. The younger members of the population move to Yugoslavia's few industrialised towns, to the tourist resorts on the coast, or seek employment as "guest workers" in Germany, Austria, Scandinavia (Sweden) and France. The result has been largely to destroy the traditional way of life of the Southern Slav extended family, which in the past has facilitated survival in bad times and in the inhospital natural conditions of this barren region. The old traditional attitudes – a mingling of poverty, generosity and pride – are now increasingly diluted by considerations of gain and practical advantage. Visitors travelling in Bosnia, Hercegovina and Montenegro are struck by their natural beauty and distinctive character; but they are now regions of rapid social change, whose inhabitants contemplate with some envy the faster development of the neighbouring republics, favoured both by nature and by history.

Around the Dinaric uplands lie three regions, each with a character and aspect of its own – to the N the Alpine foreland, merging into the Sava-Drava plain; to the W the Adriatic coastal region; and to the E the topographical patchwork of the Morava and Vardar valleys.

In the Julian Alps (Slovenia)

The northern frontier of Yugoslavia runs along the crest ridge of the southern calcareous Alps. In the **Karavanke** (*Karawanken*) range, the **Julian Alps** and the **Kamniške Alpe** (*Steiner Alps*) Yugoslavia possesses a considerable area of mountain territory of authentic Central European type, reaching its highest point in *Triglav* (9394 ft/2863 m), the country's highest peak. The pass roads running up from the Klagenfurt basin in Austria drop sharply down into the **South-Eastern Alpine Foreland**, matching the abrupt fall in the mountains themselves, which descend in one gigantic step to the karstic gateway of Postojna (1818 ft/554 m). The foothills of the southern calcareous Alps which fan out into the hill country of southern Styria (Austria) and the Sava uplands form the republic of **SLOVENIA** (*Slovenija*), in which forest-covered hills alternate with well-populated fertile plains. The natural heart of this region with its varied topographical pattern is the town of Ljubljana.

The line of the southern Alps is continued eastward by a number of horsts (areas of land thrown up between two parallel faults) made up of crystalline schists. To the N of the Croatian capital, Zagreb, is the Medvednica range. In the region between the rivers Drava and Sava rises the completely isolated range of the Moslavačka Gora. Mounts Papuk and Psunj form a substantial continuous range of medium height. The Fruška Gora, in the loess plain to the S of the Danube towns of Novi Sad and Petrovaradin, is the last of this series of "island ranges" – so called because they are bounded on the N and S by the broad water meadows of the Drava and the Sava and slashed by depressions and basins filled with late Tertiary diluvial and alluvial deposits.

Although the area between the rivers Drava and Sava forms the south-western edge of the great Pannonian plain it does not really share the continental climate of the plain. The western part of the area receives its rainfall from the SW winds of the Adriatic, and the temperature pattern begins to take on more continental characteristics only in the eastern part. The whole of the region between the rivers was an area of natural forest. In the 5th and 6th c. it was occupied by an immigrant Slav people, the Croats. During the Turkish wars, when it was a frontier region between the Habsburg and Ottoman empires, it suffered severe depopulation. Towards the end of the Turkish period the Roman Catholic Croats were joined by Orthodox refugees from the interior of the Balkan peninsula, who were settled by the Habsburgs in small fortified towns on the military frontier which ran from the Adriatic into Transylvania. Eastern **CROATIA** (*Hrvatska*), extending from the area around Bjelovar and the Sava depression to the ridge of the southern "island ranges" of mountains, was part of this frontier zone. From the end of the 17th c. many German officers and officials were stationed in the frontier territories, but German peasants did not begin to come into the area until after 1860, when settlers from the Sudenten region (now in Czechoslovakia) and the German-populated lands in the middle Danube valley established themselves in Slavonia and Srem (the region between the rivers), cleared tracts of forest and brought areas of marshland into cultivation. Large German villages laid out on a regular checkerboard plan were established in Srem (the eastern part of the region), smaller villages in the hilly country south of Osijek and Djakovo. The real Croatian heartland with its small villages and hamlets begins in the area of the rivers Čazma and Lonja.

German cultural influence is more evident in the towns of this northern frontier region of Yugoslavia than in the country areas. Purely Slav territories have relatively few towns, and the towns of present-day south-eastern Europe were originally either Roman, Byzantine, Turkish or German foundations. The areas with most towns tend to be those occupied by large German population groups; and the south-eastern Alpine foreland and Sava-Danube lowlands are the part of Yugoslavia with the largest number of towns.

Visitors entering Yugoslavia from Austria will no doubt at first be struck by much that is new and strange, but when they reach Zagreb they will feel themselves back in Central Europe. All the older public buildings, cafés, offices and private houses are in a style reminiscent of the Austro-Hungarian monarchy, and the churches and palaces are typical Austrian Baroque. This is hardly surprising, for most of the towns in northern Yugoslavia were the work of German architects and builders, following patterns with which they were familiar at home. Some of them were originally fortress towns, such as Karlstadt (now Karlovac), founded in 1579 at the junction of the rivers Korana and Kupa (Croatia). Others acquired importance as the sees of bishops. Many small towns were built along the frontier, all with a regular plan around a large square. – In more recent years developing industries have been established in these towns, and the south-eastern Alpine foreland and the region between the rivers are not merely the agricultural heartland of Yugoslavia but also its principal industrial area.

The **Adriatic coastal region**, the narrow strip of coast in Istria and Dalmatia with its fringe of offshore islands, is a world of its own. It is a coast without any hinterland, with the great limestone barrier of the Dinaric Alps rearing up only a short distance from the sea. There is only limited scope for agriculture on the rocky coastal plain and on the narrow terraces a little higher up; accordingly the people of this region have from time immemorial looked towards the sea. Of all the Slav peoples it is the Dalmatians who have produced the best seamen and ships' captains.

The much indented pattern of the coast, with its countless inlets and sheltered

Folk festival in Zagreb (Croatia)

Kotor Bay (Montenegro)

coves, was well calculated to promote the early development of seafaring. Everywhere the sea penetrates deep into the land, sometimes in a much ramified form (as in Kotor Bay, for example) reminiscent of the Norwegian fjords. These inlets, however, are of quite different origin from the fjords, for during the Ice Ages there were no glaciers in Yuglosavia reaching down to the sea as there were in Norway.

The superficial topography of the Adriatic coastal region is the result of recent folding movements. Depressions containing flysch marls (i.e. sediments produced by the erosion of fold structures) alternate with ridges of Cretaceous limestones, the flysch areas with their fertile soils and intensive cultivation contrasting sharply with the barren white hills. The *Vinodol valley* at the N end of the coast is a striking example of a cultivated area of this kind straggling between the desolate limestone ridges. The flysch depressions have frequently been much eroded by rivers, which in these areas do not seep away into the ground as in the limestone areas. As a result of the rise in sea level during the post-glacial period many of these depressions were flooded by the sea, giving rise to the channels between the islands which the limestone ridges then became. The islands and the channels show the same direction of "strike", from NW to SE, as the Dinaric mountains on the mainland. Since the gentler lower slopes of the hills have been drowned by the sea, the islands and peninsulas rise steeply out of the water in a manner characteristic of a region of marine transgression. This intimate mingling of sea and land and the alternation between the deep blue of the sea and the white of the limestone cliffs,

constantly lashed and eroded by the breakers, produce a succession of picturesque and constantly changing seascapes.

The Adriatic is a narrow offshoot of the Mediterranean, and Mediterranean climatic influences are not much felt at the northern end of the coastal region. The peninsula of **Istria** and the Gulf of Kvarner along its SE side lie in the transitional zone of the Central European mixed oak forest with its cold winters; but the olive-tree grows here, reaching a height of up to 1180 ft/360 m in sheltered situations. Farther S, particularly on the islands of **Dalmatia**, the evergreen scrub woodland or macchia of the Mediterranean predominates, producing flowers right through the winter, with tree heaths, pistachio, myrtle, strawberry tree and cistus at lower altitudes and laurel, holmoak and small-leafed lime higher up. The southern Dalmatian islands have forests of maritime pines. From about the region of Split the full Mediterranean vegetation pattern is found, with vines, figs, olives, almonds, carobs, cypresses, agaves and prickly pears. The higher slopes, however, are still covered with a sparse karstic heathland.

Cut off from inland Yugoslavia by a barrier of mountains, the coastal regions have received much stronger cultural influences from the western shores of the Adriatic than from the interior of southeastern Europe. The Slavs living along the coast were drawn into the spheres of influence of Rome and Venice, and towns such as Zadar, Šibenik, Trogir, Split, Dubrovnik and Kotor have a Romance and Mediterranean character in spite of the fact that their inhabitants were always predominantly Slavs. The coastal Slavs became Roman Catholics, while those beyond the Dinaric mountain barrier belonged mostly to the Orthodox Church.

The coastal towns, with their tall stone houses, their shady little stepped lanes and their magnificent late Gothic and Renaissance palaces, have nothing in common with other Yugoslav towns. The massive fortifications and the winged lions of St Mark which are everywhere to be seen are constant reminders of Venice's erstwhile maritime supremacy. After the fourth Crusade Venice held the whole of Dalmatia and parts of the Albanian coast, and after the fall of the Venetian republic

Dalmatia passed to Austria as Venice's heir.

Dubrovnik (*Ragusa*), the "Queen of the Adriatic", was able to hold out against the might of Venice, and developed into a powerful commercial republic which had close trading relations with all the Balkan countries, while remaining independent of Turkish political influence. But here too Venetian cultural influence was strong: the merchants of Dubrovnik were always known to the Bulgarians, for example, as the "Latins".

On this Adriatic coast of Yugoslavia the work of nature and the work of man's hands combine to produce scenery of unique beauty and harmony.

The last of the three peripheral regions of Yugoslavia is the **Morava-Vardar rift**, running for 300 miles/500 km from N to S, formed by the valleys of the Morava and the Vardar, their head waters separated by a watershed only 1510 ft/460 m high at Preševo (north of Kumanovo). The two rivers, which flow respectively into the Danube and the Aegean, thus provide a convenient and almost straight route through eastern Yugoslavia (and through the middle of south-eastern Europe) from the Pannonian plain to the sea. It is not surprising, therefore, that this route, like the other great route which runs diagonally south-eastward via Sofia and Philippopolis (Plovdiv) to Constantinople, became one of the major highways of human migration in south-eastern Europe. The two routes intersect on Yugoslav soil in the *Niš basin*, which thus occupies a key position as a hub of traffic and communications.

At the northern and southern ends of the Morava-Vardar rift are Belgrade and Salonica. The fact that these two cities are different countries, with a political boundary cutting across Belgrade's access route to the sea, obviously reduces

Dubrovnik – the pearl of the Adriatic coast

Kazan Defile on the Danube (Serbia)

the economic importance to Yugoslavia of this route; but the historical and political development of this part of south-eastern Europe had led inevitably to the drawing of this frontier line.

The Morava-Vardar rift runs through a region with a typically Balkan tectonic pattern – a patchwork of sunken basins separated and enclosed by massive horsts (upthrown areas) running longitudinally and transversely to produce alternating areas of high and low ground. The larger basins, however, with the towns on which they are sited, are by no means isolated from one another, but are linked by the Morava and the Vardar which cut through the intervening ranges of hills in deeply slashed valleys. The basins lying on either side of the N–S rift are connected with the main traffic route by side valleys of the two main rivers or by relatively low ridges of hills.

The northern part of this eastern peripheral region is occupied by **SERBIA** (*Srbija*). From the Sava and Danube lowlands the land gradually rises towards the W, S and E as if in some gigantic amphitheatre – in the W towards the Dinaric Alps, in the E towards the mountain arc linking the Balkan Mountains (Stara Planina) with the Transylvanian Alps. At first there are only individual rounded hills and upland ridges rising above the marshy meadows in the valleys; then, farther S, there follow chains of mountains rising to over 3300 ft/1000 m, such as the curving range which includes Mt Rudnik, the Gledičske Planine, the

Kučaj Planina, Mt Lisac and the Miroč Planina. The short chains of the Jelica Planina, Krivača, Jastrebac Planina and Ozren Planina reach heights of over 6500 ft/1500 m and finally the Kopaonik range rears up to over 4900 ft/2000 m.

Northern Serbia, with the plains of the lower Morava and Kolubara valleys, still shows all the characteristic features of the Pannonian plain. Large scattered villages surrounded by fruit orchards lie amid great expanses of maize- and wheatfields. The dominant base of this region is **Belgrade** (*Beograd*), in a bridgehead situation at or near the junction of the Sava, the Tisa, the Tamiš and the Morava with the **Danube** (*Dunav*). Situated just above the barrier of the Transylvanian Alps, through which the Danube carves a passage negotiable only with difficulty, the city directs traffic making for south-eastern Europe into the Morava valley: it is a gate for entry into Central Europe and for access, in the other direction, into south-eastern Europe. Its name means "white city", and during the Middle Ages it was known as the "Greek White City"; Greek merchants came here with their precious wares to negotiate their onward transmission into Hungary.

The formation of the modern Yugoslav state had its origins in Belgrade. The capital of the old principality of Serbia was Kragujevac in Central Serbia, adjoining which to the SW is the historic region of Raška. This was the area of origin of the Serbian people, and the Serbs were known to medieval travellers as Rascians. The old territory is a bleak upland region mainly inhabited by a population of stock-farmers.

In *southern Serbia* the patchwork pattern of alternating hills and depressions is particularly evident. One of the larger low-lying areas is the famous Kosovo Polje (Field of Kosovo), scene of the battle with the Turks in 1389 which destroyed the old Serbian kingdom.

Beyond the Morava-Vardar watershed is the *Skopje basin*, within the republic of **MACEDONIA** (*Makedonija*). This is the beginning of the real "Balkan" part of Yugoslavia, with its dry summers. In terms of landscape, history and culture the territory of Macedonia includes much more than the Yugoslav republic of that name: it is an extensive area which also takes in parts of Greece (Aegean Macedonia) and Bulgaria (Pirin Macedonia). The core of the population consists of Slavs, speaking a language similar to Bulgarian and Serbian, together with Turks, Albanians, Serbs and other minorities. As a result of the Balkan Wars Macedonia was incorporated in Serbia, and since the end of the Second World War it has been one of the six federal republics of Yugoslavia.

In the extreme southern tip of Macedonia is the region of the *Dessaretic Lakes*. In this area parts of the earth's crust have sunk down and formed basins which then filled with water, as happened in many basins along the Morava-Vardar line; but here most of the basins were subsequently drained by rivers, leaving *Lake Ohrid* and *Lake Prespa* as the only large basins still filled with water.

The adjoining *Bitola (Monastir) basin* still has an area of marshland in the middle, showing that it too once contained a lake. Bitola and the other towns in the southern section of the Morava-Vardar rift show all the marks of Byzantine and Old Slav culture. They are pleasant little garden cities of single-storey verandaed houses

climbing up the hillside. The intensive market gardening, the attention given to the maintenance of the irrigation systems and the costumes of the people all point to long-standing relations with the south; but these are in no sense "Greek" towns. The population is Slav, of either the Orthodox or the Mohammedan faith, with minorities of Aromanians, Albanians and a small number of Turks.

Thus the cultural geography of the Morava-Vardar valleys is more varied than that of any other Yugoslav region, extending from the Central European influences found in the N to the Greek characteristics of the S. There are also elements of Latin origin – the *Aromanians* were originally Romanised Thracians and Illyrians going back to the Roman penetration of south-eastern Europe – and also many oriental features. The Slav-populated towns with their bazaars and mosques, some based on Byzantine foundations, others newly established by the Turks in this colonial territory, reflect the very distinctive cultural synthesis achieved in this central Balkan region – for it is only within the structure of the present-day Yugoslav state that this ancient heartland of south-eastern Europe has become a peripheral territory.

Bathing beach on Lake Prespa (Macedonia)

Climate

Yugoslavia lies within three different climatic zones. Slovenia in the NW, with mountains rising to Alpine heights, belongs to the temperate zone of Central Europe; to the SE, extending to the Greek frontier, is the main part of the country, with a climate of continental character; while the Adriatic coastal strip beyond the coastal chain of mountains rising to almost 6560 ft/2000 m, with its fringe of offshore islands, is a subtropical region with a Mediterranean climate.

The climatic character of these different regions is marked by their varying patterns of temperature and rainfall over the year. Considering first the **temperatures**, the Slovenian capital of Ljubljana (alt. 1004 ft/306 m) is typical of the NW of the country with its Central European climate: annual average 48·9°F/9·4°C, January 28·8°F/−1·8°C, July 64·8°F/18·2°C, annual range 36°F/20°C. In the mountains the temperature falls by about 0·9°F/0·5°C for every 300 feet, though with a frequent occurrence of "temperature reversal" on clear winter days.

In the main part of Yugoslavia with its continental climatic pattern of warm summers and relatively cold winters average temperatures remain much the same from NW to SE, since the rise in temperature towards the S is balanced by the fall in winter temperatures towards the E, leaving the annual average unchanged. Thus Zagreb (alt. 535 ft/163 m), Novi Sad (262 ft/80 m), Belgrade (433 ft/132 m) and Niš (640 ft/195 m) have an annual average of 52·5°F/11·3°C, a January average of 32·9°F/0·5°C (Niš 31·5°F/−0·3°C), a July average of 70·7°F/21·5°C and an annual range of 37·8°F/21°C (Niš 38·2°F/21·8°C). At towns even farther S including Peć (alt. 1706 ft/520 m) and Cetinje (2202 ft/671 m), which have broadly similar temperatures, the more southerly latitude is balanced by greater altitude.

Only in Macedonia does the July average reach 75·2°F/24°C: Skopje (alt. 787 ft/240 m; annual 64·5°F/12·5°C, January 34·7°F/1·5°C, July 75·2°F/24°C, range 40·5°F/22·5°C). Ohrid (alt. 2300–2600 ft/700–800 m) has in spite of its altitude a mild maritime climate: annual average 53·2°F/11·8°C, January 37°F/2·8°C, July 69·8°F/21°C, range 32·8°F/18·2°C. Relatively extreme figures are found in the N at Slavnoski Brod (alt. 308 ft/94 m; annual 48·6°F/9·2°C, January 30·2°F/−1°C, July 72·5°F/22·5°C, range 42·3°F/23·5°C) and in the S, near the Greek frontier, at Negotino (alt. 489 ft/149 m; annual 53·1°F/11·7°C, January 28·4°F/−2°C, July 74·8°F/23·8°C, range 46·4°F/25·8°C).

Considerable variations from these average figures may arise from local weather conditions – which are also likely to have a marked effect on the rainfall – and from particular topographical circumstances. Examples of temperatures in high mountain areas are: Bjelašnica Planina (SW of Sarajevo, alt. 6782 ft/2067 m) annual 33·6°F/0·9°C, February 19·4°F/−7°C, July 48·2°F/9°C, range 28·8°F/16°C; Kopaonik Planina (W of Niš, alt. 6618 ft/2017 m) annual 39·7°F/4·3°C, January 20·3°F/−6·5°C, August 56·3°F/13·5°C, range 36°F/20°C.

The annual averages for the subtropical coastal towns are between 5·4°F/3°C and 9°F/5°C higher than for the interior of the country, rising from 57·2°F/14°C in the N (Rijeka), by way of 57·7°F/14·3°C at Pula, 59·5°F/15·3°C at Rab (at nearby Gospić, on the karstic plateau, 47.5°F/8·6°C) and 60·2°F/15·7°C at Mali Lošinj and Split, to 61.2°F/16·2°C in the S (Hvar, Dubrovnik, Herceg-Novi; Budva 60·6°F/15·9°C). The January figures range from 43·2°F/6·2°C at Rijeka to 46·8°F/8·2°C at Hvar and Budva, the July figures from 72·5°F/22·5°C at Rijeka to 77°F/25°C at Zadar, Split and Budva (Mostar and Titograd, inland, 78·8°F/26°C). The annual range varies between 27°F/15°C at Mali Lošinj (slight influence of bora) and 32·4°F/18°C at Zadar and Split (Mostar 36°F/20°C, Titograd 40°F/22·2°C).

Particularly during the winter, temperatures are depressed by the *bora*, a cold dry fall wind blowing down from the karstic plateau: annual average at Kraljevica, near Rijeka, 40·1°F/4·5°C. The *sirocco*, a hot and humid S wind which occasionally precedes cyclones, particularly during the winter months, has an enervating effect. The *maestral* is a refreshing wind which blows in from the sea on fine summer days.

The **surface temperature of the sea** in winter rises from 48°F/9°C in the Gulf of Trieste to 55°F/13°C at Budva. In summer it rises above 77°F/25°C only in the most northerly and most southerly parts of the Adriatic; between Rijeka and Split it is about 72°F/22°C, at Hvar and Dubrovnik about 75°F/24°C.

In Slovenia the **rainfall** is distributed over the whole year, with a minimum in February and a maximum in summer or autumn (Ljubljana annual 56 in./1415 mm, February 2·7 in./68 mm, October 5·9 in./150 mm). Triglav (9394 ft/2863 m) has the highest level of precipitation in the Eastern Alps, an annual 118 in./3000 mm.

In the continental part of Yugoslavia annual precipitation increases from W to E and from N to S, with a maximum in autumn (in the W) or early summer and, to a lesser extent, in autumn, and a minimum (increasingly marked towards the S) in summer:

Gospić annual 71 in./1810 mm, July and August each 3·7 in./93 mm, October 9 in./230 mm; Bihać annual 53 in./1354 mm; Banja Luka annual 42 in./1070 mm, minimum in February 2·2 in./57 mm, August 3·3 in./83 mm, maximum in May 4·9 in./125 mm, October 4·4 in./112 mm; Novi Sad annual 26 in./652 mm; Belgrade annual 26 in./655 mm, minima in February 1·4 in./36 mm and September 1·8 in./46 mm, maxima in June 3 in./77 mm and October 2·4 in./60 mm; Niš annual 21 in./530 mm; Skopje annual 17·4 in./443 mm, minima in July 0·75 in./19 mm and January 1 in./26 mm, maxima in May 2·1 in./54 mm and December 1·9 in./48 mm; Zagreb and Sarajevo annual 35 in./888 mm.

Places in the Montenegrin mountains in the vicinity of the coast have the highest rainfall in Europe: Kolašin (alt. 3104 ft/946 m) annual 106 in./2700 mm, November 14·4 in./365 mm, July 1·9 in./47 mm; Cetinje (2202 ft/671 m) annual 136 in./3452 mm, November 22 in./560 mm, August 1·4 in./36 mm, Crkvice (3610 ft/1100 m, on the slopes of Mt Orjen above Kotor Bay) annual 183 in./4640 mm, December 26 in./660 mm, August 2·8 in./72 mm – the absolute maximum for Europe. Abundant winter falls of snow in the mountains of Montenegro offer scope for winter sports even in this southern latitude.

In the subtropical coastal zone rainfall becomes lower from the N to about half way down the coast and then increases again towards the S. The maximum is in autumn, the minimum (increasingly marked towards the S) in July or August: Rijeka annual 63 in./1595 mm, October 8·5 in./215 mm, July 3 in./77 mm; Rab annual 42 in./1072 mm, October 5·5 in./140 mm, August 1·7 in./43 mm; Zadar annual 35 in./889 mm; Split annual 36 in./914 mm, July 1·2 in./30 mm; Hvar annual 31 in./781 mm, July 0·8 in./20 mm; Dubrovnik annual 54 in./1361 mm, July 1·3 in./33 mm; Herceg-Novi annual 70 in./1787 mm, November 11·8 in./300 mm, July 1·3 in./33 mm; Budva annual 65 in./1655 mm, December 8·7 in./220 mm, July 0·75 in./19 mm.

History

Occupation of the territory and establishment of the first settlements by Slavs. – The territory of present-day Yugoslavia is first occupied by Stone Age peoples. – In historical times the stock-herding and seafaring Illyrians settle in the W, the Thracians in the E.

7th c. B.C. The **Greeks** begin to found colonies on the Adriatic coast (Hvar, etc.).

229 B.C. With their war against the **Illyrians** the **Romans** set out on the conquest of the Balkan peninsula, which is completed only in the time of Augustus, after stubborn fighting. The population is Romanised: only SE of a line from Scutari via Skopje and Niš to the Balkan Mountains do Greek linguistic and cultural influences predominate. Roman provincial culture is diffused throughout the country (Split, Salona, Pula).

A.D. 395 After the division of the Roman Empire the part of the country E of a line from Belgrade to Scutari comes under Byzantine rule, soon followed by the rest of the country.

6th–7th c. The **Slavs**, advancing southward through the Carpathians from their original homeland from the end of the 5th c., are subjugated by the **Avars** in 567. From the reign of *Justinian* onwards they make frequent raids over the Danube, and later undertake joint plundering expeditions with the Avars (destruction of Sirmium in 582, of Salona in 614). In the time of *Heraclius* they establish permanent settlements in the Balkans. The Romanised inhabitants (Vlachs) withdraw to the mountain regions. On the Adriatic coast they are able to maintain their language and culture, but here too they succumb to Slav influence after the year 1000. The Slavs bring with them their tribal and family structures and their natural religion, but in their new settlements they come into the sphere of influence of the old-established advanced cultures and of *Christianity*.

8th c. Only the **Slovenes**, who have advanced deep into the Alpine valleys in the NW, establish any state of their own. They are ruled by their own dukes, but for the purposes of defence against the Avars are obliged to submit to the suzerainty of the Bavarians (Bajuwari) and from 788 of the Franks.

823 After a rising led by a Croat named *Ljudevit* the Slovene dukes are replaced by German counts. Thereafter, until 1918, the political destinies of the Slovenes are bound up with those of The German Empire or the Habsburg state.

799 After Charlemagne's victory over the Avars first PANNONIAN CROATIA and soon afterwards DALMATIAN CROATIA come under Frankish rule.

Mid 9th c. *Trpimir* establishes a national dynasty in the coastal region. Under *Zdeslav* it breaks free of Frankish rule. Under *Branimir* it casts off Byzantine overlordship and is involved in conflict with the Bulgars and with Venice.

925 *Tomislav* assumes the style of king, after incorporating Pannonian Croatia in his principality during the struggle against the Hungarians.

9th c. The **establishment of a Serbian state**, brought about by the defensive struggle against the first Byzantine kingdom and to some extent following Byzantine traditions, begins in RAŠKA (RASCIA), the upland region watered by the rivers Ibar, Lim, Tara and Piva. Among its early rulers are *Višeslav* and *Vlastimir*. *Mutimir*, submitting to

Byzantine suzerainty, makes himself sole ruler and Christianises the country.

Christianity is spread among the Slovenes in the NW by Bavarian missionaries (8th c.), among the Croats by Franks or from Aquileia (beginning of 9th c.), among the Serbs through Byzantine influence (9th c.). The Serbs are converted to the faith of the Eastern Church by *Cyril* and *Methodius*, the Apostles of the Slavs. The Slav (Glagolitic) mass also makes progress in coastal Croatia (diocese of Nin), but in association with the Western rite. At synods held in 925 and 928, however, it meets with strong resistance from the archdiocese of Split, successor to ancient Salona.

10th c. After the conquest of eastern Bulgaria by the Byzantines (972) *Tsar Samuel* establishes a powerful kingdom in MACEDONIA, which after fierce fighting is defeated and annexed by Byzantium in 1018. Its ecclesiastical heart, the archiepiscopal see of Ohrid, remains independent (autocephalous).

The medieval states until the coming of the Turks. Although externally powerful, King Tomislav's Croatian kingdom has to contend with serious domestic difficulties: the struggle for power by noble families and conflicts between Latins and Slavs and between the Latin and Slav churches give rise to continuing tensions. Under *Stefan Držislav* (969–995; crowned king of Croatia and Dalmatia c. 988) the kingdom enjoys a period of prosperity with the support of Byzantium, which makes over to it the coastal towns and offshore islands.

11th c. After suffering defeats at the hands of Venice and again coming under Byzantine overlordship (1019) the Croatian kingdom prospers under *Krešimir IV* (1058–73), though the internal conflicts remain.

1060 The Glagolitic form of worship is banned by the Papal Curia.

1090 The dying out of the native dynasty gives rise to a struggle for the throne. *Peter Svačić* is elected king, but is killed in 1097 in a battle with the Hungarians.

1102 Under an agreement with the Hungarian king *Koloman*, the "Pacta Conventa", Croatia is joined with **Hungary** in a personal union, making it increasingly dependent on that country. The nobility remain jealous to maintain Croatian rights and interests.

13th–14th c. Hungary inherits from Croatia the struggle for Dalmatia. After the Mongol incursion of 1241 *Béla IV* divides the country into the two Banats of CROATIA-DALMATIA and SLAVONIA, in which powerful noble families gain the hereditary status of Banus. *Ludovic I* brings the nobility to heel and compels Venice to renounce its claim to Dalmatia.

1409 *Ladislas of Naples* sells his rights in Dalmatia to Venice, which in the following decades takes possession of the Dalmatian towns and islands, holding on to them until the fall of the Venetian republic in 1797.

The *liberation of Serbia from Byzantine control* begins in ZETA (Montenegro), which becomes independent under *Stefan Vojislav* in 1042. His son *Michael* (1051–81) is granted the title of king by Pope *Gregory VII* in 1077. Bar is raised to the status of an archiepiscopal see in 1067. *Bodin* (1081–1101) extends Serbian territory in the E and SE at the expense of Byzantium. In the course of time the eastern upland regions become predominant.

1168 *Nemanja*, founder of the Nemanjić dynasty, becomes Great Župan of Rascia and enlarges its territory, which by 1190 includes not only Rascia but land W of the Morava, Kosovo and Zeta. In 1196 he withdraws into Studenica monastery, after strengthening Orthodoxy by the suppression of the Bogomil sect.

1217 *Stephen the First Crowned* receives the royal crown from the Pope.

1219 Nemanja's youngest son, *St Sava*, obtains from the Patriarch in Nicaea the recognition of an independent Serbian archbishopric, of which he becomes first archbishop (Žiča), and organises the new Church. The State and the Church can thus join forces to develop the separate identity of Serbia. Thereafter the young kingdom of Serbia comes into conflict with the second Bulgarian kingdom, Hungary and Byzantium, now reasserting its strength; but with large revenues from mining and trade it is able to consolidate its position, and in the reign of King *Milutin* (1282–1321) conquers northern Macedonia.

1330 After a victorious battle at Velbužd Serbia has nothing to fear from Bulgaria. It becomes the dominant power in the Balkans and threatens Byzantium's position there.

1346 *Dušan* (1331–55) has himself crowned Emperor of the Serbians and Greeks and establishes an independent Serbian patriarchate. The conquest of Byzantine provinces extending as far as the Gulf of Corinth strengthens Greek influence on the court, the administration and the whole culture of Serbia. Dušan recognises the danger of a further thrust into Europe by the Turks, who in 1354, shortly before his death, gain a foothold in the Balkans at Gallipoli.

BOSNIA, occupying an "in-between" situation, has a history of its own. The Bosnian heartland on the upper course of the River Bosna is at first under the influence of Zeta, but is conquered in 1136 by Hungary. At the end of the 12th c., under Banus *Kulin*, the Bogomil faith – the so-called "Bosnian" Church, regarded by the official Churches as heretical – gains many adherents. It finds support among the nobility and weakens the central royal authority. Bosnian rulers such as *Matija Ninoslav* (1232–50) who support Bogomilism have to contend with persecution by the Roman Curia and crusades by the Hungarians, during which the Bosnian state is reduced to the original heartland or (until 1322) is ruled by the Šubić family, a Croatian dynasty who hold the style of Banus of Croatia.

Advance of the Turks and fall of the southern Slav states. – Under Dušan's successor *Uroš* (1355–71) Serbia is split up into a number of petty states (under Vukašin in Macedonia, the Balšić family in Zeta, Prince Lazar in Morava-Serbia, etc.) which are unable to offer any resistance to the Turkish advance.

1371 The south-eastern princedoms are defeated by the Turks in the battle of the River Maritsa and their territories become Turkish provinces.

1389 **Battle of Kosovo** (the Field of Kosovo): Prince *Lazar* (1371–89), who contrives to unite and consolidate the northern territories (Kruševac, Pavanica), is defeated by Sultan *Murad I* in a battle in which both leaders are killed. The road into Europe now lies open to the Turks. After the fall of Bulgaria (1393–96) their further advance is delayed only by the defeat of *Bayezid I* at Angora (Ankara) in 1402.

First half of 15th c. Lazar's successors (with the style of "Despots") are driven steadily farther N, but by adroit political manoeuvring between the Hungarians and the Turks are able for a time to assert a measure of independence and even to achieve a fresh

cultural flowering (Manasija, Kalenić). Under *Djuradj Branković* (d. 1456), however, the situation becomes increasingly untenable after Turkish victories at Varna (1444) and Kosovo (1448), and particularly after the accession of *Mehmed II* and his conquest of Constantinople (1453).

1459 The capture of the Serbian capital, Smederevo, by the Turks marks the end of the medieval Serbian state.

In BOSNIA *Stefan Kotromanić* and, even more notably, Banus *Tvrtko* (1353–91) are able to take advantage of the situation of Serbia and Hungary to extend their authority to Hum (Hercegovina) and other areas. Tvrtko has himself crowned king of Serbia and Bosnia at the tomb of St Sava in Mileševa (1377) and conquers further Croatian territory in the W and NW. In the reign of his son, however, the decline of the kingdom begins.

1393 Hungarian suzerainty is again recognised.

1463 BOSNIA is conquered by the Turks. The northern part of its territory, with Jajce, passes to King *Matthias Corvinus* of Hungary.

1482 Hum (the "Duchy – Hercegovina – of St Sava"), which under *Stefan Kosača* had broken away from Bosnia, is conquered and annexed by the Turks.

1499 ZETA (Montenegro), ruled in the 15th c. by the Crnojević dynasty, with some degree of Venetian influence (capital Cetinje, where first printing press established 1494), is annexed by Turkey after a short period as a vassal state.

1526 The Turkish victory at Mohács puts an end to all resistance; but after the revivial of the Serbian Despotate in southern Hungary by Matthias Corvinus, the granting of fiefs to nobles and the settlement of Serbs from Hungary there is renewed resistance, led particularly by *Zmaj Ognjeni Vuk*.

1537 Death of the last Despot, *Pavel Bakić*.

At the beginning of the 15th c. the Turks thrust into CROATIA. The Croatian nobility suffer a devastating defeat in 1493. After the battle of Mohács the Turkish advance is facilitated by conflicts between the supporters of *J. Zápolya* and Ferdinand of Habsburg. Large territories (northern Bosnia, Lika, Krbava, Slovenia and the Croatian heartland as far as the rivers Sava and Kupa) fall to the Turks, so that after 1527 only a small portion of Croatian national territory (Banal Croatia, later known as "Civil Croatia") remains under Habsburg rule. Zagreb – the see of a bishop since 1094 – now becomes of increased importance as the heart of Croatian national life.

The centuries of Turkish rule. – Thus in the 15th and 16th c. most of present-day Yugoslavia is under Turkish rule. In the W only a narrow coastal strip and the offshore islands are held by Venice, while the NW is in Habsburg hands. – In the territories controlled by Turkey there is a rapid decline from the high standard of medieval culture, and their further development remains almost entirely untouched by western influences. Christians are obliged to pay a poll tax, and male children are liable to be carried off for service as soldiers for the sultan's guard (janissaries). Over much of the country, particularly in the towns, life increasingly follows an oriental pattern which has lasting effects, and the national cultural traditions are preserved only in the Church and in the extended family structure (*zadruga*) in the remoter areas. Apart from the large numbers of incomers from Anatolia (officials in the administrative areas, garrison troops, the semi-nomadic Yuruks in the Vardar valley) Islam secures many adherents among the native population, particularly in Bosnia and Hercegovina (perhaps favoured in these areas by the influence of Bogomilism), so that something like a third of the present-day population are still Moslems. Land is granted to the Turkish spahis (irregular troops) in return for an obligation to give military service. The Turkish conquest leads to a large-scale movement of population (refugees, settlers) to the N, W and NW, leading to the present-day mingling of nationalities in these areas. Off the great military highways, however, the old patriarchal national culture continues to develop its extraordinary abundance of artistic forms and traditions (heroic songs, love songs, songs for traditional occasions, folk music, folk dancing, folk art).

The re-establishment of the Patriarchate of Peć in 1557 is of great importance for the preservation of Serbian national consciousness, since its influence expands with the advance of the Turks and it comes to represent the national spirit of the whole of Serbia until 1766.

While the Church (in Bosnia particularly the Franciscans) thus acts as guardian of the national traditions, the *Uskoks*, fighting in the service of foreign powers and from the fall of Klis in 1537 until the mid 17th c. based at Senj, and the Hajduks, who keep up a running guerrilla war in the interior of the country, become the leaders of resistance and retaliation, and with the decline of Turkish power (17th–18th c.) increasingly give expression to the national aspirations for liberation. From the end of the 16th c. there are periodic risings against the Turks, stimulated by the Christian powers and sometimes supported by the Church, but these at first are unsuccessful.

In Venetian-held DALMATIA, the frontiers of which shift according to the progress of the Turkish wars, Venetian administration is introduced and Italian language and culture spread rapidly. Close cultural links with Italy lead in the 16th c. to an upsurge of humanist culture and Croatian literature, but the Turkish danger and political and economic difficulties bring on a decline in the 17th c. These Italian influences, however, leave an indelible imprint on Dalmatian life and culture.

The aristocratic republic of RAGUSA (Dubrovnik) occupies a special position. It recognises Byzantine and then (1205–1358) Venetian suzerainty, and models its administration on Venice, with a Rector (*knez*, "prince") and a council of nobles. Thereafter it is under Hungarian suzerainty until 1526, when it becomes tributary to the Turks. Throughout the centuries, however, it contrives – without any great area of territory or any considerable military forces – to maintain its *de facto* independence. Becoming wealthy through its maritime and Balkan trade and maintaining close relationships with Italy (humanism, Renaissance), it develops in the 16th–18th c. into a flourishing hub of literature (Petrarchism; Renaissance comedies by M. Držić; Baroque epic, "Osman", by I. Gundulić) and art. Its prosperity declines after an earthquake in 1667, but it remains a hub of learning and literature until Napoleon puts an end to its independence in 1808.

CROATIA suffers great loss and destruction during the Turkish wars, which hold up its cultural development. To provide protection against Turkish incursions the Habsburgs establish the "Military Frontier" in Croatia and Slavonia in the mid 16th c., manning it with Southern Slav soldier-peasants. The frontier area is under military administration and – in spite of protests by the Croatian Diet – remains outside the control of the civil authorities; it is not finally abolished until 1882.

As a result of the Turkish presence, feudal oppression and heavy financial burdens and social obligations the condition of the peasants deteriorates in the 16th c., and popular discontent finds vent in bloody risings in Carniola (1525, and again later) and Croatia (1573, led by Matija Gubec). The Reformation, coming in from Germany, finds rapid support in *Carniola*, and with the support of German Protestants *Primož Trubar* (1508–86) and his associates create a Slovenian written language and thus lay the foundations of a national literature. In Croatia (Zagreb, Varaždin) the Reformation leads to the development of a literature in the *kaj* dialect (resembling Slovene).

Decline of Turkish power: the movement for national liberation. – Apart from the major Turkish wars and the activity of the Haiduks in the interior of the country there are continual minor wars on the Turkish frontiers with Austria and Venice. At the beginning of the 17th c. (peace treaty, 1606) Turkish power passes its peak. This is the beginning of the process of driving the Turks steadily farther back which marks the history of Yugoslavia during the 18th and 19th c.

1686, 1688 Capture of Buda and Belgrade. The Imperial forces pushing forward in the Balkans are supported by the Serbs and their Patriarchs.

1690 Tens of thousands of Serbian families, led by the Patriarch, are obliged to withdraw into southern Hungary along with the troops. Thereafter the "Old Serbian" territory (now Kosovo), thus partly depopulated, is occupied by increased numbers of Albanian settlers.

1697 *Prince Eugene of Savoy*'s victories (Senta, 1698) and the Peace of Karlowitz (1699) liberate Hungary, Slavonia and part of Croatia from Turkish rule.

1718 After the war of 1716–18 northern Serbia remains under Imperial control (until 1738). During the withdrawal there is a further movement of Serbs into southern Hungary.

1766 The Serbian Patriarchate of Peć is abolished during the increased repression undertaken in reprisal for support of the Christian powers. The Turkish war waged by the Emperor Joseph II brings no change in the situation, in spite of the taking of Belgrade (1788).

In SOUTHERN HUNGARY (broadly the present Vojvodina) the Serbs are granted special privileges, in particular the autonomy of their Church. In 1699 the Military Frontier is extended to take in this area. In spite of the difficulties of the time (oppression by the Hungarian landowning nobility, efforts to secure Church unity, rising led by P. Segedinac in 1735, emigration to Russia) the Serbs are able to assert their national identity, to build up a prosperous middle class and to lay the foundations of a national culture in the fields of education, literature (D. Obradović) and the press – all of which later facilitates the Europeanisation of the non-liberated areas.

MONTENEGRO, occupying a special situation by virtue of the nature of the country and its social structure, makes successful efforts to achieve liberation, at first under Venetian influence (1684) and later, under the leadership of Bishop *Danilo Petrović* (1700–35) and his successor, in close association with Russia. The fragmentation and the feuding of the various clans are controlled by the assertion of the spiritual and political authority of the Bishop of Cetinje, leading, in the reign of *Peter I, the Saint* (d. 1830), to the establishment of a kind of theocratic state.

The Croatian territory which is liberated at the end of the 17th c., with vigorous participation by the Croats themselves, is – against the will of the Croatian Diet – incorporated in the military frontier instead of being assigned to "Civil Croatia". The absolutist attitudes of the government in Vienna and the discontent of the nobility lead in the reign of the Emperor *Leopold I* to a conspiracy by the great nobles of Hungary-Croatia and to negotiations by the magnate *Peter Zrinski* with foreign powers and finally with the Turks. For this Zrinski and *Krsto Franjopan* are executed in Wiener Neustadt in 1671. During the 18th century the popular resistance to the centralising policies of Vienna and the reforms introduced by *Joseph II* (new administrative divisions, German as official language) lead to a closer association with Hungary and (1791) the introduction of Hungarian into Croatian schools.

Emergence of the new Serbian and Montenegrin states; national "rebirth" of the Croats and Slovenes. – The decline of Turkey and the participation of Serbian irregular forces in the Austrian wars against the Turks raise the Serbs' hopes of liberation.

1804   Popular rising in the Šumadija against the rule of terror by the sultan's guard in the Belgrade pashalik (territory governed by a pasha) which had been resumed in 1799. The movement, which is not at first directed against the Porte, is led by *Karadjordje*. Victories over the Turkish army (1805–06) and the capture of Belgrade create the desire for full independence, guaranteed by one of the great powers.

In the liberated territory the elements of a national administrative organisation are established, with Karadjorje as "leader" (*vodja*); but internal dissensions and external circumstances, with Turkish superiority, lead to the collapse of the movement.

1813   Karadjordje flees to Austria.

1815   A further rising is led by *Miloš Obrenović*, who, after winning military victories, achieves by skilful negotiating tactics (with Russian support from 1826) internal self-government and a hereditary principality (1830).

1839   Constitutional conflicts lead to the abdication of Obrenović. In spite of repeated changes of ruler (1842, 1858) and constant party strife the new state is consolidated, gains the protection of the great powers in 1856 and becomes a focus for the aspirations of Serbs still under Turkish rule. At the same time *Vuk Stefanović Karadžić* (d. 1864) lays the foundations of a new national culture with his reform of Cyrillic orthography and the literary language.

1860–68   Prince *Mihailo Obrenović* pursues an ambitious policy aimed at the liberation and unification of the Balkan peoples.

1867   After the intervention of the great powers Turkish garrisons in Serbia are evacuated.

1876   Following a rising in Hercegovina an unsuccessful war is fought with Turkey for the recovery of Bosnia.

1878   At the Congress of Berlin Serbian independence is recognised and it receives an accession of territory.

1882   **Serbia becomes a kingdom.**

The unsuccessful war against a reunited Bulgaria (1885), the arbitrary rule and Austrophile policy of the Obrenovićes and the persecution of the Radical Party, which has strong support among the peasants, increasingly alienate the dynasty from the people and lead in 1903 to an officers' plot (murder of the king

Peter II Njegoš

and queen), a change of dynasty and the introduction of parliamentary government.

MONTENEGRO, which under Bishop *Peter II Njegoš* (d. 1851), the greatest Serbian poet, acquires the essential attributes of a modern state and under Prince *Danilo* becomes a secular state, carries on successful military operations against the Turks during the 19th c.

1878   Montenegro gains full independence and considerable accessions of territory in the reign of *Nikola* (1860–1918; king from 1910).

1809   Napoleon forms the **Illyrian Provinces**, with Ljubljana as their capital, from the territories acquired in 1806 and after the Peace of Schönbrunn – Istria, Dalmatia, Carniola, Gorizia and parts of Croatia.

1815   The Illyrian Provinces are returned to Austria.

IN CROATIA, in reaction against policies of Germanisation and increasingly ruthless Magyarisation, there comes into being under the leadership of *Ljudevit Gaj* the national cultural movement known as **Illyrianism**, drawing its inspiration from a variety of sources (the French Revolution, the Romantic movement, the example of other peoples), which gains wide support among the young and the middle classes for the idea of a national language and culture, solves the problem of the literary language (Serbo-Croat) in 1836 and takes as its aim the cultural unification of all Southern Slavs ("Illyrians"). With this "Croatian rebirth" it creates modern Croatian culture and political consciousness (the later National Party).

1848   The Croats, led by Jelačić as Banus, and the Serbs in southern Hungary (Vojvodina) take up the struggle against Hungarian dominance, but the neo-absolutist regime takes harsh counter-measures. Nevertheless the special privileges of the nobility are finally abolished and Zagreb is raised to the status of an archiepiscopal see (1852).

1868   After the establishment of the Dual (Austro-Hungarian) Monarchy the **Croatian-Hungarian Compromise** gives Croats in Hungary autonomy in internal affairs, education and justice. In other areas, however, the policy of Magyarisation remains in force.

Culturally Croatia makes rapid progress in the second half of the 19th c. (University, Yugoslav Academy). While *Bishop J. Strossmayer* advocates Yugoslav unity the Party of Rights led by *A. Starčević* raises the banner of Croat nationalism and the idea of Greater Croatia (1880s onward). The mass of the peasants are organised into a political movement for the first time in the Peasant Party of the brothers *Ante* and *Stjepan Radić*.

The **Slovenes** achieve their national revival, at first in the cultural field (under the influence of Baron Ž. Zois and his circle), at the end of the 18th c. Reacting against Illyrianism, they solve the question of their literary language and, by the same token, that of Slovenian cultural unity. The 1848 revolution stimulates the first emergence of the idea of political unity, which is taken up by the "Young Slovenes" in the 1860s. By the end of the century the Slovenian people is a fully formed social and political entity, with its own political parties.

In spite of differing histories and religious and cultural differences and of the political and cultural regionalism to which they give rise, the idea of Yugoslav cultural unity finds recurring expression from the period of the Reformation onwards (the idea of a common literary language, Illyrianism, "Yugoslavism"), but hardly ever gains clear political form.

First World War; the kingdom of Yugoslavia. – Under *Peter I* (1903–21) Serbia pursues a consistent policy directed towards the liberation of the territories under foreign rule. The Customs War (1906) and even more the Austrian annexation in 1908 of Bosnia and Hercegovina, which had been under Austrian administration since 1878, exacerbate relations with the Dual Monarchy, particularly since the Serbian national revolutionary movement is gaining strength there.

1912   The **First Balkan War**, in which Serbia, Montenegro, Bulgaria and Greece are ranged against Turkey, brings the occupation of Old Serbia and Macedonia.

1913   The partition of Macedonia leads to the **Second Balkan War** (Serbia and Greece against Bulgaria), in which Bulgaria is defeated. Under the treaty of Bucharest Macedonia is ceded to Serbia, but the establishment of an independent Albania frustrates the Serbian aspiration for access to the Adriatic.

1914   During the **First World War**, the occasion for which is the assassination of the heir to the Austrian throne in Sarajevo, the Serbs at first hold out against superior forces, but after Bulgaria's entry into the war (1915) are compelled to withdraw through Albania to Corfu. In 1918 they take part in the breakthrough on the Salonica front.

Serbia's military successes shortly before the First World War enhance its reputation and give a stimulus to the idea of unity. During the war the London Yugoslav Committee (1915) and the Serbian government's Corfu declaration (Pact of Corfu, 1917) call for the formation of a Kingdom of the Serbs, Croats and Slovenes. Towards the end of the war National Councils are formed which declare in favour of independence from Habsburg rule.

1918 (December 1)   **Proclamation of the new Kingdom of the Serbs, Croats and Slovenes** by the Prince Regent *Alexander*, in Belgrade.

1921   The new centralist constitution, which does not take account of the facts of history, meets with resistance, principally from the Croatian federalists. This conflict dominates internal politics and hampers the development of any clear line in foreign policy (Italy, Little Entente). After the murder of the Croatian peasant leader *Stjepan Radić* in 1928 it leads to a walk-out of the parliamentary Opposition, paralysing the working of Parliament.

1929 (January 6)   The king proclaims a dictatorship. The state is renamed the **Kingdom of Yugoslavia** and divided into nine Banats or provinces. All political parties are banned. The king seeks stabilisation in external affairs (Balkan Pact, 1934).

1934   After the assassination of King Alexander in Marseilles the regent, Prince Paul, attempts to rule with unified parties on the basis of the constitution granted in 1931.

1937   Treaties with Italy and Bulgaria designed to reduce international tensions.

1939   In a last-minute attempt to obviate domestic political difficulties an agreement (*Sporazum*) is reached granting Croatia extensive autonomy.

The international situation, leading up to the **Second World War**, allows no time for any real stabilisation. Domestic opposition grows in strength and the conflicts between the different peoples of Yugoslavia are aggravated.

1941 (March 27)   Yugoslavia's adherence to the Tripartite Pact provokes a coup d'état in Belgrade.

1941 (April 6)   German forces attack Yugoslavia.

1941 (April 10)   Proclamation of the **independent state of Croatia** under the Ustasha regime. The rest of Yugoslav territory is occupied by German, Hungarian, Italian and Bulgarian troops. After the occupation of Belgrade and the surrender of the Yugoslav army on April 17, 1941 King *Peter II* and the Yugoslav government go to London, where they form a government in exile. Large areas of Yugoslav territory are annexed by Germany, Hungary, Italy and Bulgaria, and territory ceded to Albania. In the autumn of 1941 General *D. Mihailović* organises national resistance with the aim of restoring a centralised monarchist state. He secures the cooperation for the time being of the Communist Party, led by Marshal *Tito* (*Josip Broz*, b. 1892). Agreement is reached on action by armed partisan groups.

1942   Tito forms the **Anti-Fascist Council of National Liberation of Yugoslavia** (AVNOJ) at Bihać, under his own leadership. King *Peter II*, in exile in London, does not return to Yugoslavia.

1943   After the surrender of Italy Tito's partisans are increasingly successful and the second AVNOJ session is held in Jajce.

1944 (October 20)   **Capture of Belgrade** by Soviet forces and Yugoslav partisans. Tito organises a new central government. "People's governments" are established in Serbia, Macedonia and Montenegro, and later in Croatia.

Establishment of the Federal People's Republic of Yugoslavia; its development into a socialist state. –The political and economic development of the new state bears the mark of its founder, Tito, who succeeds, in spite of continuing separatist aspirations, in unifying the country in a distinctively Yugoslav brand of socialism and in promoting its industrial development.

1945 (November 29)   Proclamation of the **Federal People's Republic of Yugoslavia**, consisting of the six people's republics of *Serbia*, including the autonomous regions of the Vojvodina and Kosmet (Kosovo-Metohija), *Croatia, Slovenia, Bosnia-Hercegovina, Montenegro* and *Macedonia*, with Tito as Premier.

1946 The new constitution, providing for a planned economy on socialist principles, is the basis for a rigorous agrarian reform and far-reaching nationalisations of industry and banking.

1947 Peace treaty with Italy: Yugoslavia receives areas in Venezia Giulia which are populated by Yugoslavs, together with Zara (Zadar).

1948 Tito's "national communism" leads to Yugoslavia's exclusion from Cominform and makes possible a cautious rapprochement with the West. There follow numerous commercial and economic treaties with the United States and other western countries.

1950 Beginning of decentralisation in the Yugoslav Communist Party and state. The establishment of a basic program for the conduct of the economy provides a basis for increased autonomy in state economic undertakings and greater decentralisation of policy and administration (federalism).

1953 New constitution: Tito is elected President of the Republic. The treaty of friendship now concluded with Greece and Turkey is directed against Soviet efforts to make Yugoslavia one of its satellite states. Tito visits Great Britain.

1954 **Balkan Pact** between Yugoslavia, Greece and Turkey, intended to last 20 years.
Under the Trieste Agreement with Italy, Zone A of the Trieste territory is to be administered by Italy, Zone B by Yugoslavia.
Beginning of policy of non-alignment.

1958 Economic agreement with the United States, following the Soviet withdrawal of credits previously offered.

1963 Change of name to **Socialist Federal Republic of Yugoslavia.** New constitution, with further decentralisation of government administration and the management of the economy.

Skopje destroyed by earthquake. Later it was rebuilt on a safer site nearby. Tito visits USA.

1964 Trade agreement with Comecon.

1968 Diplomatic relations established with Federal Republic of Germany.

1970 Tito meets Pope Paul VI.

1971 Constitution amended to provide for collective leadership (22 members).
Revival of separatist aspirations in Croatia.

1972 Political purge after unrest by Ustasha guerrillas.

1974 New constitution, making changes in the collective leadership (9 members of Presidium); Tito confirmed as President and party leader for life.
Further difficulties over Trieste (Zone B) – settled in 1975.
Tito visits the Federal Republic of Germany (agreement on financial assistance) and the German Democratic Republic.

1979 Severe earthquake on southern Adriatic coast, killing more than 90 people and destroying or severely damaging many thousands of buildings.

1980 The United States promise Yugoslavia assistance in the event of a military threat from the Soviet Union.
Belgrade Agreement with the EEC, providing for an expansion of trade.
Tito dies after a long illness (May 4).
Unrest in the autonomous province of Kosovo, the inhabitants of which (mainly Albanians) demand that Kosovo should become a seventh federated republic.

1981 After severe disturbance in Kosovo a state of emergency is declared in the province (April).

1982 12th Congress of the Yugoslav League of Communists in Belgrade (June). In October the dinar is devalued by 20%.

1983 State visit by the Soviet president, Nikolai Tichonow, with the aim of improving Soviet-Yugoslav relations (March). The Yugoslav government plans economic reform.

Art

Since Yugoslavia became an independent state only in 1918, the earlier political and cultural development of the different parts of the country showed considerable variation, making it difficult to give any unified and clearly structured account of the arts of Yugoslavia.

In 1965 excavation work for a hydro-electric power station at Kladovo, near the Iron Gates, brought to light the remains of a village (Lepenski Vir) some 8000 years old, dating from the earliest phase of the **Neolithic** period. The extraordinary and unique pieces of stone sculpture (human heads) found on this site were an archaeological sensation. In the later Neolithic period finds become more abundant. The *Danubian culture* is characterised by a type of pottery, thought to be of Near Eastern inspiration, with ribbons of parallel lines forming spirals, meanders, etc. The principal areas of this culture are in Serbian and Slavonian territory and around Butmir in Bosnia. The finds made on these sites include female idols. The hill settlements and fortified chieftains' houses protected by walls of mud-brick also show oriental influence. The finest material from this culture, which is dated between about 2500 and 1800 B.C., can be seen in the Regional Museum in Sarajevo, the National Museum in Belgrade and the Municipal Museum in Priština.

The knowledge of bronze-working travelled N from Asia Minor, influenced by Mycenaean culture. Among the principal areas of early **Bronze Age** culture (*c.* 1700 B.C.) are Ljubljana and Vučedol. From about 1300 B.C. the Bronze Age *Urnfield culture* appears, associated with the Illyrians, an Indo-European people, probably coming from the north (Únětice and Lusatian cultures), who settled in the NW of the Balkan peninsula and on the Adriatic. They are also associated with the Early Iron Age **Hallstatt culture** (*c.* 900–450 B.C.), found principally in Croatia and Bosnia. Common products of this period are long swords and situlas (bucket-shaped bronze vessels, frequently with rich relief decoration). There is interesting material of these periods in the National Museum in Ljubljana.

The area of Illyrian culture is bounded on the E by Thracian territory, and on the S it merges into the Greek sphere of influence. During the period of **Greek colonisation** from the 7th c. B.C. onwards a number of Greek settlements were founded within Yugoslavia. The most important of these was *Corcyra* (now Korčula), and there were other foundations at Vis and Hvar. Macedonia also lay within the Greek sphere. Magnificent examples of archaic Greek art were produced at Ohrid (Greek *Lychnidos*), Trebenište (gold masks and bronze vessels), Tetovo (statuette of maenad, now in Skopje Museum) and above all Novi Pazar (gold objects), and are well represented in the National Museum in Belgrade.

During its slow but steady rise to power **Rome** fought a war against the Illyrian pirates in 229–228 B.C., and by 219 the Illyrian coast was under Roman influence. The country was opened up by the construction of a dense network of Roman roads, and numbers of wealthy towns developed between the beginning of the Christian era and the period of the great migrations. Much fine Roman material can be seen in the archaeological museums of Pula (which has a large amphitheatre of the early Imperial period and a well-preserved temple of Augustus and Roma dedicated in A.D. 2 or 14), Zadar (Roman *Iaderna*) and Split and in the National Museum in Belgrade (bronze head of the Emperor Constantine, one of the three surviving copies of Phidias' Athena Parthenos).

Of particular interest, however, is the Roman site of Split. The present town has developed out of the huge palace built by Diocletian in A.D. 295–306 near the then important town of Salona (interesting remains of an amphitheatre, theatre, baths and a cemetery). After the destruction of Salona by the Avars in A.D. 615 the inhabitants sought refuge in the palace, then standing empty, and established a new town within its walls. The Palace of Diocletian is the mightiest monument of the Roman period in Dalmatia, resembling in its dimensions and layout a Roman castellum, and still houses a population of some 2500. Regular restoration work is carried on, and in recent years the imposing basement rooms have been cleared and opened to the public. Of the four gates of the palace the finest is the Porta Aurea. Diocletian's mausoleum is now the Cathedral, and the palace temple, dedicated to Jupiter, has become the baptistery.

When the Roman Empire was divided in A.D. 395 the cultural unity of the region was destroyed. In the 4th c., however, Christianity became established in the Empire, and by 600 the whole country was, more or less, Christianised. Remains of **Early Christian art** are particularly abundant in Dalmatia (Solin/*Salona*) and Macedonia (*Stobi*/Gradsko). Stobi was devastated by an earthquake in 518, but there are extensive remains of buildings on the site and much material from here can be seen in the National Museum in Belgrade and the Archaeological Museum in Skopje.

The Cathedral of Poreč (the Roman *Colonia Iulia Parentium*), the Basilica of Euphrasius, is the best preserved example of a Byzantine basilica of the 6th c., with magnificent mosaics in the style of Ravenna. At Lebane, near Leskovac, are the excavated remains of Caričin Grad, a fortified town built in the reign of Justinian (527–565), with regularly laid out streets, a forum, basilicas and a water supply system.

At the beginning of the 5th c., during the **great migrations**, there began a series of incursions by Germanic tribes, the Avars, the Huns and the Slavs. The Slavs took up settled life in the territory of Yugoslavia, laying the foundations of the population structure which still prevails. During the 6th c. the Croats were converted to Christianity by missionaries from Aquileia; in the 8th c. the Slovenes were converted from Salzburg and Aquilea. After their conversion by the "Apostles of the Slavs", *Cyril* and *Methodius*, the Serbs adhered to the Eastern Orthodox Church (*c.* 850). The political separation between West and East Rome was thus paralleled by the religious division between the Roman Catholic western Slavs and the Greek Orthodox eastern Slavs. The earliest examples of Slav art in Yugoslavia are to be found on the Dalmatian coast – still pre-Romanesque, but already reflecting Western European artistic sensibilities. The largest monument of this period is the two-storey round church of St Donatus in Zadar (now a museum), which was built in the early 9th c. on Roman foundations.

The small but finely proportioned church of St Barbara in Trogir (the Greek *Tra-*

gourion) is thought to date from the 8th c. This early architecture of the Slavs, now mingled with the Romanised urban population, shows the forms and the relatively modest dimensions characteristic of the building of this period throughout the whole of the western Mediterranean area. The buildings are decorated with relief ornament, most commonly in interlace patterns. A number of interesting items of this period are to be seen within the territory of the *old Croatian kingdom*, including the famous font of Prince Višeslav (beginning of 9th c.; now in the Yugoslav Academy, Zagreb) and various fragments of altar screens (museums in Zagreb, Zadar and Split). The earliest surviving example of *old Serbian architecture* is the round church of St Peter (Petrova Crkva) at Novi Pazar, which probably dates from the 10th c. Also found in Serbia are slabs with relief carving, dated between the 9th and 11th c., which resemble those to be seen in central Dalmatia (Kotor, Herceg-Novi). The little St Michael's Church in the small port town of Ston near Dubrovnik has remains of 11th c. frescoes in a naive style which can be recognised as early Romanesque.

In the Byzantine half of the Empire the architecture and painting are on a distinctly higher artistic level. Byzantine art, focused on the monasteries of Lakes Prespa and Ohrid, radiated over an ever wider area from the 10th c. onwards. On an island in Little Lake Prespa (now in Greece) are the ruins of the large aisled basilica of St Achilleus, built towards the end of the 10th c. The 11th c. basilica of St Sophia in Ohrid has frescoes of outstanding quality which are among the finest examples of 11th c. monumental painting in eastern Europe (narthex, 1313–14).

Romanesque art. – While 12th c. art in Macedonia is Byzantine (the little five-domed monastic church of St Panteleimon at Nerezi, near Skopje, dedicated 1164, has famous frescoes in the Comnenian style; St Clement's, Ohrid, 1295; St Nicholas's, Prilep, 1299), Serbia, Dalmatia and Istria show a mingling of Byzantine and Romanesque elements, as in St George's Church at Novi Pazar (Djurdjevi Stupovi, *c.* 1170), which suffered severe damage during the Second World War (remains of frescoes in the National Museum, Belgrade). The frescoes in the church of Sv. Krševan in Zadar

Fresco in St Clement's Church, Ohrid

also belong to the highly developed Comnenian style of fresco-painting; the church itself, dating from the 9th but mainly from the 11th c., already shows purely Romanesque forms (closed because of its dilapidated state; beautiful apse).

In the 13th c. there developed in the Ibar and Lim valleys in Serbia the *Raška school* of architecture, which shows a mingling of Byzantine and Romanesque forms. The buildings, of stone and sometimes marble, are usually aisleless and single-domed (in the 14th c. also five-domed), with rich sculptural decoration. The finest example of the architecture of this school is the fortress-like Studenica monastery, a magnificent building of white marble begun about 1190 by the Serbian ruler *Stephen Nemanja*. The principal church has a fine W doorway, sculptural decoration showing Italian influence and notable frescoes in the Byzantine style of the 11th c. The Royal Church, built in 1314, also contains frescoes of outstanding quality, reminiscent of the mosaics in the Kariye Camii in Istanbul. These frescoes date from the beginning of the development of Serbian monumental painting (early 13th c.). The finest examples of the Raška school of painting are to be seen at Mileševa, near Prijepolje (*c.* 1235), in the Patriarchate of Peć (three 13th and 14th c. churches, notably the Church of the Apostles, 1235), in the monastery of Morača (founded 1252), near Kolašin, and in the monastery of Sopoćani, near Novi Pazar, founded in the 13th c. by King Uroš I. These rank among the finest examples of 13th c. Byzantine wall painting; but towards the end of the 13th c. the quality

of Serbian monumental painting declines and gives place to the new style of the *Palaeologue renaissance,* which spreads westward and northward from Byzantium by way of Macedonia. St Clement's Church in Ohrid contains fine wall paintings in this style (1307–21).

During the 14th c. the builders working for King *Milutin* in Serbia and Macedonia developed a new architectural style which abandoned the costly material (marble) used during the Romanesque period, as well as the Romanesque repertoire of forms. Only royal mausoleums were now built in the style of the Raška school, as at Banjska near Kosovska Mitrovica, Dečani (Peć) and Sveti Arhandjel Mihajlo (Prizren). Other churches were built in stone and brick. The strongly horizontal lines of the polychrome façades found in earlier Byzantine architecture, however, give place in Serbia and Macedonia to markedly vertical lines. A fine example of this style is the monastic church of Gračanica, near Priština, a building of almost Gothic effect with its five pyramidally disposed domes, magnificent frescoes (*c.* 1321) and interesting alternation of stone and brick. Also belonging to this period are the five-domed metropolitan church of the Bogorodica Ljeviška (or Sv. Petka) at Prizren, which was used from the 18th c. to the beginning of the 20th as a mosque (frecoes covered over by the Turks, exposed 1950 onwards, showing damage from pecking to provide a key for plaster), and the church of the fine Byzantine monastery of Sveti Djordje, built in the reign of King Milutin, at Staro Nagoričane near Kumanovo (well-preserved wall paintings). The frescoes in this style are known as the *Milutin school,* the principal representatives of which were *Astrapas, Eutychius* (Eutihije) and *Michael* (Mihajlo).

At the beginning of the 14th c. a new narrative style of fresco painting, with realistic details, developed in Serbia and Macedonia.

Between 1340 and 1450 the "Greek painters" on the Dalmation coast produced large cycles of frescoes, as in the monastery of Visoki Dečani (*c.* 1330, in the reign of King Stephen Uroš III; in Romanesque-Byzantine style, with alternating courses of red, blue and grey marble), where the interior of the church with its profusion of more than a thousand frescoes is of almost oppressive effect. Similar series of frescoes can be seen in St Mary's Church in Mateič monastery near Kumanovo. This style, showing affinities with the school of Giotto, achieved a magnificent flowering at the beginning of the 14th c. In the second third of the century, however, the constant repetition of the same themes led to a certain superficiality.

Valuable examples of **icon-painting** have been preserved in Serbia and Macedonia, in particular the famous silver-mounted icons in St Clement's Church in Ohrid (12th and 17th c., period of the Byzantine renaissance; some in National Museum, Ohrid). Important icons of around 1400 can be seen in the Art Gallery in Skopje, and there are other good collections in Dečani monastery, the Patriarchate of Peč and Gračanica monastery (14th–16th c.), Slepča monastery (15th–17th c.) and Morača monastery (16th–17th c.).

Notable examples of **book illumination** are the Gospel Book of Prince Miroslav (end of 12th c.; National Museum, Belgrade), a Gospel book from Kumanica monastery (end of 14th c.; Serbian Academy of Sciences, Belgrade), the Tale of Alexander (14th c.; National Library, Belgrade) and other manuscripts to be seen at Dečani, Peć and Plevlje.

In Dalmatia the Romanesque style was fully developed by the beginning of the 14th c. (Trogir Cathedral, completed during the Gothic period; beautiful campanile; richly sculptured doorway by *Master Radovanus*, 1240; baptistery by *Andrija Aleši*, 1467; St John's Chapel by *Nikola Firentinac/Niccolò Fiorentino*, from 1468 onwards, the finest example of Renaissance architecture in Dalmatia). The Romanesque Cathedral of Zadar (Sv. Stošija), a basilica with a magnificent façade of 1324 and a separate campanile, also belongs to this period. The finest Romanesque campanile in Dalmatia is the one at Rab (12th and 15th c.); the 200 ft/ 61 m high tower of Split Cathedral, begun in the 13th c., was restored at the beginning of this century.

In parallel with the native painting school of Raška the first native sculptors of more than local significance came to the fore in Dalmatia. The great wooden door of Split Cathedral, with 28 relief panels of scenes

from the life of Christ, was carved by *Andrija Buvina* in 1214. The finest doorway in Dalmatia is the main doorway of Trogir Cathedral. The reliefs on the Split campanile are probably also the work of Master Radovanus.

In the first half of the 13th c. there developed in Slovenia an important school of Romanesque sculptors (*Virgin of Velesovo*). The Cistercian church of Kostanjevica shows the transitional Romanesque-Gothic style of the late 13th c.

Gothic. – At the beginning of the 14th c. there was a period of great building activity along the Adriatic coast (Franciscan friary in Dubrovnik, lower cloister Romanesque, *c.* 1350, by *Miho of Antivari*; Dominican friary, Dubrovnik, 1304–06). Every town of some consequence then had its own painters' and sculptors' workshops. Notable examples of Dalmatian sculpture of the 14th c. are the ciboria (altar canopies) of Trogir, Zadar and Kotor cathedrals. At the end of the century was built St Mark's Church, Zagreb, with its fine carved south doorway.

In the Morava valley in Serbia there developed between 1371 and 1459 the *Morava school* of architecture. Brick is still used, but there are richly decorated stone frames around doorways and windows. One of the finest examples is Ravanica monastery near Ćuprija, built by Prince Lazar in 1375, with the five-domed Church of the Saviour, which contains beautiful but badly damaged frescoes. Other examples are the church at Kruševac (1380), founded by Prince Lazar, with rich external decoration; Kalenić monastery, Svetozarevo; and the fortified monastery of Manasija, with its turrets and walls, which contains fine wall paintings of the Morava school.

In Bosnia, where no distinctive school of art was able to develop during the Middle Ages, a curious form of tombstone evolved in the 15th c. These *stećci* (singular *stećak*) are large roughly hewn stones decorated with reliefs, the most recent dating from the end of the 16th c. The finest examples of this crude popular sculpture, which is found in Hercegovina and parts of Dalmatia, western Serbia and Montenegro as well as in Bosnia, can be seen in the Sarajevo museum.

After the battle of Nicopolis (1396) **Turkish** influence began to extend into continental Europe. Large buildings (mosques, khans, bath-houses, bridges, etc.) began to be erected in Macedonia in the 15th c. The Sultan Murad Mosque in Skopje was built in 1430, the tall and slender Gazi Isa Beg Mosque in 1476; the Gazi Husref Beg Mosque in Sarajevo, with a beautiful fountain for ritual ablutions in the forecourt, dates from 1530. At Banja Luka *Ferhad Pasha Sokolović* built in the 16th c. the most westerly mosque in Yugoslavia, the Ferhad Pasha Mosque, with a free-standing clock-tower, the Sahat Kula. The Turks also built handsome stone bridges, usually on Roman foundations, such as the Kameni Most (Stone Bridge) spanning the Vardar at Skopje, the bridge over the old bed of the Sitnica at Vučitrn (Kosovo Polje), the Old Bridge (1566) over the Neretva in Mostar and the famous bridge over the Drina at Višegrad (described by the Nobel prize-winner Ivo Andrić in his novel *The Bridge on the Drina*). In the Turkish-occupied territories Christian art and architecture were suppressed until the beginning of the 19th c., but some modest buildings continued to be erected, including the church of Hopovo monastery with its well-preserved frescoes of the early 17th c. Applied art of the Turkish period can be seen in the Museum of the Patriarchate in Belgrade, the museum of Studenica monastery, the monastery in Cetinje (founded 1485) and the Orthodox Church in Dubrovnik.

Renaissance. – During the 15th c. major works of art and architecture were created in the Dalmatian towns, some still in late Gothic style, others already showing the

Caravanserai, Skopje

characteristics of the early Renaissance. Šibenik Cathedral was begun in Venetian Renaissance style in 1431 and completed by the Renaissance architect *Nikola Firentinac/Niccolò Fiorentino* in 1536 with a boldly contrived dome over the crossing. Other notable features of the building, which shows a mingling of Romanesque, Gothic and Renaissance forms, are the richly sculptured main doorway, the Lion Doorway in the N aisle and the 72 portrait heads by Juraj Dalmatinac on the apses. The Rector's Palace (Dvor) in Dubrovnik, in late Gothic style, was built by *Onofrio Giordano della Cava* in 1435–41; the portico was designed by the Florentine *Michelozzo Michelozzi*. The Church of the Saviour in Dubrovnik, the finest example of early Renaissance architecture in Dalmatia, was built by *Petar Andrijić* about 1520. Public buildings and private palaces were now more frequently built, usually with markedly Gothic features (e.g. the Ćipiko Palace, Trogir). The continuing threat from the Turks led the towns (including Dubrovnik in particular) to strengthen their fortifications.

Both local and Italian sculptors worked in Dalmatia in the 15th c. *Boninus* of Milan was active in Split and Šibenik, *Juraj Matejev/Georgius Dalmaticus* of Zadar in Šibenik, Split and Dubrovnik. St John's Chapel (1468) in Trogir Cathedral was the work of *Andrija Aleši, Nikola Firentinac* and *Ivan Duknović/Giovanni Dalmata*. Dubrovnik also had goldsmiths and silversmiths of outstanding quality in the 15th c., such as *Jovan Progonović* and *John of Basle*. During the 15th c., too, Dalmatian painting freed itself from Byzantine and Gothic influences. The most important native painting school was at Dubrovnik, with *Nikola Božidarović* and *Mihajlo Hamzić*. The difficult political circumstances of the time (under alien Venetian and Turkish rule) brought the development of native Dalmatian art almost to a standstill; many Venetian artists, however, worked for Dalmatia.

Baroque. – The decline of Turkish power led to a fresh cultural upswing from around 1700. In Slovenia Baroque art and architecture developed in association with the progress of the Counter-Reformation (Jesuits); but Baroque art in Yugoslavia was mainly the work of Italian artists, among them the painter *Giulio Quaglio*, the sculptor *Francesco Robba* and the architect *Marino Groppelli* (St Blaise's Church, Dubrovnik, 1706–15). While St Blaise's is in Venetian Baroque style, Dubrovnik Cathedral (Velika Gospa, 1671–1713) and the Jesuit church show features characteristic of Roman Baroque. In the course of the 17th and 18th c. native artists grew in stature, but remained of merely local significance. Real artistic individuality was shown mainly by practitioners of "rural Baroque", producing icons, under-glass paintings and wood-carving.

The first generation of late Baroque painters included native artists such as *Tripe Kokolja* (Dalmatia) and the Slovenes *Franc Jelovšek, Valentin Mencinger, Fortunat Bergant* and *Anton Cebej*, but during the second half of the 18th c. foreign artists such as the Austrian *Schmidt of Krems* were at work alongside the first trained (Serbian) artists who included *Dimitrije Kračun, Teodor Ilić-Cešljar* and *Jakov Orfelin*. They developed a new type of Baroque iconostasis which subordinated the traditional Byzantine iconography to Baroque artistic trends. The gallery of the Serbian Cultural Union (Matica Srpska) in Novi Sad has an outstanding collection of pictures of the 17th and 18th c. illustrating the development of Serbian painting from the style of the icon-painters to Baroque.

An attractive example of Baroque urban layout is provided by the little town of Perast, near Kotor, charmingly picturesque with its decaying palaces, churches, loggias and gardens.

Classicism. – In the aftermath of the Napoleonic era (Illyrian Provinces, 1809–15) there developed in the country a middle-class or bourgeois art, influenced by the ideas of the Romantic movement, which sought to give expression to the distinctive values of the Southern Slavs. A nationalist movement now set in, and Baroque – largely a feudal art patronised by the Church – gave place to classicism. A leading representative of the new trend was the Slovenian painter *Franc Kavčič* (1762–1828), who specialised in heroic and classical themes. The Biedermeier art of Vienna exerted considerable influence on Yugoslav artists, and influences from Rome also made themselves felt. Among painters of this period were *Josip Tominc* (1790–1866),

Matevž Langus (1792–1855) and *Vjekoslav Karas* (1821–58).

Historicism. – After the 1848 revolution the influence of the Romantic "historicising" school made itself increasingly felt (*Pavle Simić*, 1818–76; *Novak Radonić*, 1826–90). After 1874 the influence of the Munich Academy grew, and a school of realistic painting (landscapes) developed (*Jožef Petkovšek*, 1861–98).

In Croatia there were the beginnings of a Plein Air school (*Miloš Tenković*, 1849–90; *Celestin Medović*, 1857–1920; *Djordje Krstić*, 1851–1907).

The **Fin de Siècle** period was also characterised by the influence of Art Nouveau, which affected architecture more than painting. Leading sculptors of the period were *Robert Frangeš Mihanović* (1872–1940), *Toma Rosandić* (1879–1958) and above all *Ivan Meštrović* (1883–1962). Among the architects were *Josip Plečnik* (1872–1957), a pupil of Otto Wagner's and one of the great European architects of the early 20th c., *Viktor Kovačić* (1874–1924) and *Branko Tanazević* (1876–1945). A special position among the painters was occupied by *Anton Ažbe* (1862–1905), who founded a school of his own and became a forerunner of modern Yugoslav art of the 20th c.

Meštrović Museum, Split

Modern sculpture, influenced by the Sezession and following the model of Rodin, came to the fore in the work of Meštrović and Mihanović.

In Macedonia guilds of painters and families of artists such as the *Frčkovci* in Galičnik, the *Dičovci* in Tresonče and the *Filipovci* worked on large iconostases in the spirit of Levantine Baroque.

Slovenian architects of the 20th c. looked back to Josip Plečnik as their master and were strongly influenced by the Vienna Sezession. A school of Croatian architects was founded by *Viktor Kovačić*. *Maks Fabiani* (1865–1962) worked in Vienna, Ljubljana (particularly after the 1895 earthquake), Gorizia and Trieste. – After the Second World War each of the peoples of Yugoslavia developed a clear, modern but distinctive architectural style.

Impressionism played relatively little part in Yugoslavia (*Milan Milanović*, 1876–1946; *Kosta Miličević*, 1877–1920; *Ivan Grohar*, 1867–1911; and *Rihard Jakopič*, 1869–1943).

Expressionism was represented by *Nadežda Petrović* (1873–1915), and the Slovenes *France Kralj* (1895–1960) and *Tone Kralj* (b. 1900). The *Trojica* group, formed in Zagreb in 1929, was a variant form of Expressionism.

After 1945 Yugoslav art linked up with the international movements of the day, with such artists as *Petar Lubarda*, *Milo Milunović, Marij Pregelj* and many more.

Mladen Srbinović (b. 1925), *Boris Dogan* (b. 1923), *Stojan Čelić* (b. 1925), *Edo Murtić* (b. 1921), *Zlatko Prica* (b. 1916), *Milorad-Bata Mihajlović* (b. 1923) and *Josip Vaništa* (b. 1924) represent **Art Informel, Action Painting** and **Abstract Expressionism**.

Naive painting has been officially encouraged in Yugoslavia since 1952. The leading representative of this trend is *Ivan Generalić* (b. 1914); and although the idea of a school of naive painting may seem a contradiction in terms such a school has been established at Hlebine (Generalić's birthplace), with *Matija Skurjeni* (b. 1898) and *Emerik Feješ* (b. 1904) among its members. Other representatives of naive painting are *Ivan Rabuzin, Florica Ćet, Dejanka Petrov, Jan Sokol* and *Pal Homonai*.

Economy

The economy of Yugoslavia since 1945 has followed a very lively and distinctive course of development, largely shaped by the views of its wartime and post-war leader, President Tito. This development has been based on the theory of Titoism or National Communism, a political and social philosophy principally aimed at achieving the national unification of this multi-national state which has been so much fragmented by history, culture and religion and establishing a non-aligned communist state and economic system. In the economic field the most notable feature is the attempt to introduce elements of a market economy into the overall conception of a planned economy, in order to increase productivity and flexibility and make it possible more easily to bridge over the wide regional differences. This is also the idea behind the various amendments to the constitution during the past 30 years, all tending towards increasing decentralisation and giving even state enterprises far-reaching independent responsibility.

In contrast to what has happened in other socialist countries the agrarian reform of 1945 was followed by the redistribution of cultivable land among the peasant population but also by the recognition of the private ownership of land, with a limitation on the size of holdings. Thus today only some 10% of the total area of cultivable land is worked by agricultural cooperatives, producing mainly for commercial markets. Craft production remains in private ownership, while industry, commerce and banking are wholly nationalised.

Yugoslavia's economy, still in the course of development, shows a marked downward gradient from N to S which hampers the overall development of the economy. This is due partly to the unequal distribution of natural resources, partly to religious and sociological factors. While even the purely agricultural areas in Alpine Slovenia and Croatia, with their old-established Christian population, are fully comparable in terms of development with the neighbouring countries of Austria and Switzerland, those parts of the country which were converted to Islam after the Turkish occupation remain lamentably far behind the general economic development of the country as a whole. In these regions religious and family traditions still hinder the establishment of modern productive industry.

Roughly half the population of Yugoslavia is employed in **agriculture**; yet agricultural production is not sufficient to meet domestic consumption, and it is necessary to import considerable quantities of food, particularly wheat. Almost 60% of the country's total area is suitable for cultivation. In the NE are great expanses of plain on which wheat, maize, barley, rye, sugar-beet and fodder crops are grown by modern cultivation techniques. Other forms of agricultural production in these areas are market gardening and cattle-farming.

The Alpine regions in the NW have the same type of upland agriculture as is found in Switzerland and Austria. Here stock farming (particularly cattle in Croatia) and extensive timber-working, with their associated activities (dairy produce, meat production; furniture-making) and, in the more open valleys, fruit-growing (particularly apples in Slovenia) and wine production, have brought a considerable measure of prosperity. The forests of the Karavanke range and the Triglav massif (oak, beech, pine) provide one of the country's largest resources of timber.

The Bosnian, Serbian and Macedonian uplands account for some 40% of the total area of Yugoslavia. In these karstic hills

only the dolines and poljes and the larger depressions have enough fertile soil to grow wheat, barley, potatoes and buckwheat. The most important form of agricultural production is sheep and goat rearing, which, thanks to the practice of transhumance (seasonal migration of livestock), is highly productive. In Serbia there is also pig-rearing. The mountain foreland region, the Bosnian highlands and the Šumadija are areas of intensive mixed farming (corn, vegetables, sunflowers, fruit); and here are grown the plums used in the production of slivovitz.

Along the Dalmatian coast and in southern Macedonia mixed crops of Mediterranen type are grown – terraced vineyards, olives, citrus fruits and figs (around Dubrovnik). In Hercegovina and the Vardar valley tobacco and cotton are grown, in the irrigated plains rice.

Yugoslav agriculture suffers from a considerable drift of population away from the land, and there is little prospect, particularly in the southern parts of the country, of halting this drain, or compensating for it, by the introduction of modern methods of cultivation, since neither the necessary capital nor the skilled labour required is available. The problem is aggravated by the fact that it is the more active and energetic members of the population who are urgently needed in these areas that drift away to the industrial areas or seek employment as "guest workers" in Central and Northern Europe. The consequence is a steady ageing of the rural population.

Yugoslavia is notably rich in minerals and has considerable sources of energy – two requisites for the establishment of a flourishing industry. If industrial development has so far failed to achieve its potential, this is due partly to the lack of sufficient capital to exploit the country's resources and partly to the inadequacy of communications – an essential requirement for the development of an efficient industrial structure.

The main areas of industry, as of agriculture, in Yugoslavia are in the N of the country, which not only has the advantage of being well supplied with **minerals** but for historical reasons is better developed industrially than the S. Iron ore is worked near Vareš and Ljubija, copper in north-eastern Serbia (around

Yugoslav figs

Bor and Majdanpek), mercury (one of the largest deposits in the world) and zinc at Idria, lead in Kosovo, antimony at Zaječar and chromium in the Kopaonik range of hills.

Coal (more than 80% of it brown coal) is found in Bosnia, Hercegovina and Macedonia, lignite in northern Serbia and in Bosnia. Oil and natural gas from Croatia (Kutina, Bjelovar, Djurdjevac), the middle Sava valley, the Drava valley, the Vojvodina and north-eastern Slovenia meet roughly half the country's needs. There are oil refineries at Rijeka, Sisak, Bosanski Brod and Pančevo.

Most of Yugoslavia's requirements of electric power are met by **hydroelectric power stations**. There are hydroelectric installations on several rivers in Bosnia and Serbia (Split, at the mouth of the Cetina; Jablanica, on the Neretva; on the Rama), recently joined by the large Iron Gates hydroelectric scheme on the Danube, a joint enterprise by Yugoslavia and Romania.

Yugoslav **industry** has not yet reached its full potential. The processing industries long remained backward for lack of skilled labour and adequate capital, and after 1945 it was only heavy industry that was developed on a planned basis, following the Soviet model and with the help of Soviet capital. Most of the raw materials produced in Yugoslavia were exported in crude form and processed abroad. Since the withdrawal of Soviet capital assistance and the provision of economic help by the United States, increased efforts have been made to develop the processing industries. Here too, however, the falling gradient from N to S can be observed, requiring measures of support designed to even out the inequalities.

The main concentration of the processing industries is again in the NW. Here, in the Ljubljana, Maribor and Zagreb basins and in the Alpine valleys, the development of industry is favoured by the large rivers and by the sea. Thus in the old-established industrial areas of Slovenia, with abundant supplies of iron, coal, timber and power in close proximity and with the advantage of the River Sava (which is in part navigable), modern metalworking, electrical engineering and mechanical plants have been established. The NE (Slavonia, Osijek, Varaždin) has become

an area for the food industries and the production of agricultural machinery. On the northern and middle Adriatic coast (Pula, Koper, Rijeka, Bakar, Split) shipbuilding and mechanical engineering predominate. In Vojvodia and the lower Morava valley there are metalworking industries, textile, mechanical engineering and the construction of motor vehicles. In Serbia, particularly around Belgrade and Smederevo, there is a great diversity of industries, mainly in small and medium-sized factories. The metalworking industries are also developing rapidly in Macedonia (around Skopje).

In the field of **transport** Yugoslavia links Western and South-Eastern Europe and the Middle East. Road traffic uses the busy expressway from Ljubljana, Belgrade, Niš and Skopje, which has a railway line running parallel with it. The Danube, with the Danube–Tisa–Danube Canal and some tributaries which are navigable for varying distances, also makes a valuable contribution to transport facilities in this part of the country.

While there are good traffic routes from NW to SE, communications across the country from NE to SW are still underdeveloped. The construction of roads and railway lines through this territory is extremely costly and can hardly be contemplated without an infusion of foreign capital. – A road of great tourist importance is the magnificent Adriatic coastal highway, the Jadranska Magistrala, which extends from Rijeka to the Albanian frontier. Another recent development is the important railway line from Belgrade to the Adriatic port of Bar.

The Yugoslav national airline, *JAT* (Jugoslovenski Aerotransport), flies to all parts of the world. Domestic air services (airports at Belgrade/Zemun, Zagreb, Ljubljana, Titograd, Dubrovnik, Split, Mostar, Sarajevo, Ivangrad, Skopje and Priština) play a significant part in the country's transport system, making it possible to overcome the geographical difficulties which sometimes hamper other forms of transport.

Yugoslavia's two main Adriatic ports, Rijeka and Split, ship a high proportion of the country's exports, and there are also ferry services between Zadar and the Italian port of Ancona. Within the last few years the Montenegrin port of Bar has

Sunset over Lake Scutari, on the borders of Montenegro and Albania

been developed into one of the largest ports for container traffic in the Mediterranean; it is connected with Belgrade by rail.

The main Yugoslav **exports** are machinery and equipment for motor vehicles, which account for some 25% of total exports; others include crude steel, minerals, metals, chemicals, livestock and meat, sawn timber, textiles, tobacco, fruit and wine. Yugoslavia's principal trading partners are the Federal Republic of Germany, Italy, the Soviet Union, the United States, Austria, Czechoslovakia, France, Poland, the German Democratic Republic and the United Kingdom.

Yugoslavia has long had a considerable deficit on its balance of trade. In 1978 exports were valued at $5·254 billion, imports at $9·634 billion. It seems unlikely that this deficit will be made good in the foreseeable future, since although Yugoslav industry is growing rapidly and exports are rising the domestic demand for capital and consumer goods is also increasing steadily.

Yugoslavia is an associate member of Comecon (the Council for Mutual Economic Assistance of the Eastern European countries) and a member of the Committee for Economic Cooperation with the Soviet Union, but also maintains a continuing relationship with the EEC.

A major source of foreign currency in recent years has been **tourism**, which has developed on an unprecedented scale during the last two decades, particularly on the Adriatic coast and in the Alpine regions (which offer facilities for winter sports as well as summer holidays). Yugoslavia is now one of Europe's leading holiday countries. The country which sends the largest numbers of visitors is West Germany, followed by Austria and Italy. In the next few years along the Adriatic coast with its 725 offshore islands a uniform nautical scheme will come into existence under the title of "Adriatic Club Yugoslavia". Its aim is visibly to encourage boating and yachting.

Yugoslavia
A to Z

Počitelj, in the Neretva valley ▶

Banja Luka

Republic: Bosnia-Hercegovina (Bosna i
Hercegovina)
Altitude: 535 ft/163 m. – Population: 130,000.
Post code: YU-78000. – Telephone code: 0 78.
ⓘ **Turističko Društvo,**
  Maršala Tita 58;
  tel. 2 25 50.

HOTELS. – *Bosna*, A, 344 b., tel. 2 26 00; *Palace*, B,
160 b., tel. 2 25 50; *Slavija*, B, 88 b., tel. 2 16 76; *Motel
International*, C, 120 b., tel. 3 27 10; *Šehitluci*, D, 15 b.,
tel. 2 29 74.

CAMP SITE. – Small site with limited facilities outside
the town on the right bank of the River Vrbas.

Banja Luka, a verdant town of tree-lined avenues, parks and gardens lying astride the River Vrbas, was devastated by an earthquake on October 26, 1969; but the town, sorely tried in the past by natural catastrophes and wars, has recovered from this latest disaster. The old part of the town, with the Ferhad Pasha Mosque, one of the finest examples of Islamic art in Yugoslavia, offers visitors coming from the north their first glimpse of a typical old Bosnian town. Although neither a spa nor a port, as its name might suggest (banja=bathroom; luka=port), Banja Luka is a convenient staging point for tourists and a good base from which to explore the attractive surrounding area.

Ferhad Pasha Mosque, Banja Luka

HISTORY. – In the wars of earlier centuries Banja Luka
occupied an important strategic position at the point
where the River Vrbas emerged from the mountains
and pursued its course over the Pannonian plain to
join the Sava 19 miles/30 km N. The Romans
established a military post here on the road running
from present-day Jajce to Split on the Adriatic coast
and discovered the sulphur springs near the town,
which are no longer used for medicinal purposes. In
the 14th c. a fortress was built on the site of the Roman
station, and this still survives, though in a dilapidated
condition. In 1528 the Turks took Banja Luka and
thereafter developed it into an important town – an
outpost and a base for their further advance northward
over the Pannonian plain. In the second half of the
17th c. Banja Luka enjoyed a period of considerable
prosperity, with 3700 houses, 300 shops, more than
30 mosques and several Koranic schools.

In 1688 the Austrians briefly occupied the town.
Subsequently six major fires, four outbreaks of plague
and two floods cost the lives of thousands of its
inhabitants. In 1878 Banja Luka was assigned to
Austria by the Congress of Berlin. During the Second
World War the town was a focal point of the Yugoslav
Resistance, and the partisans established their first
airfield near the town in 1943. A huge monument on
Mt Šehetluci commemorates the fierce fighting of
these years.

SIGHTS. – The finest of the mosques in
the old part of the town on the left bank of
the Vrbas is the **Ferhad Pasha Mosque**
(*Ferhadija Džamija*), built in 1583 in the
time of the local governor, a native of the
area, Ferhad Pasha Sokolović. It was
damaged by air attack during the last war
and again in the 1969 earthquake but has
been completely restored. The slender
minaret is 138 ft/42 m high; a spiral
staircase of 128 steps leads up to the
gallery. The interior of the mosque is
decorated with beautiful arabesques and
inscriptions from the Koran. Other notable
features are the *ablution fountain* (shadirvan) and the *clock-tower* (Sahat Kula),
with what is believed to be the oldest
public clock in Bosnia.

On the banks of the Vrbas stands the
Castle, with its extensive medieval fortifi-
cations. It now houses an *Ethnographic
Museum* (interior of a Bosnian house,

local costumes, etc.) and a *Museum of the Revolution*, with relics of the Resistance.

SURROUNDINGS. – Canoeists will enjoy a trip down the River Vrbas **from Jajce to Banja Luka**, passing through numerous gorges and stretches of wild water. At a number of points the river is dammed, forming long lakes which supply power stations. There is good fishing to be had in the rivers *Vrbas, Pliva* and *Ugar.*

An excellent road, narrow in places, follows the River Vrbas to Jajce, passing between high rock walls and through tunnels and affording magnificent views.

Near Banja Luka are the spas of *Laktaši, Slatina* and *Gornji Šeher.* 19 miles/30 km N is the little town of *Bosanska Gradiška*, where a Bronze and Iron Age settlement of wooden pile dwellings was discovered some years ago; the main finds from the site are now in the National Museum in Sarajevo.

Bar

Republic: Montenegro (Crna Gora).
Altitude: 16 ft/5 m. – Population: 15,000.
Post code: YU-81350. – Telephone code: 0 85.
(i) **Turistički Savez,**
 Naselje Topolica;
 tel. 2 22 11.

HOTELS. – Following an earthquake in the spring of 1979 there are at present only a few hotels in the little township of SUTOMORE (post code YU-81355, telephone code 0 85) at the N end of the bay: *Inex – Zlatna Obala*, B, 830 b., tel. 2 24 22; *Nikšić*, B, 208 b., tel. 2 21 84.

CAMP SITES. – *Agava*, tel. 2 23 76; small privately owned site in Sutomore.

SPORT. – At SUTOMORE water-skiing, boat rental, scuba (sub-aqua) diving, table tennis, climbing (Sutorman, 3878 ft/1182 m; panoramic views of coast and Lake Scutari).

There is a car ferry service three times weekly between Bar and the Italian town of Bari, operated by the Prekookeanska Plovidba line (information and reservations: *Jugo-agent Topolica B.B.*, tel. 8 22 23). There are also car ferry services, run by the same company, linking Bar with Corfu and Igoumenitsa in Greece and with Dubrovnik. Jadrolinija provides regular services between Corfu, Bar, Dubrovnik and Rijeka (agent in UK: Yugotours, 150 Regent Street, London W1R 5FA). – There is also a *rail* service from Belgrade (see p. 51).

The bay in which Bar lies and its hinterland have much to offer the vacationer (holidaymaker), who should not be put off by the trails of smoke around the port area. There are ideal conditions for bathing on the sandy beach of Sutomore and in the sandy bay of Čanj, 2 miles/3 km N, and for the sightseer there are the fascinating ruins in the old town of Stari Bar. Once a week, too, there is a picturesque market in this ghost town, preserving intact the traditions of old Montenegrin life. On the old road to Ulcinj stands a grove of gnarled olive-trees, some of them more than 2000 years old.

There are two towns of Bar – Novi Bar (New Bar) and Stari Bar (Old Bar). The coast road from the N comes first to the newest part of Novi Bar, a rapidly growing but featureless town of tall modern blocks. The older part of the town, along the shore, was severely damaged in the 1979 earthquake.

Novi Bar cannot be regarded as a holiday resort, even though the damage to the environment from the development of industry has been kept under control. There is a sandy beach 2 miles/3 km long, used almost exclusively by local people. The harbour utilised by cargo ships and the car ferries was constructed after the last war on a virgin site and lacks the amenities of an established town: no friendly cafés or taverns, no evening promenade along the seafront as in other coastal towns. This is, however, an important hub of communications, situated at the terminus of the railway from Belgrade, which was complete only in 1976 after 25 years' work (p. 51).

Many holidaymakers come to this southern part of Montenegro for the sake of the beautiful and still uncrowded beaches, most of them sandy. The best place to stay in this area is Sutomore, a village of 600 inhabitants with the hotels mentioned at the head of this entry. The beach of fine sand is 1100 yd/1000 m long and 35 yd/30 m wide.

HISTORY. – The first town of Bar was probably on the site now occupied by the new harbour. Later the inhabitants moved their homes inland, no doubt to escape the attentions of pirates, and founded the town now known as *Stari Bar*, defensibly situated on a hill at the foot of the Rumija range. Then, after the end of Turkish rule in 1878, *Novi Bar* was built on the coast at the foot of a low ridge of hills along the bay (Luka Bar). A third district of tall modern buildings is now developing between the two older settlements.

There are various theories about the derivation of the town's name. One theory connects it with the Italian town of *Bari*, opposite Bar on the other side of the

Adriatic. Alternatively it is derived from the Latin *Antibarum* and its Greek equivalent *Antivaris*. And there are those who see the name as referring to the Avars, the barbarian people who are believed to have controlled Bar at one time.

In the early medieval period Bar was under Byzantine rule. In 1183 the Serbian župan (leader), Stephen Nemanja, captured the town. In 1443 it was taken by the Venetians, who fortified it with defensive walls and circular bastions. In 1574 it fell to the Turks, who extended the town to the SE and NW. The buildings erected during the Turkish period show a curious mingling of architectural forms and styles of local and oriental origin.

In 1877 a Montenegrin army expelled the Turks from Bar, after a massive bombardment which destroyed all the houses within the walls: whereupon the inhabitants left the ruins of their homes and built new dwellings outside the walls. This was the beginning of a general exodus from the old town of Bar. Further destruction was caused by two explosions: one in 1881, when a late Romanesque basilica used for storing ammunition blew up, and the other in 1912, when the same fate befell the late Romanesque church of Sv. Nikola, outside the oldest surviving town gate. The old town is now abandoned. The development of the new town of Bar into a large modern port began in 1952.

Ruins of Stari Bar

SIGHTS. – The principal tourist attraction in this area is **Stari Bar**. From the square in which the buses park, and in which the weekly market is held, the *ruined town on the hill opposite has an unreal spectral air, and this feeling of an abandoned ghost town is reinforced by a walk around the deserted streets, past windowless buildings overgrown with grass.

The upper part of Stari Bar, originally walled but largely destroyed by the 1877 bombardment, is now a mere field of ruins. Of more interest is the lower part of the old town, also completely uninhabited, with buildings showing oriental features. Here too are the Romanesque **St Mark's Church** (11th–12th c.), the Gothic **St Catherine's Church** (14th–15th c.), a

late medieval building which is probably the *Bishop's Palace* (remains of wall decoration, additions of the Venetian period) and a large **aqueduct** (16th–17th c.) on the N side of the town.

Sutomore also has some features of interest. Some $1\frac{1}{4}$ miles/2 km N of the village, on either side of the coast road, are two ruined **fortresses: Haj Nehaj** (of the Venetian period, later strengthened by the Turks), on a rocky hill, and **Tabija** (Turkish, 1862).

On a peninsula S of Sutomore stand the ruins of the once famous **Ratac Abbey**, a Benedictine foundation of the 11th c. – In the **Spic** area are three unusual churches, each with two altars (one for the Orthodox, the other for the Catholics).

Baška Voda

Republic: Croatia (Hrvatska).
Altitude: 16 ft/5 m. – Population: 900.
Post code: YU-58320. – Telephone code: 0 58.
ⓘ **Turist Biro,**
Obala Maršala Tita 26;
tel. 7 77 14.

HOTELS. – *Horizont*, A, 400 b., tel. 62 06 99; *Slavija*, B, 105 b., tel. 62 01 55; *Dubravka*, B, 80 b., tel. 7 77 26.

CAMP SITE. – *Baško Polje*, tel. 7 78 65.

SPORT. – Scuba diving, motorboat rental, water-skiing, tennis, tenpin bowling.

Since about 1970 Baška Voda has developed into a resort much favoured by Yugoslav vacationers. This pretty little village, lying below the Adriatic coastal highway, has only a small beach which is overcrowded during the main holiday season; but up and down the surrounding coast are many small bathing places, with access to the water over rock or shingle. The neighbouring resort of Promanja, with a pine-shaded camp site and a rocky beach, is less crowded than Baška Voda.

HISTORY. – The area was occupied in Roman times, as tombs excavated at Promanja have shown. The present village was established only in the 18th c., when the danger of pirate raids was over and the peasants moved down to the coast from the older settlements situated on higher ground amid vineyards and olive-groves, backed by the barren slopes of the mountains behind.

The beach, Baška Voda

SIGHTS. – Baška Voda has two **Baroque churches**. St Lawrence's Church (Sv. Lovro) has an unusual spindle-shaped spire; adjoining the church are a number of medieval *tombstones*.

SURROUNDINGS. – The finest walk in the area is along the shore to *Promanja* (2 miles/3 km). Climbers will find scope for practising their skills in the Biokovo range (see under Brela: also an attractive car run through the Vrulja gorge to the karstic scenery of the Imotsko Polje).

Belgrade/Beograd

Republic: Serbia (Srbija).
Altitude: 453 ft/138 m. – Population: 1,371,000.
Post code: YU-11000. – Telephone code: 0 11.
ⓘ **Turistički Informativni Centar,**
Terazije (underpass at Albanija Building);
tel. 63 56 22.
Turistički Informativni Centar,
Central Station;
tel. 64 62 40.

HOTELS. – **Jugoslavija*, L, 810 b., Novi Beograd, Beogradski Put 3, tel. 60 02 22; *Metropol*, A, 294 b., Bulevar Revolucije 69, tel. 33 09 10/19; *Moskva*, A, 218 b., Balkanska 1, tel. 32 73 12; *Majestic*, A, 135 b., Obilićev Venac 28, tel. 63 60 22; *Excelsior*, A, 130 b., Kneza Miloša 5, tel. 31 13 81; *Palace*, A, 129 b., Topličin Venac 23, tel. 63 72 22; *Srbija*, B, 612 b., Ustanička 127, tel. 41 32 55; *Slavija*, B, 492 b., Svetog Save 9, tel. 45 08 42; *Slavija Annexe A*, B, 260 b.; *Putnik*, B, 236 b., Novi Beograd, Palmira Toljatija 9, tel. 69 72 21; *Park*, B, 227 b., Njegoševa 2, tel. 33 47 22; *Šumadija*, B, 202 b., Šumadijski Trg 8, tel. 55 42 55; *Prag*, B, 191 b., Narodnog Fronta 27, tel. 32 29 01; *Turist*, B, 157 b., Sarajevska 37, tel. 68 28 55; *Toplice*, B, 149 b., 7 Jula 56, tel. 62 64 26; *Kasina*, B, 148 b., Terazije 25, tel. 33 55 74; *Balkan*, B, 140 b., Prizrenska 2, tel. 32 50 32; *National*, B, 140 b., Novi Beograd, Bežanijska Kosa, tel. 32 73 12; *Union*, B, 132 b., Kosovska 11, tel. 33 16 69; *Beograd*, B, 105 b., Balkanska 52, tel. 64 51 99; *Splendid*, B, 80 b., Dragoslava Jovanovića 5, tel. 33 54 44; *Astorija*, C, 140 b., Milovana Milanovića 1, tel. 64 54 22. – Other hotels in BEOGRAD-ZEMUM: *Central*, tel. 60 76 47; *Grand*, tel. 21 05 36; and motels in BEOGRAD-LIPOVIČKA

ŠUMA. – ROOMS IN PRIVATE HOUSES: apply to Turist Biro Lasta, Trg Bratstva i Jedinstva 1a, tel. 64 12 51.

CAMP SITES. – *Autocamp Košutnjak* (on a wooded hill 6 miles/10 km from the city), Kneza Višeslava 17, tel. 55 69 61 and 55 51 27; *Camping Nacional* (before the end of the Zagreb–Belgrade motorway), tel. 60 20 24.

EVENTS. – International Film Festival (February); "Belgrade Spring" (light music and folk music: May); performances in streets and restaurants of Skadarlija (May to October); concerts by the Kolo folk group; BITEF (International Festival of Modern Dramatic Art: September); BEMUS (Belgrade Musical Festival: October).

AIR SERVICES. – JAT, Bulevar Revolucije 17, tel. 33 10 42 and 33 03 10; British Airways, Sava Centar, Milentija Popovića 9, tel. 13 86 72.

EMBASSIES. – *United Kingdom:* Generala Ždanova 46, tel. 64 50 55, 64 50 34, 64 50 43 and 64 50 87. – *United States:* Kneza Miloša 50, tel. 64 56 55. – *Canada:* Proleterskih Brigada 69, tel. 43 45 24 and 43 45 05/07.

TRANSPORT. – Strong nerves are required to attempt your sightseeing in Belgrade in your own car. Moreover parking in the middle of the city is subject to limitations of time, and the steady extension of pedestrian precincts makes it increasingly difficult to see the sights by car. For those who are not deterred by these difficulties there are signs marked "Tourist Route" pointing the way to the main sights. The best starting point for a tour is the Kalemegdan fortress.

Public transport operates from 5 a.m. to midnight, with some tram services continuing after midnight. Taxis are almost impossible to obtain at certain times of day: there are no more than a dozen taxi ranks in the whole of the city. The best way is to call a radio taxi (tel. 76 56 66 or 44 34 43). There is a heavy demand for rental cars in Belgrade, as in the rest of Yugoslavia, during July and August, and reservations should therefore be made well in advance. City sightseeing tours are operated only from May 1 to September 30 (mornings; 3 hours; information on departure points from tourist information offices).

The historic heart of Belgrade, capital of Yugoslavia and of the republic of Serbia, lies between the Danube and the Sava, below the fortress of Kalemegdan. With its finely planned streets the modern city has the aspect of a cosmopolitan metropolis showing the influence of both East and West. In one respect, however, it may disappoint the visitor: it has preserved few monuments of the past to bear witness to its long and eventful history, since the town was repeatedly destroyed by its successive conquerors. There is scarcely another town in Yugoslavia which has suffered so severely at the hands of foreign rulers and armies.

Belgrade: view from the Kalemegdan fortress towards the suburb of Zemun.

Since the last war Belgrade has not only made good the damage it suffered during the war but has created a whole new district, Novi Beograd or New Belgrade, on the left bank of the Sava, on what was until quite recently an area of meadowland along the river. Visitors arriving at Belgrade airport can see the new residential suburbs which are extending ever farther into the countryside to the S and W of the city, their modern apartment buildings indistinguishable from those to be seen around other European cities.

HISTORY. – The high ground between the Sava and the Danube at the confluence of the two rivers attracted settlers more than 7000 years ago, and it has continued to be occupied since then. Excavations within the fortress have yielded evidence of settlement in the Bronze and Iron Ages; here too the Illyrians practised agriculture; and in the 3rd c. B.C. the area was occupied by Celts.

There is evidence that in 279 B.C. the hill now occupied by the fortress of Kalemegdan was the site of a fortified settlement known as *Singidunum* ("round fort"). At the beginning of the 1st c. B.C. this fortress was taken by the Romans, who developed it into a rectangular fort and also established a military base in the area now occupied by the suburb of Zemun. Increasing numbers of Roman citizens settled at Singidunum, and in the 4th c. it was the birthplace of a future Roman emperor, Flavius Claudius. The Roman town was laid out with wide streets intersecting at right angles – a pattern which can still be detected in the layout of the streets above the Danube.

When the Roman Empire was divided into a Western and an Eastern Empire the town lay in the frontier area between the two and was frequently the scene of conflict. It was exposed to attack by successive barbarian peoples, and in 441 the Huns captured the fortress and destroyed the surrounding settlement, dispersing the Roman population. After three further changes of rulers the town passed firmly under Byzantine control in 488. In 512 the Byzantine emperor Anastasius settled a Germanic tribe, the Heruli, in the area as a defence against barbarian attack; but only a hundred years later, when the Byzantines were waging wars in Africa and Asia, the town was occupied by the Avars, coming from Mongolia, and later by the Slavs. The conquerors now took to settled life; the town grew in size, and its modern name of Beograd ("white city") appeared for the first time in a Papal document of 878.

A period of relative peace came to an end at the beginning of the 9th c., and the town fell to a succession of different conquerors. The Avars were annihilated by Charlemagne's Franks; then the Bulgars occupied the town, and they in turn were followed by the Magyars. In 1018 Belgrade again became a Byzantine frontier fortress, which soon afterwards fell into the hands of the Hungarians and later of the Bulgars. Thereafter it was ravaged by the armies of the Crusaders, and in 1189 by the Emperor Frederick Barbarossa.

In 1284 Belgrade passed for the first time under the control of a Serbian king – Dragutin, son-in-law of King Ladislas IV of Hungary – who supported the Serbian Orthodox Church; but the brief period of Serbian development of the town's culture and economy came to an end in 1319, when it was recaptured by the Magyars. After destroying Belgrade they later rebuilt it as a base directed against the young Serbian state of Tsar Dušan.

After the battle of Kosovo (1389) the Magyars felt threatened by the Turks and allied themselves with the Serbian Despot Stephen Lazarević, who developed

In the foreground the junction of the Sava with the Danube (left) and the "Messenger of Victory" (right)

and fortified the town for them between 1403 and 1427. In 1440 and on a number of subsequent occasions the Turks tried unsuccessfully to take Belgrade, which barred the way to their northern advance; but on August 28, 1521 they finally succeeded in taking the town, which was once again burned down.

After being rebuilt Belgrade was exposed over the following 150 years to strong oriental influence. Trade and craft industry flourished, and in the 17th c. the population rose to 100,000. This period of peace ended in 1688, when Belgrade was taken by the Austrians; then in 1690 the Turks recaptured the town and destroyed it once again. In 1717 Prince Eugene of Savoy recovered it for Austria, and during the following 22 years of Austrian rule it began to lose its oriental features and come under Western European influence. Then in 1739 the Turks again regained control, and the newly built churches were converted into mosques. The Austrians remained, however, in Zemun, with the Sava as the boundary between East and West, and made a number of attempts to recover the town, with further destruction and subsequent rebuilding.

The conclusion of peace in 1791 brought Belgrade a temporary breathing space, but this was followed by a period during which the town suffered the greatest trials of its long history: mass murders and plundering by the janissaries after the death of Mustapha Pasha (1801); a Serbian rising against the Turks (1804); the liberation of Belgrade in 1806 and its reconquest by the Turks in 1813, with further devastation; a second Serbian rising in 1815, which failed to drive the Turks out of the town. The Turks did not withdraw until 1867.

In 1914 the Austrians moved into Belgrade from their advanced post in Zemun and remained there until 1918, when it became the capital of the new kingdom of the Serbs, Croats and Slovenes. The town now developed rapidly and grew still further in size. On April 6 1941 the Luftwaffe attacked Belgrade, and this was followed by the German occupation, which ended on October 20, 1944 when Tito's partisans entered the town together with the Red Army.

SIGHTS. – The fortress of **Kalemegdan**,on the high ground at the confluence of the Danube and the Sava, has played a central part in all the vicissitudes of Belgrade's history. The fortress and its surrounding *park* are the best starting point for a sightseeing tour of the town, since the whole development of Belgrade is most clearly reflected here. The name is Turkish (*kale*, "town", *megdan*, "field"). Of the Roman stronghold of Singidunum there remain only some fragments of walls. Most of the structures visible today date from the 18th c., when they were built by the Austrians on the site of older fortifications which did not match up to contemporary military requirements.

The fortress consists of two parts, an upper and a lower ward. A number of gates lead into the *upper ward*, from which we descend into a broad moat containing a display of guns and other weapons, tanks and vehicles of both world wars, including a gunboat deployed by the partisans on the Danube. Above the moat is an octagonal *clock-tower (sahat kula)* of the 18th c. The finest **view of the Danube and the Sava** is to be had

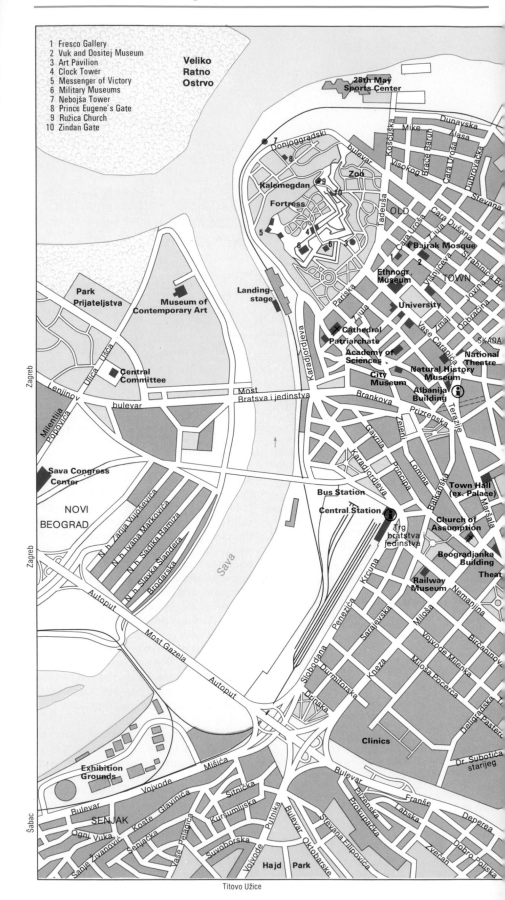

1 Fresco Gallery
2 Vuk and Dositej Museum
3 Art Pavilion
4 Clock Tower
5 Messenger of Victory
6 Military Museums
7 Nebojša Tower
8 Prince Eugene's Gate
9 Ružica Church
10 Zindan Gate

Veliko
Ratno
Ostrvo

28th May
Sports Center

Dunavska

Mike   Alasa

Donjoggradski

bulevar

Zoo

Kalemegdan

Fortress

OLD

Cara Dušana

Bajrak Mosque

Ethnogr.
Museum   TOWN

Park
Prijateljstva   Museum of
Contemporary Art

Landing-
stage

University

Cathedral
Patriarchate

SKADA

Academy of
Sciences   National
Theatre

City
Museum   Natural History
Museum

Central
Committee

Most
Bratsva i jedinstva

Brankova   Albanija
Building

bulevar

Sava Congress
Center

Bus Station   Town Hall
(ex. Palace)

NOVI
BEOGRAD   Central Station

Church of
Assumption

Trg
bratstva i
jedinstva

Beogradjanka
Building

Sava   Railway
Museum   Theat

Autoput

Most Gazela   Autoput

Clinics

Zagreb

Zagreb

Šabac

Exhibition
Grounds   Mišića

SENJAK

Hajd Park

Titovo Užice

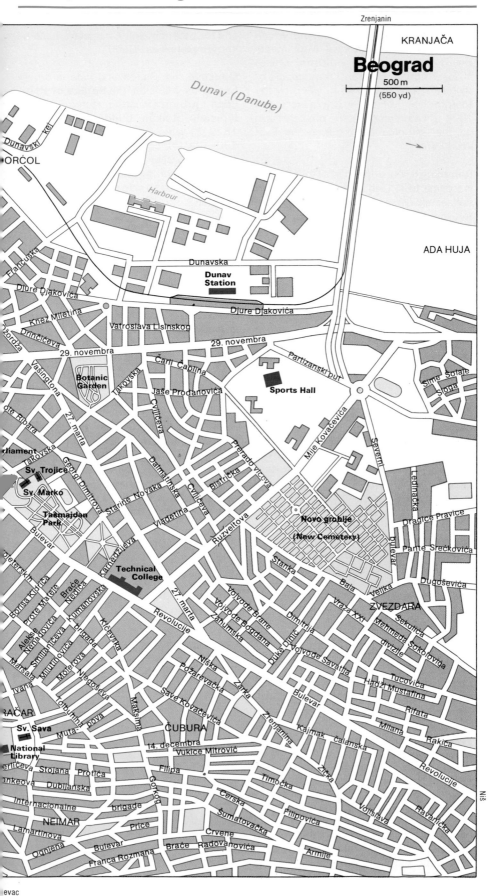

Zrenjanin

KRANJAČA

Beograd

500 m

(550 yd)

Dunav (Danube)

Dunavski kej

ORČOL

Harbour

ADA HUJA

Dunavska

Dunav Station

Flančuska

Djure Djakovića

Knez Miletina

Djure Djakovića

Vatroslava Lisinskog

Drinčićeva

Djordža

29. novembra

29. novembra

Vasingtona

Čarli Čaplina

Partizanski put

Sine Solaje

Botanic Garden

Takovska

Jaše Prodanovića

Sports Hall

Sloga

27. marta

Cvijićeva

die Ripara

Mije Kovačevića

rliament

Takovska

Georgi Dimitrova

Prerado Vrcova

Severni

Ledinačka

Sv. Trojice

Sv. Marko

Starine Novaka

Dalmatinska

Cvijićeva

Bistrička

Dragiče Pravice

Tašmajdan Park

Vladetina

Novo groblje

Pante Srečkovića

Bulevar

Karnedžijeva

Ruzveltova

(New Cemetery)

Bulevar

Petarska

Borisa Kidriča

Braće Nedića

Kumanovska

Kičevska

Stanka

Bala

Velika

Dugoševića

Technical College

27. marta

Vojvode Brane

Vojvode Bogdana

Zahumska

ZVEZDARA

Aleksa Nenadovića

prote Mateje

brigada

Revolucije

Dimitrija

Vraža XXI

Sekulica

Mehmeda Sokolovića

divizije

Maršala

Smiljanićeva

Milutinovica

Moljerova

Negoševa

Niška

Požarevačka

Žarka

Duke Dinić

Vojvode Savatija

Tucovica

Hadži Mustafina

Ivana

Maksima

Save Kovačevića

Bulevar

Rifata

RAČAR

Tolbuhina

pova

Muta

Zrenjanina

Kajmak

čalanska

Milana

Rakica

Sv. Sava

ČUBURA

14. decembra

Vukice Mitrović

National Library

Žička

Revolucije

eričeva

Stojana Protića

Filipa

Timočka

ankeova

Dubljanska

Gorkog

Cerska

Vojislava

Ravaničke

internacionalne

brigade

NEIMAR

Price

Šumatovačke

Filipovica

Lamartinova

Crvene

Armije

Ognjena

Bulevar

Braće Radovanovića

Franca Rozmana

Niš

evac

from a terrace below a building which now houses the Historical Monuments Board. Here too is a **column** with a bronze figure of the *"Messenger of Victory"* (total height 43 ft/13 m) by the sculptor Ivan Meštrović, it was erected in 1928 to commemorate the breakthrough on the Salonica front during the First World War.

Returning to the upper part of the fortress, we come to a 15th c. tower which now houses an *Observatory*. Beyond this are two other massive round towers, a suspension bridge and the former prison. On the way down to the *lower ward* we pass the *Ružica Church* (wall paintings of the Mother of God and Serbian rulers) and the *Orkva Sv*. The lower ward was built after the Turkish occupation in 1521 to provide defence against attack from the Sava and the Danube. The surviving structures in this part of the fortress were largely destroyed during the Second World War, but **Prince Eugene's Gate**, built in 1719 to commemorate the victory over the Turks two years previously, still stands by itself in a grassed-over area. A short distance away is the best preserved structure surviving from the earlier fortress, the 15th c. **Nebojša ("Fear Not") Tower**, frequently used as a torture chamber and prison.

The fortress is separated from the town by a *park* containing many busts of writers and scholars. In the main avenue is a *monument in honour of France* (by Ivan Meštrović, 1929), commemorating the alliance with France in the First World War. On the Danube side of the park stands the *Cvijeta Zuzporić Art Pavilion*, which mounts regular exhibitions of work by painters and sculptors. In the lower part of the park is the *Belgrade Zoo*.

The street below the Kalemegdan fortress and park, close to the Sava, runs into Ul. Sime Markovića, which leads into the old part of Belgrade. Here, at the corner of 7th July Street (Ulica Sedmoga Jula), stands the Orthodox **Cathedral** (1837–45), with a tall Baroque tower. Opposite it is one of the most interesting cafés in Belgrade, the *Café?*. The café was established while the church was being built and was called the "Café by the Church"; but this association of the church with a secular place of entertainment offended the clergy, and the owner was directed to change the name. This he refused to do,

and the café, remaining nameless, became known merely as "Café?"

Opposite the church and café- is a very handsome mansion, the **Palace of Princess Ljubica** (façade restored 1978), a typically Balkan building erected in 1829–31 which was occupied during the 19th c. by Prince Miloš and his family. – At the same street intersection is a fourth notable building, the **Museum of the Serbian Orthodox Church**, with material from churches and monasteries.

Parallel with Ul. Sime Markovića, also beginning at Kalemegdan Park, is *Ul. Kneza Mihajla*, Belgrade's principal commercial and shopping street (pedestrian precinct). Roughly half way along this street we come to the *Exhibition Gallery of the Serbian Academy of Sciences and Arts*. At its far end it joins the broad boulevard known as the **Terazije**, with the *Tourist Information Center* in the first pedestrian underpass. Until the first half of the 19th c. this was an area of water meadows and marshland. The street is now lined by numerous modern buildings, including the high-rise *Albanija Building*, the Moskva, Balkan and Kasina Hotels, the **Old Palace** and the **New Palace**, formerly the residence of the royal family and now occupied by the *Parliaments* of the city of Belgrade and the republic of Serbia. During the summer many restaurants and cafés set out tables and chairs in the open air.

Bearing left from the Terazije, we come into Marx-Engels Square. Immediately on the left a modern tower block houses the Trade Union Center. Opposite this are the

Parliament Building

St Mark's Church

Rector's Office to **Republic Square** (*Trg Republike*). In the middle of the square is an imposing bronze *equestrian statue of Prince Michael Obrenović* (by Enrico Pazzi, 1862); the prince, who fought for the liberation of Serbia from the Turks, is depicted pointing towards the territory then still occupied by the enemy.

On the left-hand side of the square can be seen the handsome façade of the **National Theatre** (714 seats) which was built in 1868 and has since been restored on three occasions, most recently in 1965 (drama, opera, ballet). On the NW side of the square is the ****National Museum**, one of the finest museums in Yugoslavia, which offers an almost complete picture of the country's art and culture from prehistoric times to the present day, with particular emphasis on Serbia.

The *Prehistoric Department* on the *ground floor* covers the Stone, Bronze and Iron Ages. Particularly notable items are the **gold jewelry** from Velika Vrbica and the wagon from Duplja. – Outstanding items in the *Department of Classical Antiquity* include **gold masks** from Trebeniště, a late Roman **bronze head** of *Constantine the Great* (who was born in Naissus, now Niš), one of the three surviving copies of **Phidias's Athena Parthenos** and material from excavations at Stobi, including two satyrs. – On the *first floor* is material of the early medieval period, together with copies and originals of frescoes from Serbian monasteries and icons. – *Second floor:* in the gallery to the right *pictures* by 20th c. Yugoslav artists; to the left a gallery containing works by foreign painters from the 16th c. to the middle of the 20th c., including paintings by **Tintoretto, Rubens, Claude Monet, Paul Gauguin** and **Picasso**. – In the entrance lobby and other rooms in the museum are examples of modern *sculpture*, including work by Ivan Meštrović. A large hall on the second floor is used for special exhibitions of works from foreign galleries.

offices of "Borba", the Socialist Alliance newspaper, and adjoining this, to the right, another high-rise building of rather earlier date with the **Museum of the Revolution** on the ground floor. From 1948 to 1965 the upper floors housed the offices of the Central Committee of the Yugoslav Communist Party.

On the far side of a small public garden stands the **Parliament Building** (1932), a massive structure with a central dome which houses the Yugoslav Assembly, the Skupština. In front of it is a bronze monument, the "Dance of the Black Horses" (1939). – A little way E, in Tašmajdan Park beyond the *Head Post Office*, rises the imposing **St Mark's Church** (*Sv. Marko*), built in 1932–41 on the model of the church of Gračanica monastery (see p. 189). Beyond this again is the Russian Orthodox *Church of the Holy Trinity* (Crkva Sv. Trojice), built in 1925 by the Russian general P. N. von Wrangel.

Returning to the street bordering Kalemegdan Park, we take a street which runs parallel to Ul. Kneza Mihajla, named successively Uzun Mirkova, Studentski Trg and Vase Čarapića. This leads past the **Belgrade Philharmonic Hall**, the **Open University** (concert hall, exhibition gallery, cinema) and the University

To see something more of old Belgrade we should return once again towards Kalemegdan, taking Ul. Vase Čarapića to reach Students' Square (Studentski Trg) and turning right at the far end of the square into Ul. Bracé Jugovicá to see the **Tomb of Sheikh Mustapha** (1783), one of the few relics of the Turkish period in Belgrade. Off this street to the left is 7th July Street (Ul. Sedmoga Jula), on the left-hand side of which is the **Jewish Historical Museum**, in the former Jewish quarter, one of the oldest parts of Belgrade. The museum was established by the Association of Jewish Groups in Belgrade, which began in 1945 to collect material illustrating Jewish life of the past and present.

Near the Jewish Museum, at Ul. Gospodar Jevremova 11, is the minaret of the **Bajrak Mosque** (*Bajrakli Džamija* or "Flag Mosque"), the only survivor of more than a hundred mosques which Belgrade possessed during the Turkish period. It is called the Flag Mosque because it used to fly a flag to tell the other mosques in the city when it was the hour for prayer. The mosque now stands below the present ground level, and visitors going down the steps to enter it feel themselves transported into another world within the modern city. The Flag Mosque was built in 1690, and during the Austrian occupation of 1717–39 it served temporarily as a Christian church.

Congress Center, Novi Beograd

Continuing along the street, we take the second street on the left, Ul. Cara Uroša, at No. 20 of which is the *Fresco Gallery of the National Museum. This contains copies of all the finest wall paintings of the medieval period from monasteries and churches in Serbia, Macedonia, Montenegro and Bosnia-Hercegovina.

At the end of Ul. Gospodar Jevremova is another interesting museum, the **Museum of the Serbian Theatre**, which illustrates the development of the theatre in Serbia from the earliest times to the present day; it has a large collection of portraits, busts, posters, scenery, costumes, old playbills and photographs. To the right of the Theatre Museum is the **Vuk and Dositej Museum**, in an old school-house (founded 1808).

Skadarska Street now branches off on the right, leading to the old district of *SKADARLIJA, the Montmartre of Belgrade. In this quarter live many Yugoslav writers, actors, painters, composers, journalists and bohemians. Every evening from May to September the whole district becomes a pedestrian precinct, and numbers of students, workers and others – mostly young people – gather in the streets and outside the taverns, snack bars and street stalls to talk and argue, stroll about and meet their friends. Student bands give impromptu open-air concerts, and the activity – eating, drinking, laughing, flirting – goes on until midnight. Tourists flock to the surrounding garden cafés and restaurants, which are beyond the means of the local young people. The restaurants serve local specialties from all parts of Yugoslavia, wine and beer flow in abundance, and soon the visitor ceases to care whether the gipsies, street singers and other entertainers are in the authentic folk tradition or are merely putting on a show for the tourists: at any rate an evening in Skadarlija is an experience he will not soon forget.

On the other bank of the Sava is the new district of **NOVI BEOGRAD**, which is almost a satellite town in its own right.

Crossing the river on the expressway which runs N to Zagreb, we see on the right the new Sava **Congress Center** (*Sava Centar*). Consisting of a ground floor and two trapezoid galleries, it contains ten or 12 conference halls, a variety of other rooms, a press center, post office, bank and shops, a restaurant and several snack bars. The complex is able to accommodate up to 5000 conference members at the same time.

Leaving the city by way of Ul. Brankova and turning right after crossing the Sava, we come in some 1¼ miles/2 km (on left) to the ***Museum of Contemporary Art**, a notable example of modern architecture (1960–65), with more than 3000 works by 20th c. Yugoslav artists (drawings, sculpture, pictures, etc.). The museum is designed to serve a broad-based educational purpose: its object is to introduce modern art to the public and help them to understand it. To the W of the museum is **Friendship Park** (*Park Prijateljstva*), with an area of 62 acres. From the museum can be seen the tallest building in Novi Beograd, the 24-storey tower which houses the *Central Committee of the League of Communists of Yugoslavia*. Near this is the extensive range of buildings (completed 1961) occupied by the *Federal Executive Council*, with gardens separating it from Lenin Boulevard. Farther N, on the road to Zagreb, is the *University City*.

Excavators and cranes are still busy on the left bank of the Sava, and other building sites are waiting. Attractive features of the new development are the generous spacing of the modern apartment buildings and the abundance of greenery which relieves the outlines of the new buildings. While the buildings erected in the early sixties display little architectural imagination, having been thrown up quickly in the standard Western European style of the period, the newer ones show an attempt to achieve a more personal style through the individual design of the façades and a vigorous use of colour.

SURROUNDINGS. – Leaving Novi Beograd on a road which runs past Yugoslavia's most modern hotel, the Jugoslavija, situated on the banks of the Sava, we come to **Zemun**, once the Austrian outpost confronting the Turks in Belgrade. The town is entered by way of Karadjordje Street. On a low hill can be seen the ruins of a fortress first mentioned in the records in the 9th c.; the surviving remains, however, date only from the 15th c., with a central keep built by the Hungarians in 1869. The town contains many old buildings and a number of interesting churches, the oldest of which is St Nicholas's Church, with some work dating from 745.

A popular resort of the people of Belgrade is **Topčider Park**, in the valley of the little river of that name, with the Konak (Palace) of Prince Miloš. The palace, a mingling of Balkan and Central European architectural styles, was built in 1834; it now houses a Serbian Museum. Also in the park are a House of Young Pioneers (a recreation and cultural base for young people), a sports complex, a golf club and, on the highest point, the Košutnjak camp site.

11 miles/18 km S of Belgrade, reached from the Kragujevac road, is *Mt Avala (1677 ft/511 m), to which there are daily sightseeing tours (3 hours) from May 1 to September 30. From the top there are magnificent views of Belgrade, the confluence of the Sava and the Danube, the Banat plain and the Šumadija hills. The site of an old castle is now occupied by a monumental mausoleum containing the Tomb of the Unknown Soldier, one of Ivan Meštrović's finest works. Near this rises the Television Tower, 650 ft/200 m high, with a revolving restaurant at 425 ft/130 m.

From March onwards there are hydrofoil trips daily down the Danube to the **Iron Gates** (see p. 89).

From Belgrade to Bar by Rail

The railway line from Belgrade to Bar (296 miles/476 km), carrying both passenger and freight traffic, runs through magnificent scenery and is impressively engineered, with numerous tunnels and bridges. There are several trains daily between Belgrade and Bar. From Bar to Belgrade there are organised excursions, returning by air.

The idea of constructing a railway line from Belgrade to the southern Adriatic was first conceived in 1855, but the plan was abandoned on account of the difficulty of the mountainous terrain through which the route would have to pass. It was almost another hundred years before it became possible, with modern techniques and equipment, to undertake construction of the line in 1952. The work took almost 25 years, and the line was brought into operation in May 1976. It passes through 254 tunnels, with a total length of 71 miles/114·5 km, and over 234 bridges, reaching a height of over 3300 ft/1000 m. The Mala Rijeka

From the Danube to the Adriatic
(Belgrade-Bar Railway line)

Bridge, 50 yd/500 m long, is the tallest railway bridge in Europe (660 ft/201 m).
Trains are sometimes delayed after storms in the mountains and when the snow melts in spring.

After leaving the Central Station in **Belgrade** the line crosses the *Sava* and runs through the *Šumadija* hills. From *Lajkovac* to *Valjevo* it follows the course of the River *Kolubara*, and then begins to wind its way up more steeply into the hills.

At *Titovo Užice* a branch lines goes off to Niš. The main line now runs through the beautiful *Zlatibor hills*, an area popular with walkers and climbers. Beyond *Priboj* it runs into the valley of the *Lim*, here dammed to form an artificial lake 9 miles/15 km long, and follows the river upstream. After *Prijepolje* it passes from Serbia into Montenegro and continues into the Montenegrin hills, with numerous bridges and tunnels.

Then follow the little towns of *Bijelo Polje* and *Mojkovac*, after which the line runs high above the romantic valley of the upper *Tara*. It then continues through the Biogradska Gora National Park to *Kolašin*, reaching its highest point at 3386 ft/1032 m. Thereafter it descends through the **Morača Gorge*, passing *Morača Monastery* (see p. 189), and crosses the *Mala Rijeka*, a tributary of the Morača, on a* bridge 550 yd/500 m long and 660 ft/201 m high.

Titograd (alt. 138 ft/42 m: see p. 213) lies in the marshy plain N of *Lake Scutari* (p. 186), which is crossed on a causeway. S of the lake the line again climbs steeply and after passing through the *Paštrovići* massif in the Sozina Tunnel, the longest in Yugoslavia (6750 yd/6171 m), reaches the Adriatic coast, which it follows in a south-easterly direction to the terminal at **Bar** (p. 41).

Bihać

Republic: Bosnia-Hercegovina (Bosna i Hercegovina).
Altitude: 774 ft/236 m. – Population: 35,000.
Post code: YU-77000. – Telephone code: 0 77.
(i) **Turistička Agencija Pounjeturist,**
Ulica Maršala Tita 1;
tel. 2 93 44.

HOTELS. – *Park*, B, 180 b., tel. 2 94 00; *Ada*, B, 172 b., tel. 2 93 65.

EVENTS. – *International Canoeing Championship*, held annually in summer on the River Una.

SPORT. – Good fishing in the River Una; shooting (wild pig, capercaillie) in the Plješevica range, S of the town (information from Tourist Office in Bihać).

The little country town of Bihać, on the River Una, may take some visitors by surprise. They will see brightly painted peasants' carts rattling into the town, the horses being left to graze in a shady area by the river and the peasants dragging their sacks of grain to be ground in a mill worked by water-power; and then, at the fruit and vegetable market, they will see the town's more modern aspect – women in ordinary western dress for whose business the stallholders noisily compete and swarms of girls window-shopping to keep up with the latest fashions.

HISTORY. – In the 13th c. the Hungarian king Bela IV fortified Bihać, now the most westerly town in Bosnia; stretches of wall dating from this period are still to be seen around the old town. In 1592 Bihać was taken by the Turks, who strengthened its defences, making it a powerfully fortified counterpart to the Austrian stronghold of Karlovac. During the Second World War Bihać was the hub of the Yugoslav Resistance, and the first meeting of the Anti-fascist Council of the

Tower of Romanesque church, Bihać

National Liberation of Yugoslavia (AVNOJ) was held here in November 1942. This landmark in the history of Yugoslav unification is commemorated by a number of monuments in Bihać, as well as by the Army House and the AVNOJ Museum. Both of these establishments are visited every year by many parties of schoolchildren, whom visitors will often encounter as they go about the town; they will have the same experience in Jajce, where the second congress of the AVNOJ was held in 1943.

SIGHTS. – Bihać suffered severe destruction during the Second World War. One of the surviving buildings is the **Fethija Mosque**, a Gothic church which was converted into a mosque after the Turkish conquest; it is a happy synthesis of Christian and oriental features.

The area around the **Captain's Tower** (*Kapetanova Kula*), also known locally as the Turkish Tower, has been converted into a fine museum. On the ground floor is the department of Bosnian and Turkish folk art, on the first floor material from the period of the Japodes (Iron Age), on the second relics of the Turkish period, on the third more recent material. The ruins of a *Romanesque church* damaged by bombardment have been preserved as a memorial. In front of the tower is a *Turkish cemetery*.

SURROUNDINGS. – 5½ miles/9 km SE, at *Ripač*, pile-dwellings of the Hallstatt period (800–500 B.C.) have been excavated. Near the town is the ruined Sokolac Castle.

Biograd

Republic: Croatia (Hrvatska).
Altitude: 16 ft/5 m. – Population: 3000.
Post code: YU-57210. – Telephone code: 0 57.

ⓘ **Turistički Biro,**
Obala Štampalije;
tel. 8 31 21.

HOTELS. – *Ilirija*, B, 339 b., tel. 8 31 08, with its own boating harbour, winch and ramp; *Adriatic*, B, 205 b., tel. 8 30 42; *Kornati*, 178 b., tel. 8 31 68; *Motel Biograd*, 168 b., tel. 8 31 54. – 3 miles/5 km from Biograd is the *Crvena Luka* holiday centre, B, with some 600 beds in the hotel and chalets, tel. 8 31 06.

CAMP SITES. – *Soline*; *Crvena Luka* (3 miles/5 km) from Biograd; side road off the Zadar–Šibenik coast road), tel. 8 31 06.

NATURIST FACILITIES. – Bay at Crvena Luka; on the little island of Sv. Katarina, off Biograd.

SPORT. – Scuba diving, water-skiing at Biograd and Crvena Luka, rental of row boats and canoes at Crvena Luka, rental of sail boats at Biograd.

Biograd, situated on the Adriatic coast opposite the island of Pašman, is a pleasant holiday resort with plenty of local character. It was once a place of some consequence as a residence of the Croatian kings, but there is no evidence of this in the present aspect of the town. Although Biograd is surrounded by gardens and vineyards and the coastal waters are well stocked with fish, the inhabitants of the town look to the tourist and holiday trade as their main source of income. The hotels and bathing beaches are near the ferry to Pašman.

HISTORY. – In the course of its history Biograd was twice so thoroughly destroyed that not even ruins were left to tell the tale. The first settlement, on a peninsula in the Pašman Channel 19 miles/30 km S of Zadar, was known as *Blandona*, a name first mentioned in the 10th c. by the Byzantine emperor Constantine Porphyrogenitus. Under the Croatian kings Biograd became chief town of a district and then a royal residence. In 1050 the Croatian king Petar Krešimir founded two Benedictine houses, one for men and one for women, and established the bishopric of Biograd. The town flourished, and for a time was of greater importance than Zadar. In 1102 King Koloman of Hungary was crowned king of Croatia here. In 1125, however, the Venetians captured the town and, after plundering it, burned it down. This took place on Good Friday, and the event is still commemorated annually on that day.

After the capture of Zadar by the armies of the fourth Crusade the inhabitants of that town sought refuge in Biograd, which they named *Stari Zadar* (Old Zadar). After a period during which it was governed by various local rulers, Biograd fell into Venetian hands again in 1409 and remained Venetian until 1797. Although the town walls and the castle were strengthened between 1573 and 1575 the Croatian defenders of the town were compelled in 1646 to withdraw in the face of Turkish pressure, but before leaving applied the "scorched earth" principle and reduced the town once again to a heap of rubble. Within two years much of the place had been rebuilt, but thereafter Biograd remained a small provincial township of no importance. It was only with the growth of tourism after the Second World War that this forgotten little village was to enjoy a revival of prosperity.

SIGHTS. – The two total destructions of the town have left it with no buildings of historical interest. Material of the Roman and early Croatian period which was found here is now in the Zadar museum. The local museum in Biograd displays finds recovered from a vessel wrecked off the island of Gnalić in the Pašman Channel at the end of the 16th c. (tools, jewelry, pottery, etc.). At Bošana, outside the town, the *foundations of Roman villas* have been brought to light.

SURROUNDINGS. – 3 miles/5 km SE of Biograd lies the interesting **Lake Vrana** (*Vransko Jezero*: not to be confused with the lake of the same name on the island of Cres, p. 69), 8½ miles/14 km long and up to 2½ miles/ 4 km across. The desolate surroundings, the dusty road and the reedy verges of the lake do little to enhance its scenic attractions, but it offers excellent fishing (carp, eels). – It is worth visiting the village of **Vrana**, 2 miles/3 km NE of the lake, for the sake of the Maškovića Han, one of the few examples of Ottoman architecture in Dalmatia, bearing witness to the activity of the Turks in draining this marshy and malaria-ridden area in the 17th c. Near the caravanserai are the remains of a Roman aqueduct which carried water to Zadar.

4 miles/6 km SE of Biograd on the tongue of land which separates Lake Vrana from the sea is the village of **Pakoštane**. ¾ mile/1 km N of the village is a Club Méditerranée holiday camp (not open to visitors).

Seafront, Biograd

Bitola

Republic: Macedonia (Makedonija).
Altitude: 2034 ft/620 m. – Population: 65,000.
Post code: YU-97000. – Telephone code: 0 97.
ⓘ **Turist Biro,**
Bulevar 1 Maja;
tel. 2 20 66.

HOTELS. – *Epinal*, B, 200 b., tel. 2 47 77; *Makedonija*, B, 50 b., tel. 2 29 35.

EVENTS. – "Ilinden Days" (annually at end of July and beginning of August), a festival of folk singing and dancing from all over Yugoslavia, but mainly from Macedonia.

SPORT. – Skiing complex in Pelister range.

The town of Bitola lies on the western edge of the Pelagonian plain, enclosed on two sides by hills, some of them green, others bleak and bare. It is of interest to visitors mainly as an overnight stop and for the excavations of the ancient city of Heraclea, on the southern outskirts of the town. Earlier accounts of Bitola refer to it as offering a cross-section of the artistic and cultural development of Macedonia; but the old buildings have now been swept away and replaced by modern blocks of flats, and Bitola has developed into an industrial town.

HISTORY. – Throughout its history Bitola lay in a disputed frontier region. The heart of the present town, now the second largest in Macedonia (after Skopje), lies 2 miles/3 km from the site of the ancient *Heraclea Lyncestis*, founded by Philip II of Macedonia (360–336 B.C.), father of Alexander the Great. After the Greeks came the Romans, whose great highway from Durrës on the Adriatic (now in Albania) to Constantinople, the Via Egnatia, passed through Heraclea – a circumstance which enhanced the

Roman remains at Heraclea, near Bitola

importance of the town and led to its becoming capital of the Roman province of Lyncestis. Subsequently it was ravaged by plunderers, earthquakes and finally the advancing Slavs in the 6th c. A.D., bringing its existence to an end. Excavations have been carried out since 1935, most recently on an amphitheatre discovered in 1978.

Bitola itself, which first appears in the records in the 10th c., was under Bulgar, Serbian and Byzantine rule before falling into Turkish hands in 1382. Thereafter it was known as *Monastir* ("monastery"). During the Balkan Wars (1912–13) the Turks were defeated at Bitola. There was further fighting during the First World War, then Bulgarian, German and Austrian forces clashed with French and Serbian troops, causing much destruction in the town and many casualties (German and French military cemeteries). Bitola has preserved some notable buildings of the Turkish period but no relics of medieval architecture.

SIGHTS. – The *excavations of **Heraclea** are reached from the town by taking the road which runs S to the Greek frontier crossing at Niki. A good general view can be had from the hill above the site. To the left are Roman *baths*, notable particularly for an almost perfectly preserved cold bath faced with white marble, as well as four basins for warm and hot baths. In front of the bathing establishment are the **Small Basilica** and then a group of temple columns and two statues. To the right is the *Large Basilica*, which, like the smaller one, was built on the site of earlier Roman structures. Particularly notable features of the site are the numerous *mosaics*, with ornamental patterns and hunting scenes. To the right, on the slopes of the hill, are the excavations of the *Amphitheatre*. The experts believe that so far the site has yielded up only a fraction of its hidden treasures.

In Bitola itself the most notable buildings are the **Turkish Clock-Tower** and the **Jeni Mosque** which stands opposite it. The mosque now houses a museum, with periodically changing displays. In Ul. Ivana Milutinovića (on the road to Prilep) is the brick-built **Ajdar Kadi Mosque**, the largest and perhaps the finest of the town's mosques, with inscriptions from the Koran. The Greek Orthodox **Cathedral** of St Demetrius (*Sv. Dimitrije*), in a side street near the Clock-Tower, contains many icons and a fine 18th c. *iconostasis* of gilded wood in filigree patterns. The **Archaeological Museum**, in Marx-Engels Street, which branches off Marshall Tito Street near the Makedonija Hotel, displays material from Heraclea.

SURROUNDINGS. – 9 miles/15 km from Bitola, round the highest point in the Baba range (8534 ft/

2601 m), extends the **Pelister National Park**. The forests in this area – with species which include the interesting Macedonian pine (*Pinus peuce*) – are the home of bears, foxes and wild pigs, and the rocky crags are the haunt of eagles, vultures and falcons. Walkers and climbers can find accommodation in two mountain huts, at *Kopanka* (5282 ft/1610 m) and *Golemo Jezero* (7277 ft/2218 m), and in the mountain village of *Begova Češma*, in the middle of the park. – From Bitola it is only some 25 miles/40 km to *Lake Prespa (p. 166), with its beautiful bathing beaches.

Bled

Republic: Slovenia (Slovenija).
Altitude: 1644 ft/501 m. – Population: 5000.
Post code: YU-64260. – Telephone code: 0 64.
ⓘ **Turistično Društvo,**
Cankarjeva 6;
tel. 7 74 09.

HOTELS, – *Park*, A, 338 b., tel. 7 75 21; *Golf*, A, 290 b., tel. 7 75 91; *Grand Hotel Toplice*, A, 205 b., tel. 7 72 22, with annexes *Trst*, B, 86 b., *Jadran*, C, 82 b., and *Korotan*, D, 26 b.; *Jelovica*, B, 212 b., tel. 7 73 16, with annexes *Mežakla*, C, 75 b., *Blegaš*, D, 42 b., and *Bogatin*, D, 24 b.; *Kompas*, B. 171 b., tel. 7 75 31; *Krim Neu*, B, 143 b., tel. 7 74 18, with annexe *Moj Mir*, B, 23 b.; *Krim* B, 55 b., tel. 7 74 18; *Lovec*, B, 89 b., tel. 7 76 92; *Izletniški Dom Ribno*, D, 171 b., tel. 7 74 89. – IN POKLJUKA: *Sport-Hotel*, B, 75 b., tel. 7 74 93, with annexe *Dom Jelka*, D, 40 b., and pension *Pri Mari*, D, 32 b.

CAMP SITES. – *Zaka* (on road to Lake Bohinj, on shores of lake), tel. 7 73 25; *Šobec* (1¼ miles/2 km before Bled, on a man-made bathing lake), tel. 7 75 00.

NATURIST FACILITIES. – Naturist periods daily in indoor swimming pool of Golf Hotel.

SPORT AND RECREATION. – SUMMER: shooting; climbing; tennis; golf (18-hole course); tenpin bowling; minigolf; life-saving instruction, rowing, sailing and fishing on Lake Bled; boat trips and outings in horse-carriages; airfield for light aircraft nearby. – WINTER: skating and curling on rink and on lake; rides in horse-drawn sleighs; *Zatrnik* skiing complex (2891–4147 ft/881–1264 m; ski-tows, chair-lift; mostly easy descents); *Pokljuka* skiing area (4265 ft/ 1300 m; ski-tow; cross-country skiing). Shuttle service of buses between Bled and the winter sports areas.

Bled, lying on beautiful *Lake Bled (Blejsko Jezero: motorboats prohibited), developed into a spa after the establishment of a "solar treatment establishment" by a Swiss doctor named Arnold Rikli. The spa establishments were supplied with mineral water – as the Toplice and Golf Hotels still are – by various hot springs on the shores of the lake and in the lake itself. Bled also became a

favourite summer resort with diplomats in Belgrade; and President Tito himself had a villa built on the S side of the lake, with extensive grounds. During the 1960s the new and comfortable hotels attracted increasing numbers of conferences; and finally the new skiing complex at Zatrnik, 5 miles/8 km away, has made Bled an all-year-round tourist and holiday resort, offering a wide range of facilities for visitors, both those seeking a cure and those who are perfectly well.

Church of St Mary, Lake Bled

HISTORY. – Lake Bled was formed by the action of glaciers, which left the hill now occupied by the castle and the circular island in the lake as isolated features, ground down by the ice. The shores of the lake were already occupied in Roman times. During the great migrations the region was occupied by the Slavs. In 1004 the German emperor, Henry II, presented Bled and the surrounding area to Bishop Albuin of Brixen (Bressanone). From 1803 to 1838 the territory was part of the Habsburg empire, with the exception of the seven years from 1806 to 1813, when it was incorporated in Napoleon's Illyrian Provinces. Then it came into the hands of the bishops of Brixen again for a period of 20 years. Thereafter it passed to Austria, which finally lost it, together with the rest of Slovenia, at the end of the First World War.

SIGHTS. – On a crag which rears up to a height of almost 330 ft/100 m above the crystal waters of the lake stands **Bled Castle**. Although the present structure dates from the Baroque period it has preserved the characteristic form of a medieval castle with its well-guarded entrance and two courtyards. The *Chapel* has fine 17th c. frescoes. The *Museum* housed in a wing of the castle contains material from early Slav burials, items which belonged to the bishops of Brixen and furniture and furnishings of different

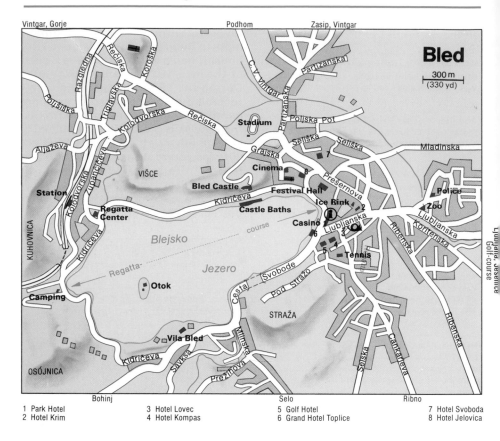

Vintgar, Gorje   Podhom   Zasip, Vintgar

Bled

⊢ 300 m ⊣
(330 yd)

1 Park Hotel   3 Hotel Lovec   5 Golf Hotel   7 Hotel Svoboda
2 Hotel Krim   4 Hotel Kompas   6 Grand Hotel Toplice   8 Hotel Jelovica

periods. – The *parish church of St Martin* in Bled, in front of which are walls dating from the Turkish period, contains modern frescoes. On the island in the lake are the Baroque *church of St Mary in the Lake* (early 17th c.) and the remains of a settlement dating from the 11th–8th c. B.C. which were excavated in the 1960s.

Lake Bled is the great Yugoslav *regatta complex*. The first rowing races were held here in 1931, and in 1966 the world championship was contested on the lake. Visitors can look around the regatta area.

In order to make fuller use of the winter season Bled established a new **skiing complex** at Zatrnik in 1972–73, easy access being provided by a shuttle service of buses. Between 2950 ft/900 m and 3950 ft/ 1200 m a double chair-lift and four ski-tows were installed, from the upper stations of which 16 trails, mostly easy descents, can be reached. Although these slopes attract few speed skiers aiming at records, all necessary safety and rescue arrangements have been provided. The essential après-ski facilities are supplied by the hotels in Bled.

The road from Bled to Zatrnik continues through dense pine forests to the **Pokljuka plateau** and the Sport Hotel. On the gentle slope in front of the hotel is a ski-tow, but otherwise this is territory for cross-country skiing. The trails are neither marked nor prepared.

Bogomil Tombs

Republic: Bosna-Hercegovina (Bosna i Hercegovina).

The best preserved necropolis (cemetery) of Bogomil tombs in the whole of Yugoslavia is near the little town of **Stolac** (pop. 2500), 13 miles/21 km off the main road from Mostar to the Adriatic coast. There are a restaurant and simple holiday chalets at the cemetery.

The largest cemetery lies between Stolac and the little village of Radimlje. It contains 133 gravestones (*stećci*), some of them weighing up to 30 tons.

A second cemetery, at *Hutovo*, can be reached from Stolac on a gravel road. A third, at *Zabredj*, is reached by leaving Stolac on the road to Ljubinje and Trebinje and turning left at the far end of the town. A fourth, containing almost 300 Bogomil gravestones, lies a little way off the road from Stolac to Hutovo.

With the exception of the first, these cemeteries are quite inadequately signposted. It is advisable, therefore, to seek directions in Stolac.

The cemeteries around Stolac are the principal legacy of a heretical religious sect which was of considerable importance in the Balkans, from the political as well as a religious point of view, from the medieval period onwards. Since there is little documentary material

on the Bogomils, as the adherents of this heresy were called, their gravestones give valuable evidence on their lives and beliefs. It is only since the last war, however, that any scholarly effort has been made even to record the tombs in the Bogomil cemeteries, most of which are in remote country areas.

It is not yet possible to interpret all the figural representations and the inscriptions in old Cyrillic script on the tombs. Visitors can, however, get a first impression of the Bogomils from the cemetery between Radimlje and Stolac, and can follow this up by visiting some of the other cemeteries which can be reached from Stolac on various by-roads.

Bogomil tombs near Stolac

HISTORY. – The religious doctrines of the Bogomils can be traced back to Persia in the 3rd c. A.D., when a Christian priest named Mani sought to achieve a synthesis between the teachings of Zoroaster and of Christianity. Although Mani himself was executed his ideas were soon disseminated through Mesopotamia. From there they were brought to Europe by Roman legionaries, but at first found few adherents. It was only at the beginning of the 10th c., when a Bulgarian priest named Bogomil ("friend of God") began to teach that the world was created not by God but by the Devil, and that it was open to man to overcome the darkness of the Devil-made world, that the old ideas

brought in from Persia took on a fresh lease of life, appealing particularly to the peasants in the country areas.

The followers of Bogomil interpreted his doctrine as a call to take an active part in the life of the world. Thus they fought against the advancing Turks as irregulars or guerrillas. Later the desire for personal gain came to the fore, and parties ranged over the countryside as robbers and bandits.

At one stage the doctrines of Bogomilism reached as far afield as the south of France. Within the territory of present-day Yugoslavia it was not confined to Bosnia

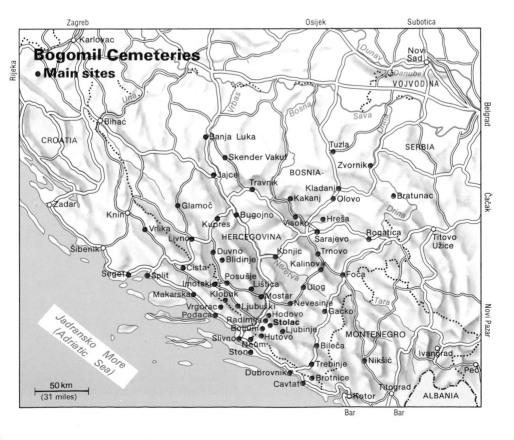

and Hercegovina but spread to Macedonia and southern Serbia. The movement died out at the beginning of the 16th c.

The first European scholar to take an interest in the Bogomil tombs was Arthur Evans, later famous as the discoverer of Knossos in Crete, but systematic study began only after the last war. So far some 5000 Bogomil tombs have been recorded. There are several hundred in the area around Stolac.

The 133 gravestones in the cemetery between Radimlje and Stolac, the one most visited by tourists, are scattered over an area of grassland bounded by cypresses. Some of the stones are carved with figures, others have geometric patterns. Only one stone in the cemetery has a detailed inscription. On one stone there is a representation of an arm raised towards the sun, symbolising man calling the powers of good to his aid; others show hunting scenes and a couple dancing.

Similar themes are found on stones in the other cemeteries mentioned above, some of them much better preserved. In these cemeteries the stones are frequently overgrown with grass and scrub, and it is sometimes very difficult to find them.

Bohinj

Republic: Slovenia (Slovenija).
Altitude of Lake Bohinj: 1716 ft/523 m.
Population of village (Bohinjska Bistrica): 300.
Telephone code: 0 64.
ⓘ Turist Biro Bohinj,
YU-64265 Bohinjsko Jezero;
tel. 7 63 70.

HOTELS. – *Zlatorog*, B, 96 b., tel. 7 63 81, with annexe *Ukanc*, B, 65 b.; *Bellevue*, C, 49 b., tel. 7 63 31, with annexe *Savica*, B, 74 b.; *Kompas-Stane Žagar*, D, 170 b., tel. 7 64 71; *Mladinski Dom*, with holiday chalets, D, 80 b., tel. 7 64 69; *Pod Voglom*, D, 58 b., tel. 7 64 61, with annexe *Rodica*, B, 52 b. – ON MT VOGEL: *Ski-Hotel*, C, 76 b., tel. 7 61 67, and pensions *Burja*, *Murka* and *Ruša*, together 60 b., tel. 7 61 67.

CAMP SITE. – *Zlatorog*, at Zlatorog Hotel, tel. 7 63 81.

EVENTS. – In winter Peasant Wedding, folk revue, Kravji Bal ("Cow Dance"); in summer Midsummer celebrations. Nordic skiing contests (FIS) in January.

SPORT and RECREATION. – SUMMER: Although *Lake Bohinj* reaches a temperature of 73°F/23°C, it is suitable for bathing only at the height of summer. Since it is surrounded by mountains for two-thirds of its extent it is not suited for sailing or wind-surfing. Motorboats are not permitted on the lake. – Rental of row boats; fishing; tennis; target shooting; riding. Mountain walking and climbing in the **Triglav** range (see under Julian Alps).

WINTER: Skiing area (no trees) on *Mt Vogel* at 4900–6200 ft/1500–1900 m (Dec.–April); cableway (limited capacity), 2 chair-lifts and 6 ski-tows; 5 mile/ 8 km run down to lake (height difference 3900 ft/ 1200 m); 9 miles/15 km cross-country ski trails, and ski trekking on *Dobrava* and *Komna plateau*.

*Lake Bohinj (Bohinjsko Jezero, alt. 1716 ft/523 m) is the central attraction of a holiday area, frequented in both summer and winter, lying some 25 miles/40 km SW of Bled. There is a commune of Bohinj, but the name is now applied to a wider area, taking in the attractive little village of Bohinjska Bistrica with its small hotels and pensions, the hotels at the outflow of the River Sava and on the S side of the lake, the holiday accommodation at the other end of the lake, at the Savica Falls, and the skiing area on Mt Vogel (with snow usually until April). The waters of the lake, which has an area of 765 acres, are rarely disturbed by a breath of wind and mirror the surrounding mountains with crystal clarity.

HISTORY. – Lake Bohinj began to attract visitors in the 19th c., and the first skiers came to Mt Vogel, using the primitive skis of the day and toiling their way up to the ski slopes on foot. Since the last war a flourishing holiday area has developed on the shores of the lake (except on the N side), with scenery reminiscent of Switzerland or Austria.

SIGHTS. – At the E end of the lake, beside the bridge over the Sava, is **St John's Church** (*Sv. Janez*), which frequently features in tourist brochures; it contains 15th and 16th c. frescoes. The road which runs past the church, away from the lake,

St John's Church, Lake Bohinj

Ski-tow, Mt Vogel

leads to the village of **Stara Fužina**, which has a *museum* devoted to the life of the mountain dairy farms. The road along the S side of the lake runs past the lower station of the cableway up Mt Vogel, then past a camp site on the shores of the lake (closed in winter), and ends at a mountain hut, the Dom Savica. From here there is a path up to the **Savica Falls**, which have a sheer drop of 200 ft/60 m. The path continues to the *Črno Jezero* (Black Lake), a 3–4 hours' climb.

Bovec

Republic: Slovenia (Slovenija).
Altitude: 1585 ft/483 m. – Population: 2700.
Post code: YU-65230. – Telephone code: 0 65.
ⓘ **Turistična Agencija,**
tel. 8 60 69.

HOTELS. – *Kanin*, B, 240 b., tel. 8 60 21; *Alp-Hotel*, B, 130 b., tel. 8 60 40.

CAMP SITE. – *Polovnik*, tel. 8 40 69.

SPORT and RECREATION. – SUMMER: climbing; walking in *Kanin* range (cableway); fishing; canoeing (white water). – WINTER: skiing in *Kanin* range (cableway in three stages from Bovec to winter sports area at 7200 ft/2200 m; chair-lift and several ski-tows); 2 mile/3.5 km long descent (difficult) to intermediate station of cableway (height difference 4265 ft/1300 m); also descents on Italian side; deep-snow trails. – Other facilities in course of development.

The village of Bovec in the Soča (Isonzo) valley, which until 1972 was known only to climbers, is due to be developed by 1992 into the leading Yugoslav winter sports complex, with accommodation for up to

12,000 visitors in hotels and pensions and on camp sites. Bovec itself is situated in the valley at an altitude of 1585 ft/483 m, where the snow lies only for a few weeks in winter. The skiing area is W of the village on the slopes of the Kanin range (highest point 8481 ft/2585 m), where the cold winds from the N meet the moister, warmer air from the nearby Adriatic, producing abundant falls of snow from November to May. The resort is still in the early stages of development.

HISTORY. – During the First World War the Kanin range lay on the bitterly contested front line between Austria and Italy. To facilitate the bringing up of supplies a road was built by Russian prisoners of war from Kranjska Gora through the Vršič range into the Soča valley.

After the end of the Second World War the fate of Bovec long remained uncertain. Both Italy and Yugoslavia claimed Trieste, and it remained an open question which side would get the Soča valley. When it was finally assigned to Slovenia there was a plan to construct a reservoir and hydroelectric station on the site of the village, involving the removal and resettlement of the inhabitants, but the plan had to be abandoned in the face of local resistance. Since, however, neither the local agriculture nor the presence of a military garrison in Bovec was sufficient to provide adequate subsistence for the local population, who increasingly drifted away from the area, a new plan was evolved to develop Bovec from its modest role as a base for climbers into an international holiday resort. In 1971 the United Nations included the development of Bovec into a winter sports complex (which will also be of benefit to the summer holiday trade) in their Upper Adriatic assisted development project.

The Town Planning Institute of the republic of Slovenia commissioned a French specialist firm to prepare plans for the development of the new resort. These were based on experience gained in France since the last war in the creation of new ski resorts. It was first calculated how many skiers the Kanin range could take; then the experts determined the number

Street Scene, Bovec

Upper station of the cableway in the Kanin range

and capacity of the cableways and ski-lifts required; and this in turn enabled the accommodation requirements and tourist infrastructure to be assessed. It is also planned to link up with the Italian winter sports complex of Stella Neva on the W side of the Kanin range, which already has a cableway running up to the Italian-Yugoslav frontier on the crest of the mountains.

SIGHTS. – There are no features of historical interest in Bovec. There is a pleasant drive up the * Trenta valley to the village of Trenta na Logu, with a *museum* containing an interesting collection of peasant implements and costumes and material on the history of the Alps. At the point where the road begins to climb to the Vršič pass a track (1 mile/1·55 km) goes off to the *source of the River Soča, gushing out of a cleft in the rock above the valley.

From the mountain restaurant in the Kanin range there are breathtaking views of Yugoslavia's highest peak, **Triglav (9397 ft/2864 m: see under Julian Alps), and the neighbouring mountain giants *Jalovec* (8672 ft/2643 m) and *Škrlatica* (8983 ft/2738 m). To the S the sky varies in hue from deep red to a delicate light blue: beyond lies the Adriatic.

Brač

Republic: Croatia (Hrvatska).
Area of island: 152 sq. miles/394 sq. km. –
Population: 12,500.
Telephone code: 0 58.
ⓘ Turističko Biro Bol,
    YU-58420 Bol;
    tel. 8 06 04.
    Turističko Društvo Sumartin,
    YU-58426 Sumartin;
    tel. 8 05 11.
    Turističko Biro Supetar,
    YU-58400 Supetar;
    tel. 8 09 17.

HOTELS. – IN BOL: *Elaphusa*, A, 568 b., tel. 8 06 17, with annexe *Pavilions*, B, 330 b.; *Borak*, B, 290 b., tel. 8 06 18, with annexe *Pavilions*, B, 96 b.; *Kaštil*, B, 72 b., tel. 8 06 06; *Bijela Kuća*, B, 52 b., tel. 8 06 05, with annexe, B, 280 b. – IN SUPETAR; *Complex Palma*, B, 592 b., tel. 8 09 17; *Kaktus*, B, 245 b., tel. 4 97 55; *Tamaris*, B, 50 b., tel. 8 09 17. – IN POSTIRA: *Vrilo*, B, 46 b., tel. 8 09 04; *Park*, C, 40 b., tel. 8 09 00, with annexes *Tamaris* and *Agava*, B, 120 b.

CAMP SITES. – *Supetar*, at Supetar; site at Bol.

NATURIST FACILITIES. – Small beach N of Supetar cemetery; beautiful sandy beach on the Bol peninsula.

EVENTS. – "Masquerades", with donkey races, at Supetar (July and August); song contests at Bol in summer.

SPORT. – AT SUPETAR: Scuba diving, water-skiing, tennis, rental of canoes and row boats, boccia. – AT BOL: scuba diving, water-skiing, tennis courts at Elaphusa Hotel, climbing (to summit of Vidova Gora). – AT POVLJA: water-skiing, handball, basketball.

BOATING and BATHING. – The light-coloured pebble beach of *Zlatnirt*, near Bol, reaching out into the sea like a curving horn, with a pine-grove at its tip, features in many tourist brochures. The beach at *Supetar* begins near the harbour and extends past the extensive range of hotels and holiday chalets, with plenty of shade. It is well cared for and kept clean, but tends to be crowded. There is a section for naturists beyond the cemetery (with mausoleum). – The other resorts do not have good beaches; there are gangways leading into the sea at some of the traditional local bathing places.

Boating and sailing enthusiasts should remember that, particularly in the channel between Brač and the mainland, the bora frequently blows up suddenly and fiercely and that the sirocco sometimes also whips up a heavy sea. The best harbour on the island is Supetar, but Sutivan, N of Supetar, also affords shelter from a sudden onset of the bora.

CAR FERRIES. – From Split to Supetar, Postira, Pučišća, Povlja and Luka; also fast hydrofoil connections.

Brač, the third largest of the Adriatic islands, was called by the Croatian writer Vladimir Nazor (1876–1949) the "island without bread, without water, without roads, without vines or olives"; and it is true that Brač is not the place for a "dolce far niente" holiday. Although the coastal areas are mostly green, the interior tends to be inhospitable, with areas of macchia and grazing for sheep, expanses of rock and bare hills. The attraction for vacationers lies in the exploration of these interior regions, still largely unspoiled by tourism. In 1977 there were only 3 miles/5 km of asphalt road on the island, but progress has been made since then and all the major road connections are now asphalted. It is now possible, therefore, to drive around the island to the best known holiday resorts – Supetar and Postira

on the N coast, Milna at the W end, Bol on the S coast, Sumartin at the E end.

HISTORY. – The island was already occupied in Neolithic times. The earliest inhabitants in the historical period were Illyrians. Later, surrounded by Greek colonies, the Illyrians traded with the Greeks but resisted Greek attempts to settle on the island. In the reign of Diocletian the Romans began to work the limestone quarries at Škrip. After a period under Byzantine rule Brač was occupied by a Slav tribe, the Neretljani, in the 9th c. Later it became part of the Croatian kingdom. When pirate raids became frequent many of the inhabitants left the coastal settlements and moved into the interior of the island. At the beginning of the 13th c. Brač came under the control of the mainland town of Omiš, and in.1240 it passed to Split. Then followed a period under the rule of the Hungarian-Croatian monarchy, after which the island was annexed by Venice and remained in Venetian hands until 1797, when it passed to Austria. Apart from a brief period of French control in 1807–15 it remained part of Austria until 1918.

During the Second World War the partisans on Brač fought against the Italian and later the German occupying forces. By 1944 Tito had gained the upper hand, and Brač became a base for partisan vessels. The holiday and tourist trade began to develop only in the 1970s. In this respect Brač was at first, and to some extent still is, overshadowed by the neighbouring island of Hvar; but the provision of a new water supply from the mainland (1977) and the improvement of the island's roads should enable Brač to catch up with its rival.

SIGHTS. – The semicircular harbour of Supetar, the administrative hub of the island, is surrounded by bright-hued buildings dating from the period of the Austro-Hungarian monarchy. The ferries and hydrofoils from Split put in here. The original settlement of Supetar is concealed from the newly arrived visitor by the buildings around the harbour; but he need only walk a few paces into the town to encounter the unpretentious single-storey houses typical of the island – huddling close to the ground to escape the fierce bora, with tiny windows and narrow roof overhangs. Typical, too, are the tall chimneys, designed to prevent the fire from being blown out in a storm.

The tourists' part of Supetar lies E of the harbour in a setting of parkland and meadows. A surprising feature at the end of the long bathing beach is the *cemetery*, with the **mausoleum** of the Petrinović family, who emigrated from Brač to Chile and made a fortune from the mining of saltpetre. The mausoleum, with oriental and Byzantine architectural features, was designed by Toma Rosandić (1879–1958). This unusual cemetery contains other tombs and works of sculpture

An inland village on the island of Brač

Zlatnirt bathing beach, near Bol (island of Brač)

commemorating wealthy inhabitants of Brač.

A narrow and winding road runs E along the coast to **Spliska**, in a bay fringed by beautiful pinewoods. Stone from the nearby quarries at Škrip was once shipped from here. In the *Roman quarry of Rasoha*, $\frac{1}{2}$ mile/800 m from Pliska, is a figure of *Hercules* carved from the rock – the finest piece of Roman sculpture on the island. The 16th c. *parish church* near the harbour has a beautiful slender tower. A minor road runs inland to the quarries.

The next place along the coast road is **Postira**, birthplace of the great Croatian writer Vladimir Nazor whose description of Brač has already been quoted. A steep street leads up from the large harbour to the middle of the little town. Below the church is a picturesque square surrounded by handsome façades and doorways. The *parish church*, with defensive loopholes in its walls, contains 18th c. Stations of the Cross. Still higher up, on Mt *Glavica*, are the primitive old houses of the peasants and herdsmen. The farm buildings are often built of undressed stone without the use of mortar; in front of them are ovens, wine-presses and old querns. – Returning to the harbour, we see

at the head of the bay the *Castle of the Lazanić Family*. Adjoining it is a *mansion* with a Renaissance gable, on the S side of which are many religious inscriptions.

Farther E, at the head of a bay reaching far inland, is **Pučišća**, which was once strongly fortified. Here too, as at Spliska, stonemasons prepared stone from the local quarries for shipment; they ranked as artists, and the local peasants were not allowed into their houses and workshops. Nowadays the stonemasons work in small industrial establishments. The *parish church* contains a fine wooden altar dedicated to St Anthony – one of the most beautiful on the island – with an altarpiece of St Roch painted by Palma Giovane, a pupil of Titian, and a carved group with a figure of St Jerome, the patron saint of the village.

The next place to the E, **Selca**, is also a stone-working village. Here the local masons have contributed to the embellishment of their own village: everything is made of stone – doorsteps, staircases, terraces, gutters, even the sinks in the kitchens and the children's toys. Croatian national aspirations and Pan-Slav ideas found expression in Selca in the foundation of a Croatian Association dedicated to maintaining the local way of life and culture. This body was responsible for the erection of a *monument to Tolstoy*, the reason for which at this particular spot is not immediately clear to visitors.

Sumartin, the newest and most easterly village on the island, had until quite recently no road usable by motor vehicles connecting it with the other villages.

Bol is now the principal tourist resort on the island after Supetar. The village huddles on a narrow coastal strip between the sea and the hills to the rear. Features of interest include a 17th c. *mansion* on the front, partly Renaissance and partly Baroque; the *Church of our Lady of Mt Carmel* (Crkva Gospe od Karmela); a large *Dominican monastery*; and a *Gallery of Contemporary Art*. The *museum* in the monastery contains prehistoric material from caves, a collection of coins, material recovered by underwater archaeologists and a collection of incunabula and parchments. Above Bol, on the road to Supetar, are the burnt-out remains of a village destroyed during the last war.

Near Bol, reached by a steep climb from the sandy bay of Blaca, is a **hermitage**, which served as a refuge for "Glagolitic" priests (see under Krk) in the 16th c. The hermitage remained in occupation until 1973, the last hermit being a well-known astronomer who had the largest telescope in the country and an extensive library. Visitors are shown the monks' cells, the observatory, a collection of old watches and clocks, weapons, etc. – Another excursion from Bol is to the summit of **Vidova Gora** (St Vitus's Hill), the highest point on the island (2553 ft/778 m), which affords magnificent views.

From Bol a road runs via **Nerežišće** (with the only industrial establishment on Brač, a chewing-gum factory), in the middle of the island, to its oldest settlement, **Škrip**. Hundreds of Roman slaves once worked in the quarries here. Numerous objects illustrating the village's long history have been found at different levels in the soil, and these are to be brought together in a local museum housed in the old Radojković Tower.

Among notable buildings in which the beautiful white limestones of Škrip have been used are Diocletian's palace in Split, the Reichstag in Berlin and the Parliament Building in Vienna.

Brela

Republic: Croatia (Hrvatska).
Altitude: 16 ft/5 m. – Population: 1300.
Post code: YU-58322. – Telephone code: 0 58.
(i) **Turist Biro,**
   tel. 8 74 13.

HOTELS. – *Maestral*, A, 118 b., tel. 8 74 40, with annexes *Mirna*, B, 91 b., and *Marina*, B, 171 b.; *Berulia*, B, 300 b., tel. 8 74 44; *Berulia II*, B, 90 b., tel. 8 74 44; *Brela*, C, 86 b., tel. 8 74 40; *Soline*, C, 44 b., tel. 8 74 40, with annexe *Primorka*, C, 70 b.

EVENTS. – St Stephen's Day celebrations (August 3).

SPORT. – Scuba diving, water-skiing, rental of motorboats and row boats.

BOATING and BATHING. – On both sides of the harbour are bathing beaches, offering holidaymakers the choice between roasting in the sun and resting in the shade of the trees which reach down to the beach. The beds of shingle which form the beaches extend for some 2 miles/3 km. Non-swimmers and children should remember that the shingle bank can suddenly give way and that only a short distance from the shore the bottom falls sharply.

The beaches are cleaned daily. The water is crystal clear; all the hotels have sewage purification plants, and the health authorities carry out regular checks on the water.

There are facilities for all kinds of water sports; scuba divers must, however, go to Makarska for cylinder refills. There are organised excursions to the islands of Hvar and Brač and to Split, 30 miles/48 km away.

Brela lies at the NW end of the 34 mile/55 km long Makarska Riviera, one of the most beautiful stretches of coast in central Dalmatia. There are really two Brelas – Donja Brela (Lower Brela), on the coast, and Gornja Brela (Upper Brela), lying inland 985 ft/300 m higher up. Lower Brela is a very popular seaside resort, lying off the main coast road with its heavy traffic and surrounded by a magnificent pine forest which extends from the edge of the bare Biokovo range down a gentle slope to the coast.

HISTORY. – Donja Brela, on the sea, came into being only in the present century, when the inhabitants of Gornja Brela and the surrounding farms in the hills moved down to the coast. The population now lives almost exclusively from the tourist and holiday trade.

Brela: holiday pleasures on the Adriatic coast

SIGHTS. – Apart from a few *Bogomil stones* (see p. 56) beside the old church in Gornja Brela neither of the Brelas has any features of historical interest.

SURROUNDINGS. – A beautiful wooded footpath runs along the coast to the nearby village of **Baška Voda**. – It is a 2 hour climb to the summit of **Veliki Kuk** (1919 ft/585 m), from which there is a superb view of the islands of Brač (in the foreground) and Hvar (to rear). – From Brela a road, stony and dusty in places, climbs up and winds its way through the *Biokovo* range in the magnificent **Vrulja Gap** to Šestanovac, continuing via Zagvozd and Grabovac to Imotski (28 miles/45 km). The old mountain village of **Imota** looks down on a fertile plain in which maize, tobacco and vines flourish. The plain is a typical karstic polje – as shown, for example, by its two characteristic lakes. (On karstic features, see p. 99.)

Brioni/Brijuni Islands

Republic: Croatia (Hrvatska).
Altitude: up to 165 ft/50 m.
No permanent inhabitants.

This group of islands is closed to visitors, and landing from boats is prohibited.

NAVIGATION. – Sailing yachts making for Pula are advised, in view of the considerable navigational difficulties and numerous prohibited zones around the Brijuni Islands, to anchor at Rovinj and take a bus or taxi to Pula. In the Fažanski Kanal between the island of Veli Brijun and the little town of Fažana on the mainland there are currents and changeable winds which can carry boats SE at 3 knots. Moreover there may be submarines in this area. The prohibited area is officially described as follows: Brijuni Islands and Fažanski Kanal within the lines linking the points Rt Barbariga light on Greben Kabula – 44° 54′ 00″ N, 13° 42′ 01 ″ E – a point 0·3 sea mile 180° from Peneda lighthouse – S tip of island of Jerolim – Rt Krišto – W coast of Istria to Barbariga.

This group NW of Pula consists of the two principal islands of Veli Brijun (area $2\frac{1}{2}$ sq. miles/6·9 sq. km) and Mali Brijun together with the islets of Sveti Marko, Gaz Obljak, Supin, Supinić, Galija, Vanga, Pusti, Vrsar, Jerolim and Kotež. Veli Brijun in particular has a luxuriant growth of vegetation. In addition to Mediterranean species such as laurel, fir and rosemary, subtropical species including cedars of Lebanon, agaves and palms flourish in the mild climate. The group of islands is now a closed area, having been chosen by President Tito as the site of his summer residence; the hotel complex on Veli Brijun has been developed to provide accommodation for official guests of the government.

The group of islands was already occupied in prehistoric times, as is shown by the tools and implements that have been found and by the remains of ring-forts, tombs and dwellings. In 117 B.C. the islands passed into Roman control, and wealthy Roman citizens from Pula soon began to build summer residences there. Thus in the bay of *Verige* on the E coast of Veli Brijun a complex of buildings was discovered, of a size and lavishness which give a striking impression of the luxury with which prosperous Romans could surround themselves. The whole complex extended for $\frac{3}{4}$ mile (1 km) along the coast, with a loggia open on the seaward side linking the various buildings – villas, priests' dwellings, stables, baths, storerooms and a palace for the reception of guests. In the middle were three temples. There were walls to protect promenaders from the wind, and the rooms of the houses were embellished with elaborate stucco ornament and beautiful mosaic pavements.

After the fall of the Western Empire the islands passed to Byzantium, then to the Patriarchs of Aquileia and finally (in 1331) to Venice. Many of the inhabitants died of malaria and most of the settlements fell into ruin.

In 1893 a Merano industrialist bought the whole group with the idea of developing the islands for the tourist trade which was then beginning to grow. He built hotels and bathing stations and laid out a racecourse, a golf-course and tennis courts; flowers were planted in profusion. The bacteriologist Robert Koch acted as a technical adviser to the enterprise. Thus Veli Brijun became an exclusive resort frequented by the nobility and financial aristocracy of Europe.

Between the two world wars the glory began to depart, and during the last war Veli Brijun in particular suffered frequent bombardment and plundering. After the war President Tito had a summer residence built on the island. Later the hotels, rebuilt or renovated, were converted into guest-houses for the accommodation of foreign statesmen and delegations.

Budva

Republic: Montenegro (Crna Gora).
Altitude: 10 ft/3 m. – Population: 3500.
Post code: YU-81310. – Telephone code: 0 86.
ⓘ Turistički Savez Opštine,
tel. 8 22 58.
Hotelsko Preduzeče Avala,
tel. 8 20 02.

HOTELS. – *Montenegro*, B, 900 b., tel. 8 21 04; *Bellevue*, B, 660 b., tel. 8 21 04; *International*, B, 580 b., tel. 8 20 24, with treatment centre for rheumatism, inflammation of the joints, etc.; *Mediteran*, B, 440 b., tel. 8 21 04; *Splendid*, B, 420 b., tel. 8 20 09; *Avala Villas*, B, 284 b., tel. 8 20 42; *Avala*, B, 168 b., tel. 8 20 42; *Mogren*, C, 284 b., tel. 8 21 05.

CAMP SITES. – *Jaz*; *Avala* (some distance from beach), tel. 8 21 04.

NATURIST FACILITIES. – Large naturist beach at Jaz camp site.

SPORT. – Water-skiing, boat rental; tennis courts, with coach at Slovenska beach; mini-golf at Bečići hotel; bowling alleys in several hotels; volleyball courts.

The Montenegrin holiday resort of Budva consists of the old town, charmingly situated on a projecting tongue of land, and a series of hotels extending to the S of the town on long sandy *beaches. The 1979 earthquake caused severe damage, particularly in the old town, which has taken a number of years to make good. In spite of this setback Budva remains a popular seaside resort for all age groups, particularly since the sea here is largely free from pollution. The hotels can accommodate considerably more visitors than there are permanent residents in the town.

The old town of Budva before the 1979 earthquake.

HISTORY. – With a history going back 2500 years, Budva is one of the oldest settlements on the Adriatic coast. According to legend it was founded by Kadmo, son of a Phoenician king. The settlement, originally Illyrian, is first mentioned in the 4th c. B.C. under the Greek name of *Buthoe*. In 168 B.C. the town, now known as *Budua*, passed under Roman control. (Remains dating from Illyrian, Greek and Roman times were found in a large cemetery in 1936 during the construction of the Avala Hotel.)

When the Roman Empire was divided into two in A.D. 395 the boundary between the Eastern and Western Empires ran through Budva; then, after the fall of the Western Empire, the town was ruled by Byzantium. Slavs and Avars settled here in the second half of the 6th c., and Budva became known for a time as *Avarorum Sinus*, after the Avars. In 841 an Arab fleet appeared off the town, and in that year, and again in 867, the Arabs plundered it and destroyed it.

In 1183 Budva came under the control of the Nemanjid dynasty of Serbia, and under their rule the town prospered, became self-governing and was granted a special status. From 1442 to 1797 it was held by Venice; but in 1571 pirates from Ulcinj captured the town and set fire to it.

After the fall of the Venetian Republic in 1797 Budva was occupied successively by the Austrians, the Russians and the French. From 1814 to 1918 it belonged to the Austro-Hungarian monarchy.

A tour of the old town of Budva has long featured in every program of excursions in Montenegro. The violent 1979 earthquake, however, caused the collapse of most of the massive old town walls and towers, and the majority of buildings in the town were damaged or destroyed. Although reconstruction is in progress it may be that Budva will never be the same again.

The cathedral (Sv. Jovan), originally built in the 8th–9th c. and rebuilt in the 18th c., contained icons and paintings of the 15th and 16th c. The 12th c. St Mary's Church (Sancta Maria in Puncta) housed an archaeological museum. From a tower in the fortifications built by the Austrians there was a fine view over the roofs of the old town.

BEACHES. – At the N end of the series of beaches is Jaz beach, with the camp site of the same name. A small cove adjoining the main beach is reserved for naturists. Both beaches have fine shingle and some sand. – *Mogrèn* beach, 550 yd/500 m NW of the Avala Hotel, can also be reached from Budva on foot. It has stretches of clean shingle and sand, reached by a narrow path running round a number of rocky promontories (admission charge). Projecting ridges of rock divide the beach into two parts: in the nearer part are changing cabins and a small restaurant, beyond this a larger restaurant. – The next little cove lies in front of the Avala Hotel, immediately adjoining the town of Budva. The beach, although clean, is not particularly inviting.

Beyond Budva is the *Slovenska Plaža*, 1400 yd/1·3 km long, with shingle and coarse sand, clean and with excellent facilities. All that is lacking is shade. At the far end of the beach is an untidy and ill-cared-for section, used by local people. – The longest beach near Budva is at *Bečići*, $2\frac{1}{2}$ miles/4 km SE of the old town. 1 mile/1·5 km long and up to 110 yd/100 m wide, it is covered with coarse sand or fine shingle. Here there are loungers, sun umbrellas, water-skiing, rowing boats and crystal clear water which makes snorkelling a delight.

Cavtat

Republic: Croatia (Hrvatska).
Altitude: $6\frac{1}{2}$ ft/2 m. – Population: 1000.
Post code: YU-50210. – Telephone code: 0 50.
(i) **Turističko Društvo,**
tel. 8 82 65.

HOTELS. – **Croatia*, L, 974 b., tel. 8 80 22; *Albatros*, A, 530 b., tel. 8 80 44; *Epidaurus*, B, 384 b., tel. 8 81 44; *Cavtat*, B, 194 b., tel. 8 82 26; *Adriatic*, B, 87 b., tel. 8 80 66; *Supetar* (no rest.), B, 76 b., tel. 8 82 79.

CAMP SITE. – *Camping Cavtat*, opposite Epidaurus Hotel, tel. 8 80 09.

SPORT and RECREATION. – Rental of motorboats and rowing boats at Albatros and Makedonia Hotels; casinos, bowling alleys and terraces for dancing at Albatros and Croatia Hotels; discotheque in Epidaurus Hotel; night clubs in Albatros and Croatia Hotels; Inex Bar.

The little town of Cavtat, situated off the Adriatic coastal highway in a beautiful bay 9 miles/15 km S of Dubrovnik, is a popular holiday resort which attracts visitors throughout the year. The quiet of the resort is unfortunately disturbed by aircraft noise, since it lies in the flight path to the nearby airport of

Cavtat Bay

Dubrovnik-Čilipi, and at the height of the holiday season the beaches are overcrowded and the water sometimes polluted. Nevertheless Cavtat offers many attractions to holidaymakers, and it is a particular favourite with German visitors.

People who want absolute peace and quiet do not come to Cavtat. It is a lively little town with a constant bustle of activity – bathing and après-bathing, daytime recreation and night life – which can be enjoyed without incurring extravagant expenditure. Pleasant evenings can be spent over a glass of wine in friendly cafés and bars, and there are casinos to satisfy the gambling instinct. But visitors who dislike aircraft noise should avoid Cavtat.

HISTORY. – In the 7th c. B.C. Illyrians settled on this peninsula – well wooded then as it is today – at the S end of the Župski Zaljev (Župa Bay). In the 4th c. B.C. Greek seafarers founded the settlement of *Epidaurus* on the same site, naming it, as a number of other sites in the Mediterranean were named at that period, after the sanctuary of Asclepius in the Peloponnese. The Romans developed the town into a staging point for trade between southern Italy and the Asiatic and Greek provinces of the Empire.

In A.D. 317 an earthquake destroyed the harbour, the quays sank under the sea and the shoreline subsided. The town was later rebuilt, but in the 7th c. was destroyed by Slavs and Avars. The inhabitants fled to the offshore islands, most of them settling on the little island of Lave, on which the town of *Ragusium*, now *Dubrovnik*, grew up. In 1427 Cavtat, built on the site of the ancient town of Epidaurus (hence its name: *civitas vetus*, "old town"), passed under the control of Ragusa. In 1451 Duke Stjepan Kosača captured and destroyed the town, but it was rebuilt by Dubrovnik as a fortified outpost. The town's great period of prosperity began only at the beginning of the 1960s with the development of the tourist and holiday trade.

SIGHTS. – On the S side of the peninsula is the **Municipal Museum**, named after the jurist Baltazar Bogišić, who was born in Cavtat in 1834. Housed in the former residence of the Ragusan governor (Rector), this contains the *Bogišić Library*, a historical collection, a *lapidarium* (inscribed and other stones) and Bogišić's notable *collection of graphic art*, consisting of over 10,000 items. In front of the museum is a monument to Bogišić. Other features of interest in the town are the Baroque *parish church of St Nicholas* (Sv. Nikola), with paintings by old masters; *St Blaise's Church* (Sv. Vlaho), with a fine Renaissance altarpiece of the Dubrovnik school; and the Franciscan friary, with a remarkable *Renaissance cloister* of 1483.

At the end of the street there is a steep climb up to the *Mausoleum of the Rašić Family (1920–22), by the internationally known Yugoslav sculptor Ivan Meštrović.

SURROUNDINGS. – There are good boat services from Cavtat to a number of small islands. Other excursions from the town are, of course, to **Dubrovnik** (see p. 75), and also to **Trebinje** (a little town which still preserves an oriental aspect), **Počitelj** (p. 158) and **Mostar** (p. 132).

Cetinje

Republic: Montenegro (Crna Gora).
Altitude: 2205 ft/672 m. – Population: 15,000.
Post code: YU-81250. – Telephone code: 0 86.
ⓘ Montenegro Turist,
tel. 2 11 44.

HOTELS. – *Park*, B, 97 b., tel. 2 19 15; *Grand*, C, 74 b., tel. 2 11 44 (a wooden building over 100 years old, the rendezvous of diplomats and men of letters in the days when Cetinje was capital of Montenegro).

The visitor who has accomplished the breathtaking drive up from **Kotor Bay on the **Lovćen road (17 numbered hairpin bends with gradients of 8–10% over a distance of 9 miles/15 km) sees this quiet little town, situated on a green plateau enclosed by rugged mountains, as no more than a convenient stopping-place with a selection of restaurants and cafés – little suspecting that it once played a part in world history.

In a sightseeing tour of the little town, its palaces now converted into museums, legend becomes reality. Visitors will be fascinated by the portrait of Peter Njegoš, prince-bishop and poet; they will admire King Nikola's collection of orders and medals; and they will see the famous billiard table which the king caused to be conveyed on perilous mule-tracks from Kotor Bay through the mountains to Cetinje. Even those little interested in history will feel the fascination of the history and the legends of Montenegro as illustrated by the remarkable collection of material (some of it damaged by the 1979 earthquake) in the National Museum. A visit to Cetinje is a journey into the eventful past of this inhospitable mountain country.

HISTORY. – Finds of Stone Age implements in a cave have shown that the Cetinje plateau was already

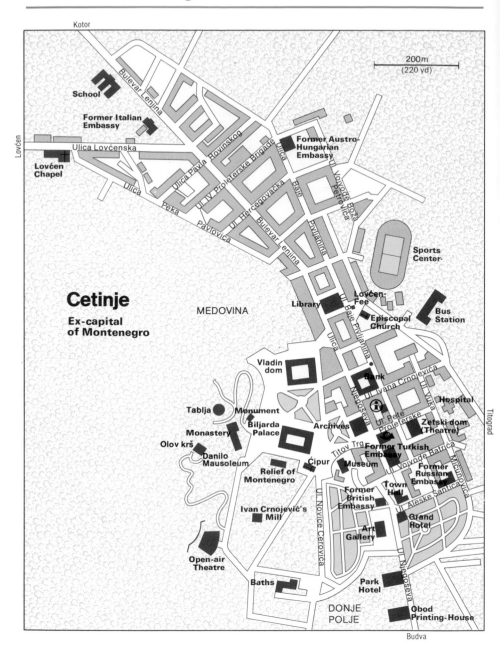

Kotor

200m
(220 yd)

School

Bulevar Lenjina

Former Italian
Embassy

Lovćen

Ulica Lovćenska

Ulica Pavla Rovinskog

Ul IV Proleterske Brigade

Lovćen
Chapel

Ulica

Peka

Pavlovica

Ul Hercegovacka

Bulevar Lenjina

Bajc

Former Austro-
Hungarian
Embassy

Voivode Boža Petrovica

Pivljanina

Sports
Center

Cetinje

Ex-capital
of Montenegro

MEDOVINA

Library

Lovćen-
Fee

Bajc Pivljanina

Episcopal
Church

Ulica

Njegoševa

Bus
Station

Vladin
dom

Bank

Ul. Ivana Crnojevića

Ulica

Hospital

Titograd

Tablja

Monument

Biljarda
Palace

Monastery

Archives

Ul. pete
Proleterske

Ul. Ivana Crnojevića

Zetski dom
(Theatre)

Olov krš

Danilo
Mausoleum

Ćipur

Titov Trg

Former Turkish
Embassy

Museum

Voivode Batrića

Relief of
Montenegro

Former
Russian
Embassy

Mitumosića

Ivan Crnojević's
Mill

Former
British
Embassy

Town
Hall

Ul Aleske Santucca

Art
Gallery

Ul Novice Cerovica

Grand
Hotel

Njegoševa

Open-air
Theatre

Baths

Park
Hotel

DONJE
POLJE

Obod
Printing-House

Budva

settled by man in prehistoric times. This green island surrounded by rugged karstic mountains must have been from an early stage in history a place of refuge for the oppressed and dispossessed: it is known, for example, that members of the Bogomil sect once sought safety here.

The principality of Montenegro and its capital, Cetinje, began to play a part in history, however, only after the Turkish defeat of Prince Lazar of Serbia in the battle of *Kosovo* in 1389. The road into Europe now lay open; but the Turks were unable to overcome the resistance of this little mountain state.

The secular rulers of Montenegro were displaced by ecclesiastical princes when the reigning metropolitan (bishop) took over power in 1499 and again in 1516. In 1687 a member of the Petrović–Njegoš family became prince-bishop. During this period the principality was repeatedly exposed to Turkish attack. On at least three occasions – in 1683, 1714 and 1785 – the Turks managed to force their way into Cetinje, plunder the town and burn down the monastery; but they were never able to maintain themselves for long in this remote mountain region, being regularly driven out by the freedom-loving Montenegrins.

Prince Peter II Njegoš, who succeeded Peter I in 1830 and reigned until 1851, was born in 1813 in the little village of Njeguši, on the road from Kotor to Cetinje; the house in which he was born is now a museum. Peter Njegoš knew five foreign languages, reading Shakespeare, the French philosophers and the German classical writers in the original, and he himself became Montenegro's greatest poet. He was also an excellent marksman with the pistol and a skilled billiard player. It was he who built the Biljarda Palace. He died of pulmonary tuberculosis at the age of only 38.

In the reign of Peter's successor Danilo II (1851–60) the combination of ecclesiastical and secular authority came to an end. Danilo handed over power to his nephew Nikola I, later known as Nikita, who ruled from 1860 to 1916. In 1910 he had himself crowned king of Montenegro.

Nikola financed the running of his country by the sale of postage stamps and by bribes from the great powers. He waged a private war against Shkodër in Albania and occupied the town. He dispensed justice sitting under a tree, and undertook a brief experiment in parliamentary government, but threw the head of the government into prison when he began to develop ideas of his own. At one time Nikola had as many as 15 foreign embassies in his little town, and he became known as the "Bismarck of the Balkans". At the beginning of the First World War he backed the Russians, but in 1916 he was driven out, together with a French expeditionary corps, by an Austrian force, which made its way up to Cetinje from the naval base of Cattaro (now Kotor) on the Lovćen road, built by Austrian engineers in 1876–81. Nikola died in exile in France in 1921.

SIGHTS. – In Trg Maršala Tita is the **Biljarda Palace**, decorated and furnished in the style of Peter II's reign. Behind it is a low building containing a *relief model of the mountains of Montenegro, made by Austrian soldiers between 1916 and 1918. To the E of the palace stands the *National Museum, with a remarkable collection of weapons, pictures and other mementoes of the reign of King Nikola. It includes the numerous orders and decorations which the king received from many different countries, as well as a present from Kaiser Wilhelm II in the form of a small-scale equestrian statue of himself.

To the W of the palace is the **Monastery of the Mother of God** (*Bogorodičin Manastir*, or *Sv. Petar*), with its square tower. Founded in 1485, the monastery

Monastery of the Mother of God, Cetinje

was later destroyed but subsequently rebuilt.

SURROUNDINGS. – One monument in the neighbourhood of Cetinje which must not be missed is the **Tomb of Peter II Njegoš**. In 1856, 14 years after his death, Peter's remains were deposited in a chapel on the summit of the Jezerski Vrh (5437 ft/1657 m). The chapel was destroyed during the First World War, and in 1917 the Austrians transferred the remains to Cetinje. In 1934 they were returned to the summit of the hill, and in 1972 were housed in a new **mausoleum** designed by Ivan Meštrović. There is a road (12½ miles/20 km) from Cetinje to the hill, from which there are panoramic *views.

The **Lovćen road** offers a succession of breathtaking views of **Kotor Bay**. At one point it affords a view of both Kotor Bay and the adjoining *Tivat Bay*. A notable feature of the road is a large double bend in the form of an M – so designed by the Austrian engineers in honour of King Nikola's daughter Marija.

Cres

Republic: Croatia (Hrvatska).
Area of island: 156 sq. miles/404 sq. km.
Population: 4000.
Telephone code: 0 51.
ⓘ **Turistički Ured Cres,**
YU-51557 Cres;
tel. 87 11 33.
Turistički Ured Osor
(in Nerezine, on the island of Mali Lošinj),
YU-51554 Nerezine;
tel. (0 51) 86 11 86.
Punta Križa: apply to office in Nerezine.

HOTELS. – IN TOWN OF CRES: *Kimen*, B, with annexe (D), 385 b., tel. 82 08 61; *Cres* and *Villa Riviera*, D, 100 b., tel. 82 08 61. – IN OSOR AND PUNTA KRIŽA: accommodation in private houses only (apply to Tourist Office).

CAMP SITES. – CRES: *Kovačine*, tel. 82 08 61, 550 yds/500 m from Kimen Hotel. – OSOR: *Adria*, tel. 86 15 95; *Bijar*, tel. 86 10 18. – PUNTA KRIŽA: see under Naturist facilities.

NATURIST FACILITIES. – Near town of Cres, *Nedomišlja* beach, opposite Kimen Hotel on opposite side of bay (reached only by sea); *Gavza* beach, reached either by land or by sea; *Baldarin* camp site, S of Punta Kirža, run by Jadranka Hotel Company, YU-51550 Mali Lošinj, tel (0 51) 86 10 11.

EVENTS. – Concerts in summer in square in front of Cathedral, Osor.

SPORT, BOATING and BATHING. – The main tourist and holiday area is the little town of **Cres**. On a hill to the W of the town is a large hotel complex. The beach below this is not particularly good, and bathers usually take a boat to the other side of the bay, where there is also a large naturist beach. The largest *naturist center* on the island, the Baldarin camp site, which extends to several square miles, with plenty of shade, lies in the S of the island; just before Osor a narrow road branches off for **Punta Križa**, a village with many private houses offering accommodation and a small harbour used by the regular boat services between Lošinj and Pag/Hvar.

There is wide scope for *boat trips* from the town of Cres; the trip to the Blue Grotto on the W coast is particularly popular. For sailing and motorboating (rental of boats in Cres) the E side of the island, with its calmer sea, is more suitable. The nearest marinas are in **Punat Bay** on the island of Krk and in the natural harbour of **Mali Lošinj** on the island of Lošinj.

CAR FERRIES. – The shortest connection with the mainland (frequent crossings) is between Brestova on the coast road from Opatija to Pula, and Porozina on Cres. An alternative route, with less frequent services, is from Rijeka to Porozina (runs only during the season). Cres is connected with Mali Lošinj by a bridge.

The town of Cres

Cres (pronounced Tsress) is the second largest of the Yugoslav Adriatic islands, measuring 42 miles/ 68 km from N to S but only 8 miles/13 km from E to W. It is an island of bare hills and plateaux, crisscrossed by low walls built to protect the crops from the wind. At some points there are small patches of woodland, but much of the island is covered with impenetrable macchia. The highest part of the island is in the N, rising to 2133 ft/650 m in Mt Sis; from there the land falls gradually away to the large valley basin around the bay in which the town of Cres lies. The most striking natural feature on the island is Lake Vrana, the green waters of which lie at 223 ft/68 m above sea level; the bottom of the lake is up to 52 ft/16 m below sea level, giving it a maximum depth of 275 ft/84 m. According to one theory the lake draws its abundance of water, which supplies the whole island of Cres as well as the neighbouring island of Lošinj, from the karstic region on the mainland by way of a channel under the sea. Another view is that the lake is fed by rainwater, which seeps down through crevices in the rock and the porous soil and is sufficient in quantity to keep the level of the lake well above that of the sea.

HISTORY. – The historical development of Cres is identical with that of Lošinj. The once flourishing town of Osor at the S end of the island, near the bridge linking it with Lošinj, was formerly the principal settlement; the island is now, however, administratively subordinate to Mali Lošinj. (On the history of both islands, see the entry for Lošinj.)

SIGHTS. – The old port of **Cres** is a picturesque little place, with towers and narrow lanes, gateways, staircases and quiet inner courtyards which show clear Venetian influence. Of the town's massive fortifications, a circuit of walls and towers enclosing a pentagonal area around the harbour, on a line now marked by the road running around the town, there survive the *Bragadina Gate* (1581) and the *Marcella Gate* (1588), with coats of arms and the lion of St Mark to commemorate the Venetian nobles after whom they are named. In the market square, with a cobbled pavement laid out in regular panels, is the **Municipal Loggia** (15th–16th c.) in which the citizens used to meet. Close by, in the line of buildings fronting the harbour, is the *Clock-Tower*, which gives access to the **parish church of St Mary of the Snows**. Its status as a cathedral is reflected in the elaborately decorated *Renaissance doorway*, with capitals depicting dolphins and fruit, symbolising the sea and the land, the town's two sources of subsistence.

Going along the side of the Cathedral, we come to *St Isidore's Church*, the oldest in the town, with the oldest bell on the island, cast in the 14th c. The church has a fine Romanesque apse with an elaborate frieze of round-headed arches.

Scattered about the town are a number of other notable buildings – the old *Town Hall*, with the municipal coat of arms under the balcony; the former *Bishop's Palace* (renovated); and various rather dilapidated *patrician houses*. The *Franciscan friary* has a fine church, the carved wooden choir-stalls (15th c.) being particularly notable; the three dolphins represent the coat of arms of a local noble.

Farther out is the *Benedictine convent*, in which the few remaining nuns let out rooms to holidaymakers. The *Municipal Museum*, in an old patrician house belonging to the Petris family, contains material illustrating the history of the two islands together with objects salvaged from a merchant ship wrecked off Cape Pernat.

Osor, at the S end of the island, is now a sleepy little village of some 100 inhabitants, but a walk around it reveals evidence of the days when it was a flourishing town with a population of 30,000. In the middle of the village is the 15th c. *Cathedral*; the little square in front of it, flanked by the *Bishop's Palace* and old burghers' houses, has excellent acoustics and is used for concerts and serenades in summer. The Cathedral, in early Renaissance style (1464–98), contains the *shrine of St Gaudentius*, bishop of Osor, who is credited with banishing all venomous snakes from the islands of Cres and Lošinj. The massive separate *tower* dates from the 17th c.

The *town walls* and *towers* now visible were not built until the 15th c., when Osor had already shrunk from its former extent. Within a few paces of the charming square in front of the Cathedral can be seen ruined churches, the façades of dilapidated old houses, the remains of a monastery.

The largest place on the island after Cres is **Martinšćica**, in a bay on the W coast. The houses of the former fishermen and farmers, now mostly working in the factories of Rijeka, have taken on a fresh lease of life as clean and attractive lodgings for holidaymakers. *St Jerome's Church*, belonging to a monastery which is still occupied, contains a notable altarpiece.

There are regular daily boat services from Cres across the bay to the little village of **Valun**, huddled under conspicuous steep cliffs, with attractive bathing beaches of light-coloured pebbles on either side. The simple *parish church of St Mary* contains in the sacristy the island's most valuable archaeological relic, the *Valun Stone* (Valunska ploča), which ranks with a similar stone from the island of Krk as the oldest Croatian text in Yugoslavia. It is particularly notable as being bilingual: the upper part has an inscription in Glagolitic (Old Slav) script, "Teha sin Vnuk Juna" ("Teha, son and grandson Juna"), while on the lower part is the Latin equivalent, "Techa et filius eius Bratohna et Junna nepos eius" ("Teha, her son Bratohna and Juna, her grandson").

From Valun a mule-track runs inland to **Lake Vrana** (bathing prohibited). The best view of the lake is from a chapel on the Cres–Osor road.

It is well worth while making the trip to the only place of any consequence on the E coast, **Beli**. At the highest point on the road which leads up into the hills from the ferry landing-stage at Porozina there is a fine view of the islands of Plavnik and Krk; a high wall protects cars from the E winds which sometimes blow violently here. A narrow road branches off at this point and runs to the N end of the island. The main road skirts areas of macchia and deciduous woodland and in 4 miles/6 km reaches Beli, on a hill high above the sea. There was a fortified settlement here in prehistoric times, and later a Roman post controlling the movement of shipping between Cres and Krk. Commandingly situated on top of the hill are the *market square* and *parish church*. There are *Glagolitic inscriptions* on a stone in the left-hand wall of a side chapel and on a tombstone set into the floor of the church. With its few surviving inhabitants, Beli is a charming little place, with narrow twisting lanes, attractive courtyards and carefully tended flower gardens. A steep path leads down to the landing-stage, with deep ruts in the paving left by the ox-carts which once transported timber for shipment to Venice: since the carts had no brakes the carters simply took off the rear wheels and let their vehicle slide down the slope.

The most northerly place on the island is the old-world little village of **Dragozetići**, perched 985 ft/300 m above the sea, with low houses, vine arbours, vaults and cisterns.

Crikvenica

Republic: Croatia (Hrvatska).
Altitude: 16 ft/5 m. – Population: 6000.
Post code: YU-51260. – Telephone code: 0 51.
ⓘ **Turističko Društvo,**
   Trg Nikole Cara;
   tel. 83 12 34 and 83 14 05.

HOTELS. – *Omorika*, B, 540 b., tel. 83 16 22; *Ad Turres Pavilions*, B, 539 b., tel. 83 14 28; *Therapia-Slavija*, B, 250 b., tel. 83 12 22; *Esplanade*, B, 155 b., tel. 83 11 24; *Mediteran*, B, 150 b., tel. 83 10 82; *Zagreb*, B, 132 b., tel. 83 13 86; *International*, B, 86 b., tel. 83 13 24; *Miramare*, C, 150 b., tel. 83 12 32; *Crikvenica*, with annexe *Viševica*, C, 72 b., tel. 83 12 38.
IN DRAMALJ: *Riviera Pavilions*, with annexe *Villa Danica*, C, 160 b., tel. 83 10 33.
IN KAČJAK: *Kačjak* tourist complex, with holiday chalets and pavilions, B, 504 b., tel. 83 11 26. – Also accommodation for 12,000 visitors in private houses (apply to Tourist Office).

CAMP SITE. – AT DRAMALJ: *Kačjak*, tel 83 13 61.

SPORT. – Scuba diving, water-skiing, rental of sail boats, motorboats and row boats; tennis courts, bowling alleys, shooting in hinterland.

The long straggling town of Crikvenica lies on the Adriatic coast opposite the island of Krk. Half way along the town a street runs down to the harbour, from which there is a car ferry service to Šilo on the island of Krk. The town has now developed into a very popular seaside resort, and the terraces of the cafés and restaurants around the harbour are always crowded with tourists in summer. The town's hotels, rooms in private houses and camp sites can accommodate a total of 15,000 visitors.

HISTORY. – Crikvenica occupies the site of the Roman settlement of *Ad Turres*. It takes its present name from the church (*crikva* in the local dialect) of a Paulite monastery (dissolved in 1786), built by Nikola Frankopan. The monastery, on the banks of the little River Dubracina, was originally a square single-storey building with a defensive tower; the church was later remodelled in Baroque style. The building of the harbour, begun in 1871, promoted the development of Crikvenica from a fishing village into a holiday resort which attracts visitors in winter as well as in summer and has an institute providing sea-water therapy for bronchitic patients.

SIGHTS. – Of the former monastery, closed in the 18th c., there survives only the *church*. An attractive *seafront promenade*, most of it tree-shaded, links Crikvenica with the resorts of Kačjak to the N and Selce to the S and provides access to a number of small coves (rocky, usually with small pebble beaches).

Harbour, Crikvenica

SURROUNDINGS. – A road, which branches off the Adriatic coastal highway at Crikvenica and climbs into the hills (signposted to Grižane and Bribir), soon comes to the ruins of the medieval **Badanj Castle**, strategically situated at the point where the vine-clad *Vinodol valley* turns towards Crikvenica and the sea. Turning left (SP Tribalj) at a road junction near the castle, in 4 miles/6 km we reach **Drivenik**, with another medieval castle built by the Frankopan family. Situated in a valley basin, Drivenik Castle has interesting cylindrical towers.

Dalmatia

The coastal region of *Dalmatia extends from the S end of the island of Pag and the Starigrad-Paklenica fjord, spanned by the Maslenica bridge, to Cavtat, S of Dubrovnik, taking in also the long string of offshore islands. On the inland side its boundaries extend from Obrovac in the N by way of Knin and Imotski to Trebinje and then down to the coast at Cavtat. This whole coastal strip forms part of the republic of Croatia, with the exception of a narrow corridor giving the republic of Bosnia-Hercegovina access to the sea near Kardeljevo (formerly Ploče), at the mouth of the Neretva. Visitors will recognise distinctive Dalmatian characteristics throughout the region, not only in the people but also in the wines, the food and the traditional costumes.

Many settlements in Dalmatia show a similar pattern of development. Pre-historic material found in caves has shown that Stone Age man had established himself at many places within the region. Later the Celts and then the Illyrians arrived. Settlements were established by Greeks and Phoenicians, first on the offshore islands and then on the coast. About 200 B.C. the Romans began to seek a foothold on the Dalmatian coast but at first had only limited success; then in 118, after a systematic campaign of conquest, Metellus brought the whole of Dalmatia under Roman control and was thereafter known as Metellus Dalmaticus.

Under Roman rule many Dalmatian settlements prospered and developed into productive colonies. Gold was still worked in this region, and other products exported to Rome included furs and fine cloth, marble, wine and oil. There was a flowering of art and architecture, and the prosperous Roman citizens in the colonies enjoyed a life of luxury and ease. The first signs of difficulty and decline appeared when the Ostrogoths and Huns came within reach of the Dalmatian coast. In A.D. 395, during the reign of Theodosius, the Roman Empire was divided into two, and Dalmatia fell to the share of Byzantium. The Slavs, who had been advancing southward through the Carpathians since the end of the 5th c. and had come under the overlordship of the bloodthirsty Avars in 567, subsequently began to harry Dalmatia with their raids. In 614 they destroyed the flourishing city of **Salona** (now Solin), to the N of Split, and later settled in the conquered territories, beginning the process of making the coastal regions Slavonic.

In 799 Charlemagne defeated the Avars and Dalmatia came under Frankish rule. Thereafter, however, the Croats gained control of the area. In 997 Venice captured many places on the Dalmatian coast, but in 1053 a Croat, Peter Krešimir, recovered the territory and assumed the title of king of Dalmatia and Croatia.

The subsequent history of the coastal regions was one of incessant power struggles. At one moment Venice gained control; then Croatian and Croatian-Hungarian kings asserted their authority, and at times various local princes ruled briefly. During this uncertain time some of the wealthier towns sought to protect themselves by paying out tributes and bribes in all directions. Then in 1301 fortune turned in favour of Venice, and

with a few exceptions, including the independent republic of Ragusa, the coastal towns acknowledged Venetian authority, while the advancing Turks occupied the whole of the Dalmatian hinterland.

With the end of the Republic of Venice in 1797 Dalmatia passed to Austria; then, under the Peace of Pressburg in 1805, Austria was compelled to cede it to Napoleon, who incorporated it in his Illyrian Provinces. This interlude, however, lasted only until 1815, when Austria regained sovereignty. After the First World War Dalmatia became part of the kingdom of Yugoslavia, except for Zadar which was assigned to Italy. During the Second World War there was fierce fighting for some of the coastal towns, which were occupied from 1941 to 1943 by Italian units and after the Italian capitulation by German troops. Split, Šibenik and Zadar in particular suffered severe destruction by bombing. Since the last war the development of the Adriatic coastal highway (*Jadranska Magistrala*) has made Dalmatia the holiday region on the Adriatic coast most favoured by foreign vacationers.

Dalmatia owes its popularity as a holiday area to its scenery, its abundance of sunshine, its many features of historical and artistic interest and not least to the tolerance and hospitality of its people. Although it has no sandy beaches sloping gently down to the sea its clean and unpolluted water, combined with its other attractions, persuades huge numbers of visitors that this is the vacation area they are looking for. The local costumes and folk traditions are somtimes decried by sceptical visitors as shows put on for the benefit of tourists; but the cheerful and friendly atmosphere of these events must surely convince them that the impulses behind them are not purely commercial.

Dubrovnik

Republic: Croatia (Hrvatska).
Altitude: 16 ft/5 m. – Population: 36,000.
Post code: YU-50000. – Telephone code: 0 50.
ⓘ Turistički Informativni Centar,
Placa;
tel. 2 63 54.

HOTELS. – *Dubrovnik President*, L, 338 b., tel. 2 26 66; *Argosy*, A, 616 b., tel. 2 29 99; *Plakir*, A, 616 b., tel. 2 29 99; *Dubrovnik Palace*, A, 600 b., tel. 2 85 55; *Tirena*, A, 416 b., tel. 2 29 99; *Libertas*, A, 400 b., tel. 2 74 44; *Excelsior*, A, 369 b., tel. 2 35 66; *Kompas*, A, 296 b., tel. 2 37 77; *Argentina*, A, with annexes *Orsula* and *Shahrazada*, 269 b., tel. 2 38 55; *Grand Hotel Imperial*, A, 181 b., tel. 2 36 88; *Villa Dubrovnik*, A, 106 b., tel. 2 29 33; *Dubrovnik Marina*, A, 26 b., tel. 8 77 22; *Adriatic*, B, 539 b., tel. 2 41 44; *Grand Hotel Park*, B, 427 b., tel. 2 56 44; *Neptun*, B, with annexe *Elita*, 419 b., tel. 2 37 55; *Lero*, B, 307 b., tel. 2 49 64; *Petka* (no rest.), B, 200 b., tel. 2 49 33; *Vis I*, B, 180 b., tel. 2 37 66; *Sumratin*, B, with annexe *Aquarium*, 123 b., tel. 2 47 22; *Lapad*, B, 120 b., tel. 2 34 73; *Splendid*, B, 115 b., tel. 2 47 33; *Jadran*, B, 110 b., tel. 2 33 22; *Bellevue*, B, 104 b., tel. 2 50 76; *Vis II*, B, 80 b., tel. 2 37 88; *Gruž*, B, 78 b., tel. 2 47 77; *Stadion*, D, 170 b., tel. 2 34 49.

CAMP SITES. – IN KUPARI (to left of road from Dubrovnik to Herceg Novi, 1¼ miles/2 km from the sea): *Kupari*, tel. 8 60 20. (The Dubrovnik/Babin Kuk site no longer exists.)

BOATING. – Yachts can be hired and moorings rented at the little *Dubrovnik-Marina Hotel*, an old house set in a park, once the summer residence of a Dubrovnik family.

NATURIST FACILITIES. – There is an official naturist beach at Mlini, S of Dubrovnik.

EVENTS. – Dubrovnik Summer Festival (usually July 10 to August 25), with a program of more than 100 events (drama, music, ballet, folk performances).

AIRPORT. – At *Čilipi*, 19 miles/30 km S. JAT office in Dubrovnik: Maršala Tita 3, tel. 2 35 75.

Dubrovnik is a unique open-air museum pulsing with vigorous life, with 220 cloudless days in the year and an average annual temperature of 61·5°F/16·4°C. Even in winter it attracts many visitors – members of the older age groups, who have discovered the advantages of Dubrovnik as a place for long out-of-season holidays. Throughout the year, too, tourists land here from the cruise ships which call in at the port, once known to the Italians as Ragusa, on their way from Venice to the eastern Mediterranean. But Dubrovnik is not merely a splendid historical showpiece and a kind of traffic junction where tourists switch between aircraft, ships, trains and buses: it is well equipped with excellent hotels, some of which

(e.g. the Babin Kuk complex at Lapad, opened in 1976) demonstrate that the creative forces displayed by the Dalmatian capital in the art and architecture of the past can still make a contribution to the "holiday architecture" of our day.

The town's program of entertainment and cultural events, which lasts into the autumn, has an international flavour and is up to the highest artistic standards; and the lighter Muse, in the field of music, dancing and folk performances, is not neglected. – There are car ferry connections with Venice, Trieste, Ancona, Bari and Corfu; the motor yachts which make the round of the small offshore islands also call in at Dubrovnik.

HISTORY. – In the 7th c. A.D. refugees from the nearby town of Cavtat settled on the island of Lausa, on the site now occupied by the old town of Dubrovnik. But this was probably not the first settlement here, since an Early Christian capital found on the highest part of the crag suggests that there may have been earlier inhabitants. On the mainland opposite the island there was also a Slav settlement with the name of *Dubrava* ("oak-grove"). Lausa became **Ragusa**, the name by which the town was known until 1918, and Dubrava gave rise to the present name Dubrovnik. In the 13th c. the citizens filled in the channel which separated the island from the mainland, on the line now occupied by the Placa, the finest promenade in Yugoslavia.

The town, which soon rose to prosperity through its trade and its shipping, was ruled by a governor (*strategs*) appointed by the Byzantine emperor. Even at this early period, however, the townspeople were able to assert their right to manage their own affairs – by adroit political manoeuvring, by deploying their economic influence and no doubt to some extent also by bribery. Thus during the first period of Venetian rule (1205–1358) Venice was not so much the overlord as the patron of Ragusa. When the town became part of the Croatian–Hungarian kingdom of 1358 it secured formal confirmation of its right of self-government. The principal organ of this self-government was the Great Council, made up of well-to-do citizens. The Great Council elected a Senate, and this in turn appointed a Lesser Council which consisted of ministers responsible for various special fields. Each month Lesser Council elected one of its members to be head of the municipal administration, the Rector, who was required to live and work in his official residence, separated from his family. (Visitors can see in the Rector's Palace the room in which he spent this period of "house arrest".)

The first Slav republic also contrived to reach an accommodation with the Turks who then occupied the mainland. Ragusa nominally recognised the overlordship of the Ottoman empire and paid tribute to the Turks; but in their own enterprises, their steadily growing trade and the maintenance and development of their fleet the wealthy merchants of Ragusa suffered no interference from the Turks.

Moreover the citizens of Ragusa had prudently set out at an early stage to convert their town into an impregnable stronghold. In 1272 they began the

◀ **Dubrovnik – the Placa**

Town walls of Dubrovnik

systematic development of the town's defences – an earlier circuit of walls and towers – into a monumental complex of fortifications.

Dubrovnik's greatest days were between the 14th and 16th c., when it was the home of philosophers, artists and famous architects, and the ideas of humanism and the Renaissance found expression in literature and art.

The municipal administration was notable for its pioneering achievements in public health and social care: it organised a central water supply and drainage system, built hospitals, an orphanage and an old people's home, and constructed a granary, the Rupe, with a capacity of 1500 tons in 15 dry chambers hewn from the rock. In 1301 a kind of health service was established, and in 1319 the first pharmacy in the Balkans was opened. In order to reinforce the town's defences the far-seeing patricians of Ragusa purchased a series of outposts at strategically important points – Ston, in the narrow channel leading to the Pelješac peninsula; the islands of Mljet and Lastovo, guarding the shipping route to Venice; and the town of Cavtat, protecting their S flank.

The 17th c. brought a period of difficulty for the shipowners and seamen of the Mediterranean, for the interest of the great powers was now turning towards overseas territories. Then on April 6, 1667 came the blackest day in Ragusa's history, when a violent earthquake almost totally destroyed the town and killed 5000 of its inhabitants. It took a long time to recover from this blow. In 1806 Napoleon's troops occupied the town, and in 1808 it lost its status as an independent republic and was incorporated in Napoleon's Illyrian Provinces. the Congress of Vienna (1814–15) assigned the town to Austria; and finally after the First World War it became part of King Alexander's new kingdom.

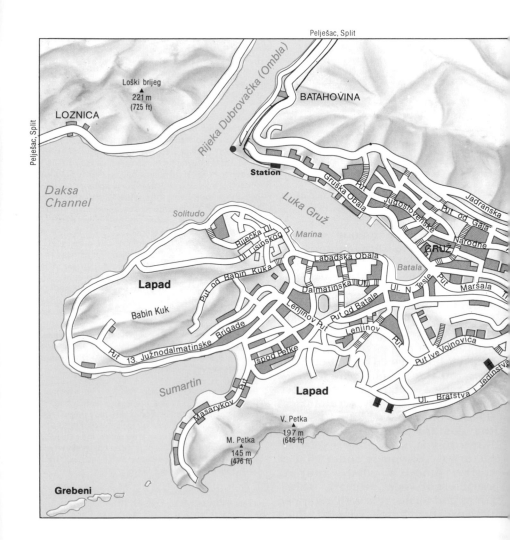

SIGHTS. – Neither a day's visit nor a sightseeing excursion from a cruise liner is sufficient to see even the principal sights of Dubrovnik. And quite apart from sightseeing, any visit to Dubrovnik is incomplete if it does not provide for a leisurely evening in the town. After a concert, a performance at the theatre or a demonstration of folk singing and dancing there should still be time to stroll along the Placa, look out over the silvery glitter of the sea from the town walls, and finally enjoy a glass of local wine in an open-air café or restaurant.

The best starting point for a tour of the town is the **Pile Gate**. Since the whole of the****OLD TOWN** is a pedestrian precinct it is necessary to park your car before setting out. During the main season the best plan is to leave it at your hotel or camp site or in one of the car parks on the outskirts of the town (there are good bus services to Brsalje Square, outside the Pile Gate).

The fortified town had four gates, two on the landward and two on the seaward side; two further gates were opened in the walls during the Austrian period, when the fortifications had lost their defensive function. As already noted, the * **town walls** and the *defence works* outside them were constructed between the 12th and 17th c. by a series of different military engineers. Behind the main wall runs a walk 2120 yd/1940 m long, still passable today. The walls on the landward side are 13–20 ft/4–6 m thick, on the seaward side 5–10 ft/1·5–3 m; almost everywhere they are 80 ft/25 m high. They are reinforced by three round and twelve square *towers*, five *bastions*, two *corner towers* and the principal defensive work, **Fort St John** (*Sveti Ivan*): an imposing and formidable complex of fortifications, representing a huge expenditure of effort which was no doubt justified as much by its psychological effect as by its military effectiveness.

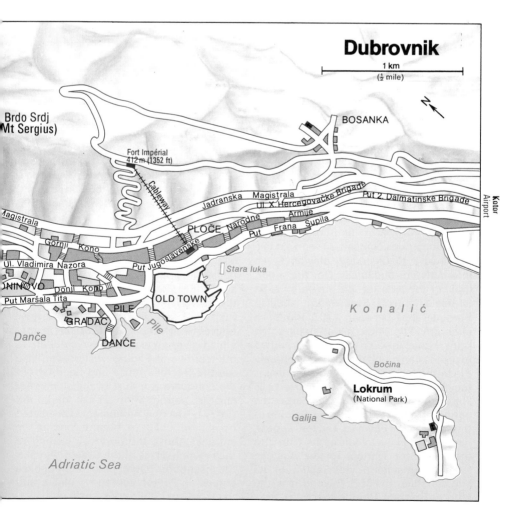

Visitors entering the old town through the Pile Gate are immediately confronted with the most evocative part of Dubrovnik, the wide street known as the Placa, paved with stone slabs worn smooth by the passage of many feet and thronged with sightseers and casual strollers. This street was not constructed by the Romans, as is often supposed, but by the townspeople of Ragusa in 1468, after the installation of a water supply system under the roadway. The stone-built houses on either side were destroyed in an earthquake in 1667, leaving only the ground floors standing, and were subsequently rebuilt in uniform Baroque style. The ground floor shops were restored, and still contribute in their colourful variety to the atmosphere of this popular promenade.

Immediately inside the gate, on the left, is the *Chapel of the Saviour* (Sveti Spas), an aisleless structure in Lombard style, and adjoining the *Franciscan friary*, with a 15th c. Pietà above the late Gothic doorway of the church. Between the church and the chapel is the entrance to the beautiful Romanesque **Lower Cloister*, which houses the **Pharmacy** founded in 1319 (see above, History), still preserved in its original state. Beyond this, to the left, rises the *Minčeta Tower*, which gives access to the wall-walk.

To the right, just inside the gate, is the *Large Onofrio Fountain* (1438), with a low domed roof and 16 water-spouts.

At the far end of the Placa is **Luža Square**, from time immemorial the hub of the town's life. Here, around the *Small Onofrio Fountain* and the *Roland Column*, groups of musicians and singers are always to be found, playing to an international audience. On the right, looking towards the old harbour, is **St Blaise's Church** (*Sveti Vlaho*), rebuilt in Baroque style between 1706 and 1715 after a fire. The 14th c. gilded statue of the saint on the high altar was formerly carried in procession round the town on February 3! On the left-hand side of the square is the *Clock-Tower* (Zvonik), whose bells were used to summon the members of the council to a meeting or to give warning of the approach of enemies. The *Bell Loggia*, demolished in the middle of the 19th c. to make way for a house for the Austrian town commandant, was rebuilt in its original state in 1952. Beyond it is the 16th c. **Sponza Palace**, once the resi-

dence of the Rector, which also housed all the municipal offices apart from the financial department and had cells for prisoners in the basement. On the first floor of the palace is a section of the *Municipal Museum*. The pillared vestibule and arcaded courtyard are particularly fine.

The lane straight ahead leads through a passage under the town walls to the old *harbour*. To the left is the **Dominican friary**, with a magnificently decorated 14th c. *cloister*. The *church*, rebuilt after the earthquake, contains many *pictures* by old masters; an altar on the N side has a painting by Titian, "Mary Magdalene between St Blaise and the Archangel Raphael" (*c.* 1554).

The lane past the Dominican church leads to the **Ploče Gate**, the second of the two main gates of the old town. Beyond the gate a bridge over the former moat gives access to *Fort Revelin* and through an outer gate one reaches the Ploče quarter of the town. From here there is a view along the coast road where Dubrovnik's older hotels are situated. To the right can be seen the whole of the *Old Harbour*, with the arched entrances to a stone-built boathouse in which the state barges used by the patrician rulers of Ragusa were kept.

We now return to Luža Square. Opposite St Blaise's Church is the ***Rector's Palace**, the finest building in the old town, with the former *Town Hall* of 1852 (now café, with a theatre) next to it. The palace was built between 1435 and 1451 by Onofrio Giordano della Cava (who was also responsible for the two fountains named after him) as the seat of the Great and Lesser Councils and the residence of the Rector, and was rebuilt in its original form after the 1667 earthquake. It now houses a *Museum of Cultural history* which gives an excellent survey of life in the republic of Ragusa. Visitors can also see the Rector's office and bedroom. In the courtyard is a bust of the shipowner and art patron Miho Pracat of Lopud (1637) – the only monument ever erected by the republic to honour one of its citizens. Above the doorway leading to, the meeting-place of the Great Council is the inscription "Obliti privatorum publica curate" ("Forget your own affairs and think only of public concerns").

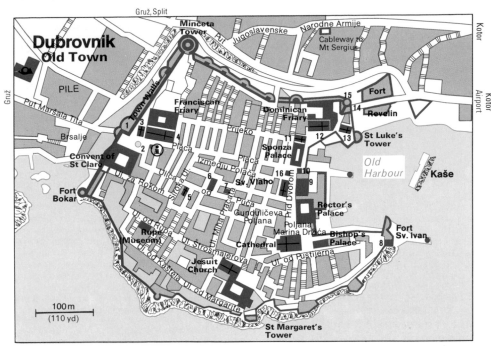

1 Pile Gate
2 Onofrio Fountain
3 Chapel of St Saviour
4 Franciscan church

5 All Saints Church
6 Serbian Orthodox church
7 Icon Museum
8 Aquarium, Maritime Museum, Museum of Ethnography

9 Town Hall
10 Clock-Tower
11 St Nicholas's Church
12 Dominican church

13 Church of Annunciation
14 Ploče Gate
15 Asimov Tower
16 Roland Column

To the right of the Rector's Palace stands the **Cathedral**, dedicated to the Assumption (*Velika Gospa*); it was rebuilt in Baroque style (1671–1713) after its destruction in the earthquake. It contains some fine pictures (including works by Pordenone and other pupils of Titian) and a rich *Treasury*, with no fewer than 138 relics dating from the 9th c. onwards. Its most precious possession is a reliquary containing St Blaise's skull, wearing a Byzantine crown. Also of particular interest is a large basin with a silver gilt ewer depicting the flora and fauna of Dubrovnik in the 16th c. The church also has a Flemish triptych which Ragusan envoys took with them on their official journeys as a portable altar.

Beyond the Cathedral, to the right, is the *Bishop's Palace*, and beyond this again, along a lane running parallel to the harbour, we reach *Fort St John* (Sveti Ivan), on a projecting tongue of land. The fort now houses an *Aquarium*, a *Maritime Museum* and a *Museum of Ethnography*.

Returning to the Cathedral, we take Ul. *Štrosmajerova* (Strossmayer St), which runs past it to the **Jesuit church** (on left), built 1699–1725. Farther along the street, also on the left, is the Rupe (state granary), now a museum. Farther left,

towards the sea, is the *Kaštel*, the oldest part of the town. From here, continuing along the walls, we come to *Fort Bokar*, the oldest casemated (casemate – a chamber, with embrasures for artillery) fort in the world, situated at the point where the rocky coast ends, and then to the Pile Gate.

Passing through the Pile Gate and keeping left beyond Brsalje Square, we arrive at *Fort Lovrijenac*, in which dramatic performances are given during the Dubrovnik Festival.

Farther W, at GRUŽ, is Dubrovnik's *New Harbour*, where the cruise ships put in and freighters discharge their cargoes. From here, too, excursions leave for the nearby islands, including the *Elaphite Islands* (see under Koločep) and **Lokrum** (luxuriant subtropical vegetation, natural history museum, institute of biology; smoking prohibited on the island).

A magnificent general *view of the town can be enjoyed from the upper bypass (access to N at Rijeka inlet, to S at Dubac). There is also a rewarding *view from **Brdo Srdj** (Mt Sergius, 1352 ft/412 m), crowned by a fort built by the French in 1809, and which can be reached by cableway.

SURROUNDINGS. – On the W side of the new harbour is the charming **Lapad** peninsula, with numerous hotels and villas and beautiful trees (Aleppo pines, cypresses, etc.). In a pretty bay on the W side of the peninsula is the popular seaside resort of *Sumartin*. On the S side, high above the sea, is *St Blaise's Chapel* (Sveti Vlaho), which affords a very fine*view, as does *Mt Petka* (646 ft/197 m; 1 hour's climb).

Dugi Otok

Republic Croatia (Hrvatska).
Area of island: 48 sq. miles/124 sq. km. –
Population: 6000.
Telephone code: 0 57.
ⓘ **Turističko Društvo Sali**
YU-57281 Sali;
tel. 8 79 33.
Turističko Društvo Božava,
in Božava Hotel,
YU-57286 Božava;
tel. 5 72 86.

HOTELS. – IN SALI: *Alga, Koral, Perla* and *Sirena*, C, 96 b., tel. 8 78 78; *Sali*, D, 100 b., tel. 5 72 81; also 300 beds in private houses (apply to Tourist Office). – IN LUKA: *Luka*, C, 126 b., tel. 2 42 55. – IN BOŽAVA: *Božava*, B, 385 b., tel. 8 63 02 (annexes, C).

SPORT. – Hire of rowing boats, canoes and sailing boats in Božava; water-skiing, scuba diving (German-run diving school). Hire of sailing boats in Sali. Water-skiing at Luka and Sali. – At Luka Hotel, beginning of June to end September, training courses for motor-boat helmsman's certificate (test at harbour office, Zadar); enquiries to JTP Turisthotel, YU-57000 Zadar, tel. (0 57) 2 42 55.

NATURIST FACILITIES. – Beaches at Sali and Božava.

BOATING and BATHING. – Almost the whole of the W coast of Dugi Otok is inaccessible, with vertical cliffs rising sheer out of the sea to heights of 330 ft/100 m or more. The most attractive holiday resort is **Božava**, in a natural bay with a small pinewood, a green and pleasant spot with its gardens, fruit orchards and fig-trees. The hotel chalets are in the woods. The bathing places mostly have rock approaches, but there are a few small shingle beaches. In a remote cove 15 minutes from Božava is an Austrian-run naturist site with sanitary installations, saunas, play areas and sports facilities (no camping). The rocky beach of the chalet hotel at **Sali** (10 minutes' walk from the village) is laid with concrete. There is also a shingle beach; in the water the bottom is sandy. At **Luka** there is only one hotel (beach partly rock, partly shingle). – Some parts of the coast of Dugi Otok are closed to divers: information from hotels in Božava.

FERRIES. – Daily services from Zadar to the island of Molat and Božava and from Zadar to Sali, Luka and the island of Iž. Cars not carried.

Dugi Otok ("long island") is 27 miles/44 km long and nowhere wider than 3 miles/5 km – at some points no more than 1 mile/1·5 km across. With

Boats in Božava harbour, Dugi Otok

an area of 48 sq. miles/124 sq. km, however, it is the largest island in the North Dalmatian archipelago. In the past the great attraction of Dugi Otok for visitors seeking a quiet and relaxing holiday was the absence of cars, but with the construction of a road between the port of Božava, in the NW of the island, and Sali, on the SE coast, it seems likely to lose this advantage. The island has no springs or above-ground watercourses, but in winter the karstic depressions of Malo Jezero, Velo Jezero and Dugo Polje fill up with fresh water, and the rainfall and ground water are sufficient to allow vines, olives, vegetables and pines to flourish. The only accommodation for visitors is at Božava, Sali and Luka.

HISTORY. – The island was already occupied by man in prehistoric times; the earliest finds, near the village of Žman, date from the Neolithic period., The remains of Illyrian forts and grave mounds can be seen on some of the hills. Roman villas, settlements and tombs have been excavated, and on the *Proversa* peninsula can be seen the foundations of a villa with its water supply and drainage system; a mosaic pavement found here is now in the museum in Zadar. The island was settled by Slavs at an early stage, and there are the remains of small churches, houses and tombs of the early Croatian period, wholly or partly preserved. From the 10th c. onwards the island belonged to religious houses or the municipality of Zadar. It first appears in the records, under the name of *Pizuh*, in a document of the Byzantine emperor Constantine Porphyrogenitus (mid 10th c.); towards the end of the 10th and during the 11th c. it begins to appear in documents as *Insula Tilaga*.

SIGHTS. – Apart from the remains of buildings and tombs which have already been mentioned Dugi Otok has few remains of the past. In **Sali**, the largest place on the island and the main fishing area of the Kornati Islands, with several fish-processing factories, there is a pleasant walk from the lower to the upper part of the village, ending at the **cemetery**, where an unusual form of burial, found nowhere else in the Adriatic islands, can be seen – stone vaults blasted out of the rock and closed with slabs of stone.

An interesting day trip from Sali by boat is to the impressive cave of **Strašna Pećina**, which has stalactites up to 40 in./1 m thick. A view of more than a hundred islands can be had by climbing the hill of *Bručastac*.

Durmitor Range

Republic: Montenegro (Crna Gora).
ⓘ Turističko Biro Žabljak,
YU-84220 Žabljak;
tel. (0 84) 8 83 31.

HOTELS. – IN ŽABLJAK: *Jezera*, A, 245 b., tel. 8 83 01; *Durmitor*, B, 240 b., tel. 8 82 78; *Žabljak*, B, 70 b., tel. 8 83 00; also 500 beds in private houses (apply to Tourist Office).

CAMP SITE. – Simple camp site for motorists at Crno Jezero.

SPORT. – Canoeing on River Tara, fishing in lakes; walking and climbing, shooting; skiing in Žabljak area four ski-tows).

Most of the *Durmitor range (highest point 8275 ft/2522 m) is a National Park. The principal holiday resort is Žabljak. The area offers magnificent scenery, with flower-spangled mountain pastures, a mountain stream pursuing a winding course into the lake and brightly painted peasants' houses. The plateau is known as the "land of the little lakes": 20 of them at heights of between 4600 ft/1400 m and 7200 ft/ 2200 m, fed by melt-water from the neighbouring glaciers.

The best known lake is the *Crno Jezero* or Black Lake, with the massive bulk of Medjed rearing 2300 ft/700 m above it. Above the Black Lake is a smaller lake, 490 yd/450 m long by 285 yd/260 m wide, which is linked with the larger one. Both lakes are surrounded by dense, dark forests. There is a road from Žabljak to the Crno Jezero, with car parking at the camp site from which a beautiful footpath makes a circuit of the lower lake.

The highest point in the Durmitor range is *Bobotov Kuk* (8275 ft/2522 m); experienced climbers can reach the summit from Žabljak in 5 hours. Other rewarding peaks are Sljene (8127 ft/2477 m), Prutaš (7851 ft/2393 m) and Soje (7835 ft/2388 m), all of which can be climbed in about 4 hours. The routes up these mountains are well marked. There are no climbing huts nor any organised mountain rescue service.

The views from these summits of valleys, gorges, winding mountain streams, snowfields and green meadowland offer an unforgettable experience. Skiing is also possible in summer in the Durmitor range

In the Durmitor range: the Black Lake, with Bobotov Kuk in the background

Guides and ski instructors can be contacted through the hotels.

The area is rich in game – bears, wild boar, deer, chamois, foxes, hares – and the lakes are frequented throughout the year by a variety of waterfowl. Visitors can fish in the two Black Lakes and in the Tara from May 1 to November 1, and shooting permits can also be obtained.

Žabljak, whose first houses date from 1871, is the principal place in the National Park which includes most of the Durmitor range. The little village first began to attract nature-lovers and climbers in the early years of this century, though originally only in summer. On average Žabljak is snow covered 120 days in the year; the average annual temperature is 41°F/5°C.

The first people to spend the winter here were the partisans of the last war, who had their headquarters in this area in 1941. The Durmitor Hotel, built in 1934 for the accommodation of climbers, was used as a hospital. Tito lived in a hut not far away.

Since then Žabljak has developed steadily into a popular winter sports resort. There are already four ski-lifts, and more are planned. There is skating on the lakes; there are a number of toboggan runs; and visitors can enjoy rides in horse-drawn sleighs.

A side road which branches to the right off the Pljevlja–Nikšić road just before the middle of Žabljak leads to a hill from which there is a fine view of the village and the surrounding lakes. The road then continues through dense forest and climbs into the Tepca area, where the steep rock face slopes down from the unmade road to the River Tara 3300 ft/1000 m below.

Žabljak

Foča

Republic: Bosnia-Hercegovina (Bosna i
Hercegovina).
Altitude: 1280 ft/390 m. – Population: 22,500.
Post code: YU-71480. – Telephone code: 0 73.
ⓘ **Turističko Društvo**,
tel. 7 22 04.

HOTEL. – *Zelengora*, B, 165 b., tel. 7 20 36.

RAFT TRIPS on the rivers Drina and Tara: for
information and reservations apply to Tourist Office.

**The little town of Foča extends
along the banks of the Drina, surrounded by wooded hills. Although
it is an industrial town, the old town
has remained unspoiled. The market
square, half way up the hill above the
main road from Dubrovnik to Belgrade, has preserved its oriental
character, with two mosques and a
number of winding lanes. The attraction of Foča for tourists lies in
the *raft trips on the Drina (it is at
the end of the trip through the Tara
gorge and the beginning of the trip
to Višegrad) and in its convenience
as a base for excursions into the
*Durmitor range, to the *Sutjeska
National Park, to the new man-made
lake on the Piva, with the Pivski
Manastir (monastery), and to the
pilgrimage church of Čajniče
(reached by way of Goražde, 21
miles/34 km away).**

HISTORY. – Foča was from an early stage a small
settlement on the old caravan road from Dubrovnik via
Niš to Constantinople. Situated at the confluence of
the Čehotina, coming from Pljevlja, and the Drina, it
developed into an important road junction and trading
post known as the "town of roses and flowers". It first
appears in the records, as *Hotča*, in 1450. In 1465 it
was occupied by the Turks, and from 1470 until well
on in the 16th c. it was the residence of a high Turkish
official. In 1590 Hassan Nazir, director of the
Hercegovina mines, financed the construction of the
Aladža Džamija, the Many-Coloured Mosque, one of
the most splendid examples of Ottoman architecture
in Yugoslavia. Since the improvement of the main road
between Dubrovnik and Belgrade in 1972 the
successful development of industry in the town has
been followed by a considerable increase in the tourist
trade.

SIGHTS. – The *Aladža Mosque (not to
be confused with the similar mosque
above the market square, built 200 years
later) stands near the bus station on the
Dubrovnik–Belgrade road.

The vestibule is notable for the richness of its
decoration. Here too is the eulogy by the Turkish
traveller Evliya Celebi, inscribed in Persian script,
which is frequently quoted in Yugoslav travel books:

"I have travelled much and visited many cities, but a
land such as this I have never seen. . . . This was written
by the slave of God, Evliya, in the year 1074." The
interior decoration of the mosque is also very
beautiful, with numerous arabesques.

Apart from the *market square* and the
oriental-style lanes around it Foča has
another feature of interest in the **Municipal Museum**, housed in an old
caravanserai (Bosnian folk art, traditional
costumes, peasant household equipment
and implements).

Foča, in the Drina valley

SURROUNDINGS. – Every year from the end of June
to the beginning of September the Foča tourist office
organises raft trips down the Drina to Višegrad, 56
miles/90 km away by road. The rafts depart on
Saturday afternoon and take 5 hours to reach the town
of **Goražde** (dinner, folk performances and overnight); the second part of the trip, from Goražde to
Višegrad, takes 8 hours. Other trips are from *Ščepan
Polje to Foča* (1 day) and from *Djurdjevića Tara to
Foča* (4 days).

For excursions to the *Durmitor range (see p. 81),
preferably spending the night at Žabljak, there are two
possible routes, both of which involve considerable
stretches of road with surfaces of sand, gravel or
stones. The first is from Foča via *Goražde, Pljevlja* (51
miles/82 km of bad road) and *Djurdjevića Tara* to
Žabljak; the other route runs via *Nikšić* (very bad for
two-thirds of the way) to Žabljak (bad for part of the
way). For detailed information see the entry on the
Durmitor range; for excursions in the National Park see
under Sutjeska.

Another attractive excursion is to the enchantingly
beautiful* *Piva reservoir, an artificial lake of deep
blue water 15 miles/25 km long which is enclosed
between mountains rising to 6560 ft/2000 m: in some
spots it is caught between sheer rock walls and shrinks
to a width of 110 yd/100 m, then opens out again as
the mountains recede. – The road from Foča is
asphalted for the first 2 miles/3 km, after which it is
surfaced with sand for 10 miles/16 km, with many
bends and the additional hazard of construction
traffic. Between the villages of *Hum* and *Brijeg* the
tumultuous River Tara is crossed on a temporary
bridge dating from the Second World War. Then
follows a stretch of excellently engineered road

running alongside the lake, with more than 50 tunnels; at one point it crosses the lake on a dam (impressive view into the valley 500 ft/150 m below). At the end of the lake the road climbs to the new tourist complex of **Plužine** (two hotels, a dozen or so holiday chalets or houses with accommodation for visitors; bathing beach, sports facilities). From here it is only a short distance to the *Pivski Manastir* (good access road branching off the road to Nikšić; signposted). The monastery, moved to its present site on a hill from its original site in the valley, now covered by the reservoir, was founded in the late 12th c. It is noted for its beautiful wall paintings, which survived the move unharmed. – From this point until shortly before Nikšić the road is surfaced with sand and gravel, with many bends and often with poor visibility when passing through the forest.

To the pilgrimage church of Čajniče. – Leave Foča on the Belgrade road, and at *Goražde* turn right into a road which crosses the Drina and comes in 12 miles/19 km to **Čajniče**, situated at an altitude of 2625 ft/800 m on the rim of a rocky gorge with almost vertical walls. Here there is a famous pilgrimage church (15th c.) containing valuable icons, the best known of which is the *Mother of God of Čajniče*, believed to date from the 1st c. and ascribed to Luke the Evangelist. It is established at any rate that the icon was brought here from a monastery on Athos in Greece. The church, in the Serbian style of the 15th c. with 14 lead-covered domes, also contains a number of valuable manuscripts. Every year on August 28, the Orthodox feast day of the Mother of God (the Virgin), thousands of pilgrims flock to Čajniče. The little town is also popular with Yugoslavs as a summer holiday resort.

Herceg-Novi

Republic: Montenegro (Crna Gora).
Altitude: 33–490 ft/10–150 m. – Population: 10,000.
Post code: YU-81340. – Telephone code: 0 82.
(i) **Turistički Savez Boke Kotorske,**
Trg Nikole Djurkovića;
tel. 8 72 51.

HOTELS. – *Villa Primorka*, A, 98 b., tel. 4 34 22; *Motel Dubravka*, on the Adriatic coastal highway, A, 70 b., tel. 4 38 33; *Topla*, B, 470 b., tel. 4 37 22; *Riviera*, B, 460 b., tel. 4 31 77; *Plaža*, B, with annexe *Villa Palma* (¾ mile/1 km from town), 387 b., tel. 4 32 22. – IN BIJELA: *Park*, A, 115 b., tel. 4 35 51. – IN KAMENO: *Borići*, A, 15 b., tel. 4 34 02.

CAMP SITE. – *Zelenika*, in the district of that name, tel. 4 33 61. Entrance on the road to Kotor (No. 10): steep access road, impracticable for large caravan trailers.

SPORT. – Water-skiing (Riviera and Topla Hotels), scuba diving, fishing, sailing, boat rental (Topla and Plaža Hotels); table tennis, bowling alley, mini-golf.

The holiday resort of * Herceg-Novi, situated in Topla Bay, an inlet sheltered by hills on the Adriatic coast of Montenegro, is noted for its extraordinarily mild climate (average January temperature 50°F/10°C) and

Herceg-Novi before the 1979 earthquake

its luxuriant subtropical vegetation. In spite of the severe damage it suffered in the 1979 earthquake the town, nestling amid greenery, is still a popular resort both in summer and in winter.

HISTORY. – The history of Herceg-Novi (previously spelled as a single word, Hercegnovi) dates only from the year 1382, when King Tvrtko of Bosnia resolved to build a port at the entrance to the bay in order to give his kingdom an access to the sea. The port was constructed in the short space of five months, and the king then established a salt market in the town. Its trade flourished, and in 1448 Duke Stjepan set up a factory here. The town, now fortified, took its name from the duke (*herceg*).

In 1483 Herceg-Novi was taken by the Turks. In 1538, however, a naval force under the command of Andrea Doria, consisting of Spanish, Venetian and Papal troops, drove out the Turks, and a fort designed by Andrea Doria himself was built above the town and named *Španjola* in honour of the Spaniards who had taken part in the attack. Furious over the loss of the town Sultan Selim II sent an expeditionary force of no fewer than 110 ships to recover it. By ill luck Andrea Doria and his fleet were elsewhere, and accordingly the defences were stormed by 8000 Turks and 3000 of the defenders were slaughtered in a single night. The battle ended after 25 days with the surrender of the town, the Spanish defenders being granted the right to withdraw; but when the Turks saw that there were only 25 of them left they offered these valiant warriors the privilege of remaining in the town as free men.

In 1687 the town passed into the hands of Venice. In 1797 it was occupied by Austrian forces; in 1806 and 1807 the Russian fleet anchored off the town; from 1807 to 1811 it was occupied by the French; in 1814 it was held briefly by the Montenegrin army; and thereafter it remained under Austrian rule until 1918.

SIGHTS. – In the market square are a graceful *Clock-Tower* and the *Karadja Fountain*, with a Turkish inscription. On a crag above the bay is a **Venetian fort** protecting the harbour, and above this again is another Venetian fort, the **Forte**

Mare, now an open-air cinema. The ruined *Kanli Kula,* another of the bastions defending the town, now contains a large open-air theatre. On top of the hill are the ruins of **Fort Španjola,** built by the Spaniards in 1538, which was completely destroyed in the 1979 earthquake. There are fine panoramic views from the summit.

To the W of the town are the **Archaeological Museum** and a holiday villa once occupied by the novelist and Nobel Prize winner *Ivo Andrić.*

SURROUNDINGS. – In a park to the E of Herceg-Novi is the Orthodox **Savina Monastery** (severely damaged in the 1979 earthquake), with two churches. The name comes from the 13th c. church of St Sava above the monastery. The smaller and older of the monastery's two churches, dating from the 11th c., has a rich *treasury,* with works of religious art of the 15th–19th c., including a crystal episcopal cross of 1219, a gilded circlet and a silver-plated reliquary of 1675. The newer church (end of 18th c.) shows a successful sythesis of Baroque forms and traditional Byzantine architecture.

Hvar

Republic: Croatia (Hrvatska).
Area of island: 116 sq. miles/300 sq. km. –
Population: 20,000.
Telephone code: 0 58.
(i) **Turistički Savez Općine Hvar,**
Trg Maršala Tita 1,
YU-58450 Hvar;
tel. 7 40 58.
Turistička Agencija Jelsa,
na Obali,
YU-58465 Jelsa;
tel. 7 56 28.
Dalmacijaturist Stari Grad,
YU-58460 Stari Grad;
tel. 7 58 28.

HOTELS. – IN HVAR TOWN: *Amfora,* A, 745 b., tel. 7 42 02; *Sirena,* A, 316 b., tel. 7 41 44; *Bodul,* A, 300 b., tel. 7 40 49; *Palace,* A, 148 b., tel. 7 43 06; *Dalmacija,* A, 136 b., tel. 7 41 20; *Adriatic,* A, 116 b., tel. 7 40 24; *Delfin,* A, 112 b., tel. 7 41 68; *Galeb,* C, 68 b., tel. 7 40 44. – IN JELSA: *Mina,* A, 400 b., tel. 7 43 20; *Fontana* tourist complex, B, 376 b., tel. 7 56 32; *Jadran,* C, 280 b., tel. 7 56 15. – IN VRBOSKA: *Adriatic,* A, 350 b., tel. 7 54 36; *Madeira,* A, 44 b., tel. 7 54 15. – IN STARI GRAD: *Arcada,* A, 580 b., tel. 7 58 22; *Helios,* B, 418 b., tel. 7 58 22, with annexe *Helios Bungalows,* B, 108 b.; *Adriatic,* B, 170 b., tel. 7 58 22; *Jadran,* C, 33 b., tel. 7 58 27.

CAMP SITES. – IN STARI GRAD: *Jurjevac,* tel. 7 58 21. – IN JELSA: *Mina* (with facilities for naturists).

NATURIST FACILITIES. – HVAR TOWN: on the offshore island of *Jerolim* and in Vira Bay. – JELSA: on the island of Zečevo. – STARI GRAD: on a nameless offshore island. Regular motorboat services to all naturist islands. – *Helios* camp site at Stari Grad.

EVENTS. – International Fashion Festival at Stari Grad in June. – Open-air performances in summer in the ruins of St Catherine's Monastery above Hvar town, in the Arsenal and in the courtyard of Sv. Marko.

SPORT, BOATING and BATHING. – Although the island offers visitors beautiful scenery, fine old buildings in the towns and a relaxed holiday atmosphere, it lacks good *bathing beaches* suitable for families with children. On the beaches in front of the hotel complexes in **Hvar town** the rock has been covered with concrete and gangways into the water have been provided; but there are only small stretches of pebbles or sand. Large numbers of sun-worshippers travel daily by boat to the naturist island of **Jerolim.** The hotels of Stari Grad have a better beach (though swimming at the head of the inlet is not recommended). Here too the naturist sun-lovers travel by boat to a nearby stretch of beach.

There are facilities for bathing in front of the hotels at **Jelsa,** but the beach is rocky. There are boat services to the naturists island of Zečevo.

All the hotels have excellent *sports facilities.* Hvar town has an Olympic-size swimming pool at the Amfora Hotel, with gymnastic and training facilities which are used in winter by Yugoslav sports teams. – Also scuba diving and water-skiing.

Everywhere boats can be rented. There are daily "pirate voyages" to bays and offshore islands for picnics. Aqualungs can be refilled in Hvar.

FERRIES. – Hydrofoils and fast motor launches from Zadir to Vira, the harbour for Hvar town (Hvar itself is a pedestrian precinct); no cars on these services. Car ferries Split to Vira, Split to Stari Grad, Sućuraj (at the E end of the island) to Drvenik. Boat services between Jelsa and Bol and between Hvar and Korčula.

**Hvar, with its flower-filled gardens, its palms, its orange and lemon groves, its fragrance of rosemary, its enchanting countryside affording glimpses of a deep blue sea, is an island of captivating charm. With 20,000 visitors at the height of the season, mainly concentrated in the resorts of Hvar town, Stari Grad, Vrboska and Jelsa, and an area of only 116 sq. miles/300 sq. km it can at times be uncomfortably crowded; but before and after the main season, particularly during the mild winter months, a holiday on Hvar will be an experience to remember. Snow, fog and frost are so rare even between December and March that the hotels are able to offer a reduction of 50%, or even to make no charge at all, on days when they occur. The climate of the island is particularly good for the asthmatic.

HISTORY. – Hvar has had an eventful history, under constantly changing rulers. Evidence of occupation in the Neolithic period has been found in caves. In 385 B.C. Greeks from the Cycladic island of Paros founded

Hvar town

the settlement of *Pharos*, and soon afterwards another settlement, *Dimos*, was established on the site of the present-day town of Hvar. In 235 B.C. an Illyrian king, Agron, gained control of the island. The Romans landed on Hvar in 219 B.C. and held the island until the 7th c. A.D. Thereafter it was occupied by Slavs from the Neretva mountains. From 870 to 886 it belonged to the Byzantine empire, and then fell back into the hands of the Neretvans. In the 11th c. it was controlled by the kings of Croatia, from 1145 to 1164 by Venice, from 1164 to 1180 by Byzantium, from 1180 to 1278 by the Hungarian-Croatian kings, then again by Venice. The Hungarian-Croatian kings regained control from 1358 to 1420, after which the island belonged to Bosnia and then to the republic of Dubrovnik. From 1420 to 1797 it was held by Venice, then from 1797 to 1806 by Austria, from 1806 to 1813 by France, and again by Austria from 1813 to 1918. From 1918 to 1922 it was under Italian occupation, after which it was incorporated in the kingdom of Yugoslavia. In April 1941 the island was occupied by Italian troops, who were replaced by Germans after the Italian surrender in 1943. In September 1944 Hvar was recovered by partisan units.

Passenger ships and freighters, and the motor launches and hydrofoils from Split, put in at the natural harbour of *Vira* on the N side of the island in order to keep cars, trucks and buses away from the town of Hvar, 2 miles/3 km S. Some vessels from Split also put in at Stari Grad, and there is a ferry service between the mainland town of Drvenik and Sučuraj, at the extreme easterly tip of Hvar.

The idea of admitting only cruising liners into the harbour of Hvar town and banning all other vessels serving more everyday purposes might have been devised by a Hollywood film director, for the lights of a great luxury liner set against the background of the old town with its carefully illuminated buildings give an incomparably glamorous effect. It is not surprising that film-makers from all over the world come here to take advantage of this beautiful setting.

The principal place on the island, **Hvar**, lies in a sheltered bay on the SW coast. The *Sea Gate* leads into the main square, paved with large slabs of white stone. To the left the 16th c. **Cathedral** with a handsome 17th c. *tower* contains a number of valuable paintings, including a "Madonna with Saints" by Domenico Umberti (1692), a "Madonna and Child" (Pisan school, 13th c.), a "Pietà" (*c.* 1520) and a "Madonna with Saints" (by Palma Giovane (1626–27). The most valuable item in the *Treasury* is the gilded staff of Bishop Pritić (1509).

In the square in front of the Cathedral stands the large *Town Fountain* of 1529. On the S side of the square is the **Arsenal** (13th–17th c.), with a wide arched entrance to admit a galley. On the first floor is a small theatre, installed here in 1612 – the first indoor theatre in the

Balkans, now a museum. The ground floor is now occupied by a supermarket.

Going towards the harbour, we see on the right the *Palace Hotel*, originally a Venetian palazzo, with a magnificent façade, loggia and clock-tower. The building was completely reconstructed and modernised in 1970, leaving the external walls unaltered.

Most of the houses in the picturesque *Old Town* have been renovated in recent years. Almost every house lets rooms to visitors, and in the evenings the inner courtyards are occupied by cheerful parties. A glass of wine, the pleasures of conversation and song, bring a fresh breath of life to the old stones.

From the hotels of the old town around the right-hand harbour basin (looking towards the sea), in the roof gardens where musicians play in the evening, footpaths lead through the beautiful *Municipal Gardens* to the modern hotel complexes to the N of the town. On the hillside is a ruined monastery in which concerts and dramatic performances are given during the summer.

Returning to the harbour, we can make our way up to the **Spanish fort** above the town (cableway planned; bus service from harbour until 1 a.m.), from which there is a superb *view over the harbour and the old town to the *Pakleni Oroci* ("Pitch Islands" or "Hell's Islands"). Farther N, a little higher up, is a well-preserved *French fort*, not open to the public (radar station, military installations).

From the main square it is 5 minutes' walk SE along the sea wall to the **Franciscan friary**, built in the 15th c. and restored after its destruction by the Turks in 1571, with a fine *church* (pictures by Bassano, Palma Giovane and Santa Croce) and a museum housed in the *refectory* (*"Last Supper" by Matteo Rosselli, 1578–1650; pictures by Titian and Tiepolo; vestments, incunabula, etc.). Behind the refectory is a small garden with a 300-year-old cypress.

A winding hill road leads to **Stari Grad**, the ancient *Pharos*, at the head of a bay which reaches far inland. The hotels lie outside the old town, which possesses five churches, three of them half ruined. Many of the old houses have been renovated to provide attractive accommodation for visitors, preserving the

original style. The town has many reminders of its long history – *cyclopean stones* dating from the Illyrian period, *Roman mosaics, Early Christian fonts*. Its most interesting building – concealed from view by a screen of palms – is a 16th c. house, built within an old Turkish fort, which belonged to the Croatian Renaissance poet *Petar Hektorović*. In the courtyard is a basin connected by a pipe with the harbour. – On the outskirts of Stari Grad is an interesting modern *winepress*. During the vintage hundreds of carts – some drawn by donkeys, others by tractors – come here every day with their loads of grapes.

Vrboska is charmingly situated amid pinewoods and vineyards at the innermost tip of a narrow inlet. It has two churches; one of them, a fortress as well as a church, contains a picture attributed to Titian. In the harbour is a beautiful little green islet.

Jelsa, half way along the island, is a quiet little place which appeals mainly to young people and senior citizens. The hotels lie on the wooded slopes on either side of the harbour. An interesting trip is to the *Grapčeva Cave*, in which evidence of prehistoric occupation was found; it is reached by boat from the harbour.

Igalo

Republic: Montenegro (Crna Gora).
Altitude: 10 ft/3 m. – Population: 600.
Post code: YU-81347. – Telephone code: 0 82.
(i) **Turistički Savez Boke Kotorske,**
Trg Nikole Djurkovića,
YU-81340 Herceg-Novi;
tel. 8 72 51.

HOTELS. – *Igalo*, B, 390 b., tel. 4 37 33; *Tamaris*, B, 280 b., tel. 4 36 66; also holiday apartments, tel. 4 32 99, and *Villa Zanjic*, 10 b., tel. 4 39 25. – *Hotel Inex Igalo*, 730 b., the largest and most modern treatment and rehabilitation complex on the Adriatic coast of Yugoslavia. Visitors from other hotels are treated on an outpatient basis.

CAMP SITE. – *Boka*, on the Dubrovnik–Kotor road, tel. 8 71 63.

Igalo's reputation as a spa is based on its radioactive mud. The first scientific investigations of its therapeutic effectiveness were carried out a hundred years ago, and from small beginnings this little place at

the entrance to **Kotor Bay, 1¼ miles/2 km from the resort of Herceg-Novi (see p. 84), has developed into a spa, using not only the mud but also a slightly radioactive mineral spring, sea water and the equable Mediterranean climate as elements in the curative process. After the establishment of the Simo Milošević Rehabilitation Center in 1949 President Tito was a regular visitor. The Inex Igalo complex was opened in 1974.

The spa of Igalo; Montenegro

The mineral water of Igalo is classified as muriatic-saline and slightly radioactive (3·7 Mache units). It is used both internally and in baths. The sea mud is an organic and mineral peloid (mud used therapeutically), also slightly radioactive.

Igalo enjoys a high reputation as a spa, attracting large numbers of Yugoslavs and a minority of foreigners. The Inex Igalo hotel is run as a sanatorium. In addition to the treatment facilities Igalo offers pleasant walking country and a variety of sports and entertainment. The damage caused by the 1979 earthquake has been almost entirely repaired.

The Adriatic coastal highway bypasses Igalo, so that although it is conveniently accessible there is little traffic within Igalo itself. Most visitors belong to the older generation.

Igalo has a beach of fine sand ¾ mile/1 km long, flanked by a seafront promenade. The radioactive mineral springs are at the mouth of the River Sutorina. To the W are large expanses of vineyards and orchards. On a hill 6 miles/10 km N of Igalo, *Debeli*

Brijeg, is the "Three Republics Corner", where the republics of Bosnia-Hercegovina, Montenegro and Croatia meet.

Ilidža

Republic: Bosnia-Hercegovina (Bosna i Hercegovina).
Altitude: 1637 ft/499 m. – Population: 2000.
Post code: YU-71210. – Telephone code: 0 71.
ⓘ Hotel Terme,
tel. 62 14 44.

HOTELS. – *Bosna*, A, 142 b., tel. 62 14 44; *Srbija*, A, 78 b., tel. 62 14 44; *Terme*, B, 353 b., tel. 62 14 44; *Hercegovina*, B, 66 b., tel. 62 14 44; *Jadran*, B, 57 b., tel. 62 14 44.

CAMP SITE. – *Autocamp Ilidža*, tel. 62 14 36, on the W side of the Sarajevo–Mostar road (noisy).

The little spa of Ilidža, set in very beautiful *scenery, lies 7½ miles/12 km W of Sarajevo, capital of the republic of Bosnia-Hercegovina. Large numbers of visitors now come to "take the cure" at its hot springs of sulphurous water.

HISTORY. – Ilidža's mineral springs were already being frequented in Roman times. In modern times its great heyday began after 1878, when the Congress of Berlin assigned Bosnia and Hercegovina to Austria. A spa hotel in neo-classical style was built; but the influence of Vienna is even more clearly evident in the Villas Dalmacija, Hercegovina, Bosna and Jadran. Until the end of Austrian rule in 1918 Ilidža was a favourite resort of the high nobility of the Austro-Hungarian monarchy. The opening of the Hotel Terme in 1971, with baths under the same roof, marked the beginning of a new era for Ilidža. A large treatment and recreation area, with an open-air swimming pool, sports facilities and a sunbathing lawn are planned.

Srbija Hotel, Ilidža

Ilidža lies in a secluded setting on the left bank of the river Željeznica. It is only a short distance from Sarajevo, to which there is a regular bus service. Sarajevo airport is also close – though, lying well away from the main flight path, Ilidža does not suffer from aircraft noise. The hotels nestle among the trees, only their façades being glimpsed from the river. Excellent facilities are available for those confined to wheel-chairs. There are both a hot bath 86–95°F/30–35°C) and a warm swimming bath (68–75°F/20–24°C); the hot spring (water containing sulphates) is just outside the baths.

100 yd/100 m from the new Hotel Terme is the older Srbija Hotel, on the edge of a circular park. Nearby are some of the sumptuous *villas* once occupied by great personages of the Austro-Hungarian monarchy; others have been pulled down to make way for the new construction which is converting Ilidža into a modern recreation centre.

On the other side of the river is the old part of the town, with a *Balneological Institute* (balneology is the science dealing with the therapeutic effects of baths and bathing) which carries out laboratory investigations for doctors working in the spa.

SURROUNDINGS. – The spa is surrounded by extensive and well-kept *parks and gardens*. Visitors can hire an old-fashioned horse carriage and drive along a poplar-lined avenue 2 miles/3 km long to the *source of the River Bosna, which gushes out of the earth at the foot of Mt Igman. The volume of water is sufficient to form a sizeable river within 220 yd/200 m of the source. The river is well stocked with fish and is the haunt of many waterfowl. Pleasant footpaths crisscross the area.

Iron Gates/ Djerdap

Republic: Serbia (Srbija).

DOWN THE DANUBE BY HYDROFOIL. – The boats operate daily from March 15 to October 1, leaving Belgrade (Sava harbour) at 6 a.m. and returning about 6 p.m. Reservations are made through the Centroturist agency: advance booking is necessary, since the trips are almost always sold out. Lunch (at Kladovo), bus transfers, a film presentation and admission to the hydroelectric station are included in the fare (about $45/£25, including pickup by bus at Belgrade hotel). Passports required.

BY CAR. – There is now a bridge over the Djerdap dam, shortening the road distance from Belgrade to Bucharest by some 125 miles/200 km: it is now only 340 miles/550 km via the frontier crossing on the dam, compared with 465 miles/750 km by the Vršac/ Moravița crossing (previously the only route between Yugoslavia and Romania) and then via Timișoara and Arad. – Leave Belgrade on the autoput (E5), take the Osipaonica exit and continue on a road which reaches the Danube at Veliko Gradište. On the return route, continue down the Danube on road 17 (some bad stretches); then S to Zaječar and W to rejoin the autoput at Paraćin (53 miles/85 km).

ACCOMMODATION. – *Karatas* tourist village, B, 750 b., with indoor swimming pool, bowling alleys, discotheque and sports facilities, tel. (0 19) 8 82 27 (immediately adjoining the hydroelectric station). – *Djerdap Hotel* in Kladovo, B, 161 b., tel. (0 19) 8 87 70.

The Iron Gates (Djerdap) are a 2 mile/3 km long stretch of the Danube some 95 miles/150 km E of Belgrade as the crow flies. This part of the river, with its dangerous rapids, had long been a hindrance to navigation on the Danube, and the problems were finally solved only in 1972 with the completion, after $7\frac{1}{2}$ years' work, of a dam which controls the river for a distance of up to 75 miles/120 km upstream. The construction of the dam was a joint project between Yugoslavia and Romania, and it was formally opened by the Presidents of both countries. Although Djerdap can be reached by road, with frequent glimpses of the Danube narrows before the Iron Gates, the most memorable experience is provided by the *day trip by hydrofoil from Belgrade.

The story of the joint Yugoslav–Romanian project is told in a documentary film which is shown to visitors at Djerdap. The film also gives an account of earlier attempts to overcome the difficulties and dangers for shipping.

HISTORY. – The 60 mile/100 km stretch of the Danube beginning at Golubac, where the river forces its way between the Carpathian and the Balkan mountains, was regarded down to Roman times as impassable. The first attempt to construct a road through the defile was made in A.D. 28, during the reign of Tiberius. Some sections were painfully hewn out of the rock face; elsewhere the roadway was carried on a kind of bridge supported on beams set into the rock. But the problems proved too great, and after some time the work was abandoned. Work was resumed about A.D. 100, when the emperor Trajan needed the road to permit rapid troop movements, and it was completed in 103. The making of the road is recorded in the *Tabula Traiana* (Tablet of Trajan), a Roman inscription carved on the rock face. The

The Tabula Traiana at the Iron Gates

By hydrofoil from Belgrade to the Iron Gates

Leaving **Belgrade** (Sava harbour), the boat sails past the *confluence of the Sava with the Danube*; to the right can be seen the fortress of Kalemegdan, to the left the suburb of *Zemun*. There is then an impressive view of the middle of the city. The river then becomes broader, reaching a width of 1 mile/1·5 km in places. To left and right are pastureland, water meadows and orchards; the hydrofoil often meets trains of barges.

Pančevo, on the left bank, at the inflow of a tributary, the Tamiš, coming from Romania.

Vinča, on the right bank: nuclear research complex, archaeological site.

inscription had to be moved from its original position before the construction of the dam and was set into the walls of the gorge some 130 ft/40 m higher up. The hydrofoils frequently sail close enough to read the inscription: "IMP CAESAR DIVI NERVAE F NERVA TRAIANUS AUG GERM PONT MAXIMUS, etc." ("The Emperor Nerva Traianus Augustus Germanicus, pontifex maximus, etc. . . . built this road after conquering the mountains and gorges of the Danube").

Until 1913 the Iron Gates were almost impassable for vessels of any size, even for ships such as paddle steamers with powerful motive force. Even smaller vessels, hauled upstream by tow-horses, were frequently pierced by rocks and sunk. During the summer the water was often too low for boats to avoid the obstacles. Accordingly in 1890 Austrian engineers began to cut a canal 1½ miles/2.2 km long and 165 ft/50 m wide on the Yugoslav side of the river. This gave ships an easier passage, with no rocks to bar the way; but the flow of water was so rapid that all vessels had to be towed upstream. A railway line was laid alongside the canal, and ships travelling upstream were hitched on to a specially designed locomotive. This reduced the time required for passing through the canal from 130 to 20 hours.

In 1964 work began on the construction of a dam above the towns of Turnu Severin (Romania) and Kladovo (Yugoslavia). When this was completed the rise in the water level drowned not only the rapids and cataracts in the river but a dozen villages in the valley. Each country constructed on its side of the dam a series of locks for shipping and a hydroelectric station. The two power stations produce some 12 billion kilowatt hours of electricity a year, giving them fifth place among the world's river hydroelectric stations.

Planning has begun for the construction of two more dams. The first dam and power station, at Golubac are due to be completed in 1985; the second dam, below Smederovo, is planned for the end of the eighties. The dammed water will then reach as far upstream as Belgrade, and other towns and villages on the banks of the river will have to be moved to new sites

Smederevo, with a *castle which is one of the greatest medieval fortresses in Europe (25 towers, walls up to 16 ft/5 m thick). The castle was built by the Serbian Prince Branković in 1428–30 in order to bar the way to the advancing Turks. After an unsuccessful first attempt to take the castle in 1453, the Turks captured it in 1459, in the reign of Sultan Mehmed, and held it, with only brief interruptions, until 1867. – Just after Smederevo the Morava flows into the Danube on the right, and

Orthodox Church, Smederevo

beyond this the 11 mile/18 km long island of *Ostrovo* is passed on the left.

Kostolac, on the right bank: an industrial town, and beyond it (barely visible) remains of the Roman station of *Viminacium*.

Ram: another old castle on the right bank. On the left bank is Romania.

Veliko Gradište: the water blocked by the Iron Gates dam reaches up as far as here. On the right bank the hills come closer to the river. Scenically this is the beginning of the finest part of the trip. In the middle of the river is the large *Moldova Island*.

Golubac, with Golubac Castle, built by the Hungarians and later strengthened by the Turks. The river now enters the first defile (Mali Djerdap), 25 miles/40 km long.

Donji Milanovac, at the end of the defile: a new village, built to replace the older settlement, now submerged by the river. Nearby was found the important archaeological site of **Lepenski Vir**, a fishing village 8000 years old: important because the excavations made it possible to fill a gap in archaeological knowledge of the period between the Mesolithic and Neolithic in the Carpathian area. Part of the material recovered from the foundations of some 70 houses, including objects of everyday use and well-preserved stone sculpture, is now in the National Museum in Belgrade; the rest is displayed in an open-air museum near Donji Milanovac.

Now begins the most impressive part of the trip, the passage through the *Veliki* (Great) *Djerdap*. The climax of this is the 5½ mile/9 km long **Kazan Defile* (*kazan*="cauldron"), in which the Danube is caught between high rock walls and reduced to a width of 185–220 yd/ 170–200 m. The river formerly surged tumultuously through the defile: it is now quiet, the water level raised by the dam. It was formerly possible to see traces of the old Roman road on the right bank, but these have now disappeared under the surface. The *Tabula Traiana* (see above, under History) can, however, be seen in its new position above the river. Just beyond this the hydrofoil puts in at the right bank and passengers are taken by bus to the *dam*. This is 260 ft/80 m high and some 1400 yd/1300 m long, with

Djerdap hydroelectric power station

chains of locks at each end and the two *power stations* in between. Before entering the complex visitors pass through a security check (passports required). Photography is strictly prohibited.

The construction workers' settlement on the Yugoslav side of the dam has been converted into a tourist village.

After the conducted tour of the power station and the showing of a film the buses continue to the town of *Kladovo*. Some of the restaurants offer a special delicacy of caviar from Danube sturgeon.

Istria

Republic: Croatia (Hrvatska).

*Istria is a large wedge-shaped peninsula at the N end of the Adriatic coast of Yugoslavia with an area of some 1220 sq. miles/3160 sq. km. The greater part of it, to the S, belongs to Croatia, the smaller northern part to Slovenia. The boundary between the two republics follows a zigzag course eastward from a point on the coast S of Portorož and cuts across the Postojna–Rijeka road just N of Rupa. The eastern boundary of Istria lies roughly along a line from Trieste to Rijeka. The largest population group is formed by 200,000 Croats; there are some 100,000 Slovenes, and, in particular places, groups of Italians.

Italian, as the everyday language of the local people has almost disappeared, although in coastal towns such as Koper (Capodistria), Piran (Pirano) and Portorož (Portorose) and road signs are bilingual and most shops advertise their wares in Italian as well as Slovene. But Italian is still understood everywhere and is used in dealings with the numerous Italian visitors who flock into Istria for the sake of its lower prices. The Italian television and radio programs do more to keep the language alive than the former Italian cultural institutes or Italian-language newspapers (now closed down) ever did. The principal foreign languages taught in schools are English and German.

settled only when the Venetians gained control of most of the W coast of Istria in the 15th c., while the E coast passed to the Counts of Görz (Gorizia) and later to the Austrians. Venetian power ended in 1797, when the Peace of Campo Formio assigned the whole peninsula to Austria. From 1809 to 1815 Istria was part of Napoleon's Illyrian Provinces, after which it reverted to Austria, remaining in Austrian hands until 1918. In 1920 Yugoslavia was compelled to cede Istria to Italy, which pursued a deliberate policy of Italianisation and had to deal in 1922 with a rising by Slovenes and Croats. During the Second World War German troops occupied Istria after the Italian surrender. For two years after the war British and American troops maintained the neutral status of the territory, still contested between Yugoslavia and Italy, until it was finally assigned to Yugoslavia. The Trieste area was divided into two parts, Zone A being administered by Allied troops, Zone B by Yugoslavia; then in 1954 Zone A, with the town of Trieste, was finally assigned to Italy and Zone B to Yugoslavia.

Limski canal, Istria

HISTORY. – The area was occupied in the Stone Age, some 5000 years ago. In the Bronze and Iron Ages Illyrian peoples settled here, operating from some places on the coast as pirates. There were also numbers of Greek settlers. In 117 B.C. the Romans set out to subjugate the Illyrians and Greeks, advancing ever farther into the interior, and the conquest was practically complete by the 1st c. A.D. Slav tribes appeared in Istria in the 7th c., first occupying the interior of the peninsula and then advancing on the old-established towns on the W coast. In 787 Istria came under the control of the Franks, while the coastal towns and the islands in the Kvarner Gulf remained part of the Byzantine empire. Duke Ivan, appointed governor by the Franks, settled Slavs in the towns in an attempt to reduce Roman influence. This policy led to conflict between the towns and the Duke, a conflict which was, however, resolved at a meeting by the River Rižana, near Koper, in presence of envoys sent by Charlemagne (804).

In the middle of the 10th c. Istria was separated from the Frankish kingdom in Italy and assigned to the duchy of Bavaria. Thereafter it belonged to various local principalities, all dependent on the German Emperors. In the 11th c. it was granted the status of an independent March (border territory) directly subordinate to the German imperial crown. Increasing influence was, however, gained by the Patriarchs of Aquileia, the bishops of the coastal towns and local feudal lords, leading to constant conflicts which were

In the post-war period Istria has developed into a popular holiday area, helped by the good communications which make it rapidly accessible from other parts of Europe. The beginnings of the tourist and holiday trade, however, go back to the Austrian period, when Portorož, Opatija and the island of Lošinj were already popular spas and bathing resorts. The principal holiday bases in Istria are now Piran-Portorož, Umag, Poreč to Rovinj, the area S of Pula and the whole stretch of coast from Mošćenička Draga to beyond Lovran. Excursions are run from the coastal resorts to the principal tourist attractions – particularly Pula with its Roman remains, Poreč with its 6th c. basilica, the picturesque little town of Rovinj and such jewels of the past in the interior of the peninsula as Motovun, Pazin and Beram, but also farther afield to the Lipica stud-farm, the karstic cave

In Vrsar harbour, Istria

systems of Postojna and Škocjan and the Plitvice lakes.

Young people will find the widest range of sports facilities around the Poreč lagoons, while naturists have the choice of almost a dozen holiday areas (Umag-Katoro, Solaris, Ulika, Istra, Koversada, Valalta, Red Island and the settlement of Rubin near Rovinj, Monsena, Medulin-Kazela near Pula). The number of winter visitors is also beginning to increase, now that there are more modern hotels with indoor sea-water baths and treatment facilities open all year round. These can be found particularly in Portorož, Rovinj, Pula and Opatija.

Fishing boats in Izola harbour

Izola

Republic: Slovenia (Slovenija)
Altitude: 197 ft/60 m. – Population: 12,000.
Post code: YU-66310. – Telephone code: 0 66.
ⓘ Turist Biro,
    Kridičevo Nabrežje 4;
    tel. 7 17 56.

HOTELS. – *Haliaetum*, B, 105 b., tel. 7 13 40, with annexes *Karola, Mirta, Palma, Perla* and *Sirena*, B, together 305 b., tel. 7 15 50; *Marina*, B, 87 b., tel. 7 13 42; *Belvedere* tourist village, C, 218 b., tel. 7 11 41; *Riviera*, D, 60 b., tel. 7 12 55.

CAMP SITES. – *Belvedere*, adjoining the Belvedere Hotel, on road to Koper, tel. 7 11 41; *Jadranka*, Polje 8, tel. 7 12 02.

SPORT, BOATING and BATHING. – The sheltered yacht harbour of **Izola** has excellent facilities for boats of all sizes. Off the beach at the Belvedere tourist village the water is too shallow for anchoring. – Facilities for scuba diving, water-skiing and sailing.

The **Belvedere tourist village**, still being developed, lies to the S of the town on a spacious beach, with areas of grass which in summer become dry and brown. There are gangways leading into the sea and a beach of imported sand with the natural stony beach below it. Farther S is a section of coast with easier access to the sea as a result of a landslip of sand from the steep face above the beach. Still farther S, in Simon's Bay, is a public bathing station with a beach of concrete and imported sand. There are boats for rent, and some facilities for sports. A pleasant evening occupation is a stroll along the seafront in Izola with its friendly little wine-shops.

The first thing a visitor sees when approaching Izola from the Koper–Pula road is a huge smoking factory chimney. This ancient little fishing town takes pride in the prosperity it has achieved since the last war by the establishment of

fish-canning plants, shipyards and metalworking industries; but it is also concerned to retain its attraction for vacationers, who are well catered for by the Belvedere holiday base to the S of the town. The old town, not unexpectedly, is pervaded by a strong smell of fish.

HISTORY. – The medieval town was established on a peninsula connected with the mainland by a narrow isthmus, now much enlarged. The first occupants were refugees from Aquileia. From 1280 to 1797 the town was held by Venice and was surrounded by stout walls for defence against Turkish attack. Subsequently the town, like the whole of the W coast of Istria, was occupied by the French and then by Austria and finally Italy.

SIGHTS. – The principal attraction for visitors is the **fishing harbour**, on the S side of the tongue of land, with the *yacht harbour* outside it. Izola still has a fleet of fishing boats, though it is much smaller than it used to be. Visitors who want to see and photograph the landing of the fish caught overnight must get up very early in the morning. The older and less active fishermen gather near the harbour and pass the morning discussing the results of the night's fishing.

By the harbour is the 16th c. **Town Hall**, and beyond it is a 15th c. church, renovated in 1821 and now awaiting further restoration. Beyond the church stands the *Manzioli House*, with fine Gothic windows and a reddish façade, similar to the Venetian palazzo in Piran and likewise showing the effects of time. Other old mansions in the town are also in a state of advanced dilapidation. – On higher ground is the 16th c. **parish**

church, three-aisled, with a dull neo-Romanesque façade. The harmoniously proportioned *interior* has numerous pictures; the *altarpieces* are by Venetian masters. The free-standing *tower* of the church is impressive only from a distance: it too is in need of restoration.

Jablaničko Jezero
(Lake Jablanica)

Republic: Bosnia-Hercegovina (Bosna i Hercegovina).

HOTEL. – IN JABLANICA: *Motel Jablanica*, B, 74 b., tel. 7 28 03.

Jablanica is a road junction, and now a rising tourist resort, at the end of the Jablaničko Jezero, a man-made lake with an area of 4½ sq. miles/12 sq. km. Just beyond the town the Sarajevo–Mostar road enters the famous *Neretva Gorge, which has already lost much of its original wilderness as a result of the road and railway and will suffer further from the construction of an underground conduit parallel to the river carrying water for the generation of hydro-electricity. Earlier accounts of the road and the river may now, therefore, strike the contemporary visitor as somewhat over-enthusiastic.

Lake Jablanica

Lake Jablanica is at the beginning of its tourist development, having become conveniently accessible only in the 1970s, when the roads to Banja Luka and to the Adriatic were improved and asphalted over their whole length, providing an alternative to the Adriatic coastal highway (Jadranska Magistrala).

HISTORY. – Evidence of Roman settlement has been found on the site of Jablanica and at Konjik, 14 miles/ 23 km up the Neretva valley, on the watershed between the zones of continental and Mediterranean climate. During the Second World War there was bitter fighting between Yugoslav partisans and the German and Italian occupying forces in the area between the two villages, both in the valleys and in the difficult hill country. When the partisans were forced to withdraw they succeeded by adroit manoeuvring in getting 4000 wounded across the tumultuous river (February 22, 1943). This operation was the subject of a film shot in 1968, "The Battle of the Neretva".

The road from Sarajevo to Jablanica (No. 10) passes the **Bjelašnica range** (on left), which rises to over 6560 ft/2000 m. From Konjic an attractive detour can be made to the **Boračko Jezero**, a glacier lake in a valley basin between the Bjelašnica and Prenj hills (small hotel and camp site). From Konjic to Jablanica the road runs at times directly alongside the lake, at other times some distance above it. It is not easy to find access roads to the lake.

The other approach to Jablanica, from Banja Luka, traverses the **Makljen pass** (3685 ft/1123 m), where the road has been improved and the gradient eased. Before reaching Jablanica the road crosses the lake on a bridge.

Between Konjic and Jablanica there are a number of simply equipped camp sites on the lake, not included in the official lists. They provide bases for anglers or climbers in the **Bjelašnica** and **Prenj ranges**.

Beyond Jablanica the road climbs again, at first following the right bank of the Neretva. It then crosses to the left bank, with a view across the river of the bare karstic slopes of the **Čvrsnica range**, rising to over 6560 ft/2000 m, with the best chamois hunting grounds in Yugoslavia. The railway continues along the right bank. The grand scenery of the gorge, with the river foaming below, ends at the villages of **Potoci** (on left) and **Raška Gora** (on right), where the road enters the *Mostar plain*, with its great expanses of vineyards and orchards.

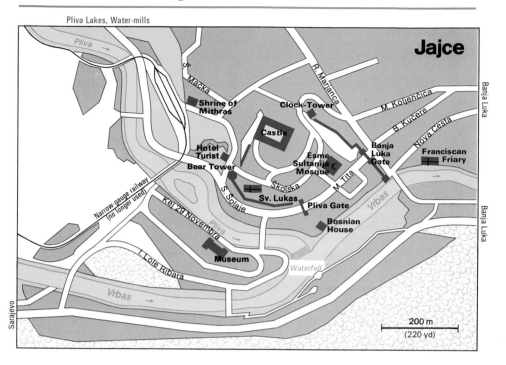

Pliva Lakes, Water-mills

Jajce

Jajce

Republic: Bosnia-Hercegovina (Bosna i Hercegovina).
Altitude: 1237 ft/377 m. – Population: 15,000.
Post code: YU-78240. – Telephone code: 0 70.
ⓘ **Turist Biro,**
opposite the road bridge over the Pliva;
tel. 2 16 30.

HOTELS. – *Jajce,* A, 155 b., tel. 2 14 26; *Turist,* B, 95 b., tel. 2 10 68; *Motel Plivska Jezera,* C, 62 b., tel. 2 11 85; *Sport* (pension), D, 130 b., tel. 2 10 67.

CAMP SITE. – *Unis-Turist* (on road from Jajce to Bihač), tel. 2 13 30.

Older books and tourist brochures all show the same picture of Jajce: in the foreground a mighty waterfall (illuminated if the photograph is taken at night) and above this houses, mosques and walls rising up to the castle. Visitors looking towards Jajce from the road E of the town, beyond the River Vrbas, will, however, no longer see this view. It is now obscured by trees and industrial haze from the nearby steelworks further blocks the view – though dust filters fitted into the stacks have reduced this hazard. The lake near the town is an attraction for holidaymakers, and the old town itself has much of historical interest to offer the visitor.

HISTORY. – There was a Roman settlement at the junction of the Vrbas and the Pliva, and it was the Romans who brought the Indo-Iranian cult of Mithras to Jajce. Visitors can see a carving of Mithras in the remains of a Roman temple below the castle hill, which was certainly already fortified in Roman times. After the fall of the Western Empire Jajce lay within the Byzantine sphere of influence. When the Slavs occupied this area in the 6th–7th c., however, little evidence was left of the former population.

The name of the town first appears in the records in 1363, when the king of Hungary set out to conquer Bosnia but was halted at Sokol, 18 miles/29 km from Jajce. As a result, when the Turks first advanced into Bosnia in 1386 they did not encounter united resistance: some of the inhabitants sought help from the Hungarians, others allied themselves with the Turkish conquerors against the Hungarians. The last Bosnian king, Stjepan Tomašević (1461–63), sought in vain for allies in the Christian world to aid him in the great decisive battle against the Turks which he planned; the Pope sent no money, but merely a crown with which Stjepan crowned himself in 1461. Two years later Stjepan was compelled to flee in face of the advancing army of Sultan Mehmed II, but was caught and executed at Jajce. In the same year, however, the wheel took another turn and the advantage fell to the Hungarians. The Hungarian king Matthias Corvinus took the town after a four day siege, and from 1464 to 1527 the Hungarians successfully defended Jajce against numerous Turkish attacks. In 1525 an army of 20,000 Turks was unable, after besieging the fortress for a year and a half, to compel its surrender; but a year later, when the Hungarian state fell to pieces after the defeat of its army, the Turks finally entered Jajce without encountering any resistance. Thereafter the town enjoyed a long period of peace, when trade and craft industry flourished. After 1878, when the Congress of Berlin assigned Bosnia to Austria, this progress continued, promoted by the industrial exploitation of the region's mineral resources which now began. Between the two world wars tourist and holiday trade began to develop, with the many natural beauties around Jajce as a prime attraction.

Jajce's great historical moment came during the Second World War, when the Anti-Fascist Liberation Council of Yugoslavia (AVNOJ), established at the nearby town of Bihać in 1942, held its second session here on the night of November 29–30, 1943. The 142 delegates resolved to form a new federal state of Yugoslavia consisting of the republics of Slovenia, Croatia, Serbia, Bosnia-Hercegovina, Macedonia and Montenegro and the two autonomous regions of Kosovo and the Vojvodina, and also to appoint Josip Broz, known as Tito, Marshal of Yugoslavia. Many of the delegates travelled hundreds of miles by foot on mountain paths and through the lines of the occupation forces. During this night the foundations of the new Yugoslavia were laid in Jajce, and the date of the Congress of Liberation is now inscribed in the middle of the Yugoslav national coat of arms.

Mithraic relief, Jajce

SIGHTS. – The best starting point for a sightseeing tour of Jajce is the Tourist Office at the road bridge over the Pliva. The finest views of the famous *waterfall, 65–100 ft/20–30 m high, are to be had from look-out points, approached by footpaths, on either side of the river. Opposite the Tourist Office, on the right bank of the river, is the **Museum of the National Struggle for Liberation**, housed in the hall (restored) in which the Liberation Council met under Tito's chairmanship in 1943. Daily throughout the year, except in July and August, the museum is thronged with parties of young people.

The street running up from the Tourist Office enters the old town through the *Pliva Gate*, a massive tower in the town wall, here completely preserved. Women

Water-mills between Jajce and the Pliva Lakes

clad in the black and white traditional local costume, still worn as their everyday dress, are almost always to be encountered in the streets. Inside the gate, to the left, are a number of old Bosnian houses roofed with shingles. The street continues up past the **Esme Sultanija Mosque** and bazaar-like shops and souvenir sellers and under the castle to the new residential quarters on the far side of the hill. (One-way traffic up the hill between 7 a.m. and 10 p.m.).

In the new district a street bears sharp left, leading to the castle entrance; the last part of the way must be done on foot. From the wall-walk of the castle there is a fine view into the Pliva valley.

Returning from the castle to the new part of the town, we take another side street which makes a wider circuit around the castle hill, running down towards the Pliva. Shortly before the Turist Hotel (on right) and the round *Bear Tower* (on left) a narrow street goes off on the right, ending at a low-lying building with the air of a military bunker. This houses the **Mithraic shrine** built within the Roman fortress, which now lies under the modern street level. The cult of the oriental light god Mithras was brought from India and Iran by Roman legionaries. Mithras himself is depicted in a well-preserved *relief* in the ritual act of sacrificing a bull. The shrine can be seen only with a guide from the Tourist Office.

Near the Bear Tower is the entrance to the **Catacombs**, which in fact are mainly an underground *burial church*. They were constructed at the behest of Grand Prince Hrvoje Vukčić ("Little Wolf"), the 14th c. ruler who built the castle. Above the entrance is carved his coat of arms, and he himself is buried here.

On the walls of the vestibule of the church are unfinished drawings. The crescent beside the cross over the altar suggests that although the Bosnians of the period had officially become Roman Catholics the Bogomil cult was still secretly practised.

Above the town looms the tower of **St Luke's Church** (*Sv. Luka*), situated inside the *town walls* and one of the most interesting medieval buildings in Jajce. The relics of the saint are said to have been preserved in this church at one time but were later sold to Venice, where they now rest in St Mark's.

SURROUNDINGS. – There is some accommodation for visitors in Jajce itself, but the main base of tourist activity is some 5 miles/8 km from the town (Jajce–Bihać road), on the shores of the **Pliva Lakes**. The road to the lakes runs past some picturesque old *water-mills*, now accessible by wooden gangways. On the largest of the lakes (with tourist hotels and holiday chalets) is a stand for spectators of the rowing and canoeing competitions that are held here. The lakes offer facilities for a variety of water sports (sailing, rowing, fishing, etc.).

9 miles/15 km away is an anglers' hotel, the Sokočnika (turn off Jajce–Bihać road at Jezero, then via Šipovo). The fishing permits issued by the Jajce hotels cover 3 miles/5 km of the river on the upstream side of the hostel of the Disciples of Peter.

An attractive excursion from Jajce is to the idyllic **Lake Balkano** (motel, restaurant), 19 miles/30 km away on the Bihać road (just off the road on the left). This also offers good fishing, and there are beautiful paths for walkers in the hills and forests.

Julian Alps

Republic: Slovenia (Slovenija).

The **Julian Alps, the south-easterly part of the Alpine chain, run eastward across Slovenia to end in the Pannonian plain. The frontier between Austria (Carinthia) and Yugoslavia (Slovenia) runs first along the ridge of the Karavanke (Karawanken) range, followed to the E by the Pohorje range and the Slovenske Gorice, opposite the Austrian province of Styria. The chain of the Alps comes to an end in the hills of the Slovenske Gorice.

The Julian Alps are separated from the long ridge of the Karavanke range by the Sava valley. The Sava, Yugoslavia's longest river, has two sources – the Sava Dolinka, in the valley between the two ranges of mountains, and the Savica springs, rising beyond the W end of Lake Bohinj in the Julian Alps.

With their dark expanses of forest, their peaks soaring up to over 9000 ft/2800 m, their mountain lakes and streams, the Julian Alps are popular both with mountain walkers and climbers and with winter sports enthusiasts. The beauty of the mountains and the routes to the summits were first described by the climber and nature-lover *Dr Julius Kugy*, whose monument stands on the southern approach to the Vršič pass.

Triglav, Yugoslavia's highest mountain

The highest peak in the Julian Alps, and indeed the highest in Yugoslavia, is **Triglav** (pronounced Triglow, to rhyme with "how"; 9394 ft/2863 m), the "three-headed" mountain, since time immemorial the sacred mountain of the Slovenes. It guards the "magical realm of beauty and wonder" (Kugy) and is believed to be the home of the mountain spirit Zlatorog (Golden Horn), a white chamois with golden horns. There is a small glacier, the Zeleni Sneg ("Green Snow"), on the mountain. On the summit is the Aljaž Tower, 180 ft/55 m below this (to left) the Stanič Cave, blasted out of the rock.

Climbing Triglav. – There are a number of different routes:

A side road off the Kranjska Gora–Jesenice road leads to the village of Mojstrana, from which a road (narrow in places, slippery in wet weather, not cleared in winter) climbs up to the two mountain inns (with overnight accommodation, renovated 1978) of Aljažev Dom (3330 ft/1015 m), where the car must be parked. From here there are two well-marked paths to the summit; one of them is narrow and runs by way of steep drops, but is provided with ropes.

A shorter but more strenuous climb starts from the Trenta valley. From the village of Na Logu, just before the road begins to climb to the Vršič pass, a by-road ascends the Zadnjica valley, where the car must be left. From here it is a 4–5 hour climb for experienced climbers.

The longest routes, but scenically the finest, start from the Sporthotel in Pokljuka or from the W end of Lake Bohinj. It is not possible to give detailed descriptions here, but local guidebooks set out the routes, indicate their degree of difficulty and list the 30 or so mountain huts around Triglav, most of them with overnight accommodation for climbers.

From Aljažev Dom the second highest peak in the Julian Alps, *Škrlatica*, can also be climbed (8983 ft/ 2738 m; 5 hours).

Some of the best known *winter sports resorts* in Yugoslavia are in the Julian Alps – **Kranjska Gora** (see p. 113), with the nearby ski-jumping station of *Planica, Mt Vogel* above Lake Bohinj, the skiing area of *Zatrnik* and the cross-country skiers' paradise of *Pokljuka* near **Bled** (p. 55), and **Bovec** (p. 59). Bovec has been developed on the model of French skiing areas with financial assistance from the United Nations "Upper Adriatic" project. On the southern fringe of the range the new winter sports area of **Kalič**, 4 miles/ 6 km from Postojna, is in course of development.

The most beautiful lakes in the Julian Alps are *Lake Bohinj* and *Lake Bled.* The most impressive scenery is to be found in the *Soča valley* (Italian *Isonzo*). This was the scene of bitter fighting between German/ Austrian and Italian forces in the First World War, no fewer than 12 battles being fought in the Isonzo valley. Kobarid (Caporetto) is associated with the Italian defeat in 1917 during the German Isonzo offensive. The writer Ernest Hemingway was involved in the fighting, and describes the country around Caporetto in his novel "A Farewell to Arms".

In a cave at Tolmin in the Soča valley (commemorative tablet in the village of Čadrg) Dante is said to have lived during his exile from Florence and to have written part of the "Divine Comedy".

Karlovac

Republic: Croatia (Hrvatska).
Altitude: 367 ft/112 m. – Population: 60,000.
Post code: YU-47000. – Telephone code: 0 47.

ⓘ **Kvarner-Express,**
Ul. P. Zrinskog 17;
tel. 2 31 17.
Turističko Društvo,
Perivoj Slobode 10;
tel. 2 57 39.

HOTELS. – *Korana*, B, 403 b., tel. 2 30 69; *Gradina Dubinac*, C, 17 b., tel. 3 24 56; *Central*, D, 68 b., tel. 2 36 94; *Mrežnica*, D, 35 b., tel. 3 13 72; *Park*, D, 33 b., tel. 2 67 17.

CAMP SITE. – *Korona* (on road to Plitvice), with holiday chalets (20 b.), tel. 2 35 27.

The spaciously planned and developing town of Karlovac lies near the

end of the stretch of highway running SW from Zagreb which is planned to continue to the Adriatic port of Rijeka. Passing motorists see only the recently built parts of the town and get no impression of its earlier character as a typical Habsburg garrison town.

HISTORY. – In the 16th c. Karlovac was selected, together with Novi Sad, to form a bulwark against the continuing northward thrust of the Turks. Both towns lie in roughly the same latitude, and Novi Sad was designed to be an advanced outpost in the E, while Karlovac performed the same role in the W. In 1579 Archduke Charles of Habsburg began the construction of a strong hexagonal fortress which, with the additional protection of a moat and the surrounding marshland, was calculated to withstand any attack. When the Turks marched on Vienna in 1683, however, they paid no attention to Karlovac, simply bypassing it to the E. After Prince Eugene's capture of Belgrade in 1717 Karlovac lost all military significance but remained a garrison town. (The old Austrian barracks are now occupied by the Yugoslav army.) Situated on the River Kupa, which flows into the Sava at Sisak, Karlovac became a trading post, with a small river harbour. In 1776 the empress Maria Theresa granted Karlovac the status of a "royal free city". The industrialisation of the town began at the end of the 19th c., and it now has a number of important factories.

SIGHTS. – The River Kupa forms the boundary between the industrial district of *Banija* and the **Old Town**. Laid out on a rectangular plan, this was formerly surrounded by fortifications; but the old moat outside the walls is now filled in, and much of the area is now a *public garden*. The old town contains numbers of handsome old burghers' houses in Renaissance and Baroque style. The Baroque

Dubovac Castle, near Karlovac

Franciscan church and a *clock-tower* date from the 18th c. The **Municipal Museum** at Štrossmajerov Trg 7 offers an excellent survey of the military and cultural history of the town and surrounding area.

SURROUNDINGS. – SW of Karlovac is **Dubovac Castle** (leave on the Novo Mesto and Ljubljana road and immediately turn off to the right). The castle, built in the 14th c., belonged to the Frankopan family, whose principality extended from the Adriatic coast far inland to the E. When Karlovac was fortified the defences of Dubovac were also strengthened.

Another Frankopan castle, **Ozalj**, lies 9 miles/15 km from Karlovac near the road to Zagreb. It has recently been converted into a hotel.

Karst

Karst in the geographical sense is an arid, stony and infertile territory near Trieste which became known for its extensive and characteristic erosional phenomena and its beautiful stalactitic caves, the result of subterranean erosion. In its geological use the term karst has been extended to cover all areas with similar "karstic" formations and underground watercourses – i.e. in Yugoslavia mainly the islands and the coastal regions.

Two types of karst are distinguished:
1. **"Naked" or uncovered karst,** found on islands and the immediate coastal area. The hills and hillsides, now bare, were not always without vegetation: the present "nakedness" has been brought about by uncontrolled deforestation, particularly by the Venetians, who needed timber for their large fleets and the piles on which their city was built, and by the destruction of large areas of woodland to provide firewood, the failure to replant trees and the use of the treeless land as grazing for sheep and goats, with all the consequences in the form of erosion that then followed.
2. **Covered karst,** found mainly in the coastal hinterland. Here the limestone rock has often been overlaid by the products of its own weathering and decomposition, and the karstic processes have then continued under the covering of humus. With sufficient rain, trees can grow – oak to about 2600 ft/ 800 m, then conifers to 5900 ft/1800 m, occasionally even higher.

How does a karstic landscape develop? Although the various karstic processes can take place relatively rapidly, karst formation is a long-continued operation, the destructive effects of which have been by no means halted by sporadic programs of reforestation and landscape protection.

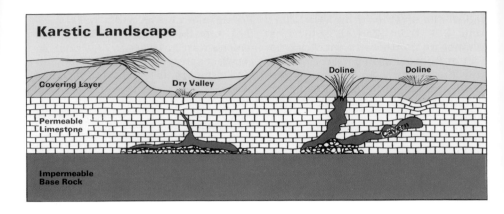

Rainwater finds its way through the cracks and crevices typical of porous limestones into the underlying rock, and the carbon dioxide contained in the water converts the solid limestone (calcium carbonate) by a chemical process into dissolved bicarbonate. The dissolved substance is then washed away, and as a result the original hair-line cracks in the rock are steadily enlarged and widened. This then produces a pattern of clefts and ridges, usually running parallel to one another. When a large area is covered with formations of this kind it is known as a karrenfeld or "pavement".

The rainwater can now penetrate even deeper into the ground, forming cavities by the chemical process of *corrosion* and filling them. Then, when the water begins to flow through these underground cavities, it continues its destructive action in breaking down and carrying away the rock by the mechanical process of *erosion*.

The water accumulating under the surface forms watercourses and currents in the same way as water on the surface. Recent research has shown, however, that the direction and speed of flow are not determined solely by gradients: in a system of linked cavities, crevices and channels pressure can build up, forming "pressure dams" which can occasionally cause water to flow uphill.

In this way subsurface watercourses develop consisting of caverns, passages and conduits; and the faster the water flows the deeper it cuts its way down. When an underground cavern is not completely filled with water the process of stalactite formation may begin, depending on the rate at which water percolates through the roof of the cavern. If the land

above the cavern is covered with woodland the flow of water with a high carbon dioxide content is much stronger than under pastureland or a completely bare surface.

The term **dripstone** is applied to a variety of different formations:

Water dripping from the roof of a cavern may form calcium "icicles" or *stalactites*, or it may build up *stalagmites* on the floor of the cavern. When stalactites hanging from the roof join up with stalagmites growing upward from the floor and then increase in thickness they form columns known as *stalagnates*.

Another type of formation which creates a particularly striking effect in illuminated caverns consists of the *sinter curtains* formed by water trickling from an overhanging rock face. This can produce canopy-like formations, like those to be seen in the Postojna caves (see p. 163).

The shape taken by the dripstone formations depends on a variety of factors, including the calcium content of the water, the amount of evaporation in the cavern and the direction of air movement. They are given their colouring by traces of metallic salts dissolved in the water.

The formations in caves which have been open to the public for a century or more often lack the brilliance of colour found in more recently discovered caves. This is because in the past the caves were frequently illuminated by torches, bundles of burning straw or oil lamps, and soot deposits have dulled the colours.

Not infrequently the roof of an underground cavern will fall in, producing a depression like a bomb crater, known as a *doline* (sink, swallowhole), which may sometimes reach a diameter of as much as 1100 yd/1000 m. Adjoining dolines occasionally coalesce, forming what is known as an *uvala*. Still larger depressions, sometimes covering many square miles and usually surrounded by hills, are known as *poljes* ("fields").

Dolines usually provide good agricultural land, since fertile alluvial soil tends to accumulate in them. Poljes with a flat floor, making them particularly suitable for agricultural use, commonly acquire a cover of reddish clay-like soil (terra rossa) deposited by the percolating water.

Typical features of **poljes** are their disappearing rivers. These usually emerge at the edge of a polje and after flowing for some distance disappear into the ground again. After heavy rain, normally occurring at the end of winter, the cavities in the ground may not be able to absorb all the water immediately. This then forms a lake, which may end by covering the whole area of the polje. The peasants therefore always have their houses at the edges of a polje, and if there is a heavy early rainfall in autumn must make haste to get the harvest in before it is covered by the rising flood-water. The passing summer tourist may be surprised to see small boats lying about among dry cornfields; but these serve a useful purpose when the poljes quickly turn into lakes after heavy rain.

A peculiarity of karstic country is the absence of rivers of any length. Along the whole length of the Yugoslav Adriatic coast only a few above-ground rivers of any size reach the sea – the Dragonja, Mirna and Raša in Istria, the Krka and Čikola at Šibenik, the Cetina at Omiš and the Neretva in the Opuzen delta. The water which seeps into the ground re-emerges at the foot of the hills in the form of large *karstic springs*.

An impressive example of karstic landscape can be seen near Dubrovnik. In the neighbourhood of the little Moslem town of Trebinje is the **Popovo Polje**, more than 35 miles/60 km long, which fills up with water every September.

Kolašin

Republic: Montenegro (Crna Gora).
Altitude: 3166 ft/965 m. – Population: 4500.
Post code: YU-81210. – Telephone code: 0 84.
ⓘ **Turističko Društvo,**
   tel. 8 71 64.

HOTELS. – IN KOLAŠIN: *Bjelasica*, B, 160 b., tel. 8 71 32, with annexe at Biogradsko Jezero (National Park), to NE; two motels; also accommodation in Morača monastery, to SW. – IN MOJKOVAC: *Mojkovac*, A, 81 b., tel. 7 21 57.

CAMP SITE. – At Bjelasica Hotel; also site near Morača monastery.

SPORT. – Mountain walking and climbing, canoeing, fishing, shooting, skiing.

Soon after reaching the Montenegrin mountains the road from

Titograd to Belgrade enters the *Morača Gorge. The rock walls come ever closer to the road, towering up ever more steeply, and finally the road disappears into a series of tunnels. Then suddenly the mountains draw back, and in the more open valley a motel is seen on the right, soon followed by the Morača monastery. The road, magnificently engineered, now climbs to the Crkvina pass (3412 ft/1040 m) and runs down into the valley of the Tara, here a slow and tranquil stream. A bridge over the river (to right) leads to the little mountain town of Kolašin, a good base from which to explore the Biograd National Park.

Kolašin, looking towards the Tara valley

The town is also a convenient staging point for visitors on their way from the southern Adriatic coast to Belgrade or Macedonia or making for the famous National Park in the *Durmitor range (see p. 81). Although the shorter road from Titograd to Nikšić and beyond is now asphalted as far as Šavnik, the stretch from Šavnik (beyond which the road is blocked by snow in winter) to shortly before Žabljak is only gravel-surfaced: from Kolašin, however, Žabljak can be reached via Mojkovac, the *Tara gorge (see p. 211) and Djurdjevića Tara on an asphalted road all the way.

HISTORY. – Kolašin was founded by the Turks in the 17th c., and ruined buildings dating from that period can still be seen. The town was named after Kolaži, its first commandant.

Morača monastery, one of the most notable of Montenegro's historic old buildings, was founded in 1252 by Duke Stephen Vukanov, son of the great prince Vukan and grandson of Stephen Nemanja. The yellow stone used in building the monastery was conveyed from Tužine, a day's journey away, by a long chain of workers passing it from hand to hand.

The monastery was richly decorated with wall paintings, only a few of which have survived. In 1504 the Turks plundered the monastery and removed its roof, and during the following 70 years many paintings were destroyed by the effects of weather. The only scenes which have survived from the 13th c. depict Elijah being fed by a raven, the anointing of kings and prophets and the birth of St John. The monastery was renovated towards the end of the 16th c. Some new frescoes were painted, those at the main entrance being the work of Gregorije Mitrofanović (17th c.). The monastery later developed into the cultural and religious heart of the region.

The little town of Mojkovac to the N of Kolašin, where the road through the Tara gorge branches off the Titograd–Belgrade road, was an important mining town in the Middle Ages, with zinc, lead, gold and silver mines. In the 13th c. the Brstvo mine was the largest in the Balkans, worked by 40,000 miners. During the reign of King Uroš I a coin was minted here which resembled a Venetian silver coin but weighed 12·5% less. The Venetian republic issued warnings about the "counterfeit dinars of Brskovo", and Dante refers in the "Divine Comedy" to "him of Rascia, who counterfeited the coin of Venice".

Mojkovac is now a rising industrial as well as a mining town, with a considerable woodworking industry. A modern gold-washing plant is in course of construction.

Kolašin is at the beginning of its development into a climbing and tourist area, following the establishment, just to the N of the town, of the *Biogradska Gora National Park (alt. 2600–7200 ft/ 800–2200 m). The park surrounds *Lake Biograd (Biogradsko Jezero), lying at an altitude of 3300 ft/1000 m, which is well stocked with trout; it can also be reached from Mojkovac. The dark waters of the lake, which is ringed by deciduous and coniferous forest, contain a salmon-like fish, the huchen, as well as trout. This is a popular excursion for holidaymakers on the coast, and the lake is also included in the tours of Montenegro run by the travel agencies.

SURROUNDINGS. – Morača monastery lies in a very beautiful setting. From the main entrance a footpath to the right leads to the edge of the gorge, which here opens out a little; far below can be seen an old round-arched bridge over the Morača, probably dating from Roman times.

The monastery church is in the style of the Raška school. The frescoes of scenes from the story of Elijah which cover the S, W and N walls of the diaconicon (to right of apse) are particularly well preserved. The little chapel to the right of the main entrance also contains 13th c. paintings.

Kolašin is a good base for walks and climbs in the wooded hills of the Bjelasica range. The hotel stands on a hill outside the town (swimming pond nearby).

Koločep, Lopud and Šipan

Republic: Croatia (Hrvatska).
Total area of islands: 9 sq. miles/24 sq. km
Population: 1600.
Telephone code: 0 50.
ⓘ Turističko Društvo Koločep,
YU-50221 Koločep;
tel. 8 70 54.
Turisticko Društvo Pracat,
YU-50222 Lopud;
no telephone.
Turističko Društvo Šipan,
YU-50223 Šipanska Luka;
no telephone.

HOTELS. – ON KOLOČEP: Koločep, with annexes, B, 296 b., tel. 2 42 44. – ON LOPUD: Lafodia, B, 302 b., tel. 8 70 02; Dubrava-Pracat, with annexe Sutjeska, B, 220 b., tel. 8 70 25; Grand Hotel Lopud, B, 220 b., tel. 8 70 44. – ON ŠIPAN: Dubravka, C, 49 b., no telephone.

CAMP SITES. – ON KOLOČEP: sites for tents (no cars or caravan trailers) at Gornje Čelo and Donje Čelo. – ON ŠIPAN: at Sudjurad.

NATURIST FACILITIES. – In many coves away from the villages and hotels (inquire at hotel reception desks).

SPORT. – Boat rental in Lopud village.

TRANSPORT. – No car ferries. Boat services from Dubrovnik. No motor vehicles on Koločep and Lopud; on Šipan only buses.

The Elaphite Islands, which are covered with subtropical vegetation, lie NW of Dubrovnik, 6 miles/10 km off the coast. Perhaps the best way of seeing the three principal islands (Koločep, Lopud and Šipan) out of the seven islands in the group is in a day boat trip. There are also a number of hotels and pensions catering to visitors who enjoy the absence of cars and noisy entertainment.

HISTORY. – The history of the various islands in the group is very similar. They are first mentioned by Pliny the Elder under the name of the Elaphites ("Deer Islands"). All the islands were occupied by Greek settlers. During the Roman period wealthy citizens of Ragusa built villas here, of which remains have been found. In the 15th c. the islands came under the control of Dubrovnik, and in 1457 Lopud and Koločep were given their own Rector (Governor). After a raid on Lopud and Koločep by the notorious pirate Ali Ulić in 1571 many watch-towers – still prominent landmarks – were built on the islands. With the abolition of the republic of Dubrovnik in 1808 the islands became part of Napoleon's Illyrian Provinces. Since then the islands have shared the history of the Dalmatian coastal regions.

SIGHTS. – The three Elaphite Islands which are still inhabited – Šipan, Lopud and Koločep – have some interesting historical remains but these alone would hardly justify a visit. The attraction of the islands lies in their natural beauty, the charm of the sea and the hospitality with which the islanders greet visitors. Here, only a few miles from a large town, the arrival of strangers is still an event.

With an area of only 1 sq. mile/2·4 sq. km, **Koločep** is the smallest island in the group. It has a rich subtropical plant life, and the inhabitants live by farming, fishing and the tourist trade. **Donje Čelo** has a *parish church* which contains fragments of Roman marble sculpture and remains of early medieval interlace ornament. Above the church is one of the watch-towers built as a protection from pirates. The road to *Gornje Čelo*, the other settlement on Koločep, passes the ruins of a considerable *castle* Like the other islands, Koločep also has a large number of ruined or half-ruined churches and chapels.

Lopud, on the island of the same name

The island of **Lopud**, with an area of 1¾ sq. miles/4·6 sq. km, is the second largest in the group. Thanks to the island's springs of fresh water the vegetation is even more luxuriant, with palms, cypresses, oranges, lemons and other subtropical species. The village of **Lopud**, the only settlement on the island, was the residence of the Rector appointed by Ragusa, and the ruins of his house, commandingly situated on high ground, can still be seen. There is an interesting little pre-Romanesque *church* dedicated to *Sv. Ilija* (St Elias, Elijah), with wall paintings. A particular attraction for visitors, however, is the *museum* adjoining the presbytery, recently established by the young local priest, who has systematically assembled here anything of historical interest left in abandoned houses or salvaged from ruined churches.

The largest of the islands is **Šipan**, with an area of 6½ sq. miles/16·5 sq. km. Its highest point is the *Velji Vrh* (797 ft/243 m). Olives, figs, grapes, carobs, almonds and pomegranates flourish here. In the principal settlement, **Šipanska Luka**, the *Rector's Palace* still bears witness to the splendours of the past; above the Gothic doorway is an inscription of 1450. The parish church contains a fine painting by the 15th c. Venetian artist Maestro Pantaleone, "The Virgin adoring the Child Jesus". The footpath to the village of **Sudjurad**, 2½ miles/4 km from Šipanska Luka, goes past the former summer residence of the bishops of Ragusa (16th c.; partly restored). Sudjurad itself has a fortified castle of 1539 with a tower of 1577.

Koper

Republic: Slovenia (Slovenija).
Altitude: 16 ft/5 m. – Population: 20,000.
Post code: YU-66000. – Telephone code: 0 66.
ⓘ **Turistično Društvo,**
Pistanski Trg 7;
tel. 2 13 58.

HOTELS. – *Zusterna*, B, 359 b., tel. 2 16 40; *Triglav*, C, 185 b., tel. 2 16 50.

CAMP SITES. – *Adria*, tel. 5 18 99; *Študentski Tabor*, tel. 7 48 26. Both are in Ankaran, on the N side of the bay.

EVENTS. – Yugoslav Folk Festival in Koper, Portorož, Izola, Piran and Ankaran (mid July).

SPORT. – Water-skiing, rental of sail boats, scuba diving; tennis in Ankaran.

Most visitors travelling from Trieste to one of the Istrian bathing resorts drive past Koper. Neither the modern part of the town nor the industrial area with its smoking chimneys invite the interest of the tourist, but it is well worth turning to the right off the main road to see the old town, originally built on an island but now only partly surrounded by water. On the outskirts of the town many old buildings were destroyed during the construction of a ring road, but the historic hub

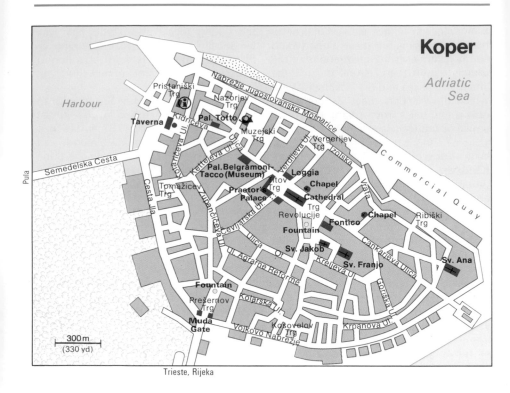

Trieste, Rijeka

has been preserved in its original condition.

HISTORY. – The island was occupied by Greek settlers, and later the Romans built a stronghold here. Under the Byzantine empire the island town was known as *Justinianopolis*. After many years of fighting, Koper fell to Venice in 1275. In 1797 and again in 1813 it passed to Austria. In 1918 the town was assigned to Italy and was named *Capodistria*. After the Second World War Yugoslavia claimed Trieste and the surrounding area, and as an interim solution the victorious powers established two zones – the Italian-administered Zone A and the Yugoslav-administered Zone B, based on Koper. Finally in 1954, under the London Agreement, Yugoslavia gave up its claim to Trieste. This political settlement stimulated the development of Koper, since ships which had previously anchored at Trieste now came to Koper, and the increasing traffic in turn promoted a considerable growth of industry. The town is bilingual, though the predominant language is Slovenian.

SIGHTS. – From the trunk road which runs between old and new Koper we branch off either on the right or the left to reach the ring road running around the OLD TOWN. In front of the white *Town Gate* (Muda Gate) is a car park where cars must be left, for only residents are allowed to drive within the old town. Going past the gate (the passageway of which is barred by chains) we come into *Prešernov Trg*, at the far end of which is a beautiful *fountain* in the form of a small bridge, erected in 1423 by the Venetian mayor Lorenzo da Ponte.

Almost all the town's streets lead to the central square, now known as *Titov Trg* (Tito Square), with the Cathedral, the Praetor's Palace and the Loggia – the point on which all tourists converge. The **Praetor's Palace**, with its imposing battlements, was the residence of the Venetian governor. As the differences in architecture show, it was originally two separate buildings which were later combined into one. The palace was the seat of the mayor of the town as well as the governor. The Façade is decorated with

Praetor's Palace, Koper

numerous coats of arms, busts and inscriptions. There is now a restaurant in the palace, and the splendid *Loggia* opposite is occupied by a café.

The **Cathedral** has an imposing but relatively plain façade, the lower part being Gothic (15th c.) and the upper part Renaissance (16th c.). The interior has an air of coolness; it contains a number of paintings by major Italian artists. To the rear of the high altar is the sarcophagus of St Nazarius, the town's patron saint (1332).

The *tower* of the Cathedral was originally a watch-tower not connected with it. While the construction of the Cathedral took roughly 100 years (15th–16th c.), the tower took much longer, having been begun in the 13th c. and completed only in 1660. Beyond the Cathedral is Trg Revolucije (Revolution Square), at the far end of which can be seen the Renaissance façade of the *Fontico Building*, originally built in the 14th c., later (and still) occupied by offices. Adjoining this, to the right, stands a little Romanesque and Gothic church, now deconsecrated, as is the former monastic church of St Francis, still farther to the right, which now houses official records. In its heyday Koper had something like 50 churches and chapels, and although many of them have been preserved, few of those which visitors will see in walking about the town are still open.

110 yd/100 m S of the Cathedral is the *Belgramoni-Tacco Palace*, now occupied by the *Municipal Museum*. The old streets and houses opposite the palace have all disappeared to make way for the new Post Office, car parks and apartment buildings. Below this residential area is the town's bathing station (not recommended: badly polluted water).

Korčula

Republic: Croatia (Hrvatska).
Area of island: 108 sq. miles/279 sq. km. –
Population: 23,000.
Telephone code: 0 50.

ⓘ **Turist Biro Marko Polo, Korčula,**
YU-50260 Korčula;
tel. 8 10 67.
Turistički Biro Vela Luka,
YU-50270 Vela Luka;
tel. 8 20 42.
Turističko Društvo Lumbarda,
YU-50263 Lumbarda;
tel. 8 36 05.

Wind-surfer, Korčula

HOTELS. – IN KORČULA: *Bon Repos*, B, 660 b., tel. 8 11 02; *Park*, B, 400 b., tel. 8 10 04; *Marko Polo*, B, 230 b., tel. 8 11 00; *Korčula*, D, 40 b., tel. 8 10 04. – IN RAČIŠĆE: *Mediteran* (pension), B, 20 b., tel. 8 38 13. – IN LUMBARDA: *Lumbarda*, B, 116 b., tel. 8 36 22, with annexes *Borik* and *Lovor*, B, 149 b. – IN BLATO: *Alfier*, B, 120 b., tel. 8 53 07; *Lipa*, B, 24 b., tel. 8 52 42. – IN SMOKVICA: *Feral*, B, 160 b., tel. 8 52 10. – IN VELA LUKA: *Poseidon*, B, 250 b., tel. 8 22 26.

CAMP SITES. – IN KORČULA: at Bon Repos Hotel. – IN SV. ANTUN: *Solitudo*, tel. 8 11 90.

NATURIST FACILITIES. – On the islands of *Velika Stupa* and *Mala Stupa* (boats from Korčula town).

EVENTS. – Every Thursday before and after the main season, twice daily in July and August, 16th c. sword dance, the Moreška. Annually on April 23 (Liberation Day), performance of the Kumpanija, a battle dance, in Blato. Summer concerts in Korčula town.

SPORT, BOATING and BATHING. – The public beach of Korčula town (pebbles) has a gentle slope which makes it suitable for children; admission charge. The hotel beaches are better maintained, but the shipping traffic in the channel between Korčula and Pelješac causes some pollution. Also in Korčula boat rental, scuba diving, water-skiing, tennis. – Lumbarda has three large coves with beaches of pebbles and sand, particularly suitable for children; scuba diving, boat rental. – Vela Luka has a long beach and many coves; boat rental; bowling alley; spa treatment establishment (curative mud), opened in 1972.

Sailing enthusiasts prefer the moorings at Orebić on the Pelješac peninsula to the harbour of Korčula town, which is frequently overcrowded.

CAR FERRIES. – Services between Korčula town and Orebić, Prigradica and Drvenik, Korčula town and Split. Passenger services from Split and Dubrovnik.

A little town of well-planned streets, backed by dark green wooded hills and looking out on to a strait only 1390 yd/1270 m wide: this is what tourists see as they pass *Korčula town, chief town of Korčula island, on cruise liners sailing from Venice to Dubrovnik and on to Greece. These ships follow the same route as the trading ships of antiquity. This jewel among the Yugoslav Adriatic islands is becoming increasingly popular with vacationers, who are attracted not only to Korčula town but to other towns and villages on the island including Vela Luka, Čara, Smokvica and Blato.

Korčula town

HISTORY. – A complete account of the various peoples who have lived on Korčula, or the rulers who have held sway there, would be a considerable undertaking. At the very outset the problem is complicated by the fact that here, in contrast to the other islands, the first settlers after the earlier Neolithic occupation were not mainland Greeks but two peoples from the eastern Mediterranean – first Trojans, led (as the legend will have it) by the hero Antenor (1200 B.C.), and then Dorians from Knidos (4th c. B.C.), who were followed by other Greeks from Syracuse. From 35 B.C. onwards the island, together with the Dalmatian mainland, was under Roman control. After the fall of the Western Empire it passed in 493 to Theodoric's Ostrogothic state and in 555 to Byzantium.

In the 9th c. a Slav people, the Neretvans, captured the island. About the year 1000 it passed into the hands of Venice, and from 1180 it belonged to the Hungarian-Croatian kingdom. In 1298 a Genoese fleet defeated a Venetian force near Korčula, and it is said to have been on this occasion that Marco Polo (1254–1324), who is claimed as a native of Korčula and not of Venice, fell into the hands of the Genoese. While in prison he dictated to a fellow-prisoner his account of his journey to China, which lasted for 24 years (from 1271). In 1390 Korčula came under the control of the kings of Bosnia; and the battles of this period against the Turks are still commemorated in the Moreška, the dance-cum-drama which was formerly performed, against the backdrop of the old town, only on July 27 but is now put on twice daily during the main season.

An attempt by the republic of Dubrovnik in 1413–17 to acquire Korčula as a further outpost in its defensive system was unsuccessful. Thereafter the island remained a dependency of Venice, with self-governing status, until 1797. It was then held in rapid succession by Austria (1797–1805), France (1805–13) and Britain (1813–15). From 1815 to 1918 it belonged to Austria; from 1918 to 1921 it was claimed by Italy, but it was finally assigned to the kingdom of Yugoslavia. From 1941 to 1943 it was under Italian occupation; then in the following year Yugoslav partisans landed on the island.

SIGHTS. – The palaces and churches of Korčula town magnificently display the whole range of architectural styles from the 14th to the 16th c. The middle of the old town is still surrounded by high walls and towers, leading the visitor to reflect with some surprise that at the beginning of the 16th c. the OLD TOWN, covering an area only 185 by 330 yd/170 by 300 m, housed a population of some 4000 people. The layout of Korčula resembles the pattern of the veins on a leaf: the main axis of the town runs from the entrance in Tito Square (triumphal arch) to the squares in front of the Cathedral and St Peter's Church, with slightly curving parallel side streets branching off at an angle.

The best starting point for a sightseeing tour of the town is the waterfront at the harbour. The route runs past two massive towers and a small and elegant 16th c. Loggia (on left); then through the Land Gate (just within the gate a handsome triumphal arch of 1650) into the main street. On the left is the Renaissance façade of the former Prince's Palace, with a 16th c. loggia, and opposite it is the 17th c. St Michael's Church, also in Renaissance style. Continuing in the direction of the Cathedral, we pass on the left a small Baroque church and on the right the former Bishop's Palace (14th c.), with a 17th c. Baroque façade; it now houses a museum containing, among much else, the Cathedral treasury and works by Italian masters. To the left is the Gabrieli Palace, a handsome Renaissance mansion which now houses the Municipal Museum. St Mark's Cathedral (to right), begun in the 13th c. and completed some 300 years later, shows Romanesque, Gothic and Renaissance features, and contains a painting ascribed to Tintoretto behind the high altar as well as some good pictures by artists of the 13th–15th c. – Beyond *St Peter's Church* (museum of religious art), on the right, is a street leading to the **Marco Polo House**, in which the great traveller is said to have been born.

Outside the town walls are two features of interest: a *Dominican friary*, on the seafront to the W, and the two-aisled *St Nicholas's Church*, which has a copy of Titian's "St Peter" above the Baroque altar.

At the SE end of the island, only 4 miles/6 km from Korčula town, is **Lumbarda**. On Koludrt Hill to the N of the village, by the medieval St John's Church, were found fragments of a stone tablet dating from the period of Greek settlement (copy in Korčula Municipal Museum, original in Archaeological Museum, Zagreb) which contained information about land ownership, mentioning Illyrian as well as Greek names. Lumbarda is also noted for its golden "Greek" wine, *Grk*, and the skill of its stone-masons. It is possible to visit the studios of some of the sculptors working here.

A drive along the 30 miles/48 km of asphalted road between Korčula and Vela Luka reveals the scenery of the island in all its variety – woodland, vineyards, olive plantations, with little in the way of inhospitable karstic terrain. Beyond the village of Pupnat the road passes the island's highest point, *Klupča* (1864 ft/568 m; good view, but strenuous climb). **Blato**, the largest town on the island (not on the sea), has its own pageant play, performed annually on April 23, the day on which the island was liberated in 1944. Here too is preserved the tradition of the "guslars", the folk singers who sing to the accompaniment of a one-string fiddle interminable melancholy sagas about battles, heroes and sorrows of long ago. The little town itself is of great interest, with numerous medieval buildings. In the *Castle* is a *Local Museum*, which also contains finds from the nearby Roman villa of Junium.

The road then continues to **Vela Luka**, which is seeking to develop both industry

(cooperative processing of agricultural produce, fish canning, small boatyards) and the tourist trade. Here the visitor is reminded that in earlier centuries foreign conquerors were attracted to Korčula not only by its fine quarries of white marble but by the shipyards of Vela Luka and Korčula town.

SURROUNDINGS. – Boat trips from Korčula town to the island of **Badija** (Franciscan friary of 1420, with arcaded cloister of 1477) and the island of **Vrnik** (limestone quarries).

Kornati Islands

Republic: Croatia (Hrvatska).
Altitude: 0–771 ft/0–235 m. – Uninhabited.
ⓘ **Turist Biro,**
B. Petranovića,
YU-57000 Zadar;
tel. (0 57) 2 26 33.

ACCOMMODATION. – Summer only, tents for visitors on a week's motorboat trip among the islands; some supply posts also operate then.

CAMPING. – Permitted everywhere. Many sheltered coves for boats (also used by fishermen).

NATURIST FACILITIES. – Everywhere.

SPORT. – Fishing (with an abundance of fish); scuba diving.

SAILING AROUND THE ISLANDS. – Boats can be rented, with or without crew. There are also motorboat trips, each lasting a week, with accommodation in tents which are pitched on some of the islands at the beginning of the season. The main food supply consists of fish caught by the members of the party.

If you are sailing on your own you will need a reliable compass and good charts. Small boats must beware not only of reefs but of the walls which run just under the water at some points between the islands.

Although the Kornati Islands are frequently described by foreign writers as comprising all the islands around Zadar, in Yugoslav usage the name is applied only to the islands of Kornat and Žut together with 145 small islets, with formidable cliffs rising to 330 ft/100 m on the seaward side and a series of small coves on the inland side. Seen from the air, the islands appear almost round, and they are covered with a sparse growth of vegetation. The whole archipelago, with an area of some 116 sq. miles/300 sq. km, is now a National Park.

The barren Kornati Islands – a bird's-eye view

The islands have none of the obvious tourist attractions, and indeed at first sight appear bleak and inhospitable. According to the Yugoslav geographer Rubić, however, the Kornati show rock forms not found on any other islands on the Yugoslav Adriatic coast. To the skipper of a boat approaching from the sea they present a harsh and forbidding appearance, but he has only to round the island to find on the other side a sheltered cove which provides anchorage for three or four boats and a safe haven in a storm. Here too land the shepherds who spend many months on the islands with their flocks, until the grass begins to turn brown. There are also a few green valleys in which olives grow, but the peasants pay only rare visits to the islands to tend them.

For many centuries the islands have been inhospitable and barren, leading such inhabitants as there were to leave them. They are believed to have once been covered with forest; and at least in Roman times they must have been green and fertile, since wealthy Romans had villas here, as evidenced by the remains of walls still to be seen under the surface. In a history of the Kornati, Amos Rube Filipi records a long series of pirate raids and occupations by foreign troops using the islands as bridgeheads for the conquest of the mainland. During the last war the

islands could not be adequately policed by the occupation forces and provided Tito's partisans with an ideal operational base. As early as 1941 the Yugoslav Resistance established their first base for fishing boats on the island of Žut, and this was soon followed by a hospital, moving from place to place on short notice, where the partisans cared for those who had been wounded on the mainland.

There are only a few houses on the islands, occupied only in summer. The most popular rendezvous for anglers and scuba divers is a restaurant in the cove on the S side of Katina, an islet between Dugi Otok and Kornat. The only source of fresh water

Cliffs on one of the Kornati Islands

is a meagre spring in the bay of Luka Žut on the island of that name. A number of inns on the islands bring in water by tanker, and in the coves used as anchorages there are cisterns which are filled in spring by the fishermen and shepherds; but these supplies are frequently insufficient to meet the increasing demand from visitors throughout the summer.

For many years now the Kornati have been popular with scuba divers, and they are also well known – and indeed, on account of their dangerous shallows and reefs, notorious – to owners of motorboats and yachts. Many wrecks, some of them dating from the Venetian period, lie off their coasts. Their waters are well stocked with fish, yielding larger catches than any other part of the Yugoslav Adriatic coast. Underwater fishing is, however, prohibited. For scuba diving a permit is required, obtainable from the harbourmaster at Zadar or Biograd.

As a vacation area the Kornati appeal to active and adventurous visitors who do not insist on all their creature comforts.

Kosovo

Kosovo is an autonomous province in the republic of Serbia, with Priština as its capital. With an area of 4203 sq. miles/10,887 sq. km, it has a population of 1,300,000, two-thirds of whom are of Albanian stock, the remaining third being made up of Serbs, Montenegrins and Turks. This region in south-eastern Yugoslavia has powerful tourist attractions in its grand mountain scenery and its churches and monasteries with their art treasures. In the towns the oriental and Moslem atmosphere of the past is increasingly giving way to modernisation and industrialisation.

The province of Kosovo is a part of Yugoslavia still relatively little known to foreign visitors. Until the end of the 1960s the bad roads discouraged even the more adventurous vacationers; but the new roads which have been built make all the main places of interest (with only a few exceptions) readily accessible to visitors, and the travel firms now include this area in their programs.

HISTORY. – Between the little towns of Vučitrn and Uroševac, in a valley 45 miles/70 km long and averaging 9 miles/15 km in width, is **Kosovo Polje**, the *Field of Kosovo* (alt. 1640–1970 ft/500–600 m), now noted outside Yugoslavia mainly for its light sweet wine. This valley, in which is the provincial capital of Priština, was the scene of two major battles. In 1169 the Serbian prince Nemanja I won a victory here which established the Nemanjid dynasty; then on St Vitus's Day (Vidov Dan), June 28, 1389, a Turkish army under Sultan Murad I defeated the Serbian forces of Prince Lazar which had sought to bar the way to the Turks' northward advance. This Turkish victory on the Field of Kosovo marked the beginning of 500 years of Turkish rule in the Balkans.

Thousands of men died in the battle, and the wild peonies which cover the Field of Kosovo with a red carpet in spring are said to represent the blood of the dead warriors. The event lives on, too, in numerous legends and heroic songs.

Murad I's mausoleum on the Field of Kosovo

Much of the province of Kosovo, including the whole of the Field of Kosovo, was originally inhabited by Serbs, but under the pressure of the civilian population which followed the Turkish army they moved ever farther northward and their abandoned villages were occupied by Turks and Albanians converted to Islam. In 1912, during the first Balkan War, Serbia, Montenegro, Bulgaria and Greece fought against the Turks, who finally lost their last strongholds in the Balkans. In 1913 Albania became independent and Serbia acquired the territory of Kosovo and Metohija, as the present autonomous province was then known.

When the Kingdom of the Serbs, Croats and Slovenes was established in 1918 this area was the most backward province of the new state – with no good roads and no industry and with much of the population unable to read or write. The Albanians ("Škipetars"), despised by the Serbs, still clung to their traditional customs, including polygamy and the blood-feud; in the towns they did the most menial work, maintaining their freedom as peasants only in the inaccessible mountain regions. A posting to Kosovo was regarded by Serbian officials and officers as a disciplinary transfer.

After Mussolini's conquest of Albania many Albanians thought that incorporation in a new state taking in the whole Albanian-speaking territory would at last bring them freedom and economic advance; but for Italy Albania was merely a colony to be exploited. In 1943 German troops occupied Albania, and thereafter there was no change in the circumstances of the region until November 1945, when Kosovo again became part of Serbia within the People's Republic of Yugoslavia.

In 1948 Stalin broke with Tito, when the Soviet Union and other Communist states aligned themselves against Yugoslavia's "own road to Socialism". In the same year Kosovo was granted the status of an autonomous province within the republic of Serbia. The Albanian language now enjoys equal status with Serbian, and all over the province signs are written in both languages. There are radio and television programs in Albanian and Albanian newspapers, magazines and books, and there is now an Albanian university in Priština.

Although the province of Kosovo has made tremendous progress in overcoming its former backwardness, with financial and material assistance from Belgrade, it still remains far behind the rest of Yugoslavia. Current plans, therefore, provide for a rate of economic development 50% above the average in order to bring the province into line with the development of the country as a whole.

The basis for this development is provided mainly by the province's rich mineral resources and energy supplies. Kosovo has large reserves of lead, zinc, nickel and almost all non-ferrous metals; and the power supplies for processing these minerals are to be increased by four thermal and two hydroelectric power stations. Agricultural production is also to be increased by 4·5% annually between 1980 and 1985; the increase is to be achieved mainly by growing more wheat and maize, but experiments are also being made in the growing of rice in Kosovo Polje.

Kotor

Republic: Montenegro (Crna Gora).
Altitude: 16 ft/5 m. – Population: 7700.
Post code: YU-81330. – Telephone code: 0 82.
ⓘ **Inturs,**
Trg Oktobarske Revolucije 437;
   tel. 2 51 13.

HOTEL. – *Borik*, B, 70 b., tel. 8 80 51.

CAMP SITES. – *Dobrota*, 1½ miles/2·5 km N of Kotor; small private site at Prčanj, on far side of bay.

SPORT. – Boat rental in yacht harbour.

EVENTS. – *"Fishermen's Nights"* at Muo, opposite Kotor on the Lepetane road.

The town of Kotor lies in a magnificent mountain setting at the SE end of **Kotor Bay. Until the devastating earthquake of spring 1979 a visit to this little medieval town, still completely preserved with its churches and palaces and its massive walls, offered a unique experience, the more so because of the long-standing ban on motor vehicles in its narrow streets. It will be years before the damage can be repaired, and some features will be impossible to restore. The newer part of the town was also damaged. Holiday accommodation outside the town, on the road to Muo and Prčanj, is again available. – Kotor is the starting point of the magnificent **Lovćen road to Cetinje (see p. 67).

(see p. 67)

Motorists coming from Dubrovnik on the coastal highway (Jadranska Magistrala) have a choice between two alternative routes to Kotor: they can drive around the wide sweep of Kotor Bay via Risan and Perast (with possible traffic light holdups) or they can take the car ferry from Kamenari to Plavda, continuing via Prčanj, a shorter route which also has numerous potential bottlenecks. – Many visitors also approach Kotor from the sea, on the cruise liners which put in to the bay.

**Kotor Bay (Boka Kotorska), reminiscent of a Norwegian fjord in its setting of high karstic hills, is one of Yugoslavia's most striking scenic attractions. The narrow entrance passage into the bay forms a natural defence against invaders, and it was no doubt thanks to this geographical advantage as much as to its stout walls that the town of Kotor was able to avoid capture by the Turks.

HISTORY. – A Greek colony was founded at the S end of Kotor Bay under the name of *Akourion*. In Roman times the town was known as *Acruvium*, and during the Middle Ages the variants *Dekadaron*, *Catarum*, *Catera* and *Cathara* arose. The Southern Slavs who settled here soon established the form *Kotor*, which became *Cattaro* in the mouths of the Venetians.

After the fall of the Western Roman Empire Kotor passed under Byzantine rule, but enjoyed municipal self-government. It preserved its privileges when it became part of the Serbian kingdom, under the Balšić and Nemanjić dynasties, between 1186 and 1366. After short periods of rule by the Hungarian king

Ljudevit and the Bosnian king Tvrtko I Kotor and the surrounding territories became independent for a time, but the local feudal lords finally compelled the town to submit in 1420 to Venetian rule, which lasted until 1797.

In 1797 the town was occupied by Austrian forces, succeeded in 1806 by Russians and then in 1807 by the French, who remained until 1813. Then came the Austrians, who based their fleet in Kotor Bay (the scene of a mutiny in 1918 very similar to the rising in Leningrad) and advanced up the Lovćen road to take Cetinje. In April 1941 Italian troops landed here, later giving place to Germans. In November 1944 the town was taken by Yugoslav partisans.

SIGHTS. – In front of the *town walls* (4400 yd/4000 m long, up to 33 ft/10 m high), opposite the quay (large car park) are the market stalls, where peasants wearing traditional costume can still occasionally be seen. The western town gate or Sea Gate leads into October Revolution Square (Trg Oktobarske Revolucije), in which stands the modern **Town Hall**. The whole of the W side of the square is occupied by an unfinished **Venetian palazzo**. A street runs past the *Clock-Tower* (1602) to *St Michael's Church*. Beyond this other streets lead past the *Bisanti Palace* (17th c.) and *Beskuća Palace* (1776) to the **Cathedral of St Tryphon** (*Sv. Tripun*). Originally dating from the 12th c., the Cathedral has two Renaissance towers (17th c.) of different heights. Over the high altar is a ciborium of 1362; the *sacristy* contains the altar silver; and in the adjoining *reliquary* are the relics of St Tryphon and an old crucifix.

Old Kotor (before the 1979 earthquake)

Farther N, reached by a lane which passes the *Drago Palace*, is the *Maritime Museum*, housed in the 18th c. *Grgurina Palace*.

Almost every building in the old town was damaged in the 1979 earthquake, and it is doubtful whether the numerous architectural details, the elaborate doorways and decorated windows and the coats of arms, can ever be restored.

From a street running parallel to the almost vertical rock face behind the town a steep flight of steps leads up to **Gospa od Zdravlta Church**, which dates from 1500. Above this is **Fort St John** (*Sveti Ivan*, alt. 850 ft/260 m), with walls 33 ft/10 m thick and up to 66 ft/20 m high. It is not known who began the building of this massive fortress nor when it was built.

The *town walls* of Kotor date in their present form from the time of the Nemanjić and Balšić families and the period of Venetian rule. They withstood many hostile assaults in the course of their history, particularly by the Turks, who directed their strongest attacks against Kotor in 1539 and 1657 but were never able to take the town.

Kraljevo

Republic: Serbia (Srbija).
Altitude: 669 ft/204 m. – Population: 50,000.
Post code: YU-36000. – Telephone code: 0 36.
ⓘ Turistički Savez,
   tel. 2 14 32.
   Informacije Agencija INEH,
   tel. 2 42 50.

HOTELS. – *Termal*, B, 200 b., tel. 7 43 66; *Turist*, B, 160 b., tel. 2 23 66.

The industrial town of Kraljevo, on the right bank of the River Ibar above its junction with the western Morava, is for most visitors merely a convenient base from which to visit the *monasteries of Žiča, Studenica, Veluće, Ljubostinja and Kalenić and the Lazarica Church in Kruševac, 37 miles/60 km away. The basin surrounding the town, enclosed by ranges of hills, is a hub of agricultural production, noted particularly for its dairy produce, including the salty cream cheese known as Kraljevački kajmak. Kraljevo suffered severe destruction during the Second World War, but no sign of this is left in the present town, now rebuilt in contemporary style.

HISTORY. – Not much is known of the history of the town, which lies at the intersection of important traffic routes. It first appears in the records in 1737 under the name of *Karanovac*. During the 19th c. the town increased in importance as a local base for trade and the marketing of agricultural produce. In the Second World War it was frequently bombed as it was not held by the partisans. The fighting of this period is commemorated in a monument by the sculptor Lojze Dolinar, "Resistance and Victory", with 20 slender bronze figures symbolising the people's resistance.

SIGHTS. – In the Municipal Park is the *konak* (residence) of the former governor, Vaso, which now houses the *Municipal Museum*. There are no other features of tourist interest. The industrial activities of this rapidly developing town are represented by a wagon-building works, woodworking factories, a metalworking plant and other factories.

SURROUNDINGS. – 3 miles/5 km from Kraljevo, to the left of the Priština road (No. 11), stands *Žiča monastery, where the Serbian kings were once crowned. This example of the work of the Raška school, in Romanesque-Byzantine style, was built in the 13th c., burned down soon afterwards in the course of a war and rebuilt in its present form in the following century. 1¼ miles/2 km beyond it, on the right bank of the Ibar, is the spa of *Mataruška Banja*.

25 miles/41 km farther on the same road, from the little town of *Ušće*, a side road (7 miles/11 km; dust-free) goes off on the right to *Studenica monastery, the finest example of the work of the Raška school. It has three churches – the Church of the Mother of God, St Nicholas's and the Royal Church – all with splendid frescoes. See the entry on Serbian monasteries.

The monasteries of Ljubostinja, Kalenić and Veluće are reached by way of the road which runs E from Kraljevo to Kruševac.

At *Trstenik*, 19 miles/30 km from Kraljevo, a road (5 miles/8 km) branches off on the left to **Ljubostinja monastery**, with a church of the Morava school built in the 15th c. by the Serbian Princess Milica, who is buried here. The frescoes are preserved only in part.

*Kalenić monastery lies well off the beaten track at the end of 25 miles/40 km of bad road running through a gorge. It is worth making the journey, however, for the sake of the well-preserved frescoes and the fine façade of the church. This monastery is also an example of the Morava school.

8 miles/13 km farther along the main road a track on the right, barely deserving the name of road, leads in 1¼ miles/2 km to **Veluće monastery**, one of the oldest examples of the Morava school. Only a few frescoes have been preserved, notable for the fact that they were painted not by artists but by untrained local painters: at no other Serbian ecclesiastical site are there so many paintings with portraits of laymen.

19 miles/30 km beyond this is **Kruševac**, resembling Kraljevo in being a developing industrial town in a flourishing agricultural region. During the reign of Prince Lazar (who lost his life at the Battle of Kosovo Field in 1389: see under Kosovo) Kruševac was capital of Serbia, and master builders from Dubrovnik surrounded it with strong defensive walls. In 1380 Prince Lazar built a castle of which little now survives (remains of a tower on the N side and staircases which once led to the upper floors). The *Lazarica church

which he founded within the castle, however, is almost completely preserved. Its decorative architecture is characteristic of the Morava school. The only surviving frescoes, some fragments dating from the early 18th c., are now in a Belgrade museum. It is suspected that there may be older paintings concealed under a layer of plaster.

Kranj

Republic: Slovenia (Slovenija).
Altitude: 1263 ft/385 m. – Population: 27,500.
Post code: YU-64000. – Telephone code: 0 64.
ⓘ Gorenjska Turistična Zveza Kranj,
Koroška 27;
tel. 2 15 39.

HOTELS. – *Creina*, B, 160 b., tel. 2 36 50; *Jelen*, C, 82 b., tel. 2 14 66; *Evropa*, D, 66 b., tel. 2 11 23.

The industrial town of Kranj lies 16 miles/25 km NW of Ljubljana and about the same distance from the Austrian frontier. 5½ miles/9 km N of the town is the junction of two Alpine pass routes, the roads from the Loibl (Ljubelj) tunnel and the Wurzen pass (Korensko Sedlo), and in the town itself a third, less frequented, pass route comes in from the Seeberg saddle (Jezerski Vrh). The road passes an ungainly shopping complex and various industrial buildings to enter the town proper, which has many relics of the Austro-Hungarian monarchy (when the town was known under its German name of Krainburg). The clientele of the hotels consists mainly of businessmen and passing travellers: few visitors stay longer than one night – though Kranj would in fact make a

Burghers' houses, Kranj

good base from which to explore the attractive surrounding country.

HISTORY. – The site of Kranj was occupied by Celtic settlers, attracted by this high promontory at the confluence of the Sava and the Kokra and by the fertile surrounding plain, the Kranjsko Polje. Later the Romans established their station of *Carnium* on the same site. In subsequent centuries the town gained importance from its situation at the meeting-place of three Alpine pass routes. The great Slovenian poet France Prešeren (1800–49) lived in the town and died there; there is an imposing statue of him in the main square. With flourishing textile and electrical industries, Kranj is a lively and expanding town.

SIGHTS. – Kranj is a busy shopping and commercial town, and the central area is closely packed with shops, offices, restaurants and cafés. From the Gothic **parish church** it is a short distance to the end of the main street, with the handsome façade of the *Ortenburg Palace*, now occupied by offices. Immediately beyond it is the **Pungrat Chapel**. From here there is a fine view into the Sava valley, with the numerous industrial establishments which have developed there in recent years. Other features of interest in the town are the *Museum of Upper Carniola* (Gorenjski Muzej) and the medieval *Council Chamber* in the Town Hall.

SURROUNDINGS. – 6 miles/10 km S of Kranj, a little way W of the road to Ljubljana, lies **Škofja Loka**, a charming little town with a history going back a thousand years and which is protected as a national monument. On a green hill rising above the town is the castle of *Loški Grad*, now housing the Municipal Museum. The town is entered over an old stone bridge, and the houses in the central part almost all date from the period after an earthquake in 1511. For centuries the town was held by the Bishops of Freising in Bavaria, to whom it had been granted by the Emperor Otto II.

Other possible excursions from Kranj are to the *reservoir on the Sava* at **Medvode** (camp site) and to the *Šmarjetna Gora* (hotel, with restaurant), NW of the town.

Kranjska Gora

Republic: Slovenia (Slovenija).
Altitude: 2658 ft/810 m. – Population: 1200.
Post code: YU-64280. – Telephone code: 0 64.
ⓘ **Turistično Društvo,**
tel. 8 87 68.

HOTELS. – *Kompas*, A, 280 b., tel. 8 86 61; *Larix*, B, 260 b., tel. 8 85 75; *Alpina Kompas*, B, 180 b., tel. 8 87 61; *Prisank*, B, 126 b., tel. 8 84 72; *Prisank Garni*, B, 98 b., tel. 8 84 72; *Lek*, B, 75 b., tel. 8 85 20; *Slavec*, C, 92 b., tel. 8 84 21; *Alpe Adria*, C, 56 b., tel. 8 85 84; *Erika*, D, 75 b., tel. 8 86 62, with annexe *Janez*, B, 54 b.; *Razor*, D, 33 b., tel. 8 84 28.

CAMP SITES. – *Špik*, tel. 8 84 15, in Gozd Martuljek; *Šranc*, tel. 8 19 91, in Jesenice.

SPORT. – Climbing, walking, tennis, bowling. In winter cross-country skiing (43 miles/70 km), downhill skiing, ski-jumping, skating, curling; cleared footpaths.

With its chair-lifts and ski-tows, its ski school, its ice-rinks and its cross-country skiing trails, its discotheques and its bars, Kranjska Gora is now the largest winter sports complex in Yugoslavia. There are also ambitious expansion plans providing for an extension of the skiing area in the direction of the Vršič pass. Winter vacationers will find an international atmosphere at Kranjska Gora, with Yugoslavs predominating only on weekends. In summer the village is full of climbers, mainly Yugoslavs, Germans and Austrians.

HISTORY. – The Sava valley, lying between the Karavanke (Karawanken) range and the Julian Alps, was already occupied by man in prehistoric times. At this altitude the valley floor was used principally for grazing, while the forest-covered slopes on either side of the valley yielded timber. In the years before the First World War Kranjska Gora had already become a climbing base, with a few inns catering to visitors.

During the First World War this little mountain village became a place of strategic importance, when Russian prisoners of war built a road over the Vršič pass (5236 ft/1611 m) into the Soča (Isonzo) valley, losing many men in the process; a chapel on the hill commemorates their sufferings. Just before the end of the southern approach to the pass is a statue of the Slovenian scholar Dr Julius Kugy, discoverer of the Julian Alps as an area for climbers, who wrote a number of guides and books on the subject at the end of the 19th c. and thus prepared the way for the later development of tourism. At present the pass road is closed in winter, but with the further development of Kranjska Gora and of Bovec (see p. 59), where a skiing resort on the French model is being established, the road will be kept open throughout the year.

The discovery of Kranjska Gora as a good place for winter sports began in 1934, when a Slovenian engineer named Stanko Bloudek built the first large ski-jump in the Alps in the nearby Planica valley. The Austrian ski-jumper Sepp Bradl, then aged 17, was the first to make a jump of over 110 yd/100 m there. Most of the hotels, as well as the cableways and ski-lifts, at Kranjska Gora were erected only after the last war. The new developments all lay outside the modest mountain village, leaving the original village unspoiled. A bypass keeps through traffic out of the village in winter; only in summer do cars making for the Vršič pass go through the village itself.

WINTER SPORTS. – Near Kranjska Gora, on **Mt Vitranc** (5351 ft/1631 m), is the highest winter sports station in the area, with a two-stage chair-lift up to the summit. The ski trails run down through

Kranjska Gora in winter

the forest (upper part, medium difficulty; lower part, with fewer trees, easy), normally with 5 ft/1·5 m of snow lying until the end of March. The ski-tows up Vitranc all start from behind the hotels. There is ample space for beginners. Ski school, with some 30 instructors.

Skaters and *curlers* can practise their sports either on a natural ice-rink on the S side of the village or on an idyllically situated lake beside an inn on the road to Vršič. For *Nordic skiers* there are trails laid out on the meadows around the village, and there is also plenty of scope for ski trekking.

The Planica *ski-jumping station* is $4\frac{1}{2}$ miles/7 km from Kranjska Gora. In addition to the original ski-jump of 1934 there are five more recently constructed jumps. Here and in Kranjska Gora itself numerous international skiing competitions take place every year.

SUMMER SPORTS. – In the mountains around Kranjska Gora there are about a dozen serviced mountain huts for mountain walkers and climbers in summer. For walkers who prefer less strenuous country there is an extensive network of paths in the Sava valley. In Kranjska Gora itself visitors can play tennis and mini-golf. There is an open-air swimming pool in

addition to the indoor pools in the hotels; and for the sportsman there is fishing to be had in the area and shooting trips are organised.

Krk

Republic: Croatia (Hrvatska).
Area of island: 158 sq. miles/409 sq. km. –
Population: 20,000.
Telephone code: 0 51.

ⓘ **Turist Biro Omišalj,**
Prikrešte 11,
YU-51513 Omišalj;
tel. 85 11 53.
Turističko Društvo Krk,
in Hotel Dražina,
Ružmarinova 4,
YU-51500 Krk;
tel. 85 10 22.
Turističko Društvo Punat,
YU-51521 Punat;
tel. 85 40 04.
Turističko Društvo Baška,
YU-51523 Baška;
tel. 85 68 17.
Turističko Društvo Malinska,
YU-51511 Malinska;
tel. 88 55 07.
Turističko Društvo Vrbnik,
YU-51516 Vrbnik;
tel. 85 11 66.

HOTELS. – IN KRK: *Dražica*, B, 320 b., tel. 85 10 22, with annexes *Dubrava*, 67 b., *Koralj*, 398 b., *Lovorka*, 218 b., and *Bor*, 50 b. – IN OMIŠALJ: *Adriatic I, II and III*, B, 572 b., tel. 88 80 15, with annexes *Bodulka*, 54 b., and *Jadran*, 20 b. IN PUNAT: *Park*, B, 423 b., tel. 85 41 40, with annexes *Kostarika*, 26 b., and *Kvarner*, 64 b.; *International*, C, 75 b., tel. 85 51 84. – IN BAŠKA: *Corinthia*, 244 b., tel. 85 68 24, with annexes *Adria*, 66 b., *Baška*, 55 b., *Mirna*, 14 b., *Strand*, 16 b., *Zvonimir*, 152 b., *Bungalows*, 40 b., and *Velebit*, 56 b. – IN MALINSKA: *Palace*, A, 464 b., tel. 88 55 66; *Tamaris*, B, 645 b., tel. 88 54 05; *Malin*, 166 b., tel. 88 55 31, with annexes *Draga*, 59 b., and *Bungalows*, 40 b.; *Slavija*, 79 b., tel. 88 55 26, with annexes *Kvarner*, 24 b., and *Marina I and II*, 105 b.; *Triglav*, 70 b., tel. 88 55 04, with annexe *Jadran*, 34 b. – IN VRBNIK: *Vrbeniče na Moru*, 27 b., tel. 85 11 66, with annexe *Galeb*, 24 b.

CAMP SITES. – IN KRK: *Ježevac*, tel. 85 10 81. – IN PUNAT: *Punat*, tel. 85 41 01. – IN BAŠKA: *Bunculuka*, tel. 85 68 24; *Zablaće*, tel. 85 68 24.

NATURIST FACILITIES. – *Akapulka* camp site at Punat, run by Park Hotel, Punat (access by land only on footpath; cars left in Punat; transport of camping gear by motorboat; caravans also transported by boat); new naturist site (1979) at Baška.

SPORT, BOATING and BATHING. – Between 1969 and 1971 the hotel board invested well over $18,000,000/£10,000,000 in the construction of the **Haludovo** resort complex, with accommodation for 1500 visitors, at the quiet little village of Malinska. An above-average standard of comfort and amenity is provided by two hotels and by various holiday chalets (bungalows), villas and apartments built in the style of an old fishing village. There are facilities for every kind of sport – tennis courts, mini-golf, a fleet of boats for rent, water-skiing and surfing instruction, even a floating stage for performances of folk dancing and singing in the evening. Included in the complex is a rehabilitation center with a staff of doctors.

Krk offers facilities for scuba diving, water-skiing, tennis and bowling; also boat rental. Owners of sail boats and motorboats prefer Punat, which has a marina with stocks of spare parts. Naturists leave their cars in Punat and take a motorboat which conveys them and their camping gear to the **Akapulka** camp site, which extends around three coves. Caravan trailers (maximum length 21 ft/6·50 m) are loaded on to a pontoon which is then towed to Akapulka by several motorboats. The restaurant and service facilities (including a number of holiday chalets) are run by the Park Hotel, Punat. A new naturist site was opened at Baška in 1979.

The bay at Punat is too shallow to allow the larger ships to come in to the quay; passengers are therefore embarked and disembarked by launch. The islands around Krk offer magnificent scope for sailing enthusiasts, with the uninhabited island of Plavnik, the larger island of Cres and Rab, to the S, all within easy reach. Landing on the island of Prvić (penal establishment) is prohibited.

ACCESS. – Bridge from mainland. Rijeka airport is on Krk.

The island of Krk in the northern Adriatic, lying opposite the town of Crikvenica, is the largest in Yugoslavia. Most of the population is concentrated in the lower and more fertile northern part of the island; the limestone hills in the S have only a sparse growth of vegetation. The chief place on the island, Krk town, is on the W coast, sheltered from the bora. The economy is based on agriculture and sheep-farming, with the tourist trade an important additional source of revenue.

HISTORY. – Krk was occupied by an Illyrian tribe, the Liburni, and there was at least a temporary Greek settlement on the island. It was taken by the Romans in the 2nd c. B.C., and during the war between Caesar

A rocky creek on the island of Krk

and Pompey there was a naval battle off the island in which Pompey's forces were victorious. In 395, when the Roman Empire was divided into two, Krk fell to Byzantium. In 480 Christians in what is now Krk town began to build a basilica on the site of a Roman bath-house, and the external walls and columns of this church, repeatedly altered and enlarged, have survived the passage of 1500 years almost unscathed.

Between the 9th and 12th c. the island was ruled by the Croatian kings. Thereafter it came under control of the Venetians, who appointed Count Frankopan, a Croatian, as ruler of the island. The Frankopan family maintained their sway from 1118 to 1480. Then, in face of the increasing danger of Turkish occupation, Venice took over the administration itself, and continued to hold Krk until 1797. Napoleon incorporated the island in his Illyrian Provinces for a brief period, after which it passed to Austria-Hungary. The treaty of Rapallo (1920) assigned Krk not to Italy, like the neighbouring islands of Cres and Lošinj, but to the new kingdom of Yugoslavia. During the Second World War it was occupied by the Italians, later (1943) replaced by Germans. After Krk became part of the new People's Republic of Yugoslavia in 1945 many of the Italian inhabitants left.

The tourist development of the island began in the late sixties, at a time when it still had no asphalted roads. The Rijeka airport is now at the N end of the island. In addition to the bridge which now connects it with the mainland, replacing the earlier ferry crossing from Črišnjeva and Voz, there are ferry services between Crikvenica and Šilo and between Senj and Baška. At Malinska, on the W coast, there is a new oil port for large tankers, from which crude oil is pumped in a pipeline over the new bridge to the mainland and on to Hungary.

GLAGOLITIC SCRIPT. – The Glagolitic script used in writing Old Slavonic, which resembles the Coptic or Armenian alphabet more than any European script, was devised in the 9th c. by Cyril, the "Apostle of the Slavs": it is not certain whether this script or the other early Slavonic script, the Cyrillic, is the older. The Glagolitic script developed two distinct forms, the angular Croatian form and a more rounded form. It spread so rapidly that two councils held at Split in 925 and 927 launched a vigorous attack on churchmen who used the script and also preached in Croatian instead of in Latin. Glagolitic soon became a symbol of the resistance by patriotic Slavs to the alien clergy under Roman control, and the pro-Slav priests, the glagoljaši, were persecuted. At a further council in 1060 the adherents of Rome finally triumphed over their opponents, but the Glagolitic script and the Old Croatian language continued in use on the islands, particularly on Krk, and in the 13th c., by Papal decree, the use of Glagolitic was permitted in the diocese of Senj and on Krk. Until the end of the 15th c. books, charters, registers and statutes were printed in Glagolitic; and the first printed book of the Southern Slavs, a missal of 1483, is in Glagolitic script. By the beginning of the 16th c. there were Glagolitic printing presses at Rijeka and on Krk; but from now on the script was used only for ecclesiastical purposes. A famous codex of 1395 on which the French kings swore their coronation oath was written in Glagolitic. One of the oldest documents in the Croatian language and in Glagolitic script is the charter, inscribed on a stone tablet, recording a donation by the Croatian king Zvonimir to the Benedictines. The original of the tablet is now in the Zagreb museum; there is a copy in Baška. Another Glagolitic tablet can be seen in the village of Valun on the island of Cres (see p. 69).

The chief place and principal port on the island is the town of **Krk**, in a bay on the W coast. It is still surrounded by remains of the old *town walls*; the watch-tower at the main entrance to the town bears a carving of the lion of St Mark, like so many other buildings on the Adriatic islands. Continuing from the gate, past stalls selling souvenirs, we come to Tito Square, beyond which, concealed from direct view by houses, is the **Frankopan Castle** (1197). To one side stands the *Bishop's Palace*, which contains a collection of 16th and 17th c. pictures. The **Cathedral**, originally built on the site of a Roman bath-house and subsequently enlarged, lies just off the square. To the N of the town is a Gothic *Franciscan church*. Life moves at a tranquil pace around the harbour, which now contains more motor yachts carrying vacationers than active fishing boats. Every evening the restaurants on the seafront promenade are lively and noisy, with music which can be heard on the opposite side of the bay.

From Krk a hilly road runs around the bay to the little town of **Punat**, with many weekend and holiday chalets on the slopes above it. Just before Punat, on the right, are a small boatyard and the boating marina, which is due to be enlarged in the next few years. – Punat's principal feature of interest, a *Franciscan friary*, lies away from the village in a wide bay on the islet of *Košljun*. Above the doorway is the Glagolitic inscription "Mir i dobra" ("Peace and goodness"). Visitors are shown the gravestone of one of the last of the Frankopan family, Princess Katherine, who died in 1529. In the *library* is a dugout canoe, of a type still used at Punat at the

Akapulka, near Punat (Krk)

end of the 19th c., together with cos-tumes, kitchen equipment and Glagolitic vestments. The *church* contains a pol-yptych by Girolamo da Santa Croce and a "Last Judgment" by Ughetti.

From Punat a donkey-track leads to the next coastal village, **Stara Baška**, whose normal communications are by boat. The village, above the sea on the slopes of the island's highest hill, Obzova (1867 ft/569 m), is in a state of decline and many of the houses are mere ruins.

Baška, on the island of Krk

The next village, **Baška**, is connected with Krk town by bus. In the church was found the oldest Glagolitic inscription (see above); the tablet now to be seen here is a copy. Baška has a long pebble beach, and there is good walking in the beautiful fertile plain inland from the village.

Vrbnik, opposite the town of Novi Vinodol on the mainland, lies at the top of steep cliffs, from which there is a breath-taking * view of the coastal mountain range. Much of the medieval town has been preserved, including old stone houses and churches. The altarpiece in the *Church of the Assumption* was painted in Venice by an artist from Kotor. Here too there are Glagolitic inscriptions – one on the sacristy window, another in the Lady Chapel and a third on the rear wall of the cemetery chapel.

Šilo, where the ferries from Crikvenica put in, is no more than a huddle of houses on the coast and along the road running up into the hills.

Omišalj, the first village beyond the new bridge, situated on the cliffs, was once a fortified settlement controlling the seaway to Rijeka. It has a fine Romanesque basilica (13th c.) with a notable treasury.

Njivice is a quiet little holiday village. Beyond it is **Malinska**, with the largest tourist complex on the island, Haludovo, notable for its ultra-modern architecture.

Krka Falls

Republic: Croatia (Hrvatska).
ⓘ **Turističko Društvo Skradin,**
YU-59222 Skradin;
tel. 7 10 90.

The *Krka Falls are one of the most notable tourist attractions between Zadar and Split, although tourist groups are usually taken to see only the last and highest of the eight cataracts on the River Krka between its source to the E of Knin (37 miles/ 60 km from Šibenik) and the town of Skradin. The river has been tamed, however, by the harnessing of its water to provide electric power, and in a dry summer it has a very scanty flow.

Knin, reached from Šibenik on an asphalted road running inland to the NE, was occupied in prehistoric times; later it was a Roman settlement, probably known as *Arduba*. On *Mt Spas* is a large and well-preserved medieval castle, which was

Skradin Falls

much enlarged and strengthened down to the 18th c. It affords a fine view of the surrounding plain. The *Franciscan friary* in the village has a fine collection of old Croatian art. On market days the local peasants still wear the old traditional costumes and sell beautiful embroidery and lace to the few tourists who come this way.

From Knin a bad road (signposted to Kistanje) goes off on the right and runs parallel with the river to the remains of the Roman fort of *Burnum*. To the right of the road, 1¼ miles/2 km from the fort, are the ruins of a fortified Roman settlement, with remains of an amphitheatre, a water supply system, a road and burial mounds. The settlement was destroyed by the Avars in 639.

The Falls. – The first fall is near the source of the river. Below Knin the little river widens into *Lake Marasović*. The lake and the next falls can be reached only on foot (narrow track on left bank).

Farther downstream is *Lake Bobodol* (Bobodolsko Jezero), beyond which are two cataracts, the *Brljan Slap* and the **Manojlovac Slap**, which has a fall of 205 ft/62 m. 1 mile/1·5 km beyond this is the *Miljačka Slap*, below which, on either side of the river, are the two ruined castles of *Trošenj* (to W) and *Nečmen* (to E).

4 miles/6 km farther downstream is the Orthodox *Monastery of the Archangel* (Sv. Arhandjel), with an interesting treasury.

4½ miles/7 km S of the monastery we come to the **Roški Slap** (main fall 50 ft/15 m high), which can also be reached from Šibenik by road (via Drniš). The river now widens to form Lake Visovac. On a small island in the lake is the *Franciscan friary* of Visovac (15th c.), a fine complex of buildings which includes a library containing Turkish firmans and early Croatian editions of Aesop's fables.

At the end of the lake the River *Čikola* flows into it from the E, and immediately beyond this is the *Skradinski Buk (Skradin Falls; also accessible by road from Skradin), where the river falls 150 ft/45 m in 17 "steps". Nearby are a camp site, a restaurant and a pumping station which supplies Šibenik with its water. The area around the falls is a nature reserve.

S of Skradin the Krka flows through the *Skradin Canal* into the 9 mile/15 km long

Lake Prokljan (Prokljansko Jezero). The river then passes under a road bridge and flows into the Adriatic at **Šibenik** (see p. 194).

It is also possible to take a motorboat trip to the Skradin Falls, walk along the falls and get a connecting boat on Lake Visovac which sails past the Franciscan friary to the Roški Slap. Visitors can sail their own boats (maximum draught 40 in./1 m) up the river and the canal to Skradin; to the N of the town the river is spanned by a bridge.

Leskovac

Republic: Serbia (Srbija).
Altitude: 820 ft/250 m. – Population: 45,000.
Post code: YU-16000. – Telephone code: 0 16.
ⓘ **Turist Biro,**
Bulevar Predsednika Tita;
tel. 4 11 00.

HOTELS. – *Motel Atina*, B, 72 b., tel. 4 16 79; *Beograd*, C, 185 b., tel. 4 20 42.

CAMP SITE. – *Atina*, tel. 4 14 71.

Leskovac, lying just off the Niš–Skopje highway to the W, is an industrial town whose economy is based on the production of textiles – an industry first established here in the 18th c. An international Textile Fair, with a reputation extending far beyond the bounds of Yugoslavia, is held here annually in July. For the ordinary tourist the town is of interest mainly as the starting point of a trip to the fascinating Byzantine ruins of Caričin Grad, 19 miles/30 km SW near the little town of Lebane.

Gastronomically Leskovac is noted for its roasts and grills, which tempt many a traveller to leave the highway at this point. A favourite speciality is Leskovačka mučkalica (grilled cubes of veal or pork, steamed in earthenware pots and seasoned with onions, paprika and peppers).

HISTORY. – Leskovac, in a fertile plain watered by the southern Morava and other rivers and now covered by tobacco plantations, fields of wheat and poppies and fruit orchards, was probably founded in Byzantine times. It first appears in the records under its present name in 1308. Then and in subsequent centuries the town was mainly a staging point for trading caravans and troops travelling between N and S. The few surviving Turkish buildings in the old town were destroyed during the Second World War.

SIGHTS. – This industrial town has little in the way of historic old buildings to attract the tourist, apart from an old *church*

In Svetoilijski Park, Leskovac

(restored 1839) containing fine beech-wood carvings, and two old *Balkan-style houses*. One of the old houses now contains the **Municipal Museum** (Uči-telja Josifa Ul. 2), with material of folk interest and finds from Caričin Grad.

SURROUNDINGS. – The site of **Caričin Grad** is reached by taking the country road from Leskovac to Priština (signposted to *Lebane*) and turning right in Lebane, from which it is 4½ miles/7 km to Caričin Grad. (19 miles/30 km beyond Lebane the road to Priština becomes so bad that it should not be contemplated: better to return to Leskovac).

The reign of the emperor Justinian (527–565) has left two major monuments in Yugoslavia, the basilica of Poreč on the Adriatic coast, with its fine mosaics, and the site of Caričin Grad (the "City of the Empress"). It is not certain whether this is the imperial city of *Iustiniana Prima*: the emperor's monogram on one of the capitals in the citadel is not sufficient to prove this.

The town, built on a plateau at the junction of the rivers Caričina and Svinjarica, was surrounded by walls and towers; so far two town gates have been discovered. It had a population of some 10,000, and the excavations have revealed evidence of a flourishing community – workshops, shops, churches, administrative buildings, cisterns, baths and a variety of other buildings.

In the middle of the town is a large circular space where four streets meet. One leads to a three-aisled cathedral, 215 ft/65 m long, with a mosaic pavement, columns and a water tank holding a reserve supply in case of siege. Another street leads to a large basilica with a crypt.

Outside the walls were smaller settlements, another church and a whole system of fortified outposts. Below the town on the River Caričina a dam was discovered which diverted water to supply a black-smith's forge on the banks of the river. The town was

destroyed in the 7th c. by Slavs, who left traces of their passage in the form of implements, weapons and coins, and hearths within the ruined buildings.

The excavations so far suggest that Caričin Grad has still many secrets to reveal. Finds made at deeper levels point to an earlier settlement here in the 3rd c.

Lipica

Republic: Slovenia (Slovenija).
Altitude: 1319 ft/402 m. – Population: 100.
Post code: YU-66210. – Dialling code: 0 67.
ⓘ **Hotel Maestoso,**
tel. 7 30 09.

HOTELS. – *Maestoso*, B, 175 b., tel. 7 30 09; *Lipica*, B, 204 b., tel. 7 35 41.

SPORT. – Riding (instruction available).

The stud-farm which breeds the world-famous white Lipizzaner horses to be seen at the Spanish Riding School in Vienna lies near Sežana, close to the Italian frontier to the E of Trieste. Visitors can see the stables with 200 horses, 20 or 25

Lipica stud-farm

of which are available at any given time for performances of dressage; but they can also learn to ride here, pass various tests of skill in riding and dressage, and they can enjoy riding in the beautiful surrounding country.

Lipica celebrated the 400th anniversary of its foundation in 1980.

HISTORY. – The stud was established in 1580 by Archduke Charles of Austria, then ruler of Carniola, Istria and Trieste. This area was selected because it had been noted since Roman times for breeding horses of great strength, speed and stamina. The stud's function was to supply good riding and draught horses for the court in Vienna and the archduke's own capital of Graz. Horses considered suitable for the new stud – white, of handsome appearance, high-stepping

– were purchased by Baron Khevenhüller in Spain, and others were later acquired at Rovigo in Italy. They were joined by horses from the royal stud at Frederiksborg in Denmark, which, like all the others, were of Arab descent.

During the reign of Maria Theresa (1740–80) Lipica had 150 stud mares. In 1796, when Austria was at war with France, the stud, with 300 horses, was moved to Székesfehérvár in Hungary. The stud had to leave Lipica again in 1805, after the French had appropriated the best of its breeding stock, and yet again in 1809, when it was transferred for the second time to Hungary. After it returned to Lipica in 1815 the emperor Franz Joseph I decided that it should stay there, and thereafter it remained undisturbed until the First World War. When Italy entered the war in 1915 the stud was moved to Laxenburg, near Vienna, while the young horses found temporary quarters at the court stud-farm of Kladruby in Bohemia. When Lipica passed to Italy in 1920 there were 107 horses on the stud-farm; Austria was left with 97, which were used to build up a Lipizzaner stud at Piber, and this stud still supplies horses to the Spanish Riding School in Vienna. A Lipizzaner stud was also established at Topol'čianky in Slovakia.

During the Second World War the stud was transferred after the Italian surrender to Hostinec in Czechoslovakia, where the Lipizzaners from Piber were also housed, together with horses from the Yugoslav stud of Duvanovo and the Polish stud of Janov. In 1945, in face of the Russian advance, General Patton transferred the horses to Schwarzenberg in Austria. In May of that year, soon after the German surrender, the director of the Spanish Riding School took over responsibility for the horses, which were moved to Italy, then to Austria and finally in the autumn of 1947 (then only 13 in number) back to Yugoslavia.

The typical Lipizzaner horse is of noble appearance and medium height, with long legs and great staying power. The head is handsome, with large lively eyes, the glance intelligent and friendly. The neck should be of medium length, set high, the back long and straight.

Visitors see the horses in the stables, ranging at liberty and also in use as draught animals, as well as in the famous displays of dressage. There are also package tours covering a week's hotel accommodation, riding instruction and a final test of skill.

Lipizzaners in the Spanish Riding School, Vienna

Ljubljana

Republic: Slovenia (Slovenija).
Altitude: 961 ft/293 m. – Population: 302,000.
Post code: YU-61000. – Telephone code: 0 61.
ⓘ **Turistični Informacijski Biro,**
Titova 11;
tel.2 32 12.
Ljubljanska Turistična Zveza,
Titova 168.

HOTELS. – *Holiday Inn*, L, 215 b., SB, tel. 2 45 07; *Lev*, A, 336 b., tel. 31 05 55; *Union*, B, 440 b., tel. 2 45 07; *Turist*, B, 260 b., tel. 32 20 43; *Slon*, B, 247 b., tel. 2 46 01; *Ilirija*, B, 216 b., tel. 55 12 45; *Kompas*, B, 122 b., tel. 32 60 61; *Gostilna pri Mraku*, B, 62 b., tel. 2 34 36.

CAMP SITES. – *Avtocamp Ježica*, Titova 260a, tel. 34 11 13 (with indoor swimming pool, mini-golf and bowling alleys); *Dragočajna*, on Zbiljsko Jezero, near Medvode.

RESTAURANTS. – *Podrožnik-Čad*, Cesta na Rožnik 34, tel. 2 01 09; *Pri Vitezu*, Breg 18–20, tel. 2 46 85; *Slon*, Titova 10, tel. 2 46 01; *Tikveš*, Draga, Ljubljana-Šiška, tel. 55 78 93. – *Šestica* (garden restaurant), Titova 6.

EVENTS. – *Ljubljana Festival*, annually in July–August; *International Biennale of Graphic Art*, June–August in alternate years (in Modern Gallery).

SPORT. – *Tivoli* sports park (indoor swimming pool, tennis courts, mini-golf, bowling alleys, keep-fit trails, skating); *Kodeljevo* (swimming pool, bowling alleys).

AIRPORT: Ljubljana. JAT office: Miklošičeva Cesta 34, tel. 31 43 40.

Visitors arriving in Ljubljana, capital of the republic of Slovenia, are greeted by extensive modern residential districts: it takes some time before they reach the old town, dominated by the castle on its hill. The city has doubled its population in the last 25 years and is steadily expanding farther N. Of all Yugoslav towns Ljubljana has the highest average income per head. This is also a town of young people, with more than 15,000 students in addition to the pupils of its numerous schools.

Ljubljana has contrived a happy synthesis between its monuments of the past and its modern buildings. That the town once belonged to Austria can be seen from the style of the buildings in its older streets, but its atmosphere has all the friendly cosmopolitanism of Slovenia. A walk along the little River Ljubljanica, spanned by arched bridges of Venetian design, is a captivating experience. The narrow little streets and courtyards of the old town

Ljubljana, with the castle

have all the charm of the past, but in the newer business streets of Ljubljana the same bustle and urgency is felt as in the cities of northern Europe.

HISTORY. – The settlement of *Emona* was founded by Illyrians in the first millennium B.C. in this valley basin enclosed by the last outliers of the Calcareous Alps, at the intersection of the "amber road" from the Baltic to the Mediterranean and the military and trade route between the Adriatic and Pannonia. In 34 B.C. Emona was granted municipal status by Augustus.

During the great migrations the Roman town seems to have disappeared, for in the 7th c. A.D. Slovenes coming from the E founded a new settlement which they called *Lubigana* – a name which first appears in the records in 1142.

In 1270 Ottokar of Bohemia captured the town, and in 1282 the province of Carniola and its capital Ljubljana passed to the House of Habsburg. During the 14th c. the town was exposed to repeated Turkish attacks. From the beginning of the period of Habsburg rule German or German-speaking citizens increasingly occupied official posts and leading positions, while at the same time Slovenian life and culture were able to develop freely. Thus in the 16th c. the Ljubljana Reformer Primož Trubar, the "Slovenian Luther", translated the Bible into his own language and, like Luther established a unified vernacular language and literature.

There was an interlude of French rule from 1809 to 1813, when Ljubljana became capital of the Illyrian Provinces. During this period an intellectual and national renewal in Slovenia began to gather strength, with the poets France Prešeren and Valentin Vodnik as its mentors.

In 1895 a devastating earthquake destroyed many of the town's old buildings, mainly those of the Baroque period. The end of the First World War saw also the end of 600 years of Austrian and Habsburg rule. In 1941 there began a further period of foreign occupation; but the Slovenes gave the Italian occupation troops so much trouble that they withdrew into the city and set up a defensive ring of bunkers and barbed wire around it.

Since the end of the last war Ljubljana has been in the throes of unprecedented industrial and economic development.

SIGHTS. – The best starting point for a walk around the town is the spacious **Liberation Square** (*Trg Osvoboditve*). The main traffic artery is the *Titova Cesta*.

At the W end of Liberation Square is the **Ursuline church** (*Uršulinska Cerkev*), the town's finest Baroque church, with an imposing facade (massive columns, Doric cornice, pediment with pointed arches). On the N side of the square lies a park, from which a pedestrian underpass leads into the more modern part of the town. At the NW corner stands the *Kazina Palace*, formerly a casino, with a frontage of Doric columns. On the S side of the square is the *Old University*.

To the W of the Ursuline church extends the large *Revolution Square* (Trg Revolucije). To the N of this, beyond Šubičeva Ulica, lies *Heroes' Square* (Trg Herojev), with the *Heroes' Vault* and a bronze statue of the Carniolan historian *Weikhard von Valvasor*. On the E side of the Square is the *Parliament* of the republic of Slovenia, on the W side the **National Museum**.

Bridges over the Ljubljanica

The ethnographic department contains Slovenian *costumes, jewelry* and *domestic equipment*. In the department of antiquities are remains of *pile-dwellings* from the Ljubljana area. A notable feature of the section of folk art is the unique collection of painted *beehive boards* (the boards above the entrance to the hive which were decorated in a naive style of painting with the idea of guiding the bees to their hive). Boards of this kind (usually modern copies, but nevertheless attractive and unusual souvenirs) are to be found in antique shops in Ljubljana.

NE of the National Museum, beyond Tomšičeva Ulica, is the **Slovenian**

National Opera House, which has an international repertoire. A little way W of the Opera House is the *Modern Gallery*.

Some 330 yd/300 m S of Liberation Square is **French Revolution Square** (*Trg Francoske Revolucije*). On the S side of this square is the former headquarters of the Teutonic Order, with the *Križanke* or Church of the Teutonic Order (13th c., remodelled in Baroque style in 17th c.), in the courtyard of which are remains of the Roman town walls. Here the Ljubljana Festival (open-air performances, folk events) is held annually in July and August. The "Peasant Wedding" (Kmečka Ohcet- with dancing) in May, in which bridal couples from all over Europe took part, is no longer held.

On the E side of the square stands the *Auersperg Palace*, now housing the **Municipal Museum**. In the square in front of the courtyard the *Illyrian Column* commemorates the period of more than four years when Ljubljana was capital of the French Illyrian Provinces.

NE of Liberation Square is the Head Post Office, and to the E of this *Prešeren Square* (Prešernov Trg), named after the poet and intellectual mentor of Slovenia, *France Prešeren* (1800–49). A bronze statue of Prešeren looks on to the busy traffic intersection of **Tromostovje** ("Three Bridges") and the swarms of people who cross the River Ljubljanica here from morning until night. The road bridge and two pedestrian bridges here link the city hub with the old town and the market. On the N side of the square stands the massive Baroque **Franciscan church** (17th c.).

NW of Prešeren Square is a modern landmark of Ljubljana, the **Nebotičnik Building**, a tower building in Titova Cesta (elevator to the top: not worth while). Most visitors confuse this with another more modern high-rise building. – To the NW of the town are various sports facilities and the *Museum of the Revolution*.

On the other side of the Ljubljanica are two notable buildings – the **Town Hall** and the **Cathedral**. In front of the Town Hall a marble *fountain*, with three dolphins spouting water, symbolises the rivers Sava, Krka and Ljubljanica. It is worth looking into the courtyard of the

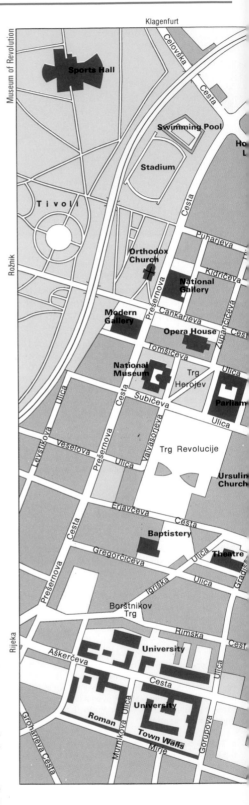

Town Hall to see the *murals* depicting battles for the town (the representation of the attacking Turks being particularly vivid). The Cathedral has *ceiling paintings* by Giulio Quaglio. Nearby in the square a

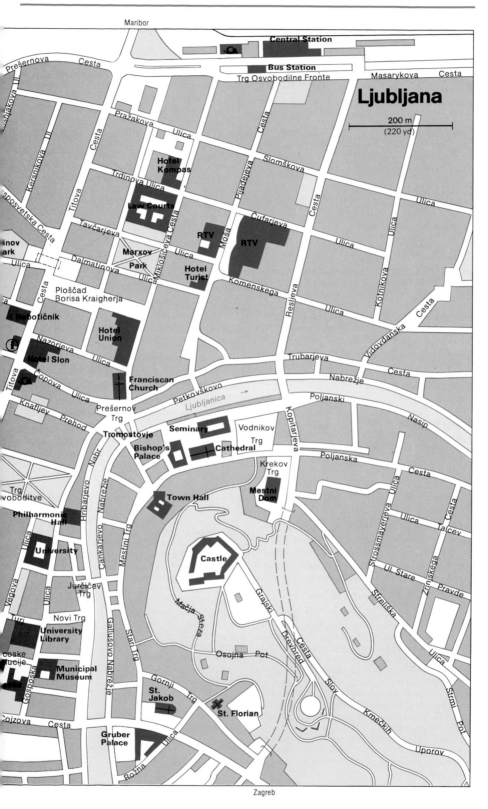

lively *vegetable market* is held every morning.

Above the city looms the **Castle**, once residence of the feudal lords of the town. It affords a magnificent *view over the *old town* to the Kamniške Alpe, the Julian Alps and the Karavanke (Karawanken) range.

Lošinj

Republic: Croatia (Hrvatska).
Area of island: 29 sq. miles/75 sq. km. –
Population: 8000.
Telephone code: 0 51.

ⓘ Turist Biro Mali Lošinj,
Obala Maršala Tita 7,
YU-51550 Mali Lošinj;
tel. 86 10 11.
Turist Biro Veli Lošinj,
YU-51551 Veli Lošinj;
tel. 86 12 83.
Turistički Ured Nerezine,
YU-51554 Nerezine;
tel. 86 11 66.
Turistički Ured Ilovik,
YU-51552 Ilovik;
tel. 86 12 31.

HOTELS. – IN MALI LOŠINJ: *Auroa* and *Vespera*, A, 1500
b., tel. 86 13 24; *Bellevue*, B, 414 b., tel. 86 12 22, with
annexe *Villa Dubrovnik*, B, 34 b.; *Helios*, B, 262 b., tel.
86 12 26, with annexes *Villa Karlovac*, B, 32 b., and
Villa Rijeka, B, 44 b., and *Bungalows*, B, 120 b.;
Alhambra, B, 86 b., tel. 86 10 50, with annexes *Villa
Sarajevo*, C, 11 b., and *Villa Zadar*, C, 19 b.; *Čikat*, C,
85 b., with annexe *Villa Flora*, C, 16 b.; *Istra*, C, 43 b.,
tel. 86 10 50. – IN VELI LOŠINJ: *Punta*, B, 315 b., tel. 86
10 22. – IN NEREZINE: accommodation in private houses
(apply to Tourist Office).

CAMP SITES. – IN MALI LOŠINJ: *Čikat*, tel. 86 14 10;
Poljana, tel. 86 10 77, with yacht harbour. – IN VELI
LOŠINJ: *Punta*, tel. 86 10 22. – IN NEREZINE: *Rapoča*, tel.
81 10 77, with a small harbour.

NATURIST FACILITIES. – Beaches at Mali Lošinj,
near Čikat Bay; other sites at Aurora and Vespera
Hotels; naturist solarium at Veli Lošinj; naturist
camping on the little island of Veli Orjul which is not
permanently inhabited (tents only; transport of gear
on fishing boats from Mali Lošinj harbour; water
supply by arrangement).

EVENTS. – *Winter Cup of Nations* and *New Year's
Cup of Cities* (international underwater fishing
contests), end of Decmber.

SPORT, BOATING and BATHING. – Scuba diving,
water-skiing; tennis; bowling; hill walking. – The best
known bathing beach is **Čikat Bay**, near the hotel
complex in a wooded coastal area SW of Mali Lošinj.
At the height of the season it is usually overcrowded.
To the S, after a number of small coves belonging to
hotels but open to the public, is a naturist area (no
shade). Beyond this, as far as the cape at the S end of
the island, are other coves, some of them with small
sandy beaches, which can be reached on bridle-paths
but are more quickly and easily accessible by boat. On
the E side of the island the bathing is not so good: the
beach at the entrance to Veli Lošinj harbour tends to
be crowded, and the only good beaches are a few near
Nerezine, to the N.

The large natural harbour of **Mali Lošinj** is popular
with sailing enthusiasts. The Privlaka Channel allows
motorboats and small sail boats to leave the harbour
basin to the E, and there is a marina here with a slip,
winch and service facilities. The sheltered E side of the
island and the proximity of other islands (Oruda, Mali
Orjul and Veli Orjul, which has a naturist camp site)
make these waters ideal for less experienced sailors.

The calm water, particularly in the Mali Lošinj bay,
provides good conditions for water-skiing. The newer
hotels all have tennis courts with artificial lighting. It is
difficult to find a motorboat for rent. There are daily
trips to the islands of Susak, Unije, Cres and Hvar. At
Veli Lošinj there is a naturist medical center for those
"taking the cure"; the largest naturist center, run and
supplied from Mali Lošinj, is opposite the town on the
southernmost tip of the island of Cres (the *Baldarin*
center).

FERRIES. – Connections with the mainland via the
island of *Cres* (bridge): car ferries Porozina–Brestova,
Porozina–Rijeka, and also Pula–Lošinj–Zadar. Passenger services: Pula–Ilovik–Unije–Mali Lošinj–Silba–
Olib–Rab; also fast hydrofoil services.

**Subtropical vegetation and a
climate in which the thermometer
never falls below freezing have
made the island of Lošinj (area 29 sq.
miles/75 sq. km), lying 43 miles/70
km S of Rijeka, a popular resort frequented throughout the year. Official statistics show that it averages
300 cloudless or practically cloudless days in the year. During the 19th
c. asthma sufferers were already
flocking to Lošinj to seek alleviation
of their complaint in a combination
of fresh sea air and aromatic vegetation. This "spa" aspect now plays a
relatively minor role: what now
attracts most visitors to the island is
the facilities for water sports.**

HISTORY. – Like the neighbouring island of Cres,
Lošinj was already occupied by man in the Neolithic
period, as has been shown by finds in caves on the
steep W coasts of both islands. From the Bronze and
Iron Ages date the remains of some 50 fortified
settlements with stone ramparts which have been
found all over the area. About 1200 B.C. both islands
were settled by Ilyrians, who are described by
contemporary writers as daring seamen and dreaded
pirates. Whether the Greeks reached as far as Cres and
Lošinj has not been established. At the end of the
3rd c. B.C. the Romans established, on the channel
between Lošinj and Cres, the fortified town of *Absorus*
(present-day Osor), which soon had a population of
30,000. After the Slav occupation of the early 7th c.
Osor continued under Byzantine sovereignty, which
came to an end only in 842 when the Saracens
captured and sacked the town. The early 10th c. saw
the establishment of the first independent Croatian
state under King Tomislav, of which Lošinj and Cres
now became part. In 1018 Doge Orseolo II took Osor
with a Venetian fleet, but 50 years later King Krešimir
IV of Croatia recovered both islands.

In the following three centuries Lošinj and Cres
alternated between Croatian and Venetian control.
The victors always established themselves in Osor, but
paid little attention to the now almost uninhabited
island of Lošinj, which was regarded as good only for
grazing sheep. In the 15th c. Osor was depopulated by
malaria. During the 16th and 17th c. the Turks did not
venture on to the islands; but there were frequent raids
on the coastal settlements by pirates from Senj. Better
days for Lošinj began only after the Congress of

The picturesque little town of Mali Lošinj

Vienna (1815) gave Austria back its former possessions in Dalmatia and the northern Adriatic.

In 1854 the Austrian authorities founded a school of seamanship on Lošinj. This was followed by the establishment of shipyards on the island, and in 1875 the emperor Franz Joseph came to Mali Lošinj for the launching of the "Imperatrice Elisabetta" ("Empress Elizabeth"). Soon afterwards, however, the age of sail ended and the shipyards fell into decline. Then phylloxera destroyed the vineyards of Cres and to a lesser extent those of Lošinj, and the inhabitants increasingly drifted away from the islands. The situation improved from about 1880 with the beginnings of the tourist and holiday trade, and thereafter Mali Lošinj and Veli Lošinj took on a new lease of life.

The treaty of Rapallo in 1920 assigned Lošinj and Cres, together with the surrounding smaller islands, not to the new kingdom of Yugoslavia but to Italy, which pursued a radical policy of Italianisation and suppressed the Croatian language and customs. In 1945 Yugoslav partisans landed on Lošinj and Cres, and under the treaty of Paris in 1947 both islands, together with Istria, were incorporated in the republic of Yugoslavia.

SIGHTS. – In **Mali Lošinj** a Venetian tower 112 ft/34 m high adjoining the

church affords magnificent panoramic *views over the sea and the neighbouring islands. **St Mary's Church** (1676), with a handsome Baroque façade, has a notable high altar, with the *reliquary* of the martyred St Romulus , the *Altar of the Cross* (by the Venetian sculptor Ferrari) and the *Patronal Altar* on the N wall, which has figures of the islands' patron saints – St Gaudentius (Cres), St Quirinus (Krk) and St Christopher (Rab). From the church a path leads up to the 15th c. **Castle**. The churchyard of St Martin's Church contains the graves of shipowners and sea-captains. A Way of the Cross, with 14 Baroque stations of the Cross, ascends the *Calvary Hill* (Kalvarija) to the SW of the town. In Čikat Bay is the little *pilgrimage church of the Annunciation*, both side walls of which are covered with ex-votos depicting ships in peril on the sea.

Features of interest in **Veli Lošinj** are the *parish church of St Anthony*; the little

A street in Mali Lošinj

pilgrimage church of St Mary on the promontory; a *watch-tower* of 1455 beyond the first row of houses on the harbour; the *Church of Our Lady of the Angels* (Gospa od Andjela), of 1510; and the old St Joseph's Monastery (Sveti Josip), now the presbytery. Above the town is a wooded park known as the Arboretum. Here in 1885 Archduke Karl Stephan of Austria built his **Wartsee Palace**, set in a beautiful 30 acre park, which now belongs to a sanatorium.

The third largest place on Lošinj is **Nerezine**, now of growing importance as a summer resort. Here and in the neighbouring village of **Sveti Jakob** there is good accommodation to be had in private houses. From both villages there are waymarked paths up to the highest point on the island, **Televrina* (1929 ft/588 m), from the summit of which there are superb views over the sea to the neighbouring islands and the mainland. Accommodation in private houses is also available in **Čunski**, 5 miles/8 km from Mali Lošinj.

The three little islands to the S – Ilovik, Sveti Petar and Kozjak – are a kind of continuation of Lošinj.

Ilovik, with an area of barely 2¼ sq. miles/6 sq. km, is covered with an impermeable clay soil and accordingly, unlike Lošinj, has a number of springs with a considerable flow of water. The only settlement, the attractive little village of *Ilovik*, offers visitors a quiet, traffic-free holiday with accommodation in private houses. The parish church (1878) contains numbers of painted wooden figures made by a woodcarver in what is now the Val Gardena in Italy and presented to the church by American immigrants during the period of Austrian rule. Ilovik produces rich crops of oranges, lemons and vegetables. There are regular boat services from Mali Lošinj and Zadar.

Opposite Ilovik lies the little island of **Sveti Petar**, covered with a rich Mediterranean flora. In the

channel between the two islands is an old watch-tower built for protection against pirates. A large house on the coast is used by Franciscans from Zagreb as a convalescent home.

The third island, **Kozjak**, is uninhabited.

Lovran

Republic: Croatia (Hrvatska).
Altitude: 16 ft/5 m. – Population: 6000.
Post code: YU-51415. – Telephone code: 0 51.
ⓘ **Turističko Društvo,**
　Šetalište Maršala Tita 68;
　tel. 73 10 41.

HOTELS. – *Beograd*, B, 191 b., tel. 73 10 13, with annexe *Villa Frappart*, B, 26 b.; *Splendid*, B, 166 b., tel. 73 11 42, with annexe *Villa Liana*, C, 21 b.; *Lovran*, B, 110 b., tel. 73 10 13; *Park*, B, 104 b., tel. 73 11 26, with annexe *Villa Danica*, C, 29 b.; *Primorka*, B, 43 b., tel. 7 31 66, with annexe *Villa Zagreb*, C, 46 b.; *Magnolia* and *Bungalows*, C, 95 b., tel. 73 10 95; *Miramara*, C, 60 b., tel. 73 11 24, with annexes *Villa Atlanta*, *Elza* and *Eugenia*. C, 95 b.; *Belvoir*, C, 46 b., tel. 73 10 13.

CAMP SITE. – *Medveja*, tel. 73 11 91.

EVENTS. – Folk evenings on open-air stage; Summer Festival in Opatija, 4 miles/6 km away.

SPORT, BOATING and BATHING. – Scuba diving; boccia, tennis, walking. – Bathers are faced with the same problem in Lovran as at Opatija: insufficient room for the number of visitors. Not surprisingly, therefore, the two small stretches of beach (admission charge) are overcrowded, even outside the two main vacation months of July and August. The hotels offer their guests private access to the rocky shore. The sea is not clean, since all the sewers in Lovran flow into it, with outfalls only 100 m from the shore.

The hotels provide full programs of entertainment, and there are also discotheques and night-clubs. Visitors staying at Lovran can also take advantage of the wide range of entertainments and cultural events offered by Opatija. In spite of the shortage of space some hotels have found room for tennis courts. Visitors' boats can be moored in the small harbour.

The camp site lies in a valley running down to the sea from Mt Učka. It suffers from overcrowding, and also has the disadvantage that the Rijeka–Pula road runs immediately in front of it and must be crossed by bathers on their way to the sea; at Opatija this two-lane road (dual carriageway) runs above the town at some distance from the central area, at Lovran it runs right through the middle of town.

Lovran was long overshadowed by the internationally known bathing resort of Opatija, with which it is connected by the finest seafront promenade on the Yugoslav Adriatic coast, running past parks and gardens filled with luxuriant subtropical vegetation. Its rise to popularity began at the turn of the

19th c. It now caters mainly to summer visitors.

HISTORY. – In the 1st c. A.D. a Roman statesman built himself a summer residence at Lovran, a building to which there is a reference in the 6th c. From 1275 the place was held by the Counts of Pazin, and later by the Counts of Görz (Gorizia). It then passed to Venice, which did nothing to help when the town was twice raided and burned down by piratical Uskoks from Senj. In 1153 the Arab cartographer El Idrisi refers to Lovran as important for trade and shipping: the former attribute appears very dubious, but the people of Lovran were undoubtedly ship-owners and seafarers. The little town began to develop a degree of prosperity only after the opening of the Rijeka–Pula road in 1843.

SIGHTS. – Lovran – like Opatija, sheltered from cold N winds by Mt Učka – has few buildings of historical or artistic interest. In the main square stands *St George's Church* (14th c., with 15th c. Gothic vaulting), which contains frescoes (painter unknown) of a quality scarcely to be found elsewhere in Istria, with a 15th c. Glagolitic inscription (on Glagolitic, see under Krk).

In the park outside the town walls is the 13th c. *Trinity Chapel*, with remains of late Gothic wall paintings (15th c.) and a 16th c. Glagolitic tomb inscription. Above the town are the ruins of *Knezrad Castle*.

SURROUNDINGS. – Experienced climbers can climb Mt Učka (4580 ft/1396 m), from the summit of which, in clear weather, there are breathtaking **views. Information about the best route, starting from the Vrata pass, should be obtained in the town.

Makarska

Republic: Croatia (Hrvatska).
Altitude: 16 ft/5 m. – Population: 8000.
Post code: YU-58300. – Telephone code: 0 58.
ⓘ **Turist Biro,**
Titova Obala 2;
tel. 61 16 88.

HOTELS. – *Riviera*, B, 506 b., tel. 61 10 00; *Dalmacija*, B, 360 b., tel. 61 10 77; *Park*, C, 160 b., tel. 61 11 11; *Beograd*, C, 80 b., tel. 61 15 22; *Osejava*, D, 76 b., tel. 61 14 33.

CAMP SITES. – *Dalmacija*, tel. 61 10 00; *Riviera*, tel. 61 10 00; *Savinja*, tel. 61 27 40.

NATURIST FACILITIES. – N of Makarska.

SPORT, BOATING and BATHING. – Makarska Bay offers suitable anchorage for larger coastal craft, but sailing enthusiasts dislike the harbour, since it offers no protection against the bora which blows down from the hills in violent gusts. A safer refuge is offered by Bol and Sumartin on the offshore island of Brač. The Dalmacija Hotel has its own yacht harbour and slip.

Makarska beach, with the Biokovo range in the background

There is a supply point for scuba divers, where gear can be rented and aqualungs refilled. Several hotels have tennis courts, and there are facilities for all kinds of water sports.

The main beach at Makarska is on the **Sveti Petar** peninsula, bordered by a shady pine-grove. Although it is over 1100 yd/1000 m long it is sometimes overcrowded during the main holiday season. The Dalmacija and Riviera hotels have their own beaches. Visitors with their own boat or a rented one will have no difficulty in finding a quiet bathing beach to the S of the town.

The little port of Makarska lies in a wide bay, surrounded by greenery on all sides, at the foot of the rugged Biokovo range, which reaches its highest point in Sveti Juraj (5781 ft/ 1762 m). The local building regulations now require all new buildings to have red tiled roofs: all the more conspicuous, therefore, are a massive concrete hotel situated directly on the coast and a number of apartment buildings behind the town, which contrast strikingly with the picturesque little town nestling at the foot of the hills. Makarska, with the "Makarska Riviera" between Brela and Ploče, offers visitors a comprehensive range of amenities – beautiful beaches, facilities for sport and recreation attached to the hotels and a varied program of evening entertainment.

HISTORY. – The early history of Makarska is obscure, though there is believed to have been a Phoenician settlement in this sheltered bay. As at so many other places along this coast, the later history of Makarska is a long record of destruction. The Roman settlement of *Muccurum* was razed to the ground by Germanicus Caesar in the 1st c. A.D., and in 548 the Ostrogothic king Totila followed his example. Later Venetian pirates found the place ideally suited to their purposes. In 887 the Venetian fleet was defeated in a naval battle off Makarska. Until the 14th c. the town was held by the Croatian and Croatian-Hungarian kings, who were succeeded from 1324 to 1563 by the Bosnian Kotromanić family. Then came the Turks, who once again reduced the town to ruins. They remained in possession until 1646, when they were displaced by the Venetians. Thereafter Makarska passed to Austria, which held it until 1918. During the Second World War the town suffered further destruction by bombing, and the reconstruction of the town suffered a setback in an earthquake in 1962. In consequence of this long series of destructions Makarska has preserved few old buildings.

SIGHTS. – Of the numerous Baroque buildings which once stood around the harbour there remains only one house, with a handsome balcony, to the N of the landing-place on the coast road. In the main square with its small Venetian fountain stands the Baroque *parish church of St Mark*, which has 16th c. icons in the sacristy. In the Jurjevićeva Poljana is the town's finest surviving Baroque building, the **Ivanišević Palace**, which now houses the *Museum of National Liberation*. – To the S of the town, beyond the Sports Complex, where teams from Yugoslavia and other countries train throughout the year, is the *Franciscan friary* (1400; twice restored since then), with a beautiful cloister, a handsome tower and (in the basement) a unique *collection of shells*.

SURROUNDINGS. – Easily reached from Makarska are two peaks in the Biokovo range which are popular with Yugoslav climbers. *Sveti Juraj (5781 ft/1762 m) and Vožac (4662 ft/1421 m). A convenient base is provided by the *Partizan* mountain inn (4495 ft/ 1370 m), which can be reached either on a path from Makarska (via Makar and Velo Brdo) or on a gravel road which branches off the road from Tučepi to the Staza pass. – The local travel agents offer a wide range of excursions by land and by sea – e.g. to Split, Trogir, Mostar and Dubrovnik by coach and to the islands of Hvar and Biševo by boat. Biševo has a *Blue Grotto*, which, like its better known counterpart on Capri, can be reached only in calm weather.

Maribor

Republic: Slovenia (Slovenija).
Altitude: 899 ft/274 m. – Population: 130,000.
Post code: YU-62000. – Telephone code: 0 62.
ⓘ **Turistični Biro,**
   Sodna Ulica 5;
   tel. 2 12 62.

HOTELS. – *Orel*, B, 228 b., tel. 2 61 71; *Turist*, B, 200 b., tel. 2 59 71; *Slavija*, B, 192 b., tel. 2 23 61; *Habakuk*, B, 75 b., tel. 3 36 81; *Motel Jezero* (chalets), C, 60 b., tel. 2 44 17. – IN POHORJE: *Areh Šport Hotel*, B, 50 b., tel. 72 31; *Bellevue*, C, 96 b., tel. 72 05; *Pajkov Dom*, 26 b., tel. 72 09; *Planika*, 26 b., tel. 72 24; *Železničarski Dom*, 86 b., tel. 72 27.

CAMP SITES. – *Bresternica*, tel. 2 44 17, 4½ miles/7 km from the town on the Drava reservoir.

AIRPORT: Maribor. JAT office: Grajski Trg 3, tel. 2 61 55.

Maribor, the second largest town in Slovenia, lies between the Pohorje and Kozjak hills straddling the River Drava. The older buildings in the central part of the town, on the left bank of the river, reflect the fact that Maribor belonged to Austria until 1918 (when it was known as Marburg an der Drau). The newer part of the town on the right bank of the Drava is steadily reaching farther out towards the villages amid the

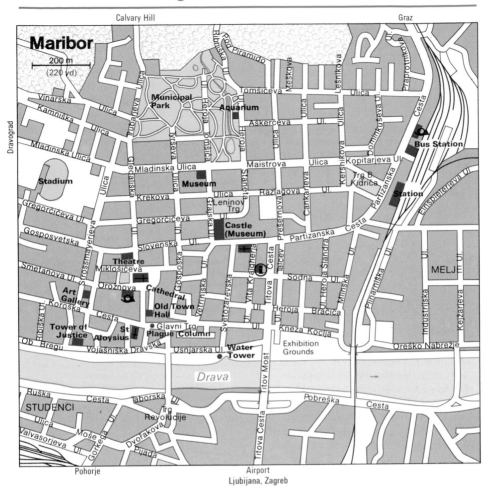

forests and meadows of the beautiful surrounding countryside.

There are relatively few tourist sights in this industrial city, which for most visitors is merely a staging point on their journey. The road from Graz and the Austrian frontier, 11 miles/18 km N, carries heavy traffic, particularly trucks, which prefer this route between Austria and Yugoslavia, crossing the frontier at Spielfeld, with the advantage of not going over a pass. This busy road can be avoided by taking the alternative route via Dravograd and Lavamünd, ascending the beautiful Drava valley, which becomes narrower just above Maribor.

HISTORY. – During the Magyar incursions into Pannonia the area around Maribor was made a frontier lordship, and at the beginning of the 12th c. Bernhard Sponheim, then holder of the lordship, built a castle on Pyramid Hill, styling himself thereafter Count of Marchpurch (the "castle on the marches"). The name *Marburg* first appears in a document of 1257 referring to the construction of a defensive wall around the town. In 1529 and again in 1683 Turkish troops advancing on Vienna devastated the town, and during the Thirty Years War (1618–48) invading armies

brought death and destruction. An outbreak of plague in 1680 is commemorated by the Plague Column in the main square (Glavni Trg) and by St Barbara's Church on the Calvary Hill. After being under Austrian or Styrian rule since 1140 the town, now known as Maribor, was assigned to Yugoslavia in 1918. Since the end of the Second World War Maribor's industries (in particular metalworking and textiles) have been successfully developed.

Plague Column in the Glavni Trg, Maribor

SIGHTS. – In the Glavni Trg, the main square of the OLD TOWN, stands the Renaissance-style **Town Hall** (1565) with its *clock-tower*, and in front of it the *Plague Column* commemorating the 1680 plague. Under the balcony of the Town Hall is a large municipal coat of arms. The Council Chamber has rich stucco decoration, with caryatids supporting the ceiling. – Also in the main square is *St Aloysius's Chapel*, preceded by a wrought-iron grille.

The pedestrian precinct beyond the Town Hall leads to the **Cathedral**, dedicated to St John the Baptist, which was originally built in 1150 as a three-aisled pillared basilica but was substantially altered in the 17th c. In the Gothic choir (16th c.) are the *Bishop's Throne* and a statue of the first Prince-Bishop of Marburg, A. M. Slomšek.

NE of the Cathedral, in the middle of the town, is the **Castle**, with a large courtyard now used for industrial purposes. In front of the castle stands a *Monument of the Struggle for National Liberation*. The castle itself now houses the *Regional Museum*. In the great hall is a ceiling painting which depicts among other things a battle with the Turks.

Passing along the street on the left bank of the Drava, at the corner of Prištaniška Street, we see a massive *round tower* known as the Tower of Justice. Going E towards the *Drava Bridge*, we pass the **Venetian House** and then, beyond the ramp leading up to the bridge, the *Jew's*

Tower and the *Water Tower*. Beyond the next bridge are the *Exhibition Grounds*.

On higher ground to the NE of the Glavni Trg lies the **Municipal Park** (*Mestni Park*), beautifully situated and carefully tended. To the right of the park is an **Aquarium**, with fish from Yugoslav inland waters, the Adriatic and the tropics.

From the NW corner of the park a handsome avenue leads in 20 minutes to the **Calvary Hill** (1240 ft/378 m), on which is *St Barbara's Chapel*.

SURROUNDINGS. – There are two routes to the **Pohorje hills** and their hotels. One way is to take the municipal bus to the lower station (3 miles/5 km away) of the cableway which runs up from 1065 ft/325 m to the upper station at 3445 ft/1050 m, close by the *Bellevue Hotel*. The alternative is a road which branches off the main Maribor–Zagreb road at Hoče and winds its way up to the summit. Both routes are well signposted from the middle of the town. At 3760 ft/1146 m is an outlook tower.

4½ miles/7 km from Maribor on the Dravograd road, on the Drava reservoir, is a **water sports complex**, with the Jezero Motel, a restaurant, a camp site and facilities for boat rental; the water of the lake is usually fairly cold.

Mlini

Republic: Croatia (Hrvatska).
Altitude: 16 ft/5 m. – Population: Mlini 200, Plat 150, Srebreno 100.
Post code: YU-50207. – Telephone code: 0 50.
ⓘ **Turističko Društvo Župa Dubrovačka Mlini,**
Srebreno 7;
tel. 8 62 54.

HOTELS. – IN MLINI: *Astarea*, A, 431 b., tel. 8 60 66, with annexes *Studenae*, B, and *Elaphity Villas*, B, together 306 b.; *Mlini*, B, 136 b., tel. 8 60 53. – IN PLAT: *Plat*, B, 1200 b., tel. 8 62 22. – IN SREBRENO: *Orlando*, B, 482 b., tel. 8 60 22, with annexes *Tamaris*, B, 108 b., *Župa*, 200 b., and holiday chalets (bungalows), 74 b.

CAMP SITE. – IN KUPARI: *Kupari*, tel. 8 60 20, 1¼ miles/2 km from sea.

NATURIST FACILITIES. – Beach at Mlini.

SPORT, BOATING and BATHING. – All the villages have broad shingle beaches, from 33 yd/30 m to 330 yd/300 m long, separated from one another by rocks. The beaches usually have a fairly gentle slope, making them suitable for children. Although the water looks clean it is not of good quality, since there is no provision for sewage treatment in the bay. The naturist section of the bay at Mlini is too small for the increasing numbers of naturists who come here in July and August. Boat-owners seeking an overall tan make for the reefs and rocky islets off the coast – though

Cableway up the Pohorje hills

these are exposed to the exhaust of numerous aircraft using the flight path which passes over them.

There are ample facilities for all kinds of sports in the bay – sailing, water-skiing, bowling, tennis (courts floodlit at night), mini-golf – and the program of entertainment is varied and noisy, with dancing, folk performances and music in the open air. There are regular bus services to Dubrovnik and Cavtat.

The beach, Mlini

Župa Bay (Župski Zaljev) lies at the end of a stretch of rocky coast S of Dubrovnik, with the Adriatic coastal highway (Jadranska Magistrala) running high above it, offering splendid views of the coastal scenery. The former villages and hamlets on the coast have now coalesced into a single holiday resort which can accommodate fully 5000 visitors in its hotels, rooms in private houses and camp sites. Although the beaches are fully occupied at the height of the season, the little places round the bay – Kupari, Srebreno, Mlini, Plat – have avoided the worst effects of mass tourism.

HISTORY. – This bay to the S of Dubrovnik was until quite recently a farming area noted for its fertile soil. The only kind of industrial activity was at Kupari, where there was a tile-works. When this had to give place to hotels two kilns were left as a reminder of the past, but with the continuing expansion of the tourist trade they too seem doomed to disappear. The history of the villages in the bay was closely connected with that of Cavtat, the little town situated on a promontory at the S end of the bay. In the 7th c. the inhabitants of Cavtat fled before the advancing Avars and Slavs and sought refuge on the little islet of Lave, where they founded their new settlement of Dubrovnik.

SIGHTS. – Near Mlini beach, part of which is shaded by pines, is the *parish church of St Hilary* (Sv. Ilar), originally dating from the 15th c. but rebuilt after an earthquake in 1687. Nearby, on the road

to Cavtat, are the remains of Roman buildings.

SURROUNDINGS. – Some 20 miles/30 km inland is the interesting little town of **Trebinje**, picturesquely situated in the hills NE of Mlini, with an old castle, a clock-tower and two mosques. From Trebinje a road runs SE and climbs, with many bends, to the *Orjen saddle* (5230 ft/1594 m), below * **Mt Orjen** (6217 ft/ 1895 m), from which there are superb views of the Adriatic and the Montenegrin mountains.

Mljet

Republic: Croatia (Hrvatska).
Area of island: 38 sq. miles/98 sq. km. – Population: 2000.
Post code: YU-50226. – Telephone code: 0 50.

(i) **Mljet National Park,**
Govedjari;
tel. 8 90 10.
Turističko Društvo Saplunara-Okuklje-Maranovići,
YU-50224 Maranovići;
tel. 8 90 19
(letting of rooms in private houses).

HOTELS. – *Odisej*, B, 317 b., tel. 8 90 10; *Melita*, B, 86 b., tel. 8 90 10, in the former monastery of Sv. Marija na Jezeru.

CAMP SITE. – *Vrbovica*, tel. 8 90 10.

SPORT, BOATING and BATHING. – A holiday on Mljet is for those who want peace and quiet, away from the usual round of tourist pleasures. In addition to the modest hotel in an old Benedictine abbey there is the new **Odisej holiday complex**, equipped with every modern amenity, including a camp site, its own private section of beach and its own motorboats and sail boats. On either side of Pomina there are coves (pebble and rock) suitable for bathing. At Saplunara there is a large sandy bay. The Vrbovica camp site and the best places for scuba diving and fishing are near the harbour on the Veliko Jezero. There is another camp site at Govedjari, in the new holiday complex.

FERRIES. – Polače–Sobra–Dubrovnik (car ferry). Regular passenger service to the Pelješac peninsula.

Mljet is noted for having "an island on the island" – the islet in the Veliko Jezero, an inlet of the sea, with a Benedictine abbey. Until quite recently the only visitors who came here were a few day-trippers from Dubrovnik. It is only in the last few years, since the two salt-water inlets at the NW end of the island became part of Mljet National Park, that visitors have begun to spend their whole holiday here.

Mljet cannot offer vacationers ideal bathing beaches: the attraction of this island, 70% of which is forest-covered, lies in its natural beauties. An asphalted road 37 miles/60 km) long runs around the two north-western inlets from Polače and eastward to Cape Gruj, passing through the inland villages.

HISTORY. – Is Mljet the island of Melita mentioned in *Acts* where Paul and his companions suffered shipwreck on their voyage to Rome and received "no little kindness" from the local people? Melita is usually identified as Malta, but some Yugoslav scholars have pointed out that Paul was later bitten by a viper – a species unknown on Malta but formerly so common on Mljet that mongooses were brought in from India by seafarers to combat them. Adders are still found on Mljet and some other Yugoslav Adriatic islands and have been known to disturb campers during their nocturnal foraging expeditions.

The island, with its landscape of limestone hills and karstic depressions, was occupied by Illyrians. In Roman times it was known as *Melita*. Its inhabitants frequently attacked Roman ships, and Augustus had to send a punitive expedition to subdue them. The emperor Septimius Severus used the island as a place of banishment.

In 536 Mljet became part of the Eastern Roman Empire. Later it was occupied by the Slavs. In 1151 the whole island was granted to Benedictines from Apulia, who established their headquarters on the little "island on an island". In the 13th c. Mljet passed to Dubrovnik, which appointed a governor (Rector) with his residence in Babino Polje. Thereafter the island enjoyed a long period of peace, interrupted only in 1572 by a great corsair raid under the leadership of the notorious Ali Ulič.

SIGHTS. – The two lakes, like Scottish sea lochs, at the NW end of the island are not in fact the result of intrusion by the sea into the land but are karstic features (see the entry on Karst). The smaller of the two lakes, the *Malo Jezero* (area 59 acres, greatest depth 97 ft/29·5 m), is linked with the larger one, the *Veliko Jezero* (358 acres, greatest depth 151 ft/46 m), which in turn is connected with the sea by a channel 33 ft/10 m wide and 8 ft/2·5 m deep. A strong current flows through this channel, altering direction every 6 hours in accordance with the ebb and flow of the tide. In the interior of the island are four other karstic depressions, with no connection to the sea, which fill up with water after rain. The two sea-water lakes with their surrounding coniferous forests and some areas of agricultural land form the *Mljet National Park*, which has a total area of 12 sq. miles/31 sq. km.

The **Church of Our Lady** belonging to the former Benedictine abbey on the island in the Veliko Jezero is in Apulian Romanesque style, an aisleless building of regularly dressed stone with an apse and a dome surrounded by a frieze of round-headed arches. In front of the church stands a Renaissance portico bearing the arms of the Gundulić family (15th–16th c.). Above the atrium and sacristy is a defensive tower of the same period, pierced by loopholes. There are two side chapels, with altars, added in the Baroque period. The monastic buildings on the harbour side of the church, with a cloister and a roomy cellar, date from the 16th c. The church was renovated in 1949 and the monastic buildings, long abandoned, were converted into a hotel.

The largest village on the island, **Babino Polje**, lies 4 miles/6 km W of the harbour at Sobra, at the foot of Mljet's highest mountain, *Veli Grad* (1686 ft/514 m). Near the village are a number of caves, the finest of which are the stalactitic *Movrica Cave*, 100 yd/100 m long, and the *Ostaševica Cave*, 440 yd/400 m long.

Polače takes its name from the remains of a Roman palace to be seen, with other Roman remains, in the middle of the village. There are also the ruins of an *Early Christian basilica*. On a hill to the E, *Nodilove Košare*, overgrown with scrub, are the remains of another Early Christian church.

Mostar

Republic: Bosnia-Hercegovina (Bosna i Hercegovina).
Altitude: 194 ft/59 m. – Population: 100,000.
Post code: YU-79000. – Telephone code: 0 88.
ⓘ **Turist Biro,**
Trg Republike 1;
tel. 2 64 75.

HOTELS. – *Bristol*, B, 84 b., tel. 3 29 21; *Mostar*, B, 60 b., tel. 3 29 41; *Neretva*, B, 60 b., tel. 3 23 30; *Hercegovina*, C, 40 b., tel. 2 13 11.

CAMP SITE. – *Buna*, tel. 7 12 01, 7¼ miles/12 km S.

AIRPORT: Mostar. JAT office: Braće Fejića 2, tel. 2 33 46.

Mostar, capital of Hercegovina, is picturesquely situated on both banks of the Neretva, here spanned by the famous Turkish *bridge. In addition to the bridge the town has a number of interesting old buildings. It is less suited for a stay of any length, having the reputation of

The old bridge over the Neretva, Mostar

architect dug his own grave, the Sultan having threatened him with execution if the bridge collapsed, and fled the town shortly before the scaffolding was removed. Since 1566, however, the bridge has survived numerous earthquakes, and in recent years the tramp of many thousands of tourist feet, without showing any signs of collapse.

The towers at either end of the bridge were built in the 17th c. The Helebija Tower on the right bank was formerly a guard-room and prison, the Tara Tower on the left bank a powder magazine.

Although two outbreaks of plague carried off almost the whole population and a violent earthquake destroyed most of the houses, Mostar developed in the 16th and 17th c. into a town of industry and craft production. The various crafts occupied their own particular quarters of the town: thus the old part of the town on the left bank of the Neretva is still known as Kujundžiluk ("goldsmiths' quarter").

being the hottest town in Yugoslavia.

The Turks left in 1877, but the old town has preserved its oriental character. 40% of the population are still Moslems, and ten of the town's 14 mosques are still in use. The industrialisation of Mostar began during the period of Austrian rule (1878–1918). Since the end of the Second World War the population has increased fourfold. The town's principal industry is aluminium production. In the plain surrounding the town agricultural combines cultivate vines, tobacco and fruit, and the earliest cherries, apricots, figs and pomegranates in Yugoslavia are grown in this sunny valley. Visitors will soon become familiar with the wines produced in the Mostar basin – Žilavka, a light white wine, and Blatina, a heavy red.

HISTORY. – Compared with other places in Hercegovina, Mostar is not particularly old. At the source of the River Buna, 6 miles/10 km away, there was a considerable settlement known as Bona (later called Blagaj by the Slavs), which became in the 15th c. the most important town in Hercegovina and the seat of Duke Stjepan Vukčić. During this period Radivoj, one of the duke's vassals, established a caravan post on the site of present-day Mostar. In 1440 the Turks took Blagaj, and with it no doubt the little supply post on the River Neretva. Thanks to its more favourable situation on the road between the Adriatic and the interior, this smaller settlement soon began to outstrip Blagaj, which is now no more than a village. The Turks built a timber chain bridge over the river, and the town's present name is derived from mostari, "keepers of the bridge".

In 1522 the town became the seat of the Turkish governor of Hercegovina, and in 1557, during the reign of Sultan Suleiman the Magnificent, the Turkish architect Hairudin was commissioned to replace the old timber bridge by a new one of stone. The new bridge, built of white limestone, was boldly conceived with a single arch 100 ft/30 m wide. When it was nearing completion, after nine years' work, the

SIGHTS. – The *OLD TOWN with its numerous mosques and oriental atmosphere must be explored on foot: the streets and lanes leading into it all end in areas closed to traffic. All visitors, of course, make straight for the *Turkish bridge, from which during the summer some of the local youths, for a suitable consideration, will dive the 65 ft/20 m into the Neretva. Every year on July 27 a diving competition is held here.

On the way to the bridge there are numerous souvenir shops, some of them fitted out as goldsmiths' and coppersmiths' workshops in which jewelry and a variety of other articles are produced. By

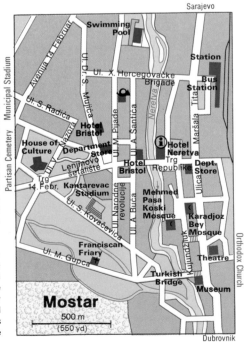

Mostar

500 m
(550 yd)

no means all the antiques sold here (jugs, pots, scales, Turkish smoking apparatus), however, are genuinely old.

From the rear of the *Helebija Tower* on the right bank a lane runs E to the **Museum of Hercegovina** (Ul. Maršala Tita 160).

To the N of this, in Ul. Braće Fejića, is the **Karadjoz Beg Džamija** (1557), the largest mosque in Mostar and the finest in the whole of Hercegovina, with a dome and a tall slender minaret. Adjoining it is a *medrese* (religious school). In the courtyard is a beautiful Turkish fountain. – Close by is the *Mehmed Paša Koski Mosque*, a massive building rising above the rocky bank of the river. The best general view of the town can be had from its minaret. In front of the mosque is a *türbe* (domed Turkish tomb) containing a sarcophagus.

Another interesting building is the **old Serbian Orthodox church** (1833), near which stands the **new Serbian Orthodox church**, built in 1873 on a site personally selected by the reigning Sultan, Abdul Aziz, who also provided money for its construction. The old church, lying below the level of the surrounding ground, is sometimes called the "underground church". it contains a fine collection of *icons* and pictures by Serbian, Russian and Italian masters.

The organised sightseeing tours of the town also include visits to **old Turkish houses** which give some impression of the way of life of merchants and senior Turkish officials in Mostar in the first half of the 19th c. These show houses are still occupied, and the families, wearing Turkish clothing, serve coffee to visitors.

SURROUNDINGS. – No visitor to Mostar should omit an excursion (6 miles/10 km) to the village of **Blagaj**, which was supplanted in the 15th c. by the much younger town of Mostar. On the hill above the village is the castle of *Stjepan Grad*. The village street ends at the source of the little River Buna, a tributary of the Neretva – a good example of a karstic resurgence. The upper course of the river, here called the Zalomka, disappears into the ground many miles downstream, to re-emerge as the **"source of the Buna"* in a great gush of water at the foot of a steep rock face. Beside the cave is one of the very few surviving dervish convents in Yugoslavia, now restored and open to visitors. This shingle-roofed building, of several storeys, is protected from rain by the overhang of the rock face. A few hundred yards from the convent, on the outskirts of the village, is a restaurant serving trout from the River Buna.

Murter

Republic: Croatia (Hrvatska).
Area of island: 7½ sq. miles/19 sq. km.
Population: 5540.
Telephone code: 0 59.
ⓘ **Turističko Društvo Tijesno,**
YU-59240 Tijesno;
tel. 7 80 46.
Turističko Društvo Jezera,
YU-59242 Jezera;
tel. 7 80 20.
Turističko Društvo Betina,
YU-59244 Betina;
tel. 7 52 41.
Kornatturist Murter,
YU-59243 Murter;
tel. 7 52 15.

HOTELS. – IN MURTER: *Colentum*, B, 208 b., tel. 7 52 55. – IN TIJESNO: *Borovnik*, B, 160 b., tel. 7 80 65. – Also accommodation in private houses (apply to Tourist Office).

CAMP SITES. – *Jazine*, at Tijesno, tel. 7 30 83; *Plitka Vala* – *Kosirina*, at Betina, tel. 7 52 31; *Lovišća*, in Jezera, tel. 7 80 15; *Slanica*, at Murter, tel. 7 52 55.

NATURIST FACILITIES. – The nearest hotel, bungalow and camping complex (*Miran*) is at Pirovac, on the mainland opposite the island. Information from Riviera hotel company, YU-59213 Šibenik, tel. (0 59) 2 28 48.

SPORT, BOATING and BATHING. – Boat rental at Murter, Betina and Tijesno. – There is adequate shelter for boats at Bora, in Koširina Bay on the SW side of the island. Anchorages for larger boats in Jezera Bay on the E side and at Tijesno. Murter is an excellent base from which to explore the Kornati Islands (see p. 107).

The only hotel in Murter village, commandingly situated on a hill gay with flowers, has a beach of clean fine sand in Slanica Bay, but it is overcrowded at the height of the season. There is almost endless scope for bathing on the much indented E coast of the island, facing the mainland.

TRANSPORT. – No car ferries; Murter is connected with the mainland by a swing bridge.

With an area of barely 7½ sq. miles/19 sq. km, Murter is one of the smaller Adriatic islands. The NW end of the island is an area of loess soil on which fruit, olives and vegetables are grown. The predominantly steep SW coast is broken up by a series of small coves. In those parts of the island which consist of limestone there is only a sparse vegetation cover, mainly grazing for sheep. The road to the island branches off the Adriatic coastal highway between Pirovac and Vodice and crosses the Murterski Kanal (Murter Channel) on a swing bridge 40 yd/37 m long at the village of Tijesno, which lies partly on the mainland and partly on

Murter, looking towards the neighbouring islands of Prišnjak and Radelj

the island. It then continues, with many bends and extensive views, to the little fishing port of Betina, skirts the beautiful sandy beach of Hramina, comes to the village of Murter (not on the sea) and ends at the sandy beaches of Slanica.

HISTORY. – Murter was occupied by the Illyrians and later by the Romans, who have left evidence of their presence at the site of ancient Colentum, where much archaeological material has been recovered. In the 13th c. there were only two settlements on the island, *Veliko Selo* (now Murter) and *Jezero*. The villages of *Betina* and *Tijesno* were established during the period of Turkish attack. Tijesno is first recorded in 1447.

SIGHTS. – **Tijesno** – a village of bright red tiled roofs, like the other settlements on the island – has a *parish church* built in 1548, remodelled in Baroque style in 1640 and enlarged in 1840, with a handsome *tower* of 1680. The other little churches in the village date from the 17th c. – In **Ivinj**, on the mainland SE of Tijesno, is the medieval *St Martin's Church* and at **Dazlina** a ruined medieval *watch-tower*.

The village of **Betina**, on *Mt Gradina*, occupies the site of the Illyrian and later Roman settlement of *Colentum*. It has a medieval *Church of the Mother of God* (Gospa od Gradina).

The main place on the island, **Murter**, lies in a fertile plain some 750 yd/700 m from the sea. The medieval *St Michael's Church* (Sv. Mihovil) was restored in 1770 and enlarged in 1847. The Baroque high altar has sculpture by Pio and Vico Dell'Acqua (1779). On a hill above the town stands the little *St Roch's Church* (1760).

Niš

Republic: Serbia (Srbija).
Altitude: 623 ft/190 m. – Population: 150,000.
Post code: YU-18000. – Telephone code: 0 18.
ⓘ Turistički Savez Opštine,
Ul. Nade Tomić 7,
tel. 2 21 08.

HOTELS. – *Ambassador*, A, 296 b., tel. 2 66 50; *Park*, B, 161 b., tel. 2 32 96; *Niš*, B, 129 b., tel. 2 26 43; *Motel Mediana*, B, 110 b., tel. 3 15 69.

CAMP SITE. – *Mediana*, tel. 3 15 69.

The industrial town of Niš, on the River Nišava, which flows into the Morava a few miles downstream, has been an important hub of communications since time immemorial, and accordingly has always been of great strategic importance. Here the streams of traffic coming down from the N divide: the highway continues S up the Morava valley towards the Greek frontier at Gevgelija, while the road to Dimitrovgrad and the frontier crossing into Bulgaria turns off to the left. The motorway bypass now draws off the heavy traffic which formerly passed through the town.

HISTORY. – In Roman times Niš (*Naisus*) was an important stronghold on the road to Byzantium. The emperor Constantine the Great (306–337) was born in the town and for a time had a summer residence here. Justinian and his successors further developed and fortified the town, but few remains of this period have survived. The armies of the Crusaders later passed through Niš several times on their way to Constantinople, and during the third Crusade the emperor Frederick Barbarossa and the Serbian Župan Nemanja met here (1189). The Turks took the town in 1385 but were later driven out by the Serbs; then in 1454 they retook it and held it until 1877. During the First World War, in 1915, Austrian, German and

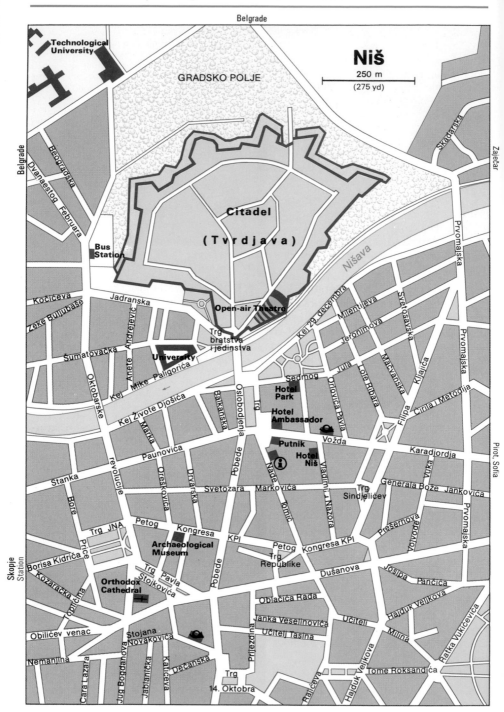

Bulgarian troops captured Niš during their campaign against Serbia, and the occupation ended only in 1918, when the French and Serbian corps which had landed at Salonica entered the town. In the Second World War Niš suffered severe destruction by air attack and bombardment, but on the ruins of the older parts of the town there soon grew up after the war a modern industrial city.

SIGHTS. – Niš's main tourist attraction lies not in the town but outside it – the **Tower of Skulls** (*Čele Kula*), which stands in a south-eastern suburb on the right of the main road to Sofia. During the first Serbian rising against the Turks in 1809 the Turkish forces finally encircled the rebels, and the leader of the rising, Stjepan Sindjelić, made his last stand in a powder tower; then, in order to avoid falling into the hands of the Turks alive, he and his companions blew themselves up. Thereupon the Turks cut off their heads, together with those of many of their comrades who had fallen in the battle – 952 in all. The Pasha of Niš had the skin flayed off their heads and filled with cotton, and then sent these macabre trophies to Constantinople in proof of his victory. He had the skulls set into the walls of a five-sided tower some 16 ft/5 m high which was built for the purpose, with 14 rows of 17 heads on each side. This Tower of Skulls was intended to deter the Serbs from any further rebellion, but it had the precisely opposite effect, becoming a memorial which strengthened their determination never to give up the struggle against alien rule. – There are now few skulls left on the walls of the tower, for many were removed by early souvenir-hunters, and in 1877, after the liberation from Turkish rule, most of those remaining were deposited in a chapel. In order to prevent further damage the whole tower is now enclosed in a protective bell of lucite.

On the right bank of the Nišava, opposite the central area of the town on the left bank, lies the **Tvrdjava**, the old Turkish citadel, occupying a site which was already fortified in Byzantine times. In its present form it dates from 1690 to 1720. After the loss of Belgrade it became the principal bastion of the Turks' strategy on their northern frontiers. Particularly impressive is the battlemented entrance gateway, the *"Gate to Istanbul"*, with inscriptions in Turkish and ornamental devices in Arabic script. Not much of interest is now left within the walls of the fortress – remains of the walls and towers of a mosque and a Turkish bath. The whole of the citadel now stands in a *park*, with an open-air theatre, several cafés and a network of attractive paths.

On the other side of the river, not far from the central area, is the **Archaeological Museum** (*Arheološki Muzej*), which has an interesting display of material recovered by excavation, mostly of the Roman period.

SURROUNDINGS. – 2½ miles/4 km E of Niš on the road to Bulgaria, to the left is the Roman site of **Mediana**, where the emperor Constantine is believed to have had his villa. The remains of a number of Roman villas have been excavated here; the lines of streets can be traced, and there are also remains of baths and a number of well-preserved mosaic pavements. The main finds from the site are now in the Archaeological Museum in Niš.

If we leave the city by the Belgrade road (to the N), turn right just after the bridge over the Nišava into the Zaječar road and then immediately left, we come to the

remains of four Christian churches and various Roman buildings which were discovered during the post-war reconstruction of the town. It is certain, too, that much still remains to be discovered in this district, the **Jagodin Mahala** quarter. The excavations – not yet open to the public – have revealed among much else a large crypt, once under a temple, and an underground chamber containing a monogram of Constantine the Great and the remains of wall paintings and drawings.

Novi Sad

Republic: Serbia (Srbija).
Autonomous province: Vojvodina.
Altitude: 245 ft/75 m. – Population: 200,000.
Post code: YU-21000. – Telephone code: 0 21.
(i) **Turistički Savez Opštine,**
    Dunavska 27;
    tel. 5 18 88 and 2 92 36.

HOTELS. – *Tvrojava*, L, 100 b., tel. 4 63 93; *Park*, B, 250 b., tel. 5 26 55; *Sajam*, B, 21 b., tel. 2 03 99; *Putnik*, C, 88 b., tel. 2 93 44; *Vojvodina*, C, 70 b., tel. 2 93 24; *Venac*, C, 46 b., tel. 4 90 06.

CAMP SITE. – *Ribarsko Ostrvo*, tel. 5 46 11, on the peninsula of that name in the Danube (sandy beach).

Novi Sad is capital of the autonomous province of Vojvodina within the republic of Serbia. Many of its inhabitants are of Hungarian descent. It is an industrial town with much recent building, revealing traces of earlier Turkish, Hungarian and Austrian influences only in the central area and the magnificent castle of Petrovaradin.

HISTORY. – The hill rising above the Danube on which Novi Sad lies, opposite the fortress of Petrovaradin, was occupied in Roman times by a fort. In the Middle Ages Cistercian monks built on the same site a fortified monastery which was later converted by Hungarian conquerors into a small fortress. In 1526 Petrovaradin was stormed by the Turks, who had taken Belgrade five years before, but in 1691 it was recovered by Prince Eugene of Savoy.

In the strategic planning for the defence of Europe against the Turks Petrovaradin was now designed to form a bridgehead in north-eastern Serbia, while Karlovac became a bar to the Turkish advance in the NW. The castle of Petrovaradin was therefore enlarged and strongly fortified. Work on the fortress came to a halt between 1717, when Belgrade was taken by Prince Eugene, and 1739, when it was lost again. Thereafter the Austrians developed Petrovaradin into a masterpiece of the art of fortification. Passages with a total length of 10 miles/16 km were constructed within the massive walls, on four levels. Loopholes for a force of 18,000 men were provided, and huge quantities of cannon and ammunition were amassed. With its formidable defences and powerful armament, the stronghold of Petrovaradin served to deter all aggressors right into the 19th c.

Novi Sad

The construction of the castle led to the growth, on the other side of the Danube, of a settlement of fishermen, craftsmen, traders and soldiers' wives, and this developed in course of time into a town which by the middle of the 18th c. had a population of some thousands. By this time the earlier military control over the settlement had been given up, and the inhabitants of the little town, who were predominantly Serbs, were allowed to manage their own affairs. In 1748 the Empress Maria Theresa granted the town, then known by its German name of *Neusatz*, the status of a royal free city. During the 18th and 19th c. it began to be styled the "*Serbian Athens*", the influx of Serbian refugees having made it increasingly the principal capital of Serbian culture. In this period too the population was increased by numbers of Germans, who had been brought into the nearby Bačka area to work the land and if necessary defend the territory, and by many Hungarians.

The development of the town suffered a setback in 1848, when rebellious Hungarians and Hungarian troops in Petrovaradin bombarded the town from the fortress and destroyed two-thirds of it. The town was relieved by an Austrian force in June 1849, and in the subsequent rebuilding Novi Sad became a larger and a handsomer town. Its development into a modern city, however, began only in the thirties of this century. Novi Sad is now the economic and cultural heart of Vojvodina, in which some 20 different population groups live and several languages – predominantly Serbo-Croat and Hungarian – are spoken.

SIGHTS. – In Freedom Square (Trg Slobode) are the **Old Town Hall** (outlook tower) and the Orthodox **Cathedral** (completed 1740), with works by one of Serbia's greatest painters, Paja Jovanović, on the *iconostasis* (1903). The iconostasis itself is made of wood from the "Holy Mountain" (Mount Athos). The **Church of the Dormition** (*Crkva Sv.*

Uspenska), a Baroque structure of 1736, also contains icons and superb wood-carving. The **Bishop's Palace** catches the eye with its Byzantine-style additions.

Petrovaradin Castle

The *Picture Gallery* of the Matica Srpska society (Trg Proleterskih Brigada 1) offers an excellent survey of the art of the Vojvodina.

A bridge leads over the Danube to **Petrovaradin Castle**, situated high above the bank of the river. Particularly impressive is the extensive system of underground passages and tunnels. Within the castle are two *museums* illustrating the history of the town and the region, as well as a luxury hotel and a restaurant. From the hill on which the castle stands there are fine *views over the town, extending to the hills of the Fruška Gora.

SURROUNDINGS. – To the N of the town, reached by the road to **Subotica** (E 5), is the Bačka region, lying between the Danube and the Tisa, the population of which until the end of the Second World War included many farmers of German stock.

Immediately S of Novi Sad lies the **Fruška Gora National Park**, a stretch of hilly country which extends along the Danube for almost 50 miles/80 km, reaching its highest point in Crveni Cot (1768 ft/ 539 m). The hillsides are covered with great expanses of vineyards and orchards, and in the valleys are fields of maize and large areas of pastureland. Within the National Park are two interesting old monasteries, *Hopovo* and *Krušedol*.

The road which runs along the right bank of the Danube from Petrovaradin towards Belgrade comes in 7½ miles/12 km to the little town of **Sremski Karlovci** (German *Karlowitz*), where a treaty with the Turks was signed in 1699, giving Austria possession of almost the whole of Hungary, Transylvania and Slavonia. Notable features in the town are the Cathedral, the Patriarch's Palace, the school and the theological seminary.

Ohrid

Republic: Macedonia (Makedonija).
Altitude: 2300 ft/700 m. – Population: 30,000.
Post code: YU-97300. – Telephone code: 0 96.
ⓘ **Turističko Biro,**
Ul. Partizanska 3;
tel. 2 24 94.

HOTELS. – *Grand Hotel Palace*, A, 274 b., tel. 2 20 30, with annexe, 148 b.; *Metropol*, A, 250 b., tel. 2 11 32, with night-club; *Slavija*, A, 107 b., tel. 2 21 98; *Orce Nikolov*, B, 242 b., tel. 2 20 36.

CAMP SITES. – *Elešec*, tel. 2 23 38, and *Gradište*, tel. 2 25 78, both on the lakeside road to the S of the town.

AIRPORT: Ohrid-Struga. JAT office: Partizanska 4, tel. 2 25 30.

*Ohrid lies in the SW of the republic of Macedonia on the shores of *Lake Ohrid. This is surely the most interesting place in Macedonia, with its numerous Byzantine churches, frequently converted into mosques during the Turkish period (1394–1912), and its characteristic old houses.

HISTORY. – The town of Ohrid, rising up the slopes of a hill from the shores of the lake to the ruined castle on the highest point, was originally founded by Illyrians in the 3rd c. B.C. During the Roman period it lay on the *Via Egnatia*, the great highway which linked the Adriatic with the Aegean. For centuries Ohrid was part of the Byzantine empire, and thereafter was held by the Turks until the end of the Balkan Wars (1912-13). In 1918 Macedonia was incorporated in the new Yugoslav kingdom. In 1941 it was occupied by Bulgarian troops. The Declaration of Jajce (1943), adopted by delegates from all over Yugoslavia under Tito's chairmanship, recognised Macedonia's national independence within a Yugoslav federation; and in 1950, after centuries of oppression, the Macedonian spoken language became a written language for the first time. Members of different racial and religious groups – Macedonians, Albanians and Serbs, Moslems, Christians and atheists – now live together in Macedonia, speaking many languages, including Greek. This mingling of races, the result of all the vicissitudes of history, ranks with the beauty of the surrounding countryside as one of the enduring impressions of a visit to Ohrid.

SIGHTS. – The best starting point for a tour of Ohrid is the car park at the harbour. The street running W past a restaurant with an open-air terrace (pedestrian precinct) is the scene of the regular evening promenade. The street ends at an ancient plane-tree, at least 500 years old, which formerly housed a café within the

Ohrid, with the ruins of Tsar Samuel's castle on the hill

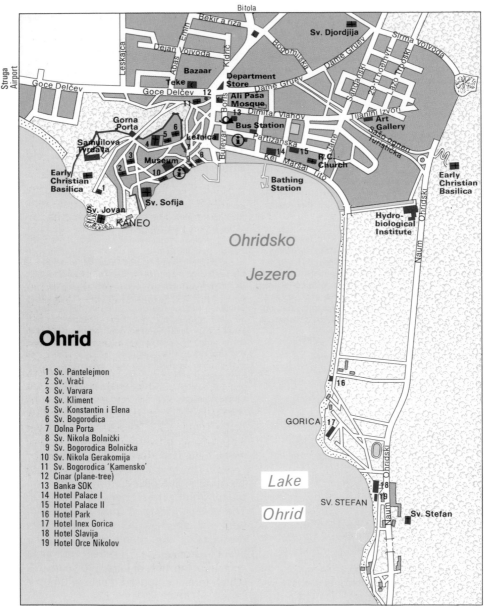

Bitola

Ohrid

Ohridsko Jezero

1 Sv. Pantelejmon
2 Sv. Vrači
3 Sv. Varvara
4 Sv. Kliment
5 Sv. Konstantin i Elena
6 Sv. Bogorodica
7 Dolna Porta
8 Sv. Nikola Bolnički
9 Sv. Bogorodica Bolnička
10 Sv. Nikola Gerakomija
11 Sv. Bogorodica 'Kamensko'
12 Cinar (plane-tree)
13 Banka SOK
14 Hotel Palace I
15 Hotel Palace II
16 Hotel Park
17 Hotel Inex Gorica
18 Hotel Slavija
19 Hotel Orce Nikolov

Lake

Ohrid

SV. STEFAN

Sv. Stefan

Peštani, Sv. Naum

different sections of its trunk (total diameter 65 ft/20 m). Bearing left along Ul. Goce Delčev, the road to Struga, we pass a row of shops which are also workshops producing the goods they sell, including pointed leather shoes (*opanci*) and copper articles. From this street various other streets go off on the right, one of them leading to the *market square*. The market, held on Mondays, is attended by many peasants wearing traditional local costume, but for colour and atmosphere the market in the neighbouring little town of Struga, held on Saturdays, is perhaps even more attractive.

From the harbour it is a short climb up to the *Castle*. The houses flanking the narrow street draw ever closer together, with the overhanging upper storeys so frequently found in the Balkans. All attempts to ban motor vehicles from this fascinating part of the old town in order to save the houses, many of them already dilapidated, from further damage have been frustrated by the resistance of the inhabitants.

After passing the *National Museum* (on right) the street continues up to the *Cathedral of St Sophia (on left), the

St Sophia's Cathedral, Ohrid

oldest surviving church in Ohrid and for centuries the seat of an archbishop. It contains a unique collection of *medieval frescoes* of the 11th–14th c. During the "Ohrid Summer", the festival held annually in July and August, concerts and recitals are given in the church by orchestras and artistes of international reputation.

Beyond the Cathedral a flight of steps leads up to a path (to left) leading round the hill to the 13th c. *St John's Church* (Sv. Jovan), in the village of Kaneo. The church stands by itself on a rocky promontory above the lake (*view). Below the church is a small beach which visitors who discover it try to keep to themselves.

Returning to the Cathedral, we continue up the hill to **St Clement's Church** (*Sv. Kliment*), which dates from 1295. Its *frescoes* are much better preserved or restored than those in St Sophia's.

St John's Church, Kaneo, Lake Ohrid

The FRESCOES mark the beginning of a new trend in Byzantine art, the so-called "Palaeologue Renaissance". The painters now depict saints in a realistic way, like portraits of contemporaries, with no signs of suffering, martyrdom or the illumination of the ascetic. In addition to the frescoes the church contains a very valuable collection of 12th c. *icons*, assembled here since the last war. Some particularly venerated icons are embellished with silver facings and ornaments.

The ruins of the **Castle** built by Tsar Samuel of Macedonia (*Samuilova Tvrdjava*), crowning the hill to the W of St Clement's, are impressive both in themselves and for the sake of the magnificent *views* they afford over the lake and the plain to the N. The castle also plays its part in the Ohrid summer festival.

Other features of interest in Ohrid are the *church of Sv. Nikola Bolnički*, with frescoes which include portraits of Archbishop Nikola of Ohrid and King Dušan of Serbia; the *church of Sv. Nikola Gerakomija*, with icons, which contains the remains of St Clement, transferred here from St Clement's Church in 1952; and the *church of Sv. Pantelejmon*, known during the Turkish period as the *Imaret Mosque*. St Pantelejmon's was originally a monastic church founded by St Clement in 893. The monastery housed the first Slav university, and St Clement himself, the first Macedonian Slav writer, wrote some of his works here, including his "Eulogy of St Cyril".

Lake Ohrid

Republic: Macedonia (Makedonija).

HOTELS. – IN PEŠTANI: *Desaret*, B, 393 b., tel. 2 24 18, with chalets. – IN STRUGA: *Inex Hotel Drim*, A, 358 b., tel. 7 21 19, 3 miles/5 km from town; *Biser*, A, 115 b., tel. 7 22 12. – IN SVETI NAUM: some hotel rooms, and accommodation in private houses. – IN OHRID: see entry for Ohrid.

CAMP SITE: – IN KALIŠTA: *Livadišta* (a new site; little shade).

With an area of 135 sq. miles/350 sq. km, *Lake Ohrid (Ohridsko Jezero) in southern Macedonia is Yugoslavia's third largest lake, coming after Lake Scutari (143 sq. miles/370 sq. km) and Lake Prespa (137 sq. miles/354 sq. km). The lake, created by tectonic movements, is enclosed by mountains rising to over 6560 ft/ 2000 m, those on the E side being in

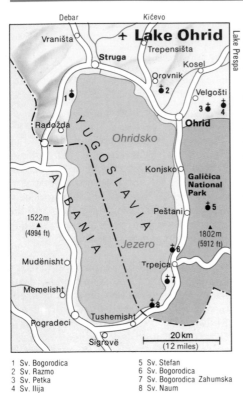

1 Sv. Bogorodica
2 Sv. Razmo
3 Sv. Petka
4 Sv. Ilija

5 Sv. Stefan
6 Sv. Bogorodica
7 Sv. Bogorodica Zahumska
8 Sv. Naum

Yugoslavia and those on the W side in Albania. It has a total length of 19 miles/31 km and a maximum width of 9 miles/15 km, reaching its greatest depth (938 ft/286 m) between Peštani and Trpejca, some 3 miles/5 km from the shore.

The lake, which is notable for the clarity of its water (visibility down to 70 ft/22 m), is fed mainly by underwater tributaries and to a lesser extent by mountain streams. The greatest inflow of water comes from springs below the monastery of Sv. Naum, at the S end of the lake, conveyed in subterranean channels under the Galičica hills from Lake Prespa, lying a few miles E and 518 ft/158 m higher up.

Two-thirds of the lake's area and shoreline are in Yugoslavia, the other third in Albania; the frontier between the two countries is marked for most of its length by buoys. The Yugoslav authorities advise against going too close to Albanian territory, though visitors require no special permit to use motorboats, sail boats or other types of craft. The lake offers excellent fishing, but fishing with nets and from boats is permitted only on Sundays and public holidays. There is a twice-daily service by motorship between Ohrid at the

N end of the lake and Sv. Naum at the S end.

The great scenic charm of Lake Ohrid lies partly in the contrasts of colour between the blue water of the lake, often turning purple in the late afternoon, and the changing hues of the mountains, now greenish-brown, now black, and in the evening often bathed in a blood-red glow; partly also on the constantly changing pattern of the shoreline – now reed-fringed, now covered with light-coloured pebbles, now edged by rugged red walls of rock, or by clumps of trees reaching down to the water's edge.

Further variety is added by the towns and villages around the lake – *Ohrid (see separate entry), with its picturesque *old town*, now protected as a national monument, huddling under Tsar Samuilo's *castle*; **Struga**, with vacationers thronging its beach or enjoying the shade of its trees; **Kališta**, towards the Albanian frontier, where the women still regularly wear the old traditional costumes and do their laundry on the shores of the lake, between patches of reeds; the village of **Radožda**, only a few hundred yards from the frontier, with its mingling of the poverty inherited from the past and the new prosperity brought by "guest workers" in Germany; **Peštani**, on the E side of the lake, with its brightly painted boats drawn up on the beach; and, farther S, the old *monastery of Sveti Naum* rising above the lake.

Tourists are attracted to Lake Ohrid, too, by its climate. The mean annual temperature is 54°F/12°C, and during the summer four out of every five days are usually hot and cloudless, with cooler air in the evenings brought by winds blowing down from the mountains.

The water of the lake frequently reaches its highest temperature only in September (75°F/24°C); between May and August the temperature ranges between 64 and 68°F/18 and 20°C. Ohrid itself has no good beaches; in the harbour is a swimming pool (clean water; admission charge), in which there are frequent swimming contests, and once a year a marathon championship, but visitors staying in Ohrid tend to make for beaches outside the town (unfortunately poorly served by buses).

The most popular beach is a mile or two S of Ohrid, between the Park and Slavija hotels. There is also a very beautiful sandy beach near the S end of the lake, where the road from Ohrid comes down into the plain before Sveti Naum; new hotels and holiday chalets are to be built here to take advantage of this still empty beach. The beach below the monastery (admission charge) is frequently crowded with local people.

To its other attractions Lake Ohrid adds that of being a kind of open-air museum of natural history, preserving in its waters primitive forms of life which have not been found anywhere else. The discovery of these forms of life in the 19th c. led to the establishment of the *Hydrobiological Institute*, which has carried out much scientific work on various species of snails, worms, small crustaceans, algae, etc. – though without solving the puzzle of how these forms arose here.

One speciality is Lake Ohrid trout, which, stuffed with sweet onions and paprika, features on the menus of the local restaurants. A variety of other species of fish are served according the season – carp (weighing up to 55 lb/25 kg), in spring and early summer; eels (up to 40 in./1 m long), mainly in autumn; bleak, with their anchovy-like taste (and with scales which are used in Ohrid to make imitation pearls), throughout the winter. Trout are to be had all year round.

The flat-bottomed boats, hand-thrown nets and other fishing gear to be seen in old photographs of Lake Ohrid are now things of the past. The fishermen now use motor-powered boats: the old-fashioned type of boat which was still in use in the sixties no longer paid for its keep and was scrapped.

Kališta lies at the N end of the lake, off the road into Albania (entry to Albania permitted only in organised groups). Here there is the interesting old *monastery of the Mother of God* (Sveta Bogorodica), with a church (restored 1978–79) containing valuable icons. Nearby is the old *hermitage of St Athanasius*, reached with the aid of ladders.

Struga (pop. 7000), one of the areas of the Lake Ohrid eel fisheries, is a little town of markedly oriental aspect. It has a *Zoological Museum*. The attractive local costumes are still to be seen on Saturday, which is market day.

From Struga the road runs 9 miles/14 km along the N end of the lake to *Ohrid (p. 139).

S of Ohrid is **Peštani**, near which are the *monastery of Sveti Stefan*, on higher ground, and the little *Church of the Mother of God* (Sveta Bogorodica).

At *Trpezica*, near the lake, is another interesting church, *Sveta Bogorodica Zahumska*.

The best known monastery in the region is ***Sveti Naum**, magnificently situated at the S end of the lake, close to the Albanian frontier. It has now been converted into a hotel, and also houses a museum.

Clement and Naum (Nahum), disciples of SS. Cyril and Methodius, had preached the Gospel without success in Moravia before coming in 886 and 900 to Ohrid, which they made a great hub of Slav literature, culture and art; and the work continued after their deaths in 916 and 910. Naum founded the monastery which bears his name about the year 900, and ten years later he was buried there. His church was destroyed during the Turkish period, but remains of the building have been discovered. The present structure is characteristic of medieval Slav architecture. In the church is a curious painting of the burial of St Naum with SS. Cyril, Methodius and Clement standing by the bier – although in fact they all died before Naum.

Market day in Struga (Lake Ohrid)

Omiš

Republic: Croatia (Hrvatska).
Altitude: 16 ft/5 m. – Population: 2500.
Post code: YU-58310. – Telephone code: 0 58.
ⓘ **Dalma,**
Ul. Šetalište Prvoboraca;
tel. 8 36 44.

HOTELS. – *Brzet*, C, 176 b., tel. 8 60 54; *Plaža*, D, 70 b., tel. 8 60 40; *Ruskamen* holiday complex (see under Naturist facilities).

CAMP SITE. – *Ribnjak*, in Omiš-Duće, tel. 8 61 01.

NATURIST FACILITIES. – *Ruskamen* holiday complex, hotel, B, 340 b., and 40 chalets, tel. 8 61 57, 4½ miles/7 km S of Omiš on right of road to sea.

EVENTS. – Folk festival, with groups from all over Dalmatia, second half of July.

SPORT, BOATING and BATHING. – Water-skiing, scuba diving; boat rental. – There is a long sandy beach with no hotels: merely one huge camp site. The beach at the town itself, with water which is not particularly clean, is used only by local people. There are no problems about pollution, however, at the *Ruskamen* holiday complex, which is reached on a road curving down from the Adriatic coastal highway. This large complex, with a hotel and chalets, lies above a clean pebble beach and is surrounded by attractive woodland. Even the dancing in the evening does not disturb those who want to sleep, since it takes place in an underground night-club.

Boats with a draught of up to 30 in./75 cm will have no difficulty in entering Omiš harbour. Skippers of larger boats should seek advice from the local people, since the River Cetina deposits considerable quantities of silt every year on the approach to the harbour.

The little town of Omiš, 16 miles/26 km S of Split, is torn between three interests – the beauty of its scenery, the tourist trade and industrial development. The town lies at the mouth of the abundantly flowing River Cetina, here spanned by two bridges, at the foot of almost ver- tical cliffs. Along the edge of the area of alluvial soil deposited by the river runs a sandy beach several miles long, but a factory at the entrance to the town colours the sky a dingy grey, and a cement works at the far end, close to a hotel, covers the surrounding area with yellow dust. Within the town itself ugly new apartment buildings clash unpleasantly with the older buildings. For the most part, therefore, Omiš is no more than an overnight stop for tourists.

HISTORY. – The Roman settlement of *Oneum*, on this site, was later occupied by Slavs from the mountains around the River Neretva; they established a pirates' lair here and gained a reputation exceeded only by that of the dreaded pirates of Senj (see p. 188). In the 12th and 13th c. the town belonged to the princely Kačić family, and in the 14th c. – by now surrounded by walls – it was held by the Šubić family. In 1444 the Venetians finally took the town and drove out the pirates, some of whom joined their fellows in Senj, and for another 200 years the piratical traditions of their forefathers were continued.

SIGHTS. – Of the medieval fortifications there remain the southern *town gate* and some fragments of walls, a square *tower* and the ruins of the fortress of **Stari Grad**, 1020 ft/311 m above the town. In the principal square stands the Baroque *parish church* (17th c.), with a handsome doorway and tower. The little *Church of the Holy Spirit* (16th c.) at the end of the main street has a picture by Palma Giovane. Adjoining the church is a *clock-tower*, from which steps lead to the upper part of the little town. In the PRIKO district, on the right bank of the Cetina, is the little pre-Romanesque *St Peter's Church* (10th c.).

SURROUNDINGS. – An attractive trip up the left bank of the Cetina, passes through a gorge to the **Radmanone mill**. On the way there are magnificent views out to sea over the river and the town. Farther upstream are the fine **Falls on the Cetina**, with a drop of up to 160 ft/48 m.

Opatija

Republic: Croatia (Hrvatska).
Altitude: 16 ft/5 m. – Population: 9000.
Post code: YU-51410. – Telephone code: 0 51.
ⓘ **Turističko Društvo,**
Ul. Maršala Tita 10;
tel. 7 13 10.

HOTELS. – *Ambassador*, L, 386 b., tel. 71 21 11; *Kvarner*, A, 101 b., tel. 71 12 11, with annexe *Villa*

Omiš, at the mouth of the Cetina

Opatija harbour

Bathers are likely to find themselves cramped for room at the height of the season. The main beach of imported sand in the centre of the town is only some 330 yd/300 m long and 22 yd/20 m wide. There are also three still smaller bathing stations (all with admission charge), while the hotels have mini-beaches and sunbathing platforms. In some places reaching the sea involves clambering down the rocks and using a ladder. The shortage of room for bathers reflects the fact that Opatija was originally established as a winter resort.

The shortage of space also limits the sporting facilities available, but there is no lack of entertainment for vacationers. There are numerous discotheques and, in the larger hotels, night-clubs.

Amalia, A, 58 b.; *Adriatic*, B, 600 b., tel. 71 13 11; *Opatija*, B, 320 b., tel. 71 27 11; *Kristal*, B, 270 b., tel. 71 13 33; *Slavija*, B, 231 b., tel. 71 18 11; *Zagreb Esplanade*, B, 198 b., tel. 71 27 11; *Palme*, B, 196 b., tel. 71 14 33; *Paris Garni*, B, 180 b., tel. 71 19 11; *Jadran*, B, 168 b., tel. 71 23 33; *Slavija-Bellevue*, B, 146 b., tel. 71 10 11; *Istra* and *Marina*, B, 140 b., tel. 71 12 33; *Grand Hotel Belvedere I*, B, 125 b., tel. 71 24 33, with annexe *Belvedere II*, B, 60 b.; *Astoria*, B, 125 b., tel. 71 14 11; *Continental*, B, 120 b., tel. 71 25 11; *Avala*, B, 114 b., tel. 71 24 11; *Brioni*, B, 104 b., tel. 71 22 98, with annexe *Miran*, C, 50 b.; *Dubrovnik*, B, 78 b., tel. 71 16 11; *Atlantik*, B, 50 b., tel. 71 21 33; *Villa Ambassador*, C, 97 b., tel. 71 22 11.

CAMP SITE. – *Preluk*, tel. 61 79 68.

EVENTS. – On the open-air stage, July to end September, chamber music, solo recitals, opera and ballet with Yugoslav and foreign artists, pop shows, folk performances.

SPORT, BOATING and BATHING. – Boat rental, water-skiing; tennis, walking. – The small harbour can take small and medium-sized yachts, but is usually overcrowded in summer. It has a slip and a winch. Boats should avoid the red buoys off the main beach, which mark the line of a steel net designed to keep sharks out, and also a stretch of water used for the landing of seaplanes.

Sheltered from the cold N winds by Mt Učka, *Opatija (formerly known as Abbazia) has a luxuriant growth of evergreen subtropical vegetation. Its equable climate led a wealthy Rijeka businessman named Scarpa to build a holiday house here in 1844, and when, 16 years later, the wife of ex-Emperor Ferdinand of Austria was looking for a quiet place for the sea-bathing which her doctors had prescribed for her he offered her the use of his house, the Villa Angiolina. This was the beginning of Opatija's rise into a fashionable seaside resort; but while in its early days it was a health resort frequented only in winter, its busiest season is now in the summer, with a total over the whole year of some two million "bed-nights".

HISTORY. – There was a small settlement here in ancient times. About the beginning of the 15th c. an abbey was built, some remains of which are to be seen in St James's Chapel (Sv. Jakov): hence the name

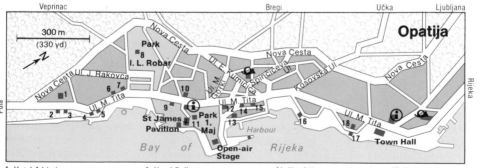

1 Hotel Adriatic	6 Hotel Bellevue	11 Hotel Kvarner	15 Hotel Soča
2 Hotel Istra	7 Hotel Slavija	12 Hotel Avala	16 Hotel Ambassador
3 Hotel Marina	8 Hotel Opatija	13 Hotel Brioni	17 Hotel Belvedere
4 Hotel Kristal	9 Hotel Atlantik	14 Hotel	18 Belvedere
5 Hotel Dubrovnik	10 Hotel Imperial	Continental	Annex

Abbazia/Opatija. In 1844 Iginio Scarpa built his neo-classical holiday villa, surrounding it with a park full of exotic plants, which flourished luxuriantly in the mild climate. Here he brought parties of friends at weekends, and soon other citizens of Rijeka began to come to Opatija for the sake of its coolness in summer and its mild winter climate. In 1854 Scarpa entertained a high Croatian dignitary in his villa, and in 1860 the Austrian empress Maria Anna accepted his invitation to come here to take her sea-water cure. This was reported in the newspapers, and soon the nobility of the Austro-Hungarian monarchy began to take an interest in Opatija. The air of the resort, with its high concentration of ozone, was certified by Viennese professors to have a health-giving effect; and the plan to develop it as a health resort was supported by the Viennese Southern Railway Company, which was in process of extending its Vienna– Trieste line to Rijeka. The first hotel was built in 1883, but in the previous year there had already been over 1400 visitors.

Thereafter further hotels were built, providing luxurious accommodation for winter visitors from the nobility and wealthy middle-class families. A medical congress in 1885 gave a further stimulus to Opatija's popularity by confirming the therapeutic qualities of its climate, and the provincial government then gave it the officially recognised status of a health resort. The resort acquired further prestige by visits from crowned heads from all over Europe and politicians who came here for conferences or to take the cure. The emperor Franz Joseph of Austria had a meeting in Opatija with Wilhelm II of Germany. The First World War put an end to this period of splendour. Under the treaty of Rapallo in 1920 Italy received Istria as a reward for its entry into the war on the side of the Allies, but it showed no interest in Opatija, preferring that visitors should patronise its own spas. During the Second World War most of the hotels were taken over by the German army for use as hospitals. The renovation of the old hotels and the building of new ones began in 1947. An establishment providing thalassotherapy (for disorders of the respiratory passages, rheumatism and follow-up treatment after coronary thrombosis) was opened in 1957, taking up the old tradition of spa treatment. Opatija has not yet, however, been included in the official list of spas in Yugoslavia.

SIGHTS. – The *Villa Angiolina*, which gave the first impetus to the development of Opatija, stands in a magnificent *park, now a Botanic Garden. Among the most notable of the species to be seen here are giant Californian sequoias, Atlas cedars, magnolias with blossoms 8 in./20 cm long, palms and camellias. The villa was sold by its original owner in 1875, and thereafter was used for conferences of emperors, kings and statesmen. It now contains a library and reading-room.

In a small park on the seafront, adjoining the Kvarner Hotel, is the little *St James's Church* (Sv. Jakov), a relic of the former Benedictine abbey. Beside the church is a figure of the Virgin, commemorating an Austrian count who was drowned in the sea. – On the rocks in Portić Bay is a bronze figure (erected in 1956) of a nymph feeding a seagull, known as the "Greeting to the Sea", which has become the emblem of Opatija.

Osijek

Republic: Croatia (Hrvatska).
Altitude: 308 ft/94 m. – Population: 120,000.
Post code: YU-54000. – Telephone code: 0 54.

ⓘ Turist Biro,
   A. Cesarca 2;
   tel. 2 37 55 and 2 39 47.

HOTELS. – *Osijek*, B, 275 b., tel. 2 53 33; *Turist*, C, 67 b., tel. 2 69 55; *Central*, C, 59 b., tel. 2 72 22; *Royal*, C, 58 b., tel. 2 60 33.

Osijek, which at one time had a large German-speaking population and was known in the time of the Austro-Hungarian monarchy as Esseg, is a rapidly growing industrial town. It is also a considerable educational area, with a university, technical colleges, scientific institutes and 34 schools. For the average tourist it is usually no more than an overnight stop, though its active cultural life would fully justify a longer stay.

HISTORY. – In the 1st c. A.D. the Romans established the fort of *Mursa Maior* on the banks of the Drava, in the area now occupied by the lower town, and in A.D. 133 the emperor Hadrian raised the settlement to the status of a colonia. During the great migrations the town was destroyed, and a new settlement grew up in the 10th c. on the site of the castle. The town is first mentioned in the records in 1196. Craft industry and trade rapidly developed.

In 1526 the town was taken by the Turks, and in 1566 Sultan Suleiman II, the Magnificent, built a bridge 5 miles/8 km long over the marshland which then lay N of the town on the left bank of the river to what is now the town of Darda – a technological achievement at which Europe marvelled. The bridge was destroyed in 1644. In 1687 the Turks withdrew, and the Austrian authorities then began to build a powerful new fortress here, similar to their strongholds at Novi Sad and Karlovac. Osijek was the birthplace in 1815 of Josip Juraj Strossmayer, the well-known bishop, writer and political fighter for the independence of the Southern Slavs.

SIGHTS. – Osijek is not a strikingly beautiful city in the traditional sense, but visitors will be impressed by the skill with which its planners have contrived, by the provision of parks and gardens, to relieve the contrast between the rapid development of the outer districts and the cautious process of change in the old town, enabling it, even in its new modern dress, to maintain a sense of unity.

The town is entered by either of two roads running parallel to the Drava, Ulica Strossmayerova (coming from Maribor and Varaždin) and Bulevar JNA, both lined by buildings typical of the Austrian period. Both streets lead to the neo-Gothic Roman Catholic **Cathedral**, near which are an *Art Gallery* (Ul. Augusta Cesarca 4) and the *Municipal Theatre*. Continuing alongside the Drava past the *Park Maršala Tita*, we reach Partisans' Square (Partizanski Trg), in the middle of which rises a Baroque *Plague Column*. On one side of the square is the *Provincial Museum of Slovenia*, which contains, among much else, an interesting collection of coins. – The remains of the *castle* of Osijek are on the other side of the Drava, near the bridge which it was designed to protect.

SURROUNDINGS. – N of Osijek, beginning on the left bank of the Drava, is the large State-run model farm of **Belje**. This former Habsburg estate (entailed so that it could be neither sold nor divided) is now the largest "agricultural combine" in Yugoslavia, with an area of 85 sq. miles.

To the E of the town, between the Danube and the Drava, is the wild life and nature reserve of **Kopački Rit**. This area of marshland, 270 sq. miles in extent, provides a unique breeding ground for many species of wild life, a territory difficult of access to man in which fish, small game and waterfowl can live undisturbed.

Pag

Republic: Croatia (Hrvatska).
Area of island: 110 sq. miles/285 sq. km. –
Population: 10,000.
Telephone code: 0 51.
(i) **Turist Biro Novalja**,
Trg Loža 1,
YU-51291 Novalja;
tel. 89 35 15.
Turističko Društvo Pag,
Obala Maršala Tita 1,
YU-51290 Pag;
tel. 89 11 31.

HOTELS. – IN NOVALJA: *Liburnija*, B, 248 b., tel. 89 35 24; *Loža*, B, 76 b., tel. 89 35 13. – IN PAG: *Bellevue*, B, 302 b., tel. 89 11 22.

CAMP SITE. – *Straško*, Trg Loža 1, Novalja, tel. 89 35 86 (part reserved for naturists).

EVENTS. – Pag Summer Carnival, with parades and folk performances, July 26–29.

SPORT, BOATING and BATHING. – Scuba diving, boat rental; bowling. – The 440 yd/400 m long pebble beach at Pag town is usually overcrowded, and the water lacks the purity and clarity usually found on the

Yugoslav Adriatic coast, since there is little movement in the water of this narrow inlet with its restricted access to the open sea. It is better to look for a bathing-place on the open W coast of the island, where boat-owners will find numerous private little coves in which no one will disturb them. There is also a public pebble beach at Novalja; and the naturist beach of the camp site can also be used by non-campers. Novalja harbour has a winch and slip. Visitors can go out with the local fishermen on their nocturnal fishing expeditions. – Every year on July 27 there is a great popular *festival* on Pag when the *kolo*, the rhythmic Yugoslav national dance, is performed by dancers in traditional costume (the women wearing small lace caps).

CAR FERRIES. – Jablanac–Stara Novalja, Karlobag–Pag. – Bridge connection with mainland.

The northern Dalmatian island of Pag, which is separated from the mainland by the Velebit Channel, 1¼–3 miles/2–5 km wide, is Yugoslavia's third longest island (37 miles/59 km). The coast has numerous bays and inlets, and the island itself is traversed by parallel ranges of bare karstic hills. Vines and olives are grown on the few areas of fertile land; apart from this major contributions are made to the island's economy by sheep-farming and fishing.

Seen from the coast road, this long stony island has a bare, featureless and barren aspect. Never wider than 7 miles/11 km, it has an area of 110 sq. miles/285 sq. km. The E side, facing the mainland, is without vegetation of any kind, as a result of the fierce onslaught of the bora: not even one of the 40,000 sheep on the island could find a blade of grass here. Even on the W side of the island the vegetation is sparse, but here at least there are a few olive-groves, fields of vegetables and areas of green pastureland.

The tourist and holiday trade is concentrated in the little towns of Pag and Novalja and their immediate surroundings. The mud baths at the Pag salt-pans have brought cure or relief to many patients; the waters around the island offer ideal sailing conditions; gourmets appreciate the local cheese (Paški sir); and the beautiful lace made on Pag is a favourite souvenir of a stay on the island.

HISTORY. – In prehistoric times Pag was occupied by an Illyrian people, the Liburni. In the 1st c. B.C. the Romans established a defensive system on the island, with a fortified post at Caska (*Cissa*), another at the harbour of Novalja (*Novalia*) and a number of smaller forts. In the 6th c. A.D. the Slavs came to Pag. In 1071

King Krešimir IV of Croatia sowed the seeds of much further trouble when he presented the northern part of Pag to the church on Rab and the southern part to Zadar, for thereafter Rab and Zadar were constantly at odds, each seeking to acquire the whole of the island. In 1311 the inhabitants of Pag rose against Zadar, but it was not until 1376 that the town of Pag was granted self-government. From 1409 to 1797 the Venetians held the island, which then passed to Austria together with the Dalmatian mainland. During the Second World War Pag was occupied by Italian and later by German troops.

Parish church, Pag

SIGHTS. – The *parish church* (begun 1443) in the town of **Pag**, the chief place on the island, is an aisled basilica which shows a mingling of Romanesque, Gothic and early Renaissance features. The same architect, Juraj Dalmatinac, designed the unfinished *Bishop's Palace* in the same square and laid out the town on an orthogonal plan based on the square. The late Gothic *Rector's Palace* is now occupied by a department store. *St George's Church* (Sv. Juraj) is also of interest. Outside the town are the salt-pans, in a lagoon which cuts many miles inland from the S. In the lagoon, when the water is calm, can be seen the foundations of a Roman settlement swallowed up by the sea.

The former fishing village of **Novalja**, now a seaside resort, has a Roman aqueduct and remains of Early Christian churches. Apart from this it is entirely concerned with the tourist trade, its mild climate attracting visitors from May to the end of October. Farther S is the fresh-water lake of *Velo Blato*, which in winter is 3 miles/5 km long but in summer shrinks to no more than $\frac{3}{4}$ mile/1 km. The reeds around the edge of the lake provide breeding places for waterfowl, and its

waters are well stocked with fish; turtles can also be seen on its shores.

From a hill NE of Novalja, *Komorovac* (653 ft/199 m), there is a fine view of the coast and the island of Rab.

Pašman

Republic: Croatia (Hrvatska).
Area of island: 22 sq. miles/56 sq. km.
Population: 1900.
Post code: YU-57262. – Telephone code: 0 57.
ⓘ **Turističko Društvo Jasenice,**
Pašman village;
tel. 8 31 25.

ACCOMMODATION. – Rooms in private houses (apply to Tourist Office).

SPORT, BOATING and BATHING. – Boats can moor in Tkon harbour, though at the height of the season it may be overcrowded. A sheltered anchorage (except when the bora is blowing) can be found in the Uvala Zaklopica, a cove just N of the southern tip of the island. Even boats with a shallow draught must keep a good look-out in the waters around Pašman, where there are many jagged rocks just below the surface.

The best bathing is at Tkon, which has a clean sandy beach. – The highest hill on the island, Bokolj (899 ft/ 274 m), can be climbed from Nevidjane.

Pašman is a good place for those interested in water sports, fishing and walking. Hotels and sports facilities are being developed over the next few years.

CAR FERRY. – Biograd–Tkon.

Pašman cannot yet compare with the neighbouring island of Ugljan in the facilities it offers to visitors. It is now, however, accessible by car, since it is connected by a bridge with Ugljan, which has a ferry service (several times daily) from Zadar, and

In Pašman harbour

there is also a direct ferry (also several times daily) from the mainland town of Biograd to Tkon, on Pašman. The island is not so green as Ugljan but has better beaches, still barely touched by mass tourism.

HISTORY. – The island has been continuously inhabited since prehistoric times. Tombs and hill-forts have yielded evidence of Illyrian occupation, and there were Roman settlements on the sites of the present-day villages of Pašman, Nevidjane and Banj. In 1050 the island passed into the hands of the Bishop of Biograd, in 1126 of the Archbishop of Zadar. During the Turkish occupation of the mainland many of the inhabitants fled to Pašman, which, like its neighbour Ugljan, was never conquered by the Turks. The channel between Pašman and Ugljan was originally so shallow that even small boats had difficulty in getting through; in 1883, therefore, a passage 13 ft/4 m deep was cut between the islands, and this is now spanned by a bridge.

SIGHTS. – Roman remains have been found near **Pašman**, a little town on the NE coast. The *parish church*, originally built in the early medieval period, has an early 18th c. nave. The *tower* dates from 1750. The church contains two late Gothic processional crosses and an altarpiece by C. Medović. – **Mali Pašman**, W of Pašman, has an aisleless medieval *church* dedicated to St Roch.

On *Čokovac*, a hill NW of the village of **Tkon**, which lies directly opposite Biograd, is a Romanesque *Benedictine abbey*. After being rebuilt in the 14th c. this became a secret base of Glagolitic worship (see under Krk). There are a Glagolitic crucifix in the church and a Glagolitic inscription in the refectory. – At **Kraj** is a 14th c. *Franciscan friary*, partly remodelled in Baroque style. – At **Nevidjane** is the early medieval *monastery of St Neviana*.

Pelješac

Republic: Croatia (Hrvatska).
Population: 3000. – Telephone code: 0 50.
ⓘ Turistički Ured Orebić,
YU-50250 Orebić;
tel. 8 30 14.
Trpanj and Ston:
inquire in hotels.

HOTELS. – IN OREBIĆ: *Orsan*, B, 196 b., tel. 8 30 26; *Rathaneum*, B, 196 b., tel. 80 30 22, with annexe, 52 b.; *Bellevue*, B, 139 b., tel. 8 31 48, with annexe, B, 82 b. – IN TRPANJ: *Faraon*, 224 b., tel. 8 34 22. – IN STON: *Adriatic*, 57 b., tel. 8 40 01.

CAMP SITE. – *Broce*, at Ston.

NATURIST FACILITIES. – Motorboat services daily from Orebić to the little naturist islands of Velika Stupa and Mala Stupa.

SPORT, BOATING and BATHING. – Scuba diving, boat rental, water-skiing; tennis, volleyball. – On the Pelješac peninsula itself there is little in the way of shelter for small boats; most yachts make for Korčula, though it becomes difficult to find a mooring there at the height of the season.

There are good scuba diving grounds all around the peninsula. Walkers are catered for by numerous footpaths.

The pebble beach at *Trpanj* is exposed to the bora and often suffers from pollution from the nearby ferry port. This beach is mainly patronised by Czech vacationers, since the only hotel in the village is owned by a Czech government organisation.

At *Orebić* the hotels outside the town have their own beaches (sand, pebbles, sometimes shelving rock), which suffer from deposits of bitumen and the growth of seaweed. The sea here is also polluted by untreated sewage from the hotels and by the numerous cruise ships which use the channel between Pelješac and Korčula. The sandy beach at *Trstenica* is also polluted. There are boat services to the two naturist islands.

There are regular ferry services (cars carried) between Orebić and Korčula, and many of the Orebić hotels also run regular boat trips to Korčula.

FERRIES. – Car ferries: Orebić–Korčula, Trpanj–Ploče, Trpanj–Drvenik; passenger services: Orebić–Dubrovnik.

The Pelješac peninsula, linked with the mainland by a narrow tongue of land, is more like an island than a peninsula; and, like an island, it is served by ferries, one at either end. These enable visitors to avoid the 45 mile/70 km long road which runs the whole length of the peninsula, through beautiful scenery but with many bends and stretches running above precipitous drops. Some parts of the peninsula are bare and infertile, others are green and attractive. The most beautifully situated place on the whole peninsula, lying opposite Korčula, is Orebić, known as the "town of the sea-captains" from the many retired seafarers who live there.

HISTORY. – The earliest known inhabitants of the peninsula were Illyrians, who were followed by Greek settlers. In Roman times Pelješac was known as *Rhatanae Chersoneus*: at any rate it is referred to by Pliny the Elder under that name. After the fall of the Western Roman Empire it passed to Byzantium. In the 9th c. the area was occupied by a Slav people, the Neretvans. Between 1333 and 1808 Pelješac belonged to the republic of Dubrovnik, which developed

Ston, at the landward end of the peninsula (where there had been a Roman fort), into a strongly fortified outpost. In 1490 a naval harbour for warships from Dubrovnik was constructed at Mali Ston. Later the strategic importance of Ston declined, and Orebić – so named in the 16th c. after a sea-captain from Bakar – began to overshadow it, enjoying a period of great prosperity in the 18th and the first half of the 19th c., when the local ship-owners transported goods between the Ottoman empire and ports throughout western Europe. Orebić is now the home of many retired Yugoslav sea-captains; and when the cruise ships on which they formerly served sail past they give a blast on their sirens by way of greeting, to which the old sea-dogs respond by waving white cloths.

After leaving the Adriatic coastal highway visitors see on the right the oyster-beds at the head of the long inlet which looks more like a lake than an arm of the sea. Beyond this, on the slopes of Mt Bartolomija, can be seen the wall built to defend Mali and Veliki Ston and keep out enemies from the mainland – a task made easier by the narrowness of the peninsula at this point.

In **Veliki Ston** there are a number of interesting old buildings, including the Gothic Chancery of the Republic of Dubrovnik; the Gothic Sorkočević Palace; the Bishop's Palace (1573); the Franciscan friary, with a cloister in Southern Italian Gothic style; and the late Romanesque St Nicholas's Church (in the sacristy a large painted crucifix, silver missal covers, a Gothic wooden statue of St Nicholas, etc.). In the little port of **Mali Ston** the main features of interest are the Great Wall and the Sea Gate of 1335.

At the NW end of the peninsula is the port of **Trpanj**, where the car ferries from Kardeljevo (formerly Ploče) put in. On the hill above the bay near a ruined medieval castle is a partly preserved Roman bath.

The road running along the peninsula now switches from the N to the S coast in order to avoid the highest point, Sv. Ilija (3153 ft/961 m). The Italian name for the mountain is Monte Vipera, after the horned vipers which were once common here but are now rare on most of the Yugoslav islands. Although visitors may not see any vipers they are likely to encounter some of the mongooses which were originally introduced to keep down the vipers. The jackals which were once numerous on Pelješac are now rare, and are only occasionally heard at night, having been almost wiped out by hunting.

There is an easy path (4 hours) from Orebić to the summit of Sv. Ilija, from which there are extensive views; overnight accommodation is available in a mountain hut.

Orebić, formerly called Trstenica, was the residence of a Rector during the period when the peninsula belonged to the republic of Dubrovnik (1343–1806). It now forms part of the commune of Korčula. The town has numbers of handsome villas. There is an interesting Maritime Museum, with old charts, navigational apparatus and pictures. It is particularly rich in material of the days when sail was giving place to steam. Other interesting material on seafaring life can be seen in the private collections of the Fisković and Župa families, which are open to the public. – 1¼ miles/2 km W of Orebić is a Franciscan friary of 1470. Above this stands a Gothic Church of the Mother of God, with ancient sarcophaguses and centuries-old cypresses. There are also remains of the old Rector's Palace. From this point there are superb views.

Perast

Republic: Montenegro (Crna Gora).
Altitude: 10 ft/3 m. – Population: 800.
Post code: YU-81336. – Telephone code: 0 82.
ⓘ **Turist Biro,**
Kap. Marjanovića 92;
tel. 7 20 22.

ACCOMMODATION. – Some rooms in private houses. Nearest hotels in Kotor.

The little town of *Perast in Kotor Bay, sometimes known as the "dead city", is protected as a national monument. Like Kotor before the 1979 earthquake, it is a picturesque little old-world town. Although many of the houses have lost their roofs and only ruins remain to bear witness to the town's former prosperity and splendour, all visitors fall under the spell of its medieval atmosphere. The 1979 earthquake added further ruins to those inherited from the past and caused severe damage to the museum.

HISTORY. – The town, built along the water's edge at the foot of Mt Sutilija (2746 ft/837 m), first appears in the records in 1326. Until the end of the 16th c. its history paralleled that of Kotor. Although the Turks occupied the whole of the northern part of the bay they were never able to take either of these towns. An inscription over the doorway of St Nicholas's Church commemorates an occasion in 1654 when the men of Perast inflicted a decisive defeat on the attacking Turks.

Since they lacked any agricultural land the people of Perast directed their energies to shipbuilding and seafaring. There is believed to have been a shipyard here as early as the beginning of the 14th c. In the town's heyday in the middle of the 18th c. the ship-owners of Perast possessed more than 50 sizeable cargo vessels plying in the Adriatic and along the coasts of Greece. The wealth of these citizens of Perast tempted the Barbary corsairs to attack the town with a well-armed fleet in 1624, but on this occasion and many other occasions in subsequent years they were driven off. In the course of these conflicts the men of Perast became experienced fighters on both land and sea, and many of them enlisted for service in Venetian ships and made careers for themselves as seamen in the service of other nations.

In 1698 a sea-captain named Marko Marinović (1663–1716) established a school of seamanship at Perast to which Peter the Great of Russia sent 17 young Russians for training. During this period Perast became increasingly prosperous, and its citizens were wealthy enough to transform their houses into splendid palaces in a mingling of late Renaissance and Baroque styles.

Above Perast is a castle, built in 1600, with the help of which the defenders of Perast are said to have driven off an attacking French warship.

SIGHTS. – It is not so much the individual palaces and burghers' houses that make an impression on visitors as the whole atmosphere of this old town. The Baroque **Bujović Palace** now houses the small *Municipal Museum.* The former **School of Navigation** is occupied by a *Museum of Seafaring*, with the war flag of the Russian navy presented to the founder of the school by Peter the Great. The **parish church of St Nicholas** has a *treasury* containing fine examples of goldsmiths' and silversmiths' work and a handsome octagonal *tower*.

In the bay, a little way out from Perast, lie two small islands – to the E Sveti Juraj, to the W Gospa od Škrpjela. There are unfortunately no longer any regular boat trips to these islands: visitors must inquire locally until they find a boat-owner willing to take them.

On **Sveti Juraj**, surrounded by dark cypresses, is a *Benedictine abbey* with its church (12th c.). The abbey was re-peatedly plundered and destroyed by earthquakes.

The islet of **Gospa od Škrpjela** was originally no more than a bare reef, on

The islands off Perast in Kotor Bay

which, it is said, two brothers out fishing on the night of July 22, 1452 discovered a radiantly shining image of the Virgin. They took it to Perast, but it returned to the reef; and when this happened a second and a third time the brothers realised that they must build a church on the reef. They brought loads of stone and sank them round the reef, and then built the church – subsequently enlarged – in which the miraculous image is still displayed.

In addition to paintings and sculpture by local and Venetian artists the church contains 2500 silver ex-votos presented by seafarers. The tablets depict many different kinds of ship, usually shown in a storm or attacked by pirates.

The discovery of the image is com-memorated annually on July 22 by a **pilgrimage** from Kotor and Perast in gaily decorated boats.

Petrovac na Moru

Republic: Montenegro (Crna Gora).
Altitude: 10 ft/3 m. – Population: 800.
Post code: YU-85200. – Telephone code: 0 86.
ⓘ **Turističko Društvo Primorje,**
tel. 8 51 34.

HOTELS. – *Castellastva*, B, 354 b., tel. 8 51 99; *Riviera*, C, 162 b., tel. 8 51 32.

CAMP SITES. – *Autocamp I,* some distance from beach; *Autocamp II,* on sea.

SPORT. – Water-skiing, fishing, scuba diving; table tennis, walking.

Petrovac na Moru is a quiet bathing resort which has the great advan-tage of being situated away from the

The beach, Petrovac na Moru

Adriatic coastal highway. This favourite family resort lies between pinewoods and olive-groves at the point on the coast where the road to Titograd and Belgrade branches off the coast road, but at some considerable distance from the junction. Its characteristic feature is its beach of sand and pebbles, ranging in colour from bright red to light brown. The little harbour by the castle is a daily port of call for excursion ships.

HISTORY. – Until 1919 Petrovac na Moru was known as *Castel Lastua*, after the late 16th c. Venetian castle at the end of the bay. The site was already occupied in Roman times, and there are the remains of a villa; fragments of a mosaic from this villa can be seen behind the church of Sv. Ilija.

Beyond this most of what we known about Petrovac is legend rather than history. There is, for example, the story of a maiden called Ruža who, fleeing from the Turks, threw herself into the sea from the highest crag to the W of Petrovac in order to avoid becoming unfaithful to her betrothed. There is also the tale of the fisherman who survived shipwreck on a reef off Petrovac and in gratitude for the divine intervention which had saved him collected enough money to build a church on the cliff. The little islet is now known as Sveta Nedelja ("Holy Sunday").

Another local legend is associated with the ruined monastery of Reževići, 2 miles/3 km N of the town near the coast road. It is said that there was once an inn here, with a thoughtful landlord who always set out a full jug of wine so that thirsty travellers could refresh themselves without more ado. In 1226 King Stephen the First Crowned passed this way, and after emptying the jug of wine thought not so much of the hospitable landlord as of the heavenly powers which had inspired him with the idea of setting out the wine. The pious king therefore resolved that the site would be better occupied by a church than by an inn. A second church was built here by the emperor Dušan in 1351. Thereafter the history of the churches tells only of

destruction – by the Turks in 1785, the French in 1812 and the Italians in 1941 – and nothing is now left but ruins.

Petrovac lies in front of the impressive backdrop of the Paštrovići massif, a karstic range rising to almost 3300 ft/1000 m through which a road winds its way inland to Lake Scutari (see p. 186). The little bay, with a beach ¾ mile/1 km long, is surrounded by hills, either forest-covered or planted with olive-groves.

SURROUNDINGS. – 2½ miles/4 km E are the ruins of the **monastery of Gradište**, which was completely destroyed in the violent earthquake of spring 1979. The wall paintings in the oldest of the three churches, Sv. Sava, were an interesting example of late medieval Montenegrin painting. Also buried under the rubble is the unusual icon of the "holy ass', depicting a monk with a donkey's head – a guise adopted by a handsome young monk to frighten off the women who ran after him. The scale of the damage caused by the earthquake is such that reconstruction of the monastery cannot be contemplated.

1¼ miles/2 km SE of Petrovac is the **Buljarica beach**, 2000 yd/1·8 km long and 33–45 yd/30–40 m wide, frequented mostly by local people and visitors staying on the two camp sites. Beyond this stretch of coast is the Vuk Bošković Tower, commemorating a Montenegrin hero who was killed in a battle with the Turks in 1685.

Piran

Republic: Slovenia (Slovenija).
Altitude: 16 ft./5 m. – Population: 6000.
Post code: YU-66330. – Telephone code: 0 66.
ⓘ **Turistično Društvo Portorož,**
Avditorij-Senčna Pot 10,
YU-66320 Portorož;
tel. 7 33 42.

HOTELS. – *Punta*, B, 136 b., tel. 7 39 51; *Piran*, B, 116 b., tel. 7 36 51; *Sidro*, D, 30 b., tel. 7 36 40.

CAMP SITE. – *Jezero*, Fiesa 57, tel. 7 34 73.

SPORT. – Rental of motorboats and sail boats; supply station at harbour entrance, to S; scuba diving; riding at Lipica; target shooting, bowling.

In the mild light of early evening the façades of the buildings fronting Piran harbour look like a theatrical setting for some historical play. At this time of day the gaudier hues are toned down and the peeling patches on the walls merge into the general effect of pastel tints. With its photogenic townscape *Piran is

The picturesque old harbour of Piran

characteristic both of Italian archi-tecture and of the atmosphere of the present-day Yugoslav region of Istria. It is not a place where visitors stay long, for it has no beaches; but a visit to Piran – still a bilingual place, known in Italian as Pirano – is highly recommended to any visitor passing within reach of the town; it is an experience not to be missed for its sounds, smells and sights.

HISTORY. – The site of Piran was occupied in pre-Roman and Roman times: this tongue of land between two bays, with a hill rising above it, must have seemed to the strategically minded Romans an ideal site for the establishment of a fortified post. The town held out for many years before finally acknowledging Venetian authority in 1283, thereafter remaining subject to Venice until 1797. From then until 1918 Piran belonged to Austria. Under the treaty of Rapallo in 1920 Istria was assigned not to the new kingdom of Yugoslavia but to Italy, which held on to it until the end of the Second World War. After Italy's surrender in 1943 its troops finally left the town, which was then briefly occupied by German forces. After the war Piran was included in the Trieste "Zone B" which was administered by Yugoslavia, and thereafter was formally incorporated in Yugoslavia. Italian influence has steadily declined, the former Italian Institute in the town has been closed, and the use of Italian on a bilingual basis is increasingly being restricted to official signs.

SIGHTS. – During the summer parking space in Piran is at a premium; the best plan, therefore, is to leave your car outside the town. The best view of the colourful and historic old buildings is from the harbour quay. The *harbour itself is no longer used by fishermen and is now filled with pleasure craft, whose owners may occasionally throw out a line or a net to catch a few fish. To the right, opposite the entrance to the inner harbour, is the *Maritime Museum*, which was originally established in 1954 as the Municipal Museum but has concentrated since 1959 on collecting material relating to seafaring in the Slovenian coastal area. Associated with the museum are an archaeological collection, a section devoted to the old salt-pans of Piran, a room containing the papers and other relics of the Piran-born violin virtuoso and composer Giovanni Tartini (1692–1770) and the municipal archives.

Tartini Square, beyond the harbour, was until 1894 a further harbour basin. Until the 15th c. this lay outside the town walls, but in later centuries the area around this second inner harbour was so densely built up that even before the coming of the automobile age it was desperately short of space. Finally, when the smell from the harbour basin became too much even for the less sensitive noses of those days, the town council had it filled in.

On the edge of the square are two *columns* topped by flagpoles (and nowadays much defaced by posters) bearing the *lion of St Mark*, the *municipal coat of arms* and a *figure of St George* (15th c.). To the left is the **Tartini Monument**, with a figure of Tartini playing the famous "Devil's Trill" sonata.

Far left, on the near side of the square where the present harbour basin ends, are the **Law Courts**, with *St George's Gate*, a 17th c. town gate, built into them on one side. Adjoining, on the W side of the square, stands the **Town Hall** (1877–79), designed by Trieste architects, which is a typical example of the Viennese monumental style, incorporating Mediterranean elements. In the atrium are various inscribed stones and coats of arms from the earlier town hall on the same site, among them a richly ornamented stone with three cavities representing the town's standard measures (1477).

At the NW corner of the square, far left, we find a mid 15th c. *palace with a red-painted façade, Gothic windows, a pretty balcony and sculptural decoration of white marble – one of the finest examples of Gothic domestic architecture in Slovenia. Between the two uppermost windows on the façade looking on to the square the figure of a lion holds between its paws a scroll with the inscription (readable from the square only with field-glasses) "Lassa pur dir" ("Let them say what they will") – a retort by the wealthy Venetian merchant who built the house to

those of his fellow-citizens who envied him his fine mansion.

Going E from this house, we see, in the street opposite *St Peter's Church* (Sv. Petar; above the altar a painting of the Virgin, said to be a copy after Titian), a low neo-classical building erected in 1818 on the site of an earlier church, the *house in which Tartini was born.*

The next street running up from the square, Boltniška Ulica, leads under a 15th c. house in Venetian Gothic style (much in need of renovation). Beyond this, on the right, is a square surrounded by old houses, with *St Francis's Church*. The church, like the monastic buildings to the right, was built in 1318 and was much altered in 1600. Its main interest lies in its pictures, in particular a "Last Supper" immediately to the right of the entrance. Its principal treasure, a "Madonna with Saints" by Vittore Carpaccio (1519), was carried off to Italy in 1940. Between the church and the monastic buildings (now a school boarding house) is the *cloister*, which was restored in 1951.

Returning to Boltniška Ulica, we see on the left, immediately adjoining St Francis's Church, the tiny *Church of Our Lady of the Snow* (Marija Snežna), built in 1404. Behind its unpretentious exterior it conceals an impressive array of religious pictures. The walls of the nave are covered with *oil paintings*, all in carved wooden frames, the work of an artist from Motovun in 1666. Under the pictures frescoes have recently been discovered which have been rated by experts as superb examples of the medieval wall painting of Istria.

At the end of the street, where the sea comes into sight, a road on the right ascends to the *Castle*, of which there survive only seven battlemented *towers* and some remains of the *town walls*.

The street on the left leads to the **Cathedral**, rearing up above the town on the cliff-fringed coast. The complex includes a tall *campanile* (1608) modelled on the one in St Mark's Square in Venice and a domed circular *Baptistery* (1650).

There were undoubtedly other churches on this exposed site before the building of the present Cathedral in 1637. A tablet on the façade refers to a church built in 1345, but the origins of this place of worship must go still farther back. The façade of the Cathedral seems overpoweringly massive when seen from immediately in front of it, but it fits into its setting on the hill when observed from farther away, out to sea. The campanile, imposingly tall and square, stands some distance away from the Cathedral. The most notable feature in the interior of the Cathedral is the treasury. – The Baptistery has a font made from a Roman sarcophagus.

From Tartini Square Levstikova Ulica, on the right, leads to a group of fine old houses with colourful façades. Particularly notable is a house at No. 8 with three Gothic windows fronting a small balcony on a blue-painted façade.

To the right of the northern harbour basin is an *Aquarium*, in front of which are the stone stalls of the former fish-market. From here a street runs past the old Theatre (now a movie house) and a hotel to the *seafront promenade*, with many fish restaurants.

Plitvice Lakes/ Plitvička Jezera

Republic: Croatia (Hrvatska).
(i) **National Park Administration,**
Nacionalni Park Plitvička Jezera;
tel. (0 48) 7 63 14.

HOTELS. – *Jezero*, A, 530 b., tel. (0 48) 7 63 16; *Plitvice*, A, 130 b., tel. (0 48) 7 63 40; *Bellevue*, B, 138 b., tel. (0 48) 7 63 44; *Garni Hotel Villa Izvor*, tel. (0 48) 7 63 06.

CAMP SITE.

TOURIST INFORMATION. – In July and August visitors flock to the lakes in large numbers – up to 10,000 every day. Day trips from the coastal resorts, allowing a stay of only 2–3 hours at the lakes, can give only a very hasty impression of these extraordinary natural wonders. The admission tickets are valid for two days; and at least that amount of time is necessary for even the most superficial exploration of the scenery and curious natural features to be seen in the National Park.

Plitvice Lakes – the lowest waterfall

There are three entrances to the National Park, with adequate car parking. Sightseeing coaches run along the old lakeside road (now closed to private cars), with recorded commentaries in several languages. There are also motor-launch trips on *Lake Kozjak*, connecting with trains on the panoramic railway.

On payment of a fee anglers can fish for trout in *Lake Kozjak*, the *Prošćansko Jezero* and *Lake Ciginovac* (rental of row boats). There is a National Park Information Bureau at Gate I. There are plans to extend the park and to exclude through traffic within the next few years.

The **Plitvice Lakes, half way between Zagreb and Zadar on the road to the Adriatic, have developed into one of Yugoslavia's greatest tourist attractions, with more than half a million visitors every year. The authorities of the National Park, within which the lakes lie, have plans to extend the park from its present area of 77 sq. miles to 127 sq. miles.

HISTORY. – The first known settlers in the area of the lakes were the Thracians, around 3000 B.C. Later, after the Illyrians, came the Romans, followed by the lapodes and the Liburni. At the beginning of the 7th c. A.D. the Slavs appeared. Living in family communities, they sought protection from frequent enemy attacks in fortified houses of a type characteristic of this region of *Lika*.

After the Turkish period the area came under Austrian rule, and it was Austrian officers who first discovered the natural beauties of the Plitvice lakes and had the first accommodation for visitors built. In 1893 the Society for the Development of the Plitvice Lakes was established in Zagreb, and three years later the first hotel was built. Other tourist amenities built after the First World War were destroyed during the Second. The area was declared a National Park in 1928, and this status was confirmed by the Croatian Parliament in 1963. Since January 1970 the park has been run by a specially established self-governing body which has largely freed it from direct state control. The government now makes no financial contribution to the running costs of the National Park, which must be met from current income.

The unique natural phenomenon of the **Plitvice Lakes consists of 16 lakes linked with one another by overflows, waterfalls and cave systems. They are divided into two groups – the Upper Lakes (*Prošćansko Jezero, Ciginovac, Okrugl-*

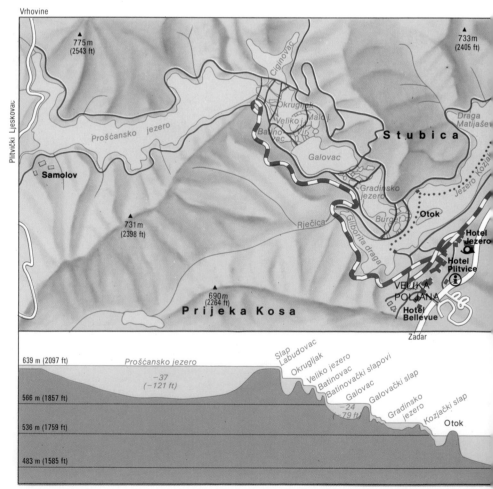

jak, Batinovac, Veliko Jezero, Malo Jezero, Vir, Galovac, Gradinsko Jezero, Burget and *Jezero Kozjak*) and the Lower Lakes (*Milanovac, Gavanovac* and *Kaludjerovac*).

The largest of the lakes is *Kozjak*, with an area of 203 acres and a greatest depth of 151 ft/46 m. 2 miles/3 km long, it is very similar to the second largest lake, the *Prošćansko Jezero*, which has an area of 168 acres. All the other lakes are quite small, with areas between 1 acre and $18\frac{1}{2}$ acres, and none of them is deeper than 33 ft/10 m.

The lakes are linked by waterfalls and by subterranean caves and channels. The waterfalls all have names: one, the *Milka Trinana* fall, commemorates a famous opera singer of the late 19th c., while the others take their names from various legends and from a monk who once lived in a cave above one of the lakes.

The distinctive feature of the Plitvice lakes is a phenomenon which has been scienti-fically studied only within quite recent years. The barriers between the lakes are not formed of natural rock but of cal-careous sinter formations known as *rauhwacke*. Unlike ordinary limestone, which is worn away by the erosional force of water, rauhwacke actually grows in size under the influence of water, as the result of a biodynamic process which involves the action of mosses, algae and minerals dissolved in the water.

Calcareous mud is deposited on the bottom of the lakes, covering submerged tree-trunks with a white coating which gives them the air of sleeping crocodiles. This mud, combined with the reflection of the sun's rays, gives the waters of the lakes their characteristic changing hues, rang-ing between green and blue according to the angle at which the sun strikes the surface.

The forests around the lakes play an important part in preserving the rauh-wacke barriers and providing them with a regular supply of water. In some parts of

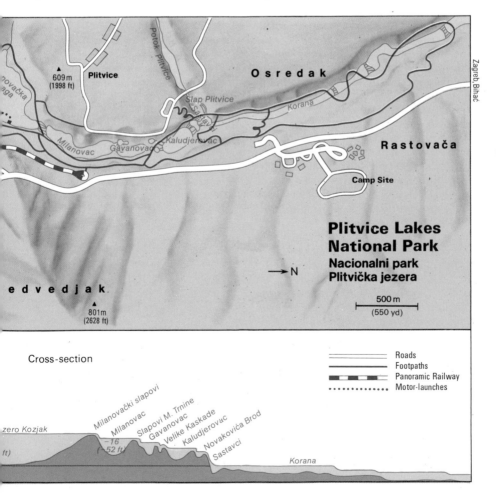

the National Park, where the dense growth of trees resembles a primeval forest, there are bears, wolves, deer, wild pigs, martens, foxes and badgers. Since some of the species cannot find enough food for themselves they have to be supplied with food by man. While the wolves remain hidden in the depths of the forest even in the hardest winter, a bear will occasionally appear at one of the hotels to rummage through the garbage cans for food. But visitors who keep to the waymarked tracks and do not venture out into the forest after dark have nothing to fear from the wild animals of the National Park.

Pljevlja

Republic: Montenegro (Crna Gora).
Altitude: 4462 ft/1360 m. – Population: 15,000.
Post code: YU-84210. – Telephone code: 0 84.
ⓘ **Turist Biro,**
    tel. 8 12 03.

HOTELS. – *Pljevlja*, B, 108 b., tel. 8 11 21; *Tara*, tel. 8 16 69.

Pljevlja, the most northerly town in Montenegro, is well worth a visit not only because it has the finest example of Islamic architecture in Montenegro, the Mosque of Pasha Gazi Husein (1562), with the tallest minaret in Yugoslavia (138 ft/42 m), but also for the sake of its very distinctive atmosphere – a mingling of the Turkish past with the developing industrial present in a magnificent mountain setting.

Although surrounded by mountains, Pljevlja is connected with the outside world by roads to N, S, E and W. There is an excellent road (some sections still in course of improvement) from Titograd via Mojkovac and the *Tara gorge; a road to the E, asphalted all the way, links Pljevlja with Prijepolje, on the main Belgrade–Titograd road; a poor road runs N to Prijeboj and Višegrad; and to the NW there is a road (unimproved) to Goražde, on the Belgrade–Dubrovnik road.

HISTORY. – There was a settlement here in Roman times, though its name is not known. In the 11th c. it was known by the Turkish names of *Taslidza* and *Kamenica*. In 1576 it became the seat of the pasha governing Hercegovina. Its present name first appears in the records in the 15th c. It was formerly a place of some importance as a staging point on the road from Dubrovnik to Skopje, and in the 16th c. there was a caravanserai here.

The town was several times destroyed by devastating fires, and in 1818 by the explosion of a powder magazine. In consequence it has few old buildings. On December 1, 1941 there was a battle here in which the partisans suffered heavy losses – an event commemorated by an impressive memorial on Mt Stražica, with an obelisk 130 ft/40 m high. Pljevlja is now increasingly developing into an industrial area. There are lignite, zinc and lead mines in the area, and the processing industries are being further developed.

Interior of the Gazi Husein Mosque, Pljevlja

SIGHTS. – In the middle of town is the *Mosque of Pasha Gazi Husein. – At Sandšak in the suburb of ŠEVARI is a 16th c. Turkish house with numerous inscriptions on the façade. – Near the village of Gosteče, in the immediate vicinity of Pljevlja, are the ruins of the town of Kukanj, founded by Duke Stephen in the second half of the 15th c.

SURROUNDINGS. – Outside the town, in a wooded gorge, is the Orthodox monastery of the Holy Trinity (*Sv. Trojica*), built in the Middle Ages, with beautiful frescoes and a treasury. It is now occupied only by a few nuns. Between the monastery and the road is a small motel with a restaurant, now monopolised by the intellectually and artistically minded younger generation of Pljevlja. Here are held art exhibitions, readings by poets and other writers and musical evenings – which in summer take place on the terrace, with wide views over the rocky country of the plateau.

Počitelj

Republic: Bosnia-Hercegovina. (Bosna i Hercegovina)
Altitude: 36 ft/11 m. – Population: 800.
Post code: YU-79400. – Telephone code: 0 88.
ⓘ **Turist Biro,**
    tel. 8 02 83.

HOTEL. – *Stari Grad*, B, 39 b., tel. 8 02 83.

*Počitelj, picturesquely situated on a rocky slope above the River

Neretva, on the road from Mostar to the Adriatic coast, is a living museum village full of memories of its Turkish past. From the banks of the river Počitelj is seen ranging down the hillside like an amphitheatre – from the castle which dominates the town, past the mosque and religious school, towers and old buildings, to the Neretva flowing between banks of white sand, often emerald green in hue. During the summer months visitors will frequently encounter artists paying for their holiday by painting. Their works can be seen in a gallery in the town.

HISTORY. – The first appearance of Počitelj in the records is in 1444, the year in which it was founded. In 1471 it was taken by the Turks, who soon began to fortify this strategically situated little town on the caravan road between Sarajevo and the Adriatic. Most of the fortifications now visible, however, date from the 17th c. The Citadel was also built during that period on the walls of an earlier castle. The Turks also built a mosque, a clock-tower (*sahat kula*), a religious school (*medrese*), an inn (*han*) and a bath-house (*hamam*).

The Turks remained in the town, with only brief interruptions, until 1878. After the last war increasing numbers of the inhabitants left the village. Then in the sixties Union Impex, a Sarajevo commercial organisation, began restoring the old buildings, providing apartments for visitors and a small hotel. The old Koranic school became a restaurant. As a result Počitelj now attracts many vistors on day trips from the coastal resorts.

SIGHTS. – The great fascination of Počitelj lies in the complete picture it affords of a little Turkish *town of the 16th–17th c. The **Ibrahim Pasha Mosque** has a slender *minaret* and contains beautiful, brilliantly coloured *carpets*. The best time to visit the town is in the morning or late afternoon, since the climb up through the narrow streets to the **castle** is a very strenuous undertaking in the noonday sun. A large house (restored) half way up the hill is occupied by the *painters' colony*. The castle is now in ruins, but the climb is worthwhile for the sake of the view.

Podgora

Croatia (Hrvatska).
Altitude: 16 ft/5 m. – Population: 1800.
Post code: YU-58327. – Telephone code: 0 58.
ⓘ **Turist Biro,**
tel. 7 78 98.

HOTELS. – *Minerva*, A, 330 b., tel. 7 78 12; *Aurora*, B, 280 b., tel. 7 78 12; *Mediteran*, B, 248 b., tel. 7 73 07;

Primordia, B, 72 b., tel. 7 73 42, with annexe *Borak*, C, 28 b.; *Podgorka*, B, 31 b., tel. 7 72 21, with annexes *Bambus*, B, 55 b., and *Lovor*, B, 64 b.; *Salines*, C, 300 b., tel. 7 78 97. – IN IGRANE: *Igrane*, C, 64 b, tel. 7 72 90.

CAMP SITES. – *Sutikla*, tel. 7 72 68. – AT DRAŠNICE: *Drašnice*, tel. 61 23 56. – AT ŽIVOGOŠCE: *Blato, Velka Duba*.

NATURIST FACILITIES. – Information from hotel reception desks.

EVENTS. – "Fishermen's Night", end of July.

SPORT. – Scuba diving, water-skiing; boat rental; bowling.

Holidaymakers strolling along Podgora's narrow seafront promenade (closed to cars) in the evening will smell the same aroma that pervades every Yugoslav Adriatic resort, from Umag in the N to Ulcinj in the S – a compound of smoke from open fires, grilled ražnjići, ćevapčići, chicken and fish. The beach below the road is also narrow, and during the day is usually crowded. Lack of space also hampers the provision of sports facilities: there is no room for tennis courts or for mini-golf. There is, however, ample scope for every kind of water sport, and the hotels provide a variety of entertainment – dancing, folk displays – for the evenings.

In the S of the Makarska Riviera, which extends for 34 miles/55 km between Brela and Ploče, lies Podgora, the last major lively holiday resort. At the end of the beautiful coastal stretch of central Dalmatia are the quieter and smaller tourist resorts of Igrane, Živogošće, Zaostrog and Gradac. To the S of Gradac the scenery

In Podgora harbour

changes; the bare mountains turn away from the coast, and the region of the Neretva estuary with its marshes, lakes and rice plantations begins. Podgora has developed from a fishing port into a popular holiday resort. Its architectural charm is best appreciated from the sea; from the main road passing close behind the hotels the motorist sees only the less attractive backs of holiday apartments and old houses.

HISTORY. – During the Middle Ages, from the 9th c. on, Podgora was occupied by Neretvans, a Slav people for whom piracy was a way of life. Until the 14th c. the little settlement of peasants and fishermen belonged to Croatia. In 1483 came the Turks. When French troops moved into this area in 1807 in order to incorporate it in Napoleon's Illyrian Provinces the inhabitants of Podgora, urged on by a Russian admiral, put up fierce resistance, but without success, and the men of the village had to flee to the neighbouring islands to escape execution. During the Second World War the people of Podgora again showed their mettle in the Resistance. On September 10, 1942, barely a year after the occupation of Yugoslavia by German and Italian troops, the partisans established their first naval unit here, earning Podgora the name of "cradle of the Yugoslav navy". The event is commemorated by a monument on the hill above the harbour, known locally as the "Gull's Wings". In 1962 an earthquake caused considerable damage in this area, and those of the inhabitants who had lived on the higher ground below the bare karstic hills of the Biokovo range left their ruined houses and moved down to the coast. The building of hotels for holidaymakers has put great pressure on space, and the communal authorities have now banned any further building of this kind.

SIGHTS. – As a result of the destructions of the Second World War – when Podgora suffered 40 air attacks – and the 1962 earthquake many old buildings have been lost. In the upper part of the village, at the hamlets of **Marinovići** and **Ruščići**, are 17th and 18th c. *watch-towers*. The Baroque *church* dates from 1764.

SURROUNDINGS. – A mile or two down the coast, on a steep-sided peninsula, is **Igrane**. On the highest point are a 17th c. watch-tower and the Baroque parish church (1752), and in the olive-groves above the village the aisled pre-Romanesque church (11th–12th c.) of St Michael (Sv. Mihovil). – At **Živogošće** are the ruins of a Franciscan friary. – **Gradac** has the finest beach on the Makarska Riviera, 2 miles/3 km long, and an old watch-tower.

Poreč

Republic: Croatia (Hrvatska).
Altitude: 16 ft/5 m. – Population: 4300.
Post code: YU-52360. – Telephone code: 0 53.
ⓘ **Turistički Biro**,
Trg Slobode 3;
tel. 8 61 26.

HOTELS. – IN POREČ: *Bellevue Villas*, B, 728 b., tel. 8 62 04; *Diamant*, B, 509 b., tel. 8 66 82, with *Diamant Apartments*, b, 560 b.; *Poreč*, B, 117 b., tel. 8 66 24; *Neptun*, C, 288 b., tel. 8 60 26; *Riviera*, C, 162 b., tel. 8 60 24, with annexes *Adriatic*, C, 33 b., and *Jadran*, C, 54 b. – IN PLAVA LAGUNA: *Parentium*, A, 573 b., tel. 8 63 24; *Lotos I, II, III, IV*, B, 1875 b., tel. 8 63 22; *Albatros*, B, 845 b., tel. 8 61 37; *Galeb*, B, 776 b., tel. 8 60 07; *Mediteran*, B, 623 b., tel. 8 64 04; *Astra*, B, 552 b., tel. 8 66 96; *Plava Laguna*, C, 1030 b., tel. 8 60 72, with chalets. – IN OTOK (Sv. Nikola): *Splendid*, B, 300 b., tel. 8 62 10, with chalets; *Dvorac-Istra*, C, 48 b., tel. 8 62 10; *Miramare*, C, 110 b., tel. 8 62 10. – IN BRULO: *Rubin*, B, 484 b., tel. 8 66 02; *Kristal*, B, 444 b., tel. 8 65 24. – IN PICAL: *Pical*, B, 620 b. tel. 8 61 87; *Pical Apartments*, B, 506 b., tel. 8 61 88; *Zagreb*, B, 502 b., tel. 8 61 88. – IN SPADIĆI: *Turist*, B, 276 b., tel. 8 62 44, with *Villas Turist*, 120 b., and *Bungalows Turist*, 436 b.; *Luna*, B, 238 b., tel. 8 62 06, with *Luna Apartments*, 352 b. – IN MATERADA: *Materada*, B, 823 b. tel. 8 62 49. – IN LANTERNA: *Lanterna Hotels*, B, 788 b., tel. 8 60 28, with *Lanterna Apartments*, B, 1292 b., and *Lanterna Villas*, B, 440 b.; *Solaris Apartments*, B, 504 b., tel. 8 63 68, with *Solaris Pavilions* (see under Naturist facilities). – IN LIM: *Motel Lim*, C, 24 b., tel. 8 63 96. – IN CERVAR: *Prat Apartments*, B, 611 b., tel. 8 62 37; *Ulika* naturist camp (see under Naturist facilities).

CAMP SITES. – *Lanterna* (6 miles/10 km N of Poreč), tel. 8 66 88; *Zelena Laguna* (1 mile/2 km S of Poreč), tel. 8 66 96. Other sites: see under Naturist facilities.

NATURIST FACILITIES. – *Solaris Naturist* (5½ miles/9 km N of Porec), with "pavilions" and apartments, 808 b., tel. 8 63 68; *Ulika Naturist Beach* (N of Poreč), tel. 8 60 05; in a cove at Zelana Laguna camp site.

Poreč, from the beach

SPORT, BOATING and BATHING. – Scuba diving, water-skiing, boat rental, wind-surfing (with instruction); hang-gliding, riding, tennis, target shooting, archery, volleyball, handball, basketball, boccia; rental of bicycles. – Sailing enthusiasts rank Poreč as the best harbour on the W coast of Istria. It is sheltered by the island of Sv. Nikola and two breakwaters, and has a slip and winch. Some of the hotels and camp sites also have slips.

Few resorts are so well equipped as Poreč with facilities for every kind of sport. Instruction is also provided in many sports: details and charges are posted locally.

A popular trip from Poreč is to the island of Sveti Nikola. The busiest beaches are the *Plava Laguna* (Blue Lagoon) to the N of Poreč and the *Zelana Laguna* (Green Lagoon) to the S.

In 1962 Poreč had only one hotel with 80 beds: only seven years later it had more hotel beds than Dubrovnik, and it now has accommodation for something like 35,000 visitors. The old town has fortunately been spared by this great building boom and now forms an oasis of peace amid the surrounding hotels in which – particularly around midday when the streets are deserted – time seems to stand still. With its fine old palaces and above all with its Cathedral, the best preserved example of a 6th c. Byzantine basilica on the whole Yugoslav coast, Poreč is a Mecca for visitors from far and wide, not merely for the local holidaymakers who swarm into the town in the evenings.

Mosaic in Poreč Cathedral

HISTORY. – The site of Poreč was occupied in prehistoric times, and in the 2nd c. B.C. the Romans established a fortified post here. The settlement was later given the status of a municipium, and in the 1st c. A.D. became the *Colonia Iulia Parentium*. After the fall of the Western Empire the town was taken by the Ostrogoths, but soon afterwards, in 539, came under Byzantine rule. In 788 it was occupied by the Franks. During the 12th c. Poreč enjoyed a period of independence, but in 1232 passed into the control of the Patriarchs of Aquileia. In 1267 the Venetians captured the town; then in 1354 it was ravaged by Venice's mortal enemies the Genoese. During the 16th and 17th c. the population of Poreč, like that of many other towns on the Istrian W coast, was decimated by plague and malaria. In the second half of the 17th c. refugees and immigrants from other regions settled here, including Dalmatians and Albanians (whose descendants now run the town's cake-shops and cafés). After the fall of the Venetian republic Poreč came under Austrian rule. In 1861 it became the meeting-place of the Istrian Provincial Assembly, which was given responsibility for local affairs. In 1918 Poreč was assigned to Italy together with the rest of Istria. In 1943, after the Italian surrender, the town was occupied by German troops. Many of the old buildings were destroyed by air attack during the Second World War. In April 1945 Poreč was liberated by partisans.

SIGHTS. – The principal feature of interest in Poreč is the *Cathedral, the *Basilica Euphrasiana*, which dates from the middle of the 6th c. It was built by Bishop Euphrasius of Poreč on the foundations of two earlier churches dating respectively from the second half of the 4th c. and the 5th c., and is of approximately the same size as these earlier structures. At the W end of the basilica is a square *atrium*, surrounded by a covered ambulatory with Byzantine columns which now houses a lapidarium. To the W of the atrium is an octagonal *baptistery*, and beyond this the 15th c. *campanile*. Adjoining the Cathedral, to the NW, is the *Bishop's Palace*.

The INTERIOR is notable for the fine **mosaics** on the upper part of the triumphal arch and in the semi-dome of the apse. They show a wide range of delicate colours, using mother-of-pearl, semi-precious stones and marble, with a gold ground. Bishop Euphrasius's monogram appears on the medallions of military saints round the church, and the bishop himself is depicted holding a model of the church in the semi-dome of the apse (left-hand group), flanked by his brother Claudius and his nephew.

In the floor of the N aisle two layers of *mosaics* can be seen, one from the 4th c. church, the other from its 5th c. successor. – Note also the very fine **altar**; the *ciborium* is decorated with mosaics from Byzantine workshops in Venice. – Built on to the S side of the Cathedral are three *chapels*, the one at the W end dating from the 17th c., the most easterly added in the 19th c. The **choir-stalls** in the middle chapel date from 1452.

Other features of interest in Poreč are a three-storey 15th c. building in Beogradska Ulica; near this a Romanesque house,

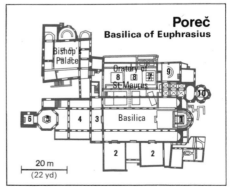

Poreč
Basilica of Euphrasius

Bishop's Palace
Oratory of St Maurus
8 8
9
6
4 3   Basilica
10
2 2

20 m
(22 yd)

1 Altar
2 Chapels
3 Narthex
4 Atrium
5 Baptistery
6 Bell-tower
7 3rd c. mosaics
8 4th c. mosaics
9 Sacristy
10 Memorial chapel

the *Kuća Dvaju Svetaca*; in Marafor Square the remains of a Roman *Temple of Neptune* and a Romanesque building, in the area once occupied by the Roman forum; and the *Franciscan church*, with a bell-tower

Portorož

Republic: Slovenia (Slovenija).
Altitude: 16 ft/5 m. – Population. 200^
Post code: YU-66320. – Telephone code: 0 66.
ⓘ **Turistično Društvo,**
     Avditorij-Senčna Pot 10;
     tel. 7 33 42.

HOTELS. – *Grand Hotel Metropol*, with annexes *Marita/Suisse* and *Barbara & Vesna*, A, together 610 b., tel. 7 35 41; *Grand Hotel Palace*, A, 396 b., tel. 7 35 41; *Park Villas*, B, 478 b., tel. 7 52 71; *Bernardin*, B, 465 b., tel. 7 52 71; *Grand Hotel Emona*, B, 420 b., tel. 7 52 71; *Palace*, B, 363 b., tel. 7 33 41, with annexes *Neptun*, B, 206 b., tel. 7 33 59, *Apollo*, B, 192 b., tel. 7 35 42, and *Mira*, B, 192 b., tel. 7 33 58; *Riviera*, B, 358 b., tel. 7 30 72, with annexes *Slovenija*, A, 272 b., and *Jadranka*, A, 175 b.; *Lucia*, B, 180 b., tel. 7 51 41, with annexes *Roža*, A, 219 b., and *Lucija Villas*, A, 164 b.; *Helios*, C, tel. 7 30 45, *Istra*, C, tel. 7 33 48, and *Virginia*, C, tel. 7 52 61, together 182 b.

Hotels, Portorož

CAMP SITES. – *Lucija*, tel. 7 50 86; *Strunjan*, tel. 7 36 07.

Casino in Grand Hotel Metropol.

EVENTS. – From 15 May to September a programme of dramatic performances, folk displays and beauty competitions; International Sculptors' Symposium, annually; Yugoslav Folk Festival, mid July.

SPORT. – There are several tennis courts and volleyball and basketball courts at the yacht harbour, on the site of the old salt-pans. The Metropol and Palace Hotels have swimming pools with heated sea water. The quiet waters of the bay offer ideal conditions for water-skiing and sailing (instruction available). There is a scuba diving station at Piran.

BOATING and BATHING. – Rental of motorboats and row boats. Good moorings in the new yacht harbour at the end of the bay. Small harbour at Bernardin Hotel; workshop with spare parts for all common types of motorboats and repair yard for small boats.

The large bathing beach (free to hotel guests) is covered with imported sand, which is kept constantly clean and is renewed every year. There are a number of gangways leading into the sea. The beach has a gentle slope and is accordingly suitable for children. Along the beach are play and sports facilities, and several restaurants and snack bars which can be patronised in bathing suits.

The waters of the bay are clean, since all sewage is properly treated. If the water is occasionally clouded this is due to natural changes in the rivers flowing into the sea: scientific investigation has shown that it is not the result of pollution.

NATURIST FACILITIES. – In the Kanegra camp site, at the end of the bay on the S side, opposite the Bernardin Hotel (from Koper–Pula road take side road for Umag, then turn off for Kanegra), stony beach, with restaurant, snack bars, etc.

Portorož, in Italian Portorose, the "Port of Roses", is a select resort which fully lives up to its name, with old-established parks full of sub-tropical vegetation and public gardens gay with flowers. The climate is exceptionally mild, since the town, straggling around the N side of a wide bay, is sheltered by the sur-rounding hills from cold N winds and also from the E wind. More than a dozen hotels of the higher cate-gories cater for visitors throughout the year, and the old Palace Hotel still preserves the splendours of the Austrian period. The beach, over $\frac{3}{4}$ mile/1 km long, is of fine sand, as is the sea bottom.

HISTORY. – The Portorož area is first mentioned in the records in the 12th c. as a property belonging to the Benedictine abbey on Cape Sv. Lovrenc. Its develop-ment as a resort began in 1830 with the building of the Villa Vesna, and by the end of the 19th c. there were several hotels, patronised mainly by visitors who came for the sake of the mud baths and the high salt content of the air. The resurgence of the tourist trade which began soon after the Second World War encouraged Portorož to expand still further its holiday amenities, the most recent development being the construction of a new sports complex on the site of the old salt-pans.

SIGHTS. – Portorož has no features of historical or artistic interest to attract visitors. There is, however, an **open-air museum**, *Forma Viva* on the *Seča* penin-sula, with a display of sculpture (mostly of Istrian marble) produced during the annual Sculptors' Symposium. The old *salt-pans* are no longer worked, but behind the new yacht harbour which now occupies part of the site, in and around an old mill, a museum of salt-working is planned. – A road runs along the coast, passing through the modern *Bernardin* resort complex, to the picturesque little town of *Piran* (see p. 152). There are many attractive footpaths around Portorož.

SURROUNDINGS. – There are numerous attractive excursions to places of interest within easy reach of Portorož – for example through the hills, with magnificent glimpses of the sea, to *Pula* and *Trieste*; to the inland villages of *Buje*, *Motovun* and *Pazin* (see under Vrsar); to the charming little coastal towns of Poreč and Rovinj; to the Lipica stud farm (see p. 119); and to the Škocjan caves (see under Postojna Caves).

Underground railway in the Postojna Caves

Postojna Caves/ Postojnska Jama

Republic: Slovenia (Slovenija).
Altitude: 1818 ft/554 m. – Population (**Postojna**): 6300.
Post code: YU-66230. – Telephone code: 0 67.
(i) **Turistično Društvo,**
Tržaška 4;
tel. 2 10 77.
Kompas Travel Agency,
YU-66210 Sežana;
tel. (0 67) 7 32 26.

HOTELS. – *Jama*, B, 134 b., tel. 2 11 72; *Kras*, B, 118 b., tel. 2 10 71; *Motel Proteus*, C, 418 b., tel. 2 12 50; *Šport*, C, 126 b., tel. 2 11 50; *Motel Erazem*, C, 29 b., tel. 2 11 09.

CAMP SITE. – *Pivka Jama*, with chalets, 2½ miles/4 km N, tel. 2 13 82.

The ** Postojna Caves (Postojnska Jama) are one of Yugoslavia's outstanding tourist attractions. This labyrinth of underground passages and chambers on two levels, with a total length of 14 miles/23 km, offers a succession of extraordinary rock formations of breathtaking beauty and colour. Since the publication in 1821 of the first guide to the caves, which were partially explored by Lukas Čeč in 1818, they have been visited by more than 16 million people from all over the world. The cable railway constructed in 1924, double-tracked in 1964 to cope with the increasing traffic, runs through the caves for a distance of 1½ miles/ 2·5 km, after which visitors have a

walk of 1 mile/1·5 km back to the entrance.

The caves contain a curious cave-dwelling amphibian, the olm (*Proteus anguineus*), which can be seen in a pool below the cave chamber known as the Concert Hall. This is a flesh-coloured eyeless salamander-like creature which has gills for breathing in water and a lung for breathing air, normally produces eggs but occasionally gives birth to fully developed young. It lives in lateral branches on the lower level of the caves, through which water flows (not open to the public).

Beyond the village of Kalce the highway from Ljubljana to the Adriatic and the ordinary road (No. 10), which runs parallel to it, enter the Planina basin, a typical karstic feature which fills with water in early spring and forms a lake up to 4½ miles/7 km long, the Planinsko Jezero. At the end of the basin are the Javorniki hills, and beyond these the Pivka basin, traversed by the little River Pivka, a stream well stocked with fish which collects most of the basin's water and directs it into the Postojna Caves.

Millions of years ago the water from the Pivka basin flowed down into the Planina basin in above-ground rivers. Then, when the ground bordering the Pivka basin rose, the rivers cut their way ever deeper down and, encountering less resistant beds of limestone, filtered down through this rock and continued on their way underground. These underground watercourses then carved out a series of caverns by the mechanical process of erosion, reinforced by the chemical process of corrosion in which the carbon dioxide in the water dissolved the limestone, enlarged existing cavities in this way and deposited limestone in the form of sinter; and these sinter deposits produced the most astonishing variety of dripstone formations (stalactites, stalagmites, etc.).

In the course of time the River Pivka carved its way ever deeper into the earth, finally forming such enormous caverns that when the caves were being opened up for tourists it was possible to construct a system of paths and gangways a whole "storey" above the river.

HISTORY. – During the Ice Age the Pivka basin was occupied by Palaeolithic man, who also left traces of his presence in the Postojna Caves. During the construction of the tourist route through the caves many remains of animal bones were found. No signs of occupation have been found, however, for the long period between the Palaeolithic and the early Middle Ages. Inscriptions and names carved on the walls of the caves, which were examined during the 19th c., refer to a variety of dates between 1213 and 1676.

The first accounts of the caves were given by travellers such as J. W. Valvasor, who claimed in 1689 to have penetrated 2 miles/3 km into the mountain, and the Viennese court mathematician J. N. Nagel, who described the caves in 1748. In 1803 the writer J. G. Seume visited the caves in the course of a "walk to Syracuse" which he described in a book of that name.

The caves began to become a tourist attraction after a local peasant named Luka Čeč climbed the rock face on the right bank of the Pivka in 1818 and discovered the entrance to the Great House. Since then the exploration of the caves has steadily advanced. In 1974 divers explored the passage linking the Postojna and the Pivka caves. The connection between the Pivka and Planina caves, which must be some 1¼ miles/2 km long, has not yet been found in spite of all the efforts made to discover it.

TOUR OF THE CAVES. – The temperature in the caves remains at a fairly steady 46°F/8°C throughout the year. Warm clothing is therefore necessary, even in summer or perhaps particularly in summer, for visitors doing the conducted tour, which takes about 1½ hours. Although the trains, each of 25 cars, leave at half-hour intervals in July and August there is sometimes a line of people to board them, since there may be up to 10,000 visitors a day at the height of the season.

After passing through the specially constructed entrance tunnel 150 yd/140 m long, the train enters the passage known as the *Upturned Ship*, up to 33 ft/10 m high, which shows clear signs of an explosion: during the Second World War the Germans used this cave for storing gasoline, which was blown up by the partisans in 1944. The stalactites in the adjoining *Great House* (130 yd/120 m long, 55 yd/50 m wide, 110 ft/33 m high) were destroyed in the explosion. Then comes the *Gothic Hall* (22 yd/20 m wide, 43 ft/13 m high), also known as the *Snow Mountain* for its beautiful white sinter covering; from the roof hang long stalactites and on the floor are tall stalagmites. The train then enters the *Congress Hall* (formerly known as the *Dancing Hall*), which was given its present name on September 12, 1965 in honour of the International Speleological Congress then taking place at Postojna. This chamber also has beautiful sinter deposits, as well as a stalactitic column 30 ft/9 m high remarkable for its fine colouring.

The route now continues into the *Washhouse* and through the *Crystal Corridor* to the *Small Caves*. On the right-hand wall is the illuminated *Curtain*, a thin layer of deposits, in colours ranging from brown to bright red and orange, formed by drops of water collecting on the sloping rock face.

The train now runs past side passages leading to the *Nameless Corridor* and the *Many-Coloured Corridor* and passes under a fallen stalactitic column 16 ft/5 m thick. The rail journey ends at the *Great Mountain* and the tour continues on foot through winding passages, reaching a height of 1835 ft/560 m. The finest chambers after the descent from the summit of the Great Mountain are the 550 yd/550 m long *Beautiful Caves*, formerly called *Paradise*.

The guides draw attention to particularly striking features, including the stalagmite known as the Leaning Tower of Pisa and the slender stalactites aptly called Macaroni. From the *Red Hall* the route continues to the *Tiger's Hall*, the *Winter Hall* and the very beautiful *Diamond Corridor*. Then comes another climb to the *Concert Hall* (70 yd/65 m long, 45 yd/40 m wide), with a snack bar and a "Cave Post Office". This chamber, which has excellent acoustics, is occasionally used for concerts. From here the train

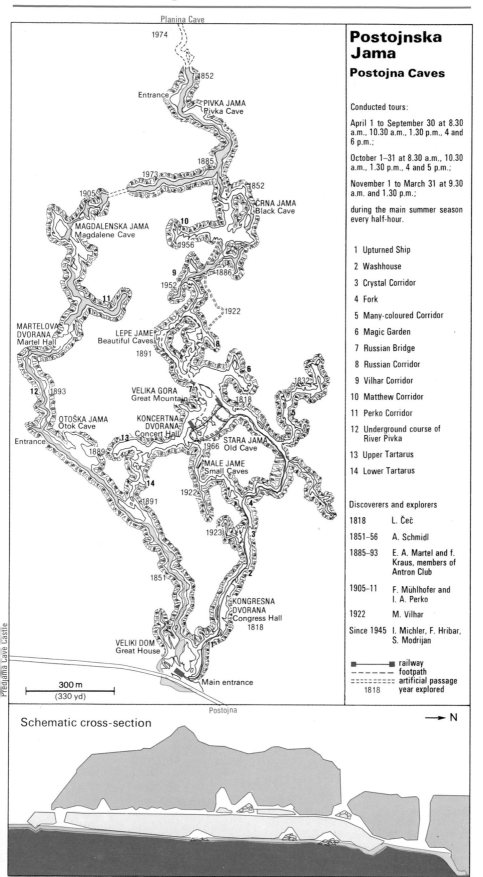

Planina Cave
1974

1852

Entrance

PIVKA JAMA
Pivka Cave

1885

1973

1905

1852

CRNA JAMA
Black Cave

MAGDALENSKA JAMA
Magdalene Cave

10

1956

9   1886

1952

11

1922

MARTELOVA
DVORANA
Martel Hall

LEPE JAME
Beautiful Caves

1891

8

6

1832

12   1893

VELIKA GORA
Great Mountain

1818

5

OTOŠKA JAMA
Otok Cave

KONCERTNA
DVORANA
Concert Hall

Entrance

13

STARA JAMA
Old Cave

1889

1966

MALE JAME
Small Caves

14

1891   1922

1923   3

1851

2

KONGRESNA
DVORANA
Congress Hall
1818

VELIKI DOM
Great House

300 m
(330 yd)

Main entrance

Postojna

Predjama Cave Castle

Schematic cross-section

Postojnska Jama
Postojna Caves

Conducted tours:

April 1 to September 30 at 8.30
a.m., 10.30 a.m., 1.30 p.m., 4 and
6 p.m.;

October 1–31 at 8.30 a.m., 10.30
a.m., 1.30 p.m., 4 and 5 p.m.;

November 1 to March 31 at 9.30
a.m. and 1.30 p.m.;

during the main summer season
every half-hour.

1 Upturned Ship

2 Washhouse

3 Crystal Corridor

4 Fork

5 Many-coloured Corridor

6 Magic Garden

7 Russian Bridge

8 Russian Corridor

9 Vilhar Corridor

10 Matthew Corridor

11 Perko Corridor

12 Underground course of
   River Pivka

13 Upper Tartarus

14 Lower Tartarus

Discoverers and explorers

1818   L. Čeč

1851–56   A. Schmidl

1885–93   E. A. Martel and f.
            Kraus, members of
            Antron Club

1905–11   F. Mühlhofer and
            I. A. Perko

1922   M. Vilhar

Since 1945 I. Michler, F. Hribar,
            S. Modrijan

■━━━━■ railway
– – – – – footpath
========= artificial passage
  1818   year explored

⟶ N

returns to the entrance after describing a great loop 490 yd/450 m long.

SURROUNDINGS. – 2½ miles/4 km from the entrance to the Postojna Caves, near the camp site, is the entrance to the **Pivka Cave** and the **Black Cave**, linked by a labyrinth of passages. There are a number of other caves which can be seen only by visitors with a specialist interest.

5½ miles/9 km from Postojna, beyond the village of Veliki Otok, is **Predjama Castle** (*Predjamski Grad*), which is built in the mouth of a cave. In the 15th c. it was the home of a robber knight named Erasmus Lueger who preyed on the merchants' caravans passing between Postojna and Trieste. The municipal authorities of Trieste laid siege for almost a year to this rocky eyrie, which could be reached only by a bridge over a 200 ft/60 m deep chasm, and was supplied by a secret passage (still in existence but not now open) ending in the forest above the castle. The predatory knight was eventually killed by a cannonball.

The castle is now open to the public. It contains an interesting *collection of archaeological material* from the cave behind the castle, which has 4 miles/6·5 km of passages. There are plans to open the cave to the public.

15 miles/25 km SW of Postojna are the *Caves and Cataracts of Škocjan, which are wilder and more romantic than the Postojna Caves, though they attract fewer visitors and the conducted tour is rather more strenuous. At the point where the highway from Ljubljana at present comes to an end, a few miles beyond Postojna, a road goes off to Kozina; then after the village of Divača a side road on the left leads to Martavun, at the entrance to the caves. The conducted tour (four times daily in summer) takes 2 hours.

This labyrinth of caves, which is referred to by Pliny and Virgil, is made accessible to visitors by a series of paths, flights of steps and bridges. For the most part the tour follows the course of the River *Reka*, which after its tortuous passage through this underground world emerges at two places, respectively 25 miles/40 km and 19 miles/30 km away – at the village of San Giovanni between Monfalcone and Trieste, where it is know as the *Timavo*, and as the *Aurisina* above the seaside resort of Grignano. Both streams then flow into the Adriatic.

The River Reka foams through huge caverns rising to as much as 330 ft/100 m, tumbles over cataracts and gathers in quiet underground lakes. The route through the caves leads to the Giant's Gate gorge, which is crossed on a bridge (viewpoint) and then returns up the other bank of the river to the entrance.

Lake Prespa/ Prespansko Jezero

Republic: Macedonia (Makedonija).

ACCOMMODATION. – IN OTEŠEVO: 11 hotels in categories B and C, with a total of 700 beds; also holiday houses and camp sites. Information: Hotelsko-Turistička Naselba, YU-97319 Oteševo/

Ohrid airport

Prespansko Jezero, tel. (0 96) 7 41 00. – A new hotel complex is being developed at *Pretor*.

*Lake Prespa in southern Macedonia belongs partly to Yugoslavia, partly to Albania and partly to Greece, the frontiers of which meet in Great Lake Prespa. Little Lake Prespa, linked with its larger neighbour by a natural channel, lies S of the Yugoslav border, mainly in Greece but with a small part in Albanian territory.

The largest lake in Yugoslavia is *Lake Scutari in Montenegro, with an area of 143 sq. miles/370 sq. km. Whether the second place is assigned to *Lake Prespa or to *Lake Ohrid in Macedonia, only 22 miles/35 km away, depends on whether or not the 27 sq. miles/70 sq. km of Little Lake Prespa (Malo Prespansko Jezero), almost all of which is in Greece, are added to the 110 sq. miles/284 sq. km of Great Lake Prespa. The justification for including the smaller lake is that it is linked with the larger one by a natural channel. Little Lake Prespa is sometimes not shown on maps.

While Lake Ohrid has drawn increasing numbers of visitors, attracted both by its historic old buildings and by its bathing beaches, since the opening of Struga airport in 1970 and the completion of the realigned road to Skopje in 1976, Lake Prespa has so far remained off the tourist track; but here too the development of the tourist trade has been in progress since the mid seventies.

Great Lake Prespa, lying at an altitude of 2800 ft/853 m, has an area of 110 sq. miles/284 sq. km and a greatest depth of 250 ft/76 m. Like its neighbour Lake Ohrid, it was created by tectonic movements. The lake is bounded on the E by the Baba range of mountains which reach their highest point in Pelister (8534 ft/ 2601 m), the favourite skiing area of the people of Bitola. On the W side, so far as it lies within Yugoslavia, is the Galičica range, with other ranges, also rising to 6560 ft/2000 m, within Albanian territory. The reed-fringed northern shores of the lake merge into the fertile plain around the town of Resen, while to the S is an expanse of marshy ground between Great Lake Prespa and *Little Lake Prespa*.

The surprising thing about Lake Prespa is that although it is fed by numerous mountain streams it has no outflow and yet its level hardly rises even when there is a large inflow of water after heavy rain. The explanation was found to be that the excess of water flows through underground channels to Lake Ohrid, lying 518 ft/158 m lower down. The water emerges in a pool at the monastery of Sv. Naum and then flows into the lake. The phenomenon can be observed from an island in the pool.

The temperature of the water in Lake Prespa ranges between 64°F/18°C and 75°F/24°C from mid June to mid September. There are relatively few really hot days during the summer, and even on hot days there is a a distinct cooling-off around the lake at night.

A glance at the map shows the division of the lake between three countries. Two-thirds of the area of Great Lake Prespa lie within Yugoslavia, the remaining third being shared about equally between Albania and Greece. Little Lake Prespa lies almost entirely in Greece, with only the south-western tip extending into Albania.

The three countries meet at a point (not marked in any way) to the S of the Yugoslav island of *Golem Grad*. Owners of motorboats and sail boats can use Lake Prespa without the helmsman's certificate and sailing permit which are required in coastal waters. They should, however, keep clear of the frontier area S of Golem Grad: boats are not allowed to cross either the Albanian or the Greek frontier.

The pass road between Trpejca on Lake Ohrid and Carino on Lake Prespa climbs in long straight stretches with sharp bends (maximum gradient 8%). From Lake Ohrid (2280 ft/695 m) there is a climb of more than (3600 ft/1100 m) to the pass (5900 ft/1800 m).

The best view of both lakes from the pass is to be had by leaving the car and

Great Lake Prespa, where the frontiers of Yugoslavia, Greece and Albania meet

climbing a little way up the hill on the N side. The lakes are, however, frequently concealed under a white blanket of mist.

From the pass the road descends to Lake Prespa through oak forests. Just before the lake a dusty road goes off on the right to the village of *Stenje*, situated on a long sandy beach, with a population consisting largely of old people. Near here is a prehistoric cemetery.

The road beyond Stenje continues towards Albania (frontier closed). Returning to the main road, we continue towards Oteševo. At a curve just before the town, below the road, is a camp site, attractively situated by a little bay. Adjoining this is another site, with more shade but not so well equipped. Then comes the tourist village of **Hotel Oteševo**, lying off the road away from the traffic.

The whole tourist complex is laid out along a sandy beach which attracts large numbers of people from Skopje and Bitola at weekends, when it tends to become crowded, in spite of the admission charges. The "free" bathing beaches outside the tourist complex are not so clean or well kept. It is advisable to wear bathing shoes when going into the water, since although there are sandy beaches around almost the whole extent of the lake the sand often gives place to sharp stones at the water's edge.

The Oteševo holiday village is well provided with facilities for a variety of sports, including football, volleyball, basketball and table tennis. A motorboat is available to tow water-skiers. Anglers can fish for carp, eels and trout, and their patience will rarely go unrewarded.

Beyond Oteševo are a number of smaller villages surrounded by fruit orchards (mainly apples), tobacco plantations and fields of poppies. The freshly plastered walls of the mosques and the brightly painted minarets show that prosperity is now coming to this region. The agricultural produce is handled by canning factories and cooperatives.

Farther around the lake a well-made side road turns right off the main road, which continues straight ahead to Bitola. $5\frac{1}{2}$ miles/9 km along this road a minor road (signposted to Asamati) goes off on the right and, running parallel to the larger road, comes to **Pretor**, another new holiday resort on Lake Prespa, with a beautiful broad sandy beach, excellently equipped camp sites and various convalescent homes and guest-houses for Yugoslav workers.

It is advisable to return from here to the main road. There is a sandy road continuing along the lake between dunes and fruit orchards, but some of the bridges over streams flowing into the lake are in a rather dilapidated state. Some 6 miles/10 km beyond Pretor is another complex of hotels and holiday chalets.

Returning to the main road, we come in another 2 miles/3 km to the village of *Kurbinovo*, with the 12th c. St George's Church (Sv. Djordje) on a hillside some 330 ft/100 m above the lake. The church contains frescoes of 1191 which are among the finest examples of medieval art in Macedonia.

Beyond the village of *Dolno Dupeni* is the Greek frontier. Although maps show the road continuing beyond the frontier, and apparently offering the shortest way to Little Lake Prespa, it is not possible to enter Greece by this route. To reach the smaller lake it is necessary to make a detour of some 60 miles/100 km via Bitola, Niki (frontier crossing) and Florina.

There are a number of islands in the lakes, two of which are of some interest – *Golem Grad* in Great Lake Prespa and *Ail* in Little Lake Prespa. Boat trips to Golem Grad are run from Oteševo and Pretor, and visitors can picnic in the ruins of a palace built by Tsar Samuilo. Golem Grad – a long ridge rising out of the deep blue waters of the lake – is notable also for its characteristic flora and fauna. On the island of Ail can be seen the ruins of St Achilleus's Church, an aisled basilica built at the end of the 10th c., when the Byzantine style was gaining ground in Macedonia.

Primošten

Republic: Croatia (Hrvatska).
Altitude: $6\frac{1}{2}$ ft/2 m.– Population: 1400.
Post code: YU-59202. – Telephone code: 0 59.
ⓘ **Turističko Društvo,**
tel. 7 00 22.

HOTELS. – *Slava*, A, 336 b., tel. 7 00 22; *Zora*, B, 336 b., tel. 7 00 22; *Raduča*, B, 200 b., tel. 7 00 22.

CAMP SITES. – *Adriatic* and *Esperanto*, both tel. 7 00 22.

Primošten

NATURIST FACILITIES. – *Marina Lučica* hotel complex, with its own yacht harbour, A, 600 b., tel. 7 00 22. – Naturist beach for guests in other hotels on an offshore island.

SPORT, BOATING and BATHING. – Yacht harbour in Marina Lučica hotel complex (naturists). **Rogoznica** has a large marina with a winch, slip and service workshop. Primošten harbour is very suitable for sail boats, since there is room to enter the harbour without the use of a motor and a depth of not less than 10 ft/ 3 m at the pier. The camp site has no sheltered moorings.

Bowling, tennis; water-skiing, scuba diving; motorboats and row boats for rental. The hotels are well equipped with facilities for various sports (including boats for rental). There is also a full program of entertainment.

The beaches consist partly of shelving rock with patches of concrete, partly of coarse gravel (bathing shoes essential) and partly of pebbles. The Marina Lučica complex also has a beach of imported sand. The shore has a fairly steep slope. The beaches are cleaned regularly and the water is clear, although the sewage from all the hotels still goes into the sea. All along the beach are trees which provide welcome shade. There is no traffic noise, since the Adriatic coastal highway is ¾ mile/1 km away.

The picturesque little town of Primošten, half way between Šibenik and Split, is built on a former islet now joined to the mainland by a causeway. This old fishing village with its red-roofed houses dominated by the tower of the church appeals to holidaymakers with its old-world atmosphere and its friendly little restaurants and wineshops.

HISTORY. – During the 16th c. Primošten, then an inhospitable rocky islet, was occupied by people from the coastal regions fleeing from the Turks, who fortified their new settlement with a wall which survived until the end of the 19th c., having outlived its purpose. The short causeway linking Primošten with the mainland was also built at that time. The picturesqueness of the view led to the first hotels being built on the peninsula adjoining during the 1960s.

SIGHTS. – Apart from the much photographed view of the town clustered around its church Primošten has little in the way of particular tourist sights to offer. The *parish church of St George*, originally dating from the 16th c., was rebuilt in 1760. The *Church of Our Lady of Mercy* (Gospa od Milosti) is first recorded in 1553. The little *St Roch's Church* was built in 1680.

SURROUNDINGS. – There are organised trips from Primošten to Šibenik, the Krka Falls and Split, and evening "pirate voyages" to some of the neighbouring uninhabited islands, with barbecue parties on the beach.

Priština

Republic: Serbia (Srbija).
Autonomous province of Kosovo.
Altitude: 1903 ft/580 m. – Population: 100,000.
Post code: YU-38000. – Telephone code: 0 38.
ⓘ **Turist Kosovo,**
tel. 2 23 73.
Turistički Savez Kosova,
tel. 2 23 75.

HOTELS. – *Grand Hotel Priština*, A, 664 b., tel. 2 02 11; *Kosovski Božur*, B, 210 b., tel. 2 44 00; *Kosovo* (Kosovo Polje), C, 35 b., tel. 8 70 17; *Union*, D, 40 b., tel. 2 49 16.

Behind the apartment houses which surround Priština, capital of the autonomous province of Kosovo, lies concealed a little reserve of oriental life – Ottoman buildings, old streets, craftsmen making baskets, pointed leather shoes, silver jewelry and the little felt caps of the Albanians. Priština is a good base from which to visit the Field of Kosovo, the *monastic churches of Peć, Prizren and Dečani and the monastery of Gračanica. 12½ miles/20 km S of the town is a marble cave recently opened up to the public.

HISTORY. – The Roman town of *Ulpiana*, several times destroyed and rebuilt, lay to the S of Priština, at the junction of three rivers. Later the inhabitants of this town moved to the edge of Kosovo Polje and, during the medieval period, established the new town of Priština. In the Turkish period this became the administrative capital for the region and an important traffic junction – as it still is – at the meeting of roads from Niš, Skopje and the Adriatic. After the last war many of the old streets gave place to modern buildings. In 1968 Priština was the scene of a demonstration by Albanian students protesting against the Serbian administration, and in the same year Kosovo was given the status of an autonomous province. A university and many secondary schools, at which the teaching is in Albanian, now reflect the recognition of this population group on the same basis as the other nationalities in Yugoslavia. In 1981 demonstrations took place against the present status of Kosovo as an autonomous province.

SIGHTS. – From the *Partisan Memorial* it is only a short distance to the **Sultan Murad Mosque**, the *Careva Džamija* or Imperial Mosque, a 15th c. structure with four domes. To the E of the mosque is a 19th c. *Clock-Tower* (Sahat Kula). An old *Turkish bath* (Hamam) of 1493 now houses a cheese-making establishment. The *Municipal Museum* displays historical and folk material relating to Kosovo ranging from earlier times to the very recent past.

SURROUNDINGS. – The *monastery of Gračanica* (see under Serbian monasteries) is reached by leaving on the Skopje road (No. 2) and taking a minor road to the left, signposted to Gnjilane.

To see the recently opened **Marble Cave of Donje Gadimlje**, leave Priština on the Skopje road and in 8 miles/13 km turn right into the Prizren road; 2½ miles/ 4 km along this road is the village of Lipljan, from which it is only 2 miles/3 km to the cave. So far only 1650 yd/1500 m of passages and chambers have been explored. The entrance, near the Gadimska Reka (river), gives access to a wonderland of beautiful stalactites and stalagmites. Hanging from the roof in the middle of the cave is a bush-like formation which is reflected in the motionless pool of water below.

N of Priština on the road to Kosovska Mitrovica (No. 11: side road on left 2 miles/3 km before the village of Miloševo) is a **Mausoleum**, with a sarcophagus which is said to contain the internal organs of Sultan Murad I, who fell on the Field of Kosova in 1389 (or according to another account was murdered in his tent before the battle by the Serbian commander Miloš Obilić); his body was sent to Constantinople for burial. Here too are the tombs of two Turkish pashas.

Near the mausoleum, 2 miles/3 km farther S, stands a **Memorial to the Heroes of Kosovo**, erected in 1953. From the platform, 80 ft/25 m above the ground, there are extensive views of the Field of Kosova.

Prizren

Republic: Serbia (Srbija).
Autonomous province of Kosovo.
Altitude: 1378 ft/420 m. – Population: 50,000.
Post code: YU-38400. – Telephone code: 0 29.
ⓘ **Turist Kosovo,**
   tel. 2 23 44.
   Putnik,
   tel. 2 22 78.

HOTELS. – *Theranda*, B, 89 b., tel. 2 22 92; *Motel Vlazrimi*, B, 50 b., tel. 2 41 22.

CAMP SITE. – *Putnik*, tel. 2 25 52.

Prizren, lying 11 miles/18 km from the Albanian frontier in the autonomous province of Kosovo, has preserved more of its oriental character than any of the other towns in the region which have been modernised in recent years. As in the Macedonian town of Struga on Lake Ohrid, the peasants of the surrounding area flock into the town, wearing traditional local costumes, every market day (Wednesday). With its *old town of narrow streets and picturesque old houses and its numerous mosques, Prizren holds an abundance of interest for the visitor.

HISTORY. – In Roman times the site of Prizren was occupied by the town of *Theranda*, situated on a road from the Adriatic to Skopje and the south. In Byzantine times the town became known as *Prizdrijan*. During the reign of Emperor Dušan (1331–55) it became an important town of the Serbian empire. In the middle of the 15th c. the Albanian national hero Skanderbeg captured the town after a heroic battle with the Turks, but soon afterwards was compelled to give it up. After the first Balkan War, which brought the final Turkish withdrawal from Serbia, Prizren again became a Serbian town, with a predominantly Albanian population.

SIGHTS. – In the central part of the town, on the left bank of the River Prizrenska Bistrica beside an old Turkish stone bridge, are the **Sinan Pasha Mosque** and the **Mehmed Pasha Mosque**. Historically the most interesting building in Prizren, however, is the **Sveta Bogorodica Ljeviška Church**, also known as Sveta Petka, built by King Milutin in 1307 on the foundations of a still older church with frescoes, covered over by the Turks, which have recently been brought to light. When the Turks converted the church into a mosque they knocked holes in the walls to provide a key for the mortar facing over the frescoes, and these holes show as white patches in the restored paintings.

Above the town, to the E, are the ruins of **Prizren Castle** (alt. 1723 ft/525 m), from which there are fine views of the surrounding country.

In the old streets of Prizren silversmiths and goldsmiths of Albanian origin offer their finely crafted products for sale – rings, bangles, pendants, etc. The prices are reasonable, offering visitors the opportunity of a bargain.

SURROUNDINGS. – The more direct and shorter road to Skopje runs via Brezovica to join road 2 at Doganović; but this road is narrow, winding and in poor condition, and the best route to Skopje is the rather longer one via Štimlje and Uroševac. – 2 miles/3 km from Prizren on the shorter road are the ruins of **Višegrad Castle**, which was already in existence in the early 14th c., during the reign of King Milutin. Nearby, in the valley, are the ruins of the **monastery of the Archangel Michael** (*Sv. Arhandjel Mihajlo*), with remains of old frescoes and the stone burial vault of Tsar Dušan. A mosaic pavement and other finds from this monastery are now in the Archaeological Museum in Skopje.

On the other road to Skopje (at first signposted to Priština) a side road on the right in the village of Koriša leads to the **Cave Church of St Mark** (14th c. frescoes), in a mountain range rising to over 6560 ft/2000 m.

42 miles/67 km NW of Prizren is the **monastery of Visoki Dečani**, on the Djakovica–Peć road (No. 17a). Here, in a green valley enclosed by forests, is one of the largest and finest of the Serbian monastic churches (see under Serbian monasteries).

From Prizren a road runs W to the frontier crossing into Albania at Vrbnica, continuing to Shkodër. The frontier is not open for tourists.

Ptuj

Republic: Slovenia (Slovenija).
Altitude: 755 ft/230 m. – Population: 14,000.
Post code: YU-62250. – Telephone code: 0 62.
ⓘ **Turist Biro**,
Trg Svobode 4;
tel. 7 75 69.

HOTELS. – *Poetovio*, C, 56 b., tel. 77 26 21, with annexe *Beli Križ*, C, 20 b., tel. 77 15 93.

Ptuj, situated on a hill on the left bank of the Drava, is a town of narrow winding streets dominated by a 12th c. castle. The old part of the town is protected as a national monument, with the varying architectural styles of different centuries combining in a harmonious and impressive whole. Visitors passing through Ptuj on their way south have an opportunity to see a number of interesting old buildings and also to sample the excellent Slovenian wines.

HISTORY. – In the 4th c. B.C. the site of Ptuj was occupied by Celts. Later, in 35 B.C., Augustus established a fortified post here to protect the military road from northern Italy into Pannonia; but since there were few hostile incursions in this area the military station soon became a colonia inhabited by time-expired soldiers, under the name of *Poetovio*. Later, on the approach of the Goths and Huns in the 4th and 5th c., Poetovio became a strong garrison town, occupied at one time by 15,000 men.

In the 6th c., after the Roman withdrawal, the area was occupied by Slavs and the once handsome town declined into a mere village. During the great migrations the last remains of the Roman town disappeared, with the sole exception of the Orpheus Monument.

The town's present name is first recorded in the 11th c., when Ptuj was held by a German margrave. In the 13th c. it passed to the kings of Hungary and later of Bohemia, and finally was granted by the Habsburgs to the bishops of Salzburg. The Turks captured the town and destroyed it, but thereafter it was recovered by the bishop of Salzburg.

During the 19th c. Ptuj was increasingly over-shadowed by Maribor. Austrian rule ended in 1918, when Slovenia was ceded by Yugoslavia, but until the Second World War the town still had many German-speaking inhabitants.

SIGHTS. – Since there is no room to park in the town's narrow streets cars are best left outside the central area. In any event the main sights lie fairly close together. – Starting from the Tourist Office near the *bridge* over the Drava (opposite the post office), we see on the right the old **Minorite convent**. The Minorite church, the oldest Gothic building in Slovenia, was burned down in 1944.

From here we make for the middle of town, turning left at the first corner, by the Town Hall, and continuing up Murkova Street. At the first turning on the right is the **Orpheus Monument**, a marble monolith 16 ft/5 m high erected in A.D. 194 in honour of the emperor Septimius Severus after his victories in Africa. The carving on the monument shows Orpheus with his lyre singing to the lions. During the Middle Ages the monument was used as a pillory.

Beyond this is the **parish church** (1125), which combines Romanesque and Gothic features. Note particularly the Gothic *choir-stalls* (1446), the Baroque *pulpit* and the *Roman gravestones* (2nd c. A.D.) built into the walls.

Near the church is the 177 ft/54 m high **City Tower**, once part of the town's defences, with fragments of Roman sculpture and inscribed stones built into the lower part. of the walls. One of the stones has an inscription mentioning the Roman name of the town: "C. CAESIUS. C.F. PAPIRIA. INGENVVS. POETO-VIONE V.F. SIBI . . .".

Ptuj – a view from the castle

Returning to Murkova Street and following it around the foot of the hill, we come in a few minutes to the **Dominican friary**, founded in 1230, with a 15th c. *cloister.*

We now climb up to the **Castle** (restaurant, with terrace; extensive views). The site was occupied until the 6th c. by the Roman castrum, which was suc-

ceeded by later fortifications directed against the Magyars and then the Turks. A notable feature is the three-storey *arcaded courtyard*. The castle now houses part of the *Municipal Museum* (weapons, goldsmiths' work, an ethnographic collection, etc.).

Now return to the square in front of the Town Hall. At the intersection of Murkova, Krempljeva and Lackova Streets, just around the corner, is a large wine-tasting establishment, which provides a suitable preparation for a visit to the **Wine Museum**, housed in the old Water Tower just before the bridge over the Drava. The museum displays old methods of wine-making, and implements used by vine-growers and vintners, wine casks and wine-dispensers.

On the other side of the river, in Spodnja Hajdina and Mariborska Cesta, are the remains of two *Mithraic temples*. To see them, turn left at the far end of the bridge in the direction of the suburb of *Breg*.

SURROUNDINGS. – 7½ miles/12 km SW of Ptuj, on a long low hill, is *Ptujska Gora*. On the highest point stands a Gothic fortified church which was surrounded with defensive walls during the Turkish advance (15th c.). Note particularly the Celje Altar, with a relief of the Virgin sheltering under her cloak a great crowd of figures – kings, church dignitaries, burghers, peasants – all depicted in the costumes of the period.

4½ miles/7 km from Ptuj on a minor road to Ljutomer is the Baroque *Dornava Palace, by the village of the same name. This massive pile, the finest late Baroque building in Slovenia, was built by Count Josef Attems in 1739–43. It has well-preserved ceiling paintings.

The main road from Ptuj to Varaždin (turn right at Zavrć) leads to **Borl Castle**, picturesquely situated on a rocky hill directly above the Drava. From the second courtyard a gateway leads on to the terrace, from which there is a fine panoramic view of the Slovenian vineyard region.

Pula

Republic: Croatia (Hrvatska).
Altitude: 16 ft/5 m. – Population: 50,000.
Post code: YU-52000. – Telephone code: 0 52.
ⓘ **Turistički Savez Općine,**
Trg Republike 1,
YU-52000 Pula;
tel. 2 26 62.
Arenaturist,
Trg Bratstva i Jedinstva 4,
YU-52203 Medulin;
tel. 2 32 76.
Turističko Društvo Premantura,
YU-52000 Premantura;
tel. 2 79 51.

Roman Amphitheatre, Pula

HOTELS. – IN PULA: *Brioni*, A, 432 b., tel. 2 38 88; *Splendid*, B, 324 b., tel. 2 33 90, with annexe *Splendid Pavilions*, 342 b.; *Park*, B, 254 b., tel. 2 23 42; *Ribarska Koliba*, 218 b., tel. 2 26 58; *Stoja*, 56 b., tel. 2 23 95; *Complex Zlatne Stijene*, B, 748 b., tel. 2 28 11; *Complex Verudela*, B, 720 b., tel. 2 28 71; *Verudela Villas*, 80 b., tel. 2 23 42.

IN MEDULIN: *Belvedere*, B, 412 b., tel. 7 60 08; *Medulin*, 356 b., tel. 7 60 66, with annexes *Medulin*, 256 b., and *Medulin Flats*, 502 b., tel. 7 60 68; *Mutila*, 322 b., tel. 7 60 04.

IN PREMANTURA: accommodation in private houses (apply to Tourist Office).

CAMP SITES. – IN PULA: *Ribarska Koliba*, at hotel, tel. 2 26 58; *Indie* (4 miles/6 km S on Premantura road), tel. 2 69 78; *Stoja*, tel. 2 39 55. – IN MEDULIN: *Medulin* (on a peninsula 550 yd/500 m from Medulin Hotel), tel. 7 60 40. – IN PREMANTURA: *Stupice*, tel. 2 28 11; *Tašalera*, tel. 2 28 11; *Runke* (rented caravans only, 1200 b.), tel. 2 89 51.

NATURIST FACILITIES. – *Kažela* (camp site and chalets, 1½ miles/2·5 km from Medulin), tel. 7 60 50.

EVENTS. – June to August in Amphitheatre, dramatic performances, ballet, folk displays, pop concerts; end July/beginning of August, Festival of Yugoslav Feature Films.

SPORT. – Water-skiing, rental of boats of all kinds; tennis, rental of bicycles, bowling; restrictions on scuba diving (since Pula is a naval port). Danger of sharks between Pula and Premantura.

BOATING and BATHING. – The approach to Pula presents considerable navigational difficulties (several closed areas, heavy traffic of excursion boats and hydrofoils). The best plan for the owners of pleasure craft, therefore, is to make for *Rovinj* harbour or, for launching a boat from a trailer, to use the fishing port of *Fažana*, which has a slip (but no winch). There is a considerable police presence at Fažana in view of its proximity to *Brioni* (see p. 64).

Bathing is not possible within the town itself; the nearest clean beaches are at *Zlatne Stije* and *Veruda*, on the coast to the S. Veruda, with its hotels and camp sites, is a busy tourist zone, and it is better, therefore, to make for the holiday resort of *Medulin*, 6 miles/10 km away. The first hotel, on the right, is the oldest, and the standard of accommodation increases steadily towards the SE. The road ends at the Kažela naturist complex, with chalets to the left and a camp site to the right. The trees which have been planted here are of rather stunted growth, in spite of the intensive care they receive, since the flat country in this area is exposed in winter to the assaults of the bora; the landscape accordingly looks bare. There is a pebble beach, but there are only a few points where it is possible to reach the water without walking over sharp stones.

Premantura, like Medulin, has a camp site with plenty of shade as well as many houses which let rooms to visitors. There are numerous restaurants in this area.

The *Medulin* hotels have facilities for all kinds of water sports; also tennis and rental of bicycles.

AIRPORT: Pula. JAT office: Mate Balote 8.

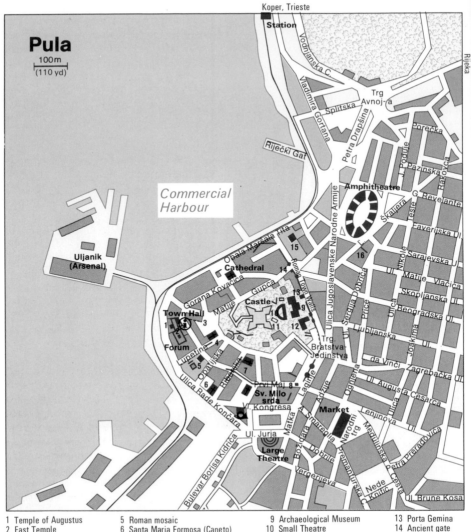

1 Temple of Augustus
2 East Temple
3 Cult building
4 Sv. Franjo

5 Roman mosaic
6 Santa Maria Formosa (Caneto)
7 Sv. Nikola
8 Porta Aurea

9 Archaeological Museum
10 Small Theatre
11 Ancient cistern
12 Porta Herculea

13 Porta Gemina
14 Ancient gate
15 Carolina spring
16 Ancient building

During the period of Venetian rule (1331–1797) Pula was treated as a kind of self-service store for the supply of building materials and sometimes whole buildings, and large quantities of stones and columns were pulled down and carried off to Italy. In 1583, indeed, the Venetian Senate conceived the grandiose idea of demolishing the whole of the Roman amphitheatre and re-erecting it in Venice – a plan which was frustrated at the last moment by a courageous senator named Gabriele Emo. In addition to the Amphitheatre, in which open-air performances are given in summer, Pula has many other interesting relics of the Roman period.

Apart from its own attractions Pula is a good base from which to visit other places of interest in the area. Excellent accommodation is available for visitors at *Veruda* (at a safe distance from the polluted water of the port) and in the hotels, chalets and camp sites of **Medulin** and **Premantura**, 6 miles/10 km away.

HISTORY. – According to the legend of the Argonauts a settlement was established in this area by Greek refugees from Colchis, and the name of the town is linked with the Greek word *polai* ("the pursued"). However that may be, it is established that there was an Illyrian fortified settlement on the hill now occupied by the castle (5th c. B.C.). Below this settlement the Romans founded a colonia, *Iulia Pollentia Herculanea*, in 44 B.C. In the reign of Augustus (30 B.C.– A.D. 14) Pula, now known as *Pietas Iulia*, became the base of Roman administration for the whole of Istria. The Amphitheatre was built by Vespasian (A.D. 69–79) under the influence of his mistress Cenida, a native of Pula. After the fall of the Western Empire (476) the town was held by the Ostrogoths for a time and then passed into the control of the ecclesiastical authorities in Ravenna. In 788 Pula, together with the rest of Istria, became part of the Frankish kingdom. In 1230 it again came under ecclesiastical control. During the period of Venetian rule (1331–1797) the town stagnated and the population was decimated by malaria and plague.

Under the Austrians, who fulfilled an old dream of becoming a major naval as well as land power by the construction of a naval port at Pula in 1848, the town enjoyed a revival of prosperity, and shipyards, factories and warehouses serving the commercial harbour were built. In 1918 Pula was occupied by Italian troops, who remained until 1943, when they were replaced by Germans. Partisan forces entered the town in May 1945, but were then displaced by British and Americans, who administered the area, disputed between Italy and Yugoslavia, until 1947. Pula then became part of the new Yugoslavia and was developed into the country's largest naval base. The shipyards have been the backbone of the town's postwar economic growth.

SIGHTS. – The best place for parking cars, reached after passing two traffic circles and the Amphitheatre, is on the quay to the right. The sights of the town can easily be visited on foot, beginning with the **Amphitheatre. Elliptical in form (435 by 345 ft/132 by 105 m), it is surrounded by a wall 102 ft/31 m high. The Venetian senator, Gabriele Emo, who prevented the whole structure from being carried off to Venice, is commemorated by a tablet set up in 1584 on the second tower facing the sea. There were originally two main entrances and four subsidiary entrances in the towers. The Amphitheatre could accommodate 23,000 spectators. There is plenty of evidence that it was intended not so much for artistic performances as for the bloodier shows in which gladiators and wild beasts took part: thus there were entrances (now missing or only partly preserved) for the wild beasts, which were brought up to the level of the arena in hoists, and a corridor through which dead or wounded gladiators could be removed from the arena. The guides who show visitors around the arena have plenty of scope for the most bloodthirsty accounts of the shows which took place here. It should be remembered, in considering the structure of the Amphitheatre, that much of it was removed by the Venetians, who particularly valued the handsome limestone blocks, and also by local people in search of building materials.

On the way from the Amphitheatre to the quay we pass through a public garden and at the far end reach, in Ul. Mate Balote,

the *Porta Gemina*, a Roman town gate of the 2nd c. A.D. Beyond this, to the left, is the entrance to the **Archaeological Museum** (open only in summer), which has a large collection of Roman remains, including many carved and inscribed stones. On the hill behind the museum are the remains of a Roman *theatre* and in the park are the foundations of a Roman *mausoleum*.

From the museum we continue down to the quay (Obala Maršala Tita). In some 220 yd/200 m we come to the **Cathedral**, an aisled church originally founded in the 4th–5th c. and rebuilt in 1640, with a detached *tower*. On the side facing the sea a number of stones with interlace ornament, evidently from older buildings, are built into the wall. The interior of the Cathedral has little of interest apart from a Roman sarcophagus now serving as the high altar and Roman capitals now used as holy-water basins in the S aisle.

After a bend in the street which follows the shore, with the shipyards to the right, a street on the left leads into the Trg Republike. Immediately in front we see the **Temple of Augustus**, appearing disproportionately high in relation to its size, with six Corinthian columns on the façade.

Adjoining the temple is the handsome façade of the **Town Hall**, which dates from the 13th c.; the *loggia* on the ground floor is probably later. To the rear is another temple, probably dedicated to Diana, which was incorporated in the 13th c. building.

Temple of Augustus, Pula

Now return to Obala Maršala Tita. To the rear of a small garden is a *Byzantine chapel* (6th c.), part of a basilica which no longer exists. Through the window at the entrance, panels of 6th c. mosaics can be seen to right and left. The architecture of the chapel as a whole is also of great interest.

Continuing through a number of cross streets in the direction of the castle, we come into the Ulica Prvog Maja (pedestrian precinct), at the end of which stands the **Porta Aurea**, a triumphal arch 26 ft/8 m high and 15 ft/4·50 m wide. The **Castle** crowning the hill, which can be reached by a number of different streets, was built in its present form for the Venetians by the French military engineer A. Deville in 1630–31. It was altered in Napoleon's time and restored in 1830.

Rab

Republic: Croatia (Hrvatska).
Area of island: 36 sq. miles/94 sq. km.
Population: 9000.
Telephone code: 0 51.
ⓘ **Turist Biro Rab,**
Maršala Tita 1,
YU-51280 Rab;
tel. 87 11 23.
Turističko Društvo Lopar,
YU-51281 Lopar;
tel. 87 11 50.

HOTELS. – IN RAB: *Imperijal*, B, 281 b., tel. 87 12 24; *Internacional*, B, 181 b., tel. 87 12 24; *Istra*, C, 192 b., tel. 87 11 33; *Beograd*, C, 94 b., tel. 87 12 66; *Slavija*, D, 42 b., tel. 87 11 15. – IN BANJOL: *Kontinental*, with annexes *Bellevue, Rio Magdalena, Margita* and *Marijan*, D, together 132 b., tel. 87 11 06. – IN BARBAT: *Barbat*, D, 30 b., tel. 87 40 63. – IN LOPAR: *San Marino*, B, 1000 b., tel. 87 11 28; *Mira*, D, 35 b., tel. 87 11 50. – IN SUHA PUNTA: *Eva*, B, 400 b., tel. 87 10 40; *Carolina*, B, 292 b., tel. 87 10 20; *tourist bungalow village*, B, 787 b., tel. 87 10 60.

CAMP SITES. – *Padova*, at Banjol, tel. 87 13 11; *Rajska Plaža*, at Lopar, tel. 87 10 48.

NATURIST FACILITIES. – In "English Bay" (reached from Rab town by boat, then footpath; admission charge); also cove at *Suha Punta*. No access to either site by car; no facilities for camping.

SPORT, BOATING and BATHING. – The shore beneath the E side of Rab town walls is not good for bathing: it is better to take a boat to some more attractive beach. Naturists also reach *English Bay* by boat (admission charge; but sanitary facilities inadequate, often overcrowded, water not clean). The beaches at the Suha Punta hotel complex are better; facilities for naturists.

Kampor Bay, shallow and silted up, is not recommended for bathing; nor is the beach at *Supetarska Draga*, where the water is not clear. *Lopar*, however, has a sandy beach 550 yd/500 m long; adjoining is a rocky stretch of beach reserved for naturists. The *San Marino* hotel complex has attractive but rocky beaches.

The harbour of Rab town is in two parts, an outer harbour (Uvala Padova) and an inner basin. The likeliest place to seek a mooring for pleasure craft is on the inner quay. – Boats sailing N must avoid the closed areas round the islands of *Goli* and *Sveti Grgur* (penal establishment); it is not permitted to approach within one sea mile of these islands.

All the larger hotels have tennis courts and mini-golf courses. The sheltered Uvala Eufemija and Barbatski channels offer excellent conditions for water-skiing. In addition the island of Rab has a wide range of facilities for sports of all kinds.

CAR FERRIES. – Senj–Baška/Krk–Lopar–Rab; Jablanac (mainland)–Rab. The fast passenger vessels from Rijeka to Dubrovnik (carrying cars) also call in at Rab.

To visitors approaching Rab from the N the dark green forest appears to rise directly out of the sea; but the E side, facing the mainland, shows a different face, swept bare by the bora. Since the 1950s the island has become one of the liveliest resorts on the Yugoslav Adriatic coast, attracting large numbers of visitors with its new hotels, bathing beaches, shady footpaths and lavish program of entertainments. But Rab also gives those with no particular interest in history some impression of the art and culture of the Mediterranean, with its old palaces, churches and picturesque little streets. The largest place on the island is the town of Rab, but there are also popular holiday resorts at

Rab, seen from the campanile

Lopar in the N and Supetarska Draga and Kampor in the NW, while Suha Punta has a whole new holiday village of hotels and villas.

HISTORY. – Rab, known in antiquity as *Arba*, was occupied in prehistoric times by an Illyrian people, the Liburni. The first reference to the island dates from 360 B.C. The Romans, who first landed here in the 2nd c. B.C., built a naval base and a number of strong points on the island. From the 9th c. A.D. to 1409, with only brief interruptions, the island belonged to Croatia; thereafter, until 1797, it was held by Venice. After a short period of Austrian rule it was incorporated in Napoleon's Illyrian Provinces in 1805, but returned to Austria in 1914. In 1918 Rab was occupied by the Italians, but under the Treaty of Rapallo was assigned to the new kingdom of Yugoslavia. – As a holiday area Rab was discovered between the two world wars. The first naturist area in Yugoslavia was established in "English Bay", so called because Edward VIII (1894–1972, king of the United Kingdom January– December 1936) is said to have set the fashion for naturist bathing on a visit here.

SIGHTS. – The island's capital, **Rab**, lies on a narrow tongue of land, with the sea on either side. The four *campaniles* which are its most conspicuous landmarks come into view as soon as the boat rounds the promontory. The tallest and handsomest (85 ft/26 m), with Romanesque windows and a short pointed steeple, stands opposite St Mary's Cathedral (Sveta Marija Velika).

From the landing-place it is a short distance, following the line of the town walls, to Tito Square, on the N side of which is the *Rector's Palace* (Knežev Dvor), with the Town Hall adjoining it. The *Sea Gate* (Morska Vrata) leads into the main square which has been the hub of the town's life since the 14th c. The principal building in the square is the **Loggia** with its eight marble columns, once used as a law court. Adjoining the Loggia are a *clock-tower* and the little Gothic *church of St Nicholas*. From here a flight of steps leads to the "Lower Street" (Donja Ulica, Ul. Marka Oreškovića), which runs past a number of fine old houses and the *Marcić Glazigna Palace* (Gothic windows and lions' heads) to the remains of the *Nemir Palace*, with a well-preserved doorway.

From the market square we continue to the "Upper Street" (Gornja Ulica, Ul. Rade Končara). To the right, adjoining the *church of Sv. Križ* (Baroque stucco-work of 1798), can be seen *St John's Church* (Sv. Ivan Evangelist). The church itself, on the edge of steep cliffs, is in ruins, but the *campanile* survives. Farther along the street is the 16th c. *St Justin's Church*, with a campanile topped by an onion-shaped stone cap. The church has a Renaissance altar of carved wood and another altar (to the left) with a picture of the "Death of St Joseph" which is ascribed to Titian but is probably by one of his pupils. Beyond this, on the right, the 11th c. *St Andrew's Convent*, a Benedictine monastery which was converted into a villa in the 19th c.

The "Upper Street" runs into the Cathedral Square, with the fine *campanile* which has already been mentioned. From the top there is an impressive view of the town, with the ruins of houses which were occupied until the 17th c. After the town was ravaged by plague the surviving inhabitants left their homes, and many houses were burned down to destroy the plague germs, or had their doors and windows walled up. The survivors then moved to new settlements to the N of the town. – **St Mary's Cathedral** (*Crkva Sv. Marija*) is a predominantly Romanesque church dating from the 12th c. The W front has a fine *Renaissance doorway* with a Pietà of 1519.

Notable features of the INTERIOR are the 12th c. silver-gilt **reliquary of St Christopher** above the high altar, carved *choir-stalls* (1445) by an unknown local master, part of a 14th c. polyptych of the Venetian school on the altar in the S aisle, an old Croatian *tabernacle c.* 1000 and a font of 1497.

At the N end of the town lies the ***Komrčar Park**. With its palms, pines, holm-oaks and cypresses this beautiful park can be compared only with the park of Gučetić family at Trsteno, near Dubrovnik (see under Slano). Walking through the park or along the beautiful ***seafront promenade**, we come to the **Franciscan friary of St Euphemia**, with a fine *cloister* and *garden*. The church contains a number of notable *pictures*, including works by Antonio and Bartolommeo Vivarini (1458). NW of the friary is the forester's house of Šuma Dundovo.

Lopar, $7\frac{1}{2}$ miles/12 km from Rab town (bus service), has only one historical association: it was the birthplace of a hermit named Marianus, who retired to the mountains for the sake of his faith and in A.D. 301 founded San Marino, the smallest and oldest republic in the world. Near the village is the hotel complex of San Marino.

Rijeka

Republic: Croatia (Hrvatska).
Altitude: 10 ft/3 m. – Population: 140,000.
Post code: YU-51000. – Telephone code: 0 51.
ⓘ Turistički Informativni Centar,
Trg Republike 9;
tel. 2 37 86.

HOTELS. – *Bonavia*, A, 289 b., tel. 3 37 44; *Jadran*, B, 145 b., tel. 4 10 00; *Neboder*, C, 97 b., tel. 4 20 71; *Park*, C, 71 b., tel. 4 11 55; *Kontinental*, D, 88 b., tel. 4 24 94. – IN RIJEKA-KOSTRENA: *Motel Lucija*, B, 150 b., tel. 4 18 86. – IN RIJEKA-MATULJI: *Panorama*, C, 78 b., tel. 74 12 22.

CAMP SITES. – *Preluk*, on Opatija–Rijeka road, tel. 61 79 68; *Kostrena*, 4½ miles/7 km S of Rijeka, tel. 86 01 34.

AIRPORT: on island of Krk (connected with mainland by bridge). JAT office: Trg Republike 9, tel. 2 55 71.

Rijeka is now Yugoslavia's largest and most important port. To the N of the town are shipyards and oil refineries, bounded by the town's main traffic artery, which is formed by the junction of the roads from Trieste and Opatija just before they enter Rijeka. This road gradually runs down from a hill just outside the town into the middle of the old town, on the level of the harbour, and then climbs again towards the S. To the rear of the industrial districts and the old town which flank the bay are hills covered right up to their bare summits with tall modern buildings. Rijeka is not a town which attracts visitors as a resort or for the sake of the bathing (though there are bathing beaches outside the town); but anyone who has occasion to come to Rijeka to catch a boat or aircraft (airport on the nearby island of Krk), train or coastal bus will find much of interest in this old town.

The municipal authorities are now actively concerned to preserve the town's historic old buildings; but many old buildings were destroyed during the last war, and compared with the numbers of new and modern buildings in the industrial and residential districts on the surrounding hills the historic core of Rijeka behind the harbour seems small indeed.

HISTORY. – The first settlers were an Illyrian people, the Liburni. During the Roman period a military base

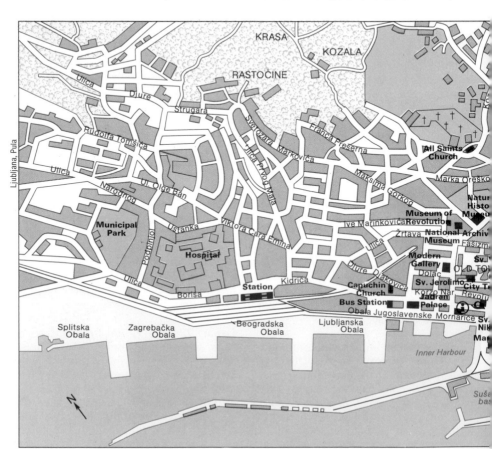

known as *Tarsatica* was built on a site at the mouth of the River Rečina, in the present harbour area, commanding the road from Rome to Salonica. Later the town was occupied by the Avars and in the 7th c. by the Slavs, who built the fortress of *Trsat* on the remains of the Roman fort. During the Middle Ages the town became known as **Fiume** (Italian, "river"), and from the 15th c. to the end of the 18th, with some interruptions, belonged to Austria–Hungary. Until 1918 Rijeka was the naval base of the Austro-Hungarian monarchy.

At the end of the First World War Rijeka became part of the new kingdom of Yugoslavia; but since the town had a considerable Italian-speaking minority and threatened to become a serious competitor to the Italian port of Trieste, farther up the Adriatic, a group of Italian irregulars led by the writer Gabriele d'Annunzio occupied Rijeka in 1919. In 1920 the Treaty of Rapallo declared it to be a free city, but in 1922 d'Annunzio and his band of adventurers again seized the town. In 1924 it was assigned to Italy, while the Sušak district to the S of the River Rečina became part of Yugoslavia. After the Second World War a plebiscite was held to decide which country the town should belong to: a majority voted for union with Yugoslavia, and many of the Italian-speaking inhabitants thereupon emigrated to Italy. – The name Rijeka, like the Italian name Fiume, means "river".

SIGHTS. – The road entering Rijeka from the W runs along the seafront and beyond the railway station becomes the broad *Obala Jugoslavenske Mornarice*, with

open-air cafés at which visitors can sit and watch the departure of the passenger ships. Parallel with this street is the town's old main street, Korzo Narodne Revolucije, and between the two is the **Jadran Palace**, flanked by a tall modern building occupied by airline offices and travel agencies.

Beyond this a quay runs S at right angles to the seafront. This leads to the offices of the harbour authorities, where sailing permits are issued for foreign craft, and to a smaller harbour basin, the *Sušački Basen*, which lay within the part of Rijeka assigned to Yugoslavia in 1924.

The Korzo Narodne Revolucije leads directly into the OLD TOWN (*Stari Grad*: to left), which is entered through the arch of the *City Tower* (Gradski Toranj). Near here, to the left, is the **Old Town Hall** (*Stara Gradska Vijećnica*), a 14th c. building with a neo-classical façade added in 1835. – From here Užarska Ulica, to the right, leads to the **Cathedral**, built in the 13th c. and later remodelled in Baroque style. The Romanesque *tower*, leaning slightly, bears the date 1377. The *sacristy* contains 15th c. reliquaries and monstrances. – NW of the Cathedral is

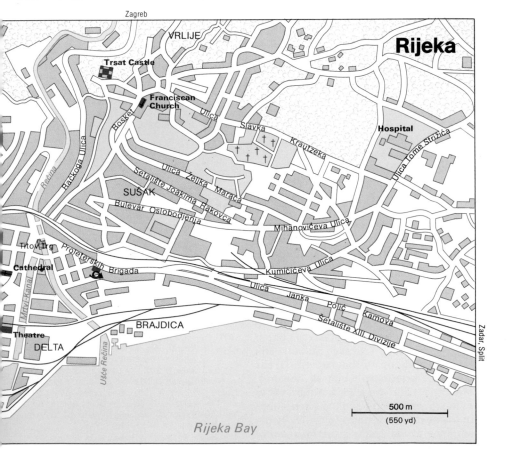

The harbour, Rijeka

St Vitus's Church (*Sveti Vid*), built in 1631 on the model of Santa Maria della Salute in Venice.

To the W, reached by way of Ulica Žrtava Fašizma, which leads past the beautiful *Vladimir Nazor Park*, is the **National Museum** (*Narodni Muzej*), which contains large collections of ethnographic and historical material and an interesting *maritime department* (ships and the sea). To the left of the entrance is a *lapidarium*, with carved and inscribed stones of the Roman period and the Middle Ages. A short distance away in the direction of Calvary Hill we come to the **Natural History Museum** (*Prirodoslovni Muzej*).

On the E side of the old town are the River Rečina and, to the S of Tito Square (Titov Trg), the *Mrtvi Kanal* ("dead channel"), crowded with boats. From 1924 to 1947 the river and the Mrtvi Kanal marked the frontier between Italy and Yugoslavia. In Tito Square is the *Liberation Memorial* (1955), by the well-known Yugoslav sculptor Vinko Matković. On the banks of the Krtvi Kanal, in Trg Vladimira Švalbe, stands the former **National Theatre** (1885) and near this the **Market Hall** (*Tržnica*).

Beyond the Mrtvi Kanal and the river lies the new district of SUŠAK. From a gateway adjoining a large bank a flight of 559 steps, the Trsatske Stube Petra Kružića, leads up to the medieval **Trsat Castle** (restaurant, open-air theatre). From the castle there are beautiful views of the town, the port and the steep slopes of the coastal mountains to the N. By the entrance to the castle is the *Museum of the National Revolution*. On the hill near

the castle are the 15th c. **Church of Our Lady of Loreto** and a *Franciscan friary* dating from the same period. The two-aisled church (conducted tours several times daily) has a fine wrought-iron screen between the nave and chancel and contains numerous large votive tablets. Above the high altar hangs a *painting of the Virgin* presented to the church by Pope Urban V (1367).

Those who do not feel inclined to climb 559 steps can reach the castle by taking the Adriatic coastal highway running S from Rijeka, turning left into a road which leads uphill, signposted to Zagreb, and then turning left again in the modern residential quarter to which this leads.

Another very fine view – but like that from Trsat Castle, liable to be obscured by industrial haze – is to be had from **Calvary Hill**.

SURROUNDINGS. – The village of **Kastav** (alt. 1106 ft/337 m), W of Rijeka, is reached by taking the Trieste road, turning right in 6 miles/10 km where the road traverses high ground and then left up to the village. Then on foot through picturesque little streets to St Helen's Church. From the churchyard wall there is a magnificent *view over the bay towards Opatija, the islands of Cres and Krk, and the eastern part of Rijeka. 29 miles/46 km E of Rijeka on road 7 (E 96) to Karlovac is **Delnice** (2290 ft/698 m), a base for climbers and winter sports enthusiasts with a cableway up Petehovac (3603 ft/1098 m). 25 miles/40 km from Rijeka on the same road is the summer and winter resort of **Lokve**, in a forest setting near the *Omladinsko Jezero* (reservoir).

A side road branching off E 96 leads to the winter sports resort of *Platak* (3645 ft/1111 m), at the foot of two mountains, Risnjak (5013 ft/1528 m) and *Snežnik (5893 ft/1796 m).

Rogaška Slatina

Republic: Slovenia (Slovenija).
Altitude: 748 ft/228 m. – Population: 2000.
Post code: YU-63250. – Telephone code: 0 63.
ⓘ **Turistično Društvo,**
   tel. 81 05 46.
TTG,
in station,
tel. 81 06 25.

HOTELS. – *Donat*, A, 208 b. and 6 apartments, tel. 81 08 31; *Park*, B, 50 b., tel. 81 00 10; *Zdraviliški Dom*, C, 188 b., tel. 81 00 10; *Slovenski Dom*, C, 118 b., tel. 81 00 93; *Soča*, C, 80 b., tel. 81 00 30; *Styria*, D, 75 b., tel. 81 00 10; *Boč*, D, 56 b., tel. 81 00 30; also annexes *Ljubljanski Dom*, D, 156 b., *Beograjski Dom*, D, 91 b., and *Slatinski Dom*, D, 66 b., all tel. 81 00 30; *Trst*, D, 34 b., tel. 81 00 30, with annexe *Turist*, 55 b.

The season at Rogaška Slatina lasts throughout the year. From April 15 to mid October most of the hotels in the high categories are fully booked months in advance. From October 16 to April 14; when there are fewer visitors, tariffs are reduced by 10%.

Rogaška Slatina, in a setting of hills, forests, vineyards and meadowland, is one of the largest and best known of Yugoslavia's spas; but even visitors who have not come to take the cure find this hill resort a pleasant place for a vacation. With a long tradition of hospitality behind it, Rogaška Slatina is particularly skilled in catering for the needs of the middle and older age groups and stimulating them to healthy activity.

Hotel, Rogaška Slatina

Visitors arriving by train via Ljubljana or Maribor alight at a small station which also houses the tourist information bureau. On the way from the station to their hotel they will pass along the shady avenues which are such an attractive feature of the town.

HISTORY. – In the year 1680 a doctor named de Sorbait successfully treated a certain Count N. for hardening of the arteries, using the mineral water of Rogaška Slatina, and wrote a book on the subject which is still displayed in the main spa establishment. There was unfortunately no opportunity of ascertaining whether the cure was permanent, for soon after his treatment the count was beheaded for treason. The first spa establishment was built in 1810, and was soon followed by the first hotels. At first there was only one mineral spring, named the Temple Spring after the temple-like building erected to house it; then in 1850 the Styria Spring was discovered, and at the beginning of the 20th c. the Donat Spring, with a pleasant taste which has made it the principal supplier of mineral water. There are now 20 springs of varying strength and composition.

The most comprehensive range of facilities is provided by the *Donat Hotel*, with an indoor swimming pool, sauna, bowling

alley, coffee-house, tennis courts, mini-golf and a fitness trail. The hotel is only a short distance away from the spa establishment, in which there are regular art exhibitions. A band plays in the park, and there is also music in the surrounding coffee-houses. There are pleasant walks along the river and up *Kapela Hill*, from which there are fine *views* of the vine-covered hills around the little town.

Rovinj

Republic: Croatia (Hrvatska).
Altitude: 16 ft/5 m. – Population: 8800.
Post code: YU-52210. – Telephone code: 0 52.
ⓘ **Turističko Društvo,**
Obala Pino 12;
tel. 8 12 07.

HOTELS. – IN ROVINJ (MAINLAND): *Eden*, A, 622 b., tel. 8 14 02; *Lone*, 325 b., tel. 8 10 70; *Park* (with annexe), B, 314 b., tel. 8 11 22; *Rovinj*, B, 150 b., tel. 8 14 08; *Centar*, C, 64 b., tel. 8 11 76; *Monte Mulin*, 230 b., tel. 8 11 30. – IN ROVINJ-POLARI: *Ruben Villas*, 2402 b., tel. 8 13 08; *Monsena* and *Valalta* chalets (see under Naturist facilities). – ON CRVENI OTOK: *Crveni Otok*, with 3 annexes, 323 b., tel. 8 11 33; *Istra*, 336 b., tel. 8 14 00. – ON KATARINA: *Katarina*, 394 b., tel. 8 14 04.

CAMP SITES. – *Polari*, 2 miles/3 km S of Rovinj, tel. 8 15 31; *Beograd*, tel. 8 12 29; *Porton Bjondi*, ¾ mile/1 km N of Rovinj, tel. 8 11 84. See also under Naturist facilities.

NATURIST FACILITIES. – *Punta Eva* beach at *Polari* camp site, and at *Rubin Villas*; naturist island of *Maškin*, linked with Crveni Otok by a causeway, for guests of Istra Hotel but also for day visitors (motorboats from Rovinj), camping not permitted; *Monsena* naturist complex, 1070 b., tel. 8 12 76, with naturist camp site; *Valalta* naturist complex, 600 b., tel. 8 13 06, with naturist camp site.

EVENTS. – Summer Festival (August); folk displays on open-air stage.

SPORT, BOATING and BATHING. – The gleaming bronze figure of St Euphemia on the campanile of the Cathedral makes a good landmark for boats approaching Rovinj. There are no problems about entering the sheltered harbour, which has a slip. There are also excellent moorings at the Valalta naturist complex, N of Rovinj at the mouth of the Limski Kanal.

Valalta, 6 miles/10 km N of Rovinj on the coast road, has holiday chalets (bungalows) and a camp site, sports facilities and play areas, some shade along the coast, a rocky beach laid with concrete, a small area of pebbles and gangways into the water. 2 miles/3 km N of Rovinj, on a site sloping gently down towards the sea from the coast road, is another naturist complex – **Monsena** – with chalets and a camp site, plenty of open space and trees providing shade. Immediately N of Rovinj is a camp site with older holiday chalets, mostly occupied by Yugoslavs.

To the S of Rovinj, in a pleasant green setting, are a number of hotels, free from the overcrowding found, for example, at Poreč. The cove at the Eden Hotel is particularly attractive. The last holiday settlement to the S is at the *Rubin Villas* (also naturist facilities). Visitors staying on the hotel island of Crveni Otok can reach the adjoining naturist island of Maškin on a causeway (no facilities; woodland, bare rocks with no gangways into the water).

In addition to all the usual water sports there are facilities for scuba divers (diving school, refilling of aqualungs). Tennis (courts at several hotels), bowling. Exhibitions of pictures by local artists; displays by folk groups on open-air stage; discotheques. A stroll by the harbour is a pleasant evening recreation.

The best view of this picturesque little town, its houses densely packed on a promontory and dominated by the 200 ft/60 m high campanile of its Cathedral, with swarms of brightly painted boats in the foreground, is from the S end of the bay containing the harbour.

Boats in Rovinj harbour

Rovinj itself has no bathing beaches, but the holiday resorts N and S of the town and on the islands of Katarina and Crveni Otok are excellently equipped for the needs of bathers and sunbathers. The town has its own attractions for sightseers and those who merely enjoy a leisurely stroll about its streets, and for the many visitors who come here on coach trips or excursions by boat.

HISTORY. – Rovinj was originally an island, which was linked with the mainland in 1763 when the channel to the E of the town was filled in. The place first appears in the records in 1218 under the name of *Ruvignio*. In the 6th c. the town belonged to the Exarchate of Ravenna; in 788 it passed into the hands of the Franks; and later it was ruled by a series of local feudal lords. From 1209 it belonged to the Patriarchs of Aquileia, and in 1283 came under Venetian rule. Thereafter it passed to Austria, and for a time, until overshadowed by Pula, it was the largest port on the W coast of Istria. From 1918 to 1943 it was held by Italy. Since the end of the Second World War the small

commercial harbour to the N of the town and the industry which has grown up around it have made little contribution to the town's economic development, which was given a rapid boost only with the construction of hotels and holiday chalets and the establishment of camp sites which began in the 1960s.

SIGHTS. – The *old town* of Rovinj, on the promontory, has preserved its old-world aspect almost intact. The handsome houses, the palazzos and the narrow streets present a typically Mediterranean picture showing strong Italian influence, and amid the swarms of gesticulating and persuasive souvenir-sellers visitors will almost feel that they *are* in Italy.

In Tito Square, by the harbour, are a red *clock-tower*, the Baroque *Balbi Arch* (1680), which occupies the position of the old town gate, and the 17th c. **Town Hall**. In the eastern part of the town, towards the mainland, is a *Franciscan friary*, and in the opposite direction, on Freedom Square (Trg Slobode), the oldest building in Rovinj, the little Romanesque **Trinity Church** (*Sv. Trojstvo*), on a heptagonal plan.

Dominating the town is the **Cathedral**, an aisled Baroque church dedicated to St Euphemia (Sv. Fuma), build in 1736 on a site previously occupied by at least two earlier churches. There is a marble relief of the saint (14th c.) on the side door on the W front (the rest of which dates only from 1861); within the church is her late antique *sarcophagus* (6th c.) and on the summit of the *campanile* (1677) her bronze statue.

On **Crveni Otok** (the "Red Island"), one of the seven little islands around Rovinj, is a Benedictine *abbey* which was occupied by Franciscans from 1446 to 1820. Part of the abbey was then converted into a private house, which later became a hotel. Of the pre-Romanesque church there survive the square central area under the dome and some 15th and 16th c. sculpture. In the dome and in a niche in the S wall are 15th c. frescoes.

Sarajevo

Republic: Bosnia-Hercegovina (Bosna i Hercegovina).
Altitude: 1762–2238 ft/537–682 m. – Population: 450,000.
Post code: YU-71000. – Telephone code: 0 71.
ⓘ Turist Biro,
    tel. 2 51 51.
    Turistički Sayez Sarajeva,
    Maršala Tita 80/1;
    tel. 3 74 86.

HOTELS. – *Bristol*, A, 506 b., tel. 61 48 11; *Evropa*, B, 395 b., tel. 2 34 81; *National*, B, 132 b., tel. 3 30 00; *Zagreb*, C, 72 b., tel. 61 21 86; *Central*, D, 65 b., tel. 3 35 66; *Stari Grad*, D, 40 b., tel. 3 66 89. – IN ILIDŽA (7½ miles/12 km from the middle of the town): *Terme*, B, 353 b., tel. 62 14 44.

CAMP Site. – At Ilidža, to the left of the Sarajevo–Mostar road (noisy, many long-term campers).

EVENTS. – Yugoslav Song Festival in April; festival of new Yugoslav folk songs and dances at Ilidža in July.

AIRPORT: Sarajevo. JAT office: Vase Miskina 2, tel. 2 49 18 and 2 45 89.

Sarajevo, capital of the republic of Bosnia-Hercegovina, is a city of the young, with 140,000 schoolchildren and students, as visitors will soon realise when they encounter the swarms of young people strolling about the town's streets and parks in the evenings and at weekends. This is a rapidly growing town, with large modern residential areas developing on its western outskirts. The old town contains many relics of Sarajevo's Turkish past, and the monumental buildings on the E side of the town recall the period of Austrian rule between 1878 and 1918. The 14th Winter Olympic Games of 1984 are to be held at various sites to the S and W of the town, all within 20 miles/30 km of the central area.

The older parts of Sarajevo, lying on the right bank of the River Miljacka between the castle in the E and the end of Ul. Maršala Tita in the W, are a curious mixture of old Turkish buildings and pompous edifices in the style favoured under the Austro-Hungarian monarchy, of dilapidation and new building. The coexistence of a variety of religions – Orthodox, Roman Catholics, Moslems and a minority of Jews from Spain – in this area is reflected in the juxtaposition of their different places of worship. Sarajevo

Husref Bey Mosque, Sarajevo

still has *72 mosques*, from which the muezzins regularly call on the faithful to turn towards Mecca in prayer (though nowadays the calls to prayer are recorded and transmitted by loudspeakers), while often the neighbouring Christian churches will be ringing the bells for their services. The number of people professing the Moslem faith has shown little change since 1977, when the government recognised the country's Moslems as a separate ethnic group. The numbers attending worship in the mosques, however, have shown a sharp decline: the congregation now consists mainly of old men.

HISTORY. – The castle which now looms over Sarajevo occupies the site of an earlier stronghold known as *Vrhbosna*. After the Turks had occupied the whole of Bosnia they built a seraglio here in 1462, and from this seraglio (demolished 1853), the residence of the Sultans, the town derives its name. It flourished particularly during the two governorships of Gazi Husref Bey (1506–12, 1521–41), at the end of which it had a population of 80,000 and 170 mosques.

After various fires, floods and epidemics of plague the town suffered a devastating catastrophe in 1697, when Prince Eugene of Savoy, advancing against the Turks, held Sarajevo for a few hours and set the whole town on fire. Two years later, when the worst of the destruction had been repaired, the governor was persuaded by the pleas of the inhabitants to move the seat of government of Bosnia N to Travnik, where it remained until 1851.

Thereafter the Southern Slav peoples manifested their opposition to Turkish rule ever more frequently and more vigorously. In 1876 Serbia, Montenegro and Russia supported a rising in Hercegovina aimed at the liberation of Bosnia, but in the subsequent war the Turks were victorious. Then at the Congress of Berlin in 1878 Bismarck sought to achieve the pacification of the Balkans; but while Serbia finally achieved independence and, like Montenegro, gained an accession of territory, Bosnia and Hercegovina were handed over to Austrian administration. The bitter disappointment of the population was reflected in bloody resistance to the entry of Austrian troops; and this bitterness grew when Austria formally annexed the provinces of Bosnia and Hercegovina in 1908. The movement for liberation of the Austrian-occupied territories grew in strength, and in 1912 and 1913 there were two Balkan wars over Macedonia.

It was against this background of the struggle to shake off foreign rule that a student named Gavrilo Princip assassinated Archduke Francis Ferdinand, heir to the Austrian throne, and his wife in Sarajevo on 28 June 1914. The fatal shots which led to the outbreak of the First World War were fired near the bridge which now bears Princip's name. On the building to the right beyond the bridge is a commemorative plaque, and on the pavement below it are two footprints marking the spot where Princip stood. The building now houses the Mlada Bosna Museum (named after the group of conspirators – "Young Bosnia" – to which Princip belonged). Princip's grave is in the town cemetery.

Since the end of the last war Sarajevo has developed rapidly as an industrial town but also as an educational and cultural area. One of the largest industrial establishments is a Volkswagen branch factory.

Souvenir stall in the bazaar quarter of Sarajevo

found at reasonable prices in a department store with the atmosphere of a bazaar.

On the edge of the bazaar quarter stands the *Husref Bey Mosque (*Begova Džamija*), one of the largest mosques in the Balkans, measuring 43 ft/13 m square, with a dome 85 ft/26 m high (interior measurement). It was built for the Turkish governor, Gazi Husref Bey, in the town's period of splendour (completed 1531).

The INTERIOR has a profusion of ornament (restored by Munich painters in 1886 after a fire). The many valuable *carpets* were presented to the mosque by distinguished visitors from various Arab countries. Outside the mosque is a *fountain* (shadirvan) for the ritual ablutions performed by the faithful before entering the mosque for prayer. In the courtyard is a *türbe* (mausoleum) containing the founder's sarcophagus, and adjoining this an *observatory* for determining the time.

Princip Bridge, Sarajevo

SIGHTS. – The *Baščaršija quarter in the OLD TOWN of Sarajevo has remained largely untouched by modern clearance and rebuilding. Originally a market for local people, particularly for the peasants from the surrounding area who used to come in on Wednesdays in their old traditional costumes, the Baščaršija is now increasingly aimed at tourists. In the streets of the coppersmiths and the vendors of pots and pans and jewelry there are still a few craftsmen who make the wares they offer in their own little workshops open to the street; and it is still open to visitors to bargain for any article that takes their fancy. Some years ago a government order requiring prices to be displayed was withdrawn since this requirement was felt to be out of character with this kind of trade. Articles of high quality, from hand-knotted carpets to elaborately decorated copper jugs, can be

A number of *old Turkish houses* have been furnished in traditional style and are open to visitors: for example the *Svrzina Kuća*, the residence of a well-to-do Turk, which shows the strictly patriarchal character of Moslem life but also the Moslem concern with the pleasures of the senses. The men lived apart from the women, who were confined to the *haremluk*. A Bosnian counterpart to this house is provided by the *Despić House*, on the banks of the River Miljacka, which shows the way of life of a Bosnian merchant in the 18th c.

To the N of the Baščaršija quarter is the interesting **Municipal Museum** (Bosnian history, culture and folk art). – On the other side of the Miljacka is the **Imperial Mosque** (*Careva Džamija*), the place of worship of the town's highest Mohammedan ecclesiastical dignitary, the Reis-

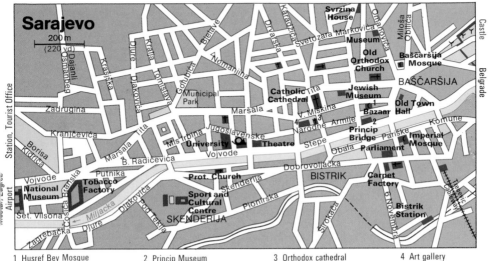

1 Husref Bey Mosque   2 Princip Museum   3 Orthodox cathedral   4 Art gallery

ul-Ulema. Not far away is the former residence of the Turkish vizier, the *Konak*, which is now occupied by the **Parliament** of Bosnia-Hercegovina. A little way S, in Ul. 6 Novembra, is the *Carpet Factory* (Tkaonica Ćilima) established by the Austrians, which is well worth a visit even if you have no idea of buying a carpet.

Other features of interest are the *Orthodox Cathedral* in Liberation Square (Trg Oslobodjenja); the *Old Orthodox Church* in Ul. Maršala Tita; the *Regional Museum* (*Zemaljski Muzej*); the **Old Town Hall** (now the *Bosnian National Library*), a building in Moorish-Byzantine style erected during the Austrian period; and the **Castle** above the town. There are also some interesting modern buildings in the new western districts of Sarajevo which

show experiments in architectural form and the use of colour.

On the left bank of the River Miljacka is the lower station of a *cableway* which runs up in 12 minutes to the terrace of a *restaurant* (3675 ft/1120 m) offering a magnificent view of the town in the valley below. The restaurant, which can also be reached by road, is on Sarajevo's own domestic mountain, *Trebević (5345 ft/1629 m), to which the town's skiers resort in winter.

WINTER OLYMPICS, 1984. – Sarajevo was selected by the International Olympic Committee in 1978 as the scene of the 14th Winter Olympics. The determining factor in the choice of this site was that Sarajevo is barely 19 miles/30 km from the Jahorina range, long a favourite skiing area, with good snow from the beginning of December until May. In preparation for the Games a large program of construction is under way – new roads, chair-lifts and

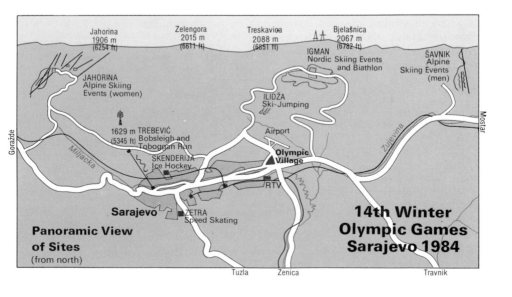

ski-tows, new sports facilities and hotels (including the *Jahorina Hotel*, 340 b., tel. 4 41 93).

The Alpine skiing events for women (slalom, downhill racing) will take place in the Jahorina range; the corresponding events for men will be held at Šavnik in the Hranisava range (reached from the Sarajevo–Mostar road). The bobsled and toboggan run is being laid out on Mt Trebević above the town (access by road or by the existing cabin cableway).

The ski-jumping contests will be held to the S of the spa of Ilidža. The Nordic skiing events for both men and women, including the biathlon, will take place at Igman, in the Bjelašnica range. The figure and speed skating events and the ice-hockey matches will be housed in the Skenderija Stadium and in a new artificial ice-rink. The Olympic Village is being built close to the airport, with accommodation for 2000 competitors and associated personnel. The hotel accommodation available in the town is also being considerably increased.

Lake Scutari/ Skadarsko Jezero

Republic: Montenegro (Crna Gora).

*Lake Scutari (Skadarsko Jezero, Albanian Liqueni i Shkodrës) is the largest lake in the Balkans and the one with the greatest abundance of fish. Of its total area of 143 sq. miles/ 370 sq. km, some 86 sq. miles/222 sq. km are in Yugoslavia and 57 sq. miles/148 sq. km in Albania. For much of its length the famous Black Mountains form an imposing backdrop to the lake, the shores of which are overgrown with water weeds. Lake Scutari's attraction lies in its unspoiled natural beauty, the constantly changing play of light and colour on its waters, its luxuriant vegetation and – not least – its great hosts of waterfowl.

The lake takes its present name from the Albanian town of Shkodër (Skadar; traditionally in English Scutari) but in the past it was known by a variety of different names – *Lacus Labeatis* (the Roman name), *Dioklit*, *Bojana* or *Blato* – some of which are still used by the local people.

There are two views about the origins of Lake Scutari. Some authorities believe that it was originally an inlet of the Adriatic which was later cut off from the sea by earth movements; others regard it as a huge karstic depression which has fallen in and sunk below sea level as a result of tectonic displacements.

The lake is some 30 miles/48 km long and up to 9 miles/14 km wide, with an average

depth of 23 ft/7 m. The level of the water is subject to sharp seasonal variations: thus after the snow melts in the mountains the level rises by 8–10 ft/2·5–3 m, while the area of the lake increases from 143 sq. miles/370 sq. km to some 212 sq. miles/ 550 sq. km, flooding up to 77 sq. miles of fertile arable land.

The great changes in water level are due on the one hand to variations in the inflow from the lake's tributary streams and on the other to a peculiarity in the outflow from the lake. During the rainy months between autumn and spring Lake Scutari receives huge masses of water, partly from the heavy local rainfall, partly from the greatly increased flow of the tributary streams (Rijeka Crnojevića, Morača, Crnica, Plavnica); and to all this is added the inflow from the numerous underwater springs in the lake itself.

The water level is normally regulated by the lake's natural outflow, the River Bojana (Albanian Buna), the middle course of which forms the boundary between Yugoslavia and Albania; in the delta at the mouth of the river is the Yugoslav naturist island of *Ada*, with a large complex of holiday chalets and a camp site. The River Bojana, however, has two tributaries within Albania, the Kiri and the Drin i Madh, which join it to the S of Shkodër, coming down from the Albanian mountains; and when these two streams are in spate they raise the level of the Bojana, which has the effect of blocking the outflow from Lake Scutari.

The *underwater springs* in Lake Scutari are a typical karstic phenomenon – depressions or shafts in the lake bottom ranging in depth from 25 ft/8 m to 145 ft/44 m and in width from 65 ft/20 m to 200 ft/60 m. The water from these springs maintains almost the same temperature throughout the year. Some of the deepest of them have been scientifically investigated (the Radiško, Krnjičko, Gradačko and Toplansko springs).

Lake Scutari is notable for its abundance of fish, and no permit for fishing in the lake is required even by foreign visitors. However good the catch, it must be for the angler's own consumption and must not be sold. 35 different species of fish are found in the lake, including whitefish, carp, trout, eels and many other edible species, but no predatory species. The professional Montenegrin fishermen take some 1000 tons of fish from the lake every year.

Lake Scutari (Skadarsko Jezero) in southern Montenegro

Lake Scutari is also one of Europe's largest bird reserves. For some species the lake is only a staging point on a longer journey; others winter here; but most of them remain in this ornithological paradise throughout the year. Wild geese and ducks also seek refuge here during the colder months. By going out at first light in one of the flat-bottomed boats which creep noiselessly through the colonies of water-lilies visitors may even hope to see pelicans.

On the Montenegrin shores of the lake there is only one place of any size – **Virpazar**, starting point of the bloody rising against the Turks in 1702 which is known as the "Montenegrin Vespers", touched off by the Turkish sacking of the monastery at Cetinje. During the Second World War, the first shots in the war between the partisans and the occupying Italian forces were fired at Virpazar on July 13, 1941; and July 13 is now celebrated in Montenegro as a national holiday.

From Virpazar a narrow road climbs up the hillside and then follows the W side of the lake, at some distance from its shores, turning S in the direction of Ulcinj shortly before the Albanian frontier. This little road, only the first section of which is asphalted, leads into an area hardly ever visited by strangers, and walkers in these hills are sure of a friendly welcome from the local people, who still preserve the old traditions of hospitality.

Off the western shores of the lake, at the foot of the Rumija Hills, are some 50 islands of varying size, known to the local people as *gorice* (hills), which are not usually shown on maps. On some of them are small 14th and 15th c. churches, now abandoned and neglected; and on the island of Starčevo is a monastery dating from the second half of the 14th c. which has recently been restored. The few inhabitants of these islets seem to the visitor to be living on the verge of another world, and it appears likely that the island of Starčevo will soon also be uninhabited.

There is one other place of some interest near the lake, situated on one of its tributary streams. This is the village of *Rijeka Crnojevića*, with the same name as the river, which lies on the Cetinje–Titograd road but can also be reached on a gravel road from Virpazar: a settlement of cube-shaped houses eaten away by the dampness, with a main street which is flooded every year when the lake rises in spring. The tourists who stop here to photograph the old arched bridge little suspect that this is a spot of major historical significance: here, in the *monastery of Obod*, founded in 1493 and now in ruins, the first Slav printing press was set up and the first book in Cyrillic script was printed. But the type, laboriously brought from Venice, remained in use for only some ten years before being melted down to make bullets when further attacks by the Turks were threatened.

There are a number of *excursion vessels* plying Lake Scutari, but there are no longer any regular services. Their routes must be kept clear by periodic cutting of the water plants which grow luxuriantly in the NW part of the lake. Information about sailings (usually only for organised parties) can be obtained from travel agencies in the coastal resorts or in Titograd.

There is no ban on the use of privately owned motorboats on Lake Scutari, but the local people do no like it; and there is always the possibility of getting into trouble through straying unwittingly over the Albanian frontier. On land, too, walkers should not go nearer the frontier than the warning signs on the Yugoslav side.

The road from Titograd to the coast crosses the N end of the lake on a causeway and a bridge, which are used also by the Belgrade–Titograd–Bar railway line. Soon after Virpazar the main road climbs, with numerous bends, to almost 3300 ft/1000 m and then descends in a series of well-engineered hairpins to join the Adriatic coastal highway at Petrovac.

Senj

Republic: Croatia (Hrvatska).
Altitude: 13 ft/4 m. – Population: 5000.
Post code: YU-51270. – Telephone code: 0 51.
ⓘ **Kvarner Express,**
Titovo Obala;
tel. 88 10 68.

HOTELS. – *Nehaj*, B, 93 b., tel. 88 12 85; *Velebit*, D, 33 b., tel. 88 13 10.

CAMP SITES. – *Camping Ujča*, 2½ miles/4 km from Senj in a small cove (road runs inland at km 284 on coastal highway); *Prva Draga II*, Istarska 16; *Škver*.

Visitors driving past this apparently insignificant little town on the Adriatic coastal highway, or waiting here for the ferry to Rab, may not realise what an eventful history it has had, or that in 1615 it was the cause of a war between Venice and Austria. The old part of the town lies above the Adriatic coastal highway, and is reached by taking the road to the Plitvice Lakes. Senj has a bathing beach, but so far it has not developed into a major seaside resort.

Senj is also notable from the meteorological point of view, since it appears to be the place of origin of the dreaded fall wind from the N, the bora (which is popularly said to be born in Senj, to be married in Rijeka and to be condemned to death in Trieste). It is certainly true that when the bora beats down on the coast it blows with particular violence at Senj, frequently causing serious accidents on the curving Adriatic coastal highway.

HISTORY. – In Roman times there was a trading station here. Later it became a place of some consequence as a town situated on the frontiers of the medieval Croatian state and the see of a bishop from 1154. In 1271 it passed into the hands of the Princes Frankopan, rulers of the offshore island of Krk; in 1469 it was taken by King Matthias Corvinus of Hungary; and in 1526 it passed to the Habsburgs. Later, refugees, including many Uskoks fleeing before the advancing Turks settled here and soon became the predominant force in the town. Thereafter, along with the original inhabitants of the town, they fought a war on two fronts, against the Venetians and against the Turks, and were consistently victorious. But their warlike activity, begun in self-defence, soon developed into piracy, and ships from Senj threatened the safety of Venetian maritime trade from Koper to the mouth of the Neretva. Their daring exploits were celebrated in many folk songs. In 1615 the people of Senj were the occasion of a war between Venice and Austria; but two years later these two great powers got together and resolved to put an end to Senj's troublesome activities; the inhabitants were captured, disarmed and resettled in the interior of Croatia. Their name is commemorated in the Uskok Hills between Ljubljana and Zagreb. After this Senj lost its previous importance, and during the 18th and 19th c. its fortifications were dismantled, leaving only a single tower in the harbour. The town's remaining historic buildings were mostly destroyed during the Second World War.

SIGHTS. – Of the 16 churches which the town once possessed only two survive in whole or in part. The **Cathedral** (*S. Marija*) was built in the 11th–12th c., suffered heavy damage in 1943 and was restored in 1947; the free-standing tower dates from 1900. The principal features of the interior are the Baroque *altars*, the *tomb of Bishop Johannes de Cardinalibus* of Senj (1392) and a 15th c. stone *tabernacle*. The *sacristy* dates from 1497.

At the W corner of the Cathedral Square stands the 15th c. **Vukasović Palace**, in a style transitional between Gothic and Renaissance, which now contains a collection of material on the history of the town. By the *Mala Vrata*, an old town gate, is an 18th c. *Baroque palace*.

Outside the town, to the right of the main road to Rijeka, is the little *St Martin's Church*, with a Glagolitic (Old Slavonic)

Nehaj Castle, above Senj

inscription of 1330. – On the hill is **Nehaj** ("Fear Not") **Castle**, built in 1558 by General Ivan Lenković, an Uskok leader. Above one of the windows are three coats of arms – the Archducal arms in the middle, flanked by those of Ivan Lenković and his wife. Also to be seen in the castle are Glagolitic inscriptions from churches outside the town which were destroyed in Turkish attacks.

SURROUNDINGS. – 6 miles/10 km S of Senj a road goes off to the ****Plitvice Lakes**. This road, asphalted and well engineered as far as the **Anići** sawmills, winds its way up from the Adriatic coast into the bare karstic hills and then descends into wooded valleys. Beyond Anići the road degenerates into a rough country track, suitable only for horse-drawn traffic but just negotiable by cars at slow speed, traversing lonely but very beautiful country. At **Otočac** it joins the main road to the Plitvice Lakes. This road, which is signposted, is no longer than the normal road to Otočac but is incomparably more beautiful.

Serbian Monasteries

SUGGESTED ITINERARY for seeing the Serbian monasteries, exploring the autonomous province of Kosovo and visiting the towns of Skopje and Niš: Belgrade – autoput to S – detours to Manasija and Ravanica monasteries – Ćićevac exit from motorway – Kruševac – Veluće, Kalenić and Ljubostinja monasteries – Kraljevo (overnight) – Žiča monastery – Studenica monastery – Raška – Novi Pazar, with Djurdjevi Stupovi and Sopoćani monasteries and the old town of Ras – Kosovska Mitrovica, with the monastic church of Banjska – Ribonice – Peć, with the Patriarchate – Visoki Dečani monastery – Prizren, with Sv. Arhandjeli and Sv. Marka – (Skopje) – Priština, with Gračanica monastery – Niš – Belgrade.

Tours of the monasteries of Serbia (including the autonomous province of Kosovo) have long been included in the programs of travel firms catering to special interests, and

with the improvement not only of the main roads but of many minor roads in Yugoslavia they are now attracting increasing numbers of individual visitors: it is no longer an adventure to visit the remoter monasteries. Visitors can also rely on finding inns and restaurants nearly everywhere.

The monasteries and monastic churches built between the 13th and 15th c. can be classified in two "schools" – the *Raška school* (from Raška or Rascia, the medieval name for the central part of Serbia in the Ibar and Lim valleys) and the *Morava school* (named after the river which is formed by the junction of the Western Morava and the Southern Morava near the town of Kruševac and which flows into the Danube at Smederevo).

The *Raška school* (13th c.) combines Romanesque and Byzantine architectural forms. The churches, built of stone or marble, are aisleless and have only one dome. The doors and windows have elaborate

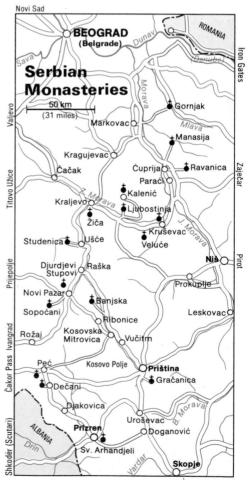

sculptural decoration. The frescoes of this school are consummate examples of Byzantine art in the time of the Latin Empire of Constantinople (1204–61).

The *Morava school* (end of 14th c. and first half of 15th c.) at first took as its model the architecture of the early 14th c. Brick is the normal building material, with richly decorated stone bases. Doorways and windows have bands of "interlace" ornament with animal and human figures. In the interior of the churches square and semicircular forms predominate. The frescoes of this period, like those of the Raška school, are of notably high artistic quality. The slender figures, set against a deep background, are of enchanting lightness.

The Raška school

The finest example of the work of the Raška school is *Studenica monastery (see under Kraljevo). There are three churches, the Church of the Mother of God, the Royal Church and St Nicholas's Church, together with Archbishop Sava's Refectory and a tower. There are believed to have originally been seven churches in this remote spot.

Studenica church

The *Church of the Mother of God* was built by Stephen Nemanja at the end of the 12th c. as his burial church. In accordance with the principles of the Raška school, it has only a single dome. The W doorway is flanked by relief figures of Christ and the 12 Apostles, and in the tympanum is a figure of the Virgin between two angels. The finest of the original wall paintings of 1208–09 is a monumental representation of the Crucifixion on the W wall of the choir. The chancel contains a magnificent series of realistically depicted figures of saints.

The little *St Nicholas's Church* also dates from the end of the 12th c. In the lower

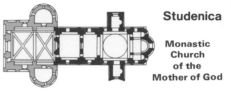

Studenica

Monastic Church of the Mother of God

range of paintings are figures of St John the Baptist and St Demetrius, in the upper range scenes from the feast-day cycle (Entry into Jerusalem, Women at the Tomb). The head of the Baptist is one of the finest examples of medieval portrait-painting in Serbia.

The *Royal Church*, dedicated to SS. Joachim and Anne, was built by King Milutin in 1314. The church is cruciform in plan, with a single dome. It has a profusion of wall paintings, the individual scenes being of relatively small size. On the S wall are portraits of the founder and his wife Simonida with SS. Joachim and Anne, on the N wall St Sava Nemanja.

Archbishop Sava's Refectory is a square building preceded by a porch with columns and marble arches. The square tower contains remains of 13th c. paintings. – Above Studenica, reached by a $2\frac{1}{2}$ mile/4 km walk, are the remains of hermits' cells probably dating from the time of Stephen Nemanja.

A further example of the work of the Raška school is the Church of the Apostles in the **Patriarchate of Peć**, a monastic house still occupied by nuns. It can be reached either from Kosovska Mitrovica or on a road from the Adriatic which until quite recently was a severe test for both car and

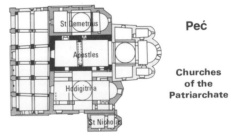

Peć

Churches of the Patriarchate

driver – running up via Titograd to Andrijevica, then over the **Cakor pass** (6067 ft/1849 m) on 25 miles/40 km of dusty road, formerly impassable for many months of the year on account of the danger of avalanches and landslides. This road is now negotiable without too much difficulty. After the pass it follows a daringly engineered route between high rock faces and through numerous tunnels, and then through the Rugovo gorge to Peć. 1¼ miles/2 km before the town, below the road on the right, is the *Patriarchate.

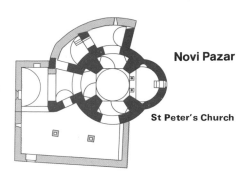

Novi Pazar

St Peter's Church

Until 1253 Žiča (see under Kraljevo) was the place of coronation of the Serbian kings and the seat of the Patriarchate; but since this monastery was in too exposed a situation Sava Nemanjić charged his successor Arsenije (1233–63) to find a safer site. The situation he chose, approaching from the inland plain, lay at the mouth of the *Rugovo gorge, then barely passable.

Looking from above, the visitor sees a complex of buildings with three domes and a tall enclosed narthex; a further structure on the S side is not visible from this viewpoint. This is not a church with three domes but a group of three churches built against one another at different times.

The first church built by Arsenije was the Church of the Apostles (with the central dome), which was completed about 1250. Archbishop Nikodim then built St Demetrius's Church next to it (on the N side, nearest the road) in 1321–24. The third church, the Hodigitrija (the Mother of God), was added on the S side by Archbishop Danilo II in 1330. Archbishop Danilo also linked the three churches by a large narthex, originally open but later enclosed, which from the outside has the air of a large barn, and added a small chapel dedicated to St Nicholas (1331) on the S side of his Hodigitrija church.

The long building period of 80 years (1250–1331) is reflected in the changing styles of both the architecture and the wall paintings. The common feature shared by all three churches is the dome over the chancel.

The *paintings in the Church of the Apostles, mostly New Testament scenes, depict figures with a severe expression, wearing simple but colourful dress. The paintings in the other two churches show great similarities, although the individual scenes were the work of different artists. These paintings are not true frescoes (i.e. they were not painted on fresh damp plaster). – The paintings in St Nicholas's Chapel date from the 17th c.

The Treasury of the Patriarchate, which has been open to the public since 1956, was founded in the 13th c. and originally contained a great store of valuable articles of gold, silver and ivory, most of which have over the centuries been stolen or destroyed. Even so the Treasury still possesses a notable collection of 89 pieces of medieval religious art – splendidly illuminated manuscript books, wood-carving, gold-brocaded vestments, icons, iconostasis doors and Bibles bound in covers of gold, silver and coloured enamel.

The whole of the Patriarchate monastery is now occupied by nuns. The seat of the Patriarchate itself is now in Belgrade.

Some 60 miles/100 km N of Peć on the road to Kraljevo is the little industrial town of Novi Pazar, which was a place of considerable consequence as an administrative and military capital in the 16th and 17th c., when it lay on the road between Dubrovnik and Niš. Its main features of interest are St Peter's Church (9th c.), built on a hill on the outskirts of the town which was already occupied in Roman times (Greek and Roman jewelry found on the site is now in Belgrade), and the Altum Alem Mosque, a well-preserved example of 16th c. Moslem architecture, with an elaborately decorated mihrab (niche indicating the direction of Mecca). In the main square is an 18th c. caravanserai, also excellently preserved.

The main reason for going to Novi Pazar, however, is to see the monastic church of Sopoćani, 6 miles/10 km W of the town on a minor road signposted to Prijepolje.

5½ miles/9 km from Novi Pazar this road passes the ruins of the old town of Ras, later called Raška, which during the 12th c., in the reign of Župan Nemanja, was the administrative heart of the Serbian state. In the 14th c., when Serbia extended steadily eastward, Raška declined in importance. The Raška school takes its name from this town (which has no connection with the town of the same name between Novi Pazar and Kraljevo).

The church of Sopoćani monastery, in a secluded valley surrounded by hills and forests, is an aisleless basilica with a single dome and a large apse. The open narthex and tower are later additions. The architecture of Sopoćani, however, is less notable than the *frescoes, which are

Sopoćani

Monastic Church

among the finest examples of medieval art in Serbia and since their restoration have become internationally known.

Sopoćani monastery was built about 1260 by King Uroš I as his place of burial. In the 18th c. it was plundered and stripped of its roof by the Turks, and until 1929 the paintings were exposed to the ravages of wind and weather. Restoration work in that year and again in 1949–58 has brought them back almost completely to their original splendour.

The particular feature of the Sopoćani frescoes is their great size. The saints are over-lifesize, though realistically depicted. Particularly notable are two masterly scenes – the Assumption of the Mother of God and a dramatic representation of the Crucifixion. Another very fine composition depicts the parable of the rich man. As in many medieval Serbian churches, the paintings also include lay figures connected with the church. Thus on the S side of the choir there are portraits of the founder, Uroš I; on the W wall are his wife Helen and their son Dragutin; and Tsar Dušan also appears, flanked by other figures. There are marked stylistic differences between the paintings in the church and those in the narthex, which are later: the scenes in the narthex are smaller, less dramatic and more matter-of-fact representations of the Biblical events they depict.

2 miles/3 km NW of Novi Pazar, off the road to Kraljevo, commandingly situated on a hill, is the monastery of **Djurdjevi Stupovi**, built by Stephen Nemanja about 1170. After 1685 the monastery declined into insignificance. The dome was badly damaged during the first Balkan War (1912), and grenades tore holes in the walls during the Second World War. The building was restored in 1947.

Architecturally the church is a particularly fine example of the work of the Raška school. It contains two layers of *frescoes*, the earlier ones dating from the 12th c., when the church was built, and the later from the 13th c., when it was restored by King Dragutin. The best preserved of the earlier paintings is a monumental and expressive figure of St George on a white horse, similar in style to the over-lifesize frescoes at Sopoćani. In the chapel at the SW corner of the church are portraits of King Dragutin with his wife Katherine and King Milutin with his wife Helen.

Later examples of the architecture of the Raška school, dating from the 14th c., are the monasteries of *Banjska* (Titova Mitrovica), *Dečani* (Peć) and *Sv. Arhandjeli* and *Visoki Dečani* (Prizren). Although not belonging to the Raška school, the finest 14th c. church in Serbia, *Gračanica*, shows links with this school.

Banjska monastery can be reached from the Kraljevo–Titova Mitrovica road (No. 11) by turning off on the right, 9 miles/15 km before the latter into a minor road to the village of Banjska. The monastery was built by King Milutin in 1313–17. The church, aisleless, has a cross-vaulted roof and a dome. Originally a handsome structure of carefully dressed white, red and blue marble, it was used as a mosque during the Turkish period and later fell into ruin. It was restored in 1938. Not much is left of the beautiful frescoes which (as we learn from a chronicler) made lavish use of gold. The village of Banjska has hot sulphur springs, which surge up in two basins, and a small hotel.

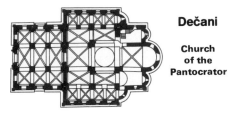

Dečani

Church of the Pantocrator

Another example of the work of the later Raška school can be seen at the monastery of *Visoki Dečani, which can be reached from Peć on the road which runs SE, parallel with the Albanian frontier, to Djakovica and Prizren. 12 miles/19 km from Peć is the village of Dečani, where a dust-free road branches off on the right to the monastery, situated in the beautiful valley of the Dečanska Bistrica at the foot of the Prokletije range. The church of Visoki Dečani is the largest monastic church in Serbia, and every inch of its walls is covered with frescoes – more than a thousand compositions in all. While most other churches were damaged, abandoned or stripped of their roofs during the Turkish period the Turks left Visoki Dečani in its original state. A plan to convert the church into a mosque is said to have been frustrated when a Turk praying in front of the doorway, in the direction of Mecca, was killed by a falling stone.

The church was built between 1327 and 1335, in the reigns of King Stephen Uroš III Dečanski and his son Dušan. In the late Romanesque-Byzantine style, it was erected by master builders from Kotor under the direction of a monk named Vito (as we learn from an inscription on the S door of the portico). Western influence can be seen in some details (e.g. the doorways with columns supported by lions).

The numerous *frescoes* were evidently the work of many different artists and, not surprisingly, are of variable quality; but the lack of unity of style which has been criticised by some experts is difficult to detect. The main problem for the visitor is to avoid being overwhelmed by the profusion of detail.

The paintings include 22 cycles of pictures and 250 figures of saints; one calendar cycle alone has 365 scenes. Every conceivable Old and New Testament scene is depicted, and there are also numerous portraits of contemporary rulers, including the whole genealogical tree of the Nemanjids from Stephen Nemanja to Dušan and his son Uroš.

Apart from the church there are other interesting remains of buildings – a tower, the old refectory and *konaks* built by princes Miloš and Leontije. 2 miles/3 km from the monastery, in the village of Ločane, is a timber-built house, older than the monastery, which is mentioned in a charter still preserved in the *library* of the monastery. The treasury also contains 150 manuscript books written on parchment and paper, many of them richly ornamented in the style of the 14th c. Among them is a biography of Stephen Uroš Dečanski by the historian Gligor'je Camblak. There is also a collection of icons and liturgical utensils. The large bronze candelabrum formerly in the treasury now once again hangs in the church.

The monastery of **Sv. Arhandjeli** at Prizren, a late example of the Raška school, is now a ruin. It was built by Tsar Dušan in 1348–52. The outer walls were of polished marble in two colours; the interior was faced with brick.

SE of Priština is **Gračanica monastery, the finest 14th c. monastery in Serbia, which is also in the tradition of the Raška school. Of the monastery, founded in 1321 by King Milutin, there survives only the church. With its five domes disposed in pyramid formation, its alternating

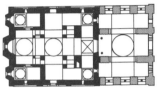

Gračanica

Church of the Annunciation

courses of stone and brick and the rich fresco decoration of the interior it is one of the finest examples of the Serbian Byzantine style. Particularly notable among the frescoes, painted by Mihajlo and Evtihije about 1321, are the Last Judgment and the genealogical tree of the Nemanjids in the narthex, the paintings in the main dome and the figures of the four Evangelists in the four smaller domes.

The Morava school

The paintings in **Ravanica monastery** are characteristic of the early Morava school. The monastery – reached from the Belgrade–Niš autoput by taking the Ćuprija exit and following the signpost for Senje and Ravanica, 6 miles/10 km away on a dusty road – was founded in 1380 by Prince Lazar, who fell nine years later on the Field of Kosova and was buried here. After the monastery had been repeatedly plundered the monks left it in 1690 and took Lazar's remains to the monastery of Vrdnik, N of Belgrade, from which they were transferred during the Second World War to Belgrade Cathedral.

Ravanica monastery is now occupied by nuns and monks, who do agricultural work. Visitors are shown the remains of the once extensive monastic complex – its fortifications, the church and the later Turkish *konak*. The monastery was originally fortified by Prince Lazar when the church was being built.

Gračanica church

The *frescoes*, which have been restored, are among the finest in Serbia. They include portraits of the founder, his wife Milica and his two sons Stefan and Vuk. Of the Biblical scenes the most notable is the Entry into Jerusalem. The frescoes in the central dome were the work of a single artist, named as Konstantin. The style is over-refined and the use of colour more restrained than in the paintings of the Raška school. Other characteristic features of the Morava school are the rich decoration of the exterior, the ornamental work of the windows and the richly embellished domes.

Other examples of buildings of the Morava school are the *Lazarica Church at Kruševac and the monastic church of Ljubostinja (for both of these see under Kraljevo).

Also E of Kraljevo, but farther N and difficult of access, is *Kalenić monastery, with a small church which ranks as the finest example of the work of the Morava school. Built in the early 15th c., this little three-apsed church is notable for the astonishingly rich decoration of the exterior – polychrome brick, intricate

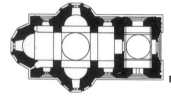

Kalenić

**Church
of the
Mother of God**

carved ornament on doorways, windows and arches and figural bas-reliefs; and the richness of the exterior is matched by the well-preserved *frescoes* in the interior, graceful compositions in delicate pastel tones. The finest is the Marriage at Cana, a scene reminiscent of a traditional Serbian wedding ceremony.

Another example of the Morava school is the monastery of **Manasija**, with its strong walls and towers, which is reached by turning off the Belgrade–Niš autoput (highway) at the Markovac exit (63 miles/101 km from Belgrade) and taking a road which runs 21 miles/33 km SE to Manasija.

Manasija monastery was built between 1407 and 1418 by Stefan, son of Prince Lazar. The church stands within the defensive walls, one of the most interest-

ing examples of medieval military architecture in Serbia, still preserving 11 of its towers. In the inner courtyard is the little stone-built church. The *paintings are not so well preserved as those at Ravanica, but the church itself is more imposing than the Ravanica church. In the dome are figures of prophets, and there is a portrait of the founder on the W wall.

In the 15th c. Manasija monastery was an important Serbian cultural base in which books in Serbian and Bulgarian were translated and copied.

Šibenik

Republic: Croatia (Hrvatska).
Altitude: 16 ft/5 m. – Population: 33,000.
Post code: YU-59000. – Telephone code: 0 59.
ⓘ **Turističko Društvo,**
Trg S. Matavulja;
tel. 2 20 75.

HOTELS. – *Jadran*, B, 81 b., tel. 2 26 44; *Krka*, B, 80 b., tel. 2 34 76; Solaris Hotels *Andrija, Ivan, Jure* and *Niko*, 4 miles/6 km from Šibenik on the Zablaće peninsula, together 2565 b., A and B, tel. 2 38 44.

CAMP SITES. – *Martinska*, Matije Gupca 50, tel. 2 28 48; *Solaris*, tel. 2 38 44.

EVENTS. – Summer Festival, June–July; Children's Festival, beginning of July.

SPORT. – Several tennis courts at Solaris Hotels, table tennis, basketball, roller-skating and target shooting in Solaris shooting range, volleyball, mini-golf, mini-football, boccia, bowling; water-skiing (instruction available), rental of motorboats and row boats, scuba diving (prohibited on certain sections of coast).

BOATING and BATHING. – Apart from the tourist attractions of the town itself, Šibenik is a good place for a relaxing stay. The hotels in the town are not particularly suitable for this purpose, but 3 miles/6 km away on the **Zablaće peninsula** (bus services from town) is the *Solaris* resort area, with hotels and a camp site. Although here too there are factories to spoil the view, the beaches are clean and there is a sewage treatment plant. The beach consists partly of pebbles, partly of imported sand and partly of large stones and shelving rock. The vegetation on the peninsula dries up in summer, but the hotels provide a full program of sport, games and entertainment.

There are pleasant trips to the island of **Zlarin**, the only island off the Yugoslav Adriatic coast with coral; the island of **Krapanj** (sponge fishing); and the **Kornati Islands** (see p. 107). Visitors can accompany the local fishermen on their nocturnal fishing expeditions. Diving equipment can be rented from a scuba club. Tennis can be played after dark on floodlit courts.

Pleasure craft making for Šibenik must watch the signal station at the entrance to the channel for signs indicating the approach of larger vessels and must not land on the right-hand side of the channel (naval base, closed area). The yacht harbour for small craft is at the head of the channel beyond the landing-stage for large vessels; it has a winch, slip and service workshop.

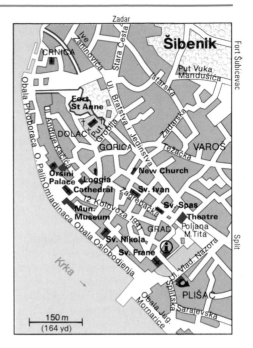

Since the last war Šibenik has developed into an expanding industrial town, supplied by new power stations. Accompanying this has been a growth in the activity of the port, which ships timber and bauxite. The effects of this industrial development on the environment can be observed both by visitors sightseeing in the town itself and by vacationers staying at the Solaris resort complex. Nevertheless Šibenik has much of interest to offer the visitor – in particular its Cathedral, which is one of the finest churches on the whole Yugoslav coast.

HISTORY. – The area around the mouth of the River Krka, with the karstic hills on which Šibenk is situated, was occupied in prehistoric times. The settlement was known to the Illyrians as *Scardona-Skradin*, to the Romans as *Rider-Danilo*. It was only in the time of the Croatian kings, however, that it developed into a fortified town. The Venetians held the town from 1116 to 1133; then in 1167 the Hungarian-Croatian king Stjepan III granted it the right of self-government. After alternating periods of Venetian, Hungarian-Croatian and Bosnian rule Šibenik finally passed under Venetian control in 1412 and remained Venetian until 1797. Thereafter, with only a brief interlude of French occupation, the town was under Austrian rule until 1918. At the end of the First World War Italy tried to seize control of Šibenik, but was compelled to withdraw its troops in 1920, when it became part of Yugoslavia under the Treaty of Rapallo. Italian troops again occupied Šibenik in 1941–43, being replaced by German forces after the Italian surrender. The partisans reoccupied the town in November 1944.

SIGHTS. – The Adriatic coastal highway bypasses Šibenik in a wide arc, and the passing motorist sees nothing of the old town, and of the newer districts only apartment buildings and factory chimneys. Motorists entering the town should drive right across it and seek a parking place for their car on the quays, within easy reach of the town's principal monument, the *Cathedral* of St James (*Sv. Jakov*).

The Cathedral took more than a century to build (1431–1555), and this is reflected in the mingling of stylistic features during the period of transition from Gothic to Renaissance. A number of different builders and sculptors were involved in the work, the two most important being

Niccolò Fiorentino, Nicholas the Florentine (see under Trogir), and Juraj Dalmatinac, George the Dalmatian, who was also responsible for the altar of St Anastasius in the Mausoleum of Split and the Minčeta Tower in Dubrovnik.

An unusual feature of the Cathedral, and a masterly technical achievement for the period, is the *roof structure*. This consists of slabs of stone jointed together which cover the nave, the two aisles, the apses and the dome without any form of support. It is no wonder that, like the master builder named Radovanus who made the proud claim to be "the best of his

Portrait figure, Šibenik Cathedral

craft" on the principal doorway of Trogir Cathedral, the architect of Šibenik Cathedral also left his signature, in an inscription supported by two putti: "Done by Juraj the Dalmatian, son of Mato".

Juraj must also have had a sense of humour, for in no other church is there such a *portrait gallery* of 74 very secular and unsaintly heads as in the frieze which runs round the outer walls of the apses – burghers, peasants, fishermen and villains, running the gamut of human features and expressions.

The most notable features of the impressive interior are the carved wooden *pulpit* by Jerolim Mondella (1624); the *singers' galleries*; the *sacristy*, with carved screens by Mondella; and the *baptistery*, circular in plan with four niches, which is roofed by a single large slab of stone.

Well in front of Municipal Loggia, Šibenik

Behind the Cathedral (looking away from the quay) is the **Municipal Loggia**, once the meeting-place of the municipal council, which was built between 1523 and 1542 and has been restored after war damage. On street level is a colonnade of nine arches and on the upper floor a further colonnade preceding the council chamber. On the other side of the Cathedral, towards the quay, stands the **Bishop's Palace** (1439–41), with a late Gothic courtyard. Beside this is the old *Sea Gate* and close by the **Rector's Palace**, which now houses the *Municipal Museum*. Farther along the quay rises a tower, once used by the Venetians as a prison. Beyond this, towards the landing-

stage used by passenger ships, is the little *St Nicholas's Church* (1451).

Immediately in from the landing-stage are the *Municipal Park* (with an open-air theatre), remains of the *town walls* and, to the left, the **Franciscan friary** and church (*Sv. Frane*). The most notable feature of this aisleless Gothic church (14th c.) is the carved ceiling. The friary contains a valuable collection of old manuscripts, books and incunabula dating back to the 11th c.

Continuing past the Municipal Park, we ccome to a spacious square, Poljana Maršala Tita. To the left, at the far end of the square, is the *Theatre*. Beyond this, in Zagrebačka Ulica, is the Orthodox *parish church*, with a spindle-shaped tower of the late 16th c. and darkly gleaming icons in the interior. From Poljana Maršala Tita a road leads up to **Fort Šubićevac**, formerly known as Fort Barone, after the Swabian Baron Christoph Martin Degenfeld, a general in the Venetian service who directed the successful defence of the town against a Turkish attack in 1647. A second fort, *Fort St Anne* (Sv. Ana), is reached by flights of steps and narrow lanes running up from the Cathedral; it affords a fine view of both the old and the new parts of the town. Below this fort can be seen a curious **cemetery** in which the remains of the dead are deposited in a series of stone pigeonholes arranged in tiers.

Šibenik's third fort, *Fort St John* (Sv. Ivan), the highest of the three, lies NW of the town.

Silba and Olib

Republic: Croatia (Hrvatska).
Altitude: up to 260 ft/80 m. – Population: 700.
Telephone code: 0 57.
ⓘ **Turističko Društvo Silba,**
YU-57295 Silba.

ACCOMMODATION. – No hotels on either island, only accommodation in private houses (apply to Poljoprivredna Zadruga, tel. 2 32 26).

CAMP SITE. – Naturist site on Silba (no caravans).

SPORT. – Scuba diving, rental of row boats.

BOATING and BATHING. – The village of Silba, on the evergreen island of the same name, has four

The little port of Olib on the island of the same name

restaurants, a pension and a shop selling all necessary foodstuffs. The naturist camp is half an hour's walk from the village: the best plan, therefore, is to arrange for the transport of your luggage on a fishing boat from the harbour, where the regular passenger boats put in, to the camp site. The two coves with bathing beaches are separated by the Laterna promontory. The sanitary installations are in the former lighthouse-keeper's house. There are many beautiful coves around the island providing shelter for small boats. Between the islands of Ilovik and Silba, to the S of Lošinj, there are frequently strong winds blowing in from the open sea and producing heavy seas which may present difficulties for small boats. Since the village of Silba lies at the narrowest point of the island and stretches from one side to the other it is possible to put in on either side of the island. The channel between Silba and Olib, the Olibski Kanal, is used only by small vessels.

The western part of Olib, which is sheltered from the bora, has a more luxuriant growth of vegetation than the E side facing the mainland. On this side there is a beautiful wood of holm-oaks. The best bathing is in the Luka Olib (bay).

FERRIES. – Passenger services from Zadar (no cars: there are no motor roads on either of the islands).

The quest for quiet little islands off the tourist track has brought a growing tourist trade to the islands of Silba and Olib, a few miles NW of Zadar, but any major expansion has been hampered by the limited amount of accommodation available in private houses. Silba, although smaller than Olib (6 sq. miles/15 sq. km against 10 sq. miles/26 sq. km), has the advantage over its larger neighbour that it possesses, in addition to the accommodation available in the houses of the peasants and fishermen, a beautiful shady naturist camp site with two large bathing beaches, both with a flat and sandy bottom. Increasing numbers of

pleasure craft now call in at Silba on their way from Lošinj to Zadar.

HISTORY. – The history of the two islands is almost identical. Both were occupied in Roman times, and both are referred to by the emperor Constantine VII Porphyrogenitus in his historical writings, under the names of *Selbo* and *Alope*. In the 15th c. the islands were leased by Venice to families from Zadar, who used them mainly for grazing sheep. During the 17th and 18th c. Silba enjoyed a considerable measure of prosperity through the activities of its seamen and ship-owners, while Olib and the small islands near it remained mere sheep grazings. No settlements of any size could develop on either island, since they had no natural springs or watercourses and depended for their water supply (as they still do) on storing water in cisterns. The decline of the Adriatic fisheries in the 20th c. led to a further exodus of population from the islands. Their prospects for the future depend on the tourist trade and the discovery of the islands as nature reserves with no motor traffic.

SIGHTS. – The *parish church* (17th c.) in the village of **Silba** has paintings by the Venetian artist Carlo Ridolfi. The Church of Our Lady (Gospa od Karmena), built in 1752, belonged to a *Franciscan friary* founded in 1660, now abandoned. Of the old fortifications there remains a ruined 16th c. *tower*. Beside the post office is a 19th c. look-out tower.

The only settlement on the island of **Olib** is in the bay of Luka Olib. The *parish church* was built in 1632 and renovated in 1858. The presbytery preserves 20 *Glagolitic codices* (see under Krk) of the 16th to 19th c. The other church in the village is older than the parish church. Outside the village are a 17th–18th c. watch-tower, the remains of a *Roman settlement* (foundations of houses), a ruined church and a monastery destroyed about 1200, in Banve Bay to the S of the village.

Skopje

Republic: Macedonia (Makedonija).
Altitude: 787 ft/240 m. – Population: 420,000.
Post code: YU-91000. – Telephone code: 0 91.
ⓘ Turistički Biro,
   Kej Dimitar Vlahov 1;
   tel. 23 84 55.

HOTELS. – *Continental*, A, 300 b., tel. 22 01 22; *Grand Hotel Skopje*, A, 274 b., tel. 23 93 11; *Olimpijsko Selo*, A, 256 b., tel. 23 17 08; *Skala*, A, 132 b., tel. 23 60 12; *Turist*, B, 162 b., tel. 23 67 53; *Panorama*, B, 157 b., tel. 23 17 08; *Bellevue*, B, 120 b., tel. 22 34 74; *Vodno*, B, 43 b., tel. 23 51 05; *Jadran*, B, 40 b., tel. 22 00 22.

CAMP SITES. – *Bellevue*, tel. 23 51 22; *Motel Katlanovi Camping*, tel. 22 32 02; *Turist*, tel. 22 30 42.

Skopje is the capital of the republic of Macedonia and its political, economic and cultural heart. For most visitors it is merely a staging point on their journey into Greece or to the new resorts on *Lake Ohrid (see p. 141) and *Lake Prespa (p. 166), now reached on an excellent new road (opened 1977) via Tetovo and Gostivar. Half the town was destroyed, and over 1000 people were killed, in a devastating earthquake on July 26, 1963, but it has been rebuilt from its ruins and is now handsomer and more modern than before. Fifteen satellite settlements are grouped around the historic heart of Skopje, from which radiate wide modern streets in a style reminiscent of an American city. But in the twisting lanes of the restored older part of the town the craftsmen still work as they always did, in striking contrast to the elegant modern shops on the new boulevards and the industrial plants belching smoke on the outskirts of the town.

HISTORY. – In Roman times Skopje (*Scupi*) was the chief town of the province of Dardania. In the 7th c. the area was occupied by Slavs, and in the 10th c. the Bulgarian tsar Samuilo (979–1014) incorporated it in his empire. A hundred years later Skopje became the capital of the enlarged Serbian kingdom of Stephen Dušan. In 1392 the Turks occupied the town during their northward advance, and under the name of Üsküp it remained one of the most important provincial capitals in the Ottoman empire until 1912. After the battle of Kumanovo in that year the Turks withdrew from the town without a shot being fired. During the First World War Skopje was occupied by the Bulgarians, then allied with the Central Powers, who held it until September 1918, when a French and Serbian force advanced N from Salonica. During the Second World War the town was again occupied by Bulgarian forces along with their German allies – a circumstance which explains the tension still existing between Macedonians and Bulgarians.

The earthquake of July 26, 1963, which found most of the inhabitants asleep, left half the town in ruins. This catastrophe gave rise to an extraordinary demonstration of international solidarity: many countries sent supplies of all kinds to help the survivors, and hundreds of caravans and temporary shelters – some of them still to be seen in the outer districts of the town – were provided to accommodate those rendered homeless. The whole population of Yugoslavia contributed toward the cost of reconstruction, and considerable sums were also provided by various foreign countries. Artists contributed pictures and sculpture for the new Skopje (now to be seen in the new picture gallery on the Skopsko Kale hill), and the United Nations sent experts to help in the replanning

Skopje – Panorama of the capital of Macedonia

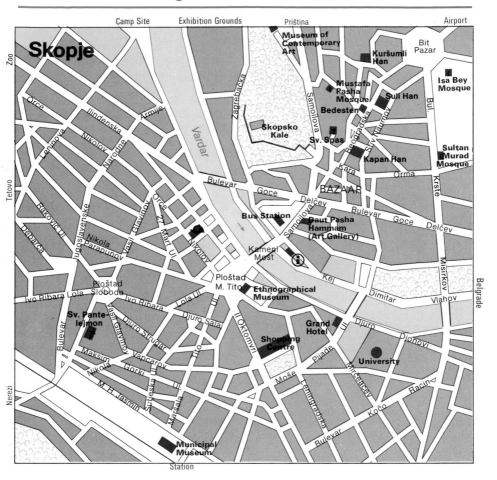

Camp Site   Exhibition Grounds   Priština   Airport

Skopje

Zoo

Museum of Contemporary Art

Kuršumli Han
Bit Pazar

Isa Bey Mosque

Mustafa Pasha Mosque
Suli Han

Bedesten

Skopsko Kale

Sv. Spas

Sultan Murad Mosque

Kapan Han

Orma

BAZAAR

Goce   Delčev

Bulevar   Goce   Delčev

Bus Station

Daut Pasha Hammam (Art Gallery)

Kameni Most

Ploštad M. Tito
Ethnographical Museum

Sv. Panteleimon

Grand Hotel

Shopping Centre

University

Municipal Museum

Station

of the town. Skopje's scars have now healed and most of the holes torn in the city's structure have been filled. Only the façade of the old railway station, with its clock still stopped at 5.16, the time in the morning at which the first tremor struck Skopje, remains to remind the visitor of the catastrophe.

SIGHTS. – The NEW TOWN lies on the right bank of the River Vardar, which flows through the town. Visitors' cars are best left in the car park in Tito Square (Ploštad Maršal Tito). On the E side of the square is the *Ethnographical Museum, with one of the best collections of its kind in Yugoslavia, concentrating particularly on Macedonia. On the S side of the new town, at the end of Ul. Maršal Tito, is the *Municipal Museum*, housed in the old railway station. From Tito Square the old Turkish **Stone Bridge** (*Kameni Most:* closed to motor traffic), of 10 arches, leads across the river into the old town. The bridge was built by Tsar Dušan in the 14th c. on the foundations of an earlier Roman bridge and was renovated by Sultan Murad II. It survived the 1963 earthquake unscathed, although the epicenter was less than 110 yd/100 m away.

Immediately beyond the bridge, on the right, is a massive domed building, the **Daut Pasha Hammam**. This is the largest surviving Turkish bath-house in the Balkans, built in 1489 and later rebuilt after destruction by fire. Since 1948 it has housed an *Art Gallery* displaying pictures and sculpture by Macedonian artists, together with a small collection of icons and copies of old frescoes from Macedonia.

Continuing straight ahead and crossing the wide Bulevar Goce Delčev, we then turn right into the OLD TOWN and the **Bazaar**. In the Old Market numerous shops and stalls offer a varied range of goods for sale – leather articles, copper ware, pottery and the usual souvenirs – and in their various workshops the metalsmiths hammer away, the cobblers work at their lasts and the carpenters ply their saws and planes, all contributing to the picturesqueness of the scene. Farther N can be seen the wooden tower of the **Church of the Saviour** (*Sveti Spas*). The foundations of the church are below

In the bazaar quarter, Stobi

street level, since during the Turkish period the roofs of Christian churches were not allowed to be higher than the gables of the houses. It contains a finely carved *bishop's throne* and a carved wooden *iconostasis* measuring 33 by 20 ft/10 by 6 m, on which three unknown artists worked for five years.

Beyond the church is the rebuilt **Kuršumli Han**, an old caravanserai which was a favourite resort of merchants travelling in the Balkans. The inner court with its smooth stone paving is surrounded by arcades which are now occupied by shops. The building now houses the *Archaeological Museum*.

SW of the Kuršumli Han is the imposing **Mustafa Pasha Mosque**, the finest example of Moslem architecture in Skopje, with a pillared forecourt, a graceful minaret and a fountain. Built of stone and marble, it dates from the 15th c.

Farther W, beyond Samoilova Ulica, rises a hill crowned by the citadel of Skopje, the **Skopsko Kale**, from which there is a fine view over the town. The severe damage suffered by the buildings in the earthquake has now been almost completely repaired.

On the lower slopes to the N of the citadel stands the *Museum of Contempo-

rary Art, built with international assistance and in accordance with the most modern ideas on museum design. The collection consists of some 3000 works ranging in date from 1955 to the present day, of which about 300 are displayed at any one time. Many of the exhibits were presented to the museum by the artists, including both Yugoslav and foreign artists, among them such distinguished names as Picasso and Vasarely.

SURROUNDINGS. – An extra day spent in Skopje will give the interested visitor an opportunity of discovering a number of monasteries and churches in the hilly country around the town – some of them well known, others obscure, and some accessible only on foot. The most important of these is the monastic church (12th c.) of **Sveti Pantelejmon**, near the village of *Nerezi* 3 miles/5 km SW of Skopje off the road to Tetovo, which is notable for its magnificent and realistically painted *frescoes*, discovered and freed from their covering of plaster only in 1926.

Other places of particular interest are *Markov monastery* (well-preserved frescoes), *Matka monastery*, the church of *Sv. Andrija* on *Lake Treska* and the monastery of *Sv. Nikita*. For information about how to reach them apply to the Tourist Office in Skopje.

One sight which should not be missed if you are continuing S on the autoput into Greece (frontier crossing at Gevgelija) is the ancient site of *Stobi*. Although it perhaps hardly justifies the title of the "Pompeii of Macedonia" which is sometimes applied to it, the remains brought to light on this site, which has still been only partly excavated, are fully equal in interest to those at the sites of Heraclea Lyncestis at Bitola and Salona, near Split.

34 miles/54 km from Skopje is the town of Titov Veles, and 16 miles/26 km farther on is the little township of *Gradsko*, beyond which a good road (No. 19) branches off on the right to Prilep, Bitola and Ohrid. To the right of this road immediately beyond the junction, on higher ground, are a motel (40 b.), a café installed in an old twin-engined aircraft and a camp site. 330 yd/300 m beyond this a mosaic inscription in white stones points the way to the site, 440 yd/400 m away.

Stobi was originally a fortified settlement of the Paeonians (a people related to the Macedonians). In

Church of the Saviour, Stobi

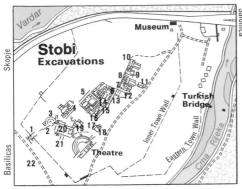

1 Porta Heraclea
2 Via sacra
3 Courtyard
4 House of the Fullers
5 Via principalis superior
6 Fountain
7 House of Psalms
8 Basilica (synagogue)
9 Public Basilica
10 Northern Basilica
11 Small baths

12 Via axia
13 Large baths
14 House of Peristerias
15 Palace of Theodosius
16 House of Parthenius
17 Via principalis inferior
18 Gaming-house
19 Bishop's Palace
20 Episcopal Basilica
21 Baptistery
22 Cemetery

168 B.C. it was razed to the ground by the Goths. In A.D. 518 the town, which had been rebuilt after its destruction, was devastated by an earthquake. In the reign of Justinian Stobi took on a fresh lease of life, but by the time the Turks arrived it was no more than a miserable little village. The site was rediscovered in 1861 by a French archaeologist named Heuzey. Excavations were begun by Yugoslav archaeologists in the 1920s, resumed after the Second World War and are still in progress.

Sculpture and mosaics from Stobi are in the Archaeological Museum in Skopje, two bronze satyrs found here are in the National Museum in Belgrade, and small finds are displayed in a museum on the site.

There is a plan of the site on the wall of the excavators' store. To the NE is a well-preserved town gate, the *Porta Heraclea*. The 2nd c. *amphitheatre*, used in late Roman times for gladiatorial games, has been completely excavated. Other remains include the foundations of five basilicas, palaces, dwelling-houses, fountains and courtyards. Of particular interest are the warm air underfloor heating systems (hypocausts) in the *House of the Fullers* and several bath-houses.

Slano lies at the head of a beautiful fjord-like *inlet 2 miles/3 km long with a narrow opening to the sea. This former fishing village is now a popular summer holiday resort, but with only three hotels (plus quite a considerable amount of accommodation in private houses) it does not suffer from overcrowding. There is wide scope for excursions in the surrounding area, notably to Dubrovnik, 15 miles/24 km away, and to Trsteno, with the beautiful *park of the Villa Gozze.

The Slano inlet is a sun-trap ideally suited for a relaxing holiday, with water which warms up more quickly than in the open sea. The pebble beaches with their gentle slope are very suitable for children, and except around Slano itself, where there is not enough tidal movement to exercise its purifying action, the water is extraordinarily clear and clean. The shores of the inlet are covered with a dense growth of vegetation, with the steep karstic hills farther inland forming a contrasting backdrop.

Slano

Slano

Republic: Croatia (Hrvatska).
Altitude: 6½ ft/2 m. – Population: 400.
Post code: YU-50232. – Telephone code: 0 50.
ⓘ Turističko Društvo,
tel. 8 72 36.

HOTELS. – *Admiral*, B, 400 b., tel. 8 72 02; *Osmine*, B, 304 b., tel. 8 72 64 (naturists only); *Rely*, B, 18 b., tel. 8 72 67. – Some 650 b. in private houses (apply to Tourist Office).

CAMP SITE. – *Admiral*; also many sites for tents and caravans on private property along the shores of the inlet.

HISTORY. – The area which is now a camp site, was once occupied by a Roman settlement, as evidenced by the sarcophagi which have been found here, and there was a Roman fort on *Mt Gradina*. There is also evidence of Illyrian settlement of this whole area. The little town which later grew up here, with its excellent natural harbour, was acquired in 1399 by the republic of Ragusa (Dubrovnik) and became the seat of a Rector (governor).

SIGHTS. – The list of tourist sights in Slano is not a long one: the **Rector's Palace** (15th c., altered at the end of the 19th c.); the *Franciscan friary*, with an Early Christian sarcophagus in front of it; the Franciscan church (1420); the *parish* *church* of St Blaise (Sv. Vlaho), of 1758; and the *mansion of the Ohmucević family*. Every year on August 2 there is a fair at which the peasants from the surrounding area wear the old traditional costumes and dance the folk dance known as the *lindo*.

SURROUNDINGS. – A steep and unsurfaced road branches off the coastal highway at Slano and runs through the karstic hills to the **Popovo Polje** area traversed by the River Trebišnjica, here twice dammed by karstic formations (see under Karst). Above the village of **Zavala** (8½ miles/14 km from Slano), where the road becomes still worse, is a rock-hewn Orthodox *Church of the Mother of God* with remains of 14th–15th c. wall paintings. Most visitors to Zavala, however, come for the sake of the nearby karstic cavern, the **Vjetrenica Jama**, one of the largest caves in the world, with a total length of 12½ miles/20 km (only 1¼ miles/2 km accessible to visitors).

The excursion can be continued to **Trebinje**, an ancient little town which still preserves its oriental character, returning to the coast just S of Dubrovnik.

8½ miles/14 km from Slano on the road to Dubrovnik is *Trsteno*, with the magnificent*park of the Villa Gozze** (formerly the *Villa Gučetić*). At the entrance to the village, on the right, are two huge plane-trees, with trunks more than 30 ft/10 m in circumference. Taking a side road to the right here, we see on the left the entrance to the park, with a sign bearing the name Trsteno Arboretum (admission charge).

This remarkable collection of Mediterranean and exotic trees, shrubs and plants is administered by the Biological Institute of the Yugoslav Academy of Sciences. On windless days the air is filled with a heavy perfume, birds flutter and swoop among the trees and the occasional snake slithers across the path. The summer villa of the family which once owned the estate now houses a small museum, in which visitors are reminded of the many famous people, from Titian to Byron, who have visited this natural paradise.

The path leads to an old mill, with oil and wine presses, and then climbs to a beautiful fountain (1736), with figures of Neptune and attendant nymphs, now rather dilapidated.

Šolta

Republic: Croatia (Hrvatska).
Area of island: 20 sq. miles/52 sq. km.
Population: 3000.
Post code: YU-58432. – Telephone code: 0 58.
ⓘ **Turističko Društvo Stomorska,**
tel. 8 08 19.

HOTELS. – IN STOMORSKA: *Olint*, C, 40 b., tel. 8 08 19. – Accommodation in private houses in Stomorska, Nečujam and Maslinica. – AT MASLINICA: *Avlija* (in castle), 120 b., no tel.

CAR FERRIES. – Split–Rogač–Stomorska–Nečujam–Maslinica.

SPORT, BOATING and BATHING. – Water-skiing and scuba diving at Stomorska.

The ferries put in at *Stomorska, Nečujam, Rogač* and *Maslinica*, making it possible to get from one place on the island to another by sea. **Maslinica** is best equipped as a holiday resort, and boats can be rented here. Eight of the islets lying off the bay are uninhabited, offering scope for naturists. Swimmers and divers are warned by the local people against swimming out from the islands towards the open sea, since in this area – near the shipping lanes to Split – sharks are frequently sighted.

Nečujam, situated in a very beautiful bay, also has ambitions as a tourist attraction. *Stomorska*, in the next large cove, has a good bathing beach.

An ideal anchorage for pleasure craft is *Maslinica Bay*, which is screened by the offshore islands and also offers shelter from the bora. The inlets at Rogač, Nečujam and Stomorska are exposed to N winds.

The little island of Šolta, an hour's sail from Split, is still lacking in the facilities for mass tourism, but for those who prefer a quiet time away from the crowds it has all that is needed within its area of barely 20 sq. miles/52 sq. km. A 9 mile/15 km long gravel road runs from end to end of the island through typical Dalmatian farming country, with groves of olives and figs, vineyards and fields of lavender. The only length of asphalted road is the short stretch between the ferry port of Rogač, on the side facing the main-land, and the largest place on the island, Grohote.

HISTORY. – Remains of Illyrian fortified settlements and burial mounds provide evidence of early settlement on the island, which was known to the Romans as *Solenta*. The present name first appears in the records of Split in the 14th c. When the Slavs and Avars destroyed the ancient town of Solina, near Split, in the 7th c. some of the inhabitants fled to Šolta. During the Middle Ages the population was exposed to frequent pirate raids and Venetian attacks. The advance of the Turks brought a further influx of refugees to the island. The island – which had served as a place of political exile in antiquity – was also used by the church during the medieval period as a place of banishment for heretics and other religious deviants, in particular adherents of the Glagolitic form of worship (see under Krk). – In subsequent centuries Šolta came under the control of Split and thereafter shared the destinies of that town.

SIGHTS. – At **Grohote**, the largest village on the island, lying a little way inland, are the remains of Roman buildings and *mosaic pavements*. Beside the parish church are the foundations of an Early Christian basilica (6th c.). The church itself has an altarpiece by the Flemish painter Pieter de Coster. There is also a 17th c. *watch-tower* in the village. In the fields outside the village stands a little

14th c. Gothic church, *St Michael's* (Sv. Mihovil), with beautiful wall paintings.

Maslinica, situated in the middle cove of a group of three at the N end of the island, has a fortified Baroque castle, now converted into a hotel. On Gradina Hill, at the little port of **Rogač**, is a *ruined castle* in which tradition has it that the Illyrian queen Teuta sought refuge when fleeing from the Romans.

Split

Republic: Croatia (Hrvatska).
Altitude: 16 ft/5 m. – Population: 224,000.
Post code: YU-58000. – Telephone code: 0 58.
ⓘ **Turist Biro**,
Titova Obala 12;
tel. 4 21 42.

HOTELS. – *Lav*, A, 666 b., tel. 4 82 88 (4 miles/6 km S on Dubrovnik road, with yacht harbour); *Marjan*, A, 394 b., tel. 4 28 66; *Split Pavilions*, B, 701 b., tel. 52 28 88; *Park*, B, 105 b., tel. 51 54 11; *Prenočište Slavija*, B, 68 b., tel. 4 70 53; *Bellevue*, C, 96 b., tel. 4 71 75; *Central*, C, 76 b., tel. 4 82 42.

CAMP SITE. – *Trstenik*, Put Trstenika 5, tel. 52 19 71.

EVENTS. – Split Summer Festival, between June 15 and August 15, with drama, opera, concert, ballet and folk performances by Yugoslav and foreign artistes; "Melodies of the Adriatic" (festival of light music) in July.

AIRPORT: Split. JAT office: Obala Maršala Tita 8, tel. 4 56 66.

CONSULATE. – *United Kingdom:* Titovo Obala 10/11, tel. 4 14 64.

Split, the largest town on the Yugo-slav Adriatic coast after Rijeka, at once reveals to the visitor approach-ing it by sea its principal historical monument: above the seafront promenade with its palms and flowerbeds rears the massive bulk of Diocletian's palace, overtopped in its immediate neighbourhood only by two church towers. Visitors ap-proaching it from the N – perhaps coming from the airport – on the Adriatic coastal highway, which passes well inland of the town, see at first only ships and shipyards on the seaward side, and to the left fac-tories and industrial haze, huge

Split

modern blocks of flats and unattractive suburbs. At Solin, shortly before the main exit road for Split, are the remains of ancient Salona, a city older than Split. Farther S the Adriatic highway passes more modern residential areas with high-rise flats on the right and Split's second industrial zone on the left. Only after another 4 miles/6 km does the road come to a resort area with hotels and a yacht marina, and only then does the sea again become suitable for bathing.

Split is now a major tourist resort. Its airport, 19 miles/30 km N, serves an extensive holiday region which extends from Šibenik in the N to Kardeljevo (formerly Ploče) in the S and takes in the offshore islands of Brač, Hvar, Šolta and Korčula as well as the Pelješac peninsula. The islands can be reached not only by car ferries but also by hydrofoils and fast motor launches. Many cruise ships make Split a port of call, and there are day trips to the town from many island and coastal resorts. Several new hotels were built here for the 8th Mediterranean Games in 1979.

HISTORY. – The early history of Split is closely bound up with that of Salona. The site now occupied by the humdrum suburb of Solin, 4 miles/6 km from the modern industrial town, was settled in the 4th c. B.C. by Greeks, who had previously established themselves on the island of Vis, far out to sea (now a military base closed to tourists). The Greek settlers displaced Illyrians who had already made their homes in this area. In 78 B.C. the Romans occupied the flourishing Greek settlement and at once proceeded to develop it further. During the civil war between Caesar and Pompey the town, now known as *Salona*,

supported Caesar, and was rewarded after Caesar's victory by being raised to the status of a colonia. In the reign of Augustus Salona became the administrative and economic hub of the Roman territories in Dalmatia, linked by important strategic roads with the main Roman bases. The population rose to at least 50,000 – an order of size reflected in the dimensions of the amphitheatre, which could seat an audience of 18,000.

The emperor Diocletian (284–305), born in Dalmatia about 245, built his palace on the sea, 4 miles/6 km from Salona, both as his imperial residence and as a home for his declining years. Although Diocletian himself persecuted the Christians, Salona had become a focus of Christianity as early as the 4th c., and in the 5th c. it was made the see of a bishop. Its end came in 614, when the town was stormed and completely destroyed by Slavs and Avars. Some of the inhabitants sought refuge in Diocletian's palace. After the withdrawal of the conquerors, however, they made no attempt to rebuild their city. The ruins were gradually buried under alluvial sand brought down by the nearby River Jadro, and the site was not reoccupied until the Middle Ages, when it was settled by peasant farmers. The excavation of the ancient site began in 1883.

When Diocletian began building his palace at the end of the 3rd c. he selected a site directly on the sea (which originally reached right up to the western wall of the palace), in the area once occupied by the Illyrian and Greek settlement of Aspalathos. After his death the palace was frequently used as a residence for dignitaries exiled from Rome. The refugees from Salona walled up the arcades on the seaward side of the palace, where once the emperor had taken his ease, to make houses for themselves; but with the influx of further refugees the palace soon became too small to accommodate them all, and new dwellings were built around it, protected in the 14th c. by the construction of a new town wall and surrounded in the 17th c. by a further system of fortifications designed for protection against the advancing Turks. After the fall of Venice (1797) the town passed to Austria along with the rest of Dalmatia. In 1805 Austria was compelled to cede it to France, but recovered it again in 1813 and thereafter held on to it

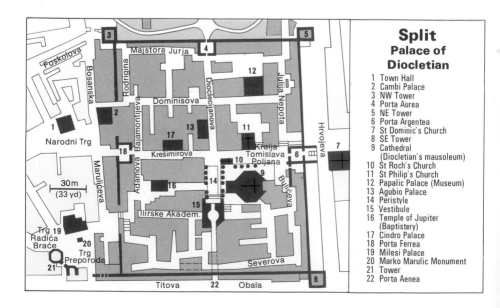

Split
Palace of
Diocletian

1 Town Hall
2 Cambi Palace
3 NW Tower
4 Porta Aurea
5 NE Tower
6 Porta Argentea
7 St Dominic's Church
8 SE Tower
9 Cathedral
   (Diocletian's mausoleum)
10 St Roch's Church
11 St Philip's Church
12 Papalic Palace (Museum)
13 Agubio Palace
14 Peristyle
15 Vestibule
16 Temple of Jupiter
   (Baptistery)
17 Cindro Palace
18 Porta Ferrea
19 Milesi Palace
20 Marko Marulic Monument
21 Tower
22 Porta Aenea

until 1918, when it was incorporated in the new kingdom of Yugoslavia. During the Second World War the town was occupied by Italian troops (1941–43) and then by Germans (1943–44). On several occasions there was violent fighting with partisan units, and considerable destruction – now made good – was caused by air raids.

SIGHTS. – The** **Palace of Diocletian**, built between A.D. 295 and 306, is the most imposing monument of the Roman period in Dalmatia. The *walls*, which now enclose part of the old town, a maze of narrow streets, measure 235 yd/215 m on the E and W sides, 190 yd/175 m on the N side and 210 yd/191 m on the S side. The emperor's residential apartments were in the southern half of the palace, towards the sea, with an arcaded portico which originally had 52 semi-columns (now only 44); the northern half was occupied by the imperial bodyguard and domestic staff.

The palace is entered from the seafront promenade (Titova Obala) by the *Porta Aenea* (Bronze Gate). To the left is the entrance to the extensive basement halls. Straight ahead a flight of steps leads up to the former *inner courtyard* of the palace, flanked by six Corinthian columns on each side, with steps which provide a shady seat for tired sightseers and a platform for groups of musicians in summer. The whole of the courtyard is an open pillared court or peristyle, the columns being linked by arches.

At the S end of the peristyle is the entrance (prothyron) to the *Imperial Apartments*, a vestibule which was formerly roofed with a dome and decorated with marble and mosaics. Nothing is now left of all this, nor of the emperor's apartments. To the E of the peristyle is the emperor's *mausoleum*, now the Cathedral. Octagonal in plan, it is surrounded by columns, and has a frieze in the interior, running around under the dome between two cornices, which contains portrait medallions of Diocletian and his wife Prisca. When the mausoleum was converted into a cathedral in the 7th c. it was considerably altered but the fine decoration was preserved. The *entrance hall* and *tower* were built at this time. The emperor's sarcophagus has long since disappeared.

The entrance hall under the tower leads into the **Cathedral** (*Sv. Dujam*), dedicated to the Virgin in the 9th c., with a dome 82 ft/25 m high. The *doors* are carved with 28 scenes from the life of Christ (1214).

INTERIOR. – The Romanesque *pulpit* (13th c.) has rich carved decoration, a consummate example of the skill of Dalmatian sculptors. The right-hand altar, with a late Gothic canopy, is by Bonino of Milan (1427); the left-hand altar (1448), with a fine relief of the scourging of Christ, was the work of a local sculptor, Juraj Dalmatinac, modelling himself on the right-hand altar. In the 17th c. chancel are finely carved Romanesque *choir-stalls*, the oldest in Dalmatia. The *Treasury* has a collection of gold and silver articles and church vestments of the Romanesque, Gothic and Baroque periods; particularly fine is a communion chalice of 1522.

The *tower* (which can be climbed: good view of the layout of the palace) was renovated in 1908, having previously been pulled down and rebuilt after earthquake damage. At the entrance are two Romanesque *lions*, and on the wall an Egyptian *sphinx* of black granite (15th c. B.C.).

On the opposite side of the peristyle from the mausoleum is a small Roman *temple*, probably dedicated to Jupiter, which was converted into a **baptistery** during the Middle Ages.

Beyond the Cathedral is the *Porta Argentea* (Silver Gate), reconstructed in 1946

Bishop Gregory of Nin (Split)

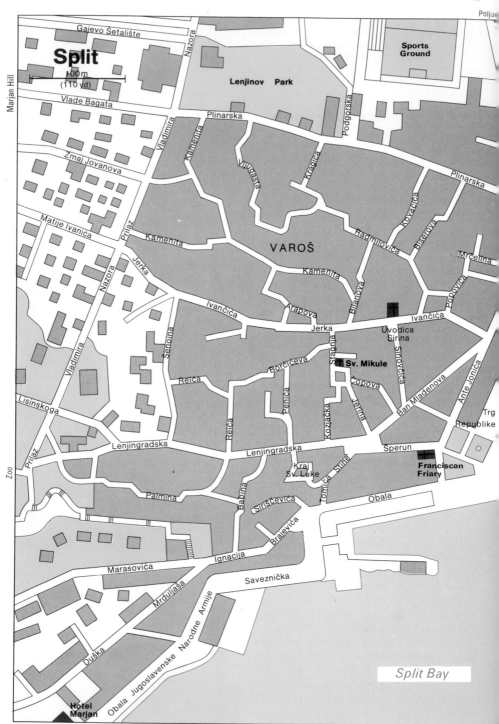

after the removal of a Venetian wall. The *Porta Aurea* (Golden Gate) in the N wall leads out of the palace into a public garden; immediately outside the gate is a massive bronze *statue of Bishop Gregory of Nin* by Ivan Meštrović (1929). (Bishop Gregory was a valiant but unsuccessful advocate, about the year 925, for the use of the Slav vernacular in church.) Nearby,

in the gardens, are the ruins of the little 11th c. *St Euphemia's Church*, with a Renaissance tower, which was destroyed by fire in 1877.

Many visitors to the palace, after seeing the many ancient palaces and houses within its precincts, are disappointed with the *basement halls* (entrance at Porta

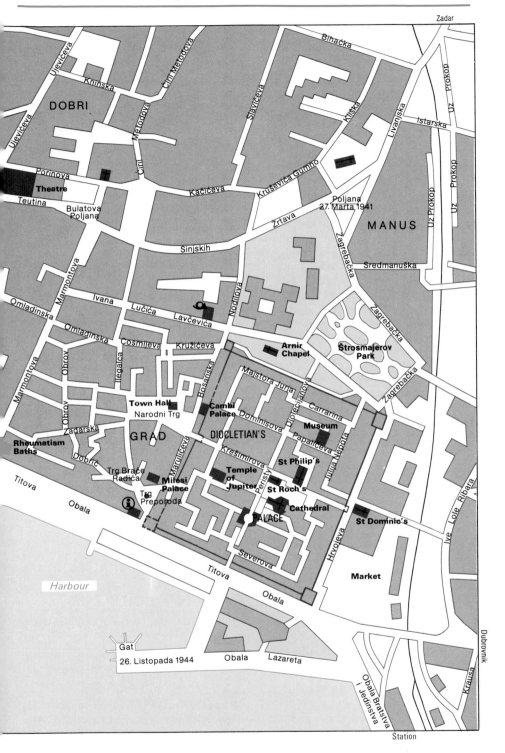

Aenea; admission charge). In these dark vaulted chambers are numerous reliefs, friezes, broken columns and fragments of frescoes, but none of the Roman furniture and domestic equipment which many people expect to see. The main interest of the basement rooms – and the reason for the excavation and clearance which is still continuing – is that they reproduce the layout and dimensions of many rooms above ground which have been destroyed or concealed under later building.

The *Porta Ferrea* (Iron Gate) on the W side of the palace leads into the Narodni Trg (People's Square), once known as Piazza dei Signori and reserved for the upper classes of the population of Split. On the

N side of the square is the **Old Town Hall** (15th c.), now housing an Ethnographical Museum (old Dalmatian costumes, domestic equipment, etc.). To the S, almost on the seafront promenade, is a square named after two Croatian politicians, Trg Braće Radića, in which is the Early Baroque *Milesi Palace*, now a Maritime Museum. The adjoining tower, the *Hrvojeva Kula*, originally belonged to a 15th c. Venetian castle of which nothing else survives.

Continuing NW along the seafront promenade and crossing Republic Square (Trg Republike) at its far end, we come to the *Franciscan friary*, with a beautiful little cloister. In front of the church stands a monumental fountain erected in 1880.

From Republic Square Ul. Heroja A. Jonića leads NE in the direction of the airport. In this street is the **Archaeological Museum*, in which most of the finds from Salona are displayed.

At the SE end of the seafront promenade (Titova Obala) is the quay from which the hydrofoils leave, and immediately adjoining is the departure point of the airport buses. The car ferries sail from a quay farther S along Obala Bratstva i Jedinstva, the continuation of Titova Obala.

SURROUNDINGS. – From the Bus Station it is 4½ miles/7 km to *Marjan Hill* (584 ft/178 m), the magnificent *view from which is unfortunately almost always obscured by industrial haze. The road skirts a park in which is the ***Meštrović Museum**, with 200

works by the great Croatian sculptor Ivan Meštrović (1883–1962), housed in the villa which he once occupied. *Holy Cross Chapel*, 550 yd/500 m from the museum, contains *wood-carvings by Meštrović. – On *Cape Marjan* is the *Institute of Oceanography*, with an *aquarium.

In the suburb of Solin, 4 miles/6 km from the town on the road to the airport and to Šibenik and Zadar, is the site of ancient **Salona** (*Colonia Martia Iulia Salonae*). Before reaching the site a long stretch of the aqueduct built to bring water to Diocletian's palace can be seen on the right of the road.

As a result of the destruction wrought by the Slavs and Avars in A.D. 614 and the subsequent silting up of the site only the foundations and the lower part of the walls of buildings have survived. The best point at which to start the tour of the site is the small *theatre*. Built on to the theatre is a temple (1st c. B.C.), and immediately adjoining is the *forum*. NE of this the remains of bridges and the foundations of Christian basilicas have been brought to light. From here the line of the town walls ran W. At the western end of the town is the large *amphitheatre*, which could accommodate 18,000 spectators. To the N, beyond the town walls, are another basilica and a cemetery, and farther along the road to Šibenik, at the car park, are the house known as Tusculum and another church. Sculpture, jewelry, pottery and other articles found during the excavations can be seen in the Archaeological Museum in Split.

Susak and Unije

Republic: Croatia (Hrvatska).
Altitude: Susak up to 322 ft/98 m, Unije up to 423 ft/129 m.
Population: Susak 200, Unije 280.
Telephone code: 0 51.
ⓘ **Turistički Ured Susak,**
YU-51561 Susak;
tel. 86 11 18.
Turistički Ured Unije,
YU-51562 Unije;
tel. 86 11 84.

ACCOMMODATION. – Only in private houses with a modest degree of comfort (apply to Tourist Office).

BOAT SERVICES. – Excursions from Mali Lošinj and Cres to Susak; passenger services: Mali Lošinj–Unije–Pula.

*Susak, lying in the open sea 6 miles/ 10 km W of Lošinj, is perhaps the most unusual of all the islands off the Yugoslav Adriatic coast. Unlike every other Adriatic island, it consists of a large hill of alluvial sand 2 miles/3 km long and up to 1½ miles/ 2·5 km wide. The only plants that will grow here are vines and reeds. The inhabitants draw their water from cisterns. The streets of the village are so narrow that there is barely room for the postman's moped to pass,

Salona
Roman Remains

300 m
(330 yd)

Trogir
Trogir
Marusinac
Manastirine
Kapljuč
Town walls
URBS NOVA ORIENTALIS
URBS NOVA OCCIDENTALIS
URBS VETUS
Gradina
Kaštelanski zaliv
Jadro
Solin
Gospin otok
Split
Klis

1 Basilicas
2 Baths
3 Five bridges
4 Porta Caesarea
5 Forum
6 Theatre
7 Temple
8 Porta Occidentalis
9 Amphitheatre
10 Basilica of Five Martyrs, cemetery
11 Porta Suburbana
12 Porta Capraria
13 Tusculum
14 Basilica, cemetery
15 Basilicas, cemetery
16 Medieval castle

and no cars have ever been seen on the island. The island of Unije, a few miles N of Susak, consists mainly of limestone, with sandhills of similar origin to those of Susak on the Poje peninsula.

Costumes on the island of Susak

In earlier days many of the inhabitants lived by fishing, but now that the upper Adriatic has been fished out, the few remaining islanders concentrate on vine-growing. The islands' vines, which were never attacked by phylloxera, yield a heavy dark red – almost black – wine with a strong bouquet. The women sell home-made souvenirs to the tourists, while the older men – many of them returned emigrants from the United States or retired seamen, with their binoculars always at the ready – live on their pensions. An attempt to bring new life to the economy by establishing a sardine factory was unsuccessful, and the ugly and aban-doned factory building remains to spoil the view of the old-world little village.

HISTORY. – Susak was inhabited in Roman times, and wealthy merchants had their country villas on the island. But of more interest than the history of its population is the question of the island's own origin. It has been established that the sand of which Susak is composed came from as far afield as the eastern Alps; but how it got here, and why it was deposited on the shelving limestone under the sea which can sometimes be seen off the island's shores, are questions that have puzzled geologists for more than 200 years. One theory is that the sand was deposited by rivers at the remote period when the Adriatic islands were still part of the mainland. Another suggestion is that Ice Age winds were responsible for building up the sand dunes which still rise to heights of 330 ft/ 100 m.

SIGHTS. – The whole of **Susak** is like an open-air museum. In the narrow streets the women knitting and embroidering souvenirs move their stools into the shade of the houses. Not a sound is heard – no laughter, hardly ever a child's voice. Time seems to stand still here. From the harbour a footpath runs past the beds of reeds to the upper part of the village, ending in an open space in front of **St Nicholas's Church** (1770), which contains a Byzan-tine *crucifix* of painted wood (12th c.) salvaged from a wrecked ship. In front of the church is one of the many cisterns scattered over the island – its only water supply, for there are no springs. The path continues to a cemetery with inscriptions in both Serbo-Croat and Italian which give a glimpse of the island's history.

Finally from the lighthouse on Garba Hill there are superb views of the numerous neighbouring islands and the open sea.

The remoteness of the island no doubt explains the fact that here – and only here – the old Croat dialect and the traditional laments for the dead have survived so long. There are traditional costumes both for everyday wear and for special occa-sions – for which the women wear wide "mini-skirts" over three underskirts.

Every day throughout the summer Susak is a port of call for numerous excursion vessels, and many sail boats seek the shelter of the harbour for an overnight stay. Visitors can find accommodation in a few private houses offering only limited comfort, but they have the lonely sandy beaches which surround the whole is-land.

Those in quest of peace and quiet will also find what they want on **Unije** (7 sq. miles/18 sq. km), which is on the route of the regular boat services between Pula and Mali Lošinj. It has an area of fertile low-lying ground with olive-groves and vineyards, 300 beds for visitors in private houses, and there is electricity. As on Susak, the only water supply is from cisterns. One can also see the remains of Roman country villas and the ramparts of prehistoric fortified settlements.

Sutjeska National Park

Republic: Bosnia-Hercegovina (Bosna i Hercegovina).

HOTELS. – IN TJENTIŠTE (alt. 1740 ft/530 m; post code YU-71490; dialling code 0 71): *Mladost*, B, 123 b., tel. 7 31 45; *Sutjeska*, B, 65 b., tel. 7 31 11, with annexe (chalets), 340 b.

CAMPING possible near hotels: no official site.

The *Sutjeska National Park, named after the stream which partly forms its boundary and partly flows through it, is one of the most beautiful nature reserves in Yugoslavia. It lies on the trunk road which links Dubrovnik with Belgrade, and accordingly its magnificent mountain scenery is within easy reach of vacationers on the coast – only 75 miles/120 km from Dubrovnik on an excellent road.

The National Park became internationally known through the American feature film "The Battle of Sutjeska", a documentary depiction of the fiercest battle between the partisans and German and Italian forces during the Second World War (May–June 1943). The battle is commemorated by a monumental **Memorial** and place of remembrance.

In May 1943 the main partisan force led by Tito was encircled by strong German forces, and even their hiding-places on the highest mountains were detected and attacked by fighter planes. The partisan

forces were threatened with annihilation, until Tito launched a spectacular counter-attack. More than a thousand partisans were killed, and their remains now lie in the memorial vault at Tjentište, above the main road, which is visited throughout the year by numerous school parties, youth groups and factory workers. Two hotels have been built to accommodate visitors to the memorial, as well as those who come here to explore the National Park.

The National Park covers an area of 67 sq. miles, based on $5\frac{1}{2}$ sq. miles of natural forest at Perućica. The park is bounded on the E by the River Piva, here dammed to form a lake 19 miles/30 km long, and on the W by the River Sutjeska and the Dubrovnik–Foča road. In the S it ends in the foothills of Mts Volujak (7540 ft/2298 m) and Bioč (7674 ft/2339 m). The highest mountain in the National Park, and the highest in the republic of Bosnia-Hercegovina, is Maglić (7832 ft/2387 m). There are footpaths through the mountains to Šćepan Polje, where the rivers Piva and Tara join to form the Drina, to the Trnovačko Jezero, to the summits of these mountains and to Perućica Forest, named after the mountain stream which flows through it. 2 miles/3 km before the Perućica flows into the Sutjeska it plunges down from a rocky plateau in a spectacular waterfall 230 ft/70 m high.

The Sutjeska National Park offers the nature-lover a paradise of wilderness and unspoiled beauty. As soon as they leave the bustle of activity at Tjentište and the Partisan Memorial and make their way over mountain meadows amid forests of Austrian pine and spruce, walkers are caught up in the tranquillity of this mountain region. Here there is none of the clutter of cafés and souvenir stalls too often found in national parks frequented by large numbers of visitors. Those who come to Sutjeska are very much on their own: in this remote natural fastness they will find no human settlements, no mountain huts; nor is there any organised mountain rescue service.

The species of *trees* vary with height. They include oak and Turkey oak, black ash, black beech, maple, Austrian pine, spruce and, higher up, juniper.

A hundred or so *bears* still live in the National Park; only two or three may be shot each year. At certain times of year wild boar, roe deer, red deer and, in the mountains, chamois can also be shot.

Partisan Memorial, Sutjeska National Park

Sveti Stefan

Republic: Montenegro (Crna Gora).
Altitude: 10 ft/3 m. – No permanent inhabitants.
Post code: YU-81315. – Telephone code: 0 82.
ⓘ **Turističko Društvo,**
tel. 8 22 33.

HOTELS. – *Sveti Stefan* ("hotel town"), L, 226 b., tel. 4 13 33. – IN MILOČER: *Maestral*, A, 294 b., tel. 4 10 13; *Miločer*, with annexes, A, 80 b., tel. 4 10 13.

CAMP SITES. – *Crvena Glavica*, tel. 8 13 15 (beautifully situated above the sea, with view of Sveti Stefan; steep approach; five small bathing coves, one reserved for naturists); *Vala*, tel. 8 22 33.

SPORT. – Boat rental, water-skiing, scuba diving, mini-golf, tennis.

*Sveti Stefan, 6 miles/10 km S of Budva, is a tourist's dream come true: a tiny island, linked with the mainland by a causeway, with all the houses on it reserved for visitors. On the mainland opposite the island is the former summer residence of King Alexander and Queen Marie of Yugoslavia, now the Miločer Hotel, which offers luxury at rates that are higher than average but not impossibly high. Although the houses on Sveti Stefan survived the 1979 earthquake relatively unscathed the little church was badly damaged.

Sveti Stefan was originally a fishing village, but the last 20 inhabitants left it in 1955 and its conversion into a vacation settlement offering a high standard of comfort and amenity then began. The "hotel town" of Sveti Stefan was opened in 1960, with the 80 houses restored and converted into 110 self-contained apartments (226 beds). The other amenities include a luxury restaurant with a terrace situated high above the sea, a casino, a night club, a snack bar and a swimming pool hewn from the rock. On the highest point in this tangle of narrow stepped lanes is the little church of Sv. Stefan.

HISTORY. – The island village, traditionally believed to have been founded by the Paštrović family, is first mentioned in the records in 1442. The inhabitants seem to have settled here for the sake of protection against hostile attack, laying in stores of provisions (old stone oil presses from this period have been preserved); but it also served as a base from which to attack Turkish ships and a hiding-place for the resultant booty. Sveti Stefan thus became an outpost of the pirates whose main base was farther S at Ulcinj.

The island maintained itself as an independent commune for 400 years; but towards the end of the 19th c. the inhabitants, finding that they could no longer make a living by fishing, began to emigrate to the United States in increasing numbers. Finally after the Second World War the plan was conceived of converting the island into a luxury "hotel town".

SIGHTS. – Tourists can visit Sveti Stefan daily from 10 to 12 and 3 to 6 (admission charge) and can thus gain some impression of this idyllic island settlement and the little houses formerly occupied by the local fishermen, now renovated or rebuilt with old stones. The beaches along the causeway leading to the island are beautifully clean, with a gently sloping bottom. The *park* of the Miločer Hotel, on the mainland opposite the island, has a network of attractive paths. Reached through the park is the *Praskvica monastery* (founded 1050), which suffered severely in the 1979 earthquake: the Trinity Church was completely destroyed and St Nicholas's Church (built 1847, with some 15th c. work decorated with frescoes) badly damaged.

Tara Gorge

Republic: Montenegro (Crna Gora).

The Tara is the longest river in Montenegro (87 miles/140 km), and the **Tara gorge between Prošćenje and the little village of Šćepan Polje is the longest and deepest canyon in Yugoslavia. Throughout this long defile the Tara pursues a winding course between sheer rock walls which rise in many places to 3300 ft/1000 m or more. From June to September raft trips are run for visitors on the 55 mile/88 km stretch between the bridge at Djurdjevića Tara and Šćepan Polje. The trip lasts 4–5 days, at a cost (including 5 days' full board) of about 250 US dollars/£165 per head (minimum number of passengers required is 10; booking through travel agencies in Yugoslavia).

The Tara gorge was regarded until the 19th c. as extremely dangerous and remained largely unexplored. Only the raftsmen who took rafts of timber down the river ventured into this wild canyon with its rapids, cataracts and violent eddies. The first foreigner to penetrate any distance into the gorge was a German

Beginning of the Tara gorge

narrow that the road has to be taken through a tunnel, with only a few yards left for the passage of the river, and the sun's rays reach the valley floor for no more than a few minutes every day.

At last the bridge at Djurdjevića Tara comes into view. 400 yd/366 m long, it spans the wide valley in five elegant arches which rise to some 490 ft/150 m above the water. A monument $\frac{3}{4}$ mile/1 km before the bridge depicts a valiant Montenegrin peasant defending the old wooden bridge against a swarm of enemies; and the new bridge too became the scene of fighting soon after it was completed in 1941.

During the Second World War the rising against the occupation forces began in this area in the spring of 1942. The territory around the mountain village of Žabljak, where Tito had his headquarters for many months, was the first part of Yugoslavia to be declared free of the enemy. When a strong force of Italians and Chetniks (troops loyal to the king) advanced from Pljevlja against the territory held by the partisans it was decided to blow up the bridge. The task was entrusted to an engineer named Lazar Jauković who only a year before had worked on the construction of the bridge and was now fighting with the partisans. He blew up the main arch of the bridge, and the advancing armoured forces were compelled to withdraw. Soon afterwards Jauković was captured by a Chetnik and Italian force, recognised and shot on the bridge (monument at W end).

named Kutschbach who had a raft specially built for the purpose in 1898; but no stranger risked entering the stretch from Djurdjevića Tara (where there had long been a bridge) to the village of Šćepan Polje, where the rivers Tara and Piva join to form the Drina – a lonely expanse of territory with no human settlements and steep rock walls hemming in the turbulent waters of the river. In 1932 canoeists traversed the whole length of the gorge for the first time.

The Tara is formed by the junction of two streams, the Veruša and the Opasnica, which rise on Mt Komovi, SE of Kolašin. It then flows past the little village of Mateševo, the climbing and tourist resort of Kolašin and the industrial and mining town of Mojkovac, where it turns NE.

From Mojkovac to the bridge at Djurdjevića Tara there is now an asphalted road running alongside the river. This at first climbs up the hillside, with the Tara flowing in the valley below, and then reaches a mountainous region resembling the Alps in character, with great expanses of green meadows providing grazing for cattle and sheep, dark forests and cool mountain streams. The numerous little cottages and huts in this area, formerly occupied by shepherds and herdsmen, are now used as vacation homes.

Then begins the passage through the gorge, which is not without its hazards after thunderstorms or long periods of rain, when there may be landslides and rock falls. At some points the gorge is so

At the junction of the road through the gorge with the Titograd–Nikšić–Žabljak–Pljevlja road is a motel. From here a road to the left ascends with numerous hairpin turns to a plateau from which the *Durmitor range comes suddenly into view, rising up in a formidable mountain barrier, its summits covered with snow almost all year round. The road to the right at the motel crosses the bridge and climbs up to the plateau on the other bank of the Tara

Hotel, Mojkovac

in a 6 mile/10 km stretch of stones and gravel (asphalting in progress).

The departure point of the raft trips on the river is below the motel, just beside the bridge. Each raft can take from 10 to 15 passengers; they are steered by experienced raftsmen and accompanied by guides speaking several languages. A separate raft carries the kitchen (housed in a tent), a bar and the passengers' luggage. The first night is spent near Tepca – the only village near the river, 2 hours' walk away – after a hair-raising stretch which leaves the passengers in a decidedly damp condition. Tepca itself is connected with Žabljak by a hazardous road. Here the raftsmen buy mutton, the local cheese and honey.

The trip ends after 4–5 days at Šćepan Polje (sometimes shown on maps under the name of Brijeg), where there is a temporary bridge. From here it is 13 miles/21 km to Foča on a road with dangerous bends.

Titograd

Republic: Montenegro (Crna Gora).
Altitude: 184 ft/56 m. – Population: 80,000.
Post code: YU-81000. – Telephone code: 0 81.
ⓘ **Turistički Savez Titograda,**
 UI. Slobode;
 tel. 5 29 68.

HOTELS. – *Crna Gora*, B, 230 b., tel. 5 25 05; *Podgorica*, B, 108 b., tel. 4 20 50; *Motel Zlatica* (with camp site), 100 b., tel. 2 21 03; *Motel Plavnica*, 14 b.

CAMP SITE. – Shady site at *Zlatica Motel*.

AIRPORT: Titograd. JAT office: Ivana Milutinovića 2, tel. 4 42 48.

This industrial town (metalworking, furniture-making, tobacco manufacture) in the plain N of Lake Scutari is for most visitors merely a port of call or staging post on their way from Belgrade to the Adriatic coast, or after the magnificently scenic ascent from Kotor Bay over the Lovćen pass to the old Montenegrin capital of Cetinje, or on the route to the Durmitor National Park. Parties making for Albania usually spend the night in Titograd before crossing the frontier beyond the Yugoslav village of Drume on the road to Shkodër. Some of the town's older houses which had survived the Second World War were destroyed in the 1979 earthquake.

90% of the old town (then known as Podgorica) was destroyed during the Second World War. Rapidly – all too rapidly – rebuilt after the war, Titograd seems at first sight a rather dull town, but it comes to life after 5 o'clock every day, when the Ulica Slobode (Freedom Street) in the middle of the town is closed to traffic and – weather permitting – is thronged with thousands of young

Titograd, the Montenegrin capital, on the Morača

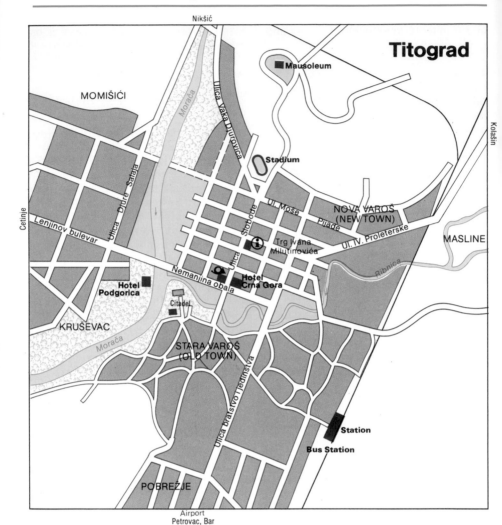

people, who overflow into the surrounding squares and parks, in groups and
couples. The passing visitor will also be
impressed by the town's broad
boulevards, planned soon after the war on
such a generous scale that they are still
fully adequate to the dense traffic of the
1980s.

HISTORY. – The history of the town which grew up in
this fertile agricultural region can be traced back for
more than 2000 years. Over the course of history it has
been known by a number of different names. It was the
Roman town of *Birziminium* or *Berzummum*, founded
after the destruction by an earthquake in 518 of the
older Roman settlement of Dioclea (the supposed
birthplace of the emperor Diocletian), 2 miles/3 km
away. Under the old Serbian dynasty of the Nemanjids
in the 13th c. the town was rebuilt and given the name
of *Ribnica*, after the river on which it lay. Why the
name was later changed to Podgorica (first attested in
1330), after the nearby Mt Gorica, is not known.

After long and bitter resistance the town, occupying
an important strategic position, fell to the Turks in
1474, and its new masters at once set about
strengthening its fortifications. The town now took on

an oriental aspect, with narrow lanes and low houses.
During the long period of alien rule from 1474 to 1879
Podgorica was a key Turkish base in the struggle with
the rebellious Montenegrins in the mountains. Relics
of the 400 years of Turkish occupation included a
handsome mosque and a bridge over the River Morača
which was of interest for its form of construction –
both destroyed during the last war. In 1946 Podgorica
was renamed *Titograd* and replaced Cetinje as capital
of the republic of Montenegro.

SIGHTS. – Little is left of the old town of
Titograd, and the few relics of earlier days
– the 16th c. *Clock-Tower* (Sahat Kula),
the *House of Paša Advović* and the ruins
of the old Turkish stronghold at the
junction of the Ribnica and the Morača –
cut a poor figure against the background
of the modern government and office
buildings, department stores and apartment buildings. Such remains of the past
can be seen, better preserved, in many
other towns in Yugoslavia.

SURROUNDINGS. – 2½ miles/4 km from Titograd, at
the junction of the Zeta and the Morača, are the

remains of ancient **Dioclea** (leave on the old road to Nikšić, then turn right into the Radovče road). Here can be seen the remains of massive ramparts, an old bridge over the Morača and the Roman law courts, together with numerous sarcophagi with carved ·decoration and gravestones with Latin inscriptions. The site of Dioclea aroused international archaeological interest in the second half of the 19th c., and Arthur Evans, better known for his work at Knossos, excavated here for seven seasons from 1875, though without making any spectacular discoveries.

7½ miles/12 km from Titograd on the road to the motel and camp site at Plavnica is **Medun**, once an advanced stronghold of the Illyrians in· their fight against the Roman invaders based in Dioclea. In the lower part of the village are remains of an Illyrian building with cyclopean walls using blocks of stone up to 6½ ft/2 m long. Marko Miljanov Popović (1813–1901), a hero of the Montenegrin struggle against the Turks, was born in Medun, and there is a small museum (opened 1971) devoted to this striking personality.

Ostrog monastery

19 miles/30 km from Titograd is **Ostrog monastery**, situated at a height of 2950 ft/900 m in a huge recess in the rock face above the valley. This is now brought within easy reach by a narrow asphalted road which winds its way up above dizzy chasms. Leave Titograd on the new road to Nikšić and at Danilovgrad turn off ˙into the old road, from which the road to the monastery (well signposted) branches off.

The greatest tourist attraction in the neighbourhood of Titograd is * **Lake Scutari** (see page. 186). To get to know the flora and fauna of the lake a stay of two or three days is necessary; and Titograd, as the only town near the lake, is a convenient base for this purpose.

Titovo Užice

Republic: Serbia (Srbija).
Altitude: 1348 ft/411 m. – Population: 35,000.
Post code: YU-31000. – Telephone code: 0 31.
ⓘ **Turist Biro Raketa**,
Maršala Tita 64;
tel. 2 13 55.

HOTELS. – *Palas*, B, 120 b., tel. 2 17 52; *Turist*, 78 b., tel. 2 45 09.

Titovo Užice, a thriving town with many modern high-rise buildings in the central area, has been from time immemorial an important traffic junction at which the road from Belgrade to the Adriatic divides into two, one road making for Dubrovnik, the other for Titograd, reaching the coast at Petrovac na Moru. The town, situated in a valley surrounded by green hills, is of interest to visitors both as a convenient staging point for an overnight stop and as a base for excursions into the nearby Zlatibor range.

HISTORY. – Archaeological evidence shows that this was already a place of some consequence as a road junction 2000 years ago. In pre-Roman times Illyrians settled in the valley basin which the town now almost completely fills. As early as the 3rd c. a fortified post was established on the rocky hill to the E of the town, above the little River Djetinja; this was destroyed and rebuilt several times, and is now represented only by ruins.

Užice fell to the Turks in 1463, and under Ottoman rule its trade and industry flourished. The town became noted for its leather goods and the long fur garments worn by the peasants. It acquired its first modern factory, a textile mill, at the end of the 19th c.

The town played an important role during the Second World War, when it became the hub of the first armed rising by the partisans in 1941 and the surrounding area was declared the first "liberated territory" in Yugoslavia. Tito and the partisans had their headquarters here for some months, after which they withdrew following an action which caused heavy losses on both sides. Tito's stay in the town is commemorated by the adjective Titovo which was added to the town's original name of Užice after the war and by a massive statue in Partisans' Square (Trg Partizana), the new and modern market square.

SIGHTS. – The road to Titograd and Petrovac leads to a point (top of hill, on right) from which there is the finest view

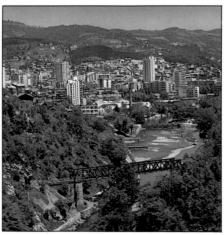

Titovo Užice

of the town and the **Citadel** to the E. The citadel can be reached, either by car or on foot, only from the left bank of the Djetinja, on which most of the town lies. The original stronghold was taken and partly destroyed in 1463 by Sultan Mehmed, who later had it rebuilt and enlarged; it was restored in 1978.

Otherwise the town has little of tourist interest to offer. It is noted for a variety of gastronomic delicacies – bacon, smoked meat and many kinds of sausage and cheese. The local distilleries produce not only the ordinary mild šljivovica (slivovitz) but also the double-distilled and therefore doubly strong *prepečenica*.

SURROUNDINGS. – The road to Titograd winds its way up out of the valley on to a plateau which has been declared a nature reserve for the protection of its distinctive flora and fauna. The hills of the *Zlatibor range* are covered with expanses of upland meadows and forest and traversed by numerous streams. The finest part of the plateau begins at the little town of *Čajetina*, 11 miles/17 km from Titovo Užice. To the right of the road are the two summer and winter resorts of **Partizanske Vode** and **Ribnica** (holiday chalets, camp sites), both good starting points for the ascent of *Mt Tornik* (4203 ft/1281 m), the highest peak in the Zlatibor range.

For art-lovers there is another sight within easy reach of Titovo Užice, the monastic church of **Arilje**. The road to this little town goes off on the right from the Belgrade road at *Užička Požega*, 15 miles/24 km from Titovo Užice, and in another 9 miles/15 km reaches Arilje. The handsome *church of Sveti Ahilije* originally belonged to a large monastery which in 1219 became the seat of a bishop – which explains the splendour of the wall paintings, some of them dating from 1296. Particularly fine are a series of figures in the narthex, including the founder, King Milutin, holding a model of the church.

From Arilje it is possible to continue along the road in the direction of **Prilike**, up the beautiful winding valley of the Moravica, past anglers sitting on the banks of the river and holidaymakers relaxing in the meadows. Soon the **monastery of Trešnjevica** comes into view on the right, high above the gorge of a rushing mountain stream. It can be reached on a steep forest track, which is just negotiable by cars. The church of the *Sveti Arhandjel* contains beautiful 12th c. frescoes.

Tivat

Republic: Montenegro (Crna Gora).
Altitude: 16 ft/5 m. – Population: 700.
Post code: YU-81320. – Telephone code: 0 82.

ⓘ **Turist Biro**,
    21 Novembra 13;
    tel. 8 62 20.

HOTELS. – *Plavi Horizont*, B, 660 b., tel. 6 13 51; *Ostrovo Cvijeća*, B, 302 b., tel. 6 13 22; *Kamelija*, B, 212 b., tel. 6 13 00; *Mimoza*, B, 126 b., tel. 6 13 44; *Tivat*, B, 60 b., tel. 6 13 24.

CAMP SITE. – *Ciparis*, tel. 6 13 59.

SPORT. – Sailing and all kinds of other water sports; walking.

AIRPORT: Tivat. JAT office: Moše Pijade 4, tel. 8 62 37.

Seafront promenade, Tivat

Tivat is a small town with a shipyard, a naval harbour and a pottery industry. It owes its development as a tourist resort to its airfield – though the number of planes using it is not so great as to cause any serious disturbance to tourists. The 1979 earthquake caused considerable damage in the town, some buildings being completely destroyed.

The bathing beaches around Tivat are of pebbles and concrete, and the sea in the neighbourhood of the hotels is notably clean. With 200 days of sunshine in the year, the resort has a season which lasts from April to the end of October. In autumn and winter it attracts many asthma sufferers.

HISTORY. – The area was occupied in antiquity, as is shown by the Greek and Roman material found here and the remains of buildings now covered by the sea. Some authorities derive the town's name from the Illyrian queen Teuta.

In the medieval and later periods noble families from Kotor Bay had their summer residences here. On the little island of Prevlaka are the remains of the old Orthodox monastery of the Archangel Michael (Sveti Arhandjel Mihajlo), headquarters of the diocese of Zeta from 1219 and seat of the bishop from 1346. The monastery was destroyed in the 15th c. The present church on Prevlaka was founded by Countess Katarina Vlastelinović, who bequeathed it in 1846 to the Montenegrin prince Njegoš. The Austrian authorities prevented Njegoš from taking up his inheritance, and his successor Danilo finally sold the island.

S of Tivat is the plain of Solisko Polje, with salt-pans which have been worked since the Middle Ages, yielding considerable quantities of salt. There were repeated conflicts between the Venetians and the Turks for control of the salt-workings, which had earlier been the occasion of a war between Kotor and Dubrovnik in the second half of the 14th c.

SIGHTS. – **St Anthony's Church** is believed to date from the 14th c. There is a beautiful **Municipal Park**, shaded by tall cypresses, in which roses bloom almost all year round. On the wooded island of *Sveti Marko*, known as Straditi during the period of Venetian rule, is a Club Méditerranée holiday village of straw huts. – Opposite Sveti Marko is the little island of *Otok*, with a monastery. A Roman altar dedicated to Juno was found here.

Travnik

Republic: Bosnia-Hercegovina (Bosna i Hercegovina).
Altitude: 1690 ft/515 m. – Population: 20,000.
Post code: YU-72270. – Telephone code: 0 72.
ⓘ **Turist Biro,**
tel. 8 14 67.

HOTELS. – *Orijent*, B, 126 b., tel. 8 12 40; *Park*, C, 44 b., tel. 7 70 44. – On Mt Vlašić, at 4134 ft/1260 m: *Babanovac*, with annexe, 200 b., tel. 8 01 71.

Travnik will be familiar to readers of the novel by Ivo Andrić (Nobel Prize, 1961), "Chronicles of Travnik", published in English as the "Bosnian Story". They will be disappointed, however, if they look for the setting of the novel in present-day Travnik, for most of the town's fine old buildings were destroyed in a disastrous fire in 1903. What survives, however, is still worth seeing.

HISTORY. – The origins of this industrial town go back only to the beginning of the 15th c., when Tvrtko II, one of the last Bosnian kings, built the imposing castle (still well preserved) above what was then a mere village at the foot of the hill. Travnik is first mentioned in the Turkish records in 1463, when Sultan Mehmed II conquered the whole of Bosnia. In 1699 the town became the seat of the Turkish viziers

A türbe (Turkish tomb) in Travnik

who governed Bosnia and Hercegovina as representatives of the Sultan until 1851. During these 150
years the European powers maintained consulates in
Travnik; and their diplomatic manoeuvrings in this
small-scale political area are depicted in Ivo Andrić's
novel. These years were Travnik's heyday, during
which many mosques, caravanserais and bazaars were
erected in the town. 6 miles/10 km from Travnik is
Novi Travnik, a satellite industrial town developed on
a virgin site since the last war, with beautiful parks and
gardens, modern apartment buildings, a hotel and a
swimming pool.

SIGHTS. – There is no published map of
Travnik, and there are no signposts to its
principal features of interest. The best plan
is to start by following the town's main
street (leave the Banja Luka–Sarajevo
road, then watch for signs to "Centar"),
which comes to the Suleiman Mosque or
Many-Coloured Mosque (*Šarena
Džamija*). The colours have now faded,
and the green meadows and ancient trees
which once surrounded the mosque have
gone. The squalid open space adjoining
the mosque is used by the local peasants
as a parking place for their carts and the
donkeys which draw them.– One handsome old building which survived the
1903 fire is the 16th c. **Hadži Ali Bey
Mosque**, which was restored in 1867. –
Under a lime-tree on the main road is a
fountain of the Turkish period.

The **Ivo Andrić House**, in which the
writer (1892–1975), author of "The
Bridge on the Drina" as well as "Chronicles of Travnik", spent his early years, is
now a museum. It is reached by turning off
the main street at the large department
store into a side street to the E.

The finest view of the town and the green
surrounding countryside is to be had from
the *Castle*.

A well-engineered road climbs up to the
holiday and recreation area on *Mt Vlašić* at
an altitude of 4134 ft/1260 m. The
Babanovac Hotel and a number of mountain huts in the surrounding area are good
bases for walkers and climbers in summer
and skiers in winter. A network of ski-lifts
is in course of development. The forests
are well stocked with game, providing an
abundant quarry for the sportsman.

Travnik is noted for its cheese (Travnički
sir), made from the milk of sheep grazing
on the lush pastures of Mt Vlašić.

Trogir

Republic: Croatia (Hrvatska).
Altitude: 16 ft/5 m. – Population: 700.
Post code: YU-58222. – Telephone code: 0 58.
ⓘ **Turističko Društvo**,
   Palača Čipiko,
   Rade Končara;
   tel. 7 35 54.

HOTELS. – *Medena*, A, 1126 b., tel. 7 37 88; *Jadran*,
B, 310 b., tel. 7 34 07; *Motel Trogir*, C, 124 b., tel. 7 34
24; chalets in *Soline* caravan (trailer) park, 120 b., tel.
7 34 24.

CAMP SITES. – *Soline*, tel. 7 36 22 (with 120 b. in
chalets); *Rozac*, tel. 7 36 62.

EVENTS. – Regular concerts of classical and folk
music during the main season.

SPORT. – Scuba diving, rental of motorboats, tennis,
bowling.

**The main doorway of Trogir Cathe-
dral has been described as the finest
example of Romanesque sculpture
in Dalmatia, the whole town as a
living museum, its **medieval townscape as unequalled in Dalmatia,
except perhaps by Dubrovnik: all
who write about Trogir, the little
town on an island 17 miles/27 km N
of Split, inevitably write in super-
latives.**

Trogir does indeed possess an assem-
blage of historic old buildings such as few
towns can claim. The guides who take
their busloads of tourists around these
treasures of art and architecture frequently
complete the course in an hour; but the
visitor who wants to see the town properly
requires a full day, and should also make a
point of spending the evening here as well
in order to observe the play of light and
shadow between these old walls. For
those who want to spend a longer time
there is the hotel settlement of Medena, 2½
miles/4 km away, with its beautiful beach.

HISTORY. – In the 3rd c. B.C. the Greek settlement of
Tragourion was founded here. Later the Romans
developed the harbour, but thereafter neglected the
town in favour of Salona, near Split. After the fall of the
Western Empire Trogir came under Byzantine rule, but
from the 9th c. onwards the inhabitants prudently also
paid tribute to the Croatian kings. In 1123 the town
was burned down by the Saracens, but was rebuilt and
then began to enjoy a period of prosperity. In 1420 the
Venetians took the town, but only after a bombardment lasting four days; and from then until 1797
Venice exerted a predominant influence on the town's
architecture. After 1797, apart from a brief period of
French occupation when Dalmatia was incorporated
in Napoleon's Illyrian Provinces, Trogir was under
Austrian rule until 1918. During the Second World

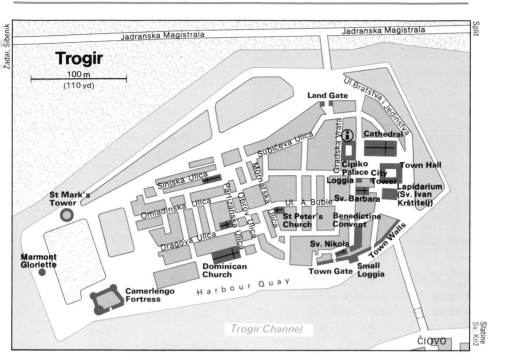

War, when the town was occupied by Italian and later by German troops, a number of handsome old buildings were destroyed in air raids. The island town is now mainly occupied by people of the older generation, while the new Trogir is expanding on the neighbouring island of Čiovo.

SIGHTS. – After leaving the Adriatic coastal highway (Jadranska Magistrala) visitors should leave their cars on the mainland. The bridge over the narrow channel separating the island from the mainland leads straight to the 17th c. *Land Gate*, topped by a statue of the town's patron saint, Sv. Ivan Ursini, once bishop of Trogir, and by the lion of St Mark. From here, bearing left through narrow lanes and past handsome palaces and Baroque houses, as well as the Municipal Museum, we reach the spacious main square of the town, the *Narodni Trg*.

The square is dominated by the *Cathedral*, dedicated to St Lawrence.

The building of the Cathedral began in 1123, but the tower was not completed until the 16th c. The undecorated external walls create an effect of great massiveness which sets off the slender grace of the three-storey campanile. Within the narthex is the *main doorway*, with a rich – and at first sight almost confusing – abundance of sculpture by a Croatian master named Radovanus and his assistants.

On either side of the doorway are lions, with figures of Adam and Eve above them. Then come three bands of sculpture extending around the whole doorway, with figures of saints in the outer band, genre scenes in the middle band and hunting scenes and fantastic figures in the inner band. The inner band in particular reflects the world of the artist's imagination, with real and imaginary figures, sometimes naked and barefooted, soldiers, shepherds, peasants – a fantastic and yet realistically detailed vision of the period. Master Radovanus himself was convinced of the quality of his achievement, for in an inscription in the tympanum of the doorway recording its completion in 1240 he refers to himself as "the most excellent in his craft, as the statues and reliefs show".

At the left-hand end of the narthex is the *Baptistery* (1464), the masterpiece of Andrija Aleši, noted also for his work in Šibenik Cathedral

The most notable feature of the INTERIOR is *St John's Chapel*, the finest example of Renaissance architecture in Dalmatia; it is dedicated to Sv. Ivan Ursini, Trogir's patron saint. The small windows under the barrel-vaulted roof of the chapel admit shafts of light which now illuminate one of the recesses in the wall, now play on the Baroque angels flanking the saint's sarcophagus. – Note also the octagonal stone *pulpit* (13th c.), the beautiful Gothic *choir-stalls* (1440) and the 14th c. *ciborium* over the Baroque high altar, with a representation of the Annnunciation. The *Sacristy* contains two pictures by Bellini and a late Gothic carved press of 1458.

City Tower and Loggia, Trogir

Opposite the Cathedral stands the **Ćipiko Palace**, which actually consists of two palaces, one large and one smaller, separated by a lane. The large palace has three late Gothic triple windows, one above the other. – The *Loggia* on the S side of the square was used both as a law court and a market hall. Offenders were chained to one of the columns immediately after sentence and exposed to public show, and the chains used are still there.

At the E end of the Loggia rises the *City Tower*. To the S is *St Barbara's Church*, the oldest church in the town (11th c.). The *Town Hall* (previously known as the Prince's Court and later the Communal Palace), facing the church has had its façade rebuilt after destruction during the last war; in the courtyard is a 15th c. staircase. S of the Town Hall is the abbey church of Sv. Ivan Krštitelj (John the Baptist), which now houses a *Lapidarium*.

To the SW, in the direction of the quay, is a *Benedictine monastery* founded in 1064; the tower dates from 1598. The monastery contains a relief (1st c. B.C.) of Kairos, the god of the "favourable moment", depicted as a young man with wings on his feet and the back of his head shaven to indicate that once he has passed he cannot be caught by the hair. There is a cast of the figure in the Municipal Museum.

Beyond the monastery is a section of the old *town walls*, followed by the old *Fish Market* (no longer used for that purpose). Along the quay to the W is the 14th c. *Dominican church*, with the funeral monument of the Sobota family (1469)

by Niccolò Fiorentino, who was also responsible for St John's Chapel in the Cathedral. The beautiful *cloister*, now in a rather neglected state, contains a lapidarium.

At the far end of the quay (and of the island) stands the massive **Kaštel-Kamerlengo**, once a formidable stronghold at the corner of the town walls; it is now used for concerts and other open-air performances. On the quay to the N, beside the large football ground, is a charming little pavilion, the **Gloriette**, named after Marmont, one of Napoleon's marshals who was appointed governor of Dalmatia. Beyond this, as the northern counterpart of the Kamerlengo, is *St Mark's Tower*.

Tučepi

Republic: Croatia (Hrvatska).
Altitude: 16 ft/5 m. – Population: 1600.
Post code: YU-58325. – Telephone code: 0 58.
ⓘ **Turist Biro,**
tel. 61 24 12.

HOTELS. – *Alga*, A, 670 b., tel. 61 18 08; *Jadran*, B, 325 b., tel. 61 22 52, with annexe *Tamaris*, B, 24 b.; *Neptun*, B, 224 b., tel. 61 18 03, with annexe *Maslinik*, C, 376 b.

EVENTS. – International Congress of Travel Journalists and Writers, May.

SPORT. – Water-skiing, scuba diving, rental of motorboats and row boats; tennis, rental of bicycles, boccia, bowling; climbing on Sv. Jure (5781 ft/1762 m) and Vožac (4662 ft/1421 m).

BOATING and BATHING. – Boat-owners looking for a sheltered anchorage will not find it at Tučepi; but boats can be rented here, and the hotels have motorboats for water-skiers. This is not good territory for scuba-divers, since there are no rocks immediately offshore. The gently sloping pebble beach is suitable for children; the pebbles here are natural and not imported as at other places on the Makarska Riviera.

Like Brela, Tučepi is really not one place but two – an old village on the hillside above and a new settlement on the coast. Although the new settlement, consisting almost wholly of hotels, is officially called Kraj the signposts bear the more familiar name of Tučepi. Here visitors will find a carefully tended park-like area of woodland, a seafront promenade lined with pines and palms, and a clean. and uncrowded pebble beach over ¾ mile/

1 km long. The hotels offer high standards of amenity and attract an international clientele.

HISTORY. – Tučepi was already the site of a settlement in ancient times. As at other places on the coast, the local people sought safety from pirate raids high up in the bare hills of the Biokovo range. The village is first mentioned in the records in 1434. During the Baroque period wealthy families discovered the advantages of this shady spot on the coast as a summer retreat and built villas here, some of which (decorated with coats of arms) still survive. An abbot, too, built himself a small summer residence on the site now occupied by the Alga Hotel.

SIGHTS. – *St George's Church*, near the hotels on the coast, dates from the 13th–14th c. and has Roman capitals built into its walls. By the church are medieval grave slabs and tombstones.

SURROUNDINGS. – It is a 2 hour walk for the more energetic visitors to the **old village of Tučepi**, situated at some 2600 ft/800 m above sea level. For other excursions from Tučepi see under Makarska.

Ugljan

Republic: Croatia (Hrvatska).
Area of island: 18 sq. miles/46 sq. km. – Population: 11,000.
Post code: YU-57275. – Telephone code: 0 57.
ⓘ **Turističko Društvo Ugljan,**
tel. 8 80 12.
Turist Biro Preko,
tel. 8 60 12.

HOTELS. – IN UGLJAN (TOWN): *Zadranka*, C, 176 b., tel. 8 80 04; also accommodation in private houses (apply to Tourist Office). – IN PREKO: *Zelena Punta* hotel complex, B, 460 b., tel. 8 72 22; *Preko*, B, 126 b., tel. 8 61 22; also accommodation in private houses (apply to Tourist Office or *Poljoprivredna Zadruga* agency, tel. 8 72 18). – Accommodation in private houses also available at Kukljica, Kali, Poljana, Sutimišča and Lukoran.

NATURIST FACILITIES. – Beach at *Zelena Punta* hotel complex.

SPORT, BOATING and BATHING. – The best bathing beaches are at **Preko**, which also has a small harbour and an attractive promenade. The beach consists partly of specially laid concrete or stones, partly of areas of grey sand. The islet of Galovac (Franciscan friary), 90 yd/80 m offshore, has a pinewood which affords shade. – The *Zelena Punta* holiday complex, near Kukljica, has facilities for a wide range of sports, a pebble beach, some stretches of sandy beach and a naturist area (reached by boat). The little town of **Ugljan** caters mainly to those seeking accommodation in private houses. Nearby are lonely coves with crystal-clear water, suitable also for naturists.

There is no fuelling point for motor boats on Ugljan. Sheltered moorings can be found on the island of Sušica (moor at the starboard-side pier to avoid the bora which blows to port within the harbour) and the harbour of Ugljan town.

CAR FERRY. – Zadar–Preko.

Ugljan has a steep and inaccessible SW coast and a N coast which slopes gently down to the sea. Its limestone hills are bare or covered only with a sparse growth of vegetation, while elsewhere the island is green and fertile, with plantations of olives, figs, vines and fruit and areas of forest. It is a densely populated island of great variety and constant surprises which attracts many weekend visitors from Zadar but has so far developed little in the way of a tourist trade, except at Preko and the fishing village of Kukljica.

HISTORY. – The island was occupied in the Neolithic period. Illyrian occupation is attested by the remains of a number of fortified settlements. During the Roman period, when the island was probably more fertile than it is today, there was a considerable population, and the remains of many ancient buildings have been found in the NW part of the island. The name Ugljan first appears in the records in 1325. After the Turks occupied the whole hinterland of Zadar and advanced to the very walls of the town Ugljan supplied vegetables to feed the beleaguered inhabitants. The two neighbouring islands of Ugljan and Pašman were originally so close together that there was no room for ships to pass between them, and a channel 13 ft/4 m deep, now spanned by a bridge, was cut to provide a passage.

SIGHTS. – On the promontory on the N side of Ugljan harbour is a *Franciscan friary* founded in 1430, with an aisleless Gothic church of 1447. The *cloister* has interesting Romanesque capitals, probably brought here from Zadar. In the courtyard of the friary is the *tomb* of Bishop Šime Kožičić Benja (d. 1536), who established a Glagolitic printing-press at Rijeka (see under Krk). Near the cove of *Bataláža* remains of a Roman villa have been found. SE of Ugljan, on *Kuran Hill*, are remains of a prehistoric fort. At *Mulin* are the ruins of Early Christian buildings of the 4th–6th c., including a memoria, a cemetery basilica and a mausoleum.

Otherwise there are only a few features of relatively minor importance on the island – the remains of Roman buildings and tombs in the farming and fishing village of *Lukoran*, a 17th c. Baroque church at *Kali* (2 miles/3 km SE of Preko). The principal holiday resort on the island, *Kukljica*, has no buildings of historical interest.

Ulcinj

Republic: Montenegro (Crna Gora).
Altitude: 10 ft/3 m. – Population: 7500.
Post code: YU-81360. – Telephone code: 0 85.
ⓘ **Turističko Biro Neptun,**
Obala Borisa Kidriča;
tel. 8 40 86.

HOTELS. – *Grand Hotel Lido,* A, 112 b., tel. 8 40 24; *Albatros,* A, 113 b., tel. 8 41 44; *Bellevue* B, 730 b., tel. 8 42 44; *Galeb,* at present closed; *Mediteran,* B, 535 b., tel. 8 41 08; *Olympic,* B, 240 b., tel. 8 40 26; *Lido Bungalows,* B, 480 b., tel. 8 40 22; *Milena Bungalows,* B, 130 b., tel. 8 41 61; *Ada Island* naturist center, B, 408 b., tel. 8 40 88; *Motel Šas,* B, 33 b. – The *Jadran Hotel,* formerly a landmark at the entrance to the harbour inlet, was destroyed in 1979 and is due to be replaced by a new building.

CAMP SITE. – *Neptun,* on the road from Ulcinj to the Lido hotel complex, tel. 8 13 60.

SPORT. – Boating, water-skiing, scuba diving (suitable conditions only at Ulcinj town). Use of boats difficult on 7½ mile/12 km long sandy beach in Lido area S of Ulcinj and on the naturist island of Ada in the River Bojana. Tennis courts at Bellevue Hotel; table tennis in Olympic and Bellevue Hotels; bowling alleys at Albatros Hotel and Lido Bungalows; walking along beach.

The most southerly holiday area in Yugoslavia extends for 9 miles/15 km from the town of Ulcinj to the Albanian frontier, marked by one of the arms of the River Bojana. It consists of three parts – the hotels and holiday chalets (bungalows) in and around the town, with facilities for bathing and sunbathing in the sickle-shaped sandy bay in the town and the shelving rocks at the hotels; the hotels in the Lido area (also a camp site), where the 7 miles/12 km of sandy beach begin; and the naturist island of Ada, with chalets and a camp site.

Fishing platforms, Ulcinj

With a mean annual temperature of 61.5°F/16.4°C and the subtropical climate of this coastal area, Ulcinj has a holiday season lasting from April to the beginning of November. It is, admittedly, farther away than other coastal resorts: the nearest airports are Dubrovnik, 88 miles/142 km away (4 hours by bus), Tivat (58 miles/93 km, 3 hours by bus) and Titograd (66 miles/106 km, 3½ hours by bus), and the distance by road from Umag at the N end of the Adriatic coastal highway to Ulcinj at the S end is some 630 miles/1000 km.

The long journey to Ulcinj, however, finds its reward in the beauty of the surrounding countryside, which strikes the visitor from farther north as different and unfamiliar, and in the many oriental features in the life of the town and – even more noticeably – of the surrounding villages. – On the excellent modern road it is now only a 20 minute drive from Ulcinj to Bar, a journey which used to take 4 hours by a roundabout inland route. At the Ulcinj gas station the road forks, the road to the right leading to the old town, the one to the left passing the curious old platforms from which fishing nets are lowered and the camp site to the Lido hotel complex. The same road, which later degenerates into an unmarked track, gives access to the naturist island of Ada. The roads are poorly signposted, sometimes not signposted at all.

HISTORY. – The ancient city of *Colchinium,* said to have been founded by seafarers from Colchis on the Black Sea, was captured by the Romans from the Illyrians in the 2nd c. B.C. and renamed *Olcinium,* a town referred to by Livy and Pliny the Elder. Legend has it that the town was swallowed up by the sea as a result of a violent earthquake in the year 444. The guides on the excursion boats show visitors the remains of houses under the sea, clearly visible when the water is calm; but since the site is some miles N of present-day Ulcinj it seems doubtful whether this can really be the lost city of Olcinium.

In the 11th c. Ulcinj belonged to the state of Zeta; in 1183 it came under the rule of the Nemanjids; and in 1396 it passed into the hands of the Balšići. From 1420 until its capture by the Turks in 1571 it was held by Venice. Thereafter, it was strongly fortified and began to take on an oriental character, acquiring mosques, Turkish baths and narrow winding streets.

In the naval battle of Lepanto (Naupactus) on October 7, 1571 a fleet of Spanish, Venetian and Papal galleys commanded by Don John of Austria annihilated the Turkish fleet. After the battle 400 survivors, Algerian corsairs, settled at Ulcinj, where they soon gained control of the town, built up a private fleet and pursued their piratical activities, threatening shipping not only all over the Adriatic but out in the Mediterranean as well, as far afield as Morocco. During this period Ulcinj became a market notorious throughout Europe not only for the disposal of the pirates' booty but for the sale of their prisoners as slaves. In 1675 Venice delivered an ultimatum to the Turks, who nominally controlled the town, to put an end to this trade, and in the course of that year the Turks destroyed the pirates' fleet by setting fire to it. The population of Ulcinj still includes some families of negroid type, descendants of negro slaves.

Ulcinj now developed into the principal port for trade between Albania and Italy. In 1878 the Montenegrins bombarded the town – as they had previously bombarded Stari Bar – destroying many houses and churches, leaving the ruins which can still be seen around the citadel. In 1880 the Congress of Berlin finally assigned Ulcinj to the principality of Montenegro.

SIGHTS. – The violent earthquake of spring 1979 destroyed almost the entire old town. Parts of the town walls on the N side of the town collapsed into the sea; the Balšić Tower was left a ruin; the Clock-Tower and the Museum were reduced to rubble; and all the minarets and towers in the town were damaged or completely demolished. Only parts of the **Citadel** survived the tremors. The hotels on the S side of the bay were damaged, but were able to reopen for business in the summer of 1979. The traditional market, held every Friday just off the main street, still brings in large numbers of peasants in traditional costumes or Moslem dress, with their donkeys, to do their weekly shopping; but it seems doubtful whether the old market can survive in the new town of modern buildings which is growing up around it.

To the S of the town, in a cove below the Albatros Hotel which is reserved for women ("Plaža za Žene"), is an *underwater sulphur spring* which is reputed to cure barrenness. Here, if the colourful stories of the local people are to be believed, old Moslem women in loose Turkish trousers and wearing veils still drive their childless daughters-in-law into the water, naked, to bathe in the sulphurous water. The cove is used by some visitors for naturist bathing.

Whatever the merits of the sulphur spring, the medicinal properties of the grey sand on the long sandy *beach to the S of Ulcinj are well established. An investigation carried out in 1932 by Dr Jovan Kujačić showed that the sand not only contained salt, iodine and sulphur but was also radioactive, and accordingly suitable for use in the treatment of disorders of the locomotor apparatus and rheumatism.

To the S of Ulcinj are various channels and lagoons in which fish are caught by a primitive method involving the use of a net hauled out of the water on a long wooden lever. Still farther S are some interesting old salt-pans, most of them no longer in use.

SURROUNDINGS. – The road towards the Albanian frontier, past the Lido hotel complex, degenerates into an unsurfaced track. Occasional side tracks lead into areas of unspoiled forest or to lonely farmsteads. Pigs wallow in the mud, and rare waterfowl scutter up in alarm when a car approaches. In 6 miles/10 km the road comes to the River Bojana and turns W to run parallel with it for another ¾ mile/1 km to the ferry just before its mouth which crosses to the island of **Ada**.

The only vegetation on this naturist paradise is along the N and E coasts. The rest of the island is sand which reflects the fierce heat of the sun. The chalet settlement in front of the restaurant consists of numbers of simple huts of dark-coloured wood and of newer buildings in light-coloured stone. Here, as on the long sandy beach to the S of Ulcinj, it is necessary to wade out for 100 yd to get enough depth for swimming. This makes it ideal for small children, but creates problems for boats of any size. In spite of the difficulty of access (though there are daily bus services from the town) and the limited amenities Ada is popular with naturists, who appreciate its seclusion and its natural beauty.

Umag

Republic: Croatia (Hrvatska).
Altitude: 16 ft/5 m. – Population: 6000.
Post codes: Umag, with Punta and Katoro YU-52394, Savudrija YU-52395. – Telephone code: 0 53.

ⓘ **Turističko Društvo Umag,**
  INA 1;
  tel. 7 22 88.
  Istratours Savudrija,
  tel. 7 45 41.

HOTELS. – IN UMAG: *Kristal*, B, 186 b., tel. 7 23 07. – IN KATORO: *Aurora*, 500 b., tel. 7 26 05; *Istra*, 228 b., tel. 7 22 56; *Koral*, 500 b., tel. 7 23 66; *Villas Polynesia*, 2716 b., tel. 7 23 06. – IN PUNTA: *Adriatic*, A, 264 b., tel. 7 22 09; *Umag*, 302 b., tel. 7 24 00; *Zagreb* hotel complex, B, 909 b., tel. 7 22 41. – IN STELLA MARIS: apartments and chalets, 1960 b., tel. 7 22 29. – IN SAVUDRIJA: only accommodation in private houses (apply to Tourist Office).

CAMP SITES. – IN PUNTA: *Arena*, tel. 7 22 41. – IN LOVREČICA: *Finida* (2½ miles/4 km away on road to Novigrad), tel. 7 21 85. – IN STELLA MARIS: site in hotel complex, tel. 7 24 24. – IN SAVUDRIJA: *Hotel-Camping Pineta*, tel. 7 45 18.

NATURIST FACILITIES. – Beach at Katoro (information from Tourist Office); *Kanegra* camp site at Savudrija.

EVENTS. – Open-air performances (plays, dancing, folk singing) daily in Mon Plaisir entertainment complex.

SPORT. – Scuba diving, sailing, water-skiing, rental of motorboats and row boats; tennis, bowling, volleyball, rental of bicycles.

BOATING and BATHING. – The tourist zone of **Umag** begins N of the town, below the hamlet of Kanegra in the double bay of Portorož. Here three disused quarries have been grassed over and now house a large naturist camp site. The beach, of small stones, has a gentle slope and is accordingly suitable for children. After this, beyond the promontory, comes the scattered settlement of **Savudrija**, with camp sites, chalets and many little holiday houses belonging to Yugoslav families. The beach is of shelving rock. The little harbour offers sheltered moorings for boats. 2½ miles/4 km S is a fascinating area for sub-aqua divers, who can explore the ruins of the village of Šipar, originally a Roman settlement, which was destroyed by pirates in the 9th c. and as a result of the subsidence of the land is now mostly under the sea.

Punta harbour and beach, near Umag

To find your way about **Katoro** it is advisable to consult the plans of the settlement which are posted. The many groups of chalets have been given a variety of fancy names but are broadly similar to one another, the older ones being more modestly equipped than the later and more modern ones. The monotony of the complex is relieved by trees and areas of open space, and there is abundant provision for sports and games of all kinds. The best general view of the whole area can be had from the roof terrace of the highest of the hotels, the conspicuous Adriatic Hotel in Punta. Nearby is a children's play area with mini-scooters, bicycles, etc.

The *Istraturist* agency in Umag (tel. 7 21 30) rents motorboats of all kinds, provides winter moorings and runs a service workshop for the repair and maintenance of motors. Temporary moorings can be found on both sides of the pier used by the ferry service, 80 yd/75 m long, directly opposite the parish church. In approaching the harbour a watch should be kept for shallows and reefs, only some of which are marked by buoys.

This ancient little town on a promontory in NW Istria, still showing the gaps left by war damage, is flanked on the S by the smoking chimneys of an industrial zone and on the N by a great conglomeration of holiday chalets and apartment buildings, medium-size hotels and camp sites. The main areas of activity in this holiday zone, from N to S, are the large naturist camp site of Kanegra, the scattered settlement of Savudrija, the Katoro area, which consists almost entirely of accommodation and facilities for vacationers, and the mixed hotel complex of Punta.

The whole zone is designed to offer holidays at the lower end of the price range and is therefore popular with young people and with families, although the rocky beaches are not ideal for their purposes. The Mon Plaisir entertainment complex, which hosts up to 3000 people every evening, is the largest of its kind in Yugoslavia.

HISTORY. – The Umag area was already settled in Roman times. In the early medieval period it was held by the bishops of Trieste, but in 1268 passed under the control of Venice, which retained it until 1797. It then passed to Austria, and apart from a brief interlude when it became part of Napoleon's Illyrian Provinces remained Austrian until 1918. Thereafter, until the end of the Second World War, it was under Italian administration, along with the rest of Istria. From 1945 it was in the Trieste Zone B, which was administered by Yugoslavia, and in 1953 was finally incorporated in Yugoslavia.

SIGHTS. – The road into the town passes through the newer districts and, bearing right all the way, comes to the spacious harbour and the large car park in front of the Baroque *parish church* (18th c.), which contains part of a 15th c. wooden polyptych. To the right of the church is the *campanile*, and beyond this a flight of steps leading up to a *cistern* which supplied the inhabitants with water during a siege. A walk through the old town reveals much faded splendour and, on the N side of the promontory (on the tip of which is a hotel), the large gap sites left by the bombing of the last war.

SURROUNDINGS. – Excursions to **Buje**, **Motovun**, **Pazin**, **Beram** (see under Vrsar), **Pula** (see p. 172) and **Piran** (p. 152). In the numerous villages in the fertile hinterland with its miles of vineyards there are many pleasant wine-shops with open-air grills.

Varaždin

Republic: Croatia (Hrvatska).
Altitude: 568 ft/173 m. – Population: 40,000.
Post code: YU-42000. – Telephone code: 0 42.
ⓘ **Generalturist,**
Trg Narodnih Heroja 7;
tel. 4 56 65.

HOTELS. – *Turist*, B, 320 b., tel. 4 64 64; *Istra*, C, 35 b., tel. 4 51 88.

CAMP SITE. – *Izletište*, at the Izletište Motel, 4½ miles/ 7 km before Varaždin on the road from Zagreb, tel. 7 11 12.

Travellers who turn off the road from Maribor to Novi Sad to enter Varaždin, park their car and make their way into the pedestrian precinct in the middle of the town find themselves surrounded by handsome Baroque buildings; and apart from the attractions of the town itself the beauty of the surrounding countryside offers an additional inducement to make an overnight stop here. For sportsmen, too, there is good hunting to be had in the neighbourhood of Varaždin.

HISTORY. – The little town on the right bank of the Drava, now surrounded by a considerable industrial zone but still preserving its historic core, is first mentioned in the records in 1181. In 1209 it became a royal free city. Strongly fortified, it withstood all assaults by the Turks and was never taken. From 1756 to 1776 it was capital of Croatia, until displaced in this role by Zagreb, and also seat of the Banus, the viceroy who governed Croatia on behalf of the Hungarian crown. Varaždin is now chief town of the Zagorje region of Croatia, and since the last war has developed textile, woodworking and leatherworking industries. The older parts of the town have largely been destroyed by fire.

SIGHTS. – In the market square and the neighbouring streets there are many handsome old burghers' houses. One of the most notable buildings is the **Patačić Palace**, with a richly decorated façade. On a hill near the middle of town stands the **Castle**, with massive walls and ramparts of the 13th c. After the Turkish danger had passed the town's fortifications were pulled down, but the castle was left. It now houses the interesting *Municipal Museum*.

In addition to its handsome palaces, Baroque churches and monasteries Varaždin has an attractive little **Theatre** in neo-Renaissance style (1873). – One unusual sight which should not be missed is the *Cemetery*, laid out in the style of the gardens of Versailles, which must be counted one of the most beautiful in Europe.

SURROUNDINGS. – 9 miles/15 km from Varaždin, at the village of **Vinica** (reached by turning left off the road to Maribor), stands **Opeka Castle**, set in a beautiful *park* which is designated as a nature reserve. In the carefully tended grounds are many exotic plants, as well as a school of horticulture and a motel. Near the castle is the *Zelendvor* hunting reserve, with its own breeding station.

9 miles/15 km SE of Varaždin, off the Zagreb road, lies the well-known spa of **Varaždinske Toplice**, with hot springs, carbonic acid springs and mud baths. The hot springs (136°F/58°C), which were already known in the 3rd c. B.C., yield an abundant supply of water and are used both internally and in the form of baths.

16 miles/25 km SW of Varaždin on a minor road which is asphalted as far as Lepoglava is the holiday resort of **Trakošćan** (Hotel Trakošćan, 100 b., tel. 0 42 – 7 51 24). Here the gently rolling countryside of Zagorje gives place to a forest-covered upland region. On a hill above a quiet and secluded lake stands *Trakošćan Castle*, one of the handsomest castles in Croatia, stored with treasures dating from the 15th to the 19th c., including a valuable collection of period furniture, a portrait gallery and a collection of arms and armour.

The area N of Varaždin known as the *Medjimurje*, between the rivers Drava and Mura, is good hunting (shooting) country, well stocked with game. Sportsmen can find comfortable accommodation in the villages of *Čakovec, Sivica* and *Otok* (apply to travel agencies).

Varaždin Castle

Višegrad

Republic: Bosnia-Hercegovina (Bosna i Hercegovina).
Altitude: 1260 ft/384 m. – Population: 25,000.
Post code: YU-71440. – Telephone code: 0 73.
ⓘ **Panos UTP,**
Turistička Poslovanica,
tel. 8 11 20.

HOTELS. – *Bikavac*, B, 88 b., tel. 8 14 24; *Višegrad*, B, 50 b., tel. 8 12 24.

Višegrad – the famous bridge over the Drina

CAMP SITE. – *Bikavac*, tel. 8 14 04.

A new resort area, at present patronised only by Yugoslavs, is in course of development near *Bajina Bašta* (beyond the dam, in the Tara Nature Park). Hotels: *Drina*, 130 b., tel. 85 14 31; *Tara*, 100 b., tel. 85 14 32 (at over 3300 ft/1000 m, ski-lifts nearby).

Višegrad, in a beautiful hilly setting at the famous bridge over the Drina, is a lively market town with little industry and which has no particular tourist sights to attract the visitor. One attraction it can offer, however, is a boat trip on the River Drina to the dam at Bajina Bašta. A few miles before the dam is the water sports complex of Perućac. Višegrad is also the finishing point of the two-day raft trips on the Drina from Foča which are run from June to September.

HISTORY. – In earlier centuries Višegrad was an important staging point on the old caravan route from Dubrovnik via Niš to Constantinople. Its name first appears in the records in 1433. After the Turkish occupation of the area it was decided to build a bridge here adequate to carry the heavy traffic on the trade route. The order for the construction of the bridge was given by Grand Vizier Mehmed Paša Soklović, who had been born a Christian but had been carried off to Istanbul by the Turks and converted to Islam. The work was entrusted to Mimar Sinan, the most famous of all Ottoman architects, whose pupil Hajrudin built the Turkish bridge at Mostar. The bridge was completed in 1571, and in subsequent centuries was several times rebuilt and restored. It was severely damaged during the Second World War. The bridge's eventful history is recounted in Ivo Andrić's novel "The Bridge on the Drina". (On Andrić, see under Travnik.)

SIGHTS. – The famous *bridge spans the Drina in 11 arches and is 190 yd/174 ·m long. (To reach the best viewpoint for a photograph, which should be taken before noon, go up the steep street just beyond the gas station on the left bank.) Half way along the bridge is a tablet recording its history.

In the village of *Dobrun*, a few miles E of Višegrad, is a 14th c. Orthodox church with a fresco of King Tvrtko and his family.

The town's bathing stations on the river are reached by taking the road down the right bank: the road on the left bank is a dead end. The excursion boats which call in at Višegrad continue downstream to the dam.

SURROUNDINGS. – Instead of making direct for Titovo Užice on the road to Belgrade it is worth while making a detour to see the **Drina** below the dam. Leaving Višegrad on the Titovo Užice road, turn left at **Kremna** into a good road which winds its way up through the forest to a height of over 3300 ft/1000 m, in an area which attracts visitors all year round (hotels, ski-lifts). The road then descends to the straggling village of **Bajina Bašta**, where the Drina, tamed and harnessed above the dam, once again recovers its full vigour.

Vojvodina

Vojvodina, like Kosovo, is an autonomous province within the republic of Serbia. With an area of 8303 sq. miles/21,506 sq. km, it has a population of two million, who all understand Serbo-Croat but among themselves speak a variety of minority languages – Hungarian, Romanian, Slovak and Ruthenian. In addition to Serbs the population includes Croats, Montenegrins and Ukrainians – all adding up to a mingling of races and languages found nowhere else in Yugoslavia.

The principal language after Serbo-Croat is Hungarian, which is the mother tongue of just under half a million people in Vojvodina. The Hungarian-speaking population have their own schools, where the teaching is in Hungarian; in the capital of the autonomous province, Novi Sad, students can take their examinations in Hungarian; there are a number of Hungarian theatres; and there are a newspaper and several periodicals in Hungarian. In general, however, the minority languages are in decline: the younger generation feel that their allegiance is to Yugoslavia and increasingly prefer to speak Serbo-Croat. German-speaking visitors are likely to find local people who understand German, particularly in the villages, less so in the towns.

Vojvodina is a region with great expanses of plain, varied by only two mountain ranges, the Fruška Gora and the Vršački Breg. It is well watered, being traversed by the Danube, the Tisa, the Sava and an extensive network of canals, and has ten lakes. It has also large areas of marshland and acidic meadowland, the best known of which is the Obed Marsh, the haunt of huge numbers of migrant birds on their journey to the south. Another infertile region is the sandy waste of Deliblato, known as the "Little Sahara".

NW of Belgrade on the autoput to Zagreb lies the little town of **Sremska Mitrovica**, on the site of the Roman *Sirmium*, birthplace of the emperors Aurelian (214–275) and Probus (232–282). Material recovered by excavation can be seen in the Municipal Museum, and there is a lapidarium in the Municipal Park. There is also a Museum of Religious Art.

Vojvodina is a paradise for fishing and shooting enthusiasts. Anglers will find no less than 247 sq. miles of fishing waters in which to try their skill. Every year thousands of sportsmen come from foreign countries, particularly from Italy, to shoot pheasants, partridges, wild duck, hares and wild pigs. The local cuisine offers a tempting array of game dishes, as well as fish and the agricultural produce of this fertile region. Vines and fruit trees have been cultivated in this area for 2500 years. The best wines come from the Fruška Gora, the southern Banat and the Subotica district.

Church, Sremska Mitrovica

Vrsar

Republic: Croatia (Hrvatska).
Altitude: 16 ft/5 m. – Population: 1200.
Post code: YU-52366. – Telephone code: 0 53.
ⓘ **HTP Anita Vrsar,**
  tel. 8 97 76.

HOTELS. – *Fontana Villas*, C, 476 b., tel. 8 97 24; *Panorama*, C, 343 b., tel. 8 97 22; *Pineta*, B, 176 b., tel. 8 97 02; *Anita* (chalets), C, 240 b., tel. 8 97 22.

CAMP SITES. – IN VRSAR-FUNTANA: *Puntica* (in a small pinewood on a promontory), tel. 8 97 33; *Valkanela-Funtana*, tel. 8 97 24. – IN VRSAR: *Turist Vrsar* (on a peninsula NW of Vrsar), tel. 8 97 40. – For other sites see under Naturist facilities.

NATURIST FACILITIES. – *Konversada* holiday area, with an island connected to the mainland by a bridge,

The old village of Vrsar on the hill above its harbour

c. 1800 b. (constantly increasing) in villas, chalets and caravans, tel. 8 98 34; several camping areas. – IN FUNTANA: *Istra* naturist camp, on a peninsula, tel. 8 98 08.

EVENTS. – Entertainment (noisy) every evening; sporting contests; "pirate voyages".

SPORT. – Sailing, water-skiing, scuba diving (dangerous on account of the numerous motorboats); tennis (lessons available), rental of bicycles, table tennis, mini-golf, volleyball, flying.

BOATING and BATHING. – Boats travelling between Poreč and Rovinj should keep at a sufficient distance from the shore, watch out for swimmers and skin divers even when they are well off shore and reduce speed, particularly off Vrsar and Konversada, for the sake of the numerous small boats. There are many bad boating accidents in this area every year. Since the construction of a bridge linking Konversada island with the mainland even boats with a shallow draught should avoid the channel (during the main holiday season they are prohibited from using it). Vrsar has moorings and a slip, and there is also a slip in the Konversada camping area – though there are no sheltered anchorages there (every year boats are driven against the cliffs and lost in heavy seas).

The bathing beaches are being improved every year, and at many places access to the sea has been made less painful on the feet by building up the beaches and provision of concreted areas on the rocks. It is still necessary, however, to exercise great caution. Although the sea looks clean, the sewage outfalls are usually only 35–55 yd/30–50 m from the shore.

During the holiday season, from June to October, the village of Vrsar, on a hill above its sheltered fishing harbour, barely seems to exist, the peaceful tenor of its life lost in the bustle of holiday activity at the huge naturist settlement of Konversada

to the S. In winter, however, Konversada with its countless chalets, villas, restaurants, places of entertainment and caravans becomes a ghost town and Vrsar comes into its own again: the local people can now spread out their nets on the quays, drink a quiet glass of wine in their favourite bar and attend to their vineyards S of the village without being .continually confronted by tourists.

HISTORY. – There was an Illyrian settlement on the hill above the bay, and the Romans established the little town of *Ursaria* here. During the early medieval period Vrsar was a fortified town, and from 983 to 1772 it was held by the bishops of Poreč, who had a summer residence in the town. The development of Vrsar into a major tourist resort began in 1960, when naturists from Munich began to pitch their tents on the islet of Konversada, 3 miles/5 km S of the village. Then a Munich travel firm persuaded the communal authorities to agree to the development of a camp site and a village of holiday chalets on the island and the mainland opposite it, up to then poor ground used only for the grazing of sheep. The holiday complex, which increases in size every year, can now provide accommodation, together with a wide range of entertainment and recreational facilities, for up to 15,000 naturist visitors.

SIGHTS. – The *parish church of St Mary (12th c.) is one of the finest Romanesque churches in Istria. The *old town* with its town gate and remains of medieval walls has lost much of its earlier charm as a result of the construction of large numbers of new buildings on the outskirts, shops and stalls for tourists, gas stations and a bypass road.

SURROUNDINGS. – One of the most attractive excursions from Vrsar is a boat trip to the **Limski Kanal**, which runs inland to the S of the village, skirting the island of Konversada. This fjord-like inlet, 6 miles/10 km long, is enclosed by forests and rugged rock walls. It is famous for the oysters which are intensively cultivated here; they can be sampled at an inn (with accommodation for visitors) almost at the head of the fjord. The inn can also be reached from the Koper–Pula road on an asphalted side road (¾ mile/1 km). – There are also daily boat trips to **Poreč** and **Rovinj**, as well as evening expeditions for "pirate picnics".

The most interesting excursions in inland Istria are to the little towns of Motovun, Pazin and Beram. – The picturesque old town of **Motovun**, 12½ miles/20 km SE of Buje on a hill (909 ft/277 m) above the Mirna valley, preserves its old town walls, towers and gates. In the main square are a massive 13th c. bell-tower, a Renaissance church and a beautiful 17th c. loggia.

11 miles/18 km SE of Motovun is **Pazin**, situated on the rim of a gorge into which the little River Pazinski Potok disappears – a typically karstic feature. This tremendous hole in the ground is said to have inspired Dante's vision of the entrance to the Inferno. Pazin Castle, the best preserved castle in Istria, is described by Jules Verne in his novel "Mathias Sandorf". The chancel of the Cathedral has 15th c. wall paintings; the free-standing bell-tower dates from 1705. This was the site of the Roman *Castrum Pisini*.

3 mile/5 km NW of Pazin is **Beram**. The font in St Martin's Church (1431) has a Glagolitic inscription (see under Krk), and illuminated Glagolitic manuscripts (now in the National Library in Ljubljana) were found here.

The main feature of interest at Beram, however, is in the cemetery, ¾ mile/1 km from the village – the *Church of St Mary in the Rocks* (Sv. Marija na Škriljinah), which has a magnificent cycle of late 15th c.* wall paintings by Vincent of Kastav (a village near Opatija). The "Dance of Death", "Adoration of the Kings" and "Wheel of Fortune" are the finest examples of medieval painting in Istria.

Beram

Chapel of Sv. Marija na Škriljinah

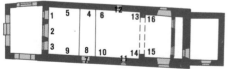

ICONOGRAPHY

1 Wheel of Fortune
2 (above door, to one side) Dance of Death
3 Tree of Knowledge
4 (above, to one side) Adoration of the Kings
5 Temptation of Christ; SS. Apollonia, Leonard and Barbara; St Martin dividing his cloak
6 St George and the dragon, Entry into Jerusalem, Agony in the Garden
7 (above door) Visitation, Annunciation
8 (framing of door) St Sebastian; Latin inscription recording foundation of church; St Michael
9 Nativity, Presentation in the

Temple, Slaughter of the Innocents, Flight into Egypt
10 Presentation of the Virgin, Betrothal of the Virgin, Christ among the Doctors, Baptism of Christ
11 (in window recess) King David, a prophet, St Ursula, St Catherine
12 (in window recess) Doctors of the Church (SS. Gregory, Jerome, Augustine and Ambrose)
13 Last Supper, Kiss of Judas
14 Nativity of the Virgin; St John the Evangelist, St Florian
15 Two saints
16 The prophets Daniel, Moses and Elijah

Zadar

Republic: Croatia (Hrvatska).
Altitude: 16 ft/5 m. – Population: 60,000.
Post code: YU-57000. – Telephone code: 0 57.

ⓘ **Turist Biro,**
B. Petranovića;
tel. 3 37 89.
Sunturist,
Narodni Trg 2;
tel. 3 36 33 and 3 37 59.

HOTELS. – *Kolovare*, B, 500 b., tel. 3 30 22; *Zagreb*, C, 190 b., tel. 2 42 66. – IN ZADARBORIK: *Barbara*, A, 378 b., tel. 2 42 99; *Novi Park*, B, 380 b., tel. 2 21 77; *Park*, B, 196 b., tel. 2 25 56, with annexe *Donat*, C, 96 b.; *Zadar*, B, 132 b., tel. 2 54 58; *Slavija*, B, 221 b., tel. 2 32 44.

CAMP SITES. – *Borik*, Vuka Karadžića, tel. 2 36 77; *Punta Bajlo*, tel. 2 32 44.

EVENTS. – Summer Festival; musical evenings in *St Donat's Church* (now an archaeological museum).

SPORT. – Scuba diving, water-skiing, rental of sail boats and motorboats at yacht harbour; tennis, bowling; fishing trips (lasting a week) to the Kornati Islands.

NATURIST FACILITIES. – Naturist hotel and chalet area at *Punta Skala* (at Petrčane, 6 miles/10 km N of Zadar on the road to Nin), 1350 b., tel. (0 57) 7 30 64.

AIRPORT: Zadar. JAT office: Natka Nedila 7, tel. 2 23 85.

CAR FERRIES. – Zadar–Ancona (Italy) daily; Zadar–Ugljan several times daily.

Despite the considerable destruction caused by air attack during the Second World War Zadar has many buildings of the Venetian period which survived unscathed or have been restored; and even where whole streets have been destroyed and replaced by new building the characteristic atmosphere of the old town has been preserved. Zadar draws its many visitors with its unique tourist attractions: although it has a number of hotels and a small beach it is not primarily a holiday resort.

There are, however, two large resort complexes within easy reach of the town. 2 miles/3·5 km away is the *Borik* holiday area with 1420 beds in five hotels of categories A and B, a camp site and a beautiful beach. On the road which runs past Borik to Nin (6 miles/10 km N of Zadar) is *Pinija*, with the *Petrčane* hotel complex, situated on a wooded promontory, and the naturist area of *Punta Skala* (2500 b.).

HISTORY. – The Zadar area was already settled in the Neolithic period, and in the 9th c. B.C. the peninsula was occupied by an Illyrian people, the Liburni. The town is first referred to in Greek sources of the 4th c. B.C. under the name of *Idissa*. In the 1st c. B.C. it was taken by the Romans, who called it *Jader* or *Jadera*. Between the 11th and 15th c. it was held alternately by Byzantium, Venice and Hungary. In the 15th c. Zadar, which had developed into a place of some consequence, began to decline when the Venetians restricted the considerable economic and political autonomy it had previously enjoyed.

The process of economic decline was accelerated at the beginning of the 16th c., when the Turks occupied the whole of the hinterland and advanced to the very walls of the town. By this time Zadar had become merely a powerful stronghold protecting Venetian trade in the Adriatic – though it remained a major focus of Croatian cultural life. After the fall of the Venetian republic in 1797 Zadar passed to Austria, and apart from a brief period of French occupation (1805–13) remained Austrian until 1918. Under the Treaty of Rapallo in 1920 the town was assigned to Italy, which thus acquired a base on the Yugoslav coast. Attempts to Italianise the population had little success. After the Italian surrender in 1943 Zadar was occupied by German troops. Partisan forces moved into the town in October, 1944.

SIGHTS. – The old town of Zadar lies on a projecting tongue of land. The road which branches off the Adriatic coastal highway runs alongside the harbour (on right) and comes to the *town walls* (on left). Cars are best parked on the quay, some distance

Zadar

Cathedral
(St Anastasia's)

Sveta
Stošija

Baptistery

10 m
(11 yd)

Church of
St Donatus

Sveti
Donat

Bell-tower

1 Altar, "Miracle of St Dominic"
2 Altar, "Apotheosis of St Dominic"
3 Altar of Holy Sacrament
4 Entrance to crypt
5 Choir-stalls
6 Sarcophagus of St Anastasia
7 Ciborium
8 Sacristy

before the bridge which spans the harbour (leading to the holiday complexes of Borik, Petrčane and Punta Skala and to the coastal town of Nin, as well as to the place where motorboats and sail boats can be rented).

Zadar itself is closed to motor traffic, although it is possible to drive around the outside of the walls to the bus station at the far end, returning along the Obala Maršala Tita on the S side of the peninsula.

The tour of the town, on foot, begins at the *Sea Gate* or *Porta Marina* (to left, in a small square). An inscription above the gate commemorates the battle of Lepanto (October 7, 1571), in which a combined fleet of Spanish, Venetian and Papal galleys commanded by Don Juan of Austria annihilated the Turkish fleet of Eulg Ali. The gate was erected (incorporating fragments from an earlier Roman building) as a triumphal arch for the reception of the victors.

Beyond the gate, on the left, is the church of St Chrysogonus (Sv. Krševan), an aisled Romanesque basilica with a beautiful W front. In the raised central apse is a Baroque marble altar (1717), behind which is a 14th c. relief of the Virgin and Child.

The third cross street, *Ul. Ive Lole Ribara*, is the main street of the old town. On the right of this street stands the *Cathedral, the finest example of Romanesque architecture in Zadar and which has a notable W front of 1324. It is dedicated to St Anastasia (Sveta Stošija), whose stone sarcophagus is in the apse to the left of the high altar. The chancel contains two marble thrones (Romanesque, 12th–13th c.) and Gothic choir-stalls (1418–50). From the campanile behind the church, 184 ft/56 m high, there are fine views of the town and surrounding area.

SW of the Cathedral, in Trg Zeleni (Green Square), is an excavated area with the remains of the *Roman forum*. The site was occupied by houses which were destroyed by the air raids of the Second World War, and the Roman remains were discovered during clearance of the ruins. The foundations of colonnades and shops can be distinguished among the litter of stones and broken columns. One ancient **column** 46 ft/14 m high, decorated with

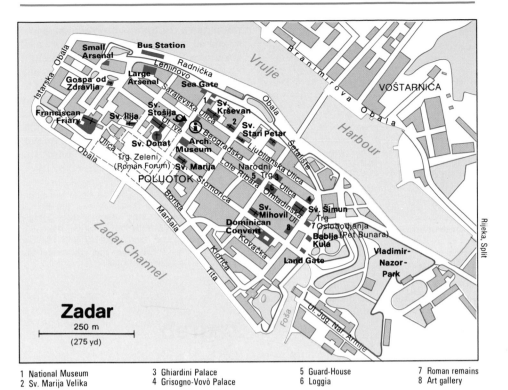

Zadar

250 m

(275 yd)

1 National Museum   3 Ghiardini Palace   5 Guard-House   7 Roman remains
2 Sv. Marija Velika   4 Grisogno-Vovò Palace   6 Loggia   8 Art gallery

pre-Romanesque interlace ornament, was left standing and was used from the medieval period until 1840 as a pillory. – On the N side of the square is the *Archbishop's Palace* (Zadar has been the see of an archbishop since 1154).

Behind the Archbishop's Palace is a two-storey round church 89 ft/27 m high, **St Donatus' Church** (*Sveti Donat*), which is believed to have been built by Bishop Donatus, on Roman foundations, at the beginning of the 9th c. The most monumental church on the E side of the Adriatic, it is circular in plan, with three apses.

Many ancient fragments (inscribed stones, columns) are built into the walls. The church was used for centuries as a warehouse and is now a museum. It has excellent acoustics, and concerts are given here during the summer. The cylindrical interior resembles Charlemagne's Palatine Chapel in Aachen, and indeed it was modelled on that church, for Bishop Donatus acted as an intermediary in negotiations between Charlemagne and the Byzantine emperors.

NW of the forum, in the direction of the open sea, stands the *church (Sveti Frane*) of the **Franciscan friary**, an aisleless Gothic church of 1283. It contains some notable *paintings*. Behind the high altar is a press containing illuminated manuscript *choral books* of the 13th–15th c. In the *sacristy* adjoining the chancel

was signed the treaty of 1358 under which Venice gave up Dalmatia. Beside the sacristy is the rich church *treasury*, with a large painted Romanesque crucifix (12th c.) among much else. In the Renaissance *cloister* (1556) grave slabs of the 15th–17th c. can be seen.

To the E of the forum we come to the 16th c. **St Mary's Church** (*Sv. Marija*), with a Romanesque *bell-tower* built at the beginning of the 12th c. by the Hungarian-Croatian king Koloman. The adjoining Benedictine convent was badly damaged by bombing during the last war. On the upper floor of the convent (not formally open to the public, but the nuns will show the treasures to individual visitors) are three rooms containing a collection of goldsmiths' work, relics and other valuable items from buildings destroyed during the war.

The **Archaeological Museum**, formerly situated on the Obala Maršala Tita, the seafront promenade on the S side of the town which is the scene of Zadar's evening passeggiata, is now housed in a new building adjoining the Benedictine convent. It contains a valuable collection of material of the Illyrian, Greek, Roman, Byzantine, Croatian and Venetian periods. Particularly notable is the collection of

The main square, Zadar

Roman glass. Associated with the museum are a special collection of gold and silver, "Zlato i Srebro Zadra", and an exhibition of local religious art.

Going SE along Ul. Ive Lole Ribara, we come to the *Narodni Trg*, the main square of Zadar, which has been the hub of the town's life since the Renaissance. On the SE side of the square is the *Loggia* (1562), once the town's law court. The *tower* dates only from the beginning of the 19th c. Facing the Loggia, in the old *Guard-House*, is the **Ethnographical Museum**, adjoining which is the **Town Hall** (1936). Within this complex is the little *church of St Lawrence* (Sveti Lovro), built in the 11th c. on the foundations of an Early Christian church. From the Narodni Trg Ul. Varoška leads N to the harbour. On the right-hand side of this street, just beyond the Guard-House, is the little *Ghiardini Marchi Palace*, with a richly decorated Gothic window.

From the Narodni Trg Ul. Ive Lole Ribara continues SE to **St Simeon's Church** (*Sveti Šimun*), on the high altar of which rests the *silver sarcophagus of St Simeon*, borne by two Baroque bronze angels. Weighing no less than 550 lb/250 kg, this was made by four goldsmiths in 1377–80 for Queen Elizabeth, wife of the Hungarian-Croatian king Ludovic I and daughter of the Bosnian Banus Stjepan Kotromanić. It is richly decorated with reliefs, including one showing Ludovic's entry into Zadar.

Beyond the church is the Square of the Five Wells, now known as Liberation Square (Trg Oslobodjenja). In addition to the wells this contains a *Roman marble column*, the remains of one of the Roman

town gates, surrounded by railings, and a medieval tower, the *Bablja Kula*, also known as Bovo d'Antona after the knight known in the English romances of chivalry as Bevis of Hampton, who is supposed to have been confined in the tower. This was part of the medieval fortifications of the town, as was the *Land Gate* (1543), commanding the only point at which Zadar was then connected with the mainland.

SURROUNDINGS. – 11 miles/18 km N is the little coastal town of **Nin** (Italian *Nona*), the Roman *Aenona*, with the little 9th c. church of Sv. Križ (Holy Cross) and remains of the Roman forum. The parish church contains many fine reliquaries (9th–13th c.). There are also the remains of an amphitheatre and the foundations of a Temple of Diana.

Zagreb

Republic: Croatia (Hrvatska).
Altitude: city centre 400 ft/122 m, upper town 518 ft/158 m.
Population: 800,000.
Post code: YU-41000. – Telephone code: 0 41.
ⓘ **Turistički Savez Zagreba,**
Nikole Tesle 14;
tel. 44 45 29.
Turistički Informativni Centar,
Trg N. Zrinskog 14;
tel. 41 18 83 and 44 18 80.

HOTELS. – *Intercontinental Zagreb*, L, 920 b., tel. 44 34 11; *Esplanade*, A, 305 b., tel. 51 22 22; *Palace*, A, 141 b., tel. 44 92 11; *International*, B, 600 b., tel. 51 15 11; *Beograd*, B, 240 b., tel. 44 10 71; *Dubrovnik*, B, 240 b., tel. 46 66 66; *Laguna*, B, 280 b., tel. 56 66 22; *Bristol*, C, 68 b., tel. 41 03 22; *Central*, C, 159 b., tel. 3 83 87; *Jadran*, C, 61 b., tel. 41 42 57; *Sport*, C, 564 b., tel. 56 42 22; *Siget*, D, 340 b., tel. 52 00 55. – IN DUGO SELO: *Park* and *Motel Ježevo* (9 miles/15 km from city centre). – IN SAMOBOR: *Šmidhen*. – IN POPOVAČA: *Stari Hrast*.

CAMP SITES. – *Mladost*, tel. 51 81 98; *Sesvete* (3 miles/5 km away on Varaždin road); *Šmidhen* (at Samobor, 14 miles/22 km W of Zagreb).

EVENTS. – Spring Trade Fair in April, Autumn Trade Fair in September (great pressure on accommodation during fairs); specialised trade fairs throughout the year; International Folk Festival (over 2000 participants), end July.

SPORT. – Trešnjevka Sports Hall (2000 seats); Zagreb Palace of Sports, Trg Sportova 11; Mladost Swimming Pool (indoor), Trg Sportova 10.

AIRPORT: Zagreb. JAT office: Zrinjevac 17, tel. 44 33 22. British Airways Offices: c/o JAT; Intercontinental Hotel, Ul. Kršnjavoga, tel. 44 84 22 and 44 85 11.

CONSULATES. – *United Kingdom*: Ul. Ilića 12, P.B. 454, tel. 44 55 22. – *United States*: Braće Kavurića 2, tel. 44 48 00.

Zagreb, Yugoslavia's second largest city and capital of the republic of Croatia, is now bypassed by the Ljubljana–Zagreb–Belgrade expressway, and motorists hastening towards the S see practically nothing of it but the recently developed districts on the outskirts. Many other visitors, particularly those travelling in organised groups, spend only a day in the city; but even a stay of three days would be barely enough for more than a superficial impression of the town and surrounding area.

HISTORY. – The site of Zagreb was occupied in Roman times by the town of *Andautonia* (finds in Ethnographical Museum), which was destroyed about A.D. 600. The next firmly established date in the town's history is 1093, when the Hungarian king Ladislas made it the see of a bishop. About 1200 the citizens began to surround the upper town (Gornji Grad) with walls, which proved their worth in 1242 when the Mongols attacked the town but were unable to take it. The Hungarian-Croatian king Bela IV found safety from his pursuers within the walls of Zagreb and showed his gratitude by granting it the status of a "royal free city".

After the establishment of the bishopric a new settlement grew up on a lower hill facing the fortified upper town, the Kaptol ("chapter") or churchmen's town. The rivalries between the rulers of the two towns degenerated on occasion into a "cold war" and influenced political developments far beyond the bounds of Zagreb. Despite these dissensions the Turks never succeeded in taking the town.

Zagreb University was founded in 1669. During the 17th and 18th c. the life of the town was dominated by the nobility, the clergy and the well-to-do middle classes. The town grew increasingly prosperous and steadily expanded, reaching out from the hills towards the River Sava. Until the early decades of the 19th c. the educated classes were almost exclusively German-speaking, but in 1847 Croat was declared the language of administration. Even today many of the older people still speak German. During the Second World War Zagreb escaped relatively unscathed. New and modern districts of the city and rapidly growing satellite towns have been developed on the right bank of the Sava. Zagreb's trade fairs are among the most important in Eastern Europe.

SIGHTS. – Zagreb is best seen on foot. The streets are heavily congested with traffic and visiting motorists are constantly frustrated by "no left turn" signs which prevent them from following their chosen route. Moreover Republic Square (Trg Republike) and a number of streets in the heart are designated as pedestrian precincts.

The best starting point for a tour of Zagreb is Republic Square, through which all the city's tram services pass. The busy activity

King Tomislav Square, Zagreb

of the square – thronged in the evening with groups of students, townspeople taking their ease and tourists – can best be observed from the terrace of the Gradska Kavana café or from the tall modern building at the other end of the square (magnificent *view of the whole city from the roof terrace).

165 yd/150 m from the high-rise building, in Tomićeva Street, is a funicular running up to the upper town. It ends at an old tower with a gun which is fired every day at noon. To the right, a few paces away, is

St Catherine's Square (Katarinski Trg), which is filled all day long with parked buses. At the corner of the square is a café with tables on the street. Adjoining St Catherine's Church is the **Municipal Gallery**, with a collection of modern art. Nearby is the *Jesuit College* (restored 1978).

The dominating feature of the UPPER TOWN is *St Mark's Church, with the arms of Croatia and Zagreb in brightly coloured tiles on its roof. Also of interest in the upper town are numbers of handsome

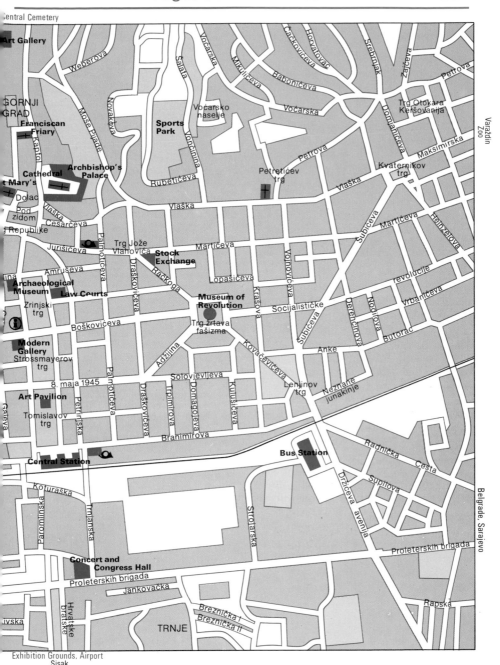

old houses, the *Stone Gate* (which contains a small Lady Chapel) and two fine mansions, the *Jelačić Palace* and the *Oršić Palace*. (As noted above, the upper town is best explored on foot: visitors driving their own cars will have difficulty in finding either of the two streets which lead up to it.)

To the E of the upper town is the KAPTOL district, the old "chapter town" or church-men's town, in the middle of which stand the Gothic **Cathedral** (13th–15th c.) and the *Archbishop's Palace*. In the square outside the Cathedral is the *Market* (*Dolac*: daily, but busiest on Fridays and Saturdays). To this market come not only the peasants from the surrounding countryside, loudly crying their wares, but also various cooperatives selling their products directly to the consumer. At the far end, where the sellers of leather goods, clothes and souvenirs have their stalls, is a small black market, tolerated by the state, in which visitors from the Eastern European countries who need Yugoslav currency sell goods they have brought with them from home.

Zagreb Cathedral

The most striking features of the LOWER TOWN (Donji Grad) are two great swathes of parks and gardens running from S to N towards the upper town. To the E, starting from the Central Station, are King Tomislav Square (Trg Kralja Tomislava), with an equestrian statue of King Tomislav, and Strossmayer Square. To the W are the *Botanic Gardens*, the *University Library* and *Marulićev, Mažuranićev* and *Marshal Tito Squares*.

In and around these "green belts" stand a variety of notable buildings and monuments. In Strossmayer Square are a **monument to Bishop Strossmayer,** the great churchman and writer who fought for the liberation of Croatia, by Ivan Meštrović, the *Modern Gallery* (Croatian painting of the last 150 years) and the **Strossmayer Gallery**, Yugoslavia's largest collection of works by old masters of the Italian, Flemish, Dutch and Spanish schools. In Mažuranićev Square is the **Ethnographical Museum**, with interesting displays of costumes, rural architecture and tools and implements from all over Yugoslavia. Ante Topic, who lives abroad, recently donated to the city of Zagreb his valuable art collection.

SURROUNDINGS. – Some 25 miles/40 km NW is **Kumrovec**, with the house in which Tito was born (visited by half a million people every year). Leave Zagreb on the Maribor road and turn off at Oroslavje. Recreation area (walking, skiing).

A few miles N of Zagreb is **Mt Sljeme** (3396 ft/1035 m), with a conspicuous television tower. Leave on the Medvednica road (many restaurants and cafés along the road); then cableway (2½ miles/4 km) or 7½ miles/12 km of mountain road followed by chair-lift.

25 miles/40 km N is **Marija Bistrica**, a place of pilgrimage which draws thousands of visitors, particularly on weekends. Leave on the Varaždin road and turn left at Sesvete. The road runs through a beautiful and typically Croatian upland region of meadows, arable fields, farmsteads and vineyards.

16 miles/25 km W on the expressway to Ljubljana is **Mokrice Castle** (16th c.), situated on a hill, with a beautiful park. It is now a hotel and restaurant (noted for its cheeses).

Practical Information

When to Go, Weather, Time
Travel Documents
Customs Regulations
Currency
Postal Rates
Travel in Yugoslavia
Sailing
Language
Accommodation
"Package" Tours
Food and Drink
Wine
Manners and Customs
Bathing Beaches
Spas, National Parks,
Climbing, Caves
Shooting and Fishing
Winter Sports
Folk Traditions
Calendar of Events
Shopping and Souvenirs
Information
Emergency Calls

Suha Punta beach on the island of Rab ▶

Time

Yugoslavia observes Central European Time, which is an hour ahead of Greenwich Mean Time and the same as British Summer Time. It has at present no Summer Time, but this is likely to be introduced.

Travel Documents

Visitors to Yugoslavia must have a valid passport. US visitors will require a visa. No visa is required by citizens of the United Kingdom and the Republic of Ireland. Foreigners entering Yugoslavia as tourists may spend up to 30 days in the country with a *tourist pass*, issued at all frontier crossings open for international traffic on payment of a nominal fee. A tourist pass cannot be extended, but visitors who want to stay longer can obtain a visa for this purpose from the local offices of the Department of Internal Affairs.

Motorists should carry their national *driving licence* and *car registration document*, which are recognised in Yugoslavia, and an *international insurance certificate* ("green card"). Cars must bear an oval *nationality plate*. If the driver is not the owner of the car he should have a written authority to drive it signed by the owner and certified by a national motoring organisation.

British citizens are entitled to receive free *medical care* (subject to a nominal fee) in Yugoslavia on presentation of their passport. Visitors not so entitled should take out appropriate insurance cover.

When to Go

Yugoslavia's great length from N to S means that the best time to go varies from region to region. Thus for Slovenia and the Yugoslav part of the Alpine chain, climatically still belonging to Central Europe, the best season is the summer, extending into September. The interior of the country, separated from the sea and its moderating influence on the climate, is very hot in the height of summer; and for most of Croatia, Montenegro and Macedonia, as well as Serbia, Bosnia and Hercegovina, therefore the best times are late spring and early autumn. Dalmatia, with its Mediterranean climate, is best visited in May–June and September–October.

Weather

In the interior of Yugoslavia, where the climate is of continental character, the summers are hot and the winters severe, with an abundance of snow. Between the Adriatic coast and the mountains the moderating influence of the maritime climate is predominant, so that in this region the summer temperatures are tolerable, while the winter months are comparatively warm but have a good deal of rain. In Dalmatia the *bora* a strong fall wind, cold and dry, can be very disagreeable, and drivers on the Adriatic coastal highway should exercise particular caution when it is blowing.

For a more detailed account of climatic conditions in Yugoslavia see p. 20.

Customs Regulations

Visitors may take into Yugoslavia, without payment of duty, clothing, toilet articles and jewelry for their own personal use, two cameras with five rolls of film, a pair of binoculars, a portable tape-recorder, a record-player with ten records, a portable radio, a portable television set, a portable typewriter, a sports boat with or without a motor, camping equipment and sports gear. There are also duty-free allowances of 200 cigarettes or 50 cigars or 250 grams of tobacco, a bottle of wine, a quarter litre of spirits, a quarter litre of eau de cologne and a small amount of perfume. All such items must be verbally declared to the customs officer and must be shown to him if requested.

On leaving Yugoslavia visitors must take out the items brought in for their personal use. Souvenirs and other goods may be taken out duty-free provided that they have been bought with imported foreign currency (as shown by receipts for money changed). Special permits must be obtained from the authorities responsible for the protection of the national cultural heritage before any works of art or antiques can be exported.

NB: Visitors entering Yugoslavia with a car showing signs of damage should have the damage recorded and certified by the police at the frontier, since they may be required to produce a certificate of damage before being allowed to leave the country.

Currency

The Yugoslav unit of currency is the **dinar** (*d*) of 100 *paras*.

There are banknotes for 5, 10, 20, 50, 100, 500 and 1000 dinars and coins in denominations of 5, 10, 20 and 50 paras and 1, 2, 5, 10, 20, 50 and 100 dinars.

Exchange Rates
(subject to variation)
1 dinar = £0·005 sterling ($\frac{1}{2}$ p)
1 dinar = 0·008 US dollar
(just under a cent)
£1 = 182 dinars
1 US dollar = 123 dinars

Visitors may take into Yugoslavia up to 1500 dinars per head of Yugoslav currency in notes of 100 dinars or less. There is a similar restriction on the amount they may bring out. There are no restrictions on the import or export of foreign currency. It is advisable to take traveller's checks which can be cashed at banks and post offices.

Foreign currency can be changed into dinars at banks and travel agencies, by money-changers on international trains and in hotels and some post offices. Receipts should be kept, since they must be presented when changing back any unspent dinars (which can be done only at authorised banks and exchange offices).

Postal Rates

Rates for destinations outside Yugoslavia:
Letters (up to 20 grams): 25·00 dinars (March 1984).
Postcards: 19·00 dinars.

Travel in Yugoslavia

Travel by Road
Map: p. 242

The Yugoslav road network has been greatly improved and developed in recent years. The main roads are all hard-surfaced (asphalt, concrete, stone setts (small, rectangular paving stones)), but there are still many minor roads without a dust-free surface. Tolls are payable on most highways.

The main trunk road through the interior of the country is the **autoput** from Ljubljana to Lavrica via Zagreb, Belgrade and Skopje to the Greek frontier. There are some sections of highway S of the capital, but between Zagreb and Belgrade the

road is merely a dual-line expressway bypassing built-up areas but with numerous junctions and intersections. This road cannot be unreservedly recommended, since it carries a heavy traffic of big trucks travelling to the Middle East and, during the holiday season, of cars belonging to "guest workers" returning from work in Western Europe. Accordingly, there is a high accident risk. S of Niš, where the road into Bulgaria (Sofia) branches off, the traffic is not so heavy.

An important tourist route is the **Adriatic Coastal Highway** (*Jadranska Magistrala*), which begins at Rijeka and follows the coast to Ulcinj in Montenegro. From Petrovac, 29 miles/46 km before Ulcinj, a road runs inland via Titograd and Priština to Skopje.

Many country people are still not used to the growing motor traffic and tend to behave with considerable nonchalance on the road. There are also the possible additional hazards of livestock on the road – even on the highway – and of vehicles driving without lights after dark. Extreme caution is therefore required of motorists, and night driving should be avoided.

> **Warning!**
> Motorists on the Adriatic coastal highway, particularly if driving a motor caravan or towing a trailer, should exercise particular care, since the dreaded *bora* – the violent fall wind which can blow up without warning out of a clear sky – can drive a vehicle off course or even blow it over. It is particularly dangerous when crossing bridges or coastal valleys. When the road is wet, too, there is a danger of skidding.

Driving in Yugoslavia. – As in the rest of continental Europe, vehicles travel on the right, with overtaking on the left. Cars must carry a *warning triangle*, and *seatbelts* must be worn. Motorcyclists must wear a helmet.

The maximum permitted *blood alcohol level* is 50 milligrams of alcohol in 100 millilitres of blood.

Road signs are broadly in line with international standards. In the larger towns there are "blue zones" in which parking is allowed only with a parking disc. Horns

═══Highways
───Trunk roads

must not be used in built-up areas. Parking is not permitted on pavements (sidewalks).

Strict *driving discipline* should be observed. Directions by the police (*milicija*) must be exactly obeyed; there are frequent radar controls. Contraventions of the road traffic regulations bring an immediate fine, which must be paid in cash on the spot.

Motorists involved in an accident are likely – at the least – to face delay and inconvenience. It is essential to make sure that they have all available evidence (statements of witnesses, sketches, photographs, etc.). All accidents must be reported to the police (summoned by dialling 92 anywhere in Yugoslavia), who will issue a certificate of damage: without such a certificate a car showing visible signs of damage will not be allowed to leave the country. A car which is a total write-off must be handed over to the customs authorities.

Motorists passing the scene of an accident are under an obligation to stop and give assistance if this is not already being provided by someone else.

Speed limits: on highways 74 m.p.h. (120 km p.h.), on ordinary roads 62 m.p.h. (100 km p.h.). in built-up areas 37 m.p.h. (60 km p.h.); vehicles with trailers 50 m.p.h. (80 km p.h.).

Fuel prices (subject to variation): *super* (98 octane) 71·00 dinars per litre, *premium* (86 octane) 68·00 dinars, diesel fuel 50·00 dinars.

Foreign motorists travelling in their own car or in a vehicle rented abroad can obtain *fuel coupons* at the Yugoslav frontier (or from their motoring organisation) which allows them a 10% reduction on the normal price. The coupons, which must be paid for in foreign currency, are sold in units of 400 dinars, up to 30 of which may be purchased for each visit to Yugoslavia. A further 30 are allowed for a motorboat.
The price of fuel coupons and the regulations on their use are subject to frequent variation.

Travel by Air

Yugoslavia is linked with the international network of air services through the

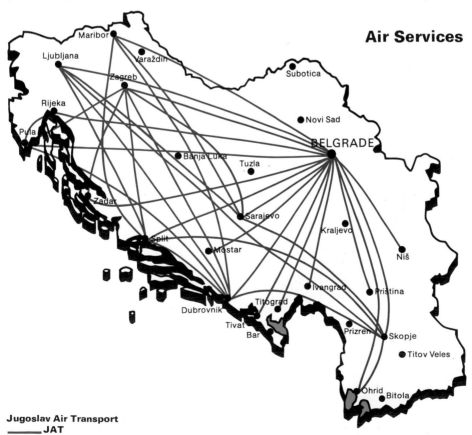

Air Services

Jugoslav Air Transport
_____ JAT

Belgrade, Dubrovnik, Ljubljana, Maribor, Pula, Split, Zadar and Zagreb airports.

The national airline, **Jugoslovenski Aerotransport** (*JAT*), flies both international and domestic services. Domestic services (including charter flights) are also provided by four smaller airlines.

There are direct scheduled services between London and Belgrade, Zagreb and Ljubljana, and seasonal services between London and Pula, Dubrovnik and Split, between Birmingham and Pula and Dubrovnik, and between Manchester and Pula and Dubrovnik. There are also direct services between New York and Belgrade, Zagreb and Ljubljana.

Within Yugoslavia there are regular services to and from the airports of Belgrade, Dubrovnik, Ljubljana, Maribor, Ohrid, Priština, Pula, Rijeka, Sarajevo, Skopje, Split, Titograd, Tibat, Zadar and Zagreb.

Air travel – the fares for which are relatively cheap – is a serious competitor to the railways for travel within Yugoslavia. In consequence the flights are often fully booked, and in order to avoid possible hold-ups it is advisable to book well in advance. It is also a good idea to check, shortly before the scheduled departure time, that the particular plane is actually flying.

NB: Before boarding a Yugoslav aircraft, for either an international or a domestic flight, passengers are required to identify their baggage. Baggage not so identified will not be transported.

Travel by Rail

The Yugoslav railway system run by the state enterprise **Jugoslovenske Železnice** (*JŽ*), has a relatively dense network of services in the N of the country, between Belgrade and the Austrian frontier, and in the SE. There are, however, relatively few lines running through the mountains from the interior of the country to the Adriatic, so that in the coastal regions bus and air services are the most used forms of public transport. In recent years, too, the railway system has been slimmed down in Yugoslavia as in other countries.

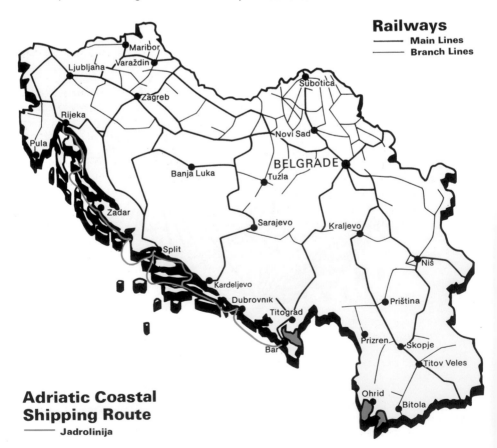

Railways
——— Main Lines
——— Branch Lines

Adriatic Coastal Shipping Route
——— Jadrolinija

But the Yugoslav railway system has one notable engineering achievement to its credit in the recent construction of the new line which runs from Belgrade through Serbia and Montenegro to the little Adriatic port of Bar. Opened to traffic on May 28, 1976, it is 296 miles/476 km long, passes through 254 tunnels (with a total length of 71 miles/114.5 km) and over 234 bridges (including the longest railway bridge in Europe, 550 yd/500 m long and 659 ft/201 m high), and reaches an altitude of over 3300 ft/1000 m. The construction of the line took almost 25 years; the journey from Belgrade to Bar, through magnificent scenery, takes 9 hours. For a description of the line see under Belgrade.

Reduced fares. – Rail fares in Yugoslavia are very reasonable, but there are also reductions for groups as well as for children. – *Children* under 4 travel free; between 4 and 12 they pay half fare. – *Groups* of ten or more adults qualify for a reduction of 25%, groups of ten or more students or young people for a reduction of 30%.

Motorail

Trains carrying cars run during the summer from 's-Hertogenbosch to Ljubljana, Brussels (Schaerbeek) to Ljubljana, Düsseldorf to Ljubljana, Munich to Ljubljana and Rijeka and Hamburg to Ljubljana and Koper. Information from Sealink Travel Ltd, PO Box 29, London SW1 1JX, British Rail travel centers or appointed travel agents.

There are also a number of motorail services within Yugoslavia.

Travel by Bus

There is a dense network of bus services in Yugoslavia, and these services have been of increased importance since the closing down of many branch railway lines. The Adriatic coast is particularly well served, with frequent fast and long-distance buses, usually running very punctually. On the long-distance services seats can be reserved.

Boat Services and Ferries

With its numerous offshore islands, Yugoslavia has a considerable network of coastal shipping services. There are ordinary passenger services, car ferries and a less luxurious kind of car ferry called a *trajekt* with a very limited degree of amenity for the driver and passengers. It is often necessary, particularly on a *trajekt*, to drive in reverse either on or off the boat

Ferry Services to the Islands

ISLAND	PORTS	
	Mainland	Island
Cres, Lošinj	Rijeka	Porozina
	Brestova	Porozina
Krk	Senj	Baška
	Crikvenica	Šilo
	(Now also bridge at N end of island)	
Rab	Senj	Lopar
	Jablanica	Mišnjak
Pag	Jablanac	Stara Novalja
	Karlobag	Pag
	(Also service from Mišnjak on Rab to Stara Novalja)	
Ugljan	Zadar	Preko
Pašman	Biograd	Tkon
Šolta	Split	Rogač
Brač	Split	Supetar
	Makarska	Sumartin
Hvar	Split	Vira
	Split	Stari Grad
	Drvenik	Sućuraj
Pelješac (peninsula)	Kardeljevo	Trpanj
	Drvenik	Trpanj
Korčula	Orebić	Dominče
	Split	Vela Luka

There are also services from Split to **Vis** and to **Lastovo**, both closed to foreigners.

– which may create problems for motorists with trailers.

At the height of the season there are likely to be lines to board the boats. Regular buses and trucks carrying supplies are always given priority, so that early arrival at the port is no guarantee of immediate departure. It is therefore advisable to buy the tickets before joining the line.

The *Jadrolinija* shipping company runs a service (four times weekly) between the following coastal ports and islands: Rijeka – Rab – Zadar – Split – Hvar – Korčula – Dubrovnik – Bar – Corfu (Greece).

Information: **Jadrolinija**, Obala Jugoslavenske Mornarice 16, Rijeka; tel. (0 51) 2 23 56.
Agent in United Kingdom: Yugotours Ltd, Chesham House, 150 Regent Street, London W1R 5FA; tel. (01) 734 7321.
Agent in United States: March Shipping Passenger Services, Suite 5257, One World Trade Center, New York, N.Y. 10048; tel. (212) 938 9300.

Ferry services between Yugoslavia and Italy: Ancona–Zadar, Ancona–Split, Pescara–Split, Bari–Dubrovnik.
Between Yugoslavia and Greece: Bar–Corfu–Igoumenitsa.
Between Yugoslavia and Turkey: Split–Izmir–Istanbul.

Sailing

The **coastal waters** of Yugoslavia offer ideal conditions and endless scope for pleasure craft, whether powered by sails or a motor. The Yugoslav Adriatic coast, with more than a thousand islands, has a total coastline of over 3700 miles/6000 km – the longest stretch of coastline of any European country.

In addition to the numerous harbours and fishing ports, large and small, there are hundreds of coves and anchorages offering shelter for small boats.

As for the **inland waters**, the following are among the large rivers and lakes open to motor-driven craft.

RIVERS: *Danube*

 Sava (between Domaljevac and Slavonski Šamac)

 Drava (between Aljmas and Be-lišće)

 Tisa (with its tributary the Bega)

 Tamiš

 Cetina (between Omiš and the Cetina Falls)

 Krka (between Šibenik and the Skradin Falls)

LAKES: *Ohrid* (frontier with Albania is marked by buoys)

 Prespa (permit required, obtainable from Tourist Office, Oteševo; frontiers with Albania and Greece well marked)

 Scutari (maximum depth only 20 ft/6 m, edges silted up; frontier with Albania not marked, risk of being fired on)

 Mavrovo (reservoir)

 Jablanica (reservoir)

 Piva (reservoir)

 Drina/Zvornik (reservoir)

Motorboats are not permitted on the Plitvice Lakes (except on Kozjak, with special permission), Lake Bled or Lake Bohinj.

Boats, with or without a motor, can be brought into Yugoslavia with special formalities or customs documents. Boats over 10 ft/3 m long or with a motor which are brought in by road must be reported to the authorities of the nearest commercial harbour, who will issue a navigation permit. Before leaving the owner should inform any port customs office.

Boats which arrive by sea must make for the nearest port handling international traffic, taking the shortest route through Yugoslav territorial waters (12 miles from the coast). Before leaving the boat must be cleared at any such port.

When a boat is reported to the authorities in this way one member of the crew must produce a "helmsman's certificate of competence" valid for similar waters in the home country. If no such certificate can be produced the harbourmaster may issue a temporary certificate, valid for the period of the visitor's stay, after an oral examination. At a number of ports it is possible to take a course leading to the issue of a certificate of competence of Yugoslav coastal waters.

In some Yugoslav ports boats can be chartered. Local tourist offices or firms such as Yugotours may be able to help in making arrangements.

●Ports with customs clearance facilities all year round

1 Koper
New Harbour, to N of town.
Provisions, water, fuel; workshop.
Jadro sailing club.
Old Harbour (sheltered). to W of town, for yachts with draught of up to 13 ft/4 m.
Provisions, water, fuel.

2 Piran
Well-sheltered harbour for small yachts.
Provisions, water, fuel; workshop.

3 Umag
Well-sheltered harbour for yachts with draught of up to 16 ft/5 m.
Provisions, water, fuel.

4 Poreč-Obala
Moderately well-sheltered harbour for yachts with draught of up to 16 ft/5 m.
Provisions, water, fuel; workshop.

Adriatic Ports of Yugoslavia

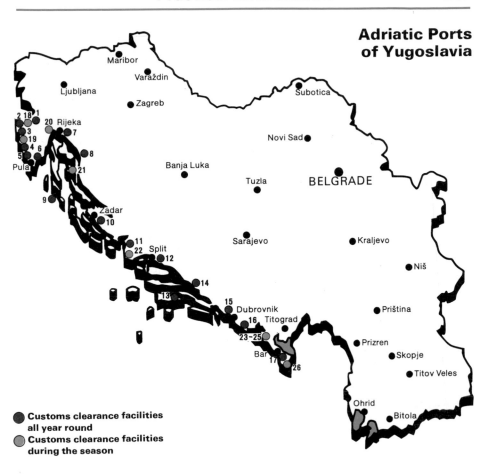

● Customs clearance facilities
all year round
○ Customs clearance facilities
during the season

5 Rovinj
North Harbour and *South Harbour* mostly sheltered.
Provisions, water, fuel; workshop.
Maistral sailing club.

6 Pula
Very well-sheltered harbour.
Provisions, water and fuel, in unlimited supply;
boat repair yards; winter storage.
Uljanik and Mornar sailing clubs.

7 Rijeka
Harbour mostly sheltered.
Long-term moorings for small yachts only.
Provisions, water, fuel; workshop.
Galeb, 3 Maj and Viktor Lenac sailing clubs.

8 Senj
Moderately well-sheltered harbour.
Provisions, water, fuel.

9 Mali Lošinj
Very well-sheltered harbour.
Provisions, water, fuel.
Jugo sailing club.

Mali Lošinj Marina, with all services (full repair and
maintenance facilities).
Long-term moorings and winter storage.

10 Zadar
Old Harbour, well sheltered.
Provisions, water, fuel.
Marina in Old Harbour for large yachts, with all
repair and maintenance facilities.
Long-term moorings and winter storage.

11 Šibenik
Sheltered harbour, accommodating large yachts.
Provisions, water, fuel; boat repair yard.

12 Split
Moderately well-sheltered harbour.
Provisions, water, fuel; boatyards.
Split Marina, very well sheltered.
All repair and maintenance facilities.
Long-term moorings and winter storage.

13 Korčula
Moderately well-sheltered harbour.
Provisions, water, fuel; workshop.

14 Kardeljevo (formlerly Ploče)
Well-sheltered harbour.
Provisions, water, fuel; boatyard.
Mornar sailing club.

15 Dubrovnik
Old Harbour, sheltered, for yachts with a draught
of up to 10 ft/3 m.
New Harbour at *Gruž*
Provisions, water, fuel; boatyard.
Dubrovnik Marina
All services (full repair and maintenance facilities).
Long-term moorings and winter storage for large
and small yachts.

16 Herceg-Novi
Harbour offering little shelter.
Provisions, water, fuel; workshop.

17 Bar
Well-sheltered harbour.
Provisions, water, fuel; repair of motors.

●Ports with customs clearance during the season

Map p. 247

18 Izola
Harbour, mostly sheltered, for yachts with a draught of up to 13 ft/4 m.
Provisions, water, fuel; workshop.
Burja sailing club.

19 Novigrad
Very well-sheltered harbour.
Provisions, water, fuel.

20 Opatija
Harbour, mostly sheltered, for small yachts.
Provisions, water, fuel; secure winter storage.
Jadran sailing club.

21 Rab
Very well-sheltered harbour.
Provisions, water, fuel; workshop.

22 Primošten
Moderately sheltered harbour.
Provisions; workshop.
Marina planned.

23 Kotor
Well-sheltered harbour.
Provisions, water, fuel; boatyard.

24 Tivat
Harbour offering little shelter.
Provisions, water, fuel; boatyard.
Delfin sailing club.

25 Budva
Harbour mostly sheltered.
Provisions, water, fuel.

26 Ulcinj
Moderately sheltered harbour.
Provisions, water, fuel.

There are also harbours for small boats at *Portorož, Medulin, Rabac, Mošćenička Draga, Lovran, Kraljevica, Crikvenica, Cres, Pag, Novalja, Nin, Biograd, Pirovac, Betina, Murter, Trogir, Omiš, Baška Voda, Makarska, Metković, Trpanj, Supetar, Stari Grad* (Hvar), *Jelsa, Hvar, Vela Luka,* etc., and modern and well-equipped marinas at *Malinska* and *Punat* on the island of Krk.

Language

In Serbia, Croatia, Bosnia-Hercegovina and Montenegro the official language, and the one spoken by most of the population, is **Serbo-Croat** (*srpskohrvatski*), in which the stress is usually on the first main syllable; in Slovenia it is *Slovene*, and in Macedonia *Macedonian*. The various ethnic minorities speak their own languages (Albanian, Hungarian, Turkish, Slovak, Romanian, Bulgarian, etc.). In Slovenia and Croatia German is understood and spoken by educated people and also by some of the older country people; and there are now also many returned "guest workers", in Serbia and elsewhere, who have brought back a smattering of German from their work in Germany or Austria.

The three official languages, all belonging to the Southern Slavonic language family, are very similar to one another, but two different alphabets are in use – the **Latin alphabet** (with some diacritics) in Slovenia, Croatia and parts of Bosnia-Hercegovina, **Cyrillic** (with some letters peculiar to Southern Slavonic) in Serbia, Montenegro, Macedonia and the rest of Bosnia-Hercegovina. In the Cyrillic areas road signs usually give place names in both alphabets.

Everyday expressions

Good morning	Dobro jutro	Tomorrow	Sutra
Good day	Dobar dan	Help!	Pomoć!
Good evening	Dobro veče	Open	Otvoren
Good night	Laku noć	When?	Kada?
Goodbye	Do vidjenja	Single room	Soba s jednim krevetom
Do you speak English?	Govorite li engleski?	Double room	Soba s dva kreveta
German?	njemački?	with bath	i kupatilom
French?	francuski?	How much does it cost?	Koliko stoji?
I do not understand	Nisam razumio	Wake me at 6	Probudite me u šest sati
	(*fem.* razumijela)	Where is the lavatory	Gdje je zahod (toaleta)?
Excuse me	Oprostite	(toilet)?	
Yes	Da, jest, je	a pharmacy?	ljekarna?
No	Ne	a doctor?	ljekar (liječnik)?
Please	Molim	a dentist?	zubar?
Thank you	Hvala	. . . Street?	Ulica . . .?
Yesterday	Jučer	. . . Square?	Trg . . .?
Today	Danas		

The Serbo-Croat Alphabet

Latin			Cyrillic		
		Pronunciation			Pronunciation
A	a	a	А	а	a
B	b	b	Б	б	b
C	c	ts	В	в	v
Č	č	ch	Г	г	g
Ć	ć	t + consonantal y	Д	д	d
D	d	d	Ђ	ђ	d + consonantal y
Dž	dž	j	Е	е	e
Đ, Dj	đ, dj	d + consonantal y	Ж	ж	zh (as in French "jour").
E	e	e	З	з	z
F	f	f	И	и	i
G	g	g	Ј	ј	y (consonantal)
H	h	h, ch (as in "loch")	К	к	k
I	i	i	Л	л	l
J	j	y (consonantal)	Љ	љ	l + consonantal y
K	k	k	М	м	m
L	l	l	Н	н	n
Lj	lj	l + consonantal y	Њ	њ	n + consonantal y
M	m	m	О	о	o
N	n	n	П	п	p
Nj	nj	n + consonantal y	Р	р	r
O	o	o	С	с	s
P	p	p	Т	т	t
R	r	r	Ћ	ћ	t + consonantal y
S	s	s	У	у	u
Š	š	sh	Ф	ф	f
T	t	t	Х	х	h, ch (as in "loch")
U	u	u	Ц	ц	ts
V	v	v	Ч	ч	ch
Z	z	z	Џ	џ	j
Ž	ž	zh (as in French "jour")	Ш	ш	sh

Travelling

airport	aerodrom, uzletište	luggage	prtljag
all aboard!	ulazite!	luggage ticket	ostavnica
all change!	preći, presjesti!	no smoking (carriage)	za nepušače, nepušači
arrival	dolazak	porter	nosač
baggage	prtljag	railway	željeznica
baggage check	ostavnica	railway station	kolodvor, stanica
bank	banka	restaurant	restoran, gostionica
boat	čamac	restaurant car	kola za ručanje, vagon-
bus	autobus		restoran
conductor (ticket-	kondukter	sleeping car	spavaća kola
collector)		smoking (carriage)	za pušače, pušači
departure	polijetanje (aircraft)	stop, halt	zadržavanje, stanica
	odlazak (train and ship)	ticket	putna karta
exchange office	mjenjačnica	ticket-collector	kondukter
ferry	trajekt	(conductor)	
flight	let	ticket office	prozorčić
hotel	hotel	timetable	vozni red
information	informacija	toilet	toaleta, zahod
lavatory	toaleta, zahod	train	vlak, voz
line (railway)	željeznička pruga	waiting room	čekaonica

Numbers

0	nula		60	šezdeset	
1	jedan, -dna, -dno		70	sedamdeset	
2	dva, dvije		80	osamdeset	
3	tri		90	devedset	
4	četiri		100	sto, stotina	
5	pet		101	sto i jedan	
6	šest		153	stotina pedeset i tri	
7	sedam		200	dvjesta, dvije stotine	
8	osam		300	trista, tri stotine	
9	devet		400	četiri stotine	
10	deset		500	pet stotina	
11	jedanaest		600	šest stotina	
12	dvanaest		700	sedam stotina	
13	trinaest		800	osam stotina	
14	četrnaest		900	devet stotina	
15	petnaest		1000	hiljada, tisuća	
16	šesnaest		2000	dvije hiljade,	
17	sedamnaest			dvije tisuće	
18	osamnaest		3000	tri hiljade, tri tisuće	
19	devetnaest		4000	četiri hiljade,	
20	dvadeset			četiri tisuće	
21	dvadeset i jedan		5000	pet hiljada, pet tisuća	
22	dvadeset i dva		1,000,000	milijun	
30	trideset				
40	četrdeset				
50	pedeset				

Ordinals

1st	prvi
2nd	drugi
3rd	treći
4th	četvrti
5th	peti
6th	šesti
7th	sedmi
8th	osmi
9th	deveti
10th	deseti
11th	jedanaesti
20th	dvadeseti
30th	trideseti
100th	stoti
101st	sto i prvi
124th	stotina dvadeset i četvrti
1000th	hiljaditi, tisući

Fractions

$\frac{1}{2}$	po, pola
$\frac{1}{3}$	trećina
$\frac{1}{4}$	četvrtina
$\frac{1}{10}$	desetina

Motoring terms

accelerator	pedal za gas
accident	nezgoda
automobile	auto
battery	baterija
bolt	vijak
brake	kočnica
breakdown	kvar
car	auto
carburettor	karburator
change (oil, tire, etc.)	mijenjati
clutch	kvačilo
cylinder	cilindar
engine	motor
fuse	osigurač
garage	garaža
gas	benzin
gear	brzina
gearbox	menjačka kutija
gear lever	uključna poluga
grease (v.)	podmazati
horn	truba
ignition	paljenje
insurance	osiguranje
jack	dizalica (za kola)
light	lampa, svjetiljka
motorcycle	motocikl
nut	matica
oil	ulje
park (v.)	parkirati
parking place, car park	mjesto za parkiranje
petrol	benzin
radiator	hladnjak
reflector	reflektor
repair (v.)	popraviti
repair garage	radionica
screwdriver	odvrtač
spanner	kluč za vijke
spare part	rezervni dio
spark plug	svećica
speed	brzina
speedometer	brzinomjer
starter	pokretač
steering wheel	upravljač, volan
tow away	odvući
tire	vanjska guma
tire pressure	pritisak zraka
valve	ventil
wash (v.)	oprati
wheel	točak

At the post office

address	adresa
air mail	avionom
express letter	hitno pismo
letter	pismo, list
letter-box, post-box	poštanski sanduk
packet	paketić
parcel	paket
postcard	dopisnica
poste restante	poste restante
post office	poštanski ured
telegram	telegram
telephone	telefon
telex	teleprinter

Days of the week

Sunday	nedelja
Monday	ponedjeljak
Tuesday	utorak
Wednesday	srijeda
Thursday	četvrtak
Friday	petak
Saturday	subota
day	dan
weekday, working day	radni dan
holiday	praznik
week	sedmica

Months

January	januar (Serbian)
	siječanj (Croatian)
February	februar
	veljača
March	mart
	ožujak
April	april
	travanj
May	maj
	svibanj
June	juni
	lipanj
July	juli
	srpanj
August	august
	kolovoz
September	septembar
	rujan
October	oktobar
	listopad
November	novembar
	studeni
December	decembar
	prosinac

Geographical and topographical terms

akvarium	aquarium
autoput	highway
banja	baths, spa
biblioteka	library
blato	marsh, swamp
brdo	hill, mountain
breg, brežuljak	hill
cesta	road
crkva	church
dolina	valley
dom	house
donji	lower
drum	road
džamija	mosque
gora	mountain, hill
gornji	upper
grad	town; fortress
groblje	cemetery
grobnica	tomb
hram	temple
izložba	exhibition
jama	pit, hole
jezero	lake
katedrala	cathedral
kazalište	theatre
konak	house, residence
koncertna dvorana	concert hall
kuća	house
luka	harbour, port
mali	small, little
manastir	monastery
most	bridge
muzej	museum
novi	new
obala	shore, coast
opština	borough
otok	island
palata	palace
park	park
pećina	cave
pijaca	market
planina	mountain
plato	plateau
plaža	beach
poljana	meadow, field
polje	field; polje (see under Karst)
potok	stream
pozorište	theatre
put	road
reka, rijeka	river
samostan	monastery
šetalište	walk, promenade
slap	waterfall
špilja	cave
spomenik	memorial
stadion	stadium
stari	old
sud	law courts
šuma	forest, wood
toranj	tower
trg	square, market
tvornica	factory
tvrdjava	fortress
ulica	street
umetnička galerija	art gallery
univerzitet	university
uvala	creek, cove (see also under Karst)
većnica	town hall
veliki	large, great
vodoskok	fountain
vrata	gate, door
vrh	peak
vrt(ovi)	garden(s)
zalic, zaljev	bay, inlet
zamak	castle
zgrada	building
zoološki vrt	zoo

Accommodation

Hotels

In recent years Yugoslav hotels have made great efforts to improve their standards of comfort and amenity and extend their capacity. In the larger towns and resorts most of the hotels are fully up to international standards of quality, and even in smaller places they are entirely adequate. There are, of course differences between various parts of the country: in the N of the country and on the coast, for example, visitors need have no hesitation in putting up at quite modest hotels, while in the S and in the interior it is better to choose a hotel in one of the higher categories.

Uvala Scott, Kraljevica

Since a considerable part of Yugoslavia's tourist trade comes to it through the large travel firms whch run package tours, it is preferable to book accommodation on an all-included basis through one of these firms if you want to be sure of getting a room in one of the popular resorts. – In many places the accommodation available in hotels is supplemented by rooms in private houses, information about which can be obtained from the local Tourist Office.

The following table gives an indication of the range of charges (in dinars) for the various categories in which Yugoslav hotels are classified – L (luxury), A, B, C and D. Prices vary widely from place to place, and at many hotels they will fall either below or above the range shown. They are, of course, also liable to be increased as a result of inflation.

Category	Single room (charge for one person)	Double room (charge for two persons)
L	1800–2900	3350–4800
A	1300–1900	2150–3100
B	700–1200	950–2400
C	600– 950	850–1550
D	350– 700	650–1300

These rates relate to the main summer season (July and August). In the "half-season" months (June and September) and out of season there are reduced – sometimes quite considerably reduced – rates. Hotel rates include service charges. Half-board and full-board terms are available for stays of three or more days.

Youth Hostels

The youth hostel (*omladinski turistički dom*) offers reasonably priced accommodation, particularly for young people. Priority is given to those under 27. There is no restriction on the length of stay. During the main holiday season advance reservation is advisable (accompanied in the case of groups by payment of 50% of the charges). Foreign visitors must have a membership card of their national youth hostels association.

Information from the **Ferijalni Savez Jugoslavije**, Moše Pijade 12/1, YU-11000 Beograd, tel. (0 11) 33 96 66 and 33 98 02.

Camping and Caravanning

Yugoslavia is a very popular camping country, although at the height of the season the sites are often filled to bursting. There are large numbers of camp sites in the N of the country and along the coast but relatively few in the S, and those mostly concentrated in towns near the main trunk roads. Although freelance camping ("camping sauvage") is officially not permitted, the local authorities and the police (*milicija*) are usually ready to help visitors who want to camp on private or communal land in areas where there are no organised sites.

Most of the camp sites are equipped with excellent facilities, supermarkets and self-service restaurants. There may, however, be difficulties in the supply of bottled gas. At the height of the season the sanitary facilities and water supply tend to be inadequate; and at sites on the coast there may not be much room for campers' boats.

A list of camp sites can be obtained from the **Yugoslav National Tourist Office**.

"Package" Tours

Most of the hotels on the Adriatic coast and on the islands, as well as large holiday complexes which let chalets and apartments, make sure of being fully booked by entering into contracts with the travel firms which run package tours for the block booking of large numbers of beds. In consequence many establishments are booked up many months before the beginning of the holiday season.

Nevertheless hotels will often accept bookings from individual travellers, on the assumption that the quotas allotted to the travel firms may not be fully taken up.

There are, of course, certain risks about this, since visitors making their own arrangements cannot expect to be given priority over the package bookings.

In addition to the usual *resorts, many travel firms offer "special interest" tours, such as *motor-yacht trips* along the Adriatic coast, *study tours* and *walks* in different parts of the country, *raft trips* on the River Drina, *riding holidays* at the Lipica stud-farm, *shooting holidays*, journeys in *gypsy caravans* "through the gorges of the Balkans" or seaside vacations with *sailing instruction* or courses leading to the acquisition of a helmsman's certificate of competence.

Food and Drink

It is not really possible to identify any typically Yugoslav cuisine: instead Yugoslavia has a great variety of regional dishes, the result of its many different ethnic groups and the outside influences to which it has been subject. In Slovenia the influence of Austrian cuisine is unmistakable; on the Adriatic coast Italian influence prevails; and in the southern regions of Serbia, Bosnia, Hercegovina and Macedonia dishes of oriental origin predominate. – In the main tourist areas, however, the hotels and restaurants are increasingly turning to internationally known dishes.

Lunch is served in restaurants between 12 and 2, dinner between 7 and 9. Meals are generally à la carte; fixed-price menus are less usual. The self-service restaurants offer meals at reasonable prices.

The Yugoslav Menu (*jelovnik*)

TABLE SETTING. – Knife, fork and spoon *pribor zà jelo*, spoon *kašika*, knife *nož*, fork *viljuška*, plate *tanjur*, glass *čaša*, cup *zdjelica*, napkin *ubrus*, corkscrew *vadičep*. – Breakfast *doručak*, lunch *ručak*, dinner *večera*. – Roasted *pečeno*, boiled *kuvano*, stewed *pirjano*.

APPETISERS (*predjela*): pâté, stuffed pasta, peppers (pickled or fried), raw ham, etc.

SOUPS (*supe*). – *Juha* soup, *riblja čorba* fish soup, *juha od povrća* vegetable soup, *pileća juha* chicken soup.

FISH (*riba*) AND CRUSTACEANS (*rakovice*). – *Grgeč* perch, *jegulja* eel, *pastrmka* trout, *šaran* carp, *štuka* pike; *bakalar* cod, *jaglun* swordfish, *orada* daurade (gilt-headed bream), *skuša* mackerel, *tunj* tunny;

hobotnica octopus, *morski rak*, *jastog* lobster, *rak* crab, *sipa* cuttlefish, *školjka* mussel.

MEAT (*meso*). – *Bravetina* mutton, *govedjina* beef, *kunić* rabbit, *odojak* sucking pig, *jagnjetina* lamb, *svinjetina* pork, *teletina* veal, *džigerica* liver, *file* fillet, *fileki* tripe, *jezik* tongue, *kotlet* cutlet, *plecá* shoulder, *pluća* lung, *rebro* rib, *šnicla* schnitzel, *srce* heart; *ćevapčići* meat balls, *djuveč* casserole of lamb or pork with rice, *hladetina* brawn, *kobasica* sausage, *pečenje* roast, *pljeskavica* a highly seasoned hamburger, *popećak* meat for roasting, *pršut* raw ham, *ranžnjići* meat grilled on a skewer, *slanina* bacon, *šunka* ham.

GAME (*divljač*). – *Jelen* venison, *srna* roedeer, *zec* hare.

POULTRY (*perad*). – *Golub* pigeon, *guska* goose, *jarebica* partridge, *patka* duck, *pile* chicken, *prepelica* quail.

VEGETABLES (*povrće*). – *Cikla* beetroot, *grah* bean, *grašak* peas, *karfiol* cauliflower, *kelj* kale, *kupus*, *zelje* cabbage, *kiseli kupus* sauerkraut, *komorac* bennet, *krastavac* cucumber, *krumpir* potatoes, *kukuruz* maize, *leća* lentil, *mahuna* bean, *modri patlidžan* aubergine, *pasulj* beans, *rajčica*, *paradajz* tomato, *pečurka* mushroom, *poriluk* leek, *rotkva* radish, *spanać* spinach, *šargarepa* carrot, *špargla* asparagus.

CONDIMENTS, SEASONINGS, ETC. – *Biber*, *papar* pepper, *češnjak* garlic, *gorušica* mustard, *hren* horse-radish, *luk* onion, *kopar* dill, *limun* lemon, *maslac* butter, *maslina* olive, *mast*, *salo* lard, *peršun* parsley, *sirče* vinegar, *so* salt, *trava* herbs, *ulje* oil, *umak* sauce, *beli luk* garlic.

ACCOMPANIMENTS, GARNISHINGS (*prilozi*). – *Knedle* dumplings, *kruh* bread, *krumpir* potatoes, *pirinač*, *riža* rice, *rezanci* noodles, *salata* salad, *žemička* roll, *žganci* polenta.

DESSERT (*deser*). – *Kolač* cake, *sladoled* ice. – FRUIT (*voće*): *dinja* melon, *grožđe* grapes, *jabuka* apple, *kajsija* apricot, *kruška* pear, *narandža* orange, *trešnja* cherry.

CHEESE (*sir*). – *Feta* (ewe's milk), *javorski sir* (ewe's milk), *dimljeni sir* smoked cheese, *kačkavalj* (cow's or ewe's milk), *skuta* cream cheese.

WINE (*vino*). – The ordinary table wine is good and reasonably priced. It is usual to order about a third or half of a pint (2 or 3 decilitres). – *Otvoreno vino* "open wine" (served by the glass), *bijelo vino* white wine, *crno vino* red wine, *trpko* dry, *slatko* sweet, *jako*

Wine-producing Areas

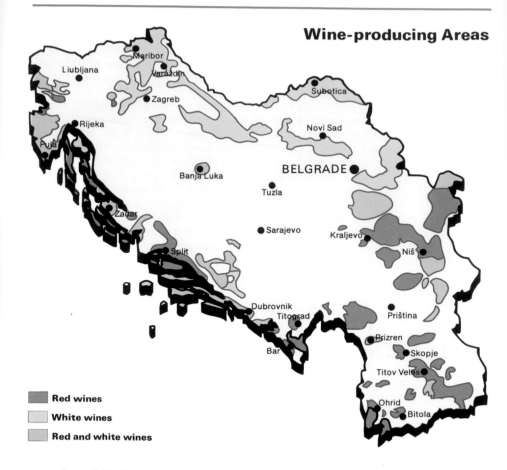

- ■ **Red wines**
- ▫ **White wines**
- ▪ **Red and white wines**

strong, *lagano* light, *domaće vino* local wine. – Older wine and quality wine is served in corked and labelled bottles (*vino u bocama*, wine in bottle).

Other popular **drinks** (*pića*) are *pivo* beer, *mineralna voda* or *kisela voda* mineral water, *limunada* lemonade and *voćni sok* fruit juice. – Popular SPIRITS (*alkoholna pića*) are *šljivovica* (slivovitz, plum brandy), *komovica* (marc), *breskovača* (peach brandy), *kajsijovača* (apricot brandy) and *vinjak* (brandy). – COFFEE (*kafa*) is often prepared in the Turkish fashion.

Cviček, a light red wine; and *Žilavka*, a dry but surprisingly fruity white wine from the Mostar region. – In southern Serbia and Macedonia most of the local red wine is made from the *Prokupac* grape. The full-bodied red *Burgundac* is made in the autonomous province of Kosovo from a grape of Burgundian type.

Wine

Yugoslavia occupies tenth place among the wine-producing countries of the world. With the exception of the great wedge of the Dinaric Alps wine is produced in every part of the country, ranging from the light fruity wines of the N and E to the heavy dark red wines of the Adriatic and the S. The label normally shows the place of origin and the variety of grape used – the grapes grown in Yugoslavia frequently being variants of those grown in the neighbouring countries (Austria, Italy, Hungary).

Among the most highly esteemed Yugoslav wines are *Pekrčan* and *Šipon*, two white wines produced in Slovenia;

The Language of the Wine Label

Bijelo vino	white wine
Biser	effervescent, semi-sparkling
Crno vino	red wine
Čuveno vino	wine made from selected grapes
Desertno vino	dessert wine
Pjenušavo vino	sparkling wine
Polsuho vino	semi-dry wine
Prirodno vino	"natural" wine (without added sugar)
Proizvedeno	produced
Ružica	rosé wine
Slatko vino	sweet wine
Stolno vino	table wine
Suho vino	dry wine
Vinjak	brandy
Vino	wine
Visokokvalitetno vino	quality wine

Yugoslav Wines and Grape Varieties

EASTERN SLOVENIA	Postup	Kevedinka
Beli Pinot	Prošek	Muškat-Ottonel
Laški Rizling	Trboljan	Plemenka
Pekrčan	Vinodolski Trbjan	Samorodno
Radgonska Ranina	Vugava	Sauvignon
(Tigrovo Mleko)	Vrnička Zlatina	Semillon
Renski Rizling		Smederevka
Rumeni Muškat	**HERCEGOVINA**	Traminac
Sauvignon	Blatina	
Šipon	Kujunduša	**SERBIA**
Traminec	Rudežuša	Bagrina
	Žilavka	Dubravka
SOUTHERN SLOVENIA		Grom
Cviček	**MONTENEGRO**	Oplenac
	Plavka	Plemenka
WESTERN SLOVENIA	Vranac	Plovdina
Merlot		Prokupac
Rebula	**NORTHERN CROATIA**	Ružica
Tokaj	Graševina	Vinjak
	Rizling Rajnski	Začinka
ISTRIA	Portugizac	Župska Ružica
Borgonja	Traminac	Župsko Crno
Cabernet		
Malvazija	**EASTERN CROATIA**	**KOSOVO**
Merlot	Bijeli Klikun	Burgundac
Muškat	Burgundac Bijeli	Cabernet-Franc
Pinot Bijeli	Cabernet	Gamay
Refoško	Graševina	Italijanski Rizling
Teran	Plemenka Ružica	
	Sauvignon	**MACEDONIA**
DALMATIA	Semillon	Belan
(Croatian coastal region	Traminac	Kavadarka
and Adriatic islands)		Krater
Barbera	**VOJVODINA**	Kratosija
Bogdanuša	Banatski Rizling	Muškat-Hamburg
Grk	Bermet	Plovdina
Dingač	Biser	Prokupac
Maraština	Čokanski Merlot	Rizling
Novalja	Ezerjo	Ružica
Opol	Frankovka	Šamotok
Plavac	Graševina	Smederevka
Plavina	Italijanski Rizling	Teran
Pošip	Kadarka	Žilavka

Manners and Customs

The people of Yugoslavia are polite and helpful to foreigners, without forcing attentions on them unasked. Visitors will also appreciate the absence of beggars and the reserved manner of guides, porters, etc., as compared with some other southern countries.

Visitors for their part should of course show tact in their dealings with the people they meet and should avoid ill-advised criticism of the country's politics or way of life.

Dress should be simple and appropriate to the season. Light summer clothing and shorts are perfectly acceptable. In churches both clothing and behaviour should be discreet. In mosques visitors should take their shoes off and should avoid stepping on the carpets to which worshippers bow their heads in prayer. When the muezzin gives the call to prayer they should wait until the prayers are over before entering the mosque.

Country people, and particularly Moslems, should not be photographed or filmed without their agreement.

Hotel and restaurant bills include a service charge. *Tipping* (*napojnica*) is officially abolished, but tips are always readily accepted, and indeed are expected by hairdressers and taxi-drivers. On the Yugoslav cruise ships the standard international 5% of the fare is collected from passengers.

Bathing Beaches

The Yugoslav Adriatic coast is mostly rocky, but almost all the coastal resorts have **pebble or sandy beaches**, either natural or man-made. In spite of the steady improvement of the beaches there are still many places where bathers entering the water may encounter jagged rocks. It is advisable, therefore, to wear bathing shoes, which will also give protection from the spines of the sea-urchins which are found particularly in secluded coves.

Other hazards for swimmers are the *bora*, which can blow them out to sea, and the *sharks* which appear sporadically, particularly in the shipping lanes around Rijeka and Split. It is wise, therefore, not to swim too far out to sea.

Scuba divers must obtain a permit from the local harbour authorities. *Underwater fishing* is prohibited, as is the bringing up of antiquities. In some areas (harbours, shipping lanes, military restricted zones) there is a ban on diving: inquiry should be made locally about such restrictions. – No permit is required for *sea angling*, but visitors are not allowed to fish with nets.

Yugoslavia has more **naturist beaches** than any other country; they are usually attached to hotels, resort complexes and camp sites.

● Bathing Beaches

1 Ankaran
Small artificially made-up beach of concrete and sand; water cloudy.
Service facilities.
Not particularly good for children.

2 Portorož
Well-kept artificial sandy beach.
Service facilities.
Suitable for children.

3 Umag
Rocky coast with small patches of sand.
Not suitable for children.

4 Poreč
Rocky beach; clean water.
Service facilities.
Not particularly suitable for children.

5 Pula
Rocky beaches, mainly S of the town.
Service facilities.
Not particularly suitable for children.

6 Rabac
Beach of rock and pebbles, reasonably well kept; water cloudy.
Service facilities.
Not particularly suitable for children.

7 Lovran
Artificial pebble beach, with areas of concrete.
Service facilities.
Not particularly suitable for children.

8 Opatija
Several beaches, some with a small strip of sand but mostly rocky; water often polluted by shipping.
All service facilities.
Not particularly suitable for children.

9 Crikvenica
Narrow strip of sand and pebble beach in town, several small coves in vicinity.
Service facilities.
Very suitable for children.

10 Island of Krk
Rocky beach at *Krk*, idyllic cove (sand and rock) at *Omišalj*, well-maintained rocky beach and small coves with artificial sandy beaches around *Malinska*.
Not particularly suitable for children.

11 Island of Lošinj
Rocky beach with made-up sandy beach at *Mali Lošinj*.
Service facilities.
Not particularly suitable for children.
Rocky coast at *Veli Lošinj*. Water clean everywhere.

12 Novi Vinodolski
Small beach of rock and sand.
Suitable for children.

13 Island of Rab
Stony beaches and many idyllic rocky coves around *Rab*; a few sandy coves on the rocky coasts in the N of the island; water clean everywhere.
Service facilities.
Not particularly suitable for children.

14 Island of Pag
Small sand and pebble beaches, with gentle slope, at *Pag* and *Novalja*.
Service facilities.
Suitable for children.

15 Zadar
Good beach (open to public) in Borik hotel complex.
Suitable for children.

16 Biograd na Moru
Rocky coast, made up in places with concrete, pebbles and sand.
Moderately suitable for children at some points.

17 Crvena Luka
Well-kept artificial beach with gentle slope.
Service facilities.
Very suitable for children.

18 Murter
Rocky coast and small gently sloping sandy cove.
Suitable for children.

● Bathing Beaches
○ Naturist Beaches

19 Vodice
Gently sloping rocky coast with some artificial sandy beach.
Not particularly suitable for children.

20 Šibenik
Several well-made-up beaches of sand, pebbles and concrete.
Service facilities.
Very suitable for children.

21 Primošten
Rocky coast, with some made-up stretches of sand and pebbles.
Service facilities.
Suitable for children.

22 Trogir
Rock and gravel beaches outside town, not well kept.
Suitable for children.

23 Island of Brač
Very narrow strip of pebble beach 550 yd/500 m long at *Supetar*; beautiful gently sloping pebble beach at *Zlatni Rat*.
Suitable for children.

24 Brela/Baška Voda
Long narrow pebble beach; clean water.
Service facilities.
Suitable for children.

25 Tučepi/Podgora
Well-kept narrow pebble beach ¾ mile/1 km long; rocky coast, with gravel beach, to S; water clean.
Service facilities.
Suitable for children.

26 Igrane/Gradac
Well-kept narrow gravel beach with gentle slope water clean.
Service facilities.
Suitable for children.

27 Island of Hvar
Rock and pebble beaches at *Stari Grad* and *Hvar*; clean water.
Service facilities.
Moderately suitable for children.

28 Island of Korčula
Several made-up beaches of rock and pebbles.
Service facilities.
Moderately suitable for children.

29 Trpanj/Orebić
Small areas of pebble beach, flat but stony, alternating with rocky coast.
Suitable for children only at certain points.

30 Island of Lopud
Gently sloping beach of fine sand; clean water.
Very suitable for children.

31 Dubrovnik
Pebble beach NW of town, usually overcrowded; water cloudy, beach not well kept.
All service facilities.
Not particularly suitable for children.

32 Budva
Small narrow pebble beach of *Avala*, at town; pebble beach at *Mogren* and sandy beach almost ¾ miles/1 km long and up to 55 yd/50 m wide at *Jaz*, to NW; pebble beach over ¾ mile/1 km long at *Slovenska Plaža*, sandy beach 1 mile/1.5 km long and up to 55 yd/50 m wide at *Beči* and pebble beach 550 yd/500 m long at *Kamenovo*, to SE. All beaches gently sloping and well kept.
All have service facilities.
Very suitable for children.

33 Sveti Stefan/Miločer
Very well-kept beaches of pebbles and sand on either side of the causeway leading to the island of Sveti Stefan.
All service facilities.
Very suitable for children.

34 Petrovac
Sand and pebble beach in town; romantic *Lučice* cove (pebble beach) to SE.
Suitable for children.

35 Sutomore
Well-kept sandy beach ¾ mile/1 km long. Water generally clean, with fresh-water spring on shore.
Service facilities.
Very suitable for children.

36 Ulcinj
Small cove in town, and 9 miles/15 km of broad beach of grey sand (not serviced or maintained), very suitable for children, extending SE to the Albanian frontier.

○ Naturist Beaches

Map:
p. 257

37 Umag
Rocky coast with small patches of sand.
Moderately suitable for children.

38 Poreč/Vrsar
Koversada and *Valalta* naturist beaches: rocky coast with artificially made-up sandy beaches.
Service facilities.
Suitable for children.

39 Rovinj-Monsena
Pebble beach.
Suitable for children.

40 Medulin
Gently sloping beach of pebble and sand.
Suitable for children.

41 Island of Cres
Sheltered pebble beach at *Punta Križa*, at the southern tip of the island, and rock and pebble beach at *Nedomišja*, to the N.
Service facilities.
Both beaches suitable for children.

42 Island of Lošinj
Rocky coast.
Limited services.
Not particularly suitable for children.

43 Island of Krk
Rock and pebble beach at *Akapulka*, near Punat, and pebble beach at *Baška*.
Service facilities.
Suitable for children.

44 Island of Rab
"*English Bay*" at Rab town (pebble beach), and other beaches at *Suha Punta* and *Draga-Lopar* cove (pebbles and sand).
Service facilities.
Suitable for children.

45 Stari Grad
Beach of sand, pebbles and rock.
All service facilities.
Suitable for children.

46 Island of Pag
Rocky beach; clean water.
Moderately suitable for children.

47 Punta Skala
Rocky coast with some made-up sandy beaches.
Service facilities.
Suitable for children.

48 Pirovac
Narrow beach of rock and pebbles, gently sloping, in a cove. Water generally clean, with springs of fresh water on shore.
Service facilities.
Suitable for children.

49 Omiš-Ruskamen
Clean beach of rock and gravel.
Suitable for children.

50 Island of Hvar
Rocky beaches on islets of *Jerolim* and *Zečevo*, beach of rock and pebbles at *Stari Grad*; water very clean.
Service facilities.
Moderately suitable for children.

51 Island of Korčula
Rock and pebble beaches on islets of *Velika Stupa* and *Mala Stupa*.
Toilet facilities only.
Suitable for chldren.

52 Slano
Beach of pebbles and sand in Osmine hotel complex; elsewhere rocky beaches.
Service facilities.
Not particularly suitable for children.

53 Cavtat
Concrete beaches in several small coves.
Service facilities.
Not particularly suitable for children.

54 Mlini
Pebble beach.
Service facilities.
Suitable for children.

55 Tivat
Naturist island of Sv. Marko (Club Méditerranée); rocky coast.
Not particularly suitable for children.

56 Ada (SE of Ulcinj)
Naturist island in River Bojana; beautiful sandy beach.
Service facilities.
Suitable for children.

Spas

Some of the medicinal springs within the territory of present-day Yugoslavia were already known in Roman times; and during the period when the country was attached to the Danube monarchy there were a number of highly fashionable spas which were frequented by the Austro-Hungarian nobility and the crowned heads of Europe. Nowadays the spa establishments, run in accordance with the principles of modern medicine, cater mainly to the ordinary citizens of Yugoslavia, with particular emphasis on preventive medicine.

It is also possible, however, for visitors to combine "taking the cure" with a vacation. Many spas offer package deals covering residence in a hotel and various forms of treatment, at rates which compare very favourably with the cost of spa treatment in Western Europe.

In addition to the spas listed below – which represent only a selection out of the total number – there are many coastal resorts which rank as health resorts by virtue of their favourable climate and other advantages.

● Spas

1 Jezersko
Altitude: 2973 ft/906 m.

2 Dobrna
Altitude: 1296 ft/395 m.
Hot springs (97°F/36°C).

3 Radenska Slatina (Radenci)
Altitude: 682 ft/208 m.
Mineral springs (carbonic acid, chalybeate).

4 Moravci
Altitude: 623 ft/190 m.

5 Laško
Altitude: 761 ft/232 m.
Hot springs (95°F/35°C).

6 Atomske Toplice
Near Podčetrtek
Altitude: 722 ft/220 m.
Hot springs.

● Spas in Yugoslavia

7 Rogaška Slatina
Altitude: 748 ft/228 m.
Mineral springs.

8 Krapinske Toplice
Altitude: 525 ft/160 m.
Hot springs (104°F/40°C).

9 Stubičke Toplice
Altitude: 551 ft/168 m.
Hot spring (149°F/65°C).

10 Varaždinske Toplice
Altitude: 650 ft/198 m.
Hot springs (136°F/58°C).

11 Šmarješke Toplice
Altitude: 554 ft/169 m.
Radioactive hot spring (91°F/33°C).

12 Dolenjske Toplice
Altitude: 587 ft/179 m.
Hot spring (97°F/36°C).

13 Čateške Toplice
Altitude: 466 ft/142 m.
Radioactive hot spring (124°F/51°C).

14 Istarske Toplice
Altitude: 820 ft/250 m.
Radioactive hot spring (95°F/35°C) with
sulphur content.

15 Opatija
Altitude: 16 ft/5 m.

16 Daruvar
Altitude: 528 ft/161 m.
Hot spring.

17 Laktaši Ilidže
Altitude: 427 ft/130 m.
Mineral springs.

18 Gradačac
Altitude: 423 ft/129 m.

19 Novi Sad
Altitude: 207 ft/63 m.

20 Vrućica
Altitude: 715 ft/218 m.
Radioactive hot springs (86°F/30°C).

21 Koviljača
Altitude: 410 ft/125 m.
Radioactive sulphur and chalybeate springs.

22 Fojnica
Altitude: 1916 ft/584 m.
Radioactive hot spring (88°F/31°C).

23 Kiseljak
Altitude: 1549 ft/472 m.
Mineral springs.

24 Ilidža
Altitude: 1805 ft/550 m.
Hot sulphurous water (131°F/55°C).

25 Visegrad
Altitude: 1260 ft/384 m.
Hot spring.

26 Partizanske Vode
Altitude: 3280 ft/1000 m.

27 Bukovička Banja
Altitude: 656 ft/200 m.
Alkaline mineral spring.

28 Vrnjačka Banja
Altitude: 755 ft/230 m.
Cold and warm mineral springs.

29 Jošanička Banja
Altitude: 1814 ft/553 m.
Very hot spring.

30 Sokobanja
Altitude: 1310 ft/400 m.

31 Žabljak
Altitude: 4790 ft/1460 m.

32 Igalo
Altitude: 10 ft/3 m.
Radioactive mineral spring and radioactive sea
mud.

33 Niška Banja
Altitude: 814 ft/248 m.
Radioactive hot spring.

34 Sijarinska Banja
Altitude: 1706 ft/520 m.

35 Debarska Banja
Altitude: 2790 ft/850 m.
Mineral springs and radioactive sulphur springs
(104°F/40°C).

36 Stari Dorjan
Altitude: 345 ft/105 m.

National Parks

Activities: walking, organised excursions and boat
trips, fishing, caving.

1 Triglav National Park (Slovenia)
Triglav Nacionalni Park
Area: 8·9 sq. miles.
In the most beautiful part of the Julian Alps,
between 1640 ft/500 m and 6560 ft/2000 m.
Activities: walking, climbing, photography.

2 Risnjak National Park (Croatia)
Nacionalni Park Risnjak
Area: 11·9 sq. miles.
E of Rijeka, between 3150 ft/960 m and 4985 ft/
1520 m.
Activities: walking, winter sports.

3 Plitvice Lakes National Park (Croatia)
Nacionalni Park Plitvička Jezera
Area: 77 sq. miles.
Lakes, waterfalls and gorges, surrounded by
wooded hills.

4 Paklenica National Park (Croatia)
Paklenica Nacionalni Park
Area: 10·8 sq. miles.
Karstic country on the southern foothills of the
Velebit range.
Activities: caving, geology.

5 Kozara National Park (Bosnia-Hercegovina)
Nacionalni Park Kozara
Forest-covered hills (1300–2800 ft/400–850 m),
lakes and streams.
Activities: walking, observation of wild life.

6 Fruška Gora National Park (Serbia)
Fruška Gora Nacionalni Park
Area: 88 sq. miles.
Hilly country up to 2300 ft/700 m, partly forest-
covered and partly under cultivation (vineyards).

In Paklenica National Park

7 Mljet National Park (Croatia)
Mljet Nacionalni Park
Area: 12 sq. miles.
On the Adriatic island of Mljet; two salt-water
lagoons.

8 Sutjeska National Park (Bosnia-Hercegovina)
Sutjeska Nacionalni Park
Area: 66 sq. miles.

Mountain country up to 7875 ft/2400 m.
Activities: walking, climbing.

9 Durmitor National Park (Montenegro)
Durmitor Nacionalni Park
Area: 124 sq. miles.
Round the Durmitor range, up to 8270 ft/2520 m;
many lakes.
Activities: walking, climbing.

10 Biogradska Gora National Park
(Montenegro)
Biogradska Gora Nacionalni Park
Area: 9·7 sq. miles.
Alpine meadows, glacier lakes, forests, gorges.
6·2 sq. miles of primeval forest; rare plants.
Activities: mountain walking.

11 Zlatar National Park (Serbia)
Nacionalni Park Zlatar
Area: 42·5 sq. miles.
Mountain country with deep gorges, lakes and
forests.
Activities: walking.

12 Golija National Park (Serbia)
Nacionalni Park Golija
Area: 67·6 sq. miles.
Unspoiled region round the Golija range, up to
5900 ft/1800 m.
Activities: hill walking.

13 Lovćen National Park (Montenegro)
Lovćen Nacionalni Park
Area: 7·7 sq. miles.
A wild and rugged region between 3950 ft/1200
m and 5900 ft/1800 m.
Activities: hill walking.

🗩 National Parks
in Yugoslavia

14 Mavrovo National Park (Macedonia)
Mavrovo Nacionalni Park
Area: 253 sq. miles.
Hills rising to 7090 ft/2160 m; Radika valley and artificial lake.
Activities: walking, observation of wild life.

15 Galičica National Park (Macedonia)
Galičica Nacionalni Park
Area: 92 sq. miles.
Between Lake Prespa and Lake Ohrid.
Activities: walking, observation of wild life.

16 Pelister National Park (Macedonia)
Pelister Nacionalni Park
Area: 46 sq. miles.
A densely wooded region E of Lake Prespa (1970–8530 ft/600–2600 m).
Activities: walking, winter sports.

17 Kornati Islands National Park (Croatia)
Nacionalni Park Kornati
Area: 116 sq. miles.
A bare and rocky group of islands off the Adriatic coast.
Activities: scuba diving.

Climbing

Slovenia has a long climbing tradition; the paths and climbing routes are waymarked, there are mountain huts and an organised mountain rescue service. In the rest of the country climbing is a relatively recent interest which is slowly developing, promoted by the establishment of National Parks in areas of particular natural beauty which call for special protection.

Caves

In the extensive karstic regions of Yugoslavia (see p. 99) large numbers of caves have been formed by the erosion of water-soluble rock. The total number of caves can only be estimated, but is certainly over 10,000. In Slovenia alone – where the exploration of caves has been most actively pursued – there are more than 3500, mostly in Triassic, Jurassic and Cretaceous limestones.

The most famous complex of caves is the **Postojna Caves** (*Postojnska Jama*: see p. 163) along the subterranean course of the River Pivka, with a number of connected caves, the *Otoška Jama, Crna Jama, Magdalenska Jama* and *Pivka Jama*. After pursuing a course which has not yet been traced the Pivka reappears in the *Planinska Jama*, where it is joined by the River Rak, which has also followed an underground course, passing through the *Zadnja Jama* and *Tkalca Jama* (Weaver's Cave). To the E of Postojna is the beautiful *Kiržna Jama* (not at present open to the public).

The most famous cave in Lower Carniola is the **Taborska Jama** (Tabor Cave), with the *Ledenica Jama* as an antechamber.

In the karstic region around Trieste are the **Škocjan Caves**, traversed by the River Reka, with a number of other caves branching off them. SW of Divača are the *Divaška Jama* and *Vilenica Jama* (Fairy Cave), still little explored, and to the SE is the *Dimnice Jama* (Cave of Mist).

Shooting and Fishing

In recent years **shooting** has become a popular activity in Yugoslavia, and a number of Yugoslav travel agencies (particularly Kompas in Ljubljana) organise package tours which include board, lodging and a game licence. There are well-equipped shooting lodges, with transport (cross-country vehicles, horses and, in winter, sleighs) and competent guides.

There is ample scope for **fishing** in Yugoslavia's lakes and rivers and in the

Still life, Vojvodina

sea. Permits are required to fish in lakes and rivers, and can usually be obtained from fishing clubs, the communal authorities and occasionally also from hotels. No permit is required for sea angling.

Underwater fishing with breathing apparatus is not permitted; and there is a general ban on scuba diving in protected areas, harbours, bathing stations and certain restricted zones.

Winter Sports

Winter sports are becoming increasingly popular in Yugoslavia, both with the Yugoslavs themselves and with foreign visitors. In addition to the well-known and easily accessible skiing areas in Slovenia and the Jahorina range near Sarajevo many smaller sites have been developed since about 1970 in other mountain regions – though lack of accommodation means that they are not at present able to handle substantial numbers of foreign visitors.

A number of international winter sports championships are already regularly staged in Yugoslavia (ski-jumping at Planica, slalom in the Pohorje hills near Maribor, figure skating in Zagreb); and the Winter Olympics to be held at Sarajevo in 1984 will undoubtedly give a further boost to winter sports in Yugoslavia.

Winter Sports Areas   Map p. 264

1 WESTERN SLOVENIA

Kranjska Gora (2658–5158 ft/810–1572 m)
14 miles/23 km NW of Jesenice.

Podkoren (2690–5158 ft/820–1572 m)
1½ miles/2·5 km W of Kranjska Gora.

Rateče-Planica (2854 ft/870 m)
4½ miles/7 km W of Kranjska Gora.

Gozd-Martuljek (2461 ft/750 m)
2½ miles/4 km E of Kranjska Gora.

Mojstrana (2103 ft/641 m)
5½ miles/9 km NW of Jesenice.

Planina-Španov Vrh (3061–4479 ft/933–1365 m)
3 miles/5 km N of Jesenice.

Bled (1644 ft/501 m)
34 miles/55 km NW of Ljubljana.

Zatrnik (2891–4147 ft/881–1264 m)
5 miles/8 km NW of Bled.

Pokljuka (4100–5250 ft/1250–1600 m)
13 miles/21 km NW of Bled.

Begunje na Gorenjskem (1896 ft/578 m)
2½ miles/4 km NE of Lesce (Bled).

Kranjska Gora

Bohinj-Vogel (1716–5906 ft/523–1800 m)
6 miles/10 km W of Bohinjska Bistrica.

Črni Vrh nad Idrijo (2241 ft/683 m)
29 miles/46 km E of Nova Gorica.

Lokve (3166 ft/965 m)
14 miles/22 km NE of Nova Gorica.

Livek (2904 ft/885 m)
16 miles/25 km W of Most na Soči.

Bovec-Kanin (1585–7231 ft/483–2204 m)
27 miles/44 km NW of Most na Soči.

2 CENTRAL SLOVENIA

Ljubelj-Zelenica (3468–5446 ft/1057–1660 m)
17 miles/27 km NW of Kranj.

Krvavec (4833–6080 ft/1473–1853 m)
8 miles/13 km NE of Kranj.

Jezersko (2973 ft/906 m)
19 miles/30 km NE of Kranj.

Velika Planina (4633–5466 ft/1412–1666 m)
6 miles/10 km N of Kamnik.

Stari Vrh nad Škofjo Loko
9 miles/15 km W of Škofja Loka.

3 EASTERN SLOVENIA

Mozirje-Golte (1148–5158 ft/350-1572 m)
19 miles/30 km NW of Celje.

Celjska Koča (2460 ft/750 m)
11 miles/17 km SE of Celje.

Mariborsko Pohorje (1065–3935 ft/325–1200 m)
3 miles/5 km SW of Maribor.

Lovrenc na Pohorju (1475 ft/450 m)
17 miles/27 km W of Maribor.

Ribniško Pohorje (2300–5020 ft/700–1530 m)
27 miles/43 km SE of Maribor.

Slovenj Gradec (1342–5007 ft/409–1526 m)
7½ miles/12 km S of Dravograd.

Mežica (1611 ft/491 m)
9 miles/15 km SW of Dravograd.

🦋 Winter Sports Areas

Črna na Koroškem (1887 ft/575 m)
14 miles/23 km SW of Dravograd.

4 GORSKI KOTAR (Rijeka)

Platak (3610 ft/1100 m)
11 miles/18 km NE of Rijeka.

Delnice-Petehovac (3610 ft/1100 m)
22 miles/35 km NE of Rijeka.

5 JAHORINA (Sarajevo)
Venue of the 14th Winter Olympic Games, 1984.
Main sites: Jahorina, Trebević, Ilidža, Igman and
Šavnik (5250–5900 ft/1600–1800 m).

6 TARA ZLATIBOR (Titovo Užice)

Partizanske Vode (3280 ft/1000 m)
S of Titovo Užice.

Zlatar (3940 ft/1200 m)
At Nova Varoš.

Tara (3280 ft/1000 m).

7 KOPAONIK PLANINA (Kraljevo)

Kapaonik (6618 ft/2017 m).

8 ŠAR PLANINA (Tetovo)

Brežovica (5580 ft/1700 m)
Kosovo (Serbia).

Popova Šapka (6152 ft/1875 m)
Macedonia.

Mavrovo (6235 ft/1900 m)
Western Macedonia.

Folk Traditions

In scarcely any other country in Europe are
the old folk traditions still so much an
integral part of everyday life as in Yugoslavia. The rich variety of Yugoslav folk art
results mainly from the mingling of the
Slav element with influences from neighbouring countries, and not least from the
East.

Visitors to Yugoslavia will still frequently
encounter, particularly in the country
areas, men and women wearing the fine
old traditional costumes, and not by
any means only on special occasions or
in special "folk" displays. The costumes
vary from region to region, sometimes
from village to village; but taken together
they form a unity which is unmistakably
Yugoslav.

In *Slovenia*, the most northerly part of the country, the **costumes** are of bewildering variety. In northern Slovenia they show many similarities to Austrian costumes, and Tirolean jackets and leather shorts for men and dirndl-like dresses for women are frequent articles of attire. Beyond the Drava the basic elements in women's dress are a bodice and skirt, usually worn with an apron and often with a laced-up corset, a leather belt falling down at the sides and decorated with little chains and ribbons, and a kerchief or cap on the head.

On the *Adriatic coast* the costumes again show an extraordinary variety. In general, however, the women wear a long, dark-coloured smock with coloured (usually red) embroidery in wool or silk on the breast and the sleeves, and over this a half-length jacket hanging loose at the waist. – In the areas inland from the coast heavy woollen garments predominate, set off by jewelry. There is a wide range of headgear, from the kerchief of Venetian origin (Istria) to the little red cap of the Dubrovnik area. The men tend to wear brightly coloured jackets and baggy breeches gathered at the knee, with wide cloth belts and caps (*kape*) reminiscent of a Turkish turban. In inland Croatia the costumes are notable for their beautiful *embroidery*. They are often made of white

Serbian countrywomen

linen, usually cut on full lines and sometimes elaborately pleated. The women wear a coloured apron over their long dress and a scarf over their shoulders, the men a white shirt hanging loose at the waist, a brightly coloured jacket and high leather boots. The women's headdress is usually a kerchief, occasionally a cap coming down over the ears.

In *Serbia*, with its geographical variety and many different ethnic groups, the regional differences are particularly marked. Hungarian influence can be detected in Vojvodina, Albanian in Kosovo. The costumes of Kosovo are particularly fine. The women wear over their long white dress a short apron decorated with bright red embroidery, silver thread and beads; they wear filigree jewelry on their breast and on their head, which is often covered with a long head-scarf hanging down behind. The costume of the men is based on Albanian models, with a white turban and a jacket overlapping in front. In central Serbia, where all the various Slav elements are mingled, the costumes show endless variety.

The costumes of *Macedonia* show strong oriental influence. The predominant colour is red, except in Skopje, where black is favoured. The women wear heavy woven aprons over their long white skirts, secured by several belts with buckles formed of three round silver discs. The men's costume is usually of white linen, with shirts – often pleated – hanging loosely over their breeches. In the Debar area they wear white felt breeches with strips of black braid.

The costumes of *Bosnia and Hercegovina* are notable for the magnificent fringed aprons woven in a carpet-like pattern. Fringes are also worn on the head or suspended from a belt. The Muslim women wear baggy white breeches; the Christian women prefer a long linen smock.

In *Montenegro* there are two kinds of costume: the elegant attire – of courtly origin – consisting of a transparent silk blouse, a long silk skirt and a sleeveless cloak, and the very plain black garments of the less prosperous. A broad leather belt studded with metal often completes the effect. The men's costume has a martial air, enhanced by a wide cloth cummerbund wound around the waist.

The usual footwear, apart from the leather boots which are sometimes worn, consists of leather sandals (*opanci*) turned up at the toes and often ornamented with coloured thongs.

In many places the costumes are still made at home.

Among local **crafts** the *lace* and *embroidery* of Slovenia and Croatia are particularly notable. Fine *carpets* are produced in Macedonia. Yugoslav *pottery* and *woodcarving* are also of excellent quality.

Traditional customs retain their vitality, particularly in the country areas. Although religious festivals are officially of no great importance in Communist Yugoslavia, they are often still celebrated in the family. Some pagan customs, including the Dodok rain dance, still survive. There are still many traditional customs and practices associated with the decisive events in human life such as birth, love, marriage and death.

Every festival is an occasion for dancing and singing. The traditional **dances** of Yugoslavia are among the most elaborate in Europe, and on occasion are choreographed with all the precision of a ballet. They have a real dramatic plot, tell of great events and the deeds of great men and symbolise ideas, feelings and customs.

The famous *kolo*, a Slav round dance in which the dancers hold each other's hands or the two ends of a handkerchief, is made up of a varied range of steps and figures. There are slow and fast forms of the kolo; and sometimes it begins slowly and increases steadily in speed. A popular Macedonian dance is the *teškoto*, which calls for great virtuosity in the dancers. The *rusalje* is an unusual dance in which the dancers carry axes and symbolically drive out the demons which have possessed a young woman.

At first hearing Yugoslav **folk music** may seem monotonous, but in course of time the attentive listener learns to appreciate its charm. In general the music of the S is more rhythmical and has more colour than that of the N, showing clear oriental influence. The folk music of central Serbia is typically Slav, of a type found in other Slav countries. Northern Slovenia specialises in music for wind instruments, similar to that of Austria and Bavaria.

The instruments used in playing folk music include the *gusla* (a single-stringed viola-like instrument), the *tambura* (similar to a guitar), the *gajde* (bagpipe), the *kaval* (a long flute), the *zurla* (a kind of oboe) and the *tupan* (a bass drum).

The Yugoslav government is making great efforts to preserve and promote the country's folk traditions in all their varied aspects. There are a number of large groups which give performances of Yugoslav folk dances and folk songs to international audiences, and folk evenings are frequently organised in the larger towns and tourist resorts, particularly during the summer. But in Yugoslavia, unlike many other European countries, visitors need not go to organised events of this kind to see something of the old folk traditions, for if they go about the country with their eyes open they will be able to observe them still being practised in the old way. – Reminiscences of folk music can often be detected in contemporary light music.

Calendar of Events

(A selection of major events)

End of March/beginning of April
Belgrade — International Motor Show

April
Ljubljana — Alpe-Adria International Trade Fair
Sarajevo — Yugoslav Song Festival

End of April
Zagreb — International Spring Fair and Tourism Congress

Beginning of May
Ohrid — Old Town Festival (music, folk singing and dancing, costumes)

May
Belgrade — "Belgrade Spring" Song Festival
Kučevo — "Themes from Homolje" (folk art of eastern Serbia)
Leskovac — International Textile Fair
Novi Sad — International Agricultural Show
Skopje — Operatic Evenings

Mid May–September
Portorož, Piran — "Events on the Coast" (fashion, sporting and cultural events, concerts, folk displays)

May 25
Belgrade — Youth Day (sporting events, folk displays)

End of May
Divčibare (near Valjevo) — Narcissus Festival

May–October
Bled — Summer program of concerts and folk displays

Folk Festival, Zagreb

May–December
Belgrade — Skadarlija Evenings (exhibitions, folk displays, music)

Beginning of June
Budva, Sveti Stefan — Musical Festival
Lipica — International Riding Tournament
Sarajevo — International Festival of Military Music

Second half of June
Istria and Croatian coastal region — Song Festival

Mid June–mid August
Split — "Split Summer" (drama, opera, ballet, concerts, folk displays)

June–August
Pula — Folk displays, concerts

End of June–September
Herceg-Novi — Theatrical performances and concerts on open-air stage

June
Skopje — Skopje Trade Fair
Zvečan — Kosovo Folk Festival

Beginning of July
Djakovo — "Djakovo Embroidery" (folk displays)
Galičnik — "Galičnik Wedding" (folk event)
Ohrid — Balkan Festival (folk singing and dancing)
Split — Festival of Light Music

Mid July
Ilidža — Festival of Yugoslav Folksongs
Koper, Portorož, Izola, Piran and Ankaran — Yugoslav Folk Festival (with participation by international groups)

End of July
Bitola — "Ilinden Days" (folk singing and dancing)
Bohinj — "Peasant Wedding"
Subotica — Dužijanca (traditional harvest festival)
Zagreb — Folk Festival

July 27
Korčula — Moreška (sword dance)
Mostar — Jumping into the Neretva from the old bridge

July–August
Bled — Folk Evenings
Dubrovnik — Summer Festival (drama, music, ballet)
Ljubljana — Program of cultural events

Ohrid — "Ohrid Summer" (cultural and tourist events)

July–September	
Arandjelovac	"Marble and Music" (show of Yugoslav art, sculptors' symposium)
Belgrade	Concerts by the Kolo folk group (three times a week)
Opatija	"Opatija Summer" (open-air performances)
Zagreb	"Zagreb Evenings" (music, drama, folk singing and dancing)

End of July/beginning of August	
Pula	Festival of Yugoslav Feature Films

Beginning of August	
Novi Sad, Belgrade and Smederevo	Danube Regatta (international rowing regatta)
Portorož	Song Festival

August 5	
Medvedje-Grmeč	Grmečka Korida (bullfights, folk singing and dancing, folk art)
Sinj (near Split)	Sinjska Alka (historic spear-throwing contest on horseback)

Mid August	
Kranj	International Trade Fair of Upper Carniola

August–September	
Portorož	"Forma Viva" (international sculptors' symposium)

End of August	
Ohrid	Old Town Festival (music, folk displays, costumes)
Struga	Poetry Evenings

End of August/beginning of September	
Ljubljana	International Wine Fair
Niš	Film Festival (review of films of past year)
Požarevac, Ljubičevo	International Equestrian Games

Beginning of September	
Krapina	Festival of "Kaj" Dialect Songs
Vinkovci	Slavonic Folk Festival

Mid September	
Ljubljana	Flower Show
Zagreb	International Autumn Trade Fair

September	
Belgrade	International Theatre Festival (BITEF) Festival of Folk Music
Vršac	Vojvodina Folk Festival

End of September	
Negotin	Mokranjac Festival (choral music, folk art, traditional fair)
Skopje	International Tobacco and Machinery Fair

Beginning of October	
Belgrade	International Festival of Children's Folk Songs and Dances
Novi Sad	Autumn Fair

October	
Belgrade	International Musical Festival (BEMUS) October Salon (fine and applied art)
Sarajevo	Slivovitz and Wine Fair

End of October	
Belgrade	International Book Fair

November	
Ljubljana	International "Ski Expo" Fair (winter sports and tourism)

December 29–30	
Mali Lošinj	Underwater Fishing Championship

Public Holidays

Throughout Yugoslavia:
January 1 and 2
May 1 and 2
July 4
November 29 and 30

Also in Croatia and Bosnia-Hercegovina:
July 27
in Serbia:
July 7
in Montenegro:
July 13
in Macedonia:
August 2
October 11
in Slovenia:
July 22

Shopping and Souvenirs

In Yugoslavia, as in other countries, it is now difficult to find souvenirs of real artistic quality which are typical of a particular place or region and can only be obtained there. All too often – at any rate on the stands of the souvenir-sellers in the coastal resorts – works of genuine craftsmanship have given place to cheap and gaudy mass-produced articles. What is extolled by the seller as a fine piece of wood-carving will often turn out to be a skilfully contrived industrial product.

In some places, however, it is still possible to find hand-made articles which are produced in such small quantities that they do not come on to the country-wide souvenir market – for example *embroidery* on the island of Susak (near Lošinj), *filigree jewelry* in Montenegro, *lace* on the island of Pag.

In the markets and on the quays of harbour towns the local peasants sell their own wine (sometimes rather sharp in taste) or their own slivovitz (usually better than that sold in the shops).

In the larger towns and holiday resorts there are state-run shops ("Narodna Radinost") selling hand-made articles of good quality, very different from the products of the souvenir industry. In these shops the prices are fixed, and there is no scope for bargaining.

Opening times. – There are no statutory provisions laying down opening times on a national basis. Since in many places factories and offices start work at 7 a.m., practically all *shops* open at 8. The smaller shops close from 12 to 4 and then remain open until 8; large shops, supermarkets and department stores are usually open from 8 a.m. to 8 p.m. without a break. On Saturdays most shops close at 1, some later. In holiday resorts shops are frequently open on Sunday mornings.

Banks are normally open on weekdays from 8 to 1 or 2.

Information

Yugoslav National Tourist Office

Turistički Savez Jugoslavije

Head office:
Moše Pijade 8/IV,
YU-11000 **Beograd** (Belgrade);
tel. (0 11) 33 90 41.

In the United Kingdom:
143 Regent Street,
London W1R 8AE;
tel. (01) 734 5243 and 439 0399.

In the United States:
630 Fifth Avenue, Rockefeller Center, Suite 210,
New York, N.Y. 10020;
tel. (212) 757 2801.

Within Yugoslavia information can be obtained from local **Tourist Offices** (some of which can also arrange for accommodation in private houses).

There are a number of **travel agencies** in Yugoslavia which can make arrangements for excursions, accommodation, car rental, etc. The following is a list of such agencies, some of which have branch offices in other towns:

Atlas
Pile 1,
YU-50000 Dubrovnik;
tel. (0 50) 2 73 33.

Centrotrans
Vase Miskina 2,
YU-71000 Sarajevo;
tel. (0 71) 2 32 41.

Centroturist
Bulevar Revolucije,
YU-11000 Beograd (Belgrade);
tel. (0 11) 45 69 25.

Dalmacijaturist
Titova Obala 5,
YU-58000 Split;
tel. (0 58) 4 46 66.

Generalturist
Praška 5,
YU-41000 Zagreb;
tel. (0 41) 44 62 22.

Globtour
Wolfova 1,
YU-61000 Ljubljana;
tel. (0 61) 2 48 41.

Inex-Turist
Trg Republike 5,
YU-11000 Beograd (Belgrade);
tel. (0 11) 62 23 61.

Interimpex-Intermakedonija
Ive Lola Ribara 10,
YU-91000 Skopje;
tel. (0 91) 2 51 24.

Intours
Autobuska Stanica (Bus Station),
YU-81000 Titograd;
tel. (0 81) 2 20 42.

Jugoagent
Knez Mihajlova 22,
YU-11000 Beograd (Belgrade);
tel. (0 11) 62 74 22.

Kompas
Pražakova 4,
YU-61000 Ljubljana;
tel. (0 61) 32 77 61.

Kosovoturist
Maršala Tita 36,
YU-38000 Priština;
tel. (0 38) 2 61 40.

Kvarner-Express
Maršala Tita 186,
YU-51410 Opatija;
tel. (0 51) 71 11 11.

Libertas
Put Republike 44,
YU-50000 Dubrovnik;
tel. (0 50) 2 40 65.

Montenegroturist
YU-81310 Budva;
tel. (0 82) 8 20 08.

Putnik
Dragoslava Jovanovića 1,
YU-11000 Beograd (Belgrade);
tel. (0 11) 33 25 91.

SAP
Titova 38,
YU-61000 Ljubljana;
tel. (0 61) 31 56 41.

Srbija Turist
Voždova 12,
YU-18000 Niš;
tel. (0 18) 2 40 71.

Unis Turist
Maršala Tita 24,
YU-71000 Sarajevo;
tel. (0 71) 3 71 55.

Vojvodina Turist
Dunavska 11,
YU-21000 Novi Sad;
tel. (0 21) 4 44 13.

Yugotours
Vasina 16-18,
YU-11000 Beograd (Belgrade);
tel. (0 11) 63 11 22.

Yugoslav Automobile Association
(*Auto-Moto Savez Jugoslavije*, AMSJ)

Head office:
Ruzveltova 16,
YU-11000 **Beograd** (Belgrade);
tel. (0 11) 45 14 86.

Branch offices:
Ruzveltova 43,
YU-11000 **Beograd** (Belgrade);
tel. (0 11) 76 27 46.

Nikole Tesle 5,
YU-50000 **Dubrovnik**;
tel. (0 50) 2 33 68.

Dalmatinova 6a,
YU-61000 **Ljubljana**;
tel. (0 61) 31 10 50.

Titova Cesta 138,
YU-61000 **Ljubljana**;
tel. (0 61) 34 23 78.

Ptujska Cesta 40,
YU-62000 **Maribor**;
tel. (0 62) 3 19 90.

Hatovska 25,
YU-79000 **Mostar**;
tel. (0 88) 2 18 84.

Marka Oreškovića 15,
YU-18000 **Niš**;
tel. (0 18) 2 22 29.

Lenjinov Trg 10,
YU-21000 **Novi Sad**;
tel. (0 21) 4 88 73.

Magistralni Put 1,
YU-38000 **Priština**;
tel. (0 38) 2 33 76.

Dolac 11,
YU-51000 **Rijeka**;
tel. (0 51) 2 28 07.

Boriše Kovačevića 18,
YU-71000 **Sarajevo**;
tel. (0 71) 3 02 00.

Maršala Tita 44,
YU-71000 **Sarajevo**;
tel. (0 71) 3 39 94.

Ivo Ribara Lola 55,
YU-91000 **Skopje**;
tel. (0 91) 5 22 16.

Obala Lazareta 3,
YU-58000 **Split**;
tel. (0 58) 4 16 46.

M. Miljanova 18,
YU-81000 **Titograd**;
tel. (0 81) 2 24 85.

Draškovićeva 25,
YU-41000 **Zagreb**;
tel. (0 41) 41 50 23.

Siget 17,
YU-41000 **Zagreb**;
tel. (0 41) 52 68 87.

Diplomatic and Consular Offices in Yugoslavia

United Kingdom
Embassy:
Generala Ždanova 46,
Belgrade;
tel. (0 11) 64 50 55, 64 50 34, 64 50 43 and 64 50 87.

Consulates:
Titovo Obala 10/11,
Split;
tel. (0 58) 4 14 64.

Ilica 12,
P.B. 454,
Zagreb;
tel. (0 41) 44 55 22.

United States
Embassy:
Knez Miloša 50,
Belgrade;
tel. (0 11) 64 56 55.

Consulate:
Braće Kavurića 2,
Zagreb;
tel. (0 41) 44 48 00.

Canada
Embassy:
Proleterskih Brigada 69,
Belgrade;
tel. (0 11) 43 45 24 and 43 45 05–7.

Airlines

Yugoslav Airlines
(*Jugoslovenski Aerotransport*, JAT)

Head office:
Birčaninova 1,
YU-11000 **Beograd** (Belgrade);
tel. (0 11) 64 34 22.
Desks at all airports in Yugoslavia.

British Airways
Sava Centar, Milentija Popovića 9,
YU-11070 **Beograd** (Belgrade);
tel. (0 11) 13 86 72.

Intercontinental Hotel,
Ul. Kršnavoga,
YU-41000 **Zagreb;**
tel. (0 41) 44 84 22 and 44 85 11.

International Telephone Codes

From the United Kingdom to Yugoslavia	**010 38**
From the United States or Canada to Yugoslavia	**011 38**
From Yugoslavia to the United Kingdom	**99 44**
From Yugoslavia to the United States or Canada	**99 1**

In dialling an international call the zero prefixed to the local dialling code should be omitted

---

Emergency Calls

Police: dial **92**

Ambulance: dial **94**

The **breakdown service** of the *Yugoslav Automobile Association* (Auto-Moto Savez Jugoslavije, AMSJ) can be summoned from 8 a.m. to 8 p.m., anywhere in the country, by dialling **987**.

Radio messages for tourists

In cases of extreme emergency the Yugoslav radio will transmit messages for visitors travelling in Yugoslavia. Information from the police and motoring organisations.

Baedeker's Travel Guides

"The maps and illustrations are lavish. The arrangement of information (alphabetically by city) makes it easy to use the book."

—San Francisco Examiner-Chronicle

What's there to do and see in foreign countries? Travelers who rely on Baedeker, one of the oldest names in travel literature, will miss nothing. Baedeker's bright red, internationally recognized covers open up to reveal fascinating A-Z directories of cities, towns, and regions, complete with their sights, museums, monuments, cathedrals, castles, gardens and ancestral homes—an approach that gives the traveler a quick and easy way to plan a vacation itinerary.

And Baedekers are filled with over 200 full-color photos and detailed maps, including a full-size, fold-out roadmap for easy vacation driving. Baedeker—the premier name in travel for over 140 years.

Please send me the books checked below and fill in order form on reverse side.

☐ **Austria** $14.95
  0-13-056127-4
☐ **Caribbean** $14.95
  0-13-056143-6
☐ **Egypt** $15.95
  0-13-056358-7
☐ **France** $14.95
  0-13-055814-1
☐ **Germany** $14.95
  0-13-055830-3
☐ **Great Britain** $14.95
  0-13-055855-9
☐ **Greece** $14.95
  0-13-056002-2
☐ **Israel** $14.95
  0-13-056176-2
☐ **Italy** $14.95
  0-13-055897-4
☐ **Japan** $15.95
  0-13-056382-X
☐ **Loire** $9.95
  0-13-056375-7

☐ **Mediterranean Islands** $14.95
  0-13-056862-7
☐ **Mexico** $14.95
  0-13-056069-3
☐ **Netherlands, Belgium, and
  Luxembourg** $14.95
  0-13-056028-6
☐ **Portugal** $14.95
  0-13-056135-5
☐ **Provence/Cote d'Azur** $9.95
  0-13-056938-0
☐ **Rhine** $9.95
  0-13-056466-4
☐ **Scandinavia** $14.95
  0-13-056085-5
☐ **Spain** $14.95
  0-13-055913-X
☐ **Switzerland** $14.95
  0-13-056044-8
☐ **Tuscany** $9.95
  0-13-056482-6
☐ **Yugoslavia** $14.95
  0-13-056184-3

Please turn the page for an order form and a list of additional Baedeker Guides.

A series of city guides filled with colour photographs and detailed maps and floor plans from one of the oldest names in travel publishing:

Please send me the books checked below:

☐ **Amsterdam** $10.95
  0-13-057969-6
☐ **Athens** $10.95
  0-13-057977-7
☐ **Bangkok** $10.95
  0-13-057985-8
☐ **Berlin** $10.95
  0-13-367996-9
☐ **Brussels** $10.95
  0-13-368788-0
☐ **Copenhagen** $10.95
  0-13-057993-9
☐ **Florence** $10.95
  0-13-369505-0
☐ **Frankfurt** $10.95
  0-13-369570-0
☐ **Hamburg** $10.95
  0-13-369687-1
☐ **Hong Kong** $10.95
  0-13-058009-0
☐ **Jerusalem** $10.95
  0-13-058017-1
☐ **London** $10.95
  0-13-058025-2

☐ **Madrid** $10.95
  0-13-058033-3
☐ **Moscow** $10.95
  0-13-058041-4
☐ **Munich** $10.95
  0-13-370370-3
☐ **New York** $10.95
  0-13-058058-9
☐ **Paris** $10.95
  0-13-058066-X
☐ **Rome** $10.95
  0-13-058074-0
☐ **San Francisco** $10.95
  0-13-058082-1
☐ **Singapore** $10.95
  0-13-058090-2
☐ **Tokyo** $10.95
  0-13-058108-9
☐ **Venice** $10.95
  0-13-058116-X
☐ **Vienna** $10.95
  0-13-371303-2

PRENTICE HALL PRESS

Order Department—Travel Books

200 Old Tappan Road

Old Tappan, New Jersey 07675

In U.S. include $1 postage and handling for 1st book, 25¢ each additional book. Outside U.S. $2 and 50¢ respectively.

Enclosed is my check or money order for $_____

NAME_____

ADDRESS_____

CITY_____STATE_____ZIP_____

THE
PAINTED
TABLE

SUZANNE FIELD

THOMAS NELSON
Since 1798

NASHVILLE DALLAS MEXICO CITY RIO DE JANEIRO

Published in Nashville, Tennessee, by Thomas Nelson. Thomas Nelson is a registered trademark of Thomas Nelson, Inc.

Published in association with the literary agency of The Benchmark Group, Nashville, TN: benchmarkgroup1@aol.com.

Thomas Nelson, Inc., titles may be purchased in bulk for educational, business, fundraising, or sales promotional use. For information, please e-mail SpecialMarkets@ ThomasNelson.com.

Scripture quotations marked NIV are taken from the Holy Bible, New International Version®, NIV®. Copyright © 1973, 1978, 1984, 2011 by Biblica, Inc.™ Used by permission of Zondervan. All rights reserved worldwide. www.zondervan.com

Other Scripture quotations are from the King James Version of the Bible.

Library of Congress Control Number: 2013949986

ISBN 978-1-4016-8970-4

Printed in the United States of America

13 14 15 16 17 18 RRD 6 5 4 3 2 1

For my Father

You prepare a table before me
in the presence of my enemies.
You anoint my head with oil;
my cup overflows.

PSALM 23:5 NIV

CONTENTS

THE BEGINNING

1858

Metal teeth rip through the rough, mottled bark and bite into white cambium. Steady strokes saw forward and back, grating, rasping. Two hands push, grate; two hands pull, rasp, lacerating the ring of yellow sapwood. The blade advances, traverses golden heartwood, more sapwood, more cambium, then needs merely to touch the last of the bark.

The sacrificial birch tips, then plummets; its startled branches cry out, rudely raking upright brothers. Severed from stump and root, the tree crashes onto the rich Valdres Valley soil—a brutal amputation, but necessary to be rendered a gift of love.

A gift that will one day be abased, and another day redeemed.

PROLOGUE

1921

A damp, colorless dress, pinned to the clothesline, tosses about in the blustery prairie wind. Arms outstretched, Joann lets the fabric flap against her thin, seven-year-old frame. She aches for her mother's hands that will never again extend from the empty sleeves that twist and turn about her head, caressing her face.

"Momma . . . Momma." The wind snatches away her whispers.

The dress belongs to Joann's oldest sister now. Evelyn began wearing it last month when her own tore beyond repair. It is an ill fit for her; Evelyn at fifteen is more plump than Clara had ever been. Seeing the dress stretching across her sister's frame is a daily offense for Joann. Joann's dress, and four others of various sizes, each faded and threadbare, flutter nearby.

Not far from the line, Evelyn, Maxine, and Dorothy bend to pick stunted vegetables. Their pa warned that the well might go dry if they watered the patch more than every few days. The heat of August is fast approaching and it hasn't rained on the North Dakota prairie since June.

Life on the prairie farm is at once strong and proud, fragile and impoverished. "Not much here today," Evelyn says. "We'll make soup again, plenty of broth." Their buckets hold a few turnips, onions, carrots, and shriveled pole beans. The potatoes are not ready to dig.

Pa and Lars and Rolf have a second pair of work clothes to wear on washday, overalls, faded and patched. But the girls, until the laundry dries, each wear only a chemise undergarment, stitched of muslin by their mother, modest enough to wear in the presence of brothers and Pa. Evelyn pins a shawl over her shoulders to conceal her already ample torso. Pa turns a deaf ear to her embarrassed, whispered requests for a brassiere from the mercantile in Steele.

In the house, carefully folded away in the big black steamer trunk, are six white batiste dresses. They were supplied by generous neighbors so the sisters had "something decent to wear" for their mother's funeral four months earlier. Shortly thereafter, Uncle Jergen, a circuit pastor, came and insisted that all his brother Knute's children be baptized at once. So the "good" dresses were worn a second time.

Beneath the tossing clothing, Joann sinks down onto prickly grass, unaware of a long, black rat snake coiled near the clothesline pole, its yellow eyes trained on her. She watches her pa's two work horses fifty yards away searching in vain for green shoots. Beyond them are fields of parched crops and boundless miles of dry grass. She shields her eyes from the sun and watches the white chickens strut daintily in the barnyard. Once, and only once, Joann had playfully imitated their jerky gait on her rickets-bowed legs.

"Look at me!" she demanded of Maxine. "I'm pretty-walking, like the chickens!"

Maxine snickered. "Those legs of yours will never walk pretty, Joann."

Lars chimed in, "*Cluck-cluck-cluck*, Joann."

Pa and the brothers unload lumber from the wagon, stacking it beside the barn. They returned last evening from a fifty-mile trip to the Valley City lumber mill. The horses had done well to pull the heavy wagonload and had earned their extra oats. Knute is proud of these black muscular giants. "A stronger pair I never seed," he often declares, his English marked by the undulant accent of his native Norwegian.

The unloading is strenuous work for Rolf and Lars, only thirteen and twelve, and small for their age. Every day tests their young muscles. But their pa, an immigrant farmer trying to survive, cannot coddle them. God saw fit to give him only two sons among seven daughters.

Knute Kirkeborg does the work of several men, in spite of one short, lame leg, but the stubborn prairie always asks for more. At times he can be a harsh man, appearing to be angry at the world, when mostly he is angry at himself. He shouldn't have taken his friends' dare to jump from the roof when he was twelve. The mishap caused his right leg to stop growing. Yet he knows it also prompted him to become clever and resourceful.

As a Norwegian boy of seventeen, he heard about earning passage to America by working in the bowels of a freighter. He could have a new life in that promised land across the Atlantic where so many Norwegians had fled. There he could till virgin flatland and grow fields of grain like Norway's mountainous terrain never could. There he could prove himself whole. His godly family was more sorrowful about their oldest son's bitterness over his short leg than his leaving. Leaving for America they could understand. They gave him their blessing.

Knute was handsome and could be beguiling. High cheekbones and an aristocratic nose distracted women from his limp. Making his way west, he met young Clara in Minnesota and quickly won her over. Part French and third-generation American, he deemed her a prize. She accepted his dreams as her own, gathered her belongings into a cedar-lined trunk, made arrangements for her treadle sewing machine to follow, and together they headed out to break the rude soil of central North Dakota.

There, in spite of ever-increasing demands of motherhood, Clara tended well to her domestic tasks. Her food preparation was in the French manner, ingredients chopped finely, not left in chunks common to Scandinavian dishes. Whenever possible, her meals had flavor and color, and she considered *lefse* a poor substitute for bread.

Knute has long talked of building an addition to the barn. Now that he has the lumber, he will need to hurry so they can store extra wheat and oats for the animals come fall. Extra, that is, if it rains. He needs more fodder; he's added a third cow.

As the three lug and pile the rough boards, they pay no heed to a mother partridge rapidly scuttling her young through tall brown grass not fifteen feet away. Neither do they notice the chickens periodically interrupt scratching to cock their heads to listen. Then, with distraught fluttering and squawking, they strut here and there in mindless circles.

Suddenly, there is a bawling. The cows, head-to-tail, are plodding determinedly toward the barn. Why? It's only been a short time since morning milking and many hours until the next. Knute notes the cows, then the frantic chickens. On his good leg, he whirls to the west. *Smoke!* An evil ribbon of black along the horizon stretches as far as can be seen to the north and south.

"Fire! Prairie fire!" he shouts. "Lars! Put da cows in da barn! Rolf! Run get da horses! Hurry!"

Rolf takes off running. Knute and Lars prod the cows. "It's still far off, but dere's a stiff wind!" Pa shouts. "We'll get dem horses harnessed, put 'em to da plow!"

Lars, pale and shaking, gathers up leather harnesses from their place in the barn. "Get da blinders," Knute barks. "Can't let 'em see da fire."

The girls in the garden, and Joann under the clothesline, hear the commotion and see the smoke. Color drains from each face. "Prairie fire! God, spare us!" Evelyn entreats. "Maxine, Dorothy, we've picked enough, we better go to the house." She can only pretend to be calm. "Joann! Joann!" she calls. "Come along now." At an early age, these prairie children learned to recoil when adults spoke of flames, hideous flames, approaching from afar, licking up all creation in their path.

Joann rises from the ground and lunges awkwardly toward the others. Her legs tremble, her heart pounds like a hammer in her chest. The rat snake races past her, slithering purposefully from west to east. Joann sees it, screams, and spurts ahead to grab Dorothy's skirt.

The washtubs and scrub boards outside the house remind Evelyn of the laundry. She thrusts her vegetable pail toward Maxine. "I'll go back for the dresses," she says. "Can't let 'em . . ." She almost says *burn*. "Girls, go in the house," she calls back over her shoulder. "Check on Helen and Francis and then stay inside."

She snatches clothing off the line with an eye on the smoke that now ascends into pillars. Not heeding instruction, the younger sisters gather into a tight huddle, mesmerized by the ominous horizon edging the flatland. Their chatter is high-pitched and nervous. Five-year-old Francis scampers out of the house and Maxine scoops her up. Evelyn hurries toward them, her arms full of laundry. She deposits it in the house and returns to stare wide-eyed with the others. Joann moans with fright and buries her face at Evelyn's waist.

Knute and the brothers manage to catch the horses' unwilling heads, strap on the blinders, and hitch the muscular animals to the plow. They whinny and paw the ground with mighty hooves. A quick check confirms that the wide leather bands are secure. Knute climbs up and stands astride. He slaps the reins and pulls right. "Haw! Haw!" he commands.

The beasts jolt forward and Knute guides them to the western edge of his cleared property, one hundred or more feet beyond the barn. He yanks the lever to lower the plow, and the pull begins. The curved metal teeth dig through the dry earth. He urges the reluctant horses to their full speed and the plow begins to cut a wide swath of ground for a generous distance north, and then south. Back and forth, back and forth he drives them, yelling, straining at the reins with all his might each time they reverse direction. The hard soil looks darker when turned, once again fertile.

Periodically Joann dares lift her head for a quick look. Each glimpse prompts an impassioned wail. "Stop! Fire, go away!"

Dorothy grips the sides of her face. "The barn and the shed," she despairs, "they'd . . . they'd burn up so fast." She doesn't dare speak of the house. Knute built the few wooden buildings with his own hands, finishing the clapboard house only four years before, so his family could finally move out of the sod house. Clara had insisted that raising children in a house of mud and grass was not civilized, even after he limed the inside walls white, hoping to placate her. He had often reminded her that sod houses don't burn.

The boys rush to join the clutch of girls and all stand close, paralyzed. The wind has increased, snatching up and whirling particles of earth. The girls feel the itching sting of dry dirt against their faces and through their thin clothing.

"What's Pa doin'?" demands five-year-old Francis, eyes wide with fright as she struggles in Maxine's firm hold.

Although they are huddled close, Lars yells to her over the howl of the wind, "He's plowin' a firebreak!"

"So we don't burn up," Rolf adds. The boys' voices, which mimic their father's "old country" speech patterns, crack with fear. Rolf is the first to note a sinister stripe of bright orange in the distant sky beneath the black smoke.

"Looks 'bout a mile out," he shouts. "Maybe closer. An' the wind's blow'n' mighty, straight outta the west." In spite of their plight, Rolf, the older brother, sounds proud to announce the information.

It isn't long until the dreaded odor of smoke whips its way across the flatland. They cover their noses. What were whimpers from Joann and Francis are now terrified sobs. Evelyn puts her arms around as many sisters as she can to prod them into the house. She doesn't try to corral the boys, who suddenly, with buffoonery and false bravado, whoop and leap, mimicking the horses, dismissing from their minds that unless the firebreak works or the wind shifts, voracious flames may devour them.

Joann tugs desperately at Evelyn's arm. "We need to run away," she shouts. "Come on, Evelyn, we need to run away!"

"No, Joann, hush now, don't pull on me. There's no place to run," she says.

Joann, in the vise of fear, breaks away from the others and darts into the house. She scuttles across the floor and dives beneath a great sturdy wooden table that dominates the room. She hunkers down on the plank flooring, surrounded by a protective barricade of rough wooden benches. Knute had made the benches crude but serviceable, like the other pieces of rudimentary furniture in the house. Not like the table, with its ornate vine motif carved into the entire length of its apron.

In the doorway, Evelyn casts a last fearful look toward their pa as he cracks his whip in the air. In spite of the blinders, the sweating horses toss their heads indignantly as they strain forward.

"Go! Faster! Faster!" she hears Pa yell.

Evelyn quickly shuts the door and turns to tend to her sisters. Although she is only fifteen, they have been her responsibility since early spring when Clara, their precious, almost continuously pregnant mother, finally proved not strong enough for homestead life. When the ninth baby came, Clara's health gave out.

Evelyn sees that sixteen-month-old Helen is still asleep in her box bed. She considers, for a moment, that she and Dorothy should prepare the vegetables for soup, carry on as if great danger were not rushing toward them. But the smell of smoke is seeping into the house, and with it, panic. Chopping vegetables is out of the question.

"God, save us!" Maxine implores.

Beneath the table, seven-year-old Joann hunches, arms tightly hugging her legs. She repeats the words in a whimper, "God, save us."

The boys tumble into the house, slamming the door behind them. Helen awakens, senses tension, and screams. Evelyn picks her up and paces back and forth, jostling the child on her hip.

From her floor-level view, Joann watches Evelyn's worn brown shoes traverse the room. Always, but at this moment more than ever, Joann craves to be held. But Evelyn, try as she may, is still a girl herself and, like her mother before her, can only do so much.

Maxine, Dorothy, and Francis shove aside the long benches in order to invade Joann's space. Perhaps their awkward runt sister has found some inexplicable safety there where she spends so much time. Joann covers her head with her hands and tries to make herself smaller, although there is room for all. The table is extended by three generously sized leaves.

The girls have noted an aura of mystery around this ancestral table that Uncle Jergen brought to them all the way from Norway some years ago. It had come by steamship, then train, then wagon. They heard Pa tell their mother he hadn't wanted to accept it. Perhaps it reminded him of things he wanted to forget. Only because his brother had come such a long way had he felt obliged to keep it.

Joann found refuge under the table long before Clara died. From here she watched her mother nurse baby Francis, then later, baby Helen. Joann didn't know that for a nutritionally depleted mother, the act of nursing is an arduous sacrifice. Although Clara had little time to give lingering hugs to the older ones, she always spoke kindly to them. No one doubted her love. But Joann's lingering ache for her mother's unavailable embrace prompted her to slip between the table benches, seeking a substitute place of comfort. Still, comfort sometimes embraces her here.

In the night, it is not unusual for Maxine, the largest sister, although not the oldest, to crowd Joann from their shared bed as she turns. In response, more than two years ago Joann began to leave the bed sometimes and, being careful not to bump and topple a bench, wrap herself in a quilt beneath the table in the main room. Here she needn't suffer a knee in her back and she can be alone, until returning before dawn. The space beneath the table, surrounded by a fence of benches, has become a haven. Other than to give occasional ridicule, her daytime visits there are generally ignored by her siblings, who are used to her idiosyncrasies. Her father has never noticed her there.

Rolf and Lars, still in a bewildered mix of exhilaration and hysteria, race back and forth between the two small west-facing windows as they report on the steadily advancing wall of flame.

"Pa's makin' dem horses fly!" Rolf yells.

"Fire's gettin' closer!" Lars screeches. Evelyn grabs his arm, pushes him under the table, and crouches down herself with the crying baby. Rolf follows.

"Don't look out!" Evelyn commands. "Stay down right here. And pray!"

"God, save us! God, save us!"

The house darkens as outside smoke swirls around it, seeps inside, hot. It feels like thistles in their throats. Fists are clenched, as they were when they came into the world.

"Mama, Mama!" Joann cries. Others join in.

"Pa!" Lars whines. "Why don'tcha come in?"

They hear the racing flames roar angrily close. Will they survive this terrible day?

Crack! The west windows, blackened with smoke, break in the heat, intensifying the children's terror. The dark room spins. Joann swoons and slumps into unconsciousness.

The others, terrorized by the sound of the inferno, cough from the smoke and sob, clinging to each other with racing hearts, keeping their eyes tightly shut. *Will the plowed earth stop the fire from reaching the house? Or will the wind carry it over? Are Pa and the horses . . . ? Oh, God!*

When the fire passes, spreading its fury eastward, the roar diminishes. Under the table, what seemed like an eternity has been close to thirty minutes.

Pa. Where's Pa?

They clamber from beneath the table and stumble toward the door, leaving Joann's limp figure behind.

"Open it real slow!" Evelyn orders, dreading what they will see. They spill into the smoke-filled yard, choking in the acrid stench. Through the haze, they see their father near the barn. Black with ash, he leans over the plow seat, retching inhaled smoke. The horses, soaked in sweat, snort as they drink lustily from the watering trough. As far as can be seen, what once were wheat fields now smolder in red and black desolation—all the way up to the freshly turned earth—*but no farther.*

"Pa!" they cry.

Knute steadies himself and raises his head.

They are safe.

"Boys," he calls hoarsely between dry coughs. "Boys. Unhitch da team. Wipe 'em down. Wipe my horses down good."

In the house, time has no boundaries for Joann in her unconsciousness. She sees herself months earlier, hunkered beneath the big table, listening . . .

Knute is urgent. Clara whimpers in protest. There is muffled struggle. What's wrong? She should help her mother—what should she do? She is bewildered, frightened, and engulfed in guilt, knowing instinctively she has heard something she was not meant to hear . . .

The voices drift and return, bringing conversation from a different night. Her father is harsh . . . *"I tell you again, Clara, if this one's a girl, we'll hafta give it away . . ."*

Her mother pleads, cries bitterly . . . *"People have a duty to keep and raise their children, Knute!"*

"I can't hardly feed all the girls I got now, and not one of 'em can do the work of a man. In town I heerd about a couple who want a baby, any baby."

"No, Knute! It will kill me if you give this baby away! It will kill me!" . . .

Joann's dream-like state meanders to a crack of lantern-glow around her father's bedroom door. The bedroom where her mother no longer sleeps . . .

The door opens. Knute, with his uneven stride, goes to Clara's trunk, not seeing that one of his daughters, wrapped in a blanket, is hunched beneath the table, watching. He places an envelope into a box in the trunk and returns to the bedroom. The light around the door goes out . . .

Joann stirs from unconsciousness. For several moments she refreshes her bearings. The fire! She jolts upright. Where are the others? Is she the only one to survive? New panic subsides when she hears her siblings outside. Joyful with relief, she dashes to join them.

Throughout the summer and long after, Joann continues to try to sort out the loss of her mother. Over and over she reviews all she knows: another baby girl was born. Her mother named her Mavis. She remembers the newborn's cry and her mother's hysterical sobs when the next day Pa picked them each up, carried them to the wagon, and drove away. There were stains of birthing blood on her mother's clothing and the bedding she left behind.

He had returned the next day without them, saying they needed to stay in a hospital for a while. He made several trips to Steele during the next weeks, and when he came home he did not answer questions. Finally, one evening Knute told them their mother had died and he had given their baby sister to "someone." He did not say to whom. When they asked Evelyn why their mother had died, Evelyn said simply, "She bled to death."

It was that same night, under the table, that Joann, stunned, had fixed her eyes on a ribbon of light around her parents' bedroom door, refusing to believe that her mother was not there, lying in bed, nursing the new baby. Then she had seen her father come from the bedroom and limp to Clara's trunk and place the envelope in it. Why had he moved so stealthily? At other times, when he rose in the dark to go to the outhouse, he was not particular about being quiet. She knew instinctively that the paper was not for her eyes, yet because it might have something to do with her mother, her curiosity became unbearable. She felt compelled to see it.

She waited several nights for an early morning when the moon was full, casting cold light through the two small west windows. She slipped from beneath the table and padded over to the trunk, cringing, fearing that her brothers in the loft or her sisters behind the blanket covering their door frame might hear. They would scoff, call her crazy, and tell Pa. He might get the razor strap he uses not exclusively on the boys.

She raised the high, curved top of the trunk, releasing the sweet smell of cedar. She saw the carefully folded white batiste dresses. Had her mother looked down from heaven and seen her girls wearing them at her funeral? In a wooden box with a slide-off lid, right on top, Joann found an envelope with handwriting on the front. Her fingers fluttered as she picked it up and tiptoed to a moonlit window. "Certificate of Death, Clara Isabelle Kirkeborg."

Death. Such a hated, incomprehensible thing that had taken her mother away. She pulled a paper from the envelope and tamped down her nervousness in order to absorb the official-looking document. Some of the words she comprehended. Others she made herself memorize, determined to understand them later—"hysteria," "exhaustion from acute mania," and "Hospital for the Insane."

Throughout the next two summers, when infrequent rains come, they often bring hail. Knute's renewed efforts to turn his girls into field workers fail, his sons prove to be barely competent. The proceeds from his farm cannot support his large family. Back in Norway, after his unfortunate accident, herding the family's sheep up rugged mountainsides became too difficult. He'd tried his hand at fishing. Whenever weather permitted, he cast his line into the swift mountain streams with great success. Now, on the parched prairie, he yearns for icy water to rush against his legs. Just a few hundred miles to the east is a place legendary for its lakes and forests. Evelyn can manage without him for a couple of weeks. He heads for northern Minnesota.

On one of the largest and deepest lakes the state has to offer, Knute finds a fishing resort for sale. He buys it on credit and sends a letter to Evelyn, with instructions to bring her five sisters on the train. He includes details of how the boys are to stay behind long enough to oversee transporting the furniture and other belongings. He writes that he is corresponding with another prairie farmer who has an interest in buying the animals. They will have a new home. Knute will be a fishing guide for tourists, his boys can look after equipment and clean the fish, and the girls, he has plenty of girls, will cook in the lodge and clean the cottages.

As preparations are made to leave, Joann stands staring at the big table. For more than two years, the space beneath the ancestral piece has beckoned her, promising solace. In this private, mysterious sanctuary, she communed with impressions and thoughts that would suddenly come to her. Soothing thoughts, she believed, came from her mother. She could not guess the origin of others, those that made her heart race and her hands clammy. Those that magnified her young life bereft of love. It has been under this table that she has seen things she was not meant to see, heard things she was not meant to hear. It is the place where the words she read on her mother's Certificate of Death embedded themselves into her psyche. Words that would hound her forever.

CHAPTER ONE

THE DRAFT NOTICE

1943

Joann looks down two stories from behind her gauze-curtained window. She watches absently as a twenty-ton behemoth snorts, grinds gears, and backs onto the sidewalk below. She often stands here, hoping to catch a cool breeze and eager for the first glimpse of her husband returning from the dairy. Even when it's too early, just seeing the street that will carry his ten-year-old Chevrolet comforts her.

Two sooty figures hasten to guide a shiny chute toward an open basement window. The beast revs, squeals, and tips its midsection high into the air. Black lumps of coal rumble, plummet, then crash through the chute. Only when lusty screams come from the nearby bedroom does Joann return to the moment and realize that the scene below is odd. A coal delivery in June? This war! Nothing is normal anymore.

She rushes into the bedroom to shut the window beyond the crib. The frightened face of her almost-two-year-old pushes against the slats. Her mother snatches her up, holds her awkwardly.

"Don't be afraid, Saffee. It's just coal to keep Daddy's little girl warm when winter comes." She speaks without mother-to-baby nuance. The screaming does not abate. Joann places her on the double bed, sits down nearby, and bounces. "Sa-ffee, Sa-ffee, Sa-ffee." The baby is not quieted.

She stops the bouncing and tries reasoning. "Maybe the coal men have to come now. They might be off to war by winter, just like . . . just like . . . your daddy."

The next afternoon when the child awakes, she screams again. Sweat-soaked, she buries her head in her mother's shoulder, hiding her eyes from the window, even though now the shade is pulled and the limp curtains drawn shut.

Why is her baby crying? "Sapphire! Stop!"

Joann hadn't desired a baby. She had never been fond of babies. But she had wanted Nels—and having a baby came along with having him. Neither gave a thought to the fact that he would be a father who had been essentially fatherless, and likewise, she a mother who had been essentially motherless.

The nurse had pestered her to declare a name for the birth certificate. From her recovery bed, Joann thought about it for three days, until the evening she peered out at a deepening blue summer sky, its first stars twinkling.

Sapphire, that's it. Like the sky. Or even better, Sapphira.

"What could be more romantic than being named for the wild beauty of a night sky?" she had gushed to Nels. He arched one eyebrow and scratched his head.

"Oh, Nels, you just don't have a flair for the dramatic like I do."

She was right. He was used to down-home names like those of his sisters, Bertha, Ida, and Cora. No highfalutin names, those. Still, he gazed at her with tenderness and pride, his wife-become-mother.

"You name 'er whatever you want, honey," he said. "Just so you like it, that's the important thing."

The nurse wrinkled her nose. "Sapph*ira*? Isn't that someone in the Bible?"

"Oh yes! I think so. Probably a beautiful queen!" Joann chortled.

"No, Mrs. Kvaale, I sort of remember maybe she was a bad person."

The hospital chaplain confirmed that the nurse was correct.

Later, when Joann noticed her baby's eyes were indeed blue, and not knowing they would soon turn to hazel, she settled on Sapphire Eve. "It was meant to be," she said. "When I saw that blue evening sky, I just knew."

The ink was hardly dry when she regretted the choice, but couldn't say exactly why. Perhaps it was the "fire" sound of it. Later, as she leaned over the bathtub, scrubbing stubborn stains from diapers and flinching at hungry cries from the crib, she decided that Sapphire was too fine a name for this baby. The beauty of an evening sky, indeed. She began to call her Saffee.

Every morning Nels leaves their small apartment before dawn to deliver glass bottles of milk door-to-door, returning in the late afternoon. The dairy job alone would be enough to cover their expenses, but the apartment building's aging owner had inquired if Nels might assist with caretaking in exchange for rent. "It'll just mean keepin' the furnace stoked in winter an' the front grass cut in summer, an' a few other things. Nothin' much," Mr. Resslar said. Nels agreed, even before asking about the "few other things," which turned out to be shoveling snow, burning trash, and trimming the front hedges.

Stoking the furnace only sounded easy. Every cold morning, which in Minnesota is almost every morning of fall, winter, and spring, Nels hurries into coveralls at 4:00 a.m. and heads for the basement. He shovels out yesterday's clinkers from the gaping boiler belly and shovels in new coal until it again belches heat. The task takes almost an hour. He barely has time to clean up, slip into his whites, eat breakfast, and get to the dairy by 5:45 a.m.

As each day wears on, Joann keeps an eye on the clock and goes to the front windows a dozen or so times. She misses him when he's gone, worries about him, craves his affection.

It's almost four o'clock. Joann tucks the ironing board into its alcove in the kitchen and lowers the burner under a simmering chicken. Cooking is a skill Joann is teaching herself. When her family moved to northern Minnesota, her older sisters cooked for the resort guests; Joann and the younger girls cleaned cottages. Knute maintained this arrangement until each girl was eighteen. Only then could they begin high school.

Those resort years, like the prairie years before, took a toll on everyone in Joann's family. And they took Knute's life—he drowned in a boating accident a month after Joann left home.

Humming along with a Sousa march, compliments of WCCO, Joann carries Nels's freshly pressed white uniform toward the bedroom.

"It's almost time for Daddy to come home!" she calls to Saffee, who is sprawled on the living room carpet, chewing and drooling on a rubber teething ring.

"Da-ddy!" the toddler says brightly through a flow of saliva.

Joann hangs the uniform in the closet and pauses at the bureau mirror to run a brush through her dark curls. She turns her face this way and that, at once vain and highly self-critical, then returns to her post at the living room window. From it she can watch mothers push babies in buggies, and men with hats and business suits hurry to what must be very important appointments. She's noted that some pass by about the same time each day. If they would look up, they might see her.

Someone is coming in the main entrance. She moves nearer the door, head tilted to one side. It's the two old gossips from the first floor. Who are they chewing up and spitting out today? Their voices fade.

With Nels due any minute, military music is not the mood Joann desires. She sits down at the desk and turns the radio dial.

"*. . . moments in the moonlight, moments of love . . . lost in the thrill . . .*"

Ahh, much better—the velvety voice of that new crooner, Frank somebody.

She draws their wedding photograph toward her across the desktop, leaning forward to give it close inspection. How many times has she wished she could readjust the veil of her white satin hat? Why hadn't the photographer told her it fell crookedly across her forehead? The gardenia corsage against the navy blue suit looks lovely. She still recalls its fragrance.

She studies the groom's solemn face and, as always, sighs. If she would have only known why her usually jovial Nels had been so out of character that day, she could have set matters straight. His mood remained alarmingly dark for two weeks after the wedding. Only a few days earlier he had been ecstatic, flushed with anticipation. But when he showed up at the church, he was irritable, said he was sick. After the ceremony he didn't want their picture taken. But the photographer was waiting.

Looking at the photo, Joann lets her mind range over the disappointing first days of marriage when she wondered why he spoke to her so harshly, wondered what had happened to his ardor . . .

"Hold me, Nels. Hold me. I thought you loved me."

Her quandary continued until the day he came home from work and found her napping on the couch. She propped herself up on an elbow, brushed away damp stray locks of hair from her face, and said apologetically, "I'm always more tired during . . . well"—she wasn't sure how to say it—"during . . . my time of the month."

Nels's jaw dropped. He fell to his knees beside her, pulled her to him, embracing her so tightly she thought he might hurt her. "I thought . . . I thought maybe . . . I'm so sorry! I've treated you so bad." A sob escaped him. He reddened and quickly wiped his eyes on his sleeve.

Joann, stunned by the disclosure, freed herself from his arms and sat upright. He took her face in his hands. "Joann, tell me you're mine, all mine, and never . . . never been with another man."

"Nels! Of course I haven't! Why did you even think it?"

He told her that when they had moved up the wedding date from

September to May, the boys at the dairy called him a "rube" and, in so many words, said she was in "a family way." They teased that her father might show up at the wedding with a shotgun. At first Nels was mad, then he began to believe them. He recalled how popular she was at the dances. There was a flirty way about her. He had seen the guys looking at her, whistling when she passed by.

Now, almost three years later, Joann is oddly conflicted. Although the memory is embarrassing, she can't resist a grin. She has to admit she enjoyed all the attention she got at the Friendship Club dances. She'd never had anyone's notice until she left home and came to St. Paul. Her bent "chicken legs" had filled out. They are not shapely, but they love to dance. When she realized her curves brought attention, she naively became a flirt, making sure it was all flash and no fire. She had never wanted to cause Nels any hurt.

Nels couldn't dance well if his life depended on it, and his grammar is atrocious. She can understand the reason for his grammar, he having been raised in a Norwegian-speaking home, but she cannot excuse it. Joann, like all of Clara's daughters, speaks good English, without the accent Knute passed on to his boys.

When Joann was obligated to exchange school for the dirty linens of fishermen, a sympathetic teacher occasionally brought her books of poetry. From then on, Joann steeped herself in rhyme. So it is not unusual that as she looks at the wedding photo she says, "Oh, Nels, 'How do I love you? Let me count the ways.'"

She's loved Nels from the beginning for his unreserved devotion to her, his sunny disposition, and his talk of getting ahead in life in spite of humble beginnings and lack of education. He was a good man, so there seemed no reason to delay marriage. She insisted on moving up the wedding date, unable to bear the thought that he might slip away. If only she had known . . . Thank goodness, since those first regrettable days Nels has continuously showered her with the affection she had hoped for, and twelve months into the marriage, their baby was born.

Saffee whimpers and looks for something else to gum. Spying the cotton teddy bear Joann made for her, she toddles across the room.

At the desk, another romantic melody scatters its stardust while Joann studies a second photograph. It is a portrait of Nels, displaying his engaging smile and prominent teeth. She had insisted he have the picture taken last summer to capture what he really looks like. With a sigh, she puts the wedding photo into a drawer. She's tired of seeing that veil askew.

She hears Nels on the stairway. Smoothing her carefully curled hair, she hurries to the door, eager for him to embrace her tightly, as he always does. She is surprised when his hug is perfunctory. He tosses his white cap and sinks into the secondhand sofa, ignoring his daughter's uplifted arms.

"It came," he says simply, waving an envelope in her direction.

"Oh, Nels." She switches off the radio and rushes to sit beside him.

"It says report for duty at Fort Snelling. Monday."

"Monday! So soon?"

Joann opens the letter addressed to Nelson Kvaale. She reads one word: "Greetings," and looks at him pleadingly.

"I was hoping . . . I was hoping you'd be deferred awhile longer . . . because . . . because of the baby . . . I don't want you to go, Nels."

"You know I hafta go, Joann . . . it's the right thing to do. But I've decided something."

He tells her that the draft board at Fort Snelling is only taking men for the army now. He's decided he wants navy and he will tell that to the board. Too many American boys are dying in foxholes over in Europe, he says. He'll take his chances in the Pacific.

The baby plops onto the floor at his feet and tugs at his shoelaces. He reaches down. "Come up here, Sapphire, up to Daddy." He lifts her onto his lap and she snuggles against him, wiping a wet chin on his shirt. Nels puts his lean, sinewy arms around his little family and holds them close. Joann begins to weep.

"Now, Muzzy." For some reason he'd given her this nickname after Saffee was born.

"Don't cry. It won't do no good." She is numb.

Saffee squirms, wiggles off Nels's lap, and slides down to the floor. Noticing her, and seeking diversion from news she cannot yet absorb, Joann bemoans her recent frustrations with the fussy baby, especially when the coal delivery frightened her.

Nels interrupts. "The coal came?" Not expecting it this early, he had pushed the bin away from the chute when he swept the basement. The floor must be covered with coal. Tomorrow he'll need to rise early and shovel it up before the building owner discovers it. He sighs.

"It's a few minutes to news time," he says. She gets up and switches on the radio again. Ever since the war started he's never missed the five o'clock broadcast.

"That's Glenn Miller," she says, trying to steady her voice. "Makes me think of the night we met." She sits down at his side, puts her head on his shoulder as they listen and remember.

"New Year's Eve, the Friendship Club," he says, stroking her arm. "As soon as I saw you, you were mine. Even if those other fellas were thick as flies 'round you. You sure had a way of attractin' 'em. But I knew you'd end up with me."

Holding his hand, Joann feels a rush of gratitude that he completely forgave her for causing suspicion in those early days. Now she is sorry she brought up the past at all. He continues the reminiscence, telling her she had looked pretty good in "that there" red sweater.

"Pretty good?"

"Well, no. Gorgeous." He turns serious again. "Yeah," he says, "and when I'm gone, promise to keep yourself, well, covered up with somethin' when you're out, okay?"

Flattered, because she knows she attracts male attention, she says, "What should I wear, a tent?"

The brief levity passes. Drafted. He'll be leaving. Joann puts her face into her hands and sobs.

At their feet, Saffee whimpers and raises chubby arms. "Up, Daddy, up!"

About nine they ready for bed, speaking low so as not to wake the little one in her crib. Nels sets the alarm clock for three thirty.

At 12:50 a.m., Joann still tosses in their bed. With whiffling snores, Nels embraces sleep with the same enthusiasm he gives his waking hours. How can he sleep tonight, knowing he's going off to war? She's already lost both mother and father. By her own choice she's essentially lost her siblings. And now Nels? She presses her hands against her face, sensing her irregular breathing. Across the room, the baby sighs in slumber.

From the start, Joann hated the idea of Nels shoveling coal into a hot furnace.

"But, Joann," he countered, "it's not dangerous. In fact, it's a *wunnerful* thing! Who else gets free rent nowadays?"

She relented, but regularly cautions him to be careful around the flames.

As she listens to his breathing, she worries that Mr. Resslar will ask her and the baby to move out when his stoker leaves for war. How will she live without Nels? She's even lonely when he's at work.

Tomorrow he'll get up . . . so early . . . She finally drifts into troubled sleep . . .

"Joann! Joann!" . . .

. . . and a new episode of her recurring nightmare . . .

Nels scoops flames, tosses, shovels, tosses, shovels . . . Joann is propelled toward the hideous conflagration . . . "Nels! Nels! Hide me!" . . . Burned faces sneer, taunt, laugh . . . Tongues of fire uncoil, lick at her . . . Armies of menacing, charred figures march lockstep . . . "Hide me! Please hide me! Where can I hide?" . . .

Joann slams upright, hands grip sheets, breath heaves to expel imagined, smothering smoke. *Who is crying? Her mother? Her sisters? Who is burning?* She bounds from the bed unsteadily, crazily.

"I'm coming! I'm coming!" With heart pounding, she snatches up her startled baby from the crib, holds her tightly in the darkness, and slumps against the wall.

Encroaching fear advances like a cancer.

CHAPTER TWO

WAR

A t the door early Monday morning, she clings to him. "Now, sweetheart," Nels pleads, "don'tcha go worryin'. Today is only the meetin' with the draft board. I'll call you before they pack me off to boot camp." But Joann doesn't try to be brave. He cups her face in his hands as they kiss; she wills it is not their last.

By the time he calls Wednesday night, she is frantic. "I've been so worried! Why haven't you called sooner?"

He tries to soothe her. Tells her that in the military everything takes a long time and there are always long lines of inductees at the telephones. "But guess what? I'm a navy man!" He sounds proud. "Took three days of arguin' with the Fort Snelling draft board, but in the end, I won." He will go to Idaho for boot camp, he says. To a place called Farragut. He leaves tonight.

"Tonight? How can you sound happy about it?" she demands, one hand gripping the receiver, the other clenching and unclenching.

"Oh, now, Joann. You know I'm not happy 'bout goin' to war or leavin' you; just happy I won the argument so I don't have to go to the fightin' over in Europe. Besides, bein' a sailor suits me more."

"*Suits* you!" She abruptly stands to her feet. "How can anything about going off to war *suit* you?" Just as abruptly, she sits again, rubbing her temple. Doesn't he understand? He is her life.

Nels tells her it must be done. "But it's going to be so *hard*!" she whines. "For me too, you know."

There's a painful silence. She attempts to pull herself together and asks how he convinced the draft board to transfer him to the navy. He says that after three days a sergeant got tired of his face and stamped his papers.

Her fingers race through her hair. "What does that mean?"

Nels hesitates. "Well, they might have it in fer me."

She tightens her grip on the receiver. "*In* for you?"

He tells her that when the navy sees that the army didn't take him, they might think he is a troublemaker. The sergeant told him that as a consequence, he might be assigned to hazardous duty.

She catches her breath. "*Hazardous*? Like what?"

He cautions her not to "go gettin' upset." He tells her, then wishes he hadn't, that he might be assigned to a ship that carries ammunition. One, he supposes, "that's a prime target fer Japs."

"*No!*" The room swims. She feels faint.

"Ah, gee, Joann, now don'tcha go worryin'. Oh, an' everythin's secret, a course, so don't go tellin' nothin' I said. It's time to catch the train. I'll write ya every day, Joann. Promise. I love you."

Joann pleads with Nels's mother. Will she keep Saffee at the farm? It won't be for long, just until she finds a job in San Francisco. She can't possibly care for a child and job hunt at the same time. Why is she going? She must be near the ocean so she can see Nels when he gets shore leave—he's on an ammunition ship and she hasn't seen him for months. She can hardly stand the worry. She'll come back on the train for her, maybe by Christmas. Saffee's well behaved for just turning three years old. She'll love the country, the chickens, the kittens in the barn. There's one thing, though—can she have her own cup to drink from instead of sharing the dipper on the water crock? Oh, and, of course, the outhouse, no place for a child—can she have a chamber pot inside? Good. It's settled then.

Good-bye, little one, be a good girl, do what your grandmother tells you. I'm going to the edge of the war to see your daddy. I'll be back for you.

CHAPTER THREE

SAN FRANCISCO

Joann had tried to make Saffee look acceptable, choosing her best dress, a blue-and-white stripe. But now it is travel-rumpled and barely reaches the top of the little girl's stocky legs. She's grown taller during their separation.

On the three-day train ride, Joann had coached her. "Now remember," she said, "you can't make any noise at Pearlmans'. They aren't used to noise. And don't make any mess—I have enough to do. I wonder if anyone's cleaned while I've been gone. I can't imagine anyone washed the floors."

They step through the service entrance into the huge kitchen of the stately house. Saffee surveys the black-and-white tile floor and whispers loudly, "Yer right, Mommy. Dis floor's dur-rty."

Maude, Joann's seventyish, aristocratic employer, is brewing tea. Hearing the comment, she looks up, startled, appraises the child, then chuckles. "Well! Joann! I daresay it's good you're back."

For three months, Joann was Maude's housekeeper and caregiver for her one-hundred-year-old mother, Grandma Pearlman, before she revealed she had a three-year-old back in Minnesota. Hoping to have proved herself an able employee, she finally dared ask to retrieve her daughter by train, promising that Sapphire would present no trouble in the home. She would be seen and not heard. Well, if they wish, her daughter would not be seen either.

Seen and not heard. Like the child Joann, under a table.

Maude and her husband, Henry, object to her leaving for even a few days. How could they get on without her? Grandma Pearlman needs constant care. And there's the cleaning and the laundry—especially the laundry—Grandma's bed needs constant attention. Well, perhaps Dora, the night aide, can stay around the clock a few days. Can Joann be back in a week?

True to the agreement, Saffee is usually hidden away in the Pearlman house. By day, she stays alone in the small bedroom where mother and daughter share a narrow bed. She gazes wistfully out the window, seeing little more than the side of the next house. She peeps out the door and listens to distant conversation and the clatter of household routine that echoes, retreats, then returns. She traces the knobby rows on the chenille bedspread with her finger, counting. But five is as far as her knowledge of numbers goes.

In other regions of the house, Joann attends to Grandma Pearlman's every need and every whim. At night, she is too exhausted to play or even talk much with a lonesome daughter.

It isn't long before Dora quits the night shift and Joann is on call around the clock. When the buzzer sounds, as it does numerous times in the night, she leaves the bedroom to attend to duty. Saffee also awakens, since she is often not tired enough to sleep deeply at the end of an inactive day.

Occasionally, as Grandma Pearlman sits staring out at the winter rain, she remembers that somewhere in the house is a child and asks Joann to bring her. When Saffee arrives, the old woman has usually nodded off, her head bent alarmingly to the side. If she is awake, she puts a dry, blue-veined hand on Saffee's arm and speaks to her briefly in a querulous voice. The conversation is always the same. Grandma Pearlman admonishes Saffee to always "be good" and obey her mother. Saffee shyly dips her head and doesn't speak.

"Well, what do you say, girlie-girl?"

Puzzled, Saffee says, "Nothin'."

"Nothing?" Grandma Pearlman furrows her brow. "Hasn't your mother taught you manners? It's best to say, 'Yes, ma'am,' not . . ." The old woman pauses, struggles to find the pocket of her black shawl, and brings forth a handkerchief to wipe away escaping spittle.

"So," she demands again, "are you going to be a good girl?"

Saffee guesses she should offer a "yes, ma'am," but the unfamiliar words won't come.

For a few moments, Grandma Pearlman's eyes seem to penetrate Saffee's face. Then the old woman sighs, again fatigued. Saffee stands quietly at her side, wondering why Grandma Pearlman looks as she does, smells as she does. She waits until the gray head falls forward in slumber and then she walks away.

When Easter approaches, Henry and Maude make plans to invite their two great-grandchildren for Easter dinner. On Saturday morning, Henry spends considerable time in the backyard. About noon, Joann rushes into the bedroom. All she can see of Saffee are her high-top white shoes sticking out from under the bed where the girl is studying a parade of ants.

"Saffee, get out from under there, quick! Mr. Henry says he wants to show you something." She pulls Saffee by the ankles, helps her up, and brushes off her dusty dress. Joann leads her daughter out through the back door, trying to smooth her hair as they hurry.

Stepping into the squinty sunlight, Saffee sees tall, bony Mr. Henry smiling proudly as he surveys a thornbush. The sun sparkles on hundreds of sugared gumdrops that the man has laboriously stuck onto every thorn he could find. Saffee catches her breath at the thrilling sight and steps closer.

"Oh! It's candy!" she says. She reaches out an eager hand and pulls off one luscious piece.

"No! No! It's not for you! It's for my Philip and Katherine. They're coming tomorrow." Mr. Henry, suddenly embarrassed, glances at

Joann. "Oh . . . well. You can keep it, of course . . . yes, you may have one."

Saffee steps back quickly and hesitantly puts the soft, sweet treat into her mouth. Although seen through welling tears, the gumdrop tree is the most tantalizingly beautiful thing she has ever beheld.

But it is for someone else.

"Saffee, hurry up now, eat your oatmeal," Joann says as she stands at the kitchen sink filling Grandma Pearlman's water pitcher. "I see Beanie coming up the walk." Even after a year, Beanie, the sizable, middle-aged Irish woman the Pearlmans call "Cook," is not used to having a child "underfoot" in her kitchen at mealtime.

Beanie doesn't usually move fast, but today she bursts into the kitchen and blurts, "Joann, where'd you say that man a yours is at?"

Alarmed, Joann almost lets the pitcher slip from her hands. "He's on a navy ship."

"I know—but where's the ship exactly now?"

"I don't know, his letters can't tell me where it goes. Everything's secret in war. What's the matter, Beanie? Tell me!"

Saffee pauses her spoon in midair listening to the distressed exchange.

"Oooh," Beanie moans, shaking her hands up and down as if that will help her to think more clearly. "Well, what's the *name* of the ship he's on?"

"Nels told me not to tell anyone. He said no reckless talk." Desperate to know Beanie's news, and knowing that his ship is the USS *Alamosa*, Joann reveals, "His ship starts with the letter *A*."

"Saints be praised." Beanie sinks into a chair at the table across from Saffee as if to catch her breath. She tells Joann that her husband, Johnny, was on his way home from the rail yards near Suisun Bay at ten o'clock the night before and heard "a terrible 'splosion." She says it was "one a them 'munition ships," but she can't remember its name. "It was *Byron* or *Bryan*, or somethin'. Yeah, that's it, the USS *Bryan*. I *knew* it din't start with *A*. Blew up high in the air when they were loadin' it. Johnny sez that's only 'bout twenty-five mile from here. Didju hear it?"

"I must have been asleep," Joann says, her head bent in relief. The pitcher is overflowing. She leans weakly against the sink and turns off the tap.

Not comprehending the conversation, Saffee says, "Mommy, when we gonna have shigger again? I like shigger on my oatmeal."

Lacking no drama, Beanie continues her report, telling Joann she heard that the explosion had lit up the sky like red and orange fireworks. Her husband wouldn't be surprised if everyone in the area had burned. Joann is shaking. She sinks into the chair beside Saffee and through clenched teeth declares, "I hate this war."

"Mommy!" Saffee hits her spoon against the cereal bowl, splashing milk.

"Saffee, stop it!" Joann snaps. "Maybe we'll have sugar when the war's over." Then more softly, "I hope."

Beanie stands and puts her plump arms around Joann. "Sorry to give ya such a scare, Joann."

"Thanks, Beanie. It's okay."

It's been a long time since anyone has offered Joann a comforting embrace. When will her man hold her again? A ship blew up, an ammunition ship. *"Hazardous,"* he had said. What an awful word.

CHAPTER FOUR

SHORE LEAVE

1944

In the middle of the night, Saffee often awakens to see Joann rereading letters from Nels. When a packet of mail arrives about every two or three weeks, Joann eagerly tears them open and cries. Having no one else with whom to share her lonesomeness, she sometimes reads to Saffee, even though all the child understands is that her daddy is gone and her mother is sad. At such times especially, Saffee, like the young Joann, yearns to be held, but her mother is too tired, too stressed to realize it.

"'The sun is so hot on deck we don't wear shirts and we look like lobsters,'" Joann reads to Saffee one evening. "'I wonder if I'll ever get used to the constant pounding of the ship's ingine and the rope hamick they spect us to sleep in.'"

Joann is sorry about her husband's discomforts, but in addition, Nels's substandard English continues to be a source of consternation. "Oh dear," she laments to Saffee, "your daddy doesn't spell any better than he talks." She'd naively assumed before they married that she would teach him a thing or two in that department.

He writes about the "rough charcters" he serves with, and how he seems to find more favor with "the brass" than they do, getting recognition for his eagerness to do well. Although the ship is camouflaged as a merchant vessel, there are opportunities to "fire our big guns" at the enemy. He's not a very good shot yet, he writes.

One letter relates that a Japanese radio station plays American music over the intercom by day and at night broadcasts the sultry voice of a woman named Tokyo Rose, who coos steamy, generalized accusations of GI wives misbehaving back home.

"I know it's propaganda to brake down our morale," Nels writes, "but sometimes the other men on bored get pretty riled up by it. I'm just glad I don't have to worry about you, Joann. I know our love will never be corrupted, no matter what crazy Rose and these guys say."

One day, poring over a newly arrived letter, Joann exclaims, "As if *being* on an ammunition ship isn't bad enough, *now* he tells me it's manned by *criminals* released from prisons!" Looking at Saffee, but not seeing her, Joann's voice falls to a strained whisper. "Japanese subs thick as the fish in the water . . . crazy bombers in the air . . . and now *criminals* right on his ship. Maybe the military doesn't mind losing *them*—but what about my Nels?"

Alarmed by her mother's distress, Saffee asks, "Mommy, what's a crim-nal?"

Joann rips open the next letter. It contains more disappointment. He's getting shore leave in Portland, Oregon, not in San Francisco! She drops the letter and puts her head into her hands.

"Joann." Maude straightens to full height, somewhat taller than her housekeeper. "Of course I understand you want to see your husband, but remember, we already let you go several days to get your girl, and now you want to leave again? I hardly think you'd expect *us* to keep . . ."

Joann interrupts, her words tumbling rapidly as she pleads. "You know that Sapphire doesn't get in the way at all and she's very quiet. The train trip only takes one day, I'll stay the next day, and then I'll come right back."

"That would be three days. My goodness." Maude folds her arms across her narrow chest and takes a few steps away as she ponders the situation. "This war is so disruptive," she says under her breath. "Gasoline rationing. Food shortages. And now the help . . ." She turns around and says more gently, "Please stop wringing your hands, Joann. I'll discuss it with Mr. Henry and let you know."

Maude and her husband give their reluctant permission for Joann to take a three-day trip to Portland, leaving Saffee at the house. Joann meets Nels and they spend fifteen hours together, mostly at an inexpensive waterfront hotel. When she returns, she is pregnant.

"Mommy! I rode an elephant! I rode an elephant with Mr. Henry!"

"I know, Saffee. I know. You've told me five times." Joann is surprised, and pleased, that Maude and Mr. Henry treated her little girl to the zoo. Saffee had had the time of her young life, and the unexpected gesture makes Joann feel less guilty for leaving "Daddy's little girl" behind when she went to Portland.

A few weeks later, when she is certain, Joann excitedly writes to Nels about the baby.

Maybe this one will be a boy! Nine months from Portland is sometime in May. Please come home by then, Darling! His name will be Nels Jr., of course. But if it's a girl, I think May would be a good name, don't you?

He answers.

A family of four—wow! I'm trying to imajine us with two kids. I hope

I'll be able to get my job back at the dairy after the war. I hear it's against the law for GI's jobs to disppear. Take good care of yourself, sweetheart. I wish you didn't have to work so hard. Remember, I'm gonna live thru this war and be back to take care of everything—and everybody. I hope I get there before the new baby does.

Joann conceals her pregnancy from Maude and the others as long as she can. But halfway into the fourth month, fatigue and a ballooning belly rule she must tell. Not eager to house a woman in "that condition," especially whose husband is nowhere to be seen, the Pearlmans quickly decide she will have to leave. They offer to help her find an apartment. Joann has saved almost every penny she has made under their employ, as well as Nels's pay that arrives every month. She is prepared to make do, at least financially.

On her last day, Grandma Pearlman is irritable and refuses to say good-bye to Joann. "Who knows what your replacement will be like?" she whines. But with her slender, blue-veined hand, she motions Saffee to draw closer and lifts a tissue-paper-wrapped package from her lap.

"This is one of my milk-glass plates," she warbles. "I'm a hundred and one years old now, and this plate is as old as I am. It's for you, girlie-girl. Don't break it." Glancing at Joann, she adds, "Your mother will take care of it for you."

Not sure how she should express her delight, Saffee grins broadly and says, "Yes, ma'am."

Joann and Saffee move to a sunbaked, stucco apartment building built into a typically steep San Francisco hillside. They settle into a top-floor, two-room unit, accessed by an outdoor stairway. When the

Murphy bed is lowered in the living room, it fills most of the space. There is a window seat where mother and daughter look far into the distance, all the way to a sliver of ocean where a man they know crisscrosses dangerous waters. The kitchen is just large enough for a two-burner stove, an icebox, and a small table. In this private, pleasant place, while they wait for the baby, and in spite of Nels's absence and the demands war has placed upon Joann, Saffee and her mother have the best months they will ever have together.

CHAPTER FIVE

THE BABY SISTER

Mairzy doats and dozy doats and liddle lamzy divvy. A kiddley divey too, wouldn't you?"

"Sing it again, Mommy! Sing it again!" Saffee begs, laughing and bouncing on the Murphy bed. Joann repeats the song, enjoying its silliness as much as Saffee.

"What are you singing, Mommy? Tell me!"

"If the words sound queer and funny to your ear, a little bit jumbled and jivey, sing, 'Mares eat oats and does eat oats and little lambs eat ivy.'"

It still doesn't make much sense to her, but Saffee happily joins in the next round of *"A kiddley divey too, wouldn't you?"*

Singing each evening as they lounge on the bed, their spirits lift in a magical way. Mixing off-key voices with laughter, Joann sings in something of an alto range and Saffee mimics with her four-year-old lilt. They sing as loudly as they dare, bouncing gently in time on the bed, in deference to Joann's "condition."

"My Bonnie lies over the ocean, my Bonnie lies over the sea . . . Oh, bring back my Bonnie . . ."

When they tire of singing, Joann reads poetry.

And they wonder, as waiting those long years through
In the dust of that little chair,
What has become of the Little Boy Blue
Since he kissed them and put them there.

Joann weaves a blue ribbon through the cloverleaf-shaped cut-outs around the edge of Grandma Pearlman's milk-glass plate and places it on a shelf above the sofa. Saffee beams. The beautiful plate is something of her very own.

While Saffee naps, Joann, a study in loneliness, spends more and more time at the window seat. Pairs of chatting women, most likely military wives, stroll with their young children along the pine-needle-strewn path of the wooded hillside next to the building. Joann notices the seeming ease in which they converse. Occasionally, at the bathroom mirror, she enters into barely audible, imagined con-versations with these unsuspecting women. She refrains from such dialogue when Saffee is nearby.

Indulging her weaknesses, Joann rarely suggests that she and Saffee leave the apartment. When they do venture out for short walks on the hillside path, Joann stays on the alert for dogs and averts her eyes from passersby. She can't hide her bulging middle, but she tries to mask her insecurities with head-held-high aloofness, all the while holding tightly to her little girl's hand.

When a friendly neighbor invites Saffee to her son's birthday party, Saffee cries and adamantly refuses to go. In front of the boy's mother, for appearances' sake, Joann briefly insists that Saffee should agree to go. But, of course, she cannot. The left-out mother has taught her daughter to be a left-out child. In her four years, she has never been in the company of other children.

It is no coincidence that one of their favorite songs goes:

Oh, little playmate, come out and play with me,
And bring your dollies three,

Climb up my apple tree.
Look down my rain barrel,
Slide down my cellar door,
And we'll be jolly friends, forevermore . . .
I'm sorry, playmate, I cannot play with you,
My dollies have the flu,
Boo-hoo-hoo-hoo . . .

To prepare for the baby, Joann and Saffee, holding hands, brave a cable car ride to a downtown department store. They return with infant clothing and diapers.

In late March, Joann feels cramping. It's too soon. She telephones a San Francisco hospital for advice and a nurse tells her to go to bed and stay there. She is not reassured.

How can she manage? Who will buy groceries? She's been concerned for some time about who will care for Sapphire when it's time to go to the hospital by taxi. She knows instinctively that this is the kind of thing family is designed for. But she, like most all her sisters, had left the family the day after graduating from high school. Run away from home and each other. Blown to the wind. For Joann, and, she suspects, for the others also, by then it was too late to bond, to behave like a family. Joann had taken a bus to a new season, a fresh life in St. Paul that brought her a little fun, a husband, and a child. She had no intention of ever again communicating with family. Especially Maxine. Especially Rolf. But now, alone and afraid, she must think about them again.

Of the sisters, Dorothy, although imperious at times, had been the only sibling who was not exactly kind, but at least tolerant. She wrote Joann a couple of letters that she has kept but did not answer. She shuffles through her stationery box. Yes, the first one has a phone number.

Perhaps Dorothy will be willing to help. She knows how hard it is to have a husband in the Pacific; her George is an officer on the

USS *Ticonderoga*. She is living, she wrote, with her two children, in the home of a cousin in Iowa for the duration of the war.

Hoping for a miracle, Joann calls and pleads with her to come. Dorothy, a more capable woman than Joann, agrees to leave her children for a short time in the care of the cousin and take the train to California. Until she arrives, Joann is beside herself. From her bed, she frets to Saffee, "*You* gave me twenty hours of hard labor, Saffee. I don't know if I can go through that again."

On a sunny spring day, Saffee watches out the window as her mother steps from a cab. The blanketed bundle in her arms is baby sister April. Aunt Dorothy carries the sleeping infant up the outer stairway as Joann relates that it was an easy birth, "compared to the first one."

"Look, Saffee!" Joann gushes. "Look at the baby. See how tiny she is. Isn't she beautiful?"

In the hospital, Joann wrote Nels the news. She tells Dorothy how she anticipates his surprise to learn he's the father of two, a whole month earlier than expected. "He probably wanted a boy this time," she says, "but I'm sure he'll be happy with a girl."

Joann places the sleeping infant on the bed and begins to unpack her small overnight bag. She thinks about her own father, recklessly sacrificing his wife's health hoping to produce male farmworkers. She knows; she had been a secluded witness. Sometime later, of course, she had understood what was happening. Perhaps that was the night her mother began to grow a seed. A girl seed. The last one. Sometimes sounds of their struggle still replay in Joann's mind, as do Clara's pleas from that other night. *"No, Knute! It will kill me if you give this baby away! It will kill me!"*

At the remembrance, a tear threatens to slide from Joann's eye. She quickly blinks it away so Dorothy doesn't see. Their mother's words had come true and explained what Joann read to be the cause of death on the certificate in the wooden box. Memorized words that have not diminished their foreboding.

Dorothy stays two more days. Joann is grateful for her help but cringes at the once-familiar caustic voice, characteristic of all her sisters. They share war information, scanty as it is, gleaned from their husbands' letters. Joann learns that two kamikaze planes hit and seriously damaged George's aircraft carrier three months earlier. Hundreds of men had been killed, burned in fires on deck, Dorothy tells her. "I'm so thankful that George was spared."

Joann trembles. A fiery attack in the same waters traversed by her Nels. The *Alamosa* could just as easily be hit and burned. Is the whole world ablaze?

Impulsively, she tells Dorothy scenes from her troubled nightmares. "It's that prairie fire. It still haunts me," she says, steadying her hands.

"Oh, Joann, it was such a long time ago," Dorothy scoffs. "We all have to move on, you know."

Joann bristles. How can her sister dismiss the horrific event? She will not mention to Dorothy that sometimes, even in *day*dreams, the fire still burns within her, visions of flames rushing over their mother's grave. What good would it do? Dorothy too is a daughter of hardship, a motherless sibling. Joann came to the conclusion some time ago that none of her siblings emerged from their needy upbringing unscathed. All of them, but less so Dorothy, were difficult people. It was with relief that Joann had left home after high school, with no desire to see any of them again.

Their conversation moves on. Dorothy speaks with sadness of their mother's death. "Can you imagine birthing nine babies at home with no medical assistance?" She recalls how weak Clara had been as she lay in bed and how they had all seen the blood. How their father, beside himself, made a pallet for her in the wagon and carried her, and then the baby, out of the house. "And then Pa wasn't able to tell us that she had bled to death, had Evelyn tell us."

Hysteria. Acute mania. Hospital for the Insane. It seems clear that Dorothy does not associate these words with their mother. Does not know the cause of her death. Just as well. They would have little impact on self-assured Dorothy. She would not relate.

"Back then," Dorothy says, "the mysteries surrounding the whole matter of giving birth prevented us from asking very many questions." Joann tries to change the subject, but her sister muses on, speculating how their lives might be different had Clara survived.

"Don't get me wrong," Dorothy says, "tragic as it was, in some ways I think her early death made me a stronger person. I became independent, and that was good."

Joann says nothing. Clearly Dorothy is contrasting herself with Joann's inadequacies. To Dorothy, she must still be the frightened girl whimpering under the table, aching for her mother's attention. Childhood emptiness rushes back and stabs her. Joann knows that she still is that little girl.

When Dorothy leaves, Joann makes a few changes. She arranges for weekly grocery delivery, and each evening she makes a bed for Saffee on the sofa. Baby April shares the Murphy bed with her mother.

As Joann strokes the downy head of her nursing baby, pleasant maternal feelings rise within her. She anticipates that this child will bring her comfort, make life good again. These are not the feelings she experienced with her firstborn, the one standing before her now, watching with her usual soberness. The newness of marriage and first motherhood, the war that made them move across the country, the months spent washing Grandma Pearlman's soiled sheets—all these had hindered closeness with the first child. But now, this new one brings hope for happier days. The war will end. Nels will come home. They will return to Minnesota.

Saffee watches her mother cuddle baby April and sing soft lullabies. She watches Joann kneel at the bathtub every day to scrub diapers, then hang them on a rack to dry. She watches her bathe April in a metal tub on the kitchen table. They no longer bounce on the bed and sing "Mairzy Doats." As April grows, Joann frequently comments that she is the "spittin' image" of Nels.

Joann is worried, then frantic, when no letter comes from Nels for four weeks, then five. Has his ship gone down and no one has told her? Finally, an envelope arrives containing an astonishing message.

Dear Joann,

　I got yer letter. So the baby was born April 11th! Swell! Wasn't it sposed to be near the end of May?

　Please don't tell me Tokyo Rose is right. When I hear that woman, I can't help having doubts—even about you. Some men out here have gotten walking papers from girlfriends back home—and there's even been a few divorce papers. How low. Its hard enuf just being out here and not knowing if I'll live thru it.

　Your all I have to live for, Joann. Thinking about some other man holding you is driving me crazy. I'm sorry to write this. I hope I'm just brainwashed and it aint true. It's hard to think straight out here.

　　　　　I still love you,

　　　　　Nels

P.S. Some nerve to name her after the month!!!

Joann is devastated, hurt, and angry. She expected him to be happy. Disregarding that he has the highest morals of any man she's ever met, and disregarding that he's written that he never takes island shore leave with the other sailors because he wants no part of their "carouzing," she retaliates.

Dear Nels,

　You're accusing me again? I thought you were over that. I thought you trusted me—as you should. And you're a fine one to talk. I read in a magazine about GIs on shore leave—taking "liberties" with those gorgeous, curvy island girls—the ones who don't wear anything but beads around their neck.

Love to you too,
Joann

She mails the letter and quickly regrets it. She writes a profuse apology. His letters from then on are few and convey no passion of a lonesome husband at sea.

CHAPTER SIX

THE HOMECOMING

1945–1946

August 15. The war is over at last. Nels will be coming home. Daddy will be coming home.

"Saffee, take this little flag, go outside, and run all the way down the hill to the end of the street," Joann instructs. "While you're running, wave the flag and shout as loud as you can, 'The war's over!' Go on, now. Run!"

"Mommy! Come with me!"

"No, I can't. I need to stay with April."

"I can't go alone!" She stamps her right foot in protest. "I won't go!" Never has she been expected to do such a public thing. Never has she been outdoors alone.

But Joann insists. After minutes of argument, Saffee grabs the flag, dashes outside, and with tears streaming, fearfully runs down the long San Francisco hill. She does not shout the wonderful news but sobs, incredulous that she must do something so intimidating.

They wait.

Nels's ship does not release him for almost ten more months. His letters during this time are lukewarm. On one hand, Joann is grieved that he doubts her faithfulness, as he had before they married. And now again, skewed by her emotional immaturity, she is not *completely* sorry for inadvertently causing jealousy, even when it is needless.

Finally, he calls to say that he's on his way from Portland to San Francisco. Joann and Saffee are beside themselves—Saffee with happy anticipation, Joann with nerves. When they hear him coming up the stairway, they expectantly open the door to a man with a heavy sea bag over his shoulder and a taut, unsmiling face that Saffee barely recognizes.

"Daddy? Daddy! You're home!" Saffee reaches for him to pick her up, but he thrusts past both wife and daughter and shows no interest in the sleeping, almost-one-year-old child on the bed. To Saffee's great dismay, her parents begin to yell angry words.

Within a few days, Joann is able to convince Nels that April is indeed his flesh and blood. "See, Nels, look at that grin. Just like yours! A baby never lived who looked more like her father."

Convinced, yes, but traumatic months of doubt at sea did permanent damage. April is a child of his flesh, but will never be a child of his heart.

CHAPTER SEVEN

ST. PAUL

1946

Saffee slouches in a living room chair, one leg slung over the armrest. As is often the case, her young mind, uncluttered by experience or preoccupation, scrutinizes the present moment. Singsong floats down the stairway as April, playing in her crib, forestalls a nap. Why is her little sister always so happy and busy?

On the floor is a rag doll that Joann made for Saffee that she has never cared for. What does one do with a doll? Why does April cuddle and coo over Saffee's neglected toy? She's dragged it around so much its yarn hair is all but gone.

Saffee listens to her parents as together they attach shelves to a kitchen wall. They aim to make their newly purchased, modest home more livable. Joann gives minute instructions and Nels tries to comply patiently and precisely, "to keep the peace." No matter what Joann and Nels are doing, decisions rarely involve discussion, since Joann usually makes up her mind quickly about things, then closes it.

After three weeks back in St. Paul, the Kvaales, other than Saffee, are fairly comfortable. It's their first house and their first backyard. April finds delight toddling barefoot in the grass, picking dandelions and chasing squirrels.

"Watch your sister," Joann often says. Saffee doesn't mind being in the backyard, but she's uneasy in the front. She's seen older children in the vicinity, to say nothing about a few dogs. She is comfortable with neither.

As she slumps in the chair, idly bouncing a leg, laughter from outdoors interrupts her boredom. Curious, she steps out onto the screened front porch, just far enough to investigate unobserved, as her mother might have done. In the adjacent yard, five girls in summer dresses, perhaps slightly older than Saffee, giggle and shout, jump and run, as they bat about a blue rubber ball, the largest ball Saffee has ever seen. She does not yearn to join them, but is curious enough to watch.

"Here. Send it over here. It's *my birthday*, you know!" a bubbly blond girl cries. The frivolity continues until an aproned woman steps out of the house and calls, "Midgie! Everyone! Come in for cake and ice cream." The laughing girls skip and tumble into the house.

Saffee remembers that her own birthday is coming. The one, she's been told, that means she must soon attend something called kindergarten. She goes inside to the kitchen. Nels is nailing shelf supports onto a wall according to Joann's carefully considered pencil markings.

"Daddy, when it's my birthday, will you buy me a big ball?" Saffee asks.

Nels pounds the last nail and laughs. "A ball? What would you do with a ball?" he teases. He lifts a shelf to its place. "Balls are fer boys, ain't they?" Teasing is Nels's usual mode of communication with Saffee. It amuses him and aggravates her.

She turns to her mother. "Mommy, I saw some girls next door having a party. They were playing with a big, big ball. The girl who lives there is Midgie."

"Nels!" Joann exclaims. "That top shelf tips to the right. Anything I'd put on *that* would roll right off."

Saffee ambles out the back door to sit on the steps. She idly watches a robin hopping here and there in the grass. He cocks his head to listen, then pecks the ground. Hop, cock, peck. She admires his orange breast and beady, bright eyes and most of all his perkiness. If she could have this incredible creature for a pet, she would not be lonely.

At supper, Saffee asks Nels how she might go about catching a robin. He tells her the only sure way is to put salt on its tail. So easy! She is thrilled with the anticipation of capturing a friend.

The next morning Saffee finds Joann stirring bright yellow dye in a steaming galvanized tub that covers two burners of the gas stove. Eagerly, Saffee asks if she might have some salt. "Don't bother me, Saffee. I'm dyeing sheets to make curtains and this dye's very hot—stay away now."

"But, Mommy, Daddy says if I put salt on a bird's tail I can catch him! Pleeease give me some salt?"

Joann reaches into a cupboard. "Here," she says, sprinkling a few stingy grains from a shaker into Saffee's ready hand. "That's enough."

Saffee skips outside and sits on the step, waiting for her robin. Presently, a wren swoops down onto the grass and begins to search for tasty morsels. Well, any bird will do. Saffee darts at the wren, tossing salt in its direction. The bird takes flight, carrying with it Saffee's hope for a friend. She tears back into the house.

"Mommy! It didn't work, my bird flew away!"

Joann, stirring intently, doesn't seem to hear.

"Happy Bir-ir-thday, Sa-pphire! Happy birthday to you!"

The family sits in the kitchen alcove brightened by windows newly curtained in yellow. Saffee blows out five candles. While Joann cuts the cake, Nels brings in a large pink balloon from the next room. Granted, it's the biggest balloon Saffee has ever seen, but there is no escaping the fact that it is not a ball.

When their cake is finished, Joann washes April's sticky fingers and Nels lifts her from her high chair. Brownie box camera in hand, Joann says, "Saffee, let's go outside now and take a birthday picture of you and the new ball."

Saffee picks up the balloon with both hands and follows. Under her breath she says, "It's not a ball."

"Me ball, Saffee?" April begs. "Pleeease?"

Nels notices a girl in the next yard and calls to her, "Are you Midgie? Come on over here. Have your picture taken with Saffee."

Saffee pulls her shoulders up toward her ears. "Daddy! No!" she hisses. As far as Saffee is aware, no one in the family, least of all her, has yet spoken to anyone in the neighborhood.

Midgie slowly crosses to the Kvaales' yard with a wary smile.

"Oh!" Joann has an idea. "Midgie, I've heard you have a great big ball too. Go get it for the picture."

Midgie glances at Saffee's balloon. "Well, okay," she says hesitantly. The young neighbor goes back to her house and returns with her blue ball. Joann poses the two older girls and April, and then prominently places the ball and balloon in front of them on the grass.

"Smi-ile! Saffee, I said smile. Come on, *big* smile." She snaps the picture. "There. Now, girls, you play nice," Joann directs over her shoulder as she and Nels turn back to the house.

April jumps up and down, squealing, "Me ball! Me ball!"

Saffee picks up her balloon and steps a few feet away from Midgie. "Want me to throw it at you?" she asks.

"Sure," says Midgie.

Saffee lifts her birthday present over her head and gives it a toss. "There."

Immediately, a gentle breeze catches the balloon. The girls watch it float to the top of a tree and alight on a branch. *Pop!*

April stretches her short arms to the sky, calling, "Come back, ball! Come back, ball!"

"Be quiet, April." Saffee seizes her sister's hand and retreats across the yard and into the house.

Midgie watches them go.

The kindergarteners, their faces full of dreams and wonder, sit on the floor and sing with high voices, hardly in unison, *"Si-ilent night, ho-oly night . . .'round yon vir-ir-gin mother and Child."*

Singing along, and contentedly rocking with the rhythm, Saffee admires the lopsided green paper wreaths adorning each of the classroom's tall windows. *It's Christmas!* She's not quite sure what it's all about, neither the tinsel part nor the spiritual part, but this year she's been touched by the magic of it. On sudden impulse, she purses her lips and begins to blow with enthusiasm.

Astonished, Miss Jessup says, "Sapphire Kvaale! We don't whistle Christmas carols! Go stand in the cloakroom!"

Hot tears of mortification and contempt flow freely as Saffee buries herself behind her wool winter coat that hangs alongside a forest of others. Hadn't her mother said that kindergarten would be fun? On the first day, Saffee knew she had been duped when she and her classmates had to tearfully bare their arms for polio vaccinations. Every morning boisterous, chattering children hurry by her as she dawdles four blocks to the intimidating redbrick building. She is usually late. The heavy outside door never yields to her pull. She leans against it, nose running from the cold, until someone passes by in the hall and opens it for her. In the classroom, she is tongue-tied when others speak to her. If forced to reply, she mumbles, hiding her face in her hands.

But this morning she had not been late because speculations about Christmas prompted her to be happy. Her father had placed a tree right in their living room and her mother had strung it with colored lights and added silver tinsel. There had been talk of a baby named Jesus and Christmas presents. How wonderful it all was. Why wouldn't whistling be an appropriate expression of joy? Now she hears her classmates sing, *"Oh, what fun it is to ride in a one-horse open sleigh."* She stares at the wood floor, made muddy with melted snow from eighteen pairs of rubber boots.

That evening Saffee sits at the supper table stirring patterns of gravy into her mashed potatoes, round and round, round and round, until she has a plateful of uniformly brown mush. Her right foot kicks a steady tempo against the table leg as she broods over the morning's humiliation.

She had been so proud of learning to whistle, and she didn't have that many things to feel proud about. Certainly not the playground races she always lost or the paintings she always smeared. But she had learned to whistle! . . . and foolishly dared reveal her new talent. During naptime, snot-nosed Alan had pointed a pudgy finger at her and sing-songed, *"Saffee's sappy, Saffee's sappy,"* and then, *"Sappy, sappy, sappy."*

She formulates a desperate emergency plan: she will stop going to kindergarten. Of course, she'll need parental cooperation.

"Mommy?" She waits for a reply, but Joann stares into some middle distance between here and there and doesn't respond.

"Mommy, listen." Still no answer.

"Mommy!"

"Eat yer potatoes, Saffee," Nels says.

"Mommy! *Please*, listen to me!"

April bangs a spoon on her high chair. "More?" she begs, pushing her bowl around the tray.

Saffee watches her mother absentmindedly spoon another helping of applesauce from a serving dish and plop it onto April's "no-touch" plate, divided so that foods don't mix.

"Mommy! I need to talk to you!"

Her father frowns. "Don't bother your mother, Saffee," he says sternly.

In spite of Nels's jovial, back-slapping ways in public, his unmistakable message to Saffee is that she must suffocate all spontaneity. Spontaneity is a problem. Bland is good. So be as bland as cold mashed potatoes. Therein is safety; safety is a virtue; risk is not to be tried. Saffee instinctively knows that his instructions are meant to avoid igniting her mother's "nerves," and she is sure he would also want her to exhibit this restraint at school. Whistling had violated her father's limiting philosophy.

Saffee shovels potatoes as fast as she can, swallowing with difficulty around the growing lump in her throat. She must get away from the table, but will be prevented if her plate is not clean.

"I'm done!" she blurts and tramps from the kitchen.

Her tears are angrier now than they were in the cloakroom. She's always hated her mother's silent staring. And she hates kindergarten. She will *never* go back.

Saffee stands biting her lip in the middle of the darkened living room, lit only by the strings of lights glowing on the Christmas tree. She stares at their reflected colors on the light gray carpeting that her mother is so proud of. Joann never misses a chance to comment, "It's a Gulistan, you know!" Whatever that means, it must be something wonderful.

Saffee quietly opens a drawer of the corner desk and pulls out her cigar box of crayons. She holds up a fat one to catch a glimmer of light. Purple. Her chin trembles and her heart beats wildly as she presses the crayon in a diagonal line from corner to corner across her mother's gray carpeting.

In the dim light, unaware that the waxy crayon has failed to leave any mark on the carpet, she dashes up the stairs to her bedroom. Under the covers, she waits for the desperate deed to be discovered.

She sleeps.

CHAPTER EIGHT

THE HIGHWAY MAN

1948

A gurgling radiator in the girls' bedroom struggles to keep January drafts at bay. Joann tucks blankets securely around April as Saffee stands at her sister's crib, watching. "Mommy, can I stay up later tonight? A second grader shouldn't hafta go to bed same time as a three-year-old."

"I suppose, for a while, but put your nightgown on now."

Joann goes downstairs. Saffee sheds her wool sweater and corduroy overalls and dives into a flannel nightgown, a quilted robe, and a pair of matted slippers.

She scampers out of the bedroom and creeps down the stairway. She loves to lie on the carpet and listen to her mother read, but it isn't a time of closeness, like those first happy weeks in the San Francisco apartment. Nowadays, when she reads verse, Joann communes only with her own melancholia. Tonight perhaps she will read "The Raven," Saffee's favorite, although very scary, poem.

"The moon was a ghostly galleon tossed upon cloudy seas . . ."

Saffee recognizes "The Highway Man," a poem that, in Saffee's opinion, is almost as good as "The Raven."

Joann sits in the armchair on many lonely winter evenings, wrapped in a blanket, lost in melodramatic rhyme. To her consternation, Nels is only home on weekends now. The dairy is rapidly expanding across the state, much of its success due to Nels, the milkman-become-sales-manager. In this new position, he acquires country dairies, hires distributors, and keeps grocers happy with the dairy's service.

Nels believes that his work is of more benefit to his family than his presence. The division of labor—he brings home the bacon, Joann raises the girls and runs the house—is taken for granted and never discussed. Nels is quite capable of doing his part, he assumes Joann is likewise. To him, his diligence through winter's cold and summer's heat means they will have all they need to live on, plus savings in the bank. To Joann and his girls, it means he is little more than a stranger. Once again, Joann feels empty.

> *The road was a ribbon of moonlight over the purple moor,*
> *And the highwayman came riding—*
> *Riding—riding—*
> *The highwayman came riding, up to the old inn door.*

Lying on the floor, her chin cupped in her hands, Saffee listens to the familiar story of tragic Bess, the innkeeper's black-eyed daughter who pulls the trigger bound to her bosom, sacrificing her own life to signal a warning of danger to her lover.

"The man is a thieving scoundrel," Joann has explained to Saffee, "but he's so-o-o handsome that he steals her heart away."

Saffee doesn't understand the nuances of the story, but no matter, poetry is, for Saffee, at least, distant communion with her mother. With increasing passion, Joann continues . . .

Then look for me by moonlight,
Watch for me by moonlight,
I'll come to thee by moonlight . . .

The poem grows long. Saffee's head sinks onto the carpet. She can't stay awake to hear the familiar, gripping climax, when the highwayman rides at a gallop brandishing his rapier high, only to be *"shot . . . down like a dog on the highway . . . with the bunch of lace at his throat."*

Several poems later, Joann hears Saffee's gentle snore and looks her way. "Saffee . . . Saffee," Joann orders from her chair, "go to bed now; you've been up way too long. There's school tomorrow." Saffee yawns and climbs the stairs. Joann goes back to her poem and reads so late she's too sleepy the next morning to ready her daughter for school.

"Get your own cereal, Saffee," she calls from her bed. "Button your coat and zip your boots. I'm going to sleep 'til April wakes up . . . don't be late now."

Saffee doesn't need the last reminder. She no longer dawdles along the four blocks to school nor plops down in the snow halfway to consider whether to go on at all. Now that she's learned to read, a skill that makes her feel alive, bordering on important, she finds security sitting in her own desk, part of an orderly row of other desks. At home she has a small collection of children's books, pages tattered from turning.

At the same time that books become doors promising light for Saffee, her mother begins to spiral downward into darkness.

CHAPTER NINE

DISCONTENT

Throughout the winter, Joann grows more resentful of Nels's absences. She broods. She frets. She gives minimal attention to her daughters, choosing instead radio episodes of *The Guiding Light*, *The Right to Happiness*, and *The Romance of Helen Trent*. The romantic poets continue to be her nighttime companions. She asks Nels to buy her a spiral-bound notebook. In it she tries her hand at her own poetry. At times throughout the day she whispers a word or phrase that fancies her, rolls it around in her head, tries it out on the mirror, and when satisfied, scribbles in the notebook, murmuring. At first her poetry dissects loneliness. The loneliness she learned as a child. Then she begins to fantasize what her life would be like with a man more handsome, more entertaining than Nels. She wonders if perhaps he also desires . . .

As is Saffee's habit, she watches her mother. She notes that Joann's hands, when quiet, are fists. Not fists that pummel, but neither do they stroke, or pat, or beckon. Their clench seems to restrain something within. At other times the same hands are fastidious, precisely stacking towels for the shelf as if on display, then moving on to pound flour with the edge of a saucer into sinewy round steak until it is pink and flaccid.

It's not unusual that when Nels returns home from work, Saffee hears her parents argue.

"Don't you forget, Nels," her mother will say, "I was *alone* all those years you were at sea, working my fingers to the bone and so worried about you. When the war was over, I thought you'd stay *home*."

"I work hard for *you*, Joann," Nels will counter, "so we can have things. Don'tcha understand?"

On weekends, Nels pays bills, buys groceries, and tends to neglected household chores.

With little to occupy her time and mind, baseless suspicions spread across Joann's void. She quizzes Nels about what he does at work each day and what he does each night.

Exasperated, Nels sputters, "If you'd just git out, Joann, *meet* folks, make some women friends—"

She cuts him off. "Gregarious is for *you*, Nels"—she tosses her head—"*not me*."

In February, Joann declares, "If I don't see more of you, Nels, I'm going to die! So I've made a decision—I'm going to travel with you."

"Joann, don't talk nonsense. What about the girls?"

"I don't know about them, Nels, but I'm just *not* going to be alone in this house anymore."

Nels knows that his wife's feelings, although not understood, cannot be treated casually. Wearied by her discontent, he offers a compromise. "How 'bout if we move, then? If we get a place more the middle of my territory, I can be home more."

Joann agrees and shakes off some of her recent melancholy. The next three Saturdays, with Saffee and April in tow, they travel miles of highways, bordered by drifting snow, to evaluate small towns that dot the interior of the state. On the third week, they consider Miller's Ford, a community of four thousand residents, where fathers work, mothers keep house, and children grow up to follow suit.

"I can see it's a decent place," Joann says as they explore. "Churches outnumber beer joints more than two to one." She's made a careful count. "And there's a minimum of garish neon signs," she adds. Nels notes there seems no need for traffic lights. "Uptown," Main Street has a variety of stores, a movie theater, and a bank. They drive past a two-story redbrick school, a small hospital, and a Carnegie library.

The following Saturday they find a six-bedroom, fifty-year-old house for sale on the west end of town. With great enthusiasm, Joann recognizes its potential and leaves behind her season of inertia, replacing it with one of creativity.

"Look, Nels. This huge kitchen could be made into an efficiency apartment to rent out." In her exuberance, she fairly flies to the next room. "The big dining room can be divided, making a small dining room for us, with a new kitchen at that end."

With ideas bubbling like a percolator, Joann quickly notes that the four upstairs bedrooms are large enough to make two more apartments. "And, oh!" she gushes. "The living room French doors downstairs can be closed to give the upstairs renters private access. We won't even have to see them at all," she says, "except to collect the rent, of course." Eventually, however, she will make sure that through those French doors she is able to see and hear *them*.

Nels, more cautious than his wife, tries to temper her, commenting that such a huge remodeling project is beyond him and would need to be hired out. While April scampers with delight from room to room, Joann solicits Saffee's support. "Saffee, wouldn't you just *love* to sit and read on the wraparound screened porch? And here, look out this window, there's a river down that hill, right across the street. You can learn to swim in the summer and skate in the winter." Saffee looks dubious.

The cost of the house, plus the remodeling, would hardly be offset by the monthly rent it might generate, but Nels's new job has increased their income. Encouraged by Joann's sudden buoyancy, he agrees that the purchase is feasible. Does she understand that she will have to oversee the carpenters, electricians, and plumbers? She paces here and there in the empty dining room, takes a deep breath, and assures him she will.

Back in St. Paul, even before the purchase is complete, Joann begins meticulous drawings, detailing her ideas for change. Saffee surveys her work and asks, "Will I have my own bedroom?"

"No. All the extra rooms will be apartments."

Eager to move and begin the work, Joann decides that Saffee can miss the last two months of second grade.

The packing of their belongings is well under way when Joann receives word that Evelyn, her oldest sister, had a heart attack and has died. The news prompts Saffee to ask questions that mostly go unanswered. Other than Dorothy, who came to San Francisco when April was born, her mother never mentions siblings.

After Nels and Joann attend Evelyn's funeral, Joann's ebullient mood plunges. The next day, and the day after that, she sits in the armchair, immobilized, staring into the mists of memory. Partly filled boxes lay neglected in every room.

"Oh, Evelyn . . ." It is a quiet moan, barely audible. "Only fifteen and had to raise us . . . like a mother hen . . . took care of everyone when that fire came . . . except the baby."

Saffee leans against her mother's shoulder and thrusts her face close to Joann's, demanding attention. "*What* baby, Mommy? *What* fire? Who are you talking about?"

Joann, far away, responds in a monotone, "Mother's last little girl . . . and Pa gave her away."

Saffee struggles to grasp the idea of a motherless family—and giving away a baby.

"Mommy, how little were you when"—she flutters her hands—"you know, when your mother . . ."

Joann continues her whispered thoughts. "Hospital for the . . ." Suddenly she exclaims, "No!" causing her focus to momentarily sharpen. "Seven," she says to Saffee. "I was seven when she died. Same as you."

"Not like me," Saffee says quickly, "because I'm almost *eight!*"

Joann reenters her distant place; her hands tighten their grip.

"Mother was delicate . . . surely not cut out to live in a sod house," she whispers. "Not meant to have nine . . . Pa insisted . . . I heard him. He only wanted boys . . ."

Saffee sinks to the floor and sits very still. Joann's emotions surge as she continues, "Then she was gone! Left Evelyn . . . left her to do the work and put up with the boys . . ."

Nels, who has taken a week off from work for the move, comes into the room and interrupts. He reminds Joann that it is Wednesday and the moving van comes Friday morning. She seems not to hear. By Thursday, with little assistance, Nels manages to fill the boxes and make all the necessary preparations.

That afternoon a battered pickup truck stops in front of the house. Saffee doesn't recognize the barrel-chested man in overalls and faded shirt who comes to the door. He removes his dusty cap and fingers it in a self-conscious manner. Nels shakes his hand. "Samuel! What brings you here?"

The man greets Nels, then looks beyond him to where Joann stands. "Hello, Joann. My Ev'lyn"—the big man's face goes red—"she wanted you ta have our ol' table, so I brung it to you." His speech is the dialect of Minnesota Norwegians. "When I heerd"—he puts his cap back on and just as quickly removes it—"at the fooneral that you bought yerselves a place out in Miller's Ford, I din't want you leavin' without it."

Joann sucks in her breath. "Oh my," she says. "The table?" She lowers herself onto a closed packing box.

"Me an' the boys, we're thinkin' a movin' to the cottage on the west side a the farm. It's right on the lake, don'tcha know. Boys, dey like ta fish a lot. Without Ev'lyn, we don't need no big place, don't need no big table. Won't have room. Anyways, it needs ta stay in Ev'lyn's side of the family, don'tcha know."

He apologizes for not bringing the chairs. His boys had been rough on them, and anyway, he adds, they were not the originals. Evelyn told him that when the table was in her childhood home, her father had made benches for it.

Joann looks pale and makes no comment.

CHAPTER TEN

THE TABLE

S affee and April follow Samuel and their dad to the truck where they watch the unloading of the heavy, disassembled relic. In addition to two large squares for the table's top and four sturdy legs, there are three good-sized leaves and several lengths of apron with a wide pattern of carved vines on each length. Although the finish has been rubbed away, the color of the old scarred wood is still warm, neither light nor dark. Samuel, puffing from the lifting, says he reckons the wood is birch.

"'At's not a tabo," says April, regarding the various pieces of wood piled on the ground.

"When it's all put together it is," Saffee informs her. April squats to get a closer look.

Nels admires one of the legs. "I think maybe this here is called dovetail joinery?"

Samuel agrees, saying that the design allowed the table's disassembly, which made it possible to transport it to America from Norway. He adds that, according to Evelyn, one of her father's brothers brought it from the family homestead to North Dakota for Knute and his family.

"That was quite a trip in those days," Nels says.

Joann has followed them outside and stands expressionless several yards away. "It was Uncle Jergen," she says in a flat voice. The men turn to look at her. "He brought it to our pa, the oldest son. But he didn't want it. And I don't want it either. Our brother Rolf should have it," she says.

Samuel runs sizable fingers through his thinning hair and repeats Evelyn's wishes on the matter. "She had her reasons. Somethin' 'bout it bein' special to you, Joann. You playin' under it or somthin'. All I know, she said it should be yers. The brothers, they ain't married, ya know. It's a piece fer a family."

Joann returns to the house without responding.

Saffee joins April's inspection. She runs her fingers over the tooled vines, tracing the intricate pattern, then turns over an apron piece and studies some lettering on the back. She strains to lift up a length of wood for Nels to examine, asking him to explain what the numbers and words mean.

"Thought you learned how to read, Saffee," he teases. Nels gives the wood a close look and reads a date, "1865. Guess that's when somebody made it. Here, Samuel, can you read it? The words are in Norwegian." Samuel props his glasses atop a large bald place on his head and squints at the lettering.

"Always heard it was Ev'lyn's grandpa who done made it, don't know for sure," says Samuel. "Yup. Here it says, 'Anders Kirkeborg'— that's Knute's father all right—'and Maria Kirkeborg.'" Samuel tilts the wood to catch more light. A twitch of head and shoulders shows discomfort. "Den I think it says somthin' like, 'God . . . is . . . glor-ious,' or some such." It isn't usual for a Minnesota man to speak of God or His attributes, no matter what his personal convictions might be.

The big man suddenly slaps his thigh. "Uff-da! Almost forgot the box." From the truck bed he pulls a wooden box somewhat less than eighteen inches long, tied with sturdy twine. Its top fits snugly between grooves. He extends it toward Nels. "Here's some of her ol' family stuff we had makin' clutter. Found it in Ev'lyn's"—he swallows with difficulty—"closet. Not much in it, just ol' records, baptizim and marriage 'tificates, that kinda thing. Maybe you 'n' Joann won't mind takin' it off my hands?"

"You betcha," Nels says. "I'll just put it with all the other boxes we've got there on the porch 'n' let the movers take care of it tomorrow."

After Samuel instructs Nels how to fit the table parts together for reassembly, the two men make trips into the house, placing the wood on the living room carpeting.

Joann is upstairs.

"My Ev'lyn . . ." Samuel chokes and looks embarrassed for it. "She told me there was somthin' special 'bout this table. Guess lot a life went on 'round it when she was a girl. Then our three put *their* feet under it fer a good while. Well . . . it's yerz now. Thanks for takin' it off my hands."

"We'll take good care of it," Nels promises. With solemnity, they thump each other on the back.

That evening Joann stands in the living room among the packing boxes. A strange, magnetic pull that she had all but forgotten draws her to the piled pieces of birch wood. Her eyes are fixed on the past . . .

Under the table, young Joann silently presses fists against streaming eyes, taking in great gulps of air, until she can breathe normally again. She wonders why the older siblings no longer cry. Don't they care their mother is gone forever? Where did they put their pain? "Come on out, and don't act like a baby, Joann," Maxine scoffs. "You're too old for that." From the floor-level view, she watches Evelyn's worn brown shoes traverse the room, ministering to the needs of the younger ones . . .

Part of Joann still longs for a place of safety. As a child, under the table she found an inconsistent safety that alternated with fearful discovery. She claps her fists together. How can a piece of furniture be so bewitching?

Saffee skirts around the cartons, lightly touches Joann's arm, and looks inquiringly into the drawn face and red eyes. Joann has two modes; Saffee dislikes them both. The first is hurry and scurry—washing, straightening, folding, peeling, stitching as if prodded and timed. Now Joann occupies her other mode, marked by an unwavering stare into some middle distance. When there, is she in a silent, vacant universe, or a cacophony more frenzied and peopled than the first? No one knows; she goes there unaccompanied.

"Mommy . . . Mommy, why are you so sad?"

Joann sinks into a chair. Her whispered words drift without direction. "We were under that table . . . hoping to stay alive."

Saffee doesn't ask what she means.

Suddenly, Joann tips her head back and gives a loud, hooting laugh. Her young daughter senses its inappropriateness and draws back, startled.

"They say . . ." Joann's eyes are again fixed, her voice low, but the words tumble fast. ". . . there were curses spoken around this table. They say Pa stood *cursing*"—she spits out the word—"*cursing over each girl* as Mother, lying in their bed, gave birth to one girl after another. He said he needed *farmworkers*, not seven *girls*!"

Saffee doesn't move.

Suddenly, Joann rises and shakes her upper body as if to cast off something distasteful, something that clings.

"I don't think I packed all the towels from the upstairs bathroom cupboard," she says. "I'll go see."

She disappears up the stairway and calls over her shoulder, "Saffee, look around for another empty box and bring it up."

Later, emotionally exhausted by the events of the day, Joann goes to bed early. In her midnight dream . . .

She rushes to her place of refuge, her head and shoulder bump and scrape against a table leg. She cries out in pain. Her mother is there, with her, under the table, soothing her, cooing. Above, Maxine yells, "You clumsy girl! What are you trying to do? Knock over the kerosene lamp? Burn down the house? It's all your fault, Joann! It's your fault!" Flames encroach. She is in her mother's arms . . .

CHAPTER ELEVEN

REMODELED

Joann's spirits lift once the family completes their move to Miller's Ford and Nels is out of town only two nights a week. For the first time in her life she becomes slightly acquainted with a few neighbors, and she and the carriers, Saffee and April, walk uptown once a week to buy groceries. Each trip is an occasion that requires special attire and grooming for all three. The family joins the First Methodist Church, demanding more attention to appearance, never forgetting white gloves.

Most important, in Nels's opinion, is that Joann has something to do that she thoroughly enjoys—remodel the old house. Her mood sobers noticeably, however, the day Nels assembles the Norway table, as they have come to call it.

"Your grandfather was a real craftsman," Nels remarks as he fits the puzzle-like pieces together without nails or glue.

Joann's appraisal is different. "It's ugly," she says. "I'll need to cover it."

Ignoring the remark, Nels places four of six chairs around it. They are old chairs of traditional style he bought at a yard sale. Joann looks at them with disinterest. In contrast to the table, anyone who knows furniture would say that the chairs have no "presence." Nels planned to put two of them in the basement, but when it is obvious, even to him, that four look lost around such a large table, he adds the others. Now that Joann seems to have come alive again, perhaps they might even have guests.

"Mom? What are you making?" Joann holds up white sheeting that she has sewn together into sections.

"It's a playhouse," she tells Saffee, pointing to the doorway and two green-shuttered windows. Each window has a cross of framing in the center to create four "panes." A row of tulips has begun to "grow" along the bottom edge.

"Oh! Mom!" Saffee dashes back to the bedroom. "April! Wake up! You won't believe what Mommy made us!"

Yesterday April had cajoled Joann into a short game of hide-and-seek. April hid under the Norway table. "You can't find me, Mommy! You can't see me!"

Of course Joann did see April, and remembered another girl. A girl with her own face, looking out from behind a barricade of heavy benches. She, too, was hiding and, like April, others knew she was there, but she wasn't playing.

"Whatcha doin' under there, Joann? Think I can't see you? You're crazy, Joann, crazy."

She thinks about nights in her childhood, under the same table, when she had sensed a light touch on her arm, or her hair, sometimes her legs. She would jerk to wakefulness, hear a scuttling away in the dark, and the creak of the ladder to the brothers' loft. Or did she dream it?

When she discovered that the offender was Rolf, she tattled to her pa. With vehemence Rolf denied it. "She's crazy, Pa, you know that! I done nothin', she's crazy!" Later he yelled louder under the razor strap. Rolf didn't bother her in the night again but took to tormenting her in other ways. It was contagious. Soon Joann, an oddly withdrawn child, became the object of the other siblings' ridicule.

"You're crazy, Joann. Just plain crazy."

In the wake of these and other unwanted memories, Joann relived her hurt and loneliness for the rest of the day. Under the table she had been a child without love. To be a child without love is a transgression. She must find a way to cover the table—this symbol of transgression against a child.

Last night the thought came to her that if April wants to play under the table, it must be made into a pleasant place. She would make a playhouse cover.

She rose early and sewed the sheets together, making them fit perfectly. Now, with crayons, she finishes the tulip border.

Throughout the weeks ahead, until the carpenters arrive to turn the house upside down, the playhouse cover is usually in place. Underneath, April tends her dolls and Saffee colors in her Jane Powell coloring book.

"A little camouflage goes a long way," Joann is heard to say.

The table would be hidden every day if Nels didn't insist that the cover come off for their Sunday after-church pot roast.

"It's not right to eat in the kitchen on Sunday," he says. Joann glumly obliges, tossing a green percale tablecloth over the relic from her childhood.

No matter what or where the Kvaales eat, chewing takes precedence over conversation—especially on Sundays when the stringy, inexpensive roast presents a challenge for all. Joann reminds her daughters that God gave them their father's big strong teeth and they should use them without whining. Neither parent is qualified to teach the girls the art of table talk. Joann's studied vocabulary and love of poetic phrases is for impressing herself and doesn't usually fit into mealtime conversation.

Joann's creative accomplishments are inconsistent with someone born in a poor prairie sod house and who has only a high school education. But she has a natural talent for design and renders precise drawings for the main-floor efficiency apartment. There will be compact built-ins, including an eating table, hinged to raise and fold up into a wall. She makes a movable, paper model. "Look at this, Saffee. It'll disappear just like the Murphy bed we had in California."

"I liked that bed," Saffee says, glancing at April.

It appears that all the necessities of a one-room apartment will fit into the allotted space—except a refrigerator. Joann is stumped. Reluctantly, she makes an unsatisfactory decision. Since there will be a door between the apartment and the Kvaales' new kitchen, the tenant will have to come into their place to share the refrigerator.

When the downstairs plans are complete, Joann turns to the upstairs. Nels gives her full rein. The only matter they take care of together is hiring the workmen.

"A person can't be too careful nowadays," says Joann. "Can't trust just *any*one coming into the house, you know."

The sawing and pounding begin and Joann keeps a critical eye on the crew, following them from room to room, peering over their sweat-soaked shoulders.

"They better not steal any materials when my back is turned!" she declares to Nels. If it seems that wallboard or trim is wasted, or too many good nails are left on the floor at night, she gathers them up and doesn't hesitate to mention it. If framing doesn't look square to Joann's eye, it's done over. As the project proceeds, the workers try to sidestep the lady of the house, but sometimes tempers flare.

"Don't those men realize that I have it hard too?" she frets. "I carry the responsibilities of management, to say nothing of noise from power tools, and how about *all this dust*!" Her frustrations alternate with exhilaration, however, as she watches her well-thought-out plans take shape.

Joann's preoccupation with the renovations allows Saffee and April, now eight and four, more freedom than they had in St. Paul.

April makes friends with neighborhood children and Saffee explores the shallows of the Blue River down the bank across the street. She steps timidly into the dark, cavernous spaces under the bridge that spans the river and, from a distance, peers warily as water crashes over the dam. When a truck rumbles overhead, her heart pounds and she scrambles up the side of the bank. More to her liking are the safe treasures found in the public library.

The cloth playhouse cover has done nothing to change Joann's sub-conscious perception of her unwillingly inherited table. It continues to feature prominently in her disturbing dreams. Perhaps if she would alter . . . In a moment of clarity, she knows what she must do.

CHAPTER TWELVE

THE FIRST COAT

Joann throws aside a worn-smooth piece of sandpaper and swipes her damp forehead with the back of her hand. Her fingers are stiff and her back aches, but she hardly notices. She selects new sandpaper with rougher grain and rubs the tabletop with intensity. Rubs away scratches. Rubs away scars and stains. Nearby, a can of primer and a gallon of fresh paint wait unopened.

Nels had objected to her plan. "You've got enough goin' on with all this remodelin'," he said, when really it was her inordinate intensity over the idea that concerned him. It had taken some persuading on Joann's part to get him to drive to the hardware store to buy supplies. He almost always complies with her wishes eventually.

Nels. She applies more pressure to her strokes. Why can't he understand that she must do what must be done? And why hasn't she thought of doing it before? She welcomes the thought of permanently obliterating the anxieties of childhood that for years have taunted her, haunted her with hellish visions in the night. They will be gone.

Or will they?

Is she doing the right thing?

This table . . . why, oh why is it such a puzzle? She gives her head a jerking twitch as if to shake herself free of confusion, and once again she reviews the past. As an insecure child, the table beckoned her. Sometimes it offered her a place of privacy, where she had hopes and good thoughts. Those times made it sacred to her. At other times, under the table, she was betrayed by darkness and foreboding. A paradox. But perhaps sanding and painting—honest toil—will bring about some understanding, maybe even some peace.

She rearranges the drop cloth she's placed on the floor to catch sanding dust and paint, then rubs a stubborn mar with intensity. Her loose, uncombed hair falls forward, a labyrinth through which she must look. When scratches diminish, she is heartened. The water stains, however, formed years ago when water splashed from laundry tubs and washboards, resist obliteration. No matter, the paint will do its work.

Yes. This labor will be worth it. She rubs feverishly, prompting quizzical glances from the two workmen who paint window trim in the adjacent living room. They make excuses to walk through the dining room to get a better look at this peculiar woman. She pays them no heed.

When the tabletop is sanded, Joann decides the vine-covered apron needs no attention. Its original varnish is mostly gone, but it has escaped the ravages of time and misuse. She alternately kneels and sits on the floor, sanding away blemishes on each leg. Fatigue takes hold. She'd intended to prepare a more perfectly smooth surface for the primer coat. Perfect, because everything Joann does must meet her standards. But in her eagerness she concludes that the paint—the paint!—will cover all remaining blemishes. She eats a few crackers to renew her energy, then opens the can of primer.

By late afternoon, the primer is dry. The day's surging emotions and the physical labor have sapped her strength. She will apply the topcoat early in the morning. But she can't resist prying open the lid, just to look at the paint she has such high hopes for. Its smell assaults her. Why did Nels buy oil-based paint? Doesn't he know it has a noxious odor? The color, however, is perfect, soft, reassuring. It seems to have a certain quality—a presence. She will dip her brush into it tomorrow.

But first comes night, and another dream . . .

A little girl on a plank floor . . . crude benches . . . whispered conversation . . .

"Lars, Pa's got the farm insured for lots a money. Hunderds, I'd guess."

"Hunderds? This here place? You know what boys like us could do with money like that? We'd be rich!"

"It's not for us, you dummy. It's fer if somthin' happens to it, you know, like a cyclone."

"Cyclone? How 'bout a fire, like another prairie fire?"

"Yeh, Lars, like a fire . . . But it don't have to be no prairie fire, ya know."

"Whatcha sayin', Rolf?" . . . Red-orange flames leap . . . "Whatcha sayin', Rolf?"

Billows of black smoke mushroom, rise, drift . . . The girl chokes, screams . . .

At 2:00 a.m., Joann, sweat-soaked, rises from her bed and writes shaky lines in her notebook.

What is it, who is it that lifts the torch and bids fire rage from the horizon? Who strikes the match to destroy a farm?

The next morning Joann strokes with wide, sweeping motions. She imagines herself an orchestra conductor, directing, not music, but a flow of color. A flow of healing color. An ointment. Oil-based? Perhaps that was meant to be after all. In spite of its odor, she will believe it to be anointing oil.

Saffee sits on a stool and watches, fascinated, as paint flows from her mother's brush onto the Norway table. "Can I help?" she asks.

Her mother's all-consuming expression does not change.

"Let me help, Mommy."

Joann is curt. "No."

Her mother's unpredictable moods and preoccupations make no sense, but Saffee knows when to be quiet. She retreats to her bedroom with a book under her arm.

As she works, Joann is at first pleased with the effect. The glossy shine of wet paint holds promise. The conductor strokes carefully, rhythmically, for almost twenty minutes. Then the smell begins to bother her. "Noxious." She speaks the word, rolls it around in her head.

Last night's dream troubles her. The North Dakota farmhouse and barn had in fact burned to the ground. There had been suspicion that her pa had arranged the fire and collected the insurance money. How else had he been able to purchase the fishing resort? She doesn't want to think that her brothers had had something to do with it. She doesn't want to think that it was arson at all. Arson was criminal. Rolf and Lars were just pathetic boys. Uneducated, overworked, buffoonish boys.

She plunges the brush into the paint too deeply. Paint rises up to the handle, irritating her. She lets it drip a moment over the can, but is too impatient to wait long enough, choosing instead to slop the excess onto the table, smearing it around into a thick mess. She tries to smooth it over with wider strokes. Like a flash of black lightning, the fire and smoke of last night's dream return. Brushing becomes erratic. Perhaps, after today, there will be no more nightmares. When the tabletop is completely covered with its coat of gray, she kneels to slap the brush back and forth onto the legs. Ample and thick. Smelly. But with promise.

CHAPTER THIRTEEN

PSYCHOLOGY

It takes three days for the paint to dry, and for three days Joann studies its effect. It had been a bold thing for her to do, paint the Norway table, but she had felt a distinct compulsion to do so. And for two nights her sleep has been dream free.

It's past time to find a place for the supplies. Again she pushes down on the cover of the remaining paint and carries it with the cleaned brush and canvas drop cloth to the basement. She will put them with Nels's collection of assorted necessities on the shelving near his workbench.

She notices his rows of tools, neatly categorized, and is grateful that he is handy, can fix almost anything. It pleases her to know that her in-house repairman loves her, adores her. Or does he? Lately, ever since she told him she wants another baby . . .

Her train of thought is interrupted as she searches for a space to store the paint can. On the highest shelf there are a number of medium-sized boxes. She recognizes that two of them store Nels's war mementos, but a third one startles her. An old wooden box, about the size of a bread box, tied with twine. How could that box turn up in her basement? Surely it isn't . . .

Her heart thumps as she lifts it down. She unties stubborn knots and removes the slide-off lid. Newspaper clippings, receipts, bills of sale, tintypes of people she doesn't recognize. She cautiously thumbs through until she finds a yellowed envelope. Scrawled across the front is "Certificate of Death, Clara Isabelle Kirkeborg." In spite of painting the table, or perhaps because she painted the table, suddenly Joann fears more than ever that the certificate inside foretells her own fate. She pulls her hand away from the damning piece, as if it were on fire. She does not need to read it. She hastens to return the box to the highest shelf and covers it with the drop cloth.

Wouldn't having another baby, a final baby, prove her stability, change her fate? Unlike what happened to her mother, this baby would not be taken away. And then the words *hysteria* and *acute mania* or words like them would never condemn Joann, would never blaze across her death certificate.

Lodging for newcomers is scarce in Miller's Ford, so the Kvaales' upstairs apartments bring in a steady income. The main floor share-the-refrigerator apartment is harder to rent until, just before the first snowfall, a shy, dithering gentleman named Henry Clement comes and stays for six months.

Mr. Clement is rarely seen, except at suppertime, when the family is seated at their new kitchen's "breakfast" bar. Most evenings, after the "God is good, God is great, we thank Him for our food. Amen," their tenant enters the kitchen with apologetic noises. His slight frame squats before the open refrigerator. He contemplates the items on his designated lower shelf while annoyingly clucking his tongue. It's not clear whether he speaks to himself or to the Kvaales when he inevitably says, "I just can't decide what to have for supper."

From where Saffee sits, she can see there is usually little for Mr. Clement to choose from—perhaps a package of bologna, a carton of eggs, butter, and maybe a head of aging lettuce. As a rule, on his first exploratory visit, Mr. Clement chooses nothing and returns to his apartment, only to reappear once or twice before making a selection.

Saffee and April find Mr. Clement's mid-meal visits amusing, but Joann is put out. One evening, as the Kvaales enjoy pork chops, scalloped potatoes, green beans, and homemade applesauce, the hapless tenant lethargically stares at his near-empty shelf. Saffee wonders if he has fallen asleep in his hunkered-down position. Suddenly Joann blurts, as if to a naughty child, "Henry! You're letting all the cold out! Our electric bill will be sky-high if you keep that door open much longer!"

Mr. Clement's shoulders slump. He stands slowly and turns toward her, his face beet-red. "Oh, I-I'm sorry," he stammers, "I'm so sorry," and makes an empty-handed retreat. "I . . . I just couldn't decide . . ." The door closes softly behind him.

From then on, it seems Mr. Clement makes an effort to shorten his refrigerator gazes, but the number of his mealtime appearances remains about the same.

"Mom, what's this pile of books?" Saffee asks one day as she passes through the dining room. She puts down her opened copy of *Heidi* and riffles through pages of an imposing textbook. "Did you go to the library without me?"

Joann looks up from her study and tells her that the books are Mr. Clement's college books about psychology. She has borrowed them. She glances toward the door that leads to Mr. Clement's apartment and whispers, "I want to find out if our tenant suffers from *neurosis* or *psychosis*." She speaks in an airy way that signals delight in a new word or two.

Joann's married years have been filled with self-education. She no longer resents her father for preventing her from going to high school until she was considerably older than her classmates. By the time she enrolled, she had matured to the point that learning fascinated her.

"What's *'chology* mean, and that other word?"

"*Psy*-chology, Saffee. And you're too young to understand."

But Joann is very intent on understanding. Perhaps it will help her avert her own mother's fate. She pores over Mr. Clement's books for days. But to Joann's disappointment, her study comes to a halt when Henry Clement and his books move away.

"Maybe he moved because he wanted his books back and was too *neurotic* to ask," says Joann.

"Maybe he wanted his own refrigerator," says Saffee.

They were both wrong, of course. What Mr. Clement wanted was something the Kvaales were not skilled in giving—friendship.

CHAPTER FOURTEEN

UP AND DOWN

1950

All spring and into the summer, Joann sews draperies, tries her hand at upholstery, and adds touches that give the main floor of the old house a certain distinction, albeit homemade. As she bends over each task, she often repeats scraps of high-minded poetry and melancholy song.

> *Sweet sounds, oh, music, do not cease!*
> *Reject me not into the world again . . .*

After this brief hiatus, Joann's nightmares resume, and something within her urges that she employ her brush again. Although disappointed, she almost dutifully removes her portable sewing machine from the table and spreads the canvas drop cloth beneath. After all, the experiment had brought relief for a while. As does the next application. For a while. And the next.

Baffled by what now seems to have become his wife's obsession, Nels tries to dissuade her, but makes no headway. The sober intensity with which she works restrains the girls from asking questions. Her colors of choice are first yellow, and then red. Now, in late summer, Joann dips her brush into chartreuse.

Nels watches his wife's fervent splattering.

"How do you like it?" she asks with a smirk. "It's vomit green."

"Joann! What's got into you?"

She glares at him. Paint drips from the brush. "This is *my* business, Nels. You stick to *yours*."

He retreats, shaking his head.

Curious about the exchange, Saffee appears in the doorway between the kitchen and dining room. She leans against the wall and watches her mother's deliberate stroking. She recalls how that morning Joann had poured the last of the milk from its waxed carton onto April's cornflakes. When the carton was empty, Joann continued to hold it tipped in midair over the bowl. One more drop finally appeared, then none. Still her mother held the carton, motionless. Was that her frugality or, like it seems now, had she been rendered immobile, abducted into some invisible lair?

Saffee is tired of her mother's complexities. She has always hated the trance-like staring. And now, after months of her mother's painting obsession, which Saffee can't possibly understand, she has grown to hate the Norway table. She heads out the front door and crosses the screened porch. April and her neighborhood friend, Marilyn, are busily drawing stick figures with chalk on the cement walkway.

Saffee says, with disgust in her voice, "Did you see Mom, April? She's painting the Norway table again."

"Yeah, I saw her. It's gonna be green."

"No, not *green*, April." Saffee mimics Joann's I-know-a-new-word voice. "It's *vomit* green."

"The king is having a ball!" April chortles as she dashes through the kitchen one afternoon. "The king is having a ball!"

She turns around and demands of Saffee, "Wash the floor, Cinderella! The king is having a ball!" and scampers away. April has recently seen a Disney matinee and ever since, her play-acting has been insufferable, at least to her big sister. Saffee looks up from her Etch-a-Sketch and appeals to Joann.

"Mother, can't you make her stop? She's bothering me." But Joann's expression says, "Isn't she cute?" Saffee can't help but notice that her mother's cares curiously fade somewhat in the presence of her younger daughter's merriment.

Later, when Nels comes home, April is still at it. "Dance with me, Prince!" she calls, stretching her arms toward him. Nels looks quizzical and scratches his head.

Joann comes from the kitchen, laughing. "April, haven't I told you before your father has two left feet? Here"—she grabs April's waving arms—"I'll dance with you." Giggling and singing, the two twirl together across the living room and out onto the screen porch.

The Miller's Ford residents who venture to make Joann's acquaintance are, for a while, fascinated by her posturing ways and unexpected pronouncements. But it doesn't take long for her singular manner to create a space between them. A young grocery store employee one day asks Joann, with Saffee by her side, if she would like him to carry her two bags of groceries to her car. Joann doesn't drive. With an upward twitch of her head she delivers an outlandish retort.

"Alas, my chariot awaiteth not at the door, young man, and my strength comes from sources you are obviously unfamiliar with." She sweeps a bag from the counter and, with a self-satisfied snicker, floats with majesty to the door. She is oblivious of his puzzled look, as well as gasps from two middle-aged women in the checkout line.

Saffee's face burns. She snatches the other bag from the checkout counter and hurries out. What fantasy world does her mother live in? Why didn't she just say, "No, thank you"?

People of the town, unsure how to cross the divide between stable and unstable, learn to avoid this strange woman. Neither they, nor her family, nor Joann herself, can fathom the nuances of a darkening mind.

CHAPTER FIFTEEN

THE SEWING CLUB

1950

Saffee tightens toe clamps around her saddle shoes and buckles brown leather straps. The cement bridge spanning Blue River is ideal for roller skating. Swinging her arms back and forth, Saffee scrapes and slides along the sidewalk, bumping over every crack. The skate key sways on its string and lightly thumps against her chest.

On the sidewalk ahead, Saffee recognizes Mrs. O'Reilly, the mother of a fourth-grade classmate. Saffee drags a front wheel. The narrow concrete walkway, and Mrs. O'Reilly's deluxe size, oblige them both to stop to avoid collision. Saffee would have preferred to zip quickly by. Mrs. O'Reilly greets her pleasantly and admires her polka-dotted shirt and matching shorts.

"So cute. Does your mother sew your clothes?"

Saffee nods.

"What's your mother's name? I wonder if she'd like to join the sewing club. I'll call her."

At supper, Saffee mentions that Mrs. O'Reilly might call.

"A sewing club? Hmm," Joann says. "More likely a *gossip* club, I suppose."

"Why don't you go?" Nels urges. "It'd be good fer ya ta get out, meet some other women."

To Saffee's surprise, Joann does attend the sewing club. Once.

The following morning at breakfast the girls are eager to know about her uncharacteristic foray into small-town society.

Joann, holding her coffee cup with a raised pinky, tells them that it was at a Mrs. Birdwell's house where everything was "hoity-toity." Mrs. Birdwell, she says, collects ceramic parrots of various sizes and colors. Joann laughs with amusement and butters her toast. "Really bad taste."

When asked about the food, she grins and reports that there was pink punch, way too sweet, and little square cakes called *petits fours*. It seemed no one knew the French pronunciation that Joann later found in the dictionary.

The women worked on "silly stuff," like crocheted doilies and pot holders with ruffles. Joann doubts that they know how to make *useful* things, like clothes and curtains. She had let down a hem on one of Saffee's skirts.

Saffee glances at April's red-checked pinafore, proud that her mother sews so ably.

"I bet ya met some nice ladies, Joann," Nels says, obviously hoping she had.

"Nice? Well, maybe, but short on looks, shorter on brains," she scoffs. Joann scoops the last of the scrambled eggs onto her plate and declares, "I won't be going back."

Nels knows it is useless to argue.

That afternoon, flushed from the July heat, Saffee hurries into the house with an armload of books and heads to the kitchen for a glass of water. Which should she read first? *Kon-Tiki* or *Pygmalion*? Her mother, at the breakfast bar, does not acknowledge her. She is scribbling in a spiral notebook, imagination meeting memory, a wry smile on her face. More and more she dashes off lines of doggerel, revising for a number of days until a piece gives her pleasure.

"The library was so nice and cool," Saffee says. "Wish our house was air-conditioned. Most of all, I really wish I could have a bike, Mom. I'm tired of walking all the time. I could have a basket on the front for books and stuff."

Whenever Saffee asks for a bicycle, her parents remind her they live on a "very steep hill," and she'd probably "break her neck."

Gulping water, she watches her mother. "Whatcha writing, Mom?"

Engrossed in her own drama, Joann does not respond. Saffee asks again.

"Talk, talk, talk," says Joann, still not looking up.

Saffee stamps her right foot on the floor and sets the glass on the counter a little too firmly. "I have *not* been talking!" she blurts. "I haven't even been in the house! And all I did was ask for a bike."

"Clean up the water you spilled, Saffee. No, I'm *writing* about talking. All that *yak-yak-yak* last night at the sewing club got me started on a poem." She surveys the page, nodding slightly, clicking her tongue. "Actually, it's turning out kind of good. Maybe I'll read it to you when I'm finished." She bends to resume. "Now, let me be so I can follow where my mind is going."

Over the next two days, Joann labors on what she calls an "essay poem." When relatively satisfied, she summons Saffee and April to a dramatic reading in the living room. Joann sits with one leg elevated on a hassock; her varicose veins are "killing her." The girls sit at her feet.

"The title is 'Ensnared,'" Joann says. "There are three parts. Here's the first one." She reads,

> *Advance. Retreat.*
> *Offend. Defend.*
> *Bumper cars converse, reverse.*
> *Teasing push here, sudden jab there.*
> *Touché! Good hit!*

For a while, April is swept into Joann's theatricality, which is much like her own. She bobs and sways to the rhythm of the words. Her sister sits very still.

> *Smiling masks belie sweaty palms, stiff necks.*
> *Stupid! I knew I should not have come.*
> *Stomachs knot.*
> *Voices blabber.*
> *Batteries rush toward their own extinction.*
> *Blam! Quiplash! Cornered!*
> *. . . At last, they slither away.*
> *Smoke and mirrors.*
> *Forgettable . . .*
> *But not forgotten.*

The confrontational words startle Saffee. She eyes her mother doubtfully. "What's that got to do with sewing club, Mom?"

"That part just sets the stage for the next two parts, so listen." Joann resumes reading.

> *We bring to the table the raw material of unspoken thoughts . . .*
> *The fabric of our words becomes weightier. Riskier . . .*

The essay poem drags on and on. By the time Joann reads the last part, she is giggling, thoroughly enjoying her own melodramatic absurdity.

> *Beware! Beware the delicate dance! The delicate verbal*
> *dance! . . .*

April has become disinterested and has left the room. Saffee listens, hoping to understand even a little about her mother's stinging reflections on the "verbal dance" and the "raucous undercurrent and pieties" at the sewing club.

. . . Naïveté trampled, again . . .
Rude cacophony retains its rule . . .
The Lord is in His holy temple.
Let all the earth keep silent before Him.

When the work finally concludes, Joann continues to edit, energetically inserting a new word here, hazarding a new line there.

Saffee sits silently. She's too young to fully comprehend that what her mother has read from the notebook reflects a growing paranoia that writes on the tablet of her mind. Yet, on a simple level, Saffee relates.

"Like you said, that was about talking, right, Mom?"

"Right," Joann answers, intent on her editing.

"I don't like to talk to people much either, Mom," Saffee says quietly.

Joann stops writing, looks down at her, and says, "Well, of course, the other night wasn't really *quite* that bad. I *made up* some of it."

"Oh." Saffee pauses. "But still, I don't think I'll ever go to a sewing club."

CHAPTER SIXTEEN

TREE OF LIFE,
TREE OF EVIL

1951

M iss Eilert, a cherubic-faced pillar of the First Methodist Church, sits facing the row of three girls and two boys in the basement Sunday school room. The chilly stone walls suggest a cave unsuccessfully disguised with yellow paint. A labyrinth of ancient, patched pipes and heating ducts crisscross overhead. The children, all eight or nine years old, wear coats dusted by snow during their short walk from school.

To Saffee's relief, a navy blue cape with silver buttons at each shoulder disguises Miss Eilert's prodigiousness. Barrel-bosomed women always embarrass her. But worse, Joann's insistence that Saffee attend this class meant she had to give up her usual after-school ice-skating on the Blue River. Saffee had put up a fuss to no avail, and now she sits hunched in a straight wooden chair, scowling.

"I'm sorry it's chilly," Miss Eilert says. "They don't turn on the furnace during the week."

Hearing her pleasant voice, Saffee's impression of Miss Eilert softens. The woman seems intent, yet kind. The children fidget but show respect.

Miss Eilert begins by holding up a paper cutout from a pile on her lap. "When God created the world," she says, "He placed the first man and the first woman in a beautiful garden called Eden." She presses the cutout of Adam and Eve, discreetly standing behind a bush, onto a flannel-covered easel. Saffee's face flushes pink. She's glad no one in the room knows that her full name is Sapphire Eve, not after this obviously naked Eve, but after an evening sky.

"This is the Tree of Life," Miss Eilert continues. "God planted it in the middle of the garden." Up goes the tree onto the easel.

"And God put another tree in the garden. The Tree of the Knowledge of Good and Evil." Up goes the second tree.

Saffee wonders if there might be a stick of Doublemint in her coat pocket. She fishes. All she feels are wet mittens.

"God instructed Adam and Eve not to eat fruit from the Tree of the Knowledge of Good and Evil. But they disobeyed." Miss Eilert covers the cutout figures with a large black circle.

"This black spot represents sin. When we do something God has instructed us not to do, that is sin. Ever since Adam and Eve, every person born, except One, has sinned. We are not allowed to carry that sin to heaven. We can't live with God unless that sin is washed away while we still live on earth."

The five children wiggle but are still attentive.

Miss Eilert smiles at them. It is a pretty smile. "God has a loving plan to take away sin and make us clean." She removes the black circle and says, "God sent His Son, Jesus, to live as a perfect man on earth."

Saffee listens to the familiar story of the birth of Baby Jesus. She was part of a speaking chorus in the church Christmas program last month. Although she diligently practiced her short solo line, she almost fainted with fright when the moment came to speak it.

As Miss Eilert displays more flannel-backed images, Saffee is able to disregard the unpleasant smell of her wet wool coat. She is startled by the picture of Jesus nailed to a wooden cross and wearing a crown of thorns, His body blood-streaked.

"Jesus allowed Himself to be nailed to a cross to die because He loves us." Miss Eilert's voice is slow, as if to let her words sink in. "The sins of the whole world, even yours and mine, were put on Jesus when He hung on the cross . . ."

Saffee perspires inside her heavy coat.

"Jesus was willing to be punished for *our* sins, even though *He* never sinned. Then . . . three days later . . ." Miss Eilert's smile widens as she presses a picture of an empty tomb onto the board. "He rose to life again . . . and He lives today."

After a brief pause, Miss Eilert and her cape stand up. "Children," she says, "we're going upstairs now. Please follow me." *What is this?*

The sanctuary feels even colder than the basement. Late afternoon light hardly penetrates the stained glass windows. Miss Eilert indicates that the children are to kneel along the curved altar rail.

Before them, lining the back of the altar, vertical brass pipes of the organ stand as if sentinels in the Sabbath-like stillness. Saffee considers the organ to be magnificent. She loves its complex sounds and routinely counts pipes during long Sunday sermons. Now, in the dusk, rising high above her, they create a mysterious holiness.

Miss Eilert whispers, "I've told you about Jesus. I've told you that He died on the cross because He loves us. When we trust our lives to Him, He forgives our sins and His Spirit comes to live inside us. Then God sees us as completely clean. Pure like Jesus. Pure enough to someday live with Him in heaven."

Softly, Miss Eilert begins to sing, *"Into my heart, into my heart, come into my heart, Lord Jesus. Come in today, come in to stay, come into my heart, Lord Jesus."*

The children squirm and don't dare look at each other.

"Jesus loves you," Miss Eilert says. "He wants to wash away your

96 | SUZANNE FIELD

sins, and live in your heart, and be with you always. With Jesus, you will never be alone. When you are happy, He will be there. When you are sad, He will be there." She pauses. Saffee senses that the moment holds inexplicable significance and that her entire life has purposefully led her to it. "If you want Jesus to be your wonderful Savior," Miss Eilert says, "please sing with me."

Miss Eilert begins the song again. With hands clasped, and audible only to herself, Saffee sings, *Come into my heart, Lord Jesus.*

And He does.

Although it is somehow more understood by her heart than her head, she knows He does. She feels an exquisite happiness.

Minutes later she steps outside and stands still in the gathering darkness. Even though she has often sought to be alone, she experiences a curious relief that she will never be alone again.

She hears the slow-moving, heavy church door close behind her. She looks up and sees menacing snow clouds. Her chest tightens. Within her is a new, wonderful, and undeniable presence of love. But in the air there is another presence that scorns the words she has sung.

CHAPTER SEVENTEEN

NANCY DREW

T urn off the light. I wanna sleep!" April mumbles.
"Gotta finish this page."
"No! I'm gonna tell!"

Saffee snaps the book shut, just as Nancy Drew's blue roadster is about to zip past the suspicious man with the scar on his left cheek. With a sigh, she turns off the flashlight and flings the sheet from her head.

Every window of the house is open but not a particle of stuffy air moves. Saffee squints across the hallway to her parents' bedroom. Rats! The door is open. But it's late; they're probably asleep. She slides out of bed, careful not to let the springs squeak. Tiptoeing past their door, she hears her father's whiffling snore. With pillow and flashlight, Saffee imagines she looks like her favorite sleuth and suppresses a giggle.

Faint rays of moonlight fall on the playhouse cover over the Norway table. Perfect. She crawls under, clicks on the flashlight, and plumps up the pillow for her head. An area rug that she and April have dragged in makes this a comfortable place to lie. As flashlight shadows play on the white fabric walls, Saffee and Nancy Drew resume a thrilling ride around hairpin mountain curves. Suspense mounts as headlights from behind grow closer in the rearview mirror. Saffee perspires.

Z-z-z-z. The high whine of a mosquito blood-hunt. Without taking her eyes from the page, Saffee swats at the pest with the flashlight. The annoying sound gathers volume. She trains the light at the underside of the table, searching for the little demon. Two of them. She slaps and misses. Watching for another chance, she wonders why her mother never paints the underside of the table. The latest topside color is buttery cream and she had carefully painted around the vine, leaving it, well, green.

Z-z-z-z. Saffee swats again. Another miss. Following the speedy buzzers, her eyes settle on lettering burned into the back of the apron above her and to the left. She has often read the engraved names of her great-grandparents on the apron's right side, but has puzzled over these words that end with numbers: 128 and 3.

Maybe a cryptic message from Viking days?

She feels a bite on her thigh and slaps. *Z-z-z-z.* Missed again. Irritated, she gives the playhouse fabric a smart tug in order to lift the opposite side, hoping the hungry pests will fly out and away.

Crash! A pile of books and Joann's metal box that stores hundreds of buttons land on the hardwood floor not far from Saffee's head.

In the bedroom, a malignant voice whispers, *"Joann! Joann!"*

Saffee's adrenaline spikes and she gives a startled yelp. She rolls to the right, out from under the table, only to become hopelessly entangled in sheeting and slide around on the skittering buttons. She struggles to free herself. Her right hand still holds the flashlight, its rays ricochet off the dining room walls.

Roused from the stupor of sleep, Joann stumbles into the dining room, her face a gash of fright. "Fire! Fire! Come, children!"

On her knees, Saffee still struggles to extricate herself from the shroud of sheeting. Joann impatiently gives her a downward shove. "Get under!" she orders. "It's coming! It's close!"

"Mother!" Saffee yells, dismayed at Joann's delusion. "What are you shouting about? It's nothing! Some stuff just fell off the table!"

Joann, desperate to escape whatever pursues her, slips on the scattered buttons and falls to her hands and knees. Her eyes blaze. "Hurry! Everybody! Get under the table or we'll all burn! It's whipping in the wind, coming for us . . . the *inferno*! Get under the table!"

Nels strides into the room. "Joann! Joann! Whatcha doin'? Whatcha yellin' about?" With effort he pulls his wife to her feet and tries to subdue her flailing arms.

"Saffee, get to bed. Right now!" he orders, as if embarrassed that his daughter is witnessing Joann's unnatural behavior.

Instead, her heart racing, Saffee flips the wall switch. Joann wears a stranger's face as her wild eyes dart around the illuminated room. There is no fire. She ceases her frantic reeling, whimpers, and crumples into Nels's arms.

He guides her back to their bedroom, where disguises of childhood trauma continue to torment Joann's midnight hours. Soon they will lurk by day.

Trembling, Saffee turns out the light, retreats to her own room, and slumps onto her side of the bed. It looks as if April has not moved.

The troubling scene lasted mere moments. Would Nancy Drew be able to unravel the meaning of it? Drama and mystery, so exhilarating on the written page, seem only to plunder real life. Although Saffee is confused, tonight she realizes, with maturity beyond her years, that her mother suffers seriously from some irrevocable trauma from her past.

As she lies in the darkness, listening to the high-pitched whine of a mosquito, it dawns on her that Joann's obsession with painting the table has nothing to do with decorating.

The next morning, after Saffee has picked up all the scattered buttons, according to her father's instruction, she wants to question her mother about last night's peculiar excitement. She stands in the kitchen several minutes, watching Joann intently ironing Nels's work shirts to a shine. It would be of no use to inquire; she is unapproachable. Saffee goes outside.

No one is in the neighboring backyard. She crosses over and climbs into the tire swing that hangs from a limb of a towering elm and idly scuffs her feet in the dirt. The tire spins in lazy circles. Saffee daydreams that her mother smiles, puts down her iron, goes to the back door, and calls her. Invites her to sit down beside her on the step, strokes her hair, and talks to her. Explains things about life and life's mysteries.

She pumps her legs vigorously. Extending her arms and leaning far back, she looks at the pattern of the leafy canopy against the bright blue summer sky. Dapples of warm sun kiss her face and she remembers that she is not alone.

Into my heart, Lord Jesus . . .

She smiles and whispers, "Jesus, You're swinging with me."

CHAPTER EIGHTEEN

PALM SUNDAY

1952

$\int$ affee kicks off her wet boots in the entryway and hears the familiar whir of the Singer sewing machine. She pushes through the French doors and hurries to the dining room where Joann bends over her work. Multiple yards of polished cotton splash pink cabbage roses across the Norway table and spill onto the floor.

"Mom, I need you to make something for the concert."

Joann glances up.

"Hang up your coat. Make what? You know I'm busy trying to finish these draperies for the living room."

Saffee pulls a length of white fabric and a mimeographed paper from a bag and shows them to her mother. The paper has a simple drawing of a square with a hole in the center. Below, it says, "Sirplus, 28 inches."

"What's this?" Joann asks. "What's a sirplus?"

"I don't know, but Mrs. Knudsen says everyone's gotta wear one on Palm Sunday for the *Messiah* concert."

Joann's studied vocabulary is a source of pride. She keeps a note-book of newly learned words she finds in *Time* magazine and practices them on the family. Once, when Saffee questioned this preoccupation, Joann gazed at the ceiling and replied, "Well, Saffee, while I would never promote pretension, a certain erudition has always been considered a virtue." But now, erudition or not, here is a word that puzzles her.

She leans to pick up a well-thumbed dictionary from the shelf of the telephone table, a book the family uses more frequently than the phone directory.

"Of course," she huffs with indignation. "It's sur*plice*. S-u-r-p-l-i-c-e. 'A loose white vestment worn by clergy and choristers at Christian church services.' You'd think that people who aspire to communicate would also aspire to spell. What kind of people are up at that church?"

White lilies, their blossoms like trumpets, edge the entire choir loft. The burgundy-colored robes of First Methodist's chancel choir serve as their dramatic backdrop. Although small in number, the choir sings from Handel's magnificent work with as much passion as larger groups of renown.

"Comfort ye, comfort ye, My people, saith your God . . ."

As the adults sing, eighteen fidgety grade-schoolers, each wearing a square white surplice, whisper in the vestibule, waiting to make their entrance. Monitored by their director, Mrs. Knudsen, the children nervously swish green palm branches, shipped specially from Florida. A boy covertly distributes sticks of Black Jack to grinning friends.

Through the glass doors, Saffee stares at the back of the congregants' heads. It is a fearful thing for Saffee to "perform" like this before the whole church. If she didn't love the music so much, she could never do it. Her dad and sister are seated out there somewhere. Her mother is not. Everything went wrong this morning. April spilled her grapefruit juice and had to change clothes. Saffee arrived at breakfast wearing her concert attire—a white blouse and dark skirt, topped, of course, by the surplice.

"Saffee!" her mother had exclaimed. "It's all wrinkled! I pressed it so nice last night; what did you do?" Nels said he thought it looked fine, but Joann pulled the garment over Saffee's head and set up the ironing board.

After that, Joann fretted for fifteen minutes at the bathroom vanity mirror, struggling to make her newly home-permed hair behave. Battling frizz with her green-handled hairbrush, she grumbled, "What good is going to church anyway? Bunch of unfriendly, snooty people. The only time anyone from church calls is when they want me to bake a cake. Lot of work and no thanks."

"Joann! We're late!" Nels said. "What's holdin' you up?"

She declared that she would not be going, but Nels insisted.

"Didn't you hear me? I'm not going!" Nels dodged the green-handled hairbrush as it flew in his direction. Joann slammed the bathroom door. Containers were heard toppling, clattering across the vanity counter.

Nels shook his head and yelled, "Joann, I'll never understand you!" He took off his suit coat and threw it across a chair.

April looked pale and started to cry.

"Daddy, we have to leave *right now*," Saffee insisted. "I can't be late for the lineup."

"We can't go to church without your mother."

"Why not?"

"People . . . people would think somethin's wrong."

"But, Daddy, today's the *Messiah* concert. I'm in the junior choir processional. We've *gotta* go."

Nels reached for his coat and as the three strode toward the garage he muttered, "Can't figger out what makes yer mother *so irritable*."

"Every valley shall be exalted, and every mountain and hill made low, the crooked straight and the rough places plain."

The words, sung by the chancel choir, pulse through the transom above the door. The fugue-like interplay of voice and organ refreshes Saffee, exhilarates her. She presses her face to the glass for a better view of the director. His robed arms beat the air with contagious confidence. His curly black hair bounces with each bob of his head.

Equally animated, the organist, wearing a bright purple suit (she insists she cannot navigate the organ in a robe), commandeers the tiered keyboards flanked by the tall brass pipes reaching heavenward. On the bench she scoots energetically from side to side because her legs are too short to reach the extreme left and right pedals.

"And the glory, the glory of the Lord shall be revealed . . ."

"Everybody! We're next!" Mrs. Knudsen whispers. "Take your places!" She matter-of-factly holds an opened concert program under various chins, into which some of the children spit wet wads of black, chewed gum.

The organ swells. The double doors open and smiling children spill into the sanctuary, branches aloft. Their young voices combine with those more seasoned at the front . . .

> *Lift up your heads, O ye gates,*
> *and be ye lift up, ye everlasting doors,*
> *and the King of Glory shall come in.*
> *Who is the King of Glory?*
> *The Lord strong and mighty, the Lord mighty in battle.*

As best she can, Saffee puts aside the mishaps of the morning and the disappointment that her mother is not present. She sings with feeling, sensing a thrill of kinship with the words, remembering that she had opened the door of her own heart to Jesus when she knelt at the altar a year ago.

"Lift up your heads, O ye gates."

The joyous words are about Jesus' entry not only into Jerusalem but also into her own life. For an instant, she sees her mother behind closed gates, confined, imprisoned. Saffee sings louder, pushing the picture away.

A number of flailing palms skim ladies' spring hats and gentlemen's heads. April grins and gives Saffee a discreet wave with a white-gloved hand as she passes. Nels smiles too.

After the concert, crescendos of "Hallelujah" continue to resonate within her. She asks Nels for permission to walk the six blocks home rather than ride in the car.

Her shiny black shoes step lightly along the wet pavement, skirting narrow, hurrying rivers of melting snow. The exquisite melodies will soon vanish into the spring air, no matter how fervently she bids them stay. She walks the quiet Sunday streets, palm branch in hand, embracing the aura of the music, embracing the closeness of God.

CHAPTER NINETEEN

APRIL

J udy Bellingham's light blue eyes are the oversized, pop-out kind that look like they might when she's afraid.

"Saffee, why is your mother yelling so much?" Judy's voice is muffled from under a pillow. "I want to go home!" She pulls up her head.

"You can't," Saffee says, watching Judy's eyes. "Your parents are gone. Your mom wants you to stay here overnight."

"I don't care, I want to go!"

"Judy, I can't sleep with the light on," says April from the floor where she has made her bed, pretending she is venturing to the center of the earth.

"When I'm scared I gotta have the light on," the guest whines.

The verbal altercation between Joann and Nels continues through the closed bedroom door.

The next day, Mrs. Bellingham retrieves Judy from the inhospitable home. When they are gone, Nels draws Saffee and April aside. "Don't be bringin' people in our house," he says. "It's not a good idea."

❧

"Look at me, I'm Queen Esther!" April sings, waltzing through the living room. A strap of Joann's old pink nightgown clings to her small right shoulder; the other side has slipped to her elbow. A gauzy purple scarf flutters from her blond curls. "I'm Queen Esther, the most *bea-oo-tiful* woman in the *whole* Bible!" Joann and April share a love for theatricality.

"Oh brother, April." Saffee sits on the living room floor braiding a bracelet of plastic gimp. She snaps the green-and-white laces in her sister's direction as April lifts the nightgown high for a pirouette. "Get outta here! You're acting dumb again. Mother!" Saffee yells. "April's annoying me!" She often whines this refrain to no avail.

She knows rudeness toward April is not right, but it's a habit she has little inclination to change, since it usually goes unnoticed by her parents. On that snowy afternoon last winter, Miss Eilert said that God's love can change people's hearts. Learning what this means is taking Saffee some time.

Nels is known in the coffee shops of Miller's Ford for his jovial, jester-like personality. Yet at home, spontaneity in his daughters has never been appreciated. "Don't make noise; don't make a mess; don't get your mother upset," he warns. The last is the reason for the first two. Saffee long ago bought into his rules, even though it is obvious their mother is charmed, not disturbed, by her little sister's antics. Antics that continue to befuddle Nels.

"Esther," ignoring Saffee's exasperation, prances out the door and across the porch to the front yard, in search of neighborhood children to join her fun.

Let chatterbox April be entertaining, enjoying quantities of attention and affection at home and elsewhere. Saffee needs none of it. She can't control her unpredictable family environment, but to a certain extent, she can control April. When parents are elsewhere, Saffee is not beyond giving her sister a lecture and a shove. But each rejection only seems to encourage April to annoy the one who refuses to give her adulation.

On a serene, small-town evening in late summer, dark green maple leaves whisper and swish against the side porch screens as if to celebrate the orange and magenta sunset that stretches along the river beyond them. The sounds of baseball faintly ebb and flow from Nels's radio in the kitchen. Saffee is curled up in a wicker porch chair with her current book, *The Wizard of Oz*. Books are her friends. She lives within their characters, looking for her own life. Such fantasy stays in her head and is not "performed" as April would.

From the corner of her eye Saffee sees shadowy movement. The bent form of Lena Bevins slowly climbs four steps and peers through the screen door. Saffee has never been near this woman who lives alone across the street. Both she and her tall, narrow house of weathered gray boards are easily ignored. In summer, if one would notice, Lena, day in and day out, pulls weeds and gathers produce in her half-acre garden of vegetables and flowers. Few know, or stop to wonder, what Lena does in winter.

"I come to take April for a walk," Lena says through the screen. Her monotone is deep, her shy grin reveals gaps between teeth.

Saffee hesitates, stays curled in her chair, then calls, "April!"

April immediately comes leaping onto the porch. "Hi, Lena! You came!"

Before Saffee can think what to say, the two take hands and head toward the brilliant pink and orange sky over Bridge Street. For a moment, Saffee watches them. Lena shambles, April jigs.

Miller's Ford offers indifference to Lena Bevins and other quiet, reclusive women like her, while Joann, voluble and apt to be bizarre, feeds the town's appetite for gossip. This matter, however, is beyond Saffee's young perspective. She resumes her own travel, down a yellow brick road. When it becomes dusk, she squints at the pages as long as possible, then retreats to lamplight in the house, where she is terrorized along with Dorothy by the Wicked Witch of the East.

April! How long has she been gone? Lena is *not* the Wicked Witch, she tells herself, but still, weren't the two headed toward the bridge over Blue River? Saffee has glimpsed the cavernous, spooky spaces between the massive cement supports under the bridge. She had shrunk away, recoiling at the mysterious graffiti emblazoned on the giant slabs of concrete. It is a place where a little sister could be swallowed up in darkness in the company of . . .

In a storm of anxiety, she runs to the kitchen. "Mother! Daddy! April's gone, it's dark!" Nels turns off the radio. "She went with that Lena. That strange woman from across the street. And they've been gone a long time. Maybe Lena's going to kill her under the bridge!"

Joann rushes from the bedroom. "Nels!" she shrieks. "What should we do?"

The three stride through the living room and across the porch— just as Lena and April, still hand in hand, come up the walk.

"Here they are," Nels says so only Joann and Saffee hear. "Now, botha you, don't look so upset. It's nothin'." Lena looks intimidated as Joann, arms outstretched, hurries down the steps toward April. Nels and Saffee remain at the open screen door.

"Mommy! I visited Lena in her garden this morning, so now she came to visit me." As is common with April, she doesn't merely speak, she chortles, adding her signature bouncy dance. "We saw the most bea-oo-tiful sunset."

Saffee fumes within; April hasn't an inkling that she has caused her family to worry.

"Tomorrow Lena's gonna let me find ladybugs on her potatoes!"

"The girl sure can sing," Lena intones, it seems with some fondness. "Well . . . bye." She turns and shuffles away into the twilight.

Now that it has turned out to be "nothin'," her parents don't seem concerned that April went off without informing them. Instead, to Saffee's chagrin, Joann says as they enter the house, "Nels. Did you hear how upset Sapphire was? She *does* love her sister. She just *acts* like she doesn't."

Saffee is surprised to hear that her mother has even noticed her lack of sisterly affection, especially since her rudeness has never been corrected. But it is true, something different (perhaps caring?) *had* bubbled up quite unexpectedly during April's brief disappearance. Saffee is profusely embarrassed and determines not to let it, whatever it was, show again.

A few days later, on a bright steamy morning, one of April's play-mates dashes into the Kvaale house, yelling, "April's been hit by a car!"

Joann bolts outside and dashes around the house to cross the alley parallel to Bridge Street, the main road that leads through town. Saffee follows close behind. It's true. Vernon, an attendant at the intersection's service station, saw the impact. He rushed into the street and now kneels beside April's unconscious form. Her custom-ary morning curlers are flattened over the top of her head, forming a crude metal helmet. A tan and maroon Oldsmobile, motor still running, is stopped nearby and its elderly driver stands wringing his hands.

April moans and, with help, is able to sit up. Watching intently, Saffee trembles but this time does not speak out her relief.

CHAPTER TWENTY

MR. MASON

1952

man. Her sixth-grade teacher is a man! Saffee is dumbstruck by the novelty of it. And Mr. Mason is not just any man, but a beautiful man who looks steadily into faces and speaks with an arrestingly gentle voice. The best part is Mr. Mason refers to and addresses each student as "young man" or "young lady." To Saffee, to be so addressed is stunning, revelatory, and dignifying. For the first time in her life she considers that perhaps she is a person of worth. No one before, certainly not her parents, has made an effort to convey that she is.

Furthermore, Mr. Mason goes beyond the customary rote teaching that the class is used to. Instead, he opens to them a world of historical and current events and encourages them to form opinions on issues. Saffee's undeniable crush causes her too much fluster to permit more than minimal classroom participation, but her homework has never been so carefully prepared.

When Mr. Mason teaches the class how to do a simple research paper, Saffee writes about the Battle of Gettysburg. "Well done!" Mr. Mason writes atop her paper. "Gripping! You made me feel like I was there!" Saffee hugs the handwritten pages and determines to keep them forever.

However, when school resumes after Christmas break, the bubble bursts. Mr. Mason announces he has been asked to join the school's administration. He introduces Miss Reynolds, who will finish the year in his stead. In shock, Saffee scans Miss Reynolds: tall and slender, long red hair, very high heels, and, worst of all, fluttering eyelashes. It is hard to miss that Miss Reynolds also is smitten with Mr. Mason.

Saffee walks home in a frozen daze. The first adult in the world to show her respect as a person—gone. For a few months, Mr. Mason had brushed a tint of color onto the dull canvas of her life. Now, the color is expunged. Betrayed, she sits on the edge of her bed and sobs.

Curious, Joann comes into the bedroom. Saffee can hardly speak. She manages to sputter enough information so that Joann realizes, with surprise, that Saffee is experiencing the bitter taste of lost first love. Mother stands staring at daughter.

Finally, she says, "You'll get over it soon enough." She begins to leave the room, then stops.

"It's time to burn the trash, Saffee. Collect everything that's paper and go out with it. Take some matches from the drawer."

Saffee swipes both her hands across hot wet cheeks. "Daddy does that. I've never started a fire." Neither has Joann.

"He's not home. If you're old enough to have a 'flame' at school, you're old enough to light a match."

Saffee cringes at the pun. Still crying, she dumps wastepaper into the oil drum in the backyard near the alley, then timidly strikes match after match against the rough, rusted inner side. Finally, one ignites. She stands still, holding her coat tightly against the winter air, staring through tears at the spreading fire . . .

We saw it far off, whipping in the wind, coming . . . coming . . . an inferno . . .

Newspaper becomes cinnamon brown and curls, crackles and turns black.

Heat dries the tearstained face.

CHAPTER TWENTY-ONE

VOICES ON THE STAIRS

1953

"W hy don't they stop yelling?" April whimpers.

"Give them time." Saffee masks her own nervousness with big-sister superiority. Her first week without Mr. Mason is finally over, but as she and April sit tensely, halfway down the chilly basement stairway, life heightens its gloom. Their parents' strident, garbled voices ricochet in the kitchen above, fade as deliberate footsteps take them into the living room, rise once again as they return.

Nels is no match for Joann's verbal skills. She skewers him in every argument. Saffee recalls that when she did research for her "gripping" paper for Mr. Mason, she read about President Lincoln's volatile wife and thought of her mother.

Catching a word here and there, Saffee realizes this argument is related to Joann's demands that Nels give her another child. A boy, for him, she says. But it is apparent that the desire is more for herself; April is growing up. Saffee has heard Nels tell her mother that her "nerves" couldn't take having another baby.

For some time, Nels has been sleeping on the foldout couch in his den. Of course, no explanation for that has been made to the daughters, but Saffee has speculated. His move from their bedroom has increased Joann's accusations of infidelity. Saffee has seen the hurt in her father's eyes when she hurls barbed remarks. He is a simple, transparent man who lives by a rigid moral code. Her mother's imaginative claims are ridiculous.

Even though it is January, the stairway heat register is closed. Higher up the wall, black windows of night are frosted over. A slit of light comes from under the kitchen door, giving scant illumination. The girls could turn on the back hall ceiling light, but semidarkness seems more comfortable, protective. Saffee stares hard to distinguish the back of her sister's head. April's blond curls pooch out on both sides where her fingers try to stop her ears.

Ever since "April's car accident," Joann has been more diligent than ever to put metal curlers in her hair. The doctor said that she had had a concussion and that those curlers may have saved her life.

Joann's doting has multiplied. April can do no wrong and her every move is reason for applause. At the same time, it seems as if Joann detects some ominous handwriting on the wall. She says because the accident must have done irreparable internal damage, fragile April will need protection forevermore.

"I didn't mean to drop my ring down the sink," April laments. "My hands were soapy—it just slipped off. Why did that make them so mad? Will Daddy have to take the sink apart?"

Saffee sighs. "April, that's not what they're fighting about."

"Really?"

"Aren't you listening? Mother's accusing Daddy of looking at some woman today when they drove to the grocery store."

"So what's wrong with Daddy looking at someone?" April asks.

"Nothing. Unless she's pretty."

During summertime treks to the grocery store, Saffee notices with discomfort how men of the town ogle her mother's curvaceous torso. It seems Joann knows it too and doesn't mind. Doesn't mind at all. But even the thought of Nels ogling another woman, that's a different matter.

In the kitchen, Nels yells, "Joann! I tol' you, I din't even *see* no woman!"

"Sure, Nels, sure," she retorts. "And you never see me either, do you? To me you are cold, withdrawn. You know all I want is—"

"Be quiet, Joann. Keep yer voice down." Their steps retreat again.

From a greater distance, Joann is heard to shout, "My own mother was deprived of her baby too, Nels. Are you aware of what happened to her because of it, Nels? Are you . . . ?"

"Stop," April whines.

Saffee slips into a practiced state of detached loneliness, locking others out, locking herself in. In this place, she is able to endure the din. Then, without warning, she is thrust from her hazy bubble to a heightened sense of awareness. She hears another voice, prominent, yet at the same time quiet and comforting. It enters not through her ears but is present deep within.

Watch . . . Listen . . . Learn. Your life will be different. Watch . . . Listen . . . Learn.

Her eyes widen. The moment and the voice are freeze-framed to be remembered all of her life.

Somewhere, probably in sermons, she's heard that God speaks in a still, small voice. Could this be? She takes a deep, uneven breath.

The kitchen door bursts open, spilling harsh light onto the stairway and rudely jolting Saffee back into the tension of the moment. Nels's footsteps are quick.

"Move over," he orders, thumping past them down the steps into the basement. They see him stride in the direction of his workbench.

Guns. Beyond the workbench are his hunting rifles. Saffee springs to her feet and races up the steps to the kitchen. "Mother! Mother! Stop arguing!" she screams.

April spurts past them and disappears down the bedroom hall.

White-faced and trembling, Saffee slumps against a wall. "He's getting a gun! This is your fault; why are you always fighting?"

Joann lurches to the stairway railing. Her rashness melts to a whimper. "No, Nels," she calls. "No. I didn't mean it. Everything's okay; don't be mad. Come up, honey. It's okay."

Nels comes up the steps looking puzzled at her change of tone. This woman he loves so deeply bewilders and frustrates him so. There is not a gun but a wrench in his hand. "Gotta take the P-trap off to get the ring," he says gruffly, striding into the kitchen.

Weak with relief, Saffee realizes how out of character it would be for her father to reach for a gun in anger. Countless ensnaring arguments with Joann must sadden him, madden him, make him yearn for peace. "Your mother is never happy unless she's mad about something," he has more than once lamented to his girls.

Saffee trudges to the bedroom and shuts the door. April is face-down on their bed, crying. In keeping with the crummy evening, it would be fitting to say something ugly to April, such as, "Shut up, crybaby." But she doesn't. Instead, she jerks the curtains over the dark windows, hiding icy patterns traced with frost, and lies down on her back beside her.

She stares at the dark ceiling for a long time, wondering about the quiet, straightforward words that were birthed inside her on the steps. *Watch. Listen. Learn. Your life will be different.* She strains to hear more, eyes and ears searching the darkness, but there is nothing.

From Mr. Mason she learned that people have value. That she has value. This simple but profound revelation is changing her thinking. And now a voice—*God's voice?*—seems to confirm Mr. Mason's view. But how could she be worthy of personal words from God? And what is she to do with them?

Three imperatives. *Watch, Listen, Learn.* Maybe she is to recognize some sort of lessons in the unsatisfactory life around her. What is she to learn from her parents' volatile behavior? That parents can scare the bejeebers out of children? Perhaps if one realizes that all people have value, one doesn't carry on so. What with youth's way of taking life as it comes, and no other life to personally compare it to, up to now it has seemed she's had little recourse but to conform to her parents' model. But the words promise change, not conformity. What was it that Mr. Mason said one day about conformity? She struggles to recall a somewhat disgusting image. Oh yes. "Dead fish flow with the stream," he had said. Perhaps she is not destined to flow in her parents' stream.

Your life will be different.

Saffee lives within a colorless present that has evolved from her lackluster past. She has never been creative enough to imagine a future that would be any different. But tonight she dares to think that God has.

Minutes pass. She studies April's fully clothed, sleeping form. She slowly pulls up blankets to cover her.

CHAPTER TWENTY-TWO

RAGS TO RICHES

1954

While a second load agitates in the humming Maytag washer, together Saffee and Joann match sheets corner to corner and pin them to the taut rope lines Nels has rigged between basement rafters. This morning's threat of rain prevents them from hanging clothes out of doors.

Joann demonstrates the art of pillowcase hanging. "First, be sure to shake out all the wrinkles," she says, giving her sample a smart snap. She limps to a chair to adjust the unsightly rag bindings that have slipped to her ankles. Only because her varicose veins are "killing" her today did she enlist help. Saffee whips a pillowcase through the air as shown and glances at her mother's ropy, swollen legs, then down at her own. She remembers a short, unexpected visit a year ago from Joann's second-oldest sister.

"Saffee, you've certainly got your mother's legs!" Maxine had chortled as she surveyed the hapless girl. Saffee's eyes had narrowed. Why did Aunt Maxine, a virtual stranger, sound delighted by her observation? Was Saffee doomed to hobble around like her mother, legs tied with rags?

Maxine had been horrified when she saw the Norway table of her childhood sporting splotchy paint. The older sister demanded to know why Evelyn had passed the table on to Joann when she had expected to get it herself. "I *never* would have painted . . . Who would want it now, completely ruined?"

Saffee pins laundry to the line, hoping for a rare mother-daughter conversation as they work together. "Mom, I'm reading your book, *Giants in the Earth*," she ventures.

Joann is busy rehanging crooked pillowcases. "I guess life was pretty hard back then." Joann nods her head in agreement but does not elaborate. Saffee is hesitant to ask a pressing question—did Joann know anyone like the book's character named Beret? Isolated Beret, tragically gripped by elements of a dark spiritual world until she was driven insane. Instead, she asks why her mother's family left North Dakota for Minnesota.

Before answering, Joann circulates items in the rinse water with a stout laundry stick and begins to feed heavy wet towels between the washer's slowly rolling black cylinders. "I guess mostly because of the prairie fire," she says. "After that, the prairie was . . . inhospitable."

Casting for safer ground, Saffee asks about washing clothes "back then." She's willing to talk about any neutral subject with her mother, but right now one seems hard to find.

"Well, let's see," Joann says. "I'm not sure if Pa and the boys took their clothes off at all in winter. Of course the girls . . . we did ours more often." She picks up a basket of wrung towels. "Those awful brothers . . ." Her voice trails off . . .

"I tell you, I saw it. It was all over some ol' rags she had! I think she was bleedin' ta death or somethin'!" "Lars, you peekin' at the girls in the outhouse agin? Don'tcha know nothin'?" "Sh-sh! Crazy Joann'll hear. She's unner da table down there . . ."

"What about your brothers?" Saffee asks.

"Well . . ." Joann pauses a moment, as if she'd rather not explain what she is remembering. "We'd hide our red-stained rags on thorn-bushes in the brush until they dried . . . could never get the stains out. The boys would find those rags . . . run after us with them, yelling and teasing. It was . . . so *embarrassing*."

For a moment, Saffee is puzzled. When understanding dawns, she stares at her mother with incredulity. Her sense of modesty, even around her mother, prevents her from speaking.

Red rags? Oh, Mother. There will be no rags in my life. I will be different. Different.

As fall approaches, Joann once again becomes irritable. She is increas-ingly oversensitive to even the subtlest adversity, such as tenants "tramping overhead." She fuels her suspicious nature by complaining, "Sometimes I see them lingering behind the French doors, peer-ing through the lace curtains into our living room. I'm absolutely shocked at the things they say about us."

While at her sewing machine, making opaque shades for the doors, she is heard to mutter, "Watching me . . . all the time, watching me . . ." At her insistence, Nels installs additional locks throughout the house.

When Nels receives a pay raise in September, mercurial Joann brightens.

"Your daddy makes ten thousand dollars a year now!" she whis-pers to the girls. "But don't tell anyone. Money is a family secret, you know."

Saffee knows. She remembers the day Joann, resembling last year's rummage sale, took her and April to the doctor to update vac-cinations. When Saffee looked in dismay at Joann's faded housedress and unraveling laundry-day sweater, Joann said the doctor would "soak them good" if he thought they were even a little prosperous.

But now, with more income and savings from the rentals, Joann decides it is time to put appearances of poverty aside and build a new house. Five years has been long enough to put up with snoopy tenants. Secure in his career with the dairy, which is rapidly expanding across the state, Nels, a man of easily summoned good nature, agrees to at least look for land. Two miles north of town they find a spacious lot in a newly subdivided area of Miller's Ford called Cottonwood Point. It sits high, overlooking a wooded valley that currently wears radiant colors of autumn.

"We'll have an absolutely *marvelous* view from picture windows in the back!" Joann exclaims as the family walks the property. She whirls in the opposite direction. "And the front will look onto that wonderful grove of cottonwoods. Look how the yellow leaves glitter in the sun!" Her enthusiasm rivals that of when she had found their current house.

To the south is an old apple orchard. Fallen fruit litters the ground. "Our own orchard!" she gushes.

Nels grins. "Does that mean apple pie?"

Saffee and April, comfortable on Second Street, are adamantly against the move. Saffee doesn't want to give up the convenience of ice skating across the street and roller skating on the bridge. April is disappointed to leave neighborhood friends for a place with few houses in sight. The move also means they will suffer the humiliation of riding a school bus.

"Don't be whiney, girls," Joann admonishes them. "It's still the same town, but just far enough out so it won't seem so hoi polloi." Joann has continued to study her dictionary.

The girls appeal to their dad, but he commends Joann's enthusiasm. It seems to confirm his belief that she is stable, merely "nervous" at times. If building a new house will bring her happiness, he says, so be it.

There might be one consolation. "Will I get to have my own room now?" Saffee asks. "I'm *thirteen*, you know."

"No."

Saffee is so indignant that Joann dismissively agrees to compromise. "All right, we'll put twin beds in your room."

All winter Joann draws house plans. When she shows them to the contractor, he is surprised at their precision and says there will be no need for professionally drawn blueprints. Pleased by his approval, she summons the courage to select brick, fireplace stone, and the right windows to frame the "exquisite" views. She can hardly wait for the excavation to begin come spring.

CHAPTER TWENTY-THREE

GONE WITH THE WIND

1955

In January, Hollywood's rerelease of *Gone with the Wind* finally arrives in the small town. The *Gazette* touts the classic film with a half-page review. On a blizzardy evening, Joann suggests that she and Saffee go uptown to see it. Nels says they should wait a day and hope for better weather.

"No, now is a good time to go," Joann insists. "On a night like this there will be good seats available." Saffee knows this means she hopes to avoid an intimidating crowd. Saffee is not sure she wants to be seen at the Roxy with her unpredictable mother, and she knows Joann would not go without her. Because she too is very eager to see the popular film, she agrees to go. Ordinarily, they would have walked the three and a half blocks to the theater, even in winter, but because Nels put tire chains on the car that afternoon, and enjoys overpowering snow-packed streets, he drives them uptown through the white flurry.

Ever since she skipped down the yellow brick road of Oz at her first movie, Saffee has determined that flashes of Hollywood magic would ornament her life as often as possible. Over the years, the Roxy has become a retreat where Saffee escapes a humdrum existence and feels very much alive. An assortment of schoolmates often sits on the right side, near the front. With that in mind, Saffee routinely chooses a seat in the middle section, farther back. In the dark, licking a Holloway, she's danced in the rain with Gene Kelly, perplexed the King of Siam, swum with Esther Williams, dressed as stylishly as Audrey Hepburn, and ridden in James Dean's Corvette—all the while looking like Grace Kelly.

"Call me when it's over," Nels says as they exit the car. He drives off, tire chains clanking through fresh drifts and Saffee's mittens left on the backseat.

Joann agrees to split a fifteen-cent box of popcorn but objects to Saffee's request for a Holloway, which, she says, would loosen her teeth. Saffee's tongue explores to see if the damage has already been done. She follows Joann into the darkened, half-full theater and is relieved when her mother selects a row near the back. When seated, Saffee slouches low in her seat.

The red velvet curtains open, and Saffee is willingly abducted into Scarlett's capricious world of extravagant gowns, plantation garden parties, and covert romance with roguish Rhett Butler. When Melanie suffers premature labor and Scarlett must deliver the baby, Saffee covers her eyes. But this discomfort is nothing like what is to come. When the Union Army burns Atlanta and the angry inferno backdrops Scarlett's perilous wagon ride, Joann gasps. She grips Saffee's arm and drags her out of the row of startled viewers, stepping on toes with no apology.

"Mom!" Saffee hisses. "What are you doing?"

"Shh! Sit down!" someone demands.

With Saffee still in tow, Joann shoves through the swinging doors to the lobby. Her eyes dart, looking for a place of refuge, but she sees none.

"Mother! What's going on?"

Joann's face is flushed and her breathing rapid. She stumbles to a far wall and weakly slumps to the floor. Her unbuttoned coat slips from her shoulders. On the wall above her is a framed poster of bare-chested William Holden. He looks down on lovely, placid Kim Novak seated on the ground, encircled by a flowing pink gown. The scene, from a coming attraction called *Picnic*, mocks the show of real life playing on the lobby carpeting below it.

Joann's nervous hands clench and unclench. Fire, again, has triggered a fearful episode.

Seeing her mother's terror, Saffee feels a mixture of compassion and mortification. She looks around, hoping there is no one else in the lobby. Mr. Jenkins, the theater manager, watches them from behind the concession stand with his cleaning rag paused in midair.

"I have to get out of here." Joann's voice is desperate but quiet. She seems to be making an effort to calm herself. "Saffee, help me get home." She waves an arm. "Pull me up."

Saffee steadies the arm and lifts upward but is unable to bring Joann to standing. She is afraid the movie will be over before they can get out the door. She can't let classmates see her struggle with a disoriented mother.

"Come on, Mother. Get up. Let's go."

Joann maneuvers to her knees and with Saffee's assistance inches up the wall, knocking Holden-Novak askew. Once upright, she smoothes her hair and orders imperiously, "Saffee, go to Mr. Jenkins over there. Tell him to give you money back for two tickets."

"No, Mother, I'm not going to do that. We need to leave." Saffee straightens Joann's coat, buttons it, and hurriedly guides her to the front double doors. With a bare hand, she pushes against the cold glass patterned with swirls of ice. The winter storm, which for more than ninety minutes had been forgotten, assaults with cruelty.

Saffee remembers that her dad expects them to call, but she cannot bear the thought of returning to the lobby, soon to be full of people who would gawk at them. They lunge into the wind. Saffee glances back over her shoulder and sees Mr. Jenkins peering out, his face distorted by the ice on the glass door.

Joann, her bare head lowered, heedlessly strides through the drifting snow. Wind quickly penetrates their clothing. Saffee holds Joann's arm firmly with two hands as if worried she might run off, but also to keep them warm. As they hurry along, she is stricken by the role reversal. How has it happened that she, the daughter, is caring for her bewildered mother?

By the time they reach home, Joann's exertion in the cold has restored her senses. Nels, surprised they hadn't called for a ride, meets them at the door.

"We came home early, Daddy, because Mother . . . she didn't like the movie."

Without a word, Joann heads to the bedroom and begins to undress for bed.

Saffee follows. "Mom, do you want me to help you?"

Joann shakes her head no.

Later Saffee lies awake, replaying the frightful evening. It didn't seem that Joann believed she was in real danger from the fire on the screen, unlike that summer night when she tried to push Saffee to some kind of safety under the Norway table. But again flames had triggered irrational behavior.

She's heard that it's illegal to yell "Fire!" in a crowded theater. Saffee shudders. The nightmare could have been even worse.

Movies! Perhaps she will never go to another one. By extension, tonight's experience has eclipsed her fantasy. Phooey on Southern plantations. Phooey on make-believe that has nothing to do with her. For years she has wasted her time being amused, amazed, and aroused by what is not real. She has foolishly built her own dreams around adventures in books and spectacles of Hollywood that will never come true for her.

Real life is the icy sting of cold glass on a bare hand, the lonely darkness of a theater's middle section, a ridiculous movie poster swinging by its frame, and, most of all, a peculiar, tormented mother, crumpled on the floor.

No wonder Joann scolded her last summer. After an engaging matinee of *Daddy Long Legs*, Saffee had parroted Leslie Caron all the way home and neglected to drop the impersonation when she walked in the door.

"And why are you acting so uppity?" Joann demanded. "Don't you come home from a movie and be a smarty. What kinds of things are you seeing there, anyway? That's not how we act in this family, and don't you forget it." Evidently an imaginary life was only for Joann, not for others over whom she might lose control.

Tonight, Saffee sees that her mother was right, and maybe it doesn't matter. When they move to Cottonwood Point, they will live too far from the theater to walk. She sees herself as too old to be driven.

However, when it comes to Saffee's love for movies, tomorrow is another day.

CHAPTER TWENTY-FOUR

COTTONWOOD POINT

s the snow melts and the ground thaws, Joann frets about how she will get to the construction site to keep an eye on daily progress of the new house, as she had the remodeling on Second Street. She decides she must learn to drive, something she has previously refused to do.

"Well, Muzzy." When Nels is pleased, he calls Joann by the pet name he gave her years ago. "I been expectin' that ever since I seen you drawed plans for a two-car garage!"

It's no secret that Nels hopes the new house project will help Joann shed some of her other idiosyncrasies as well and "become more like other women."

"Mom? Learn to drive? Good," Saffee says. "Then maybe she'll take me to chorus practice. There's no other way I can get there by seven thirty when we move out to the *sticks* and I have to ride the *bus*!"

April rattles off her list of activities that will also require transportation, including after-school tumbling. Joann reminds her there will be no such dangerous endeavor for her. "You might fall and absolutely *ruin* your kidneys," she warns.

On Saturdays and Sundays, with Nels at her side, Joann nervously nudges a new maroon Ford along nearby country roads. When she ventures onto the streets of town, she traces over and over the route from Second Street to the Cottonwood Point subdivision. The day she returns from her first solo outing, it would be hard to say whether she or Nels is more proud.

Building the new house facilitates a recovery of something that had been stolen from Joann. A driving back of evil gives her renewed vigor for life, at least temporarily. In spite of cold weather, excavation is completed by mid-April. For a few hours each day, Joann, wrapped in a long parka, stands like a sentinel, watching the construction crew lay the cement block walls of the basement. Under a cheerless sky, with the wind wrapping her in its arms, she has plenty of time to think about things—past as well as present.

Receiving compliments from the contractor for her precise drawings and learning to drive have done more to boost her well-being and perspective on life than anything for a long time. So when she remembers her childhood days, when life was observed from under a table, she evaluates the memories more circumspectly than in the past. She remembers the nights her brother Rolf trespassed her shelter, had not molested her but touched her, scaring her. Screams had brought her father, and in the morning, Rolf felt his leather strap. The brothers, both of them, were ignorant and overworked. Now she feels sorry for them.

She thinks about Maxine, the large and bony sister. Maxine, who often hurled scathing and hurtful words and jeered at Joann after incidents with Rolf. In the bed they shared, Maxine, likely troubled, thrashed around in her sleep so much that Joann often had no recourse but to leave it. Today, Joann sees Maxine, in fact all her motherless siblings, as bereft as herself.

Most vivid in her mind is her mother, feeding, clothing, and trying to placate her demanding brood. Joann's pain of neglect had been real but, she decides, it had not been unreasonable to ache for her mother's attention. It is a need she has carried into adulthood. Today, she aches for Nels. He gives her hugs before he heads out the door and again when he returns. She *knows* he loves her, but at night, nothing, depriving her of one last baby. Her mother too had been deprived of her last baby . . . Joann stamps her cold feet and swings her arms not only to keep warm but also to make sure her presence is recognized by the workmen, who probably would take off for a smoke if she weren't around.

Never far from her mind since it reappeared, and even now as she stands watch, is the old wooden box that found its way to their basement shelf and holds her mother's death certificate.

Today, maybe not tomorrow, but today, standing at the building site in the chilly air, she declares that her fate will not be like her mother's. She has designed a wonderful house. She can drive. Nels has often told her there is "nothin' wrong" with her so she "shouldn't act like there is." Today, she believes it. Yet, why then won't he give her another baby?

Looking around her post, she has time to wonder what will eventually be built on lots adjacent to the new house. She decides that Nels should plant a stand of evergreens on the north side of their property to create a privacy screen as well as a windbreak. To the south is the apple orchard. Let people build what they want beyond those trees; the Kvaales won't be bothered.

When the bricks she carefully selected arrive, four burly men unload heavy pallets of red bundles. Joann scrutinizes the delivery. She had imagined a more massive stack. She counts the bricks in one bundle, counts bundles, and multiplies.

"The cheats! They shorted me sixty bricks. They're robbing me blind."

The error is soon corrected. As time goes on, the construction project brings an assortment of such concerns, as well as exhaustion, to Joann. And, as always, when she is stressed, everyone suffers. But in October the Kvaales manage to move into their new ranch-style house.

❋

Later that month, on a gray afternoon when the girls step off the school bus, they are disheartened to see their mother in the open garage, furiously slapping tan enamel onto the old wooden Norway table. They are stunned by her disheveled appearance, her unpinned dark hair falling over her face as she leans into every stroke. She mutters to someone they cannot see and does not look up as the girls approach.

"Why are you making demands again?" they hear her say. "*Yes.* I'm painting. Can't you see? But you lied. *It does no good!* . . . Comfort. *Comfort?* Layer upon layer has given me no comfort. *Won't I ever be free? . . .*"

Alarmed at her mother's mental disarray, and recalling previous histrionics, Saffee hugs her books to her chest. April huddles against her and whispers, "What's she saying, Saffee? Who's she talking to?"

Saffee doesn't answer.

"*Smoke!* The shadow of death." Joann's alarm intensifies. "You are marking me for hell!"

Joann abruptly raises her head and emphatically shakes a heavily laden brush in the girls' direction. "*Stop tormenting me!*" she yells at an invisible phantom. Paint drips down her arm and splatters across the table. The girls want to flee, but their feet will not move. April buries her face in Saffee's sweater.

Suddenly weak, Joann drops her brush and crumples forward, forearms flattened against the wet, glossy table as she continues her garrulous talk. "What's that?" she demands. "You say *He* prepared a snare for me? *He* prepared a trap? *No!* It's not true! *Go away!*"

Slowly, slowly, she strokes with her hands and arms as if fashioning finger paint. She sways back and forth. She no longer smears, she caresses. Her voice, a whisper, turns resolute. "It wasn't a snare. I know it wasn't. 'He . . . prepareth . . . a table' . . . A table before me. *To deliver me from the presence of my enemies!*" She looks heavenward. "Oh, God . . . help me!"

The daughters bolt into the house to elude the disarray that countermands their mother's once rational mind. Behind them, Joann droops over the enigmatic table and cries.

They hang their jackets in the hall closet and dumbly sit on the new kitchen chairs that still feel foreign. Saffee wishes they were in their old house on Second Street.

"You know what I was thinking about on the bus?" April sounds wistful.

"What?"

"I was hoping when we got home Mommy would be in the kitchen, making chocolate chip cookies."

"Sure, April." Saffee rolls her eyes. "Might as well hope for the moon."

April wilts. She sinks her head into folded arms on the kitchen table and begins to cry. Saffee watches her dully.

Suddenly, April raises her tear-streaked face and demands, "Why doesn't she just *get rid* of that awful table if it makes her so upset?"

Lately, Saffee has felt more sympathetic toward her sister, but as usual, she can't resist an opportunity to flaunt her wisdom, valid or not. Furthermore, sniping at April relieves her own tension.

"Get rid of a holy thing? Don't be stupid, April. Why would anyone do a blasphemous thing like that?"

By the time Nels comes home, two days later, Joann has returned to her usual preoccupied, but less episodic, self.

"Muzzy," Nels calls out as he comes in the door. "I see you've been busy. I bet it's nice to have a big garage to paint in, and park your car too."

Since her dad is gone much of the time, Saffee concludes that he must be unaware of the extent of her mother's disturbed behavior. She decides to inform him.

On Sunday afternoon Joann is in her bedroom nursing a headache. Although Saffee is hesitant to talk behind her mother's back, she marks her page of *David Copperfield* and summons courage. She trudges to the living room and plops onto the sectional beside Nels, who is reading the newspaper.

"Daddy," she says, hushed, "I need to talk to you about something important."

Nels shifts his toothpick to the other side of his mouth and glances at her.

"Mother was really scary the other day when you were gone, all mixed up."

"Whatdya mean, mixed up?" He puts down the paper.

"In the garage, painting the table *again*, she was talking *crazy*, and paint was flying all over. It was awful, Daddy. I didn't like it!"

"Ahh. She's okay. Dere's nuttin' wrong. She even learnt how to drive."

"*Daddy, listen!* It wasn't normal. April was scared too. Mother acts *so strange* sometimes."

"Nah. She jus' gets nervous and excited about things. Her biggest problem? She thinks too much." He reopens his paper. "You jus' be sure to be a good girl. Don't go gettin' edgewise with 'er. Everything'll be fine."

"*Daddy.*" Saffee is indignant at his assessment and warning. "It's not *my* fault she's so mixed up." Although conversations with her father are usually less than satisfying, she is not going to give up. "I think she needs to go to some kind of doctor or something."

Nels, who doesn't know anyone who medicates mood changes, and wouldn't think much of anyone who does, scowls. "*Nah.* Listen, I tol' you." He takes the toothpick from his mouth and jabs the air for emphasis. "Dere's nothin' wrong with her."

Saffee reminds him that he isn't here all the time to witness his wife's behavior. She complains that she and April are at a loss to know what to do when she gets "all funny." She suggests that perhaps there are hospitals for . . .

"Now don' talk nonsense. She's never goin' to one a *dem* places."

Nels returns to his paper and toothpick. Saffee knows when to say no more but her mind churns. David Copperfield meets a world full of curious people. Had Dickens known her parents, perhaps he would have numbered them with the lot.

In November, the girls take their first ride in the car with their mother at the wheel. She drives at a careful speed, pumping the accelerator. Saffee, up front, hears April whisper in the backseat, "Wow, herky-jerky." They both notice that Joann looks in the rearview mirror almost as much as out the front window. Is she afraid someone behind is following too closely? Or criticizing the way she drives? Twice Joann activates the windshield wipers instead of the turn signals and, worse, doesn't seem to notice them scraping back and forth.

"Mom!" Saffee yells, embarrassed that someone might see them. "It's not raining."

Later Joann asks, "Saffee, what about that morning chorus practice at school? I suppose I could take you."

"No. I don't think I'll go this year, Mom. Maybe next year."

A few days later Joann's right ankle is in a plaster cast. While looking in the rearview mirror as she approached an intersection, she hit a stopped car.

She never drives again.

CHAPTER TWENTY-FIVE

RESPECTFULLY YOURS

. . . and then the tree caught fire and the whole school burned down to the ground . . ."

In the next room, Saffee surrenders her concentration. Even the great Captain Ahab, harpoon in hand, must defer to Joann when she mentions fire.

It seems that Joann is suggesting to April that out of respect for all who have perished in fires ignited by candles on Christmas trees, the Kvaales should no longer plug in strings of electric bulbs on their tree.

"Never?" April asks.

"Well, I think not," her mother says.

"Let's go tell Saffee," April says, and hurries into the living room, followed more slowly by Joann, on crutches.

"Saffee, Mom thinks . . ."

"I heard, but we don't use candles," Saffee scoffs. "That was the olden days."

"But houses and schools and nursing homes and everything burned to the ground!" April says.

Saffee doesn't understand what good it would do to dispense with pretty lights in order to remember tragic fires, but she also knows it will make no difference what she thinks. Joann's ideas quickly fossilize.

April says, "Mommy, I've always liked Christmas lights."

"A little sacrifice might be a good thing for people nowadays," Joann says. "In fact, this might catch on like wild . . . I think I'll dash off a letter to the *Gazette*."

The day before Christmas, Saffee swishes a dusting cloth over the living room's built-in bookcase. One shelf holds a few knickknacks, always arranged just so. A sunshine-yellow dancing girl lunges diagonally from the right corner as if with rapid dash she will thrust herself to center stage. The ceramic figurine has been on display since Saffee can remember and, for some reason, seems to convey more significance in the room than its five inches would indicate. Always running, never arriving, her gown revealingly presses against her upper body. She carries her yellow skirt high with outstretched arms, creating wings of perpetual flight.

Saffee has never liked the piece. The form-fitting gown is immodest. Early in their marriage Nels had purchased the unabashedly seductive piece as a gift for his wife, the dancer. Nels's "two left feet," and Joann's encumbrances, emotional and varicose, had eclipsed their dancing together long ago.

Saffee has memories of her nightgown-clad mother during the St. Paul years, swaying, swirling, twirling alone across the living room, dream-like, as Nelson Eddy and Jeannette McDonald belted, *"O sweet mystery of love at last I've found you . . ."*

"Dancing embraces the light fantastic," Joann would gush. "It's so romantic." To Saffee, it seemed like carrying on. To young April, it was an invitation to mimic her mother until she collapsed with laughter onto the carpet. The gray Gulistan carpet.

During their first weeks in the new house, veins and emotions permitting, and with the phonograph on high volume, a seductive dance from the second act of *Carmen* could still lure Joann into its spell. The staccato rhythms and frenzied climax rewarded her with delight. Saffee chose not to observe these "performances." In her bedroom, trying to ignore the music, she wondered if there had ever been another mother like hers and thinks that if anyone found out about Joann, she would die. But Joann's car accident, coupled with her increasingly pesky veins, knocked the dance right out of her.

Saffee returns the figurine to its place. There has always been a kind of paradoxical exhibitionism in Joann that makes Saffee uncomfortable. Although her mother is increasingly fearful of people, when given the opportunity, her posture continues to tease, "Look at me. Please look at me. See how well I'm built." There is much about Joann, and her own discomfort, that Saffee does not understand. All she can do is accept things as they are.

Joann slides a red curly ribbon from a small package and drops it into the reuse bag. She lets the wrapping paper slip to the floor, then scrutinizes a three-piece manicure set in a cellophane package: scissors, cuticle nipper, and file.

Saffee watches her. As a rule, she and April don't buy Christmas presents for their parents or each other. It has never been expected. But now that Saffee is fourteen, it seems right that she should try her hand at gift giving. She nagged her dad for an increase to her twenty-five-cent weekly allowance, keeping it secret that she planned to buy gifts.

"What?" he teased. "You're overpaid already!" In the end, he gave her three dollars. She added the bills to her savings without a thank-you, frustrated and angered by his teasing.

After purchasing a pair of socks for Nels and a book for April, with four dollars remaining in her billfold, she went to Walgreens and spent over forty minutes trying to select the perfect gift for her mother.

Now she can tell by her mother's upraised brows and downturned mouth that she had chosen unwisely. "I already have a manicure set," Joann declares. "And it's a far cry better than this one. These scissors couldn't cut a thing." She turns over the package. "I could have guessed," she says. "Made in Japan." She sets the gift aside and rolls her eyes. "Where'd you get it, Saffee? I hope you saved the receipt."

"Aw, Joann. It's Christmas. The first one in our new house. Now don't go ruinin' it."

Saffee bends over a good-size box on her lap and fumbles with its ribbon. She is glad her dad has spoken up. Still, she wants to throw him an accusing look because he had not supplied enough money to buy a better gift for her critical mother. Looking up would reveal her tears.

April provides distraction as she squeals with pleasure over a wine-colored outfit for her Ginny doll. There are a number of gifts under the tree that bear Saffee's name, but by its size and shape, she knows that the one she holds contains her every-Christmas ice skates. Since moving to Cottonwood Point, she's been unable to skate on the Blue River, but she hopes her dad will drive her there during Christmas vacation. She rips off the paper and lifts the lid, welcoming the smell of new leather. She holds up a white skate by its shiny runner.

"Mom. This looks so *big*." She peers at the number stamped onto the lining. "Size *nine*? I wear size seven. I'll *never* grow into *these*."

"Yes, you will," Joann assures her. "I'm tired of buying new skates every year; we've already spent a fortune on them."

CHAPTER TWENTY-SIX

SPEAKING TRUTH

1959

J oann! Joann!"
Another pitiless dream. The same voices.

Sweat-soaked, Joann shoves blankets and sheets aside. Lying immobile on her back, staring at the invisible ceiling, she tries to regain control of her breathing. Fear subsides and discouragement takes its place. Why does the specter refuse to loosen its grip? She must not sleep. She lowers her feet into slippers. The night air is cool but her skin fever-hot. Clad in her nightgown, she makes her way down the hall, tiptoeing past the closed den door, where Nels sleeps. In the dining room she stands immobile, staring at the barely visible, brooding table. Minutes pass. Still she stands; she could not say how long. Finally, she goes into the kitchen, turns on a light, and begins to write in her always-ready notebook.

The odor of a noxious pyre dogs me.
A measure of its ash pesters, clings, settles.

Exchange this curse, O God
For the fire of Your Holy Spirit,
For the fragrance of Your Christ.

After dinner, when the dishes are wiped and put away, Joann scours the sink and Saffee retreats to the dining room. At the Norway table, which has been sloppily dressed in charcoal gray for over a month, Saffee intends to hurry through an algebra assignment, then resume chapter six of *Les Miserables*. In the living room, April struggles with the left hand arpeggios of "Für Elise," despairing that her piano teacher expects all pieces first be learned hands separately.

Joann bought the spinet piano shortly after April's concussion and both girls, in spite of their lack of natural talent, began lessons. It was an obvious tactic to keep April, who thrives on active outdoor play, indoors.

For Saffee, playing the piano, even badly, becomes almost as liberating as reading. Joann's recorded music has always captivated her. From what magical places does such music spring? Reproducing even the simplest of melodies stimulates within her a strange desire to someday know the bigger life beyond the insipid Kvaale household.

April's playing, of course, is not for herself, but for performance, and she obliges anyone, not minding at all to play for their few and far between invited guests. When Joann directs Saffee to play for outsiders, sudden queasiness prevents her from playing even one measure.

"Saffee." Joann appears, removing her apron. "Come down to my bedroom."

Annoyed by the interruption, but wondering what the summons is about, Saffee follows Joann down the hall. She notices her mother's slight limp. Joann blames it on childhood rickets and on her ankle, which she says didn't mend properly after her driving accident years before. Joann shuts the door behind them, muting the piano, and sits on the edge of the bed. She indicates a chair for Saffee and gets right to the point.

"I'm going to ask you a question, and I want you to tell me the truth," Joann says. "I want to ask you . . ." She pauses, her hands twist. "I want to ask you if you think there's something wrong with me."

The question stuns. "Wha-what do you mean, wrong?"

"You know, *different* from other people, funny."

Saffee has an urge to be rude. To perhaps say, "Duh."

"I don't know . . ."

"Just tell me, Saffee. Tell me if you think there's something *wrong* with me, not normal."

Not normal? What an understatement. Disturbing memories flicker in Saffee's head like a black-and-white news reel. Her mother's trance-like staring. Conversations with an invisible someone. Hallucinations.

Oh, what she could say. Saffee has witnessed her mother's emotional gymnastics most of her life, but a valid evaluation is beyond her. And why is she asking? Joann never seeks her daughter's opinion. Now that Saffee is about to graduate from high school, does Joann consider her finally capable of *having* an opinion?

"Well?" Joann says, impatient. Saffee notes the familiar clenched hands, the pursed lips. She feels cornered.

"I don't know what to say, Mother."

At the piano, April has also become impatient. Discordant notes and premature tempo race through the walls, further scrambling Saffee's thoughts. Doesn't April know that "Für Elise" should float, not gallop?

"I guess I'm not sure what normal is, Mother," she says, knowing she sounds lame. "And anyway, why are you asking?"

Joann takes a deep breath, looks at the ceiling, and says, "I want to know because I want to have another baby, and your father is denying me that . . . pleasure."

"What? A baby?" Saffee doesn't let on she has heard them argue about this. "Don't you think, I mean, do you think you should? I mean, Mother, what are you saying?"

"I want a boy. A cute little boy, fun, energetic. For Nels. It would bring me, us, new life. April is growing up, thirteen already. I know a baby would be a male version of little April."

Nels, Joann tells Saffee, insists that her "nerves" wouldn't take having another child. But that's just an excuse, Joann scoffs. "The truth is that he doesn't find me attractive anymore."

Saffee feels intensely awkward. Shouldn't this conversation be had with a girlfriend, not a daughter? Of course, Joann has no girlfriends.

Joann gets up and goes to the bureau, preens a bit before her mirror, and asks weakly, "Am I, Saffee? Am I still attractive?"

Saffee takes a deep breath and lies. "Mom. Of course you are attractive. And there's nothing wrong with you. You're just *fine*, just *fine*, Mom."

"Are you sure?"

Saffee is unnerved. Her mother is calling for help and she doesn't know how to give it. Worse, she doesn't want to hear any more. She stands, thrusts her hands into her pockets, and takes two or three steps to nowhere.

"Mom, I just told you what I think, but as for having a baby . . ."

Joann sighs, as if resigned that she will get no acceptable answers. She tilts her head back and again looks at the ceiling. "I hope April is almost through practicing," she says, giving closure to the conversation.

"I've got a lot of homework, Mom," Saffee says quietly and turns to leave the room.

"Fine. No, wait, Sapphire." In an instant, Joann's focus has changed. "Come back, one more thing."

"What?"

"Promise me that when I'm old and infirm you'll do something for me."

"Do what?"

"Cut the hairs on my chinny-chin-chin. Promise me now."

No response seems appropriate. Stunned that one minute her mother regarded her as confidante and the next as future caregiver, Saffee quickly retreats to the dining room.

April tries harder, slowly combining arpeggios with melody.

Saffee stares at her algebra book. Her conscience overrides both piano and equations. Guilt about lying crowds out the slight flattery of Joann's asking for her opinion. Of course Saffee believes there is something "wrong" with her mother. Another baby? Absurd. But what could she have said? Both girls have noticed that their dad has been sleeping in the den. Maybe he isn't as oblivious to their mother's mental condition as they had thought.

Saffee copes with her mother by disregarding her, not analyzing her. She consoles herself with the thought that it is mere months until she goes off to college and her own life, one she anticipates will be "different" and, she hopes, better. For now she waits, detached and self-focused.

Bass and treble begin to mingle. April's "Für Elise" flits, almost charmingly, through the air.

CHAPTER TWENTY-SEVEN

THE CATAPULT

It is July; college looms. One moment Saffee's heart races with heady anticipation, the next she's filled with suffocating fear.

Clothes are a concern. She needs clothes that give the impression that she belongs at a state university. What do such clothes look like? She has no one to consult and a mother who is unpredictable in stores. Years ago, important shopping was done in Minneapolis, but Saffee is hesitant to take the bus there alone. She will try to piece together what she needs in Miller's Ford's limited dress shops.

At Gilbert's Fine Fashions, she timidly admires neatly folded stacks of sweaters in luscious colors. Any one of them would be a pleasure to own.

A tall, angular clerk, stylishly dressed and coiffed, brows raised, hovers nearby.

"You're the Kimball girl, aren't you?" she says.

"Well, ah . . ." Would it be wrong to correct her? And what does that name, right or wrong, mean to the woman? "No, I'm . . . it's Kvaale and I'm going off to college and—"

The clerk interrupts, "What kind of sweater are you looking

for?" She straightens a perfectly folded stack that Saffee had ever so slightly touched. Saffee feels like a cat at a dog show.

"Kind? Well, I . . . I mean, I don't know. Um, these here are pretty."

"Well"—the clerk sounds impatient—"do you want a cardigan?"

Saffee perspires. Her mother continually spouts obscure vocabulary, but Saffee has never heard her use this word. Everyone else in town probably knows what "cardigan" means.

"Well, uh, I don't know . . . I mean, I don't really care."

The woman gives her a withering look.

"I mean, I guess . . . I'll have to think about it." Red-faced, Saffee rushes for the exit and home to ask her mother what the word means.

"Cardigan? It's a sweater."

"I know it's a sweater, but what kind? A clerk at Gilbert's asked me if I wanted a cardigan and I didn't know what she meant. I was so embarrassed! You're forever using big words, why not that one?"

Joann reaches for her always-handy dictionary.

"You overestimate my erudition, Saffee," Joann says, searching.

Saffee rolls her eyes.

Joann finds that her dictionary defines *cardigan* as a sweater named after a Welsh earl. Not much help.

"I must need a new dictionary," she says, checking the copyright date. "1951." Her face lights up. "I'll get a new one and send this one to college with you."

With the help of a Sears Roebuck catalog, Saffee deduces that sweaters with buttons down the front are called cardigans. Joann orders one for Saffee in tan, "a good neutral color that goes with everything," and then adds another item to the form—the most recent edition of *The American College Dictionary*.

Four more days. Saffee considers each garment as she slides it across the closet bar. On her bedroom floor are two almost-full suitcases, miscellaneous boxes, a portable typewriter, packages of typing paper, carbon paper, and Joann's old dictionary.

April, sprawled across Saffee's bed, watches her sister sort remaining items on the closet shelves. Years of habit prompt Saffee to give her a get-off-my-bed look and April scoots over to her own.

She has packed a new gray tweed suit, a coordinating sweater—pullover—and sensible pumps. Joann surmises that this is what well-dressed coeds wear to class. They had shopped together at Gilbert's to purchase these and other items. To Saffee's relief, her mother was, for once, on her best behavior, and the aloof clerk must have had the day off.

In sportswear, when Joann noticed a mannequin wearing Bermuda shorts and knee socks, she sputtered, "Wool shorts? One might say that's an oxymoron."

"Only you, Mother," Saffee whispered.

"Saffee, that beautiful womanhood would succumb to such outrageous whims of fashion is counterintuitive," Joann huffed.

Saffee doubts she would have the nerve to display her thickish legs in shorts on campus, but if that is the rage, she wishes she could.

Completing her assistance, Joann made Saffee a brown wool straight skirt, and from a sewing magazine, she ordered a lifetime supply of personalized labels: SAPPHIRE E. KVAALE. She stressed how important it is to label every item to be taken. Saffee is grateful for her mother's help.

"I know you don't want me to tell you this, Saffee," April says, "but I'm going to miss you."

Preoccupied with sorting through a bureau drawer, Saffee does not respond.

April continues, "I saw Mother in the basement yesterday, opening up paint cans, checking colors or something. I just hate it when she gets in one of her painting moods. I woke up in the middle of the night because she and Daddy were arguing about it. Did you hear them?"

"No."

April buries her face in her pillow for a few moments and then says, "Saffee, when you're here and they fight it's not so bad, but when you're gone . . . I don't know . . . Maybe we can talk on the phone?"

Saffee is too preoccupied to be sympathetic. "I don't think so. It'd be long distance, you know. They wouldn't allow it." Kvaale long-distance calls are reserved for passing along only the gravest news, such as the death of a relative the girls have never heard of.

"Well, how about letters?"

The coed-to-be ignores the fact that April's voice is cracking. "I'm going to *college*, April. I'll probably be way too *busy* for letters."

"Well, *I* can still write to *you*," April says with resignation and leaves the room.

Saffee pushes April from her mind. She catches a reflection of her furrowed brow in the mirror and leans closer to inspect her face. Will she be the only girl on campus who still must conceal purply-red pimples with pasty-pale medication?

She plops down onto the floor and leans back on her elbows. Idly wagging her feet back and forth, she tries to imagine what lies ahead. She is leaving an insular, unsatisfying home life, but it has been safe, making few demands. Mr. Mason's convicting truism has flashed into her mind lately: "Dead fish flow with the stream." The image sickens her. She does not want to be a dead fish any longer. She wants to get out of the home stream that goes nowhere. But she is afraid.

She might be ready for college academically, but in addition to learning, she supposes that college years are a time to cultivate new relationships and have fun. These things her family has not taught her, while books and movies have only given passive instruction. She hopes to forget her acutely self-conscious years trudging the hallways of Miller's High. She critically views herself as unattractively large, which she is not, and boorish and dull, which, arguably, she can be. Can such a person ever have friends and fun?

Mulling the question, she surveys the familiar bedroom—the white-painted furniture, the homemade flowered curtains, the bedside table with its shelf of books. There she notices the black Bible presented to her at confirmation six years ago.

She was taught that the Bible contains the Word of God, so two or three times she tried to read it. She started at the beginning and soon became bogged down by its unfamiliar style and lists of odd names. The last time she opened it, she found that years before April had glued Green Stamps onto several pages, rather than into a Green Stamp redemption book. Irate, Saffee showed the desecrated pages to Joann, who breezily dismissed the deed. "Well, that just proves the Bible is a redemption book too!" she said, chuckling at her own wit.

Saffee considers that perhaps this is her last chance for some time to look into the old book, since she does not plan to pack it. Maybe there is some encouragement in it for her. Not knowing where to look, she decides to read whatever first meets her eye. She lets the book fall open, beyond the green pages, to near the middle, and reads:

Thou art my hiding place; thou shalt preserve me from trouble;
Thou shalt compass me about with songs of deliverance.

She reads the sentence again, changing *thou* to *you. You are my hiding place . . .* She reads it a third time.

She knows that, much like her mother's life, hers has been spent in hiding places, private and alone, not risking to unveil her innermost being to anyone. Perhaps not even to herself. The verse seems to say that there is some kind of protective place in God. A place away from trouble. This appeals to her reclusive tendencies. But what are songs of deliverance?

She recalls the tense night on the basement stairway, listening to her parents argue. There she heard God's voice: *Watch. Listen. Learn. Your life will be different.* At the time, the promise did not seem to be a song, yet since then, it has lent a certain ever-so-personal lyric to her life. Intrigued, Saffee continues to read.

> *I will instruct thee and teach thee in the way which thou shalt go: I will guide thee with mine eye.*

Saffee stares at the words. She had no idea the Bible would, or even could, communicate to her so directly. Instruct? Teach? Guide? How she desires these things. As strong as her eagerness to leave home is her fear of doing so. She has wondered if she will be able to maintain her comfortably safe distance from people. Will she be expected to speak in classes? Then there is the matter of a roommate. She attached a note to her application requesting a private dormitory room but is afraid it will not be honored.

She reads on.

> *Be ye not as the horse, or as the mule, which have no understanding: whose mouth must be held in with bit and bridle . . . Many sorrows shall be to the wicked: but he that trusteth in the Lord, mercy shall compass him about.*

If God cares enough about her to communicate like this, at the very moment she needs it, maybe she can leave home less afraid. She tucks the Bible between layers of clothes in a suitcase.

CHAPTER TWENTY-EIGHT

WHAT'S IN A NAME?

In a sense, Saffee's new life begins because of her name. "Kvaale" places her in the *J* through *L* group for five days of freshman orientation. Somewhere between Monday's health forms and Friday's convocation, she meets Mary, Mary Kvaale, who pronounces her own name as if it is an appellation of honor, even beauty.

"Hello. My name is Mary Kvaale," she says, politely extending her hand, her serene, blue eyes looking confidently into Saffee's. To others, it would have been such a minor thing. But Saffee is stunned. All her life she has painfully resented being stuck with this funny last name, and her first is not at all better. When she cannot avoid admitting to Kvaale, she distorts her mouth and quickly rolls her eyes, showing how distasteful it is to claim. In contrast, Mary speaks the very same name with seeming pride, suggesting that her Kvaale-ness is a sacred trust. Saffee appraises an aura of loveliness that envelops the girl simply because she speaks so softly, so self-assuredly.

Later, when alone, Saffee examines her own reflection in a mirror and says quietly, "Hello. My name is Sapphire Kvaale."

Amazing. Her old life is still written on her face, but something of promise shines in her eyes. She resolves to believe the words she read in the confirmation Bible.

College propels Saffee, a quirky, small-town introvert, into a culture quite foreign. But, from orientation week on, the girl who from childhood has said, *I can't, I won't, I'm afraid*, decides to plant a tiny seed of confidence. However, for some time, as she hurries to and from classes along the crowded mall that flows with a great swell of humanity, she feels empowered, not by confidence, but by her own imagined invisibility. She can't help but wonder what others might notice about her, if anyone bothered to look. Does she bear a physical stamp of her sterile, crazy upbringing? What expressions or gestures reveal her dullness to those who make slight, friendly advances in classes and the cafeteria? She chooses to be polite, but wary.

October 14, 1959
Dear Family,

What should she write? That she is thrilled to be away from the vacuum of her former existence? So thrilled that she has been "beyond words" for almost a month and therefore has been unable to write? It is duty that prompts her to write now; after all, her dad is paying.

I love it here! The campus is full of wonderful people and everyone is so nice to me.

Should she write that after days of observation she does not yet know how to embrace the new, exhilarating life around her? In the past, boredom was so easily obtained. But here, one can hardly be passive; participation is required. In her heart of hearts, how she would love to be swept up in the myriad of activity, the frivolous as well as the seriously academic.

I have a roommate. Her name is Gloria Karson. She's from the suburbs, obviously well-to-do, and has a great personality. I'm sure we'll get *along fine, even if she is a Lutheran. She reads the Bible every morning before she even gets out of bed!*

For roommates, Saffee has gone from bubbly, extroverted April to bubbly, extroverted Gloria. April, Mother's little pet, Saffee resented. Beautiful, self-assured Gloria, with curly red hair and porcelain skin, she admires and yearns to be like. Gloria's advice on makeup—"That gloppy cover-up makes you look like death warmed over"—was said with humor, not ridicule. "Let me show you what real makeup can do for you, Saffee."

Seeking approval on all fronts, Saffee doesn't want her roommate to think she's a heathen, so she tells her that years ago she tried to make sense out of the Old Testament. Gloria suggests Saffee try the book of Psalms and the accounts of Jesus in the New Testament.

Gloria thinks my gray tweed suit is quite appropriate.

"Well, if we ever have to go to a funeral, you'll be all set!" Again, her statement held humor, not sarcasm, her dimples deepening as she laughed. "If you'd like, you can borrow some of my pleated skirts and sweaters until you get more of your own."

She doesn't write that Gloria thinks it's funny that Saffee's every possession is labeled. "Did you think your roomie was going to steal your underwear?" she teased, putting her arm around Saffee's shoulders with a friendly squeeze.

Down the hall is a nice girl named Kathy. We are in some of the same classes, so we sometimes walk across campus together. Across the hall are Charlotte and Jillian from Atlanta, Georgia. I've never known Negroes before. They sure have accents! But that hasn't hindered them from already making a hundred friends! They know some university football players from their hometown. I guess coming from Miller's Ford means I've got a lot of learning to do about different kinds of people.

Saffee considers that she represents a sort of minority on campus—an outsider by personality and deficient in life experience. One reason she is drawn to Charlotte and Jillian is that they too are from a minority, albeit a different kind. She has been surprised how easily they have assimilated into activities and relationships. Under the influence of Gloria and these other new friends, Saffee begins to discard her insulated, egocentric tendencies.

The best thing: Robert Frost was the convocation speaker yesterday—in person! He's pretty old, with a shock of white hair, just like his pictures. His voice was weak until he started reading "Birches." He actually read "Birches"! (Thank you, Mother, for making it one of my favorites.)

As she listened to the revered poet, Saffee imagined the little old man, once an impish boy, clinging to a bending branch, whooping and hollering, bouncing through the air, then dropping to the ground to watch it spring back. A poem about risk. A poem about fun. A poem that did not at all resemble her own childhood.

About my classes: Psychology 101—The professor is boring, but the subject is fascinating. Mother, years ago did you read about Skinner boxes in Mr. Clement's psychology books? What terrible things. He actually put babies in boxes!

French—Pretty hard, but I like it. Let me tell you about the huge linebacker (second string) who I sometimes sit next to in class. Last week we started talking—in English, of course. Later, I ran into him (not literally, or I'd be dead) in Dinky Town (the quaint shopping village across University Ave.). We went to Bridgeman's and had a cherry Coke. He paid, so I'm calling it my first date!

She doesn't write that when she is called on in class, her face reddens and a shy dumbness comes over her. Twice in French she answered questions with Spanish vocabulary learned in high school.

And her "date" with the linebacker? She was hardly able to say an intelligent word and was so nervous she spilled her Coke on his books, and ever since she makes a point to sit at least three rows behind him in class.

Well, that's all for now. Gotta work on a four-page paper for history.

Why mention that her first and only venture to do research for that paper, in the vast, mysterious library, so intimidated her that she did not dare inquire how to locate information?

Hope you understand I don't have time to write often.
            Love,
            Saffee

She posts the letter, not imagining the kind of ruckus it will cause when it arrives.

CHAPTER TWENTY-NINE

SAPPHIRA

affee answers the phone in the hallway booth. "Hello?"

"Saffee."

"Oh!"

"This is your mother."

"Yes. I know. Did you get my letter?"

"Yes, it came today, and we want you to come home Friday night on the Greyhound."

"What? *Home?* I just got here!"

"We expect to see you Friday."

"But there's a dorm party Friday night. I've been thinking about going."

"Your dad will pick you up at the station when the bus gets in. Ten o'clock."

"Mother!"

"This is long distance. We'll talk when you get here. Good-bye."

The next day there is a letter from April. In it is no indication that she knows Saffee has been summoned home.

October 21, 1959

Dear Saffee,

I read your letter. College sounds so great! Can't wait to get there myself. What's a Skinner box?

Things around here aren't very good. Mom's been mean to me lately. She calls me bad names and then gives me the silent treatment. It really hurts the way she's changed toward me. And her arguments with Daddy are getting worse. Mom's mostly on her high horse about religious stuff now. Daddy tells her to stop talking foolishness, and that makes her madder. She's bent over her Bible all the time, writing in it. It's like when she wrote a lot in a library book and they made her pay for it. She told them she was translating the words into what they really meant and they should thank her!

With you not here at night I can't sleep very well. I lie in bed thinking about climbing out the window and leaving. I suppose that's ridiculous. When are you coming home?

Love and XXX,

April

Saffee has been away for six weeks. Now she stands in the middle of the living room, hugging her arms to her chest. Why is she uneasy in her own home? Because . . . it is *not* her home anymore. But until she feels less like an interloper on campus, she has no home. She glances around, reabsorbing familiarity: the Audubon Society magazine on the marble-topped coffee table, put there five years ago because its cover coordinates with Joann's décor; the pink fluted candy dish three inches to the left of the crystal lamp, still empty; the yellow ceramic dancing girl, still maniacally lunging on the bookshelf, and no closer to the edge.

Looking out the picture windows to the south, she sees frost-nipped hydrangeas, bent over and dead brown. The apple trees in the orchard have all but shed their leaves. During the summer, a couple named Peterson built a house, then hidden from view, on the lot beyond the orchard. Now, through the bare branches, Saffee can see it clearly. A black Labrador romps in the new neighbors' yard.

Instinctively, she knows that the proximity of the new house and its color are a significant offense to Joann. She can almost hear the protest: "Blue! Have they no sense of propriety?"

Saffee remembers once standing at this window watching April and two young town boys scoop up fallen apples. Their faces glowed with mirth as they shrieked and whooped, lobbing them over the bank into the valley below.

She visually sweeps the living room again, feeling uneasy. It is unusual that the double doors to the dining room are almost closed; it looks dark beyond. She smelled the sickening odor of wet paint when she arrived last night, the smell synonymous with her mother's periodic anguish over the Norway table. She doesn't want to see what new graffiti is there. A familiar, paint-spattered canvas drop cloth extends a few inches out the doorway. She gives it a kick so she can close the doors and sees that the room is dark because newspapers are taped to the windows. She quickly pulls the doors shut. New, worn, track-like marks on the carpet catch her eye.

Her parents are in the bedroom. What's keeping them? Her father said little when he picked her up at the bus last night. This morning they shared a breakfast of cold cereal, and again, he gave no clue as to why she was told to come home. She guesses that it was not his idea. April, he told her, stayed overnight with a friend.

As she waits, she wonders what they will want to know about college life. Her letter mentioned a number of things she is eager to elaborate on, especially her classes. Not that she has ever been in the habit of sharing with them, but now she hopes to be more open, more adult to adult.

She hears a slow shuffle coming down the hall.

"Sit down, Saffee."

Saffee is stunned by Joann's appearance. Her longish dark hair falls free, unkempt. She wears an old, matted chenille robe and supports her body with a crutch.

"Mother. What happened?"

"You mean you don't even remember my car accident? You know very well my broken ankle never healed right."

Saffee wants to mention that the accident was long ago and for years there has seemed to be no need for a crutch. She connects the track on the floor to her mother dragging one foot.

Nels and Joann settle themselves.

"Sit *down*, Saffee," Joann repeats and gives Nels a distinct glare, which tells Saffee she wants him to conduct the proceedings, "as a father should."

Nels is nervous, gruff, and to the point. "Your mother, we, don't want you datin' no colored boys," he blurts.

"Wh-what?"

"You heard me."

Saffee stares from one to the other.

"That's why you made me ride more than four hours on the bus? Date, as you say, 'colored' boys? What are you talking about? I haven't even met any."

Nels looks relieved. Joann looks skeptical. Saffee realizes they must have thought the linebacker she had written about was a Negro. He wasn't.

"Those . . . southern girls introduced you. You wrote it in your letter," Joann says. "Get it straight now, we won't allow it!" Saffee knew Joann's intention that Nels lead the conversation would not last.

"Mother, you've got it wrong. I haven't gone out with a Negro, but don't you want me to get along with everybody at school?"

"Getting along is one thing—dating is another," retorts Joann. "We're talking *Negroes* here and you've been fraternizing with them."

Saffee winces; she is committed to telling the truth. She represses last spring's conversation when she insisted there was nothing "wrong" with Joann. "No, I haven't." Saffee looks appealingly at her dad, who sits with head bowed, pinching the bridge of his nose. She wonders if either of her parents has ever even spoken to a person of color.

Joann straightens and tilts her face, posturing regal authority. "*Sapphira!* You are an astonishment!" Her pitch rises. "One's appearance, manner, and behavior should not bring disgrace to one's church, family, school, or God! Sapphira, you have not lied to man but to God."

"What?" Saffee feels sick to her stomach. Moments blur. "Sapphira? Who's Sapphira?"

"I know by your name that you are a liar," Joann insists. She turns to Nels and orders him to get her Bible.

"Aw, Joann, just let 'er be. She says—"

"Get my Bible, Nels!"

He looks at Saffee apologetically and retrieves the book from the bedroom. Joann quickly flips through the pages. Saffee sees they have been heavily annotated.

"Look here, Sapphira . . ."

"Mother, why are you calling me that? You know that's not my name."

"Here you are, right here—read this." She thrusts the worn book toward Saffee, indicating an area marked with red crayon. Joann's unmistakable scrawl almost obliterates many of the words, and sections of the page are shaded with green or yellow.

Saffee reads about a woman named Sapphira, who, after lying, falls down dead. Saffee is speechless. She has been reading the Bible, because of Gloria's encouragement, and has found it instructive and encouraging. How can her mother misuse it? Her mother is not merely eccentric, she is seriously crazy.

Nels clears his throat with a nervous, rough growl.

"See what happens to liars?" Within Joann's irrationality is a note of triumph.

"Mother, you've sent me to a school where there are all kinds of people. They come from all over the country, even the world, and I

think they are all quite wonderful—with probably lots to teach me."
She is fuming. "It never occurred to me to go out with somebody
brown, or pink, or green, but actually, I don't know why not." She is
careful not to say she won't. She needs to think about it.

Joann is not used to being refuted. She looks confused as if
unable to comprehend the show of strength. She struggles to stand,
adjusts the crutch, and rapidly drags herself across the room. Going
down the hall, she shouts, "Sapphira! You are an astonishment! You
have lied to God and man!"

Her mother's irrational theatrics have left Saffee weak, her face
drained of color. She slumps into a chair and looks at her dad. His
shoulders droop, his head is bent. For the first time in her life she is
sympathetic for the burden he carries. She leans forward and says
quietly, "Daddy, Mother needs help. She's *sick*."

Nels raises his head. Struggling for composure, he counters, "She
has good days and bad. Today's a bad one, but she'll be okay."

It baffles Saffee that he continues to deny the obvious.

"I'm so sorry . . . ," he says. "I'm so sorry you had to see her this
way. But there's nuttin' to worry about."

"But, Daddy, what about the crutch? Her ankle is just fine, don't
you think? And you know the crazy way she paints that stupid table
all the time—that's *not normal*, Dad. You know it isn't. Isn't there
someplace you could take her to get some—"

"No! Those places are terrible. She'll be okay," he insists. "I'm
thinkin' of buyin' a trailer in the spring. Maybe we can travel some
on weekends. It'll do her a world of good to get outta the house more.
She'll be okay." He seems to believe it. "Don' worry about it. When
you're home at Thanksgivin', things'll be better."

Saffee studies him as he drums his fingers on the armrests of the
chair.

"You wanna go back to school on the noon bus?" he asks. The
question sounds like an apology. "I'll take you to the station."

Chapter Thirty

Thanksgiving

Nels sits at the Formica table sharpening knives, a task he has perfected to an art. He deftly circles each blade against the whetstone. "It's all in the angle of the knife against the stone," he says. He holds up a sheet of newspaper to test the butcher knife. When the blade slices razor-perfect, without so much as fluttering the paper, he is satisfied. He will use this knife on the turkey; he has no use for fancy carving sets.

He glances up at Joann, standing at the sink scrubbing the turkey with such vigor it may be in danger of losing skin. "Quill tips," she says, patting the naked bird dry with a clean towel. "Never know when they'll get stuck in a person's throat."

Even though she is stressed over the task of preparing a holiday meal, and has even asked for assistance from her girls, overall she has a little more buoyancy than Nels has seen recently. She did not criticize the produce he bought for the Thanksgiving meal (he has purchased all the groceries for some time), not even the size of the turkey (she had requested sixteen pounds, not seventeen). She limps with determination between stove, sink, and refrigerator, giving instructions to Saffee about making cranberry sauce and April peeling potatoes. Nels notices that her crutch leans against the pantry door, handy but unused. He drums his fingers and clears his throat.

"Joann." At his stern tone, Saffee glances at him over her shoulder. "Joann," Nels repeats, "you've gotta tear them newspapers off them windows before we eat Thanksgivin' dinner."

Joann's demeanor changes. She throws him a scathing look. "What? And let those snoops next door press their blue nosey faces against the window to watch us? Let them criticize how we carve turkey? Spread lies all over town that we blow our noses on our napkins? No sirree, Nels, not on your life."

"Joann, hush! The way you talk. They're nice folks, those Petersons, nice as all get-out. You should meet 'em."

"*Nice?*" Joann fans her irritation, grips the edge of the countertop, and glares at him. "How can you say they're *nice*? I've heard all about them. Don't you ever bring them over here, Nels."

Grimacing, Saffee wipes her hands on her apron and hopes the exchange is not a preview of things to come. She finds it curious that neither parent has mentioned her recent summons to come home. As for her mother meeting neighbors? Fantasy. Joann's disordered thinking has made her unable, or unwilling, to do that since they lived on Second Street. She's heard "all about" the Petersons? From whom? She can't possibly be privy to any information that warrants her mind-set. Nels sits, pinching the bridge of his nose, his eyes closed. There is nothing more to say.

Saffee has avoided looking into the dining room since she came home from school yesterday afternoon. But if the family is going to eat Thanksgiving dinner around the Norway table, as they always do, she had better assess its condition and deal with whatever she finds before the time to set it.

She opens the door to the darkened dining room, switches on the light, and shudders at a hodgepodge of color. Her mother must have had quite a flicking, dribbling frenzy to achieve this random mess. But when it suggests Jackson Pollock's work that she's seen in *Life* magazine, she decides to view it as merely an oddly whimsical mess and tries to forget that it was probably executed during a deranged episode. She opens a china closet drawer to select a suitable tablecloth.

In the afternoon, Saffee mashes potatoes, both white and sweet, drawing only a minimum of correction. But April, Saffee notes, comes under repeated fire.

"April," Joann says, "if that cream is ever going to whip before the cows come home, you'll have to turn the beater like you mean it."

The sisters have long coveted some guise of normalcy within the household, but a clear understanding of what normal is eludes them. So, in spite of a few caustic exchanges, and the usual idiosyncrasies notwithstanding, to their eyes Thanksgiving Day progresses without serious incident. The only noticeable change is Joann's heightened criticism of April, her child who could, at least in the past, do little wrong.

At four o'clock, they sit around a table laden with heaping bowls of holiday fare. Four lime Jell-O trees, topped with stiff peaks of whipped cream, jiggle on salad plates. The feast distracts attention from what they all know: Saffee has covered a white sheet with an ecru lace tablecloth, hoping to hide from sight, if not mind, the splattered paint beneath.

"God is good. God is great. We thank Him for our food. Amen."

It is the same brief prayer that Joann has intoned over every meal since Saffee can remember. Now, as in childhood, she cracks her eyes to watch her mother's face, the uplifted eyebrows above closed lids, as beatific as a Hollywood nun. Saffee does not doubt her mother's sincerity, but its mix with affectation has always been a curiosity.

They all consume large quantities of food. Surely a "normal" American Thanksgiving requires a measure of gluttony. But the eating is only done as ritual. In the absence of conviviality, their eyes do not shine with delight. Instead, intentional carefulness prevails. To be sure, there are no spills of gravy or cranberry sauce on the lace cloth. No one mentions that the rose pleated draperies are pulled at an earlier hour than necessary, covering windows darkened by issues of the *Gazette*. Who knows if lighting by chandelier on a holiday while the sun still shines may also be normal?

Three of them pretend not to notice that Joann holds each forkful slightly aloft for inspection before it enters her mouth. Morsels that do not meet approval are discarded onto a salad plate that overflows by meal's end.

There is no mention of the holiday's origin. Kvaale life mostly senses the present. But no mention either that now there is a college girl in the family. Important matters, such as the food before them and Tuesday's ice storm that caused havoc in the orchard, eclipse other topics. By the time they indulge in slices of pumpkin and pecan pie, Joann has angled her body away from the window and her arms are around her plate.

The next day Joann is reclusive. In the late morning, Saffee catches a glimpse of her in the master bedroom. Wrapped in an old pink chenille robe, she bends over her small desk, intently writing. Not an uncommon posture. Later she hurriedly hobbles by crutch through the living room, abruptly shutting the double dining room doors behind her.

Back to school tomorrow; again Saffee counts the hours. She tries to read assignments for her world history class. Coming upon an unfamiliar word, she takes Joann's new dictionary from its place on a bookshelf. Thumbing through, she is disheartened to see handwritten commentary on page after page. Under *V*, words referring to truth are highlighted: *verify, verisimilitude, veritable*. In the margins are tightly scribbled words. Among them, "truth will liberate you" and "truth without fear." But also "deceiver," "conniver," "hoax," "impostor," "defraud," "sucker." Together, they seem to spell confusion.

Earlier in the day, when she saw Joann writing in a book, it did not appear to be this dictionary. Had it been her Bible? Hadn't April mentioned that in a letter? She remembers how her mother had clobbered her with Sapphira's story. Reinterpreting the dictionary seems foolish enough.

In the late afternoon, Saffee looks out the living room windows toward the orchard. She guesses that her mother has spent considerable time this fall standing here, watching leaves drop from the apple trees, each gust of wind exposing more of the Petersons' blue house, invading more of her privacy.

The weather has reversed itself, turning warm for a Minnesota November. Saffee notices Nels stacking dead branches beneath the apple trees and sees both opportunity and excuse to leave the house. She slips on a windbreaker and knitted gloves with leather palms and goes outside. April soon follows.

Saffee can't remember if she and April have ever helped their dad outdoors. He seems surprised and pleased when they join him.

"The Winesaps got the worst of the storm," he says, as together they pile splintered limbs on the edge of the west bank that overlooks the long, sweeping valley. The orchard is narrow and deep, stretching from the road to the bank, with five rows of apple trees parallel to the house.

April drags a large fallen limb she finds beside the road. As Saffee and Nels carry armloads of brittle branches toward the bank, she broaches the topic of hospitalizing her mother again. "Dad, have you reconsidered taking Mom to see a doctor?"

"Now don't go talkin' that way again. She was fine at Thanksgivin' yesterday, wasn't she? Just fine. See? There's nothin' wrong with her."

Overhearing him, April says, "You call that fine? I guess yesterday could have been worse, but now, one day later, anyone can see she's not fine."

No one has a heart to say more. They continue to gather and lug branches, noting that the sun will soon be down. April scoops up a few rotted apples, recently frozen and now thawed, oozing brown. She flings them into the valley.

"I used to get a royal stomachache from eating green ones," she says.

"I remember seeing you throw apples with some little boys one summer. It looked like fun," Saffee says. "I wanted to do it too."

April gives her a puzzled look. "Well, why didn't you?"

Saffee doesn't answer. April, who lives life exuberantly, not unlike, it seems, the nameless, swirling masses of people on the college campus, would not understand.

With a decisive move, Saffee picks up an apple, reaches back her arm, and flings with all her might. The soggy fruit plops not far from her feet. She is embarrassed, furious with herself.

"It's okay," April says. "Try again. Let your fingers open sooner."

The second toss arches high, streaks across the setting sun, and skitters through brush far below. The sisters' eyes meet. Saffee suppresses a giggle, and then, with impulsiveness, both girls scamper to gather a reserve and begin a competition.

Saffee throws with uncharacteristic abandon, disregarding brown, mushy stains collecting on her jacket and gloves. She wonders if Joann might have made a tiny rip in the newspaper and is watching them, disapprovingly, through the dusk.

Nels joins in. "Let's see who can hit that there willow way down at the bottom." He hurls a missile that flies twenty yards beyond what had been the girls' best shots.

"I can beat that, Daddy!" April challenges. "Just watch!"

They scramble for more ammunition and throw furiously. Unused to such camaraderie, or perhaps solidarity, Saffee's face flushes. Throwing apples, laughing, with April and Dad. At every toss, Saffee's delight is coupled with an inner grief that cries, *Why didn't we do this long ago, Daddy? Why didn't we play? Why didn't we ever, ever have fun together like this?* She is pink from exertion, as well as emotion.

Their diversion is interrupted by a police car. Was there a siren? Afterward, they can't remember. Through the dusk and bare branches, they sense a commotion at the blue house. A man yells; the black Lab barks.

"Wonder what's going on!" April takes off running through the fallen leaves. Nels and Saffee follow until they see a figure in pink chenille, spotlighted by a harsh yard light.

Horrified, Nels shouts, "Joann! Whatcha doin'?"

Disheveled, and with wild-eyed terror, Joann lunges here and there at things invisible in the Petersons' yard, her crutch discarded on the ground. She brandishes a butcher knife, stabbing the air with delusional drama. Brown dormant chrysanthemum plants lie strewn haphazardly at her feet.

CHAPTER THIRTY-ONE

ROTTEN APPLES

Blue tares, blue tares," Joann shouts. "The axe comes to lay at the root of blue tares!"

A man and woman, presumably the Petersons, cower on the porch. "Be careful, Officer, she's got a knife," the man calls out.

Joann veers toward the approaching policeman. "The axe is laid . . ." He advances slowly.

"Get back!" Joann screams at him in manic alarm. "Don't come near me. Don't touch me. Leave the blue tares alone. I must get rid of them."

The frenzied dog behind the backyard fence barks and growls.

The officer takes another step. "Mrs. Kvaale, stop right there." He is calm, but firm.

"Joann," Nels shouts, striding across the Petersons' yard.

"Get back! Stay away! Our God is a consuming fire! Get back, Nels." She grips the knife with both hands, bayonet style, pointing it at the policeman's stomach. He darts forward and grabs one of her arms, applies pressure until she drops the knife. The sharp knife. The knife that carved yesterday's turkey.

Saffee's heart pounds. Her feet are rooted to the edge of the

Petersons' yard as if paralyzed. She presses her fists hard against her cheeks, not believing the surreal nightmare unfolding in the glare of the yard light. How can this wild woman be her mother? The woman who bore her, raised her, has gone completely mad. "Mother, stop!" she yells. "Daddy, do something!"

April clings to her sister and cries. Joann struggles with the policeman as he tries to guide her toward the squad car. A second car arrives and another officer hastens to assist.

"Bingo! Quiet!" Mr. Peterson yells.

Nels, breathless and pale, circles his arms around his wife. "I've got 'er," he shouts over the din. "I'll take 'er home now."

"No, Nels," the officer says, trying to still Joann's writhing while his partner clamps cuffs around her wrists, "not this time. I'm sorry. Assaulting an officer, destruction of property—that's criminal offense. I have to take her in. We'll hold her until you get arrangements with one of the hospitals."

With tears in his eyes, Nels looks at his wife already in the squad car, secured behind a black grill that separates the backseat from the front. He sees terror on her face and he stretches his arms toward her. "Oh, Joann," he says, his voice a mixture of grief and helplessness. "Why didja do it, Joann?"

The policeman looks sympathetic. "I'm sorry, Nels. We'll take her to the holding tank at the jail for now and we'll see she gets transportation to some place. Like I told you before, you'll first have to get a court order from a judge to commit her. Too bad it's the weekend."

The officer's voice carries to April and Saffee in the crisp night air. Too horrified to go closer to the police car, closer to their mother, they have not moved. They know their dad is mortified. Keeping Joann's peculiarities out of the public eye has always been imperative. It's obvious now that others know; the policeman called her by name. Saffee's teeth chatter. She feels as if she might vomit.

Mr. Peterson leaves his porch and hurries across the yard. "I'm sorry, Nels. We had to call them, you know. I tried you first, but there was no answer. Look!" He sweeps his arm over the side yard. "She pulled up all Millie's chrysanthemums, right up by the roots. They was growing right over there." He points to the foundation of his house. "When I let Bingo out, he started barking like crazy, and then I saw her slashing that knife around, hacking away at them plants." Mr. Peterson swings his arms back and forth as if he needs to help Nels imagine the scene. "You know, Nels, I couldn't go deal with nobody with a knife. I had to get help. You understand, don'tcha, Nels?"

"Yeah. Sure." Nels shakes his bent head. "I unnerstan' . . . I'll make up the damage to ya, Peterson."

An officer suggests that Nels ride in the other car to the station. As he gets in, he calls over his shoulder, telling his daughters to go home. They needn't be told. Sobbing, adrift in swirling emotion, Saffee and April run back into the dark orchard, toward their empty house, as if pursued. Black low-hanging limbs reach out to scratch them. April trips and falls, face to the cold ground.

"Ick! Yuck!"

"What's the matter, April? Get up."

"It's the rotten apples!" On her knees, April scrapes soft mush from her face in disgust and whimpers, "This is what our life has become, Saffee, rotten apples!"

Looking down at her, never-before-opened floodgates of caring swell within Saffee. Sniffling, she pulls off her gloves, kneels, and wipes away tears and musky apple flesh from April's cheeks. She sinks to the ground and the older cradles the younger in her arms. Tells her not to cry. Tells her everything is going to be okay.

"No, it's not. They took Mom to jail!" April burrows her head in Saffee's chest. "Saffee, I don't get it. Mommy's always treated me . . . sort of special. I always used to feel like, you know, like I was her pet or something. We had good times together. But now she's changed. Now she's so mean, but I don't want her to go to jail. It's so confusing and awful."

Saffee slowly rocks her sister back and forth. Dry leaves, carried in sudden, crazy whirlwinds, pelt their faces. She reminds April that the policeman said something about having their mother committed, and that must mean to a hospital. Perhaps there she will finally get some help. "I know things will be better, April—sometime."

"How do you know?"

"Because God told me."

April looks up. "What do you mean?"

Saffee tells her about the voice she heard on the stairway, saying that her life was going to be different and better than what it had been. Different and better than their parents' lives. "It was a long time ago, and I still believe it. Now, April, I'll believe it for you too."

CHAPTER THIRTY-TWO

TASTE AND SEE

1960

January 1, 1960

Dear Saffee,

Happy New Year! And hope it's happier than the last one. Seems an odd beginning, though—me at Marilyn's and Mom still in the hospital. Thanks for your letter. I'm glad you had a good time at Gloria's for Christmas, in spite of the circumstances. I talked to Daddy on the phone after he visited Mother on Christmas Day. He sounded discouraged.

Mrs. Johnson, Marilyn's mom, is a great cook—couldn't leave her Christmas cookies alone. She even gave me presents, a red sweater and a charm bracelet. And Marilyn gave me a jewelry box and a game called Password. I pretended I was part of the family. I think Daddy's paying them to let me stay here until Mother gets out of the hospital.

Some people named Franken live next door to Marilyn. They

have twin girls, two years old. So cute! Marilyn and I babysat for them on New Year's Eve—it took two of us!

Love,

April

Over the next months, Joann has multiple "visits" of varying length to a state mental hospital. Each time she is treated with a different high-powered, experimental drug, each one producing intolerable side effects when she returns home. She alternates between lethargy and agitation, weight loss and weight gain, dry mouth and drooling. She has little choice but to conceal the hated pills under her tongue and spit them out when Nels is not looking. Invariably, irrationality returns.

More than once, when Nels is at work, Joann wanders through the neighborhood knocking on doors, warning of coming apocalypse. And once, just about dawn, a policeman finds her scantily dressed crossing the Blue River bridge, a great distance from home. One Saturday night, she orders April, now a high school sophomore, to go to bed at seven o'clock. When April refuses, Joann strikes her legs several times with a broom handle.

In response to such behavior, Nels has little recourse but to secure another court order to have his wife once again "treated" in confinement.

"The rings, Joann. I forgot to take off your rings." He'd remembered as he drove the fifty miles following the police car. The police car in which his wife, his beloved, deranged wife, was again seated, restrained in the backseat behind the black metal grate. Aching, for almost an hour, he'd watched the back of her head, bobbing indignantly back and forth.

"No!" she howls. "No! You can't have them!"

"Come on, Joann. Don't make no trouble. I always keep 'em at home, but I'll put 'em in the bank if ya want. Now give 'em to me."

She lunges at him, pummels his chest, yelling, "I am a married woman! I should wear my rings. You gave them to me, Nels. What is it? You want to give them to somebody else?"

Nels controls her flailing arms. "It's the rules, Joann. Ya gotta follow the rules! Be good now, so you don't hafta stay so long this time."

"Abandonment! That's what it is, abandonment!"

An orderly appears with the garment. Straps and ties.

"Don't worry, Mr. Kvaale. We know how to do this." His voice is brusque, not sympathetic. Joann Kvaale is part of his day's work.

Nels usually makes it back to the car before he breaks down, but not today. He leaves the tiny room, heads for the exit, and crumples against a door frame in the entry. Sobs of grief and guilt.

April's letters continue to keep Saffee informed about ups and downs on the home front. She writes that she spends more and more time in their old neighborhood with Marilyn Johnson's "normal" family, and she continues to babysit the young twins next door to them. Nels only summons her home whenever he has some confidence that Joann's latest treatment will this time bring them peace.

Although Saffee still feels like "a fish out of water" at school, she too gets a taste of normal family life when roommate Gloria invites her home some weekends. She writes to April how strange it is to experience a household "full of little brothers that make noise and mess, while the family takes it all in stride." Gloria is teaching her how to play a few board games, something Saffee has been embarrassed to know nothing about.

She surprises herself by going to Friday night mixers at the student union to learn the lindy and cha-cha. She writes, "It's not exactly 'tripping the light fantastic,' like Mother used to do, but still lots of fun. And get this, you know how only classical music used to interest me? I've found out that rock 'n' roll is okay too!"

Saffee is quite sure her parents expect her to return home during the summer break. But by February, she knows that she will not. She can never go back "home." Academics and a fledgling social life have ushered her into a different world. She refuses to consider that by staying away she is abandoning April.

During Saffee's second year at school, April writes:

Life here is crazier than ever. You won't believe what happened now—Mother and Daddy went up to the church and signed some papers to withdraw membership from the Methodist church! They say I can't go to Sunday school or youth meetings.

Here's what happened. Daddy was out of town (I hate it when he's gone), and when I came home from school, Rev. Blakley was here arguing with Mother. She told me to go to my room and shut the door, so I did, but their voices were loud so I could still hear. Mother insisted that the end of the world is coming soon and Rev. Blakley had better do his part to warn the congregation. She said she hears information from "those who know" and that she's a messenger to warn people, especially him. Rev. B. told her that she's just an ordinary person and not a prophet, and she shouldn't listen to voices, and the Bible says only God knows when the end of the world is coming.

Then he read her some verses out of the Bible. I only remember a little of the one that made her the maddest. It was something about when she dies she's going to fade away and wither just like flowers and grass, but that God's Word will still be around. She shouted that she will never be dead grass because dead grass is for burning and God told her she won't burn and he better leave the house FAST! Which he did. She probably chased him out with her crutch. I stayed in the bedroom 'til suppertime. That's when she told me none of us will be going to the church anymore.

When Daddy came home she made Rev. B. sound really bad and he believed her. Now he's mad at the minister too!

Saffee, it was so upsetting. Write to me—at Marilyn's.

Saffee writes back, "Hang on, little sister, your life will get better too before long. College in just three years." That must seem like an eternity to April, but what else can she say? She encourages her to attend a different church.

Even though their mother has never embraced much that is offered by the organized church, and often distorts truth, Saffee wants to believe that her trust in Jesus Christ is genuine. Saffee rarely thinks to spend much time talking to God, but the mounting tensions at home that April writes about remind her that He is available. She begins to pray regularly for both parents and April, chastising herself that this has not been her habit.

Saffee checks the clock and scans her biology notes one more time. "Evolution is the cornerstone of modern biology"—a quote from her professor the first day of class. She glances at a few underlined words: *mutation, natural selection, genetic drift, evolutionary lineage.* The last term is underlined twice. Some things about biology puzzle her. She entered college not doubting, "In the beginning God . . ." But how does *He* fit into all of *this*? In particular, does "evolutionary lineage" mean that she is trapped by a predestined genetic makeup to be like her mentally ill mother? What about "Your life will be different"? In spite of this promise, she'll have to write a test the professor agrees with.

The last Sunday morning in November is clear and cold. Bare tree branches and street signs look as brittle as icicles. Saffee and Gloria hurry along neighborhood streets wondering why they had thought sheer hose would keep their legs warm and they didn't need boots. Their black pumps skirt drifted snow. What was it that Joann had said when they shopped for school clothes? Something about womanhood succumbing to outrageous whims of fashion. Saffee chuckles to herself.

In her fourteen months away from parental expectation, Saffee has never accompanied her roommate to church, enjoying instead Sunday morning slumber, completely alone in the dorm room they now share for a second year. But after receiving April's letter about the sisters' involuntary excommunication from their Miller's Ford church, today it seemed important to join her roommate on this frigid hike.

She's never shared with Gloria, or anyone at school, for that matter, that her mother has psychiatric problems. Wouldn't they look at her through different eyes, perhaps attribute every mannerism, maybe every word, to the possibility that she too must be . . . crazy? Other parents visit their offspring at school once in a while. Saffee is good at making excuses for hers—obligations, terribly busy all the time, you know.

Inside the chilly sanctuary, congregants wear their coats. Saffee heads for a back pew, but Gloria prods her halfway down to the front. Unfamiliar with Lutheran liturgy, Saffee mimics her roommate, like she still does concerning many aspects of life.

When the robed minister, Dr. Price, ascends the pulpit, Saffee takes it as a signal to daydream, but within moments she is arrested by his eloquence and resonant baritone voice.

". . . He could have made us into lumps of stone to line up and admire. But He chooses to give us the breath of humanity.

"He fashions ears to hear, not merely for self-defense, but to welcome the patter of rain, the trill of a robin.

"He could give us noses with which to merely draw air, but He gifts us with the exquisite perfume of blossoms.

"He could give us skin sensitive only to pain, but He accommodates our desire to receive a loved one's tender caress."

Oh, Mother, how could you misunderstand and distort such a God?

"He could have made eyes that see only light or dark, but He created a world with an immensity of color.

"And taste. Are we bored by flavorless nourishment? No! He made tiny taste buds that differentiate exquisite delicacies from land and sea!

"Beloved! *Taste* and *see* that our Creator God is good! Drink from His river of life . . ."

Soft light filters through the stained glass windows and hovers overhead. Saffee is comfortably warmed. In her heart, she thanks God for His creative goodness. She resolves to trust Him to teach her more than the professors she esteems.

At the same time, she is saddened that her mother, who would have once loved this sermon, has perhaps banished herself from ever hearing another.

That night, as Saffee lies awake in bed, three words from the sermon replay in her head: *Taste and see, taste and see.* Isn't this the opposite of how she lives? In spite of Gloria's tutoring on campus social skills (Gloria even arranged a couple double dates), Saffee still prefers cautious anonymity, devising excuses why she can't do various things that others seem to do so easily, such as ask a professor a question or learn to play bridge. Gloria, on the other hand, is running for student council and has planned a trip to New York City with friends over spring break.

God's directives—*Watch. Listen. Learn*—have been instructive, but they are passive assignments, requiring only observation and thought. Now it seems He's added a fourth instruction, one that will call for involvement, expecting her to abandon her familiar role as left-out child.

For her Shakespeare class, she's memorized a sonnet. What is that line? Something about killing the spirit of life (or is it love?) with perpetual dullness. She's tired of dullness.

Taste and see. A new mandate.

❧

After forty minutes in the phone booth down the hall, Gloria twirls into the room. "Saffee, it's going to be such a great party. I hope you decide to come."

Taste and see.

"I'll be there," Saffee says.

She combs her straight, wet hair, conscious of her roommate's exuberant countenance beside her own more sober expression in the mirror. Gloria shares the plans for a surprise birthday party she and various friends and relatives are to give her mother. As she talks about cakes and decorations and entertainment, Gloria's joyful face sometimes comes a little too close, invading space, and contributing to Saffee's envy of porcelain skin.

"That's nice," Saffee says, moving a few inches away to reach into her bag of prickly brush rollers. "How old is your mom going to be?"

"Forty-six." Gloria's natural red hair bounces without the benefit of rollers. "She's ancient."

"Yeah. Same as my mom." It's a slip. Saffee, to avoid questions, makes a point not to ever mention that she even has a mother. She's relieved when Gloria bubbles on.

"I made Dad promise to keep everything secret from the brothers. If they told, I'd . . ."

Gloria says she expects at least thirty people to attend.

Thirty! Saffee doesn't think she even knows that many people.

"Gloria, why are you doing this?"

"Why? Because it's her birthday! And to honor her, of course, for being such a great mom."

Saffee looks into the mirror, unseeing, while Gloria itemizes the menu for the buffet dinner. Saffee interrupts, "Would you do this if she weren't? A great mom, I mean." Now she's really said too much.

Gloria raises her eyebrows. "Well," she says slowly, "the commandment isn't to honor *great* mothers and *great* fathers, it's just—"

"Yeah, I know. You're right." Saffee selects another roller and wishes she could stuff the question back into her mouth.

Gloria doesn't let it drop. "I mean, well, if my mom were"—she says the next word delicately—"incarcerated, or something, I'd have to find some different way to honor her." She takes a package of party invitations and an address book from a drawer and prepares to write. Saffee detects embarrassment.

Incarcerated. Has Gloria assumed that Saffee's reticence is because her mother is in prison? Stunned, she winds a too-large section of brown hair around a roller and anchors it firmly with a plastic pick. Incarcerated.

Well, yes, Joann *is* in a sort of prison, not physically—although Saffee imagines that the state hospital is much like one—but emotionally for sure. For a long time Joann has been in a sort of prison, not entirely of her own making. Saffee doesn't have any more insight into mental illness than her dad does and, if she were honest about it, she doesn't want to know more. At any rate, Saffee will have to find a different way to keep the commandment about honoring one's mother. It is unlikely that prisons of any kind cater to birthday parties. She won't set Gloria straight on the facts. Her roommate can think what she wants.

"Oh! One more thing—a present," Gloria says, reaching for her to-do list.

"Isn't giving a party enough of a present?" Saffee asks.

"Oh no, I want to give her a gift too. At Dayton's I saw a manicure set with oodles of nifty tools . . ."

No! Saffee wants to shout. *Not a manicure set!* She remembers the scene in Technicolor. *Anything but that. Mothers don't like them.*

She winds the last roller extra tight and jabs it with a pick.

CHAPTER THIRTY-THREE

JACK

1961

"You're going to *Paris*? April, that's amazing."

April's phone call catches Saffee by surprise. Europe. Saffee wouldn't even consider something so daring. April's capricious tendencies have always served to liberate her from various restraints. Now, since the latest shred of Joann's stability has again disappeared, she no longer tolerates any independence in April, and April's creativity resists a harness. Her only recourse is to flee; to remain would be to break.

April explains that Mr. Franken, the father of the twins she babysits, is Miller's Ford's city planner. He and his family have been invited to a small French city as part of a six-month exchange program and have asked April to accompany them as their nanny. Mr. Franken is arranging a correspondence course for her to keep up with school.

"It's not Paris exactly," she says. "I think it's a little town south of there, or maybe north. I don't know. I don't really care. Saffee, I've been hoping and hoping for some miraculous opportunity like this, and now it's come. For six whole months I'll be away from all the nonsense at home."

"But, April, how about Mom and Dad . . . ?"

"That's the biggest shock. Dad says I can go. I guess he thinks if I'm gone I'm one less thing for him to worry about. Mom's in the hospital again, and I get the idea she doesn't comprehend much right now. I think Dad will just tell her later. Saffee, it's going to be a blast!"

Saffee gives her red scarf a toss over her shoulder as she and her friend Kathy meet on the campus mall. They hug hello, then head toward a costume jewelry store they both love. "So, Saffee, I'm so excited to tell you that I have a really nice guy to set you up with . . ."

Saffee laughs. "No way, Kathy, no more matchmaking. I'll never forget that last weirdo. You told me he was, what did you say, sensitive? Yeah, like a gorilla is sensitive! That one made me swear off blind dates forever."

"Yeah, I'm sorry about him, but I know, I really know you'd like Jack. He's just like you, serious about stuff, but interesting, and fun too. I think he likes to go to the theater. I have this feeling you were made for each other!"

"And why do you think I'd like to go out with someone like *me*? Is this the same Jack you told me about months ago? I thought he graduated."

"Yeah, Jack Andrews, he did graduate. So what?"

"Sorry, Kathy, not interested. I'm still trying to fit in with college age, don't care anything about older men out of school. Fix him up with one of your sorority sisters if he's so wonderful."

"He's not an 'older man.' He just graduated at the end of last quarter. And I would fix him up with a Tri Delt in a heartbeat, except for one thing."

"So, what's that?"

Kathy grins in her impish way. "I think he's meant for you."

They walk in silence for a while.

"Kathy?"

"Yeah?"

"This Jack Andrews. Is he a good dancer?"

She's just making sure. Joann had told her never to marry a man who can't dance.

When he calls, they talk for half an hour. Small talk. Investigating. He sounds polite. He works for a St. Paul insurance company in their work/study actuarial program—whatever that is. He explains, but she still isn't sure. "Okay," he says, "just think that an actuary is a place where they bury dead actors." She laughs.

He serves in the National Guard. His favorite movie is *High Noon*. His favorite activity? Playing football in the snow with buddies from high school.

He asks if she plays golf. "No? Too bad," he says. "Putting green underfoot is the best feeling on earth."

She doesn't see that they have anything in common and wonders why he hasn't already ended the conversation.

"What's your favorite food?" she asks, hating herself for the dumb question.

"Steak," he says. "Sirloin, of course."

"Of course," she says.

"And yours?"

"Vanilla pudding."

"Vanilla pudding?" He sounds amused. "Of all the food in the world, don't you like anything better than that?"

Now she's stupidly given him a clue about her life. Her vanilla life. "Well," she hastens to add, "I mean, it's white, and Norwegians eat a lot of white food and I'm Norwegian, second generation, or, I guess third . . . white potatoes, white gravy, creamed vegetables . . . and, of course, if you mix strawberries into the pudding . . . Doesn't that sound good?"

"Mmm," he says. "I'd rather have ice cream."

"Vanilla?"

"Chocolate."

"Of course."

She avoids asking about his family for fear he'd ask about hers. She chatters on about being a small-town escapee who loves college and the big city and has never missed a performance of the university's theater company. An ideal afternoon might be a walk in a park or exploring an art gallery. He says he likes those things too. How about a movie Friday night?

Suddenly she feels bold—how about the mixer at the Union instead? No? Well, okay, movie it is.

Wearing a new red angora sweater and gray pleated skirt, Saffee goes to the dorm lobby at the appointed time. She looks for someone of football player girth. Didn't Jack say that playing football is his favorite activity? But even with an overcoat, the dark-haired young man who approaches her appears to be slender. She doesn't miss his look of approval as he helps her with her coat.

They head toward his Volkswagen and then decide instead to walk the four blocks to the Varsity theater. Speaking only when necessary, they crunch through an inch of new snow in winter night stillness. Saffee continues to size him up: nice-looking, well-groomed, and mannerly—intentional about walking on the street side of the sidewalk. Best of all, and most telling, he laughs easily, not nervously or inappropriately, but comfortably.

No sooner do they sit down in the darkness, popcorn in hand, than one of Jack's new contact lenses pops out and falls somewhere at their feet. They spend ten minutes on hands and knees gingerly feeling the cement until they find the hard, no-longer-clean lens. He had not brought his glasses. Since Jack now has clear vision in only one eye and they've missed the beginning of the movie, they go to the box office and request a refund. *Gone with the Wind*. She quickly pushes the memory aside.

Jack seems to accept the awkward situation with aplomb; Saffee is impressed. They walk back toward campus under a cold, starry sky. He is witty, self-deprecating.

"'My contacts fell out!' Tom said *ex-sightedly.*"

"What?"

Jack repeats the pun. She still doesn't get it.

"What are you talking about?"

"Haven't you heard of Tom Swifties?"

"No. Who's he?"

Jack laughs. "It's a kind of joke that links an adverb to a quote in an unusual way."

He tells her that Tom is a character in a book and that there is a Tom Swiftie contest running in the newspaper. He says he makes them up, even when he doesn't want to.

Saffee tries to decide if this makes Jack wonderfully clever or a little strange. Whichever it is, for a date, she is uncharacteristically comfortable.

"So, you like living in the dorm?" He asks, as it turns out, not because he wants to know, but so he can follow her answer with: "I could never live in one. 'I need accommodations that will accept Rover,' Tom said *dogmatically.*"

She groans, but at the same time leans slightly toward clever.

The night is beautiful, the air is mild, tall lamps illumine the wide campus mall. When they reach the end, they decide to double back.

When he asks about her family, she tells him she has one sister named April and turns the inquiry onto him. He has a married older brother, Danny, who lives in Michigan with his wife and two children.

Jack tells her about his new job and offers opinions on sports and politics. It must be obvious she knows little about either one. He answers her questions, never giving her the idea that he finds her stupid. With his range of interests and knowledge, could he ever be interested in *her*? A nobody, from a strange family? Kathy seems to think so, but Saffee doesn't dare hope.

Later, at the dorm door, she says sincerely, "I've really enjoyed the evening. You know so much about so many interesting things."

"I like the way you laugh at my jokes," he says. Would she like to try the movie again the next night?

On Saturday, another pesky contact lens falls out onto the carpeted aisle, even before they are seated. Again unruffled, Jack guides her into a row, pops out the other lens, and reaches for his glasses. They laugh throughout the comedy until the house lights come on. When the crowd thins, Saffee insists they again search on hands and knees. This time the lens they find is shattered. Like the night before, Saffee notices that Jack is matter-of-fact, does not get mad or seem embarrassed, does not blame his eye doctor or optician. This is not the way she is used to handling the unexpected.

In the middle of the next week, they go to a Minnesota/Michigan hockey game. She's never watched a hockey game, or any kind of athletic contest, long enough to catch on to how it's played. Pleased to be with him, she feigns interest as he explains game strategy; he's played hockey most of his life.

"On your high school team?" she asks.

"No," he says, seeming flattered to be asked, "just pickup games."

"I love to skate," she tells him, happy there is something to mention that she does fairly well.

He suggests they return to the rink Saturday afternoon during open skating.

On Saturday, in spite of her still-too-large size-nine figure skates, she takes secret satisfaction that she's more graceful on ice than Jack. Grace obviously isn't necessary to chase a hockey puck. He compliments her skill.

Later, with two plastic spoons, they share an entire pint of chocolate ice cream in the Union lounge, laughing, talking with their heads together. His good humor makes her laugh from a deep place unfamiliar with laughter. It seems even his slightest phrase brings her an overflow of spirit. In return, yet unaware, she gives him a wisp of her heart.

He asks her if she believes in God.

"I do," she says.

He suggests they go to church together on Sunday.

CHAPTER THIRTY-FOUR

THE VALENTINE

affee's cheeks flame. She leans against the drugstore card display and reads the simple, romantic words again . . .

When you entered my life
My world became more beautiful.
You gave me your friendship
And now I know what it is like to be truly happy.

Inside . . .

I Think You're Wonderful!
Happy Valentine's Day

This is how she feels about Jack. This is the card she wants to give him. But how can she? It seems unbelievable that Kathy might be right, that they are "made for each other." And these words that coax tears, aren't they too forward? Jack hasn't suggested he has a romantic interest in her. All she knows is that she's never felt more comfortable, or happier, around any other male. Not that she's been

| 189

acquainted with that many. Steady, purposeful, so . . . so . . . gentlemanly Jack. All right, he doesn't dance at all, but his sense of humor, sometimes witty, sometimes dry, makes her laugh. Laugh! What a wonderful thing, in which she has had way too little practice. He *has* painted her world with beauty.

With her finger she traces the card's two red intertwining hearts. Is it *proper* to give a Valentine to someone she's only known for *two weeks*? Two weeks, yes, but *five* dates—if going to church counts. But what if he never asks her out again? And if he does, maybe he won't give her a card at all. But if he does, shouldn't she be prepared? With a sigh, she reads the dreamy sentiment again, replaces it on the rack, and searches for something . . . safer.

On the phone, Jack learns that Saffee has never had Chinese food. He says chow mein from a can doesn't count. He suggests that their next date ("How about Valentine's Day?") should be downtown at the Nankin restaurant.

They indulge in generous quantities of crab Rangoon, sweet-and-sour pork, and steamed rice (for a while they fumble with chopsticks), and drink green tea. The unfamiliar exotic flavors, décor, and tonal music spur an adventurous side Saffee didn't know she had.

Jack tells her about Kenny, an ingenious friend from high school days who has worked for months constructing a hot-air balloon. After sewing silk parachutes together and rigging up a propane burner, he's spent several weeks perfecting flights, tethered in a meadow behind Jack's parents' home.

"So far he's been carried along beneath the balloon and the burner in a lawn chair," Jack tells Saffee. "Now he's working on a basket to hold the burner and he says there will be room for two passengers."

"It sounds so dangerous!" Saffee says.

"Probably not as dangerous as sky diving."

"You mean, jumping out of a plane? Don't tell me you've done that."

"A couple times," he says.

"Why?"

"Just to see if I could do it. I admit, it was a little scary, but fun."

Saffee is amazed. Risk avoidance has always been one of her priorities. She's overwhelmed by the thought that she doesn't know a blasted thing about what people call fun. For others, fun just seems to naturally happen.

On sudden impulse she says, "'How high can the balloon go?' Tom asked *loftily*!"

Jack laughs; she loves his laugh. "Bravo!" he says. "Good one!"

Saffee blushes and self-consciously glides her fork around the edge of her plate, capturing the last tangy morsels. After they compare suspect fortunes from odd little cookies, Jack removes an envelope from a pocket of his sport coat. "Read it out loud," he says.

"Out loud?" Nervous, she makes a ragged mess of the envelope. She's flabbergasted. It's the same card she wanted to buy for him.

"Read it," he prompts, leaning forward, watching her.

Turning a deeper shade of red, she reads . . .

When you entered my life
My world became more beautiful.

When she stops, he says, "Go on."

You gave me your friendship
And now I know what it is like to be truly happy.

She doesn't dare look up.

"Read inside," he says.

She already knows what is there.

I Think You're Wonderful!

Happy Valentine's Day
Love, Jack

She meets his eyes. His expression says he intends the sentiment to speak for him. She remembers the card tucked in her purse and is furious with herself. She has misjudged his feelings and now will miss an opportunity to express her own. Presumably he is hoping she will also reveal romantic interest. She struggles not to show embarrassment as she hands him his card. What else can she do?

Jack opens the envelope to find a cartoonish picture of a towering ice-cream sundae. Saffee squints, wishing she were elsewhere. "'I like you better than ice cream,'" he reads. Is that a look of disappointment? She quickly attempts to defend her choice.

"Because we bought that pint of chocolate and shared it at the Union, remember?"

"Sure," Jack says.

"Well, you saw how *much* I like *ice cream*!" Saffee says.

She drops her eyes to the gift of poetry he gave her. "I just didn't expect such a beautiful, I mean, well, romantic card from you, Jack." She smiles at him. "Thank you."

"'I like yours too,' Tom said *sweetly*."

She grins and sighs with relief. After a childhood where nothing emotional, good or bad, was handled well, maybe she's learning a thing or two from Jack.

CHAPTER THIRTY-FIVE

THE COCOON

can hardly believe it, Jack. I was skiing! Buck Hill isn't the Rockies, but I was actually skiing."

Saffee is rarely this pleased with herself. She lifts her sock-feet up onto the dashboard and rubs sore ankles, chafed by ill-fitting rental boots. The pain is worth it. "I need more work on traversing, but don't you think I pretty much mastered the snowplow?" she says, angling for a compliment.

Jack turns on the headlights as the brief twilight gives way to a cloudy darkness releasing buckets of snow held back all afternoon. He tells her she did great and sounds like he means it. The windshield wipers swish and scrape. Jack boosts the blades to their dizzying limit.

They pull onto the highway and pick up speed. Hypnotic flakes rush like pinpoints of light pelting the windshield, pulling Saffee into reflection. Today she did not shrink from challenge, in spite of repeatedly falling off the T-bar lift while small children around her had little trouble. She had persevered. Too many times she has said, "I can't." Today was different.

"Who would ever think that I could ski?" she says, more to herself than Jack.

"Seems to me you're naturally coordinated," he says.

She steals a glance at him. "Really? Do you mean that?"

"I think you could learn any sport you set your mind to." Her heart swells and she sucks in her breath. She's not used to such a thought.

Keeping his eyes on the road, he says, "Sometimes I get the idea you've been in a cocoon most of your life." Whether Jack means it to be an observation or a question, it exposes her reality. She swings from the warmth of his compliment to embarrassment. She pulls her feet down from the dashboard. Cocky posture no longer seems appropriate. It is true. Most of her life she has lived in a stifling cocoon where normal things didn't happen. Things like learning to play.

Saffee used to reason that if she didn't try new things, technically she wouldn't fail. Now, with Jack, she has begun to try a little, but her lifelong reality has been found out—her cocoon. The word makes her squirm and threatens to ruin a good day. Neither one speaks for several moments.

"I didn't mean to be rude or critical," he says. "Cocoons are good things, you know."

"No. I don't know." She is curt. "Why?"

He gives her the unself-conscious smile she's come to love. "Because from cocoons come lovely butterflies."

If she had been frozen to the bone on Buck Hill, his fact-become-poetry would have melted her entire being.

Inspired by what sounds like approval, she dares ask, "The cocoon is opening a little, don't you think, Jack?"

"Yes," he says, "I think so."

A few weeks later, after several more dates, Jack says he won't be seeing her during the month of April because of an intense study schedule prior to his May actuarial exam. Throughout the month she misses him terribly and worries he'll forget her. But when the exam is over, and the trees are beginning to show spring buds, he calls. They go biking along trails bordering Minnehaha Creek. She doesn't tell him that she didn't learn to ride a bike until after sixth grade.

The summer before her senior year, Saffee again doesn't consider going home to Miller's Ford. Even another summer of typing catalogue cards sounds more appealing.

CHAPTER THIRTY-SIX

LOYALTY

1963

affee and Nels sit in a back booth of a Dinky Town hamburger joint. This is the first time Nels has visited his daughter at college, even though the hospital Joann frequents is only about an hour from the university. During infrequent telephone calls, Saffee has sensed it is even harder than before for him to communicate with her, a college girl. When he's not telling jokes, he has never had much to say. It was a surprise when he called to take her out to eat.

She will inquire about her mother first—because that's the right thing to do—then she'll tell her dad about Jack. She reaches for the ketchup. "What's going on with Mom, Daddy?"

Until April went to France, she had supplied Saffee's only updates on her mother. Saffee has not been back to Miller's Ford since the disastrous Thanksgiving her freshman year, more than three years ago. She almost never has taken the initiative to inquire about Joann by phone. To her, her mother is dead. No one asks about the dead. By extension, neither has her father occupied much room in her thoughts. She rarely remembered her past resolve to pray for them.

Instead of answering her question, Nels eats his coleslaw. He looks downcast. His left arm is deeply tanned from hours out the open window as he drives day in and day out for his job.

"Daddy?" she repeats.

"Ahh," he says, shaking his head. He puts down his fork and crumples a paper napkin. "She's back in the hospital. She was doin' more awful stuff."

"Like what?"

Nels takes a deep breath and glances at the ceiling, the way he does when pushed to confide and doesn't want to. "She was throwin' stuff away."

"What stuff?"

"Stuff that shoulda been saved, important papers, like insurance policies, bills . . . the pitures."

"What pictures? Our baby pictures?" Other than a box full of photos of April and Saffee when they were very young, she recalls few pictures in the house.

He nods. "Plus other things," he says. "The toaster, the radio, perfectly good lamps, anything she thought might be dangerous to her." He sighs heavily. "I'll never understand her. When she don't take her medicine, she talks to things, listens to things." He drops the shredded napkin onto his plate and drums the table. "It's good April's gone. Home ain't no place for her no more."

In July, Saffee had received a postcard from April. "I've decided to celebrate my seventeenth birthday in Switzerland!" Later she wrote that with the money she had earned during the nanny stint, she planned to backpack through Europe. She saw no reason to return home for school. "What could be more educational than climbing the Alps?" she wrote.

"How did you find out about her throwing things away, Daddy?" More pain crosses his face. He tells her that he realized various things were missing, and eventually the garbage collectors noticed and started saving "the garbage" for him. And now, he laments, the whole town knows and that was the last straw.

"So I come here to tell you—we ain't gonna live in Miller's Ford no more. I can't take this kinda embarrassment."

He seems to be imploring her to understand. It stings that her mother would throw away baby pictures, but their loss is of little consequence in the face of the shame and frustration her dad carries. It seems he is sharing the news of moving because he considers the Miller's Ford house to still be her home, but it is not.

"Oh, Daddy." Her compassion triggers anger. It rises up, overflows. She knows she shouldn't say it, in this public place or anywhere, but she does. She leans forward and hits the table with an open hand. "Daddy!" She doesn't care if others hear. "Why don't you just leave her?"

It is as if she slapped him. His stricken face turns deeper red and he glares at her. Placing both hands on the table, he leans forward and declares, "When I married your mother, I promised to stick with her through thick and thin, and I will."

It is a defining moment that Saffee will never forget. She is ashamed of herself, saying what she had no right to say.

She has never been prouder of her father.

Oh, God, in spite of me, redeem the time for my family.

A few moments pass as both struggle to regain composure. In those moments, she sees him as more than her teasing but sometimes stern father. More than the back-slapping, extroverted, good-old-boy he shows the world. Beyond his simple ways, he is both tragic and noble. He will not chuck his burden, he will shoulder it.

Finally, she says, "You've been 'batching' it for a long time, haven't you, Daddy?"

"I get by," he says.

Saffee once heard when a classmate's mother was dying of cancer that for weeks friends and neighbors brought the family casseroles and home-baked bread and desserts, showing love and support. Various afflictions seem to merit this kindness, but not mental illness. Secrecy doesn't lay groundwork for others to reach out.

Saffee pushes her hamburger aside and circles a french fry in a blob of ketchup. Memories flash. Vivid is the day her father returned from the navy and he and her mother needlessly argued about April's paternity. Saffee has long suspected that Joann naively planted the suspicion with unfounded innuendo. Now Saffee sees that those hot words in San Francisco, that branded her earliest remembrance of him, had come from his hurt, and hurt had come from his love.

Until this moment, youth's capacity for ingratitude had hidden that it was out of love and duty that Nels worked so diligently to provide a comfortable material life for his disabled family. She also sees that, wise or unwise, his denial of Joann's need for psychiatric help, allowing skepticism of the treatment she might receive, had also stemmed from love. He had only been trying to protect her.

What unfulfilled expectations had her dad brought to marriage? What were his dreams? She had never thought to ask or even wonder. But here, across the table, his impassioned declaration of loyalty has shown her what she did not understand in her youth—that his love for her mother superseded any dream.

Conviction stabs her. How much greater is this love from husband than has been from daughter? Daughter, who tries to hide the very existence of an unfortunate mother.

Nels interrupts her reflections. "Actually," he says, "I've been thinkin' for some time we better move. Last summer, when Mother was doin' good, we picked out a trailer in Red Bridge."

A french fry stops midway to Saffee's mouth. "A trailer?"

"Guess they don't call 'em trailers no more—mobile home, I mean."

Nels tells her that the house is jointly owned and Joann, in her current state, refuses to sign over the papers. He'll move to Red Bridge anyway and sell the house later. It will be more convenient because the mobile home park is only eight miles from the state hospital.

The conversation has drained them both. It is clear that Saffee won't be telling her dad about Jack today. It doesn't seem to be the right time to bring up a boyfriend. A boyfriend she really cares about, who has hinted at marriage. Anyway, how could anyone marry Sapphire Kvaale, the girl with the deranged mother? If Jack knew about her, he might run the other way. Her dad has been the epitome of loyalty to a demented wife. If need be, could she expect that of Jack? Or any man?

CHAPTER THIRTY-SEVEN

FLOATING FREE

More than once Jack has said that he'd like to meet Saffee's parents. She's been to his home several times—James and Harriet Andrews are gracious and lovely. Shouldn't he know that her family members, now more like acquaintances than intimates, are not like his? Not like his at all. Saffee is longing to be known, yet frightened to be known. Finally, she resolves to quit sidestepping her family credentials and tell him all.

After their next movie date, they sit in the VW in front of the dormitory, idly chatting, watching light snow fall. It's an hour and a half until curfew.

Saffee takes a deep breath and begins. "From the day we met, you've shared your good life with me, but I've, well, I'm sure you've noticed, I'm evasive sometimes."

"I figured you'd tell me what you want me to know when the time is right," Jack says.

She suddenly sees a measure of absurdity in her reticence. Does he think she might have a sinister past, raised by the Mafia or something? Just as Gloria believed her mother . . . For a moment, the humor of the situation eases her discomfort.

She begins by telling him that her mother is mentally ill, and although she understands little about her condition, a childhood trauma, a prairie fire, seems to have been a contributing factor. Trying to be light on details, but not completely succeeding, she tells him what she knows about her mother's nightmares and how for years Joann obsessively painted a table she had hidden beneath during the fire. She recounts her mother's temper tantrums and some of the aberrant episodes that finally led to repeated hospitalizations.

Summoning such scenes from the past puts Saffee's stomach in knots. Her mouth is dry and she feels like a traitor. Even though most of her hometown probably knows about Joann's unfortunate condition, Saffee, until now, has guarded the "family secrets."

Jack listens, takes her hand when she falters, wipes a tear.

She tells him about some of the by-products of living in close quarters with mental illness—her own inadequacies and fears, both perceived and real; her sister essentially running away at the first opportunity; and her father's denial and inability to help his very troubled wife. She is quick to add her admiration for his fidelity.

After several minutes of monologue, Saffee's head tells her to stop. But once unbridled, she continues at a gallop, launching into the similarities she often notes between herself and her mother. Her mother imagines things. Saffee confesses she used to imagine herself to be every female character she met in books and movies. It's, well, crazy. (Why did she use that word?) She tells him how, like her mother, she has always preferred a life hidden away. And also, like her mother, she is critical and negative. Her self-condemning litany goes on and on.

Finally, out of breath, she drops her tense shoulders and quits. She has finally exposed her troubled mother. And herself. She threads her long wool scarf in and out around her fingers and waits for him to respond, dreading what he might say.

He says nothing. In the silence, an ugly, condemning word throbs. *Stigma.* Association with mental illness always carries stigma.

Jack continues to look out the window while silence continues to crash the hated word.

A hand-holding couple walks by headed for the front door. The door opens. The young man returns to his car and drives away.

"Let's get out and walk," Jack says. "Shouldn't waste this snowfall."

She wraps the scarf loosely around her head and begins to open the car door, but Jack has already come around. Perhaps this will be their final walk together.

"Looks like we'll have a white Christmas," he says as they walk through gentle mounds that powder the sidewalk.

"Jack"—she can't help but sound impatient—"I thought you might have something to say about what I've just told you. It was very hard for me to share those things."

"Well. Okay. First of all, what's wrong with dreaming about being someone else?" he says. "Imagination spurs achievement. And second, *you* weren't in your mother's prairie fire."

She's taken aback. He's so dismissive. Doesn't he realize that she just spilled her guts, her entire emotional being? "Of course *I* was not in the fire, but I grew up in a house contaminated with the memory of its trauma. It was not a good place, Jack."

"I heard that. So what are you going to do about it?"

"*Do?* I don't know. All I *do* is try to hide our family secrets and their influence on me and April and Dad. But I thought"—she whips around to face him—"I *thought* you'd want to know. In fact, I thought you had a *right* to know, because it seems to me"—she takes a softer tone mid-sentence—"it seems to me that we've become more than just two friends having fun times. I guess it all boils down to this: I've been hoping that our friendship will continue, even though now you know that I come from an odd family and I have . . . some hang-ups."

She's weak from being so bold. She's afraid he will say something meaningless, like he understands, and then disappear.

Guilt rolls in. "Jack," she begins again, "I never tell anyone about my family, and now I feel terrible that I told you. Especially about

Mother. She doesn't deserve my talking about her like she's some kind of freak or something. As her daughter, I'm supposed to honor her, not disparage her."

Again, Jack doesn't respond quickly. His silence convinces her that they will never again be together on a beautiful snowy night. Disappointment, anger, and guilt collide. She feels ill.

Finally, he says, "It seems to me . . ."

She waits.

"It seems to me that maybe the best way to honor your mother is not to become like her."

"But isn't it a little late? I lived at home under Mother's influence for seventeen years. I see her when I look in the mirror. Her tense expression, her narrowed eyes."

Jack looks at her face and grins. "Mmm, you mean the way you look right now?"

She's infuriated. "Jack! I'm telling you serious stuff. Of course I look tense now. And I even talk like her. I open my mouth, my mother comes out. Her emotions, even her vocabulary."

Once again the words tumble—about funny looks she receives when she innocently uses pretentious words learned at her mother's knee.

Why does she keep blabbing in this argumentative way? Why stupidly try to convince him that she is strange? At the moment, she does sound like Joann, Joann who always has to win an argument. But this is an argument Saffee should not want to win. She again gentles her voice, but continues the self-incrimination.

Finally, Jack takes charge, ropes her in. "What's so hard about changing facial expressions and choosing words more carefully if you think you need to?" he says. "Shouldn't be hard. Your fault, Saffee, is that you run yourself down. Sounds like you've rehearsed saying negative things about yourself for so long that you believe them. But if you have your mom's bad temper, I haven't seen it. Well, not much, until tonight."

"I do have a temper, just not as volatile as hers. And you know very well that I'm pretty opinionated and . . ." She's about to launch into another list of faults.

"Saffee"—he lightly touches two fingers to her lips—"stop." He takes her mittened hand.

"The question is *how* to honor your mother. Obviously she has, or at one time had, lots of good qualities that you'd be wise to retain."

"How can you say that? You haven't even met her."

"No." Jack looks full into her face. "But I've seen them in you since the day we met."

She reddens. She will not put him on the spot by asking what he has seen. She only hopes it's true. For an hour she's been babbling about her family and her burdens. But Jack, with his customary few words, has again pronounced a compliment that soothes her pain and washes her with happiness.

The streetlights showcase a sidewalk scattered over with glistening gems. They walk hand in hand in the white silence.

How long have I made huge mountains out of molehills, she wonders, *and missed gemstones at my feet?*

Jack looks high into the dizzying flakes. "Hey," he says, "it's coming down pretty good. You know what we should do tomorrow? I've got an old toboggan . . ."

Click-click-click. Kathy's oversized knitting needles gobble up lumpy red Scandia yarn. Kathy dates a hockey player who is huge even without his game pads. She's been working on a sweater for him for over two weeks.

"You make it look easy," Saffee says. "How about teaching me?"

"Sure. You want to make a sweater for Jack?"

"Well, if I can do it, it would solve the gift dilemma." She doesn't mention that Christmas giving in her family always triggered tension.

Saffee buys a simple pattern for a man's pullover, large needles like Kathy's, and skeins of bright blue Scandia yarn. Soon her needles click in concert with her friend's. Since Jack seems half the size around as Kathy's friend, it shouldn't take long. His arms are pretty long, though.

"I sure hope he likes this," Saffee says for the third time.

"If he doesn't, it's '*Hit the road, Jack*'"—Kathy breaks into a zany rendition of the popular song—"'*and don'tcha come back no more, no more . . .*'"

"Stop!" Saffee laughs. "You made me drop a stitch! Sweater or no sweater, I don't want him to go away." Then she adds, "But . . ."

"But what?"

"But I can't figure out what he sees in me. Really, I can't."

"Well, why don't you ask him?"

"Oh sure, and risk embarrassment when he can't tell me?" She remembers Jack's comment about cocoons. She's not sure if Kathy would appreciate the poetry of what Jack said, but she blurts it anyway.

"He said it seems like I was raised in a cocoon, but that was okay because, get this, from cocoons come butterflies." She sighs. "Wasn't that lovely?"

Kathy rolls her eyes and says, "Oh brother! So why didn't he just say he thinks you have potential?"

"Potential! That sounds clinical. Jack obviously knows the right thing to say to an English lit major."

During the next days, Saffee fills every available minute coaxing the blue yarn into the shape of a wearable garment. As she knits, she gives serious thought to Jack's advice that she honor her mother by not becoming her. As they had parted at the door that night, seconds before curfew, he added, "God knows the ways you should be like her and the ways to avoid. Let Him help you."

Yes, God, help me, she breathes as her needles click.

She had often tried to please her mother by copying ways she did things. Little things, like folding laundry with precision, ordering her world, as much as possible, with neatness and cleanliness. Wouldn't it be dishonoring not to be like her in these ways? But to Joann, simple tasks often became obsessions. Saffee thinks about other, more vital qualities that might put her on the right path.

She must make an effort to shed her mother-like aloofness. It's good to have friends—why scare them away? And she must temper her critical nature. What was that her dad used to say? Something about her mother never being happy unless she was complaining. She gives the yarn a tug, unwinding the ball, and adds becoming generous and courageous to the list. It will take a lifetime of amends. Yes, she will need God's help to make His promise of a "different" life a reality. She dares to hope that Jack is not only a heaven-sent reminder of God's promise but also part of its fulfillment.

Saffee and Kathy continue to knit, sometimes laughing with nearly every stitch. Knitting is giving. Giving to Jack. He has given her priceless gifts of friendship, approval, encouragement, and happiness. These have planted a desire to give in return: appreciation, admiration, affection—knit together into a tangible gift, right here in her hands.

Saffee finishes the sweater by Christmas. When Jack tries it on, the sleeves dangle almost to his knees.

"I was trying to adjust for your long arms," she moans.

"'I don't know where all this wool could have come from,' Tom said *sheepishly*."

"Jack! How can you make jokes when I've ruined your Christmas present?"

"It's not ruined, it feels nice and warm," he says, grinning, trying to roll the sleeves into thick cuffs. "Maybe I'll grow into it."

Gratefulness warms Saffee to the core.

The day finally comes (Saffee had hoped it wouldn't) that Jack's friend Kenny invites them to go up in his homemade balloon.

"I'm sure it's safe," Jack assures Saffee when she questions him. "My pesky vertigo wouldn't like riding in that flimsy lawn chair of his, but in the basket I think we'll feel contained."

"Wait a minute. If you have vertigo, why do you want to go way up in the air, hanging under a balloon?"

Jack grins. "Life's too short not to enjoy it."

Saffee is quick to jump on that one. "Yes," she says with a smile, "life is short; why make it shorter?"

"Without a few risks, it would be downright boring."

Boring? Saffee hates the word that has typified her life. And she wishes she had more courage.

Not a single sparrow can fall to the ground without your Father knowing . . . Don't be afraid; you are more valuable to God than a whole flock of sparrows . . .

How many times has she been grateful that she read the Psalms and New Testament during her freshman and sophomore years? Although at the time her motivation was to receive approval from her roommate, nevertheless, the wisdom of the Scriptures made a lasting impression.

"All right. I'll go," she says. *With the sparrows.*

The white parachutes Kenny has sewn together mushroom like a silken cloud, then rise plump and firm sixty feet above them. To control altitude, the enterprising pilot regulates propane from a tank in the center of the basket. Standing arm in arm, Saffee and Jack cautiously look down over the side. The trees and snow-covered fields are a startling distance away and rapidly getting farther.

"Kenny, where's the rope? You know, the whatcha call it, the tether." Saffee tries not to sound alarmed.

He tells her he only used a tether while perfecting the burner regulator, but not anymore. The three are cramped for space. When he's licensed, Kenny says, the FAA will probably limit him to one passenger. The information does not give comfort.

Saffee grips Jack's hand more tightly. The January air is cold; the silence is startling. She tugs the hood of her oversized, fake fur parka more tightly around her head.

"What are we, Kenny, about three thousand feet?" Jack asks. Saffee notices that Jack's glances to the ground are brief. *He's doing this, even though he's afraid.* Kenny agrees with Jack's estimate.

In the past, Saffee's fears have generally been about silly things—speaking to teachers, dogs yipping at her heels. She used to be afraid of the cavernous university library—and now she works there. Progress. But free-floating in a hot-air balloon? Her heart beats quickly—strangely, she senses that exhilaration is ruling over fear.

When Saffee asks if Kenny has had any close calls, he is dismissive. "The basket touched power lines once," he says. "They arced, but it was no big deal." Saffee and Jack squint at the ground below, looking for telephone lines.

There is a singey smell and a flicker of sparks on Saffee's shoulder.

"Oh no!" she yelps. Jack and Kenny slap her parka several times with their leather gloves. It happens quickly, and then is over.

"No worry—just sparks from the burner," Kenny says.

There are two quarter-sized black spots where the "fur" has burned away. She doesn't miss that Jack looks relieved. So is she.

"As if dangling from a balloon under a winter sky isn't thrill enough, *now* this adventure will be even more exciting to tell my grandchildren," she says, then gulps, mortified. Her face turns hot, not because she imagined falling in flames three thousand feet, but at the thought of grandchildren. She is careful not to look at Jack. She's never thought of herself with children, and certainly not grandchildren. Anyway, one story of fire in a family is enough.

Thirty minutes later they touch down on the frozen ground and help Kenny coax air out of the collapsing billows, until a friend, his spotter, arrives with a pickup truck to assist with the loading. Saffee and Jack thank their trusty pilot; Jack thumps him on the back. Saffee can tell he's as happy as she to be on the ground. Hand in hand, they begin the mile trek back to Jack's car, walking over lumpy black furrows of earth spotted with light snow.

"I'm proud of you, Saffee," he says. "That was a challenge. And you did it."

Saffee bubbles over. "Well, you did too. Today will always be a special memory."

He gives her a significant look and then says he's disappointed about one thing. He had wanted Kenny to let them go up in the air alone.

"*Alone?* Are you kidding? We wouldn't have known how to fly that thing!"

"I wanted him to show us and then just let us go. Wouldn't that have been more romantic, just the two of us? The silence. The view." Jack stops walking. "You see, well, I mean, up there I wanted to give you this"—he reaches into an inside pocket of his jacket—"instead of in the middle of some farmer's field of dirt. But I guess it is better to propose with both feet on the ground."

Her breath catches. Jack hands her a small white drawstring bag made from kidskin and closed with a satin ribbon. She takes off her gloves and opens it with shaking hands. Inside is the most beautiful diamond ring she has ever seen.

"It was my grandmother's wedding ring," he says. "I hope you don't mind."

"Mind? It's *so* beautiful."

"My mother inherited it when Grandmother died about three years ago. I bought it from Mother. For you."

He slips it on her finger. Saffee's feet are *not* on the ground. The field around them spins. Is this too good to be true?

"Why, Jack?" she demands. "Tell me, why in the world would you want to marry me?"

"Because I love you, of course."

"And I love you, more than you could ever know. And I'd love to marry you. But why in the world would you want to marry me after all I've told you?"

"Well, let's see." He pretends to be deep in thought. "I guess, like I've told you before, I like the way you laugh at my jokes."

"Be serious! You're the one who taught me how to laugh and how to have fun, but marriage is more than jokes and fun. I hope there's more reason that that." She smiles. "You better not be counting on my cooking, because I don't know how."

He momentarily feigns alarm, then says, "I've admired how you strive to learn new things. I'm not worried."

She looks down in disbelief at the sparkling diamond.

"Saffee." Jack takes her face in his hands. "You are everything I want in a wife. You're smart. You're sensible. You're honest. You're real. You're responsible. And not last, and not least, you're beautiful."

His kiss rules out rebuttal.

CHAPTER THIRTY-EIGHT

THE WEDDING

Reverend Price raises his shaggy eyebrows and looks over his glasses. "Which one of you will be taking care of the finances?" he asks.

They answer together, "I will," and exchange looks of surprise.

"*I* will," Jack repeats.

"But I'd be happy to," Saffee insists, not because she's given it any thought or is qualified (she's not), but just because she wants to be agreeable to do her part.

Jack, the math whiz and business major, looks slightly perturbed. Reverend Price, senior minister of the Lutheran church Saffee had attended with Gloria, is familiar with naive young lovers on their way to the altar. He smiles a bit wearily.

"How about children?" he continues. "How large of a family do you plan to have?"

Neither one answers. *None* goes through Saffee's mind. They haven't talked about this either. Not that Jack was unwilling to talk about it, but because she found ways to change the subject.

"Mmm." Reverend Price taps his fingertips together. "Perhaps you two have a few things to discuss before we meet again next week."

They planned to eat out after the counseling session, but when they get into the car, Jack doesn't even start the motor. They both feel impressed to immediately discuss the matters Reverend Price brought up.

Saffee apologizes about her presumption to take care of their finances and assures him that she knows he can do it better than she. Saffee's dad sent her signed checks throughout college and she's never even balanced a checkbook.

"How about children?" Jack asks.

Children? Saffee become a mother? Unimaginable. She looks down at the diamond engagement ring. A lump rises in her throat. It seems that children often do go along with marriage. What is she getting into? She decides to be noncommittal but is curious to know what Jack's view is.

"Well, um. What do you think?"

He tells her that it would be unwise to have children until he is finished with actuarial exams. "I couldn't study after work all the time and be a good father too," he says. For his age, Jack is ahead in the program. Of the ten examinations, he has five to go, which, if he passes each one as it comes, will take two and a half years. She is relieved; that sounds like a long way off.

"So, after that, just for conversation, how about one?" he suggests.

"One? An only child might be pretty lonesome, don't you think?" She wants to sound open to possibilities. "If we ever have one, maybe there should be two," she says recklessly. "I've never liked uneven numbers."

"So then, two? And what if there's a number three?"

"Oh no. Then we'd have to have four. That's way too many." She looks him squarely in the face. "Actually, Jack, don't you think *no* children would be best? Why do we need more than just you and me?"

"I guess that sounds okay with me too," Jack says, pulling her close. "We can always change our minds."

It doesn't seem necessary to tell him that her mind is already made up.

They move on to another topic—handling disagreements. Neither one imagines they will have any.

My life will be different.

Supporting themselves? Jack's job is going well; Saffee plans to continue working at the university library. She's switched from typing cards to locating items in the stacks and checking out materials at the front desk. They were both raised to be frugal; financially, they'll get by.

Getting along with in-laws? Mr. and Mrs. Andrews have embraced Saffee with cordiality. After the engagement was announced, they invited Nels to come to their home in Minneapolis and they all had an enjoyable dinner together. Jack has not met her mother. Saffee hopes to forestall that until the wedding.

At the second meeting with Reverend Price, Jack and Saffee clarify their decisions, making an effort to cover their former naiveté. The hour passes quickly. Reverend Price prays over them and they prepare to leave. He motions them to wait.

"On your wedding night," he says, "before you get into bed, get down on your knees. Thank God for each other. Thank Him for your marriage. Ask Him to bless it."

At the back of the sanctuary during the rehearsal, Reverend Price gives instructions to Jack, bridesmaids Gloria and Kathy (vagabond April could not be located), and groomsmen, Jack's brother, Danny, and Kenny. Saffee and Nels stand in the vestibule, her arm encircling his, waiting for their cue to walk the aisle.

The organist runs through pieces she has chosen to play. Saffee, not knowing the names of traditional wedding music, has given her free rein, only specifying classical. She has only attended a couple of weddings in her life and, unlike her friends in the dormitory, never tried to imagine her own.

The mother of the bride sits alone in a pew down in front, to the right of the aisle. From time to time, Saffee casts a worried look in her direction.

"Daddy, I'm so nervous I can hardly stand up."

"Why? Jack is a good man." He pats her hand. He has misunderstood her, but the unusual, small gesture makes her feel close to him.

"Not nervous about being married, but about getting married. Mostly I'm worried Mother will do something to ruin the ceremony."

"Don't worry. She's doin' fine. I'm makin' sure she's takin' her medicine." He sounds matter-of-fact, then becomes more serious, his voice husky. "Anyway, a weddin' ceremony's short. It's the marriage that's . . ." He doesn't finish. The reference to his own experience is obvious. Was it an attempt to caution her? Counsel her? If so, it would have been a first.

Since the last hospitalization, Joann has rallied, enabling her to be present at this first family wedding. The hiatus has allowed her and Nels to move into a double-wide mobile home in Red Bridge, leaving wagging tongues behind. The Miller's Ford house sold two weeks ago.

When they arrived at the church a half hour earlier, Saffee immediately introduced Jack to her mother. Joann's pale countenance bore the marks of illness. She extended her hand, laughed nervously, turning her head to the side. Saffee sensed that she might be pleased about the marriage but was too self-conscious to say anything appropriate to her almost-son-in-law. Perhaps it had been unfair that Saffee had not arranged for them to meet earlier.

She looks down the long center aisle, flanked by empty pews. Tomorrow evening most of the guests will be Andrews family friends and relatives, people Saffee doesn't know. The ushers, Jack's cousins, have been instructed to seat guests on either side of the aisle.

Following instructions, the attendants move to the front of the church. Saffee continues to wait at the back beside the man she has always called "Daddy." Years ago, didn't Joann often refer to her as

"Daddy's little girl"? He has been a long-distance father, preoccu-pied with necessary matters, but as her daddy, he has been the most important man in her life. Tomorrow, a different man will claim that place. In spite of her eagerness, her hands are clammy. She wipes them on her linen skirt.

"We've already took everythin' we're gonna need outta the house," Nels tells her. "We give possession in about ten days. You and Jack should drive over to Miller's Ford, see if there's anythin' there you want. 'Fraid we din't leave much. What you don't take, I'll try to sell."

"Thanks, Daddy. We've taken a week off work, you know. Going to spend three or four days at a place near Wisconsin Dells," she says. "We'll try to drive over when we get back." Saffee has no intention of dragging any reminders of her childhood into her new life.

"Did you take the Norway table with you?" She could have asked about any number of items, why does she wonder about this one?

"No," he says. "Way too big. The new place is pretty small."

Saffee survives the wedding. Barely. The mother of the bride shows little interest in the groom and has a vehement temper tantrum about her corsage in the bridal dressing room moments before the ceremony. Saffee had no idea that certain flowers have a snoot factor and those she had selected for Joann were "low class." The altercation makes Saffee's nose run and tears stream as she walks down the aisle on her father's arm, devastated. By the time she joins Jack at the altar she is still sniffling, but wears a smile that says she has never been happier.

At the reception in the church parlor she stands dazed and as close to her new husband as possible. She does her best to greet each guest, cut the cake, and pose for pictures. Terribly uncomfortable being the center of attention, and on impulse after forty minutes, she whispers to Jack, "Let's go."

"You mean leave? Already?"

"Yes, really."

Jack is all for it. They duck out a side entrance.

In the bridal suite at the Holiday Inn, Saffee reaches to turn back the sheets. Jack takes her hand.

"We told Reverend Price that we'd pray," he says. Saffee has forgotten. She is amazed and impressed that Jack has not. They kneel, as self-conscious as they will ever be.

"Lord Jesus, thank You for Saffee, my wonderful, beautiful wife. May we always love each other and please You in our marriage."

Her heart swells. All she can say is, "Thank You, God."

CHAPTER THIRTY-NINE

LEGACY

Jack guides the borrowed pickup through countryside dotted with tidy farms. God has gone before them, embroidering His early-morning beauty all around. Diaphanous ribbons of fog silently disperse to reveal a rosy dawn. Their spirits are high and banter comes easily. Jack's laughter is Saffee's favorite sound.

Although she has dreaded this trip back to Miller's Ford, here she is, sitting next to her husband of one week, wishing the drive would never end. She'd watched the clock most of the night. At 5:00 a.m. she woke him. "Let's go," she said. "If we get an early start, we can get back and still enjoy the afternoon. It's a three-hour trip each way."

Thirty minutes later they left the modest duplex that became their home after a brief honeymoon at the Dells. At first, Saffee was doubtful about renting a duplex. Would she like sharing a house with neighbors? Because the two single garages make a separation between the units, and the rent is reasonable for a two-bedroom place, she agreed.

She had looked forward to shopping with Jack for furniture, but, as keeper of the budget, he sees no possibility of that for some time. They will get by with basics from his parents' attic until there is some reserve in the bank, he says. There they found a double bed frame, a love seat in need of a slipcover, two mismatched Danish modern chairs, and a small Formica table with tubular aluminum legs. Their only major purchase was a mattress for the bed. Various household items from Kmart filled in where the attic and wedding gifts left off.

"I don't think my parents left much in the house," she says as they draw near the town she has avoided for four years. "We can probably check it out pretty quickly." Maybe there are some dishes, she says. They could use cereal bowls and maybe a chair for the bedroom. She wants to sound as if she's open to taking away something. After all, Jack borrowed the truck.

When the Miller's Ford water tower appears on the horizon, Jack is more eager than Saffee. "I want to see where my wife grew up," he says.

As they cross the bridge over Blue River, she tells him it is where she used to roller-skate in summer and ice-skate below in winter. She directs him to turn right, then left onto Second Street, and points out a large white house on the corner.

"That's where we lived until I was in ninth grade." Any number of memories could have come to Saffee as they drive by the house, but the one that comes is of her mother vigorously sanding the Norway table. Saffee's been trying to figure out how they can avoid seeing it when they get to the "new" house.

The pickup ascends Second Street hill—she marvels that it no longer seems particularly steep. She guides him through the uptown business district, with its familiar storefronts she hurried by for years on her way to school, yet felt like a stranger if ever she entered. She points out the library and, around the corner, the aging Methodist church with its splendid pipe organ. The church where her family no longer holds membership. This guided tour has been a delaying tactic.

They drive along Cottonwood Point Road and turn into the small subdivision with its valley view that so captivated Joann years ago. Saffee eyes the Peterson house. It appears to have a new coat of blue paint. Carefree daffodils bloom along the foundation.

On the adjacent lot, leaves on the ancient apple trees are sparse. Beyond, the redbrick house and yard her parents had once taken pride in looks unkempt. They pull into the driveway. Saffee can't name her emotion, but it is not a sense of homeness. The garage door needs paint. Nels had been so meticulous. She is glad the house has sold.

"Looks like the new owners will have some work to do," she says as they walk toward the back entry door. She takes a deep breath and turns the key. Inside, the air is stale and chilly. Saffee pulls back the faded, sun-damaged kitchen curtains to let in light. She remembers Joann sewing them, red-checkered with rickrack trim.

They open cupboards and find most of them empty, other than a dozen or more jelly jars.

She explains that they were used for "everyday" drinking and that, of course, her mother also had nice goblets for guests. Meaning the jelly jars were used every day.

Jack wanders into the living room and pulls cords to open the heavy, rose-colored draperies along the wall of windows. In several places the aging *peau de soie* fabric hangs fragmented by vertical splits.

"Wow," he says. "What a beautiful view down in the valley." Saffee stands close to him. It is beautiful. But she doesn't miss it. The dirty windows are stuck with tape residue, but Jack doesn't seem to notice.

Poor Daddy.

She remembers to add, *Poor Mother.*

The double doors to the dining room behind them are closed. Let them be. She has told him about the table, that should be enough. He doesn't have to know that being in the house with this element of her mother's aberrations is making her heart race.

The only item in the living room is the piano. "It's always been considered April's," she tells Jack.

"You girls shoulda taken accordeen lessons instead of piano," Nels had said to Saffee when he gave her the house key. "An accordeen, now, you can take that around with you easy. What am I s'posed to do with April's piano? Can't send it to her." There has been no word from April for several months.

Saffee pulls Jack toward the hallway. "This was Daddy's den," she says, opening more drapes. She doesn't mention that for years it was here her father slept. It was not to spite her mother, Saffee has come to realize; it was one of the sacrifices he had made for her.

The master bedroom is empty except for a bedside table. "Maybe this would be handy in our bedroom?" Jack asks.

"No," she says quickly, "they'll probably come back for it. It matches their bedroom set."

They cross the hall to the bedroom she had shared with April. She surveys the white twin beds and the bureau that once had been a dining room piece, until Joann saw its bedroom possibilities.

"I guess we don't need more old furniture," he says, "but maybe we could find a place for the matching lamps." To be reasonable, she agrees.

Saffee slides open the closet door and finds two cardboard cartons. One is labeled "Saffee," the other "April." Uncovering the first, she sees school mementos. She shows Jack her senior picture in her high school yearbook.

"Why the solemn face?"

She mugs a frown. "I'm a sober person, you know that."

Saffee suggests they put both boxes into the pickup; she'll sort through hers at home and save April's. *Home!* She already calls their duplex *home*. The word has taken on a new, positive meaning.

Minutes later, as they venture to the basement, Jack stops. "Is this where God spoke to you?" On their honeymoon trip she told him about God's promise, *Your life will be different.*

"No," she says, wrapping her arm around his, "that was when I was younger, in the house on Second Street." She grins. "And now I know He had you in my mind, way back then." He grins back.

In the first room below, a row of high, glass-block windows gives filtered light. "We called this room the family room," Saffee says. "But I can't remember one time when all the family was together here."

"Was it the TV room?" Jack asks.

Mom, who's Elvis Presley? Everyone at school is talking about him. I think he's on TV.

"Don't worry about it. With a name like that, he'll never amount to anything. And, no, we don't need a TV."

"No," she says.

In the unfinished half of the basement, the Maytag wringer washer still stands near the laundry tubs. One of the lines sags, supporting the weight of a full bag of clothespins.

In Nels's workshop, Jack picks up pieces of lumber. "Think he'd mind?" he asks. "Never know when a man needs some wood."

She is amused and tells him to take all he wants. *You never know what will interest a man.* Jack sets aside a few two-by-fours and miscellaneous pieces of plywood and looks pleased. He sees a wooden box on a shelf, lifts it down, and slides off the lid. "This would be just the thing for small tools," he says. "Looks like some old documents inside."

"Take it," she says. "Daddy said anything we want is ours."

In a far corner he sees a child's high chair and asks if they should put it in the truck.

"You've got to be kidding. What for?"

"Suit yourself," he says. She can see that he was teasing her.

They carry up the wood and the box and put them in the pickup. Maybe they can leave now, without either of them seeing the Norway table. If she can avoid it today, chances are she will never have to see it again.

"We should shut all the curtains like we found them," Saffee says. "Will you check the rooms down the hall, Jack? I'll do the living room." It is a mistake.

In her haste, the drapery cords tangle. Jack finishes in the bedrooms and den and comes to help her. He gestures toward the double doors. "The dining room?"

"Oh. Yeah," she says. "But it's probably empty. Jack, um, I think we could use some extra spoons. Should we look through the kitchen drawers again?" She reaches for his hand as if to lead him there but is too late. He crosses the room and opens the dining room doors.

"Saffee. Look at this table. I've never seen anything like it."

She continues to walk away. "Right. Come on, Jack, let's get going."

"No. Come here, Saffee."

"Jack, I . . ." Reluctantly she joins him. The Norway table still wears the multicolored splatter of four years ago, when she had compared it to a Jackson Pollock. Today it seems closer to some putrid disease.

"Oh, you told me," he says. "This must be the table your mother—"

"Yes." She tries to sound dismissive. "Let's get going."

Jack, not listening, is down on one knee. "Saffee, I can't believe they left this unusual table. Look at the carving on the side."

His interest irritates her. Does he think she has never seen it before? She tries to sound offhanded. "Well, it's big. They moved into a trailer, you know." She suggests they get back on the road in time to do something special with the afternoon.

"If your parents don't want it, our dining room is completely empty. We could take this leaf out—"

"No!" She stamps her foot. "I don't want this table."

He looks up, startled by her change in tone. "Why not?"

"It's ugly, Jack. Really ugly."

"Well, I don't think so." He crawls under. "There's no paint on the underside," he calls, as if she is far away. "It's beautiful wood! Light-colored. Ash, or maybe birch. Hey! Here are some words burned into the back of this side piece, but they're not English. Norwegian maybe?" He begins to read, laughing as he guesses the pronunciation. *"'Din hustru er som et frukbart vintre der inne i ditt hus . . .'"*

Saffee stands with knees locked and arms crossed over her chest. Why is she so tense? It's just a table, an inanimate object with history . . . lots of history.

Jack continues to muddle through the inscription. "'. . . *dine barn som oljekvister rundt om ditt bord. Salmenes 128:3.'"*

Why is he reading those funny words? When he finally finishes, she thrusts her hands into her pockets and takes a deep breath. "Jack," she says deliberately, trying to contain rising impatience, "I have bad memories associated with this old table. I never realized the extent of how much it affected me until now. Listen to me. *I don't want it.*"

He backs out and stands up, giving her a questioning look.

She struggles to find the right words, tries to explain how it had been frightening to see her mother obsessed with painting. That it seemed as if someone or something compelled her. She laments that her family was baffled by Joann's irrational mind. Was she trying to cover over her trauma? Some secret sins? Pain that was never shared?

"I never understood her, Jack. All I know is that I hated to come home from school and smell paint."

"So, if this table caused her so much grief, why didn't she just get rid of it?"

"Good question. And I don't know the answer. It seemed to have some kind of power over her. At times it seemed something to fear. At other times she treated it as if it were a gift from God that had sheltered her during that fire."

She takes his arm as she speaks, gently trying to pull him out of the room, but he resists. "At any rate," she continues, "painting was probably her attempt to expunge bad memories, real or imagined, and I have bad memories too—of being surrounded by her misery. Frankly, it was sometimes scary in this house."

She leans against a wall, scans the room, then looks at him imploringly. "Now can you see why I don't want it around? Let's

leave it here for my dad to take care of. Please. It's not my problem."
The lump in her throat can no longer be put down. The dam bursts.
Hating herself, she burrows her head in that comfortable place just
below his right shoulder and cries. He holds her close and rubs her
back.

"Saffee. Look at me." He tilts her chin. "All this emotion says
that it *is* your problem. I think the best thing to do is to take the table
home with us . . . and conquer it."

She pulls away. "Jack, surely, now you understand why we've got
to leave it. I don't want to ever see it again!"

Jack is not deterred. "What I mean is, what if you would strip
off all the paint, Saffee? Every layer. Strip it away, scrape it off, right
down to the raw wood." He runs a hand over the speckled top. "It
would be a really big job, of course, but as you did it, I bet you'd get
a fresh perspective. You'd be an overcomer. It would be a sort of, well,
cleansing."

Now she is furious. "There you go with your psychology." She
usually appreciates his analytical comments, but this is going too far.
"I told you, I just want to walk—"

As he has done before, Jack gently touches her lips with two fingers. "But that's not victory, Saffee. Don't you see? That's letting a
wooden table haunt you like it haunted your mother. Right now it *is*
ugly, covered over by your mother's agony. But underneath, judging
by what I saw, there lies a piece of beautiful, redeemable work. By
restoring it, I have an idea there will be benefits for you too."

He talks as if she has agreed to do this harebrained thing. Slave
over this table? That is the last thing she wants to do. However, a
degree of release has accompanied her outburst, and because of it,
and because of her trusting love for Jack, she melts. She agrees to take
the troublesome table home. Perhaps they can store it in the garage.

Together, they force apart the tabletop to release the extra leaf. It
is obvious that they will be unable to load the table into the pickup
themselves. To Saffee's chagrin, Jack says he will go to the house next

door, that blue house, he says, to enlist help. Saffee is too disconcerted to object.

While he is gone she leans against a wall, staring at the table in disbelief. How could she have agreed to take it home to their honeymoon cottage? What peculiar hold does it have over people? Over her to make her so emotional, and now, over Jack, that he would be so drawn to it he would even knock on a stranger's door in order to move it?

As they drive back to Minneapolis, Saffee is silent in disbelief. Here they are, rolling down the highway with the paint-splattered Norway table, of all things, in the truck bed. She had not expected to be dogged in marriage by anything so painfully tangible from the past.

Ten miles from Miller's Ford, Saffee blurts, "Jack, can't we turn around and put it back in the house?"

Jack says he loves her so much that he doesn't want her to carry around "memory baggage" for the rest of her life. "Don't you think everyone has something they want to forget?" he asks. "No one can completely unplug unpleasantness of the past, but sometimes actions help deal with it."

Her temper flares. "And how would you know?" Their first week of marriage not over and she sounds ugly. "You, with the perfect childhood and natural abilities and talents galore, you're lecturing me about memories!" She glares out the window, sickened that she yelled, yet not willing to retract her words.

Jack says something about as a young boy not being good in sports, having a bodybuilding regimen, compensating his inadequacies with good academic habits. She hardly listens. How can he compare her upbringing to some mere struggle with male ego—even if male ego is something she knows little about?

"I don't know about your, well, challenges," she says, "but I can't see how they compare to growing up in a home as crazy as mine and wanting to forget about it, and certainly not wanting symbols around like that old table."

"I am sympathetic, Saffee, really I am, and of course I can't completely identify. But I'll just say again that running away from memories doesn't leave them behind."

Inwardly she huffs.

CHAPTER FORTY

WEEDS

The next day Jack tinkers with the lawn mower Nels had left behind in the Miller's Ford garage. Mrs. Corbet, the duplex owner, had made it clear that both tenants were to care for half of the yard. Saffee leans against the Volkswagen parked in the driveway and watches him fill the mower with gas. She looks askance at the Norway table's disassembled parts taking up most of the floor space of the single-car garage. There is no other place to put them. She wonders how long Jack will be happy to leave the car outdoors. Maybe by the time winter comes he will agree to throw the table away.

The spring grass is hardly long enough to cut, but Jack is eager to try. "Mowing might become a chore someday," he says, "so right now I think I'll enjoy it." He pulls the starter cord and roars off. She lowers the garage door.

Enjoying the warm sun, Saffee surveys their new neighborhood. She notices that the yard fronting the other side of the duplex is perfectly groomed. The tenants have yet to be seen. Across the street is a dense wooded area that runs the length of three blocks. She admires a stand of white-barked birch trees exactly opposite the duplex. They bend and mingle like whispering old women, then shake with laughter in the breeze. Jack thinks the Norway table might be birch. It is hard to believe that the table she has grown to despise in its ugliness was once a lovely tree, or, more likely, trees free to yield their branches to the wind, free to shake their leaves.

She catches a glimpse of Jack as he heads around the corner of the house. Already, streaks of sweat on his shirt validate his effort. In the Kvaale household, she was a spectator to domestic life, rarely doing, certainly never sweating. Not knowing how to share responsibility, she has little confidence she can contribute acceptably to any task, but it seems important that she try.

Making a quick tour of the yard, she notices an unsightly brown brush along the entire east side of the house. It wouldn't require any expertise to rid the area of last year's weeds. With bare hands—she has no work gloves—she begins to remove tangles of debris. The roots are fairly deep and the stems dry and rough, but hard work feels good. Maybe they can plant some petunias here. Or geraniums? The thought energizes her. She gives Jack a wave as he roars past; he gives her a thumbs-up.

After about thirty minutes of work, a two-foot strip of brown earth is freed along the house between the lawn and the cement block foundation. Her burning hands and damp shirt give satisfaction, and she knows that Jack will approve her minor accomplishment. She jauntily heads toward the garage for a rake, stopping when she hears voices and laughter. Who could Jack be talking to? She has a familiar but unwelcome mental flash of her mother's slightly bent listening posture. Determinedly, Saffee rounds the corner. Jack is on the shared driveway shaking hands with a smiling young couple and a little girl.

"Honey," he calls, "come meet the neighbors!"

With an arm Saffee wipes perspiration from her forehead. She is relieved the garage door is still down, concealing a peculiar pile of spotted wood.

"Saffee, this is Gail and Bill." Gail holds the hand of dark-haired Jenny Rose, who, her proud mother says, is four years old. Saffee notes immediately how jovial they are.

"I'm awmost five!" Jenny Rose declares. "An' I'm gonna have a brudder! Oh, or maybe a sister!" Gail's round middle confirms the fact.

"Not due until the end of August," Gail pretends to lament, "and it's only May."

Saffee slaps her grimy hands on her jeans and apologizes for not shaking hands. She tells them she's just pulled up all the weeds on the side of the house and is about to rake.

Gail's dark eyebrows go up. "Weeds?" she says.

"Yeah. Lots. Want to see?" Saffee is pleased she can share her first visible contribution to their household.

The two young neighbors go around to the side of the house, Jenny Rose in tow.

"Oh dear," Gail says, then hesitates, eyebrows up again. "Saffee, I hate to tell you, but those weren't weeds, they were chrysanthemums. They did need cutting back, but not pulling up. I think Mrs. Corbett, the owner, was sort of proud of them."

Chrysanthemums? Any plant pulled in error would be bad, but *chrysanthemums?*

. . . the butcher knife . . . the blue house . . . the police . . .

Later that night Saffee lies awake. Her intentions to do a bit of honest labor had been innocent. She jerks over onto her side and pulls the pillow tightly around her head. *Think about things that are good. Think about ways I am not like her. Think . . . Think . . .*

CHAPTER FORTY-ONE

SOFTBALL RELIGION

What do you want on your waffles?' Tom whispered *syrup-titiously*."

"Oh, Jack, now *that's* a funny one," Saffee says, throwing her arms around him.

Looking pleased, he says, "I'll scramble the eggs."

Having been married for a week, they celebrate with a late Sunday morning brunch. The waffles drip with melted butter and maple syrup. Happy, they sit in the kitchen at the little red Formica table, knees bumping. With second cups of coffee, they move to the love seat that faces a small alcove meant to serve as dining room.

"When are you going to start taking paint off that old table in the garage?" he asks.

"Jack," Saffee sighs, "we're having a lovely morning, let's not break the mood." She pulls her legs up under her. Honeymoon contentment, other than their trip to Miller's Ford, has made her feel as if they are the only people in a world that has stopped. Nothing else, especially issues of the past, could possibly be important.

Not reading her, he says that if their neighbor, Bill, is around this afternoon, he will ask him to help assemble the parts. "It will be easier to work on if it's upright," he says.

"I'd guess the scraping is going to take some time." He catches her expression. "Just hoping there'll be room in the garage for the car by winter, that's all."

"I don't know, Jack. Maybe later, when summer comes."

"Are you saying you want to *table* the project?"

She grins.

He doesn't wheedle, cajole, or manipulate. In return, she does not argue.

On Monday morning, Saffee walks two blocks to a neighborhood shopping center where she has noticed a hardware store and buys the supplies she'll need for stripping the table. For when she gets around to it.

Back home, she pulls up the garage door and dumps her purchases onto the offending piece. She stands for several moments, arms crossed, staring at it, then brings down the door and goes into the house.

She's never been fond of talking on the telephone.

She doesn't want to call. She must call.

"Hello, Mrs. Corbett? Hi, this is Saffee Andrews . . . Saffee—Mrs. Jack Andrews . . . We rented your duplex on . . . Yes, that's right, it is Sapphire, but I don't use . . . Yes, the duplex . . . Oh no, uh, there's nothing wrong . . . No, it didn't . . . Anyway, I'm sure my husband could fix it if it . . . The plunger? Oh yes, I saw it right behind . . . No, no, I'm not calling about the lease either, we *love* living here . . . Oh, I'm so sorry . . . Shouldn't call you before 10:00 a.m., then. I'll remember that . . . Mrs. Cor . . . Mrs. Corbett, the reason I'm call-ing . . . The sink? *No!* It's fine too. I'm calling about the yard. There's something you should . . . Yes, Jack has already cut the grass, a couple times . . . Oh yes, he does the edging too. But, Mrs. Corbett, I'm calling to tell you about the chrysanthemums . . . Oh, they were? Best ever last year . . . Burgundy. Bronze and gold too. Yes, I bet they were lovely. Mrs. Corbett, did you have any white ones? . . . You don't like white? Doesn't show up against the white siding . . . You go for drama. I see. Well, Mrs. Corbett, my husband and I spent half of Saturday replacing . . . Yes, I said replacing . . . Why? Well, because I pulled them up . . . Yes, roots and all; I thought they were weeds . . . Perennials? No, I don't know the difference . . . Aha! Come back every year. I'm so sorry, Mrs. Corbett. I really . . . should have just cut them back? Yes, I see. What colors? Well now, I'm afraid they're all white, Mrs. Corbett. That's the only color the nursery had . . . No. No burnished bronze . . . Yes, they were sold out . . . No, Mrs. Corbett, really, I'm not calling about the lease . . ."

Saffee watches the liquid bubble. Is this what is supposed to happen? She reads the directions again. "Brush on, wait ten minutes, scrape off." Sounds easy. She anchors her ponytail more securely to the top of her head and waits. Shouldn't the remover come with a clip for her nose? Time to scrape. It's immediately apparent that the project will take much more effort than she expected. She repeats the process and sighs. She hates the table. She will remove the paint only because Jack wants her to. Only because underneath it all, *he* sees beauty.

Robert Scott, also an aspiring actuary who works in Jack's office, invites Jack to play on his church softball team. "No practices, just games on Saturday afternoons," he promises.

Jack digs through still-unpacked boxes to retrieve his ball and glove, and that evening, taking more study breaks than usual, he sits on the love seat, slapping the ball into the pocket. *Thwap, thwap, thwap.* Saffee finds the repetitive noise an irritating intrusion into their almost blissful state of marriage. But on Saturday, she has to admit it is fun to watch her husband run around the bases like a happy kid.

After the second game, Robert walks with Jack and Saffee to the parking lot. He says that someone has made some new rules at his church. Now, everyone who plays on the team has to attend church, at least Sunday school.

"Ah," says Jack. "What church do you go to?"

"Baptist."

"Okay," Jack says.

When they are alone in the car, Saffee exclaims, "Baptist? I didn't know there are Baptist churches in Minnesota. Aren't they like holy rollers?" She says she doesn't think she'll be going with him . . .

"I'm not going!" Joann's green-handled hairbrush flies through the air . . .

On Sunday, when Jack comes home, he tells Saffee that the adult Sunday school class was interesting. He stayed for the service too because it seemed like that was what was expected of him. He assures her he saw no unusual behavior.

The following week, when he returns, he says he thinks she would like the church and that the preacher gives a good message from the Bible.

She disagrees but senses it would not be wise to contradict Jack without knowing what she's talking about. She'll go. Once. Why couldn't it be a Lutheran ball team?

Brother Fred *(Whose brother? And don't Baptists believe in last names for their clergy?)* wears a suit rather than a robe; a tie, not a clerical collar. The sermon *is* thought-provoking—something about not burying a kind of money, called talents, in the ground. However, some of the congregants are huggers, and visitors are asked to *stand and announce their names*. Why hadn't Jack warned her?

Sunday afternoon Saffee answers the doorbell and is taken aback to find Brother Fred on the front step. He wears a short-sleeved shirt just like plain folks. Saffee invites him, their first guest, to come into the living room and calls Jack to join them. She doesn't think to offer any refreshment.

Although the preacher is friendly and nonthreatening, Saffee plunges into nervous chatter. She tells him that she was "saved"—the Baptists seem to like that term—in fourth grade, read *Egermeier's* as a child, and in college began a habit of Bible reading. She neglects to mention that the habit had not taken a full hold and has been sorely neglected for some time.

Sounding hopeful, Brother Fred tells her that the church needs help with the fifth-grade Sunday school class. Would Saffee like to "volunteer"? The morning at church *had* been fairly pleasant—nice people, good sermon, a choir that sang with gusto. But what kind of a church invites perfect strangers to teach their children? Her opinion plummets.

"Me? Well, I'm not sure . . ." She backpedals. "I don't really know the Bible very well at all," she says. "I wouldn't be able to teach it. You wouldn't ask if you knew how unqualified I am."

"Wonderful," Brother Fred says. "This is your opportunity to learn. We have teaching guides for every lesson, and as you prepare by studying the Scripture, just think how much you'll learn."

Saffee is speechless. She has never taught anything to anyone in her life. She is shy. She knows little about the ways of children, having had practically nothing to do with them when she was one herself. Why is this "brother," whom she has just met, smiling at her with an expression that says he knows she will do it?

He tells her that she would not be the lead teacher, rather an assistant to Robert Scott's wife, Mary. Nice woman. Saffee wouldn't have to do much teaching the first few weeks until she is comfortable.

She remembers her mother's lament that the only time anyone from church called her was when they wanted her to do something. In her case, to bake a cake.

On the other hand, hasn't God said . . .

Saffee hears herself agree to help, at least to try. How much more intimidating will this new life become?

CHAPTER FORTY-TWO

GIRL TALK

The open garage door, necessary for ventilation, must look inviting, but Saffee wishes Gail, her bubbly, chatty neighbor, hadn't popped into the garage unexpectedly. As usual, Saffee prefers to be alone . . .

"Don't be bringing people into our house. It's not a good idea . . ."

. . . but she tries to be gracious.

Her college dorm room had seen a parade of girls—drawn into her roommate's circle of affection, certainly not by Saffee's aloof manner. She wishes she were warm and welcoming like Gloria, whose influence seems to have only gone so deep, her mother's much deeper. Can't Gail see that Saffee is preoccupied with an arduous project? She's worked four mornings to remove layers of paint from a very small square of surface and her attitude rivals the chemicals for unpleasant.

Saffee suggests that Gail could sit in a lawn chair a couple of feet outside the small garage to distance her pregnant self from noxious fumes. Then she turns down the volume of a favorite string quartet playing on the radio.

Gail launches into a cheery monologue about a recent family

wedding. The smitten mother gushes about Jenny Rose scattering rose petals down the aisle, describes in detail what the attendants wore, how she always gets emotional at weddings, and on and on. The neighbor pauses for breath, smoothes her maternity shirt over her prominent belly, and encircles her unborn child with her short arms.

Saffee wishes she knew how to say that she too feels a little emotional at the moment and would like to be alone. But Gail would want to know what is so emotional about stripping paint and she'd never understand. Saffee isn't sure she understands either.

She tugs another roll to the sleeves of Jack's old white shirt, too worn at the collar for the office, and wonders what she should say if Gail inquires how the table came to have such inordinate layers of paint. With a quiet sigh, she counsels herself to be polite and scrapes with determination at a patch of glutinous red as Gail recounts more wedding details. They thread Saffee back to her own wedding . . .

"The flowers you got me . . . Look! . . . Brown, ugly carnations! Dead! . . . I saw the gorgeous orchids you got for Jack's mother! Shows what you think of me! . . ."

"Saffee?"

Saffee looks up at Gail and realizes she's asked a question. "I'm sorry, Gail. What's that?"

"Your wedding cake, when you got married, what was it like? Who made it?"

Embarrassed, and trying not to sound it, Saffee explains to Gail that the church secretary put her in contact with the special events committee who took care of all the details. She must have sounded like an idiot. She doesn't suppose that other brides pass on decisions to strangers. At the time, however, she had been grateful.

"Oh! Well, that's one way to get married, I guess." Gail sounds surprised, but not critical. "Bet you had classical music," she says, nodding toward the radio that plays a dramatic piece suddenly unsuitable for garage background music. Saffee turns it a notch lower.

She tells Gail that there had been a trumpet and organ processional.

"Trumpet? Cool!" says Gail. "I'll have to remember that for Jenny Rose's wedding."

Saffee, with a change of heart, flashes a smile at her neighbor. Gail's good-humored banter is entertaining, taking attention off her stiff hands. She scrapes with renewed energy.

It becomes Saffee's routine to coax paint off the Norway table for about two hours each morning before she catches the bus for work at noon. Returning to the duplex about 8:00 p.m., she usually finds Jack studying dull-looking graphs and formulas as he prepares for exams late into the night. She decides that it is good they both have challenging projects.

Gail's husband, Bill, occasionally persuades Jack to leave his books long enough to take in an evening baseball game. They are becoming good friends. Saffee has proved to be what every talkative female needs—a good listener—and somehow Gail seems to know when Saffee is in the garage. With Jenny Rose in a preschool two mornings a week, and pregnancy sapping her energy, she seems to relish spontaneous forays next door. Saffee's mother's word for Gail would be *loquacious*, and Joann's voice whispers the label every time Gail appears.

One day, as Saffee vigorously rubs a rough surface with sandpaper, Gail interrupts her own monologue to ask why Saffee doesn't rent an electric sander.

"Guess that would make the job easier," Saffee says, considering. "But for some reason, I just need, well, I mean, I have to put my own sweat into this project."

Another day Gail asks sweepingly about Saffee's childhood. Saffee remembers childhood in moments, disquieting, specific moments she does not want to share. Since the inquiry was not about moments, she replies in kind.

"Fine," she says with a warm smile in hopes to disarm Gail. "It was fine." She wonders how much trust is needed in a girlfriend relationship before she can speak freely about moments. It might be soon.

"You know, Gail, how I always have the radio tuned to a classical station when you come by, and then after a while I turn it off?"

"Yeah, I guess you do," Gail says. "How come?"

"Because having you here is never a Mozart moment—you always put me in a rock 'n' roll mood."

Gail sputters apologetically and Saffee clarifies, "Don't worry, Gail, rock 'n' roll is always more fun. It's definitely a compliment."

The demonstration draws to a close. Party guests complete their orders for Tupperware essentials that perky saleswoman Lucy has convinced them no kitchen is functional without. More than bowls and such, Lucy's effervescence and bouffant hairdo, purple miniskirt befitting a slimmer woman, and white go-go boots have held the roomful of young women in her spell for the last hour.

Gail had invited Saffee to the event, which is hosted by Gail's cousin. Seated beside her neighbor-become-friend, Saffee checks "Large Mixing Bowl Set," turns in her order form, and waits for the others to finish. She watches Gail's attractive cousin carefully arranging multicolored napkins into a fan design on the refreshment table. The young woman wears a satisfied expression as she surveys a stunning floral centerpiece and tiered serving plates piled with dainty confections.

"All right, ladies, are we ready?" Lucy inquires, collecting the last of the order forms. "Before refreshments, it's that time we've all been waiting for—the drawing for the door prize!" The guests, still atwitter under Lucy's spell, admire an arrangement of gifts from which a lucky one will choose her prize. Saffee eyes a set of red gelatin molds. They would be perfect to shape Christmas tree salads, a Kvaale tradition she thinks she can comfortably carry forth.

But there is a "catch" to the drawing. The winner not only goes home with a gift but also promises to host a Tupperware party within the next three months. For Saffee, this is out of the question. Host a party? She has almost no one to invite, she doesn't have any experience baking, and she can't accommodate a group in her small living room. Those guests who for some reason are unable to host a party are asked not to draw. Saffee counts the women present and notes she has a one in thirteen chance of being the winner. The odds are good. Why not at least play along for the fun of it? And who knows, maybe if she wins, Lucy might let her keep . . . without . . .

The slips of paper are randomly selected. Saffee's is marked "Winner!" There are "ohs," "ahs," and expressions of disappointment.

"Ladies"—Lucy squints at the winner's name tag—"Sapphire here is the next Tupperware hostess!" There is a polite clap. "And here are your lovely Jell-O molds, dear, just sign the date of your party on this clipboard."

"Oh. Well . . ." Saffee stretches upward in her chair toward Lucy's ear to address her as confidentially as possible. "I . . . but I really don't want to have a party. You see, I . . . I just wanted to play the game. I took a chance and . . ." How she yearns to run out the door.

Lucy stiffens and the room goes silent. Her expression changes from aren't-we-having-fun to a drama of disbelief. "One of the most significant responsibilities in life, Sapphire," Lucy intones, "is to be a woman of truth. A woman's word is her bond." She punctuates each word as if she holds a judge's gavel. "Her yes must be yes, and her no, no. A civil Christian society depends upon it."

Saffee is mortified. No one yells, "Preach it!" but from the wide eyes and ever-so-slightly tilted noses, there is no mistaking what the women are thinking.

Her face burns. She is shocked, but stupidly so, to be taken as a liar. Truth telling is part of her life. (She had sorely repented for lying to her mother, telling her she was "fine.") But who would believe that now? Hasn't it just been proven otherwise? To be a part of the fun, and foolishly hoping to get something for nothing, she had played her chance without considering the consequences. Harmless intentions or not, she'd been wrong and is exposed.

Coming to her rescue, dear Gail whispers, "No problem, Saffee. I can have it at my house, we'll do it together. I'm sure my bridge club will come."

Saffee doesn't dare look at Lucy, who quickly snatches the set of Jell-O molds from Saffee's hands and gives it to Gail. Before leaving, Saffee makes heartfelt apologies to Lucy.

A few weeks later the two neighbors host ten women in Gail's living room, which is identical in size to Saffee's, and serves well as a venue for Lucy's animated sales pitch.

With the help of Betty Crocker, Saffee contributes two layer cakes. One, coconut lemon; the other, chocolate marble. Two guests ask for her recipes.

CHAPTER FORTY-THREE

THE WOODEN BOX

affee has evaded Gail's questions about the table, but as their friendship grows, she begins to share snatches of its history. She relates that her great-grandfather made it in Norway and that it traveled from there to North Dakota, then Minnesota. She tells how a prairie fire prompted eight terrified siblings, her mother among them, to seek refuge under it.

Eventually she confides that her once clever, talented mother fell into a disturbed mental state and how the old table seemed to prompt within her confusing delusions of good and evil. Under its strange influence, real or imagined, Saffee says, she obsessively applied the layers of paint.

"So, why are you stripping it?" Gail asks.

Saffee sighs. "Well, it's hard to explain, and sometimes I'm not sure myself. But Jack says restoring the table will help me not be mired down by memories of being raised in a troubled home—more than I already am. I trust his judgment," Saffee says, giving her scraping tool an extra hard push. "I just hope that something good comes out of all this labor."

After the conversation, Saffee feels lighter, just as she had when she first shared her life with Jack.

Throughout the summer, the two neighbors share a certain joy as each new area of raw wood becomes completely exposed. In hot July, during a mini-celebration with glasses of Gail's lemonade, Saffee blurts, "Gail, thanks so much for being my cheerleader. I've really needed one." And she means it.

How odd it is to share this closet, this *small* closet. Business suits and sport coats and half a dozen dress shirts cram against her wrinkled blouses. A number of ties drape over her green silk dress. Black and brown wing tips jumble with pink slippers, red and navy pumps, and basketball high-tops. Removing the three boxes carted from Saffee's former life might make room for a little order. She slides them out.

Sitting on the floor, she shuffles through mementos that mean little to her now.

She finds her sixth-grade report on the Battle of Gettysburg, with Mr. Mason's affirming inscription, "You made me feel like I was there!" The words still make her feel warm. She replaces the paper and pushes the box under the bed.

She finds that the second box is mislabeled. Perhaps once it did hold April's keepsakes, but now it contains her mother's spiral notebooks. Over a dozen of them, filled with poems, short stories, and who knows what else. It was logical that her dad left what he thought was April's box with Saffee's. Reading the notebooks would be a journey into both her mother's joys and angst. Someday. She shuts the box and shoves it, too, under the bed.

The third box is the one made of wood they had found in the basement. Inside are newspaper clippings, turned brown, dating from the 1920s and '30s. Beneath them, dating from the late 1800s

244 | SUZANNE FIELD

and into the next century, is a pile of yellowed papers, most of them
legal documents.

She finds several birth certificates, vaguely recognizing the names
of her mother's siblings. One is for Joann Mabel Kirkeborg, born
March 4, 1913. There is a manifest from a cargo ship that lists her
grandfather, Knute Kirkeborg, age eighteen, as a worker on board.

And here is her grandparents' marriage license.

She opens an envelope that contains her grandmother's certificate of death.

"Clara Isabella Kirkeborg . . . Cause of death . . . exhaustion from
hysteria and acute mania. Place of death . . . State Hospital for the
Insane, State of North Dakota, May 4, 1920."

Saffee's heart thumps. Hysteria? Acute mania? Hospital for the
Insane? The words glare like neon lights. Her mother *and* her grandmother? Insane? What was that term she learned in psychology?
Evolutionary lineage. For an instant, for only an instant, her chest
tightens.

But God.

God has promised her—her life will be different. She must
believe that this box contains a view into other people's lives, not
hers. At the same time, she is saddened to learn about her grandmother. Exhaustion would be expected after bearing, how many
children? Nine? Maybe there were also miscarriages. Joanne had told
her that her mother's last baby, a girl, was given away. What happens
to a mother who carries a baby within her body and then it is taken
from her? What might she be driven to? In her grandmother's case, it
seems to have been mania.

Another question burns within Saffee. Had her mother ever
looked into this box? Had she read the "Certificate of Death of Clara
Isabella Kirkeborg"? She probably had. If so, maybe she concluded
that mental illness was very likely her destiny also.

Saffee goes to the kitchen, pours a glass of iced tea, and sits for
a while on the back step. Perhaps Saffee's grandmother Clara was

at wit's end trying to love and care for all of her brood. She thinks about her mother's decline into darkness and kinship with the table. By default, perhaps Joann was unloved, or at least felt so. What could give greater pain? Pain so deep it could never be covered over, least of all by paint.

Painting was Joann's intentional action, as Jack calls it, against powers that beset her. But painting the table hadn't spared her from mental illness. Has Jack been wrong?

Words of comfort from the past return. *I will lead you and guide you with my eye upon you.*

Saffee concludes that action in and of itself is not the answer. It must be the right action. Her mother's painting was done in torment. It created ugliness—for the painter, and for the painted. Saffee's work, in contrast, is to search for goodness and to restore beauty.

Her perspective renewed, she goes back to the bedroom, wondering what else is in the old wooden box. In a yellowed paper folder, she finds six fragile pages printed in Norwegian that look to have been torn from a magazine. A faded photograph of a weathered, somber-looking man and woman appears on the first page. The names beneath are Anders and Maria Kirkeborg. She recognizes them as the names burned into the underside of the Norway table, her grandfather Knute's parents. Another generational jump backward, to what?

Saffee looks into the rugged face of the man who, in a sense, she already knows. A sensitive artist, the skilled craftsman who many years ago labored to make a table. She hopes that the wife beside him was a good woman, a woman of strength and wholeness. The pages appear to be biographical. If only she could read them.

Seated at the circulation desk, Saffee looks up to see a graduate student she recognizes in line. She rightly assumes that Leif Bergstrom is waiting to check out research materials on plant pathology, as he often does. She's been hoping for days, ever since she opened the old wooden box of papers, that he would show up again. It's Saturday morning, a time she usually doesn't work, but today she agreed to substitute for a coworker and now is glad she did. The folder, with the article featuring her great-grandparents, is in a paper bag at her feet.

She has never spoken to this student, other than to answer his brief questions, but by his name, and more so his accent, she is fairly certain he is Norwegian.

"Mr. Bergstrom?" she says as he reaches the desk. "I was wondering, I mean, are you, I mean, do you ever . . ." She takes a deep breath and begins again. "I have something I need translated. You are Norwegian, aren't you?"

Leif Bergstrom looks a little surprised and says, "Yah. I am from Norvay."

Saffee removes the folder from the bag and hands it to him across the desk. "Is it possible that you, or do you know someone, who could translate this for me? It's six pages. I think it's a biography of my great-grandparents, and I'd love to know more about them."

The student looks at the article and politely tells her that he is way too busy to help. He's preparing his dissertation for his PhD, he says, but perhaps his wife, Ingrid, would be interested. How much would she pay?

They agree on twenty-five dollars and he looks pleased. Leif Bergstrom leaves the library with the old folder tucked into his Scandinavian-looking knapsack. She had not had the presence of mind to get his phone number.

CHAPTER FORTY-FOUR

NEWLY WED

affee returns home from the library in the early afternoon. She finds Jack studying baseball stats, his lanky body draped over the end of the love seat. She drops her purse, leans over, and pecks him on the forehead.

"Hi," she says, tousling his thick brown curls.

"Hi, sweetie." His eyes only momentarily leave the sports page.

She's eager to tell him about perhaps finding a translator for the biography, but he looks preoccupied. "I'm starved," she says. "Have you had lunch?" Three steps take her into their tiny kitchen, and from the clutter she knows the answer. Her hands go to her hips.

"You wouldn't make a very good Indian," she says under her breath.

"Mmm?"

"Jack, do you know you leave a trail *anyone* could follow?" Her head does an upward twitch.

"Yeah, it was an amazing graze," he quips, without looking up.

Mess had never been tolerated in Saffee's upbringing and was certainly no joking matter. Its appearance catches her off guard. "I bet I can tell you *everything* you've done while I was gone."

Not inquiring if he wants to hear, she begins a litany. "For start-ers, you ate some of the leftover meatloaf." She claps down the cap on the ketchup bottle, shrouds the remaining inches of meat with plastic wrap, and spirits them both into the refrigerator, shutting the door with enough vigor to rattle the jars inside.

"Aha! It was a meatloaf *sandwich*," she says, shoving slices of bread back into their bag. Gathering momentum, Saffee addresses the saltshaker as she thrusts it into the cupboard. "Just in case the pepper misses you," she says with animation.

Clunk. She throws a Pepsi can into the wastebasket. Hard. Soft drinks were only allowed for the most special of occasions in her home. She probably had only three or four in her entire childhood. And those certainly did not contain caffeine. Saffee darts a glance at oblivious Jack, who must be focused on something of great impor-tance. *Is he even listening?*

"You sat here at the table," she continues, a little louder, jerking one of the stainless steel chairs into place and snatching up a hand towel that dangles from its red plastic seat.

She picks up a postcard from the table. It's from April, the first one in months.

Hey, you two Love Birds! I called Daddy and he told me you got married. Congratulations! So sorry I couldn't be there. Hope you understand I'm pretty busy looking for my own Romeo—I sure dig these Italians!

Love and Kiss, Kiss!

April

Saffee's eyes do a big-sister roll. She drops the card and continues her mission.

"Ah! A crossword puzzle while you ate," she chortles, picking up the completed work, a ballpoint pen, and a smeary plate.

"I *am* impressed you do crosswords with a *pen*," she huffs. "I'll give you credit for *that*." She carries the plate to the sink where a bar of soap has slid off the counter, leaving a sudsy path before plopping into a puddle of water.

"Jack washed his hands. Give him another point. Only *three* cupboard doors open?" *Slam. Slam. Slam.*

With this, Jack turns his head and gives her a long, quizzical look.

She waits, daring him to respond.

Finally, he says, matter-of-factly, "I live here," and returns to his reading.

Saffee is muzzled. She pours herself a glass of milk, picks up a box of graham crackers, and goes out the back door. She sits on the top step to munch and mull. This isn't the first time she's been huffy about Jack's disregard for keeping their small house tidy. Weren't husbands, as well as wives, responsible to keep things neat?

It wouldn't be difficult to pick up after him—but would that be *fair*? She doesn't like to think he regards her as his maid.

Her mother was employed as a maid when she and her father met, and again maid and caregiver during the war years in San Francisco. As in other things, she isn't eager to follow suit. But throughout Saffee's childhood there was little need for Joann to pick up after Nels. For all his lack of polish, he was as fastidious as she. Certainly no crumbs ever fell off *his* plate.

A magazine lying on a chair flickers in her memory. Young Saffee had carelessly left it there. "How can anyone sit in this chair if you don't pick up after yourself?" her father had demanded, shaking his finger at her. The reprimand had stung and helped to foster a lasting conviction of how things "ought to be."

But wait. Why would she want to perpetuate a mind-set now that had, in part, made childhood so unpleasant? The troubling thought plays over and over in her mind. She flinches as her own petty, disapproving words ring in her ears.

She thinks of Jack's mother. From the first time Jack had taken

Saffee home to meet his parents, she couldn't help but notice how Harriet adored her less-than-orderly husband and attended to his needs without complaint. It seemed to give her joy to serve him. Of course, Saffee had heard no complaint from James either.

Roles and rules in Jack's home were quite different from those in Saffee's. So . . . Jack must presume . . . while Saffee presumes . . . oh dear. Her shoulders slump; she takes another cracker.

Okay, not so fast. The new bride juts out her chin. Jack lives here, but she does too. Why is *she* the one expected to change?

"Your mother ain't happy unless she's mad about somethin'."

. . . Your life will be different . . .

Again, recollections bring a clarifying moment. Saffee considers that there are times in life when she will have to *make* things different, *make* things better. It will not just happen with a touch of some celestial wand. Change might involve struggle, might take time. Hadn't she watched her mother take the trivial things of life way too seriously, leaving no energy to deal properly with matters that were truly important? What terrible thing had Jack done? Merely made a bit of a mess. While she—she had smattered an unredeemable half hour with rubbish much more difficult to clean up.

From her perch on the step, she has been staring into the back-yard, not seeing it. Now the lawn mower, covered with grass clippings, comes into focus. While she was gone, Jack had cut the grass. That was nice. But he could have cleaned the grass off . . . *Stop! It's trivial.*

Saffee hurries around the house to the garage and finds a broom. Returning to the backyard, she is arrested by its charm. Jack had not only mowed that morning but edged the perimeter. And she sees a mound of pruned, dead branches, tied and stacked against the house. The redbud trees proclaim a flurry of spring color—color that, in her bad mood, she hadn't noticed. She admires the thriving, newly planted young chrysanthemums they had put in the ground *together*, even though she alone had done the prior ruin.

She leans on the broom beneath a brilliant blue sky, drinking in the heady scene. Their first yard. Even if it is rented, it is, for this time, their yard. Her whole life is filled with beautiful gifts—Jack being the best. How could she have been so easily seduced to criticize him?

She looks down at the broom.

"Did I tell you that she hit my legs with a broom handle?"

Saffee quickly brushes grass off the mower and pushes it around the house and into its place in the crowded garage. She'll go in immediately to apologize.

Exiting the garage, she collides with Jack coming around the corner.

"Hey, hon, how about going to the baseball game tonight?" he says. "Bill's got some extra tickets." In one hand he holds the broom she had dropped in the backyard and in the other is her forgotten milk glass. The box of graham crackers is under one arm. She looks into his face and grins sheepishly.

"I'd absolutely love to," she says, taking the broom. "Who's playing?"

Maybe she will go to the concession stand. Maybe she will drink a Pepsi.

CHAPTER FORTY-FIVE

TENDRIL TANGLE

Early on an August Saturday, Saffee slips out of bed, being careful not to disturb Jack. He had grappled with actuarial formulas until 2:00 a.m., and she had worked until nearly eleven under lamplight in the garage, enjoying the cool evening silence. When she saw a celebration of fireflies blinking in the velvet dark, she rushed inside and pulled Jack away from his books out into the diamond-studded night.

They stood close, surrounded by the enchantment, until Jack said he must go back in.

"Aww," she objected, "you know what they say, 'All work and no play makes Jack . . .'"

"So, 'they' think I'm a dull boy?" He laughed.

"Never," she said emphatically, planting a kiss on his lips.

Now, in robe and slippers, she pads into the dark garage and raises the door. The morning sun, as if eagerly waiting, floods inside.

She turns and admires the tabletop, finally free of its multicolored past. She glides a hand along the silky surface. Last night she sanded its fine grain until it yielded a delicate sheen. Its daylight debut is even better than she'd hoped. But there is much more to do.

Today she'll begin restoring the apron, that intimidating four-inch-deep carved piece that rims the perimeter.

At eight o'clock, Saffee drives the VW to the hardware store and outfits herself with two gallons of stronger, smellier remover, a wickedly stiff wire brush, and a blunt probe to remove loosened paint from deep crevices. And more gloves. And more sandpaper.

Back in the garage, Saffee clips her swinging ponytail to the top of her head and pours a quantity of the new remover into a work bucket. Wrinkling her nose, she drags a brush full of the amber liquid onto a small area of carved vines. The serpentine twists and turns have always suggested to her some struggle between good and evil. They probably represented something similar to her mother. Joann frequently had pointed out dualities, such as truth versus lies, beauty versus ugliness.

She imagines her great-grandfather Kirkeborg coaxing the wood to release the enigmatic motif with his chisel. She wonders if he, like her mother, had imagined a certain presence. Her talented ancestor would undoubtedly be terribly disappointed to know that his lovely work had been reduced to a trap for paint.

The remover bubbles. She tries the new brush, applying pressure to the stiff bristles to test them. She's learned that many layers of paint can be scratched and grooved without jeopardizing the wood beneath. Progress is almost imperceptible and Saffee has abundant time to muse while she scrapes. Being unfamiliar with Norwegian lore, to her the design suggests something Shakespearean.

Whose reptilian head lurks in yonder braided vine?
Whose sin'ster eye leers my very soul?

She chuckles, just like her mother used to, entertained by her own strung-together words. Jack advised Saffee to be grateful for gifts from her mother. She's not sure if composition is one of them. Did Joann write something about this vine? If so, it might be in one of those spiral notebooks. Saffee debates again whether or not she wants to read them.

She wonders if the vine has a botanical name. She'll have to ask Leif Bergstrom, the Norwegian plant pathologist (pathologist, how fitting)—if she ever sees him again. He seems to have disappeared.

How many times as a young girl did Saffee see her mother apply wet paint over dry with the intensity of a combatant? Her mother's every stroke seemed to increase her agitation. But conversely, as Saffee wages a new war, this one to loosen and remove those painted layers, she senses liberation. In fact, a triple liberation. She dares believe that the wood, and she herself, and her mother also . . . "Oh, God," she whispers. "Please, Lord, set her free!"

She's trying to establish a habit of calling her dad every Sunday afternoon. She's learned that Joann seems to be coping acceptably well and showing interest in minor decorating of their new mobile home. He does not suggest that she and Jack visit. Neither does Saffee.

Coming from their street-side mailbox, Jack appears on the driveway. He steps into the garage, waving a postcard.

"A princess!" He sounds amused. "They made her a princess!"

"Who? What are you talking about?" She puts down the bristle brush and takes the card from him, trying not to stain it with her gloves.

It's from April. Saffee recalls that the last they had heard she was in Italy. Wrote she couldn't get an audience with the pope, so she settled for a Swiss guard or something like that.

Saffee reads aloud, "'I'm on Samos—a tiny, picturesque Greek island. Gorgeous. The villagers have made me their princess because of my blond hair.'"

"Well, that sounds like April," she says. "She was always pretending something."

"I look forward to meeting her someday," Jack says. "She sounds pretty adventurous."

On the driveway, Jack raises the small hood at the back of the

VW in order to change the oil. Saffee slops more remover onto a layer of cracking blue paint and continues to think about April. She regrets her own years of rudeness designed to keep kissy-huggy April at arm's length. But if her postcards are to be believed, April sounds okay and Saffee is happy for her.

A song she heard on the radio a few days ago has since been maddeningly stuck in Saffee's head. Pouring more remover into the bucket, she absentmindedly sings,

> *Sometime an April day will suddenly bring showers*
> *Rain to grow the flowers for her first bouquet*
> *But April love can slip right through your fingers*
> *So if she's the one don't let her run away . . .*

CHAPTER FORTY-SIX

JOANN'S NOTEBOOKS

affee pulls a box from beneath the bed and removes a pile of spiral-bound notebooks. Her fingers are sore from working so long on that stubborn carved vine. Today she will give them a rest. She turns pages of familiar handwriting that ranges from neatly penned to scrawls of jumbled emotion. Hatch marks slash through paragraphs deemed unacceptable.

Saffee skims the rambling "essay poem" Joann had written after attending the Miller's Ford sewing club—*"rhythms of boisterous chatter . . . raucous undercurrent . . . guttural pieties . . . boorish sticks and stones . . . rude cacophony . . ."*

She shudders at the display of criticism. What insidious powers had countermanded Joann's gifted mind so that a few women gathered to gossip had prompted this troubled torrent? She quickly exchanges the notebook for another and reads curious lines entitled "Night, From Under a Table."

> *Benches bar the world; benches mark the dark.*
> *A snore. A rustle. The last ember falls.*
> *Who whispers there?*

Will Someone come?
Or will she always be alone?
Pull the blanket tight, child.

Saffee can only guess what the words refer to. Any reference to a table must indicate the Norway table. Why would her mother have spent the night under it?

The cover of another notebook reads, "Herein lies evidence to hang, beatify, or bore."

She grins. There was no denying that Joann could sometimes be witty. Inside, she reads a scathing account of her altercation with the minister and subsequent withdrawal from the church. A poem follows:

My days are troubled and few
Am I but a flower that fades?
Is there not hope for a tree cut down to sprout again?
Its root may grow old in the earth
Its stump may burn
Yet, at the scent of Water it will bud!
Oh, God! Hide me!
Conceal me 'til your wrath is past that I may not be burned
Find my transgressions sealed, O God
My iniquity covered over
My flesh pains; my soul mourns
Your holy fire purifies

The last line is scrawled to be almost unreadable—

Or is the inferno meant for me?

Saffee rereads the muddled words. Does "a tree cut down" refer to the wood of the Norway table as well as to Joann herself? By scraping away the desecrating paint from the dead table, Saffee hopes, like the poem says, to make it "sprout" and "bud" again. The process is giving her, too, a sanding and scrub, stretching her to bloom. Yes, Jack was right.

Oh, Lord, forgive my lack of love and sympathy for my ill mother. For years I practically denied her existence. Remove my own ugly, self-centered layers—and thanks for not using a wire brush! Bring forth new life in me. And the table. And Mother.

Although she is emotionally exhausted, Saffee moves on and finds what she has been hoping for, a poem called "The Vine." It is dated shortly before the fateful Thanksgiving Day now so indelibly stamped into family memory. A catch in her chest makes her momentarily hesitate to read what might trigger the emotion of that night, but she is too curious not to.

> *The vine, that vigorous vine*
> *has gone astray*
> *Has become foreign to Him*
> *The outcast vine grows with the tares*
>
> *Shoots, planted by abundant waters*
> *Spread branches turned toward Him*
> *And commune with the stars*
> *Roots, turned toward others*
> *Will not thrive*
> *Joy, sorrow*
> *inextricably*
> *intertwined*
>
> *He will pull up the roots*
> *Cut off the fruit*
> *Leave it to wither.*
> *The vine, that vigorous vine*

has gone astray
Has become foreign to Him
The outcast vine grows with the tares

It seems possible that the table's carved vine had suggested these words. Considering what happened in the Petersons' yard, Joann must have meant them to be literal. That night it seemed as if she were fulfilling some personal directive to uproot the plants, the "tares."

Saffee reads the enigmatic poem to its conclusion, aware she will never fully understand words sprung from Joann's delusions:

The pruning shears
will come
must come
The cast-out branch is thrown into the fire!
I cling to the vine!
The pruning shears
will come
must come
"I give unto them eternal life; they shall never perish,
Neither shall they be plucked from my hand."

Saffee whispers, "Oh, Lord, I pray that in spite of her delusions, Mother knows that You are the Vine, and that You are truth."

CHAPTER FORTY-SEVEN

STUFFED RIBS

What began as a relaxing evening catching up with the newspapers suddenly changes when Jack looks up and suggests they should invite his boss and wife to dinner. Saffee, lounging on the love seat, drops her paper and sits up straight. "You're kidding, right?"

After Saffee's angst when she cohosted the Tupperware party with Gail, he knew he could expect some hesitancy. "It would be a good way to get to know them," he says. "Good for all of us. And you'll like Leonard Johnson. He's a really nice guy. I'm fortunate to work for him." Jack tells her that his boss was recently transferred to Minneapolis, so he and his wife probably know few people in the area and would appreciate the invitation.

"Where are they from?"

"Louisville, Kentucky, I think. Somewhere down south."

"Southerners? Oh, Jack. I'm not ready to compete with southern hospitality yet."

"But, Saffee . . ."

"No, Jack. I'm sorry."

Jack settles back into the turquoise vinyl chair and picks up his softball and glove. He thwaps the ball into the pocket a few times, a habit Saffee is still trying to get used to. She knows the matter is not settled.

Her memory shuffles through snapshots of her mother's pathetic attempts to entertain. She feels a queasiness not unlike that she used to experience before playing in a piano recital.

From the lumpy love seat, she scans their hand-me-down furniture.

"Honey, look at this place," she says. "You know I love it—it's great for you and me, but . . . your boss? They probably live in a very affluent neighborhood."

Jack says nothing.

Then she looks into the nook they call a dining room and knows the clincher. "Look, Jack, all we have in our so-called dining room is a Modigliani poster that's not even framed." The stylized, long-necked portrait seems to smirk at her, daring to be compared to the "real art" that must hang in the Johnson home. "We absolutely can't have company for dinner without an appropriate table. The stripping won't be finished for weeks . . . maybe months. We'll just have to wait on entertaining."

Jack's expression says he doesn't accept her arguments. He gestures toward the kitchen and their small Formica dinette set with its tubular stainless steel legs and four matching chairs with red plastic seats.

"Honey, *that* table works just fine. Don't *we* use it every day? We'll just carry it into the dining room and throw a tablecloth over it."

He moves to sit beside her. Crestfallen, she drops her head onto his shoulder. He doesn't get it. Neither one speaks for a few moments. In his gentle way, Jack asks, "Did you ever have any *good* times around the Norway table?"

"I . . . I can't remember any."

"Let's change that."

She looks dubious.

Family tables are more than just places to eat, he says. Much of his young life was around a table. Jack laces his fingers behind his head and gazes upward, as if childhood scenes replay on the ceiling. The dining room table was where he glued balsa airplanes together, he tells her, and where he played a million games of cribbage with his brother. His mother did her daily crossword puzzle there, and his dad paid bills and studied the stock market.

"When we had company," he says, "I remember more than the food. I remember my uncle recounting the same war stories over and over. And my cousins telling such unfunny jokes we howled." Jack's eyes linger for a moment, the corners of his mouth turned up. "Oh yeah, and Mother always cautioning me not to eat so fast—when sometimes I was slipping my food down to the dog. What a great place it was to be—for all of us, not just the dogs."

She is jealous beyond words of his memories. She can't believe he has even more to tell.

"When Danny and I got older," Jack says, "after meals we all lingered at the table drinking coffee, talking about life—God, politics, philosophy. I've realized that those conversations became foundational to my entire belief system. It was the place where Dad encouraged us to formulate what he called a worldview. Oh, if tables could talk," he says, summing up his reverie.

Jack's account helps her to better understand why he has a social consciousness, as well as an intellectual life. It had been built over the years with the help of his family and their guests, and now he was sharing it with her. Saffee is relieved tables can't talk.

"Oh, Jack," she blurts, turning to face him, "I really want to have what you describe. It's silly to be afraid of good experiences." She swallows the lump in her throat. "I must get over this."

Jack puts his arms around her. "Honey, you'll do just great . . . I can hardly wait for the boss to meet my lovely bride."

❖

Saffee finds the recipe in Sunday's *Minneapolis Star and Tribune*. Stuffed pork ribs. It shouldn't be difficult. With the addition of chopped apple, the stuffing is similar to the dressing her mother always made at Thanksgiving. She will make it Saturday—for the Johnsons.

That morning she swishes a dust cloth over the furniture. The carpet looks the same whether vacuumed or not . . . she chooses not. Vacuuming that doesn't show might be considered a trivial thing.

Later, as she begins to prepare the meal, she hears the *thunk, thunk* of Jack's basketball on the backboard that he and neighbor Bill put up at the edge of the driveway. Their masculine exuberance as they contend makes her happy. She so much wants the coming evening to go well, and to make Jack proud of her.

She chops an onion. A childhood scene flickers through her mind . . .

"Nels!" In the kitchen, Joann stares aghast at the irregular chunks of meat he has cut. "This is a rump roast!" she hisses so guests don't hear. "People slice rump roasts, not hack them! Don't you know the difference between a rump and a chuck?"

Saffee lectures herself. *I'll cry over an onion, but nothing else! Not even when eight legs bump under that little table . . . Having company for dinner only requires common sense.*

Oh, God, help me emulate only what Mother did right, and do other things better. Let this day honor her . . . and You.

Leonard and Betsy Johnson are warm, unpretentious, and chatty. They sip iced tea and tell about their experiences adapting to northern ways. Betsy recounts recently ordering a meal at a restaurant.

"The waitress came to our table and said, 'So, whatcha want?'"

Leonard laughs heartily and adds, "In the South, they ask me, 'What'll you have, *honey?*'" Now they both are laughing.

"I wouldn't like someone speaking that way to *my* husband," Saffee says with a smile. "Northerners aren't used to speaking with familiarity to strangers."

Leonard nods with understanding. "You'd probably want to 'wop her upside th' haid,' as they say in Loo-ih-vuhl!"

"That's for sure. I don't mind people being friendly, just don't call my husband 'honey'!"

The conversation drifts to other matters. The queasiness in Saffee's stomach has all but gone away. She sighs with relief and excuses herself to serve the meal, still within earshot of the conversation. *God, help me do this.* She tosses the salad and carefully lifts the hot pan of savory ribs from the oven. Perfect. She divides generous portions onto four plates. The Formica table is too small for a platter.

She can hear the living room talk return to eating out. Jack recommends Minneapolis restaurants the newcomers might enjoy. "There's a great barbeque place just a little to the west," he says. "Best ribs in town."

"Now that's the only way to have ribs," Leonard gushes. "Barbequed! Not the way *we* had them last night!" It is clear he is teasing Betsy.

"Oh, Leonard." Betsy laughs. "I know they were terrible! I found a new recipe in Sunday's paper," she explains to Jack. "Maybe I didn't cook them long enough."

"That wasn't the only problem, my dear. There was some kind of *mush* in between the ribs! And no barbeque sauce at all!"

"Mush!" Betsy chortles. "Leonard, it was called stuffin'!"

In the kitchen, Saffee freezes. She grips the edge of the counter for several moments until she can think.

Saffee senses that Betsy is used to her husband's humorous chiding, but she must be careful not to embarrass Jack's boss. She takes a deep breath. Here goes.

She pokes her head around the corner. Jack gives her a weak smile. Summoning her best southern accent (having college friends from the South can come in handy), Saffee announces, "Y'all're gonna love this new recipe for ribs! Ah found it . . ." She gulps. "Ah found it Sunday . . . in the *Stahr and Tribune*!"

Leonard groans. "Oh no!" With a red face, he tries umpteen ways to backpedal. Both he and Betsy insist that although something had seriously gone awry with their dish, they are sure Saffee's pork ribs and stuffing will be marvelous—it certainly smells wonderful!

That night Jack holds her tightly in his arms and whispers, "I'm so proud of you. You made the best of a delicate situation . . . and the ribs, the whole meal, it was delicious."

"Thanks, hon, but I'm afraid I didn't manage to spare the Johnsons from embarrassment."

"That would've been impossible, and I bet it won't be long 'til they laugh about it."

Encouraged more than he will ever know, Saffee smiles in the dark.

CHAPTER FORTY-EIGHT

RAINBOW HEART

B y late August, fall threatens an early appearance. The garage floor feels chilly. One day the cap from the paint remover can slips from her stiff fingers and rolls under the table. Retrieving it, she catches a glimpse of the words burned into the underside. She gets a pencil and tablet and carefully copies them. More Norwegian that needs translation, but Leif Bergstrom has not reappeared.

That evening she and Jack carry eight discarded cement blocks from the back property line into the garage. Jack, with Bill's help, lifts the table onto the stacked blocks. Saffee watches them, disappointed that her project is going so slowly. At least now she can work from a chair rather than the floor.

While Bill and Jack are discussing the upcoming football season, Saffee hears the phone ring and hurries inside to answer. She learns that Mary Scott is sick. Can Saffee teach the Bible lesson to the fifth graders on Sunday? She feels obligated to say yes, even though she too will be ill, from nerves, long before the class begins. So far, she has only helped by playing the piano and assisting with crafts.

Each morning during the remainder of the week's tedious work on the table, she has plenty of time to think about teaching the Old

Testament story of Joseph. The thrust of the lesson, according to the teacher's guide, is forgiveness, and Joseph had a lot to forgive. She runs through the injustices he suffered: sold into slavery by his brothers, falsely accused of assault by his employer's wife, thrown into prison for years, forgotten by man—but not by God.

She considers the summary points she'll make: Joseph persevered in hardship and was greatly honored; he forgave his brothers; he understood that his trials were part of God's plan for the preservation of nations.

Saffee wants the children to know that God can give them, like Joseph, a good future. That with Him good things can come from bad. Or, as the lesson book says, beauty from ashes.

As she slops more chemical remover on a paint-encrusted area, she thinks of the blessings that have come into her own life. This table, for example. It could have become ashes when flames whipped across the prairie. If it had burned, her mother would not have survived, and she and April would never have been born. The table endured considerable misuse, yet, like Joseph's honor, its former beauty is being restored.

By the time Sunday morning comes, Saffee has thought a lot about Joseph the overcomer.

Warmer weather returns. Gail sits in her usual place in the late summer sun. Saffee realizes she's never told her neighbor about the words inscribed on the table's underside. She crawls beneath and tries to read them out loud. The foreign sounds make them laugh, and they wonder about their meaning. Saffee says when she was young she imagined the words chronicled Viking conquest and buried treasure.

"No way," says Gail. "It's prophetic. It says"—she puts her hands around her mouth like a megaphone—"'There will be eight Andrews children eating at this table.'"

"No way yourself, Gail, but I guess it's no surprise you think like a mother," Saffee says, glancing at Gail's ever-growing belly that at the moment has a naked baby doll perched precariously on its slope. Jenny Rose, the doll's barefoot owner, scampers after yellow butterflies in the grassy front yard.

In privacy, Saffee has catalogued the reasons she feels negative about having a child. Her baby sister, April, had taken Saffee's place in her mother's heart. In various ways, babies had complicated Joann's life. Her mother suffered an early death because of the tragic circumstances of her last baby. Then there was Saffee's distasteful memory of Joann begging Nels for a baby, long after there was hope of offering another child a normal home. No, having a baby holds little appeal, but there had been no reason to share why with Gail, or even Jack.

Suddenly Jenny Rose bounds into the garage, throws her arms around Saffee's neck, and proclaims, "I love you, Miss Saffee!" Saffee, kneeling on the cement floor, wire brush in hand, is so startled she sinks backward onto the cement and the little girl settles into her lap.

"Oh! Jenny Rose!" Saffee has never held a child before, never felt a child's hug. The little girl is warm and soft and smells of fresh air. "Oh my!" is all Saffee can say. As quickly as the little sprite had come, she is off to twirl and play in the summer sun.

Gail wears an amused expression, then nods toward the table. "Saffee," she says, "when I look at this big wonderful table, I can't help but think about what its future will be like."

Saffee is puzzled. "What do you mean?"

"Events around it, you know, fun things, like birthday parties, children coloring Easter eggs, your kids sorting out their Halloween loot and . . ."

She's reminded of what Jack shared of his childhood. "Gail . . . I just don't know."

"Aren't you and Jack going to . . . ?"

"Jack and I are fine without any children," Saffee says, trying not to sound curt.

Gail's imagination is not deterred. She says in her mind's eye she sees a high chair pulled up alongside and a little one kicking the table with her foot.

Saffee makes it clear that after all her hard work she wouldn't appreciate anyone kicking her beautiful table. Gail rattles on, naming kinds of shoes there will be, or at least could be, sharing space underneath during meals—sneakers, sandals, little slippers with bunny ears . . .

Saffee joins in. "Don't forget *adult* high heels and black wing tips."

"Right. And don't forget the bare feet," Gail goes on, "big ones, little ones, long legs and short, all under this table."

Jenny Rose's doll tumbles from its perch. Saffee picks it up and asks Gail if she had played with dolls as a child.

"Of course. Why?"

"Just wondering," Saffee says. For some reason she's wondered if playing with dolls taught a girl how to be a mother. She grins at her neighbor. "Anyway, if we ever decide to have a baby"—even the word is hard to say—"which I doubt, you'll be one of the first to know."

"Miss Saffee! Miss Saffee!" Another day Jenny Rose comes running across the driveway and into the garage where Saffee is peeling off another pair of shredded rubber gloves. It has been a productive day.

"Look, Miss Saffee, I made you a heart!" Jenny Rose waves a crayon drawing in the air.

Saffee kneels down and puts one arm around the exuberant little girl. "I like all the colors. It's *so* pretty, Jenny Rose. Tell me about it."

"Well, this is the 'splanation . . . My heart is a *rainbow* heart!"

"Jenny Rose, what a beautiful thing. A rainbow heart."

"You can put it up in your garage and look at it while you work."

"I will. I promise."

Jenny Rose skips out of the garage. "I gotta go now. I love you, Miss Saffee! Gonna make a heart for my daddy! G'bye!"

Saffee calls after her, "Thank you, Jenny Rose." Silently, with a lump in her throat, she adds, "I love you too, Jenny Rose."

Saffee suddenly feels unsteady. She sits down in "Gail's chair." How can one's long-held, stubborn mind-set change in an instant, making all of her reasons for it completely invalid? Her heart, her "rainbow heart," feels ready to burst—all because of love. Motherhood no longer seems out of the realm of possibility. Not at all.

Saffee is at the stove browning chicken when she hears the VW pull into the driveway. Before Jack can put down his briefcase, she meets him with a warm embrace.

"Mmm, don't you look happy," he says, pulling off his tie.

"Well, I should."

"Why?"

"It's because," she says, smiling, "I have a rainbow heart."

"A what?"

She kisses him. "Come in. I'll 'splain it to you."

CHAPTER FORTY-NINE

THE WEDDING GIFT

Saffee hastens toward the library exit after a day's work.

"Mrs. Andrews?"

She stops abruptly. "Oh! Hello!" She is pleased that Leif Bergstrom remembers her name.

"I'm sorry I did not return this to you earlier," he says, pulling her folder from his knapsack. "I have been so busy . . . My wife, she wrote it all out. She said it vas interesting."

Saffee opens the folder and sees the original article along with a stack of handwritten pages. She rummages in her purse to find the folded bills she's carried for some time, waiting to see him again.

"Ingrid, my wife, she said it vas a good vay to practice her English. She didn't use the typevriter because she had to revise a lot. It vas easier to use a pencil . . . vit eraser."

"This is wonderful. Please thank her for me." Saffee presses the money into his hand.

"Thank *you*," he says. "I'm glad I see you today; ve go back home soon."

Going home? Saffee remembers the inscription she copied from the table and pulls the piece of tablet paper from her purse. "You're leaving? Oh, but there's something else . . . um . . . something short . . ." She hands him the paper.

"It is from the Bible," he says. "Do you vant me to translate? It vill just take a minute." Together they find an empty library table and sit across from each other as he writes. Upside down she reads two words: *wife* and *vine.*

Saffee curls up on the love seat with a cup of tea and the handwritten, translated article about her great-grandparents, Anders and Maria Kirkeborg. It is a compilation of interviews with their children and various acquaintances from their Valders Valley community. She skims the words, hoping to find a reference to Anders's woodworking skill and maybe even a mention of her table.

She reads at length about their being a hardworking couple whose days were filled with the arduous tasks of farming and raising children. In addition, Anders and Maria "were known as 'the hands and feet of Jesus,' as they attended to the needy. The salvation of every soul in the valley was the passion of their lives." Saffee is so warmed by numerous such glowing accounts, she forgets her tea.

"Anders was a master craftsman . . ." Ah, here's what she is looking for. She reads about her great-grandfather's ability to make his own farm implements, sleds, carriages, and . . . fine furniture. He used "neither nails nor glue, but fitted one piece into another so snugly they stuck fast. He frequently ornamented his work with traditional decorative designs. No one else in the valley carved with his skill."

Saffee marvels. One piece of this man's artistry stands in their garage. She reads quotes from a daughter: "Mother and Father led prayers after each evening meal. All the family feared God's name. We and the hired help and their families gathered at the table . . ." *Around the Norway table!* ". . . and that was the best time of the day.

Everyone was welcomed and loved. We sat crowded on long benches, parents holding children. We sang psalms, followed by Father's Bible reading and prayer. Thus we carried on our heritage . . ." Saffee thinks about how in contrast this is to what happened later.

Other pages record that the oldest of the family's seven children was Knute, who emigrated to America. Anders wrote in his testament that the family table, "the wedding table he had made for Maria," would pass to Knute. "Jergen, the second son, took the table to his brother when he too went to America in 1910."

Wedding table! The inscription that Leif translated today now makes a little more sense. Saffee pulls out the tablet paper. How does it begin? "Your wife shall be like a fruitful vine . . ." She blushes.

Smiling, she cannot sit still, but jumps up and spontaneously twirls. Originally, the atmosphere around the Norway table was one of happiness and hospitality. No longer will it suggest darkness to her, but a symbol of flourishing life.

"Jack!" Waving the pages, she hurries to his study. "The table, our table, it was made as a gift of love, a wedding gift!" She holds the pages against her chest, grinning. "This article, along with all my work, of course, has lifted all the heaviness I've experienced over it."

He gives her a loving hug and his pleased look says, "Didn't I tell you?"

The next day, as she heads to the garage, Saffee catches her smiling reflection in the hall mirror. Funny thing, smiles. They seem to be standard adornment on some faces—lately they often appear on hers too. She lifts the garage door and pulls on yet another new pair of rubber gloves. She thinks about the portrait of her great-grandparents on the front page of the biography.

The text revealed that there was a special joy in Anders and Maria Kirkeborg's Norwegian home. Their sober faces probably reflected the hard times they lived in, when smiles indicated foolishness. But nowadays, smiles are commonplace. She is filled with gratitude that her new way of seeing things, thinking about things, is not only an *internal* exercise, but shows on her face. Also, she is grateful for Jack. Sometimes so much so that her smile muscles ache.

She looks out at the birches across the street. All summer she has fancied them to be kin to her table. Their limbs, changing into yellow garb, sway in the light wind, sweeping wispy clouds from the morning sky.

Today she will coax away another layer of paint.

CHAPTER FIFTY

THE STROKE

Machines gurgle, beep, and whirr. Tubes regulate fluids. Saffee watches Nels gently massage her mother's motionless arm. Nels called her four days ago from the hospital, the day Joann had a stroke. She could tell by his voice that he wanted her to come. Needed her with him. She felt guilty that she hadn't seen either of them since the wedding. She hurried to the hospital, through a cold October rain, filled with anxiety, hating that she was nervous to see her mother—in any condition.

The doctor called the stroke massive. It remained to be seen, he said, if she will ever speak again, or move.

Today, as she lies there, Joann looks much older than fifty. Her hair, once strikingly dark, is ribboned with gray. Her face is sallow, her eyes closed. Does she hear them? A place in Saffee's heart, long fiercely guarded, is broken into unexpectedly. "I'm so sorry, Mother. I'm so sorry." The words come forth with sobs. Nels puts his arms around her. She tells him she'll be back the next day.

The next day, with cold, sore fingers, Saffee wraps fine sandpaper around the end of a screwdriver and absentmindedly rubs along the contours of her great-grandfather's carved masterpiece. Outside it has begun to rain.

"*I'm sorry, Mother.*" The words Saffee spoke in the hospital reverberate in her head. Joann's eyelids had fluttered for an instant. Her small dark eyes pierced Saffee's with an accusing look that seemed to say she took Saffee's apology to be an admission of guilt—guilt of conspiring against her, of being the perpetrator of her miserable years. Saffee is still stunned. Does Joann believe that her own daughter was the villain?

In spite of two layers of clothing under her sweatshirt, Saffee shivers. Her intent had been to express that she was sorry her mother has suffered, sorry that her life has been haunted and crazed. The apology also meant, "I'm sorry I didn't come home to see you during the college years. Surely I could have done something to ease your pain. Surely I could have helped you, my own mother. I'm sorry I did not. I'm sorry!" But she hadn't said that. Jumbled emotion, and her mother's unexpected glare, stifled the words.

Perhaps Saffee's neglect did contribute to Joann's pain. If so, she *was* the villain. If so . . . Now she whispers, "Oh, Mother, forgive me."

Saffee looks back into her childhood. She had been sullen and pouty. "Owly" had been her mother's word. But are these signs of villainy?

Her eye catches Jenny Rose's "rainbow heart" taped to the garage wall. Had Saffee ever scribbled such a gift for Joann? Once, when she spilled similar self-condemnation to Jack, he said, "Saffee, it was never your job to fix your mother, only to love her."

Well, she hadn't done a good job of that either. Hiding away at college wasn't loving. Rarely writing a letter, never calling on the phone wasn't loving. Perhaps she should have persisted in nagging her father to seek help for his sick wife. Why had she stopped? Saffee's thoughts jump to the day Joann demanded Saffee to assess if there was something wrong with her. *No, Mother, you're just fine!* The words choke her, as if she is swallowing sand. What could she have said?

Saffee is learning to interact better with others, but any opportunity to establish a satisfying relationship with her mother was lost long ago. In the chilly garage, she listens to a steady drizzle patter into the gutters. She drops the screwdriver to the floor and cries.

Late Indian summer suddenly becomes wintry. From the kitchen window, Saffee watches the first snowfall begin to blanket the grass. The warmer asphalt driveway is still bare, but it too will be white by the time she and Jack come home from work tonight. Then they will enlist Bill's help to disassemble a table that now displays a split personality—three legs still suffer variously colored layers of paint, while the rest of the table breathes free. They will prop its pieces against a garage wall for a few months and, for the first time, drive the VW inside. She has done her best to finish the project before winter. Come spring, she will.

CHAPTER FIFTY-ONE

CHRISTMAS

In early December, Jack tells Saffee there is an office Christmas party planned for the sixteenth.

She momentarily squints her eyes, wrinkles her nose, and then asks calmly, "What in the world should I wear?"

He looks at her blankly.

The next Saturday Saffee takes the bus downtown. At Peck and Peck, she finds an emerald green silk suit. It fits like a glove.

Back home, she models the new outfit for Jack and receives his unreserved approval. She reads a tag attached to the label. It says, "Love me for my imperfections." She guesses it refers to the slubby silk fabric. She wonders why it doesn't say, "Love me in spite of my imperfections."

Saffee muses over the notion. Sometimes she still wonders what her husband sees in her. "Jack," she says, reaching for a hanger, "do you love me for my imperfections, or in spite of them?"

Jack admires her reflection in the closet door mirror. "You're testing my powers of self-analysis," he says. "I'll say I love you just as you are. Not perfect, of course. Perfection would be boring."

She considers the thought. Her former life had been boring, but such a far cry from perfect. She hangs the suit in the closet. "Well, Mr. Andrews, I think *you're* perfect and not at all boring," she teases, remembering how this morning he'd left shaving cream slopped on the bathroom counter and toothpaste spattered on the mirror. Other than that, what could she fault?

At the party, holiday merriment has a life of its own and makes few demands on her. The executives' wives are older than she and seem to have known each other for years. Saffee's modest efforts to join in are only somewhat successful. She exchanges pleasantries with Leonard and Betsy Johnson, who again praise that never-to-be-forgotten meal of stuffed ribs. Smiling, but self-conscious, she stays fairly close to Jack most of the evening, listening as he banters with coworkers.

A couple of days later an invitation arrives for a New Year's Eve party given by some of Jack's high school classmates. Forgetting former resolutions to rise above old fears, Saffee considers that she has paid her party dues for one season. This time she'll stand her ground. But Jack insists they go, saying that his friends are her friends too. Hadn't they come to their wedding? Her memory of that day is a blur; she'd have to check the guest book. She tells Jack that she had endured the office party because she rightly assumed that group would have little interest in her and expect little in return. A party with people near her own age was another matter. There she would face unspoken competition, and she would lose.

Happy-faced Jenny Rose bursts in the door about noon. Gail has asked Saffee to keep her an hour or so after morning kindergarten until she returns from her baby's medical checkup. "Thanks, friend," Gail had said, "there's no one else I'd rather trust her to than you."

The little girl's cheeks are flushed, and dark curls spill across the shoulders of her bright pink jacket. "Look, Miss Saffee, I made a present for Mommy and Daddy for Christmas!" With mittened hands she holds up a green gift bag tied shut with a red ribbon.

"Nice, and what a pretty bow, Jenny Rose. Did you tie it yourself?" Saffee unzips the girl's jacket.

"Sure I did. And it's a really good present . . . but don't ask me what it is," she whispers loudly, her eyes dancing. "It's a secret!" Jenny Rose carefully places the gift bag on the coffee table and slides out of the jacket, mittens dangling from the sleeves. Saffee pulls off her matching pink boots.

"I bet you're going to put the present under your Christmas tree."

"Of course, if I can find room. There's lots and lots of presents under there!"

They go to the kitchen, Jenny Rose cradling the green bag in her arms. Saffee ladles hot soup into two bowls, puts crackers on a plate, and pours glasses of milk.

"Miss Saffee, now remember, don't ask me what this is, okay?" she says, stretching to place her gift in the center of the Formica table.

"Okay."

"Cuz I can't tell you!"

They both gently blow on spoonfuls of soup to cool it and Jenny Rose says, "Well, I can tell you"—her voice becomes mysterious—"it's something white!"

"The gift is white? That's nice."

As she munches a cracker, Jenny Rose contentedly kicks a rhythm on a table leg. "I guess I'll tell you one more thing," she says, her eyes on the bag. "I made it out of *wax*."

"Mm, wax?"

"And I can tell you something else . . . There's a string in the middle of it!"

Saffee laughs and says, "Now I really wonder what it could be."

Jenny Rose looks thoughtful. "Miss Saffee . . . well . . . maybe I can tell you one more thing." She whispers, "You're s'posed to put *fire* on top of it!"

"Ohhh," says Saffee, "fire!"

"Now don't ask me any more questions. You'll just hafta see it after Mommy and Daddy open it up." With this final pronouncement, Jenny Rose drains her milk glass, picks up the gift, and, with a self-satisfied look, holds it against her chest.

Gail had said there was no one else she would rather entrust this treasure of a child to, at least for these few minutes. Saffee found that surprising, but she can remember few compliments that have given her more pleasure.

"Okay. Let's see if I've got the lineup straight," Saffee says as the last hours of their first Christmas together wane. "The first row: rook, knight, bishop, queen, king, bishop, knight, rook. And pawns across the second row."

"Right. And remember, the white queen goes on white, and black on black."

"Got it." She knew if she bought this elegant chess set for Jack he would love it—and she would need to stretch again. Games. She's trying so hard to like them, to see the point.

When it's almost ten o'clock, Saffee figures she's spent enough time for one night learning chess strategy, but she doesn't want the day to be over. Outside it's snowing. Jack suggests a walk and she happily agrees.

They decide to walk along the mini-forest of birch trees across the street. But first, holding hands, they stop to admire their Christmas tree, twinkling through the front window. Saffee recalls the year her mother made the solemn decision to refrain from turning on holiday lights out of respect for those who had perished in tree fires. It had not seemed like one of the "good things" Saffee wanted to retain.

They cut across the yard until they are in front of Bill and Gail's corresponding window. Below it, surrounded by unblemished snow, are the kneeling, life-sized forms of Mary and Joseph keeping watch over Baby Jesus. Saffee stops to brush white flakes from the holy family's heads and shoulders, and then she and Jack walk diagonally toward the street. She turns to view the tableau again. From this angle, a vigorous flame atop a white candle inside refracts bold rays of light toward the nativity. Jenny Rose's secret gift now proclaims its surprise. More than a candle—her gift is the radiant star of Bethlehem.

At six twenty on New Year's Eve, Saffee, wearing a blue quilted robe, removes eight jumbo, prickly rollers and finds her hair more unruly than usual. Winter's furnace-dry air makes it flyaway, snapping at the brush with static electricity. She puts the brush down in chagrin and glares into the bathroom mirror. She still has about twenty minutes before they need to leave. Maybe they can be late.

She begins to apply makeup, unable to avoid seeing her mother's resemblance in her reflection, hearing her parents' voices . . .

"Joann! We're late! What's holding you up?" "I'm not going! You and the girls go."

"Joann! It's Palm Sunday! Now put yer coat on . . ." Nels dodges the green-handled hairbrush as it flies . . .

Joann is in a nursing home now, only thirty minutes away. The hospital helped Nels make the arrangements two months ago when it became clear that she would not return home after the severe stroke. She has regained partial use of one arm, but the rest of her body shows no sign of recovery. Saffee takes the bus to go sit by her side as often as possible; there is no certainty that Joann recognizes her. The visits bring back the past as Saffee sits there, trying to sort things out. They take an emotional toll on her. Sometimes these emotions, in various forms, spill over at home.

Even though Saffee is twenty-two, some of her teenage complexion lingers. She impatiently dabs eruptions with cover-up. "Glop!" she addresses the mirrored face.

"What did you say?" Jack calls from the living room. He's watching the evening news on their small black-and-white television, a Christmas gift from his parents.

"Nothing," she replies.

She plans to wear a black sheath that often brings compliments. Then again, tonight black might look like death-warmed-over.

Saffee begins to cry. What has happened to the modicum of composure and confidence that she had achieved over the past months? The office Christmas party, by no means a disaster, had seemed to set her back. She had been tongue-tied, afraid she reflected poorly on Jack. She crosses her arms and hugs the robe as if to prevent her body from falling apart. Sniffling up tears, she goes to Jack. Surely he will understand why she can't, they can't, go. She wouldn't even mind staying home alone, but she knows he wouldn't leave her on New Year's Eve.

Surprised, Jack makes room for her on the love seat. Before he can ask her what's wrong, the phone rings on the small table beside Saffee. Instinctively, she wills her voice to be normal and answers, wishing she hadn't.

"Oh. Hi, Daddy."

Nels says he will be spending the evening with Joann at the nursing home. His drive from Red Bridge takes a little less than an hour. Will Saffee and Jack join him, at least some of the evening? "Unless you have plans," he says.

Saffee's mood tempts her to retort that of course they have plans—it's their first New Year's Eve since they've been married, they're young, they like to go places. She reddens. Why would she pretend she has become some *bon vivant*?

"We're going to a party, Daddy," she says, "but it doesn't start 'til late." She casts Jack an inquiring look. He nods. "We can meet you for a while first at the nursing home."

"It's New Year's Eve, Muzzy. Nineteen sixty-four already!"

Saffee has not heard her dad use that nickname for years. The three visitors sit flanking Joann's bed in the warm, cramped room, Jack at the foot. Their winter coats drape over the backs of the chairs.

Nels pats Joann's good arm. "You know what? The world still celebrates this night, the night we met. And that was twenty-five years ago."

Her head turns. Dim, watery eyes appear to fix on him. It has been determined that Joann is blind in one eye from glaucoma; she had refused vision tests for years. The stroke affected the other eye; her distorted mouth sags to one side.

"Do you remember that night, Muzzy?" He looks with hope into her vacant face, even though he knows there will be no answers to his questions. In spite of his years of matrimonial trials, it is typical of Nels to bring up only good memories.

Several times Saffee has heard the story of her parents' first meeting, at a dance, of course. With pride, Joann told her how popular she had been at dances, and how Nels had quickly claimed her as his own.

"You sure look nice, Joann," Nels says. "You always did look good in red." She wears a shapeless bed jacket. "Someone's cut your hair." The salt-and-pepper hair is short, very short. "When it grows a little I'll give 'em some extry cash to give you a permanent," he says. He's always liked curls.

"Sapphire! When I'm old and infirm, promise you'll cut the hairs on my chinny-chin-chin. Promise me now . . ."

Since their arrival, Joann's face has been without expression, but her eyes slide from side to side. Saffee picks up her chair and carries it around the bed, placing it near Nels where perhaps her mother can see them both at once.

What goes on in her mother's head now? If the stroke quelled her delusions, as the doctor seems to think, perhaps it was a blessed thing. Too long was she caught in cycles of fairly acceptable behavior when medicated and full-blown schizophrenia when she refused drugs. No longer will there be scandal because she runs down the street scantily clad or knocks on neighbors' doors to warn of apocryphal dangers. Nels no longer will suffer the humiliation of obtaining court orders to recommit her to the state mental hospital. No more calls for police assistance. At great cost, it appears her torment is swept away.

"Mother . . ." Saffee's words have come with great difficulty during prior visits. Tonight she must try harder to bridge an emotional hurdle. Ignoring how warm she is in her black sheath, she begins. "Mother, I just want you to know that I'm fine, being married and all, I mean. I'm really good. I have a good life . . . and . . . a lot of credit for that goes to you."

There is no indication that Joann comprehends, but Saffee continues, "Mother, remember the vegetable soup you always made for us? Now that the weather's cold, I make it too. Just like you did. Jack really likes it."

Saffee glances at him. She knows he must be a little uneasy, but he smiles and says, "That's right, Joann, it's very good."

"I just want you to know that I appreciate that you always made us good meals." Nels nods at her, approving her effort to communicate.

Joann's eyes steady on her daughter's face. Saffee searches for more, anything more. "I remember once you told me to never serve liver and brown beans and chocolate cake at the same meal—too much brown."

"Ugh!" she hears Jack breathe. "Please don't!"

Saffee laughs. "Funny, the things that stick with a person, right, Mother?"

She searches how to extend her awkward, one-way chatter.

"Oh! Guess what Jack bought me for Christmas—a sewing machine. Singer, of course. You always said they're the best. I'm going to try to make curtains for our kitchen. Like you did. I couldn't begin to count all the curtains and draperies you made over the years."

She feels a duty to carry on the stilted conversation. Nels, never much of a talker, probably runs out of things to say during his frequent solo visits. Jack is quiet. Saffee crosses and uncrosses her legs, being careful not to brush against the bed rail. A run in her sheer black hose would not be good at the party.

"Remember when you used to draw a lot, Mom? Even tricky things like faces and cute little squirrels and rabbits. And all those floor plans for the Cottonwood Point house. You were so good at it. I'm planning to learn calligraphy. If I do it well, it will probably be because you passed on some of your artistic talent."

Saffee's heartfelt urge to inventory her mother's contributions to her life surprises her. She wants to continue. Wants to tell her gifted, fractured mother that she loves classical music because of all the records Joann used to play. But the eyes have closed. They hear a soft snore. Music can wait until another visit.

Jack looks at his watch and Saffee reaches to retrieve her coat. Then suddenly she knows there is one more thing she must say, even if it is not heard.

"Mother," she declares, "I'm taking the paint off the Norway table." She would not be surprised if Joann's eyes popped open at this announcement. But there is no movement.

"I hope that's good news, Mother. I . . . I hope you're glad about it. I never understood why you painted it all the time, but I just know that paint must come off." Saffee rambles a bit, saying that she suspects painting the table served to heighten her mother's trauma. She tells her that the removal is not a defiant or rebellious act, but a necessity. "The work is, well, therapeutic for me." She glances at Jack. "It's been healing, and I didn't even know I needed healing. And also, Mom, I began to imagine, and hope, really hope . . ." She chokes, making it hard to go on. "I hope that as I release layer after layer of paint, you, too, might be released from the grip of . . . well . . .

"I'm sure some people might think this sounds strange, Mom, but out there in the garage all summer, I felt that the presence of God was with me, showing me things." She takes a deep breath. Mentioning God in this familiar way is so un-Minnesotan. "I've asked Him to heal you of the emotions and agonies of the past. I really, really hope He has, and will." Saffee leans to give her mother a kiss on the forehead. "I love you, Mom. I'll be back soon."

Nels reaches out and squeezes Saffee's hand, then plants his own kiss on Joann's cheek.

Hurrying across the parking lot, Saffee holds tightly to Jack's arm. She's unsteady, not only from emotion, but also her black suede, toe-pinching high heels.

"Careful, it's getting icy," he says.

When they get to the car, he reaches into his coat pockets. Then into the right pocket of his blue blazer, and the left.

"The directions to the party," he says, "they were right on the dresser. I must not have picked them up."

He starts the motor and switches on the heater. "It would be a lot of driving to go back to the house, then back this way, and then to the party."

He looks at her and says, "You know what? There'll be other parties and I'm starving. Let's get some Chinese takeout and go home." He laughs. "We can watch the Times Square celebration on TV—like a couple of old folks."

"Okay," she says, trying not to sound relieved. Seeing her helpless mother confirmed that life needs to be lived fully and enjoyed, parties and all, while a person is able. But, as Jack says, there will be other parties.

Jack eases the car over icy patches on the road. He reaches for her hand and offers her a smile filled with love and approval.

CHAPTER FIFTY-TWO

WAITING

1964–1976

Dim, misty years drift by in monotonous discomfort. Joann can manage to slowly turn her head and raise one arm in response to those around her but is unable to speak. Throughout endless, wakeful nights she revisits regrets. Slumber disjointedly jumbles the pleasures and pains that were . . . and calls of things yet to come . . .

. . . *The soft touch of her mother's hand . . . "Joann . . ."*
        . . . *The harshness of her father . . . "High school? Not yet, Joann, not 'til eighteen . . . You'll clean da guest cottages four years, just like da odders done." . . .*

"Where are her partials? I've looked everywhere. I'm sure I put them in this morning. Look at the chart—she's hardly taking any food."

"Her partials? Do you think she dropped them in the—no, how could she?"

"That's it! I wheeled her into the bathroom, had to leave for a minute before I got her on the commode . . . maybe she leaned forward, just let them fall out."

"Only strained food for you now, Joann. Can't fit new dentures for someone who doesn't talk, you know . . . Have you seen the abscesses on her gums?" . . .

. . . "Mom? Are you awake? I've come to read to you . . ."
The Lord is my light and my salvation; whom shall I fear?
The Lord is the strength of my life; of whom shall I be afraid? . . .

. . . *"Oh, Nels! The pain was fierce; I didn't think I'd live through it! Who'd think a baby would put me through such pain. I feel so weak . . . I'm going to be a modern mother—no nursing for me. Bottle-feeding's the rage . . . I'll get some rest that way." . . .*

. . . "Joann. Wake up. Nels is here, your daughters too. Look, see how much your grandson has grown." . . .

. . . *"Rolf! Get away from me! Stop it! I'll yell for Pa!" . . .*

. . . "Mom? Can you hear me when I read?"

When the wicked . . . came upon me . . . they stumbled and fell. Though an host should encamp against me, my heart shall not fear . . .

. . . "The psychotropics, we've tried them all, Joann, none seem to have helped . . . all that's left is shock . . . If you don't consent, it will be a long trip through the courts . . . It's the only way you have a chance, Joann." . . .

. . . "Saffee's a Kirkeborg through and through, Nels, but this one, look at those blue Kvaale eyes! This one takes after her daddy." . . .

. . . One thing I have desired of the Lord, that will I seek after; That I may dwell in the house of the Lord . . . to behold the beauty of the Lord . . .

. . . "Joann . . ." The soft touch of her mother's hand . . .

. . . Memorize the words, memorize the words . . . Hysteria . . . Acute mania . . . Hospital for . . .

. . . "Open up, Joann, here comes the applesauce. Mmm. Now, Joann, don't push it away, see there, you've spilled on your bib! Here, let's try again." . . .

. . . *"Yes, Joann. You're beautiful. You always will be."* . . .

. . . "Mom, listen to these words." . . .
When my father and my mother forsake me,
Then the Lord will take me up . . .

. . . *Hospital . . . Hospital for . . . Hospital for the Insane . . .*

. . . "I see your pictures on the board, Joann. You were some looker! Nice family. Can you see them up here? Look, I'll point." . . .

. . . "It's Sunday, Joann. Nels will be coming. He always does, you know. Let's see . . . what should we wear? You look nice in this flowered blouse, and here're some matching beads." . . .

. . . "Mom, the Scriptures I always read to you are from the book of Psalms. They're wonderful words, Mom. I hope they comfort you." . . .

For in the time of trouble he shall hide me in his pavilion:
In the secret of his tabernacle shall he hide me . . .

. . . "Hungry? Sure you are. Let's roll to the dining room. Here, Joann, right up to the table now." . . .

. . . *Wait on the Lord: be of good courage, and he shall strengthen your heart;*
    Wait, I say, on the Lord! . . .

CHAPTER FIFTY-THREE

KITE LESSONS

1964

S andpaper in hand, Saffee kneels on the garage floor. Nels's car
pulls into the driveway and she gives him a wave.

"Hi, Daddy," she says as he approaches, "Look, I'm working on the third leg." Since the first real thaw of spring, she has
devoted more time than ever to the table project, terribly eager to
be finished.

Nels admires her progress and finds a tarp on a back wall shelf.
He folds it into a cushion. "Here," he says. "Save your knees."

Last summer Nels didn't seem to fully understand her zeal for
restoring the table. Saffee wasn't surprised. He's never been one to see
connections between emotion and action. For years his assessment of
Joann went no deeper than to observe, "She thinks too much." But
ever since New Year's Eve, when he heard Saffee share with Joann
about stripping the table, he's concluded that his daughter is the best
judge of how she must deal with the past.

He settles into the webbed chair.

"How was Mother today, Daddy?" He often comes from the nursing home after visiting her.

"She looked good. Dressed in a nice blue blouse and pants." These days, if Joann is awake and able to train her one dim eye on him during visits, Nels is happy. If she is asleep, or struggles to lift her left arm as if to wave him away, he is disappointed.

"I've been reading the Bible to her when I visit," Saffee says. "I hope she hears me." Nels looks appreciative.

There's a streak of moving color in the yard. Saffee waves to Jenny Rose.

"Miss Saffee! Come see my kite!" the child calls.

"Dad, there's the adorable little girl from next door I've told you about."

Nels steps onto the driveway. Jenny Rose beams contagious delight.

"See my kite!" She holds it out for inspection. "My daddy got it for me."

"It's very pretty, Jenny Rose," Saffee says, joining Nels in the sunshine.

"Daddy's gonna show me how to fly it *way, way* up in the air!"

Bill appears from the adjacent garage with twine and colorful strips of plastic. "Hey, Jenny Love," he says, "I found the string and just what we need for the tail." He notices Saffee and Nels. "Hi, Saffee. What do you think of our kite?"

"Perfect for this breezy day." Saffee introduces Bill to her dad.

"Nice little girl you have there," Nels says, smiling.

Bill agrees. Saffee and Nels watch the pair kneeling on the grass. Patient, large hands show smaller ones how to tie the plastic tail strips. Bill attaches the line to the frame and unwinds a length from the spool.

"Are we ready, Daddy? Let's make it fly!"

Bill gives the kite a strong toss into the wind.

"Look!" Jenny Rose exclaims as she runs beneath the rising,

twisting kite. "It's so high!" She scampers back to Bill, her long dark curls tossing in the breeze. "Daddy, can I fly it?"

Together they hold the spinning spool. The kite soars and dives like a magnificent bird. Saffee tries to remember if she has ever flown a kite. She doesn't look at Nels.

"Hold tight, Jenny!" she calls.

The kite loops crazily in the wind, gently tugging Bill and Jenny Rose into the next yard. Saffee returns to the garage and picks up her sandpaper. Nels follows and sits without speaking in the webbed chair. The scene of devoted father and carefree daughter replays in Saffee's mind. She wonders what her dad is thinking.

Nels clears his throat like he does when he's embarrassed. "Saffee," he says. There is a long pause. "They were . . . those two . . . I mean." More silence. He clears his throat again. "Saffee. I know I wasn't the best father."

She stops sanding. He's apologizing. The few words are all "Daddy's little girl" needs to hear. The humble admission fills her heart with love.

"Oh, Daddy." She rocks back from her knees to sit on the floor and looks up at him. His eyes get teary so easily nowadays. "You didn't have a father to teach you how to be one, just like Mother had no mother. But you did fine. Look at me, Daddy. Didn't I turn out okay? You must have done a good job."

"Yes, I know, you're fine, but . . ." Nels shakes his head. "But I shoulda done better . . . Mother, she . . . but it's not Mother's fault. I . . ." He leans forward with head down, hands on knees. "And April . . . goin' off like that. She needed a mother . . . and a father."

"She's okay, Daddy. I'm excited that she's found Kyros. He sounds pretty special. And I'm sure you're happy they're planning to move to the States when they can."

Over the winter there had been a flurry of letters from April, extolling her newfound Greek friend, Kyros, who soon became more than a friend. In February, April wrote that they had been married on the island of Santorini. The sisters had missed each other's weddings but promised by mail to make amends in the future.

"Mother's condition made your life really hard, Daddy, and . . . and sometimes it was hard for April and me too. Mother was too broken to love us well. But for us, everything is okay now. Really, Daddy."

I am loved. My life is different. I am not my mother. I am different.

Nels pulls out his handkerchief and blows his nose. "I dunno what else to say. But you're a good girl, Saffee. I, well . . . I dunno what to say." The handkerchief goes back to its pocket. Nels drums the arms of the chair for a moment, then stands abruptly. "Wonder if there's some coffee left?"

She smiles. "Sure, Dad. In the kitchen."

He ducks into the house and Saffee goes out to catch another glimpse of the kite. It flies like young Jenny Rose, wonderfully tethered, wonderfully free.

Saffee has commented more than once that she and Jack would be "just fine" with no children. But now, after watching Gail and Bill nurture their daughter and new baby, she can see that life is supposed to be more than just fine. Investing, *investing*, in a child is an opportunity to give the world a Jenny Rose. Again, Saffee has watched, and listened, and learned.

An early morning rain stops abruptly and moves on, leaving behind an overcast sky and a vigorous cool wind. Saffee switches on the garage ceiling light. The Norway table, its rich honey-toned wood finally bare but for a fresh coat of varnish, stands as if on center stage. The heirloom piece closes a circle begun years ago when a young man planed hand-hewn planks of birch and carved an enigmatic vine. The circle has compassed spiritual blessings, hardships of everyday life, terror, shelter, and demonic delusion. It survived the tyranny of a paintbrush and the excoriation of chemicals and sandpaper.

Clouds begin to part in the eastern sky. A strong shaft of yellow sunshine bursts onto the table, as if blessing it.

Saffee spins the radio dial until orchestral magic befitting celebration fills the air. She's grateful for the day at Joann's bedside when she thanked her for imparting love of classical music. For years, mother and daughter shared this spiritual grace, this communion, unspoken. She boosts the volume, exhilaration surging with the harmonies. She gathers empty paint remover cans and newspapers that litter the floor and throws them into the trash.

Saffee looks out across the road where the stand of young birches bend and sway as if in rhythm with the music. Shimmering green leaves fling showers of raindrops into the air.

"Oh," she breathes. "God, You have choreographed the trees to worship You."

She lifts her arms to join them.

"Thank You, Lord, for Your gifts," she whispers. "I have seen Your Spirit at work. You have ushered goodness and healing into my deepest being, giving my life a new lyric. You have chosen my inheritance. I needn't fear." She lowers a hand to touch the restored wood—wood that once had stood in sun and rain and swayed in the wind.

As rings mark the age of a tree, circles of life also close and begin again.

Tonight, the Norway table will take its welcome place in their home.

CHAPTER FIFTY-FOUR

REDEEMED

1975

I made this egg into a bunny. Look, Mom, he's got ears and a cotton tail." Seven-year-old Grace holds up her creation for Saffee to admire. The Norway table, covered with a vinyl cloth, is littered with containers of dye, stickers, crayons, and other essentials for Easter egg decorating. The children's enthusiastic creativity gives Saffee great pleasure.

Nels is napping, but she knows he would not want to miss out on the traditional fun.

Saffee asks Daniel, age nine, to keep an eye on Benjamin, three and a half, whose enthusiasm matches his brother's and sister's but, of course, not his skill. Saffee goes to her dad's room to see if he has awakened. His face looks peaceful; how can she interrupt him?

Thinking how pleased she is that he is part of the household, she stands for a moment watching his chest rise and fall. When Saffee and Jack bought the four-bedroom home eight years ago, they thought there was a possibility Nels would move in with them. Soon after Grace was born, he did.

For a moment, her eyes scan the room. On the bureau is the yellow ceramic dancing girl Nels gave Joann in her happier days. Saffee wonders what he thinks when he looks at it now. Her thoughts are interrupted by screeching protests in the kitchen and she quickly returns to investigate.

A cup of purple dye somehow was spilled across the table. Daniel, rather than minimize the mess, is smearing his fingers through it and exuberantly flicking purple dye onto his sister and brother. In a flash Saffee yells, "Daniel, stop! Stop! Stop!" Grabbing his arms, she glares at him. "Daniel, that's hateful! What are you doing? Are you crazy?" Her outburst surprises the children, and later prompts her own discouragement.

That night when the children are asleep, Saffee and Jack hide the eggs. When they finish, Saffee sinks into a chair and relates the afternoon's unfortunate scene.

"Daniel reminded me of Mother, madly smearing her hands and arms through paint on that same table. I could almost see her spattering colors through the air with those Jackson Pollock results. The memory stabbed right through me, Jack, and before I could think, I lost my temper.

"He wasn't being hateful, just childish," Saffee continues. "He thought I was mad about the mess. But I guess some old table angst reared its ugly head and I fell for it."

"Don't be so hard on yourself, Saffee. I don't suppose unpleasant memories ever completely go away."

"Maybe not, but I don't want the children to be affected by my sensitivity to the past."

Jack bends down and tilts her face up to his. "You've learned that lesson very well and I'm proud of you. But you're human—a wonderful wife and mother who can make a mistake." She gives him a grateful smile and relates how she and all of them cleaned up the mess together. Both Daniel and Saffee had sincerely apologized.

Jack wraps his arms around her. "You might even get Mother of the Year award!"

"Ah, go on," she chuckles, rolling her eyes.

Sunday morning Saffee sits at the Norway table, reviewing the Easter dinner menu. The table, without yesterday's paraphernalia, is the stunning centerpiece of the spacious room. She makes a note to ask Jack and Kyros to add all three table leaves before dinner.

She'll put the glazed, spiral-cut ham into the oven before the guests arrive at one o'clock; scalloped potatoes are under way; April is bringing her broccoli cheese casserole and homemade rolls. Did Kyros say he's making baklava? She smiles. April's lovable Greek husband of nine years never passes up the opportunity. Grammy Andrews promised two lemon meringue pies and a fruit salad; the green salad can be tossed at the last minute.

What else? Oh yes, the coffee, and the molded Easter bunny chocolates she couldn't resist at a candy store.

She pauses to admire the white trumpeting blossoms in the center of the table. Jack has brought her a lily every Easter since the table made its debut in the dining alcove of their rented duplex twelve years ago. Yesterday the family took an Easter lily, the symbol of resurrection, to Joann, as they always do. Joann's condition has improved little since she was admitted to the nursing home. Several times a week, month after month and year after year, Nels sits by her side. He whispers sweet love words and massages her hands and feet.

"Your dad's a prince," an aide more than once has commented to Saffee. "A lot of the residents here go for months without even one visitor. We've never seen a man as loyal as Nels."

School pictures of Saffee and Jack's three children smile down from a bulletin board, and the walls display their artistic endeavors. When they visit, the children sing or recite poems and Bible verses. They can only hope Joann enjoys their efforts.

Saffee removes the lily and folds away an embroidered runner she made, thanks to Joann, who years ago insisted she learn to embroider dish towels. The tabletop reveals accumulated blemishes. Among them, a phone number carelessly impressed through a piece of paper, irregular printing that spells "Daniel," a divot from a slip of an X-ACTO knife, and at least two white rings from sweating water glasses.

When she notices the flaws, which she rarely does, she thinks of the maxim "Love me for my imperfections." The layered paint of years ago, and these more recent scars, are mere neutral reminders of where life has been. She needn't go back to them emotionally. Long ago she decided this.

She spreads a white paper tablecloth, coaxes its stiff edges to drape downward, and places a gumdrop tree, made from a brambly branch, at the center. One more thing. She puts boxes of crayons handy on the buffet.

It is eight o'clock; the hot cross buns go into a pan to warm; she hears Nels puttering in his bedroom. The children will be waking soon. Anticipating the impending merriment, she rearranges the cellophane grass nestled in straw baskets. Any moment her tribe will fill the house with glee as they scamper to hunt for eggs. There will be just enough time for breakfast before the eleven o'clock church service.

Saffee hears Benjamin's infectious laughter as he comes scooting down the hall from his bedroom. "I found a egg! I found a egg! Grandpa Nels! Get up, get up!" He appears, one hand clutching his slipping pajama bottoms, the other holding aloft a blue and yellow egg. "My first one! It was under my pillow!"

Jack returns from walking Skye, their Scottish terrier, leaving him in the backyard. "Look, Daddy!"

"Good find, Benji," his father says. "Mom's got a basket here for you to collect more," he says, bending to tousle Benjamin's hair.

Grace appears. "Mom! Me too, where's my basket?" She's closely followed by the oldest pajama-clad child.

"I'm gonna find the most, cuz I'm the tallest and can reach the highest," Daniel boasts.

"Daddy! Daddy! I found the one with my name on it. See how nice I wrote it?"

"Good going, Amazing Grace," Jack says.

Nels, unshaven, joins the happy throng. Benjamin crawls under the rocker, although it's clearly not a hiding place that Saffee and Jack selected.

"Benji, you're gettin' warmer," Nels hints. "In fact, you might get burned around that there rocker." The little boy wriggles backward and quickly snatches a yellow egg from under the rocker cushion.

"Thanks, Grandpa!" He races elsewhere.

The hunt is in full swing. Saffee watches the hurry and scurry, joins in the banter, lives the moment.

When no more eggs can be found, Saffee pours orange juice, puts the hot cross buns on a platter, and summons her family to the table. "Mommy, I'm so hungry!" Daniel rubs his stomach. "Can I have *three* hot cross buns and *three* eggs this year?"

"Me too," says Benjamin. "Grandpa Nels, can I sit on your lap?"

"Right here, Benji, up you go. Say. You're gettin' heavy."

Saffee makes a mental note that they'll need four additional chairs for the dinner guests. They won't match, but so be it. Years ago, when she and Jack bought six ladder-back chairs, she couldn't imagine they would ever need *that* many.

They join hands and Jack prays.

He thanks Jesus, the Christ, for His sacrifice of death on the cross and His resurrection from the grave. He thanks Him for promising and providing eternal life. He thanks Him for the family gathered around the table and those who will arrive later. They all chorus, "Amen!"

The children *tap-tap-tap* eggs against their plates, breaking and scattering shells. The youngest licks frosting from the top of his hot cross bun.

Grace asks if they can decorate the paper tablecloth like they had at Christmas.

"That's why I brought the crayons," their mother says, reaching for the boxes.

"One of the best things I like about Easter is getting gumdrops for breakfast," says Daniel, his teeth sticking together as he speaks. Saffee smiles as she refills Jack's and Nels's coffee mugs. Someday she'll tell her children about the gumdrop bush of her own childhood.

The crayon boxes are passed and everyone, young and old, selects a handful. Between bites of food they scribble and draw, with no regard for lack of artistic talent. It isn't long before mostly recognizable brown bunnies, yellow chicks, and lengthy daisy chains abound across the paper. Together, Daniel and Grandpa Nels draw a large cross. It is yellow, outlined in brown.

"We drew the cross window at church," Daniel says. "It's yellow cuz the sun is shining through it."

"Gracie, what's those *green* things you're makin'? Green eggs?" Benji asks, his mouth full and a splash of juice on his chin.

"I know what they are!" Daniel says. "Green eggs and ham, like in the book."

Grace shakes her head and continues to make circles with a fat green crayon, first stretching her arm in front of Saffee on one side, and then in front of Daniel and Grandpa Nels on the other, so as to rim the table edge. Coming to the extent of her reach, she jumps up to color the paper in front of Jack.

"Okay, finished!" Gracie says when she has encircled the entire table, obviously enjoying that she has puzzled the others. "Give up?"

"I think you drawed a necklace, Gracie," Grandpa Nels says.

"No-o-pe."

"It's a train!" exudes Benji.

"No-o-pe."

"We give up. Tell us, Grace," Jack says.

"Olives!" Grace sings out in triumph.

"Olives? Don'tcha know olives are black?" says her big brother.

"Not *mine*! Cuz mine are still *growing*!"

Smugly, Grace waves her crayon in the direction of the framed calligraphy that Saffee penned for the wall—the ancient blessing that Leif Bergstrom had translated, the words Saffee's great-grandfather had burned into the wood under the table almost one hundred years ago.

"I made lots of green olives around our table, just like Mommy's picture says!"

Saffee is more pleased than Grace could know. She looks at Jack; he winks back. Saffee has read the words to her children, telling them it means they are a special promise from God.

"Why don't you read it to us, Gracie?" Saffee says.

Grace pushes her chair to the wall and stands on it for a better view, and also, Saffee suspects, for effect, reminiscent of her theatrical Aunt April.

Grace reads:

Your wife . . .

"That's Mommy, Benji," she informs him.

. . . shall be like a fruitful vine
in the very heart of your house.
Your children . . .

Grace expansively gestures toward her brothers. "And that's *us!*"

. . . like olive plants around your table.
Psalm 128

1976

She sleeps in earth's darkness . . .

"Joann, My beloved, Joann, My Joy!"

. . . and awakens to brilliant Light.

Jesus takes her hand. "Come, My Joy. Come to My banqueting table."

Kant

The unread morning paper rests on Nels's lap as he sits in his recliner. From the kitchen, Saffee watches her father, wanting to share new happiness with him, waiting for the right moment. Although he is looking in the direction of Benjamin who is revving matchbox cars over and under sofa pillows, she suspects he is lost in sadness and sees nothing. Skye sleeps on the floor beside him. Nels's right arm extends downward, his hand slowly strokes the dog's black fur. Saffee suspects that her father has been thinking about what might have been and wondering why.

The midnight call from the nursing home came two weeks ago. Nels's vigil by his wife's side was over. Regarding her father's long devotion, "Love me for my imperfections" is an adage that Saffee has replaced with another:

People are not perfect—until you fall in love with them.

The funeral was small. Attending were Nels, Saffee's family, April and her husband, and two caregivers from the nursing home. Also, out of respect for Saffee and Jack, Gail and Bill and a few people from church were there. When it was over, Saffee and April fell into each other's arms.

"I think we'll always have a part of Mother tugging at us," April said.

"That's right," Saffee agreed, "the best part."

Since April returned from Europe, still her perky self, but more worldly-wise, she and Saffee have become best of friends.

"Want to join me for a cup of tea, Dad?"

He snaps out of his reflection and takes on his usual lighthearted voice. "Nah . . . you know I don't drink that stuff. Tea's for women-folk. I had my coffee."

"I knew you were going to say that." Saffee draws up a chair beside him. "It's been a sad time, hasn't it? I can see it in your face today." He nods in agreement.

"Tell me something, Saffee." He interrupts himself to search through his pants pockets for a handkerchief. "Here it is." He doesn't use it, just holds it at the ready and continues, "Tell me"—another pause—"tell me why you think your mother had to go through so much hell."

"Oh, Daddy. I don't know. But, Daddy"—she covers his hand with hers—"I want to tell you about a wonderful dream I had about her last night."

"Oh yeah?" He looks into her eyes, eager to hear anything that is wonderful.

"It was about Mother in *heaven*, Daddy. And, Daddy, get this." Saffee squeezes his hand. "She was *dancing*!"

"Dancin'?"

"Yes, Daddy, it was a marvelous sight, since she hadn't even *walked* for years, had hardly even *moved*, couldn't smile or say a word. But, Daddy, I saw her dancing. Twirling round and round and laughing, Daddy, *laughing*!"

Nels tries to say something, clears his throat, and tries again. "She . . . she . . . when we was young . . . she loved to dance, just like that yellow, whatcha call it, figurine I got her. I still got it, you know." He looks into the distance. "That's how I like to remember her."

"I know."

Nels refocuses. "She was laughin', you say?"

"Yes, Daddy. But that was the end part. The beginning of the dream was when Jesus, surrounded by brilliant light, walked toward her, stretched out His arms, and embraced her. Then, get this, Daddy, He gave her a sparkling white stone and told her to read what was written on it. She was smiling so big when she read the stone. And then I heard *her voice*—that none of us heard for years. She said, 'It says "Joy"!' And Jesus said, 'Yes, Joy is your new name. You are *My Joy*!'"

Nels sits a little straighter, his eyes wide. "What happened then?"

"That's when she started dancing, and oh, Daddy, she was so happy. And there was music like you've never heard. Beautiful, beautiful music I can't describe. I wanted to stay right there in the middle of it myself—but that's when I woke up. Then I just had to wake up Jack to find out if *he'd* heard the music of heaven."

"Did he?"

"No, but I wish he had. I will *never* forget it."

Nels's closed eyes are brimming. Saffee wraps her arms around him and their wet cheeks touch. They rock a little, back and forth.

Nels smiles. "Dancin'," he says hoarsely. "She's dancin' to music . . . Dancin' . . . in heaven."

Reading Group Guide

1. How does Joann's mental illness affect Nels, April, and Saffee?

2. Discuss the role of fire in Joann's life.

3. What are the consequences of emotional neglect?

4. In what ways is it possible to avoid taking on the negative aspects of the people who raised you?

5. How does Saffee honor Joann? How does she dishonor her?

6. Birch trees appear throughout the novel. What might they represent?

7. Joann, Nels, and Saffee are each restricted by personal fears. What fears play a part in your life? How might this story help you deal with them?

8. Discuss the Norway table and its symbolic role in the story.

9. What leads to Saffee's growth and wholeness? Do any of Saffee's

experiences or moments of enlightenment apply to your family legacy?

10. Discuss how the main characters find redemption.

ACKNOWLEDGMENTS

Heartfelt thanks, Sandi and Scott Tompkins. Your professional expertise and encouragement made a way for me and many others to take the first steps toward becoming published authors. Your perceptive, gentle counsel was vital to this work.

Thank you, all my writing friends in the remarkable Kona Writers' Group. Your support and helpful criticism were beyond value.

Patti Hummel, my creative, tireless agent: you recognize possibilities and then make them happen. I am deeply grateful.

Thank you, Daisy Hutton and Ami McConnell of HarperCollins Christian Publishing for believing in me and my story. Also, thanks to Ruthie Dean, Becky Monds, Zachary Gresham, and Kristen Vasgaard. Each of you played a part in nurturing the various aspects of the book.

Nicci Jordan Hubert, you understood my heart and the nuances required to convey it. Your sensitive edits were appropriate and welcome.

To my Norwegian cousins, Leif and Anders, *Tusen takk!* Your gracious hospitality inspired me to learn and write about my ancestry. I am blessed to be part of the same family.

Thank you, Nancy Ann Field. When you cried in all the right places, you became one of my first encouragers. You were joined early on by Irene Periera and Barbara Fessendon. Thank you, dozens of friends and acquaintances, who went out of their way to spur me on. Particularly, Pat Weed, Vicky Scott, Joanne Archerd, and Carey Haivala. Also Judy and Gary, Rose and Jerry, Bob and Joan, Skip and Jerrien, Debra and Dennis, as well as the Prairie Life Center friends. Your interest and enthusiasm were unexpected and wonderful.

Thank you, Carol Lamse and Janet Kronemeyer and Ruth Arthurs, for believing in the message enough to share it with others.

How amazing it has been that several diverse groups of people have met to explore the story. Thank you, organizers and hosts: Linda Swygard, Char Grothues, Susan Befort, Debbie Ball, Sharon Bighley, Kathy Bondurant, Lee and Gwen Cure, and the other gatherings of readers I have never met.

Thank you, Mary Ann Shotzko and Mary Mathowicz and your staffs at St. John, for your sacrificial benevolence to my loved ones. By extension, you are part of the story.

Thank you, Holly, for your always patient, uncomplaining techy help. You knew how much I needed it. Thank you, Meeja, for your very enthusiastic promotion. And Andrew, for your expression of chagrin about a different table. Your comments planted ideas. Thank you, Sarah, for your willing support and interest. Also, thank you, Cammie. Because you lived it, you were often the only one I could consult for advice.

Thank you, Ted, my loving husband. You patiently endured, listened to me chatter endlessly about the writing without complaint, read every word, and gave me your valued perspective. You never complained when dinner was in doubt.

Most of all, I acknowledge God the Father, Son, and Holy Spirit, in whom I live, and breathe, and have my being.